BRITISH WRITERS

BRITISH WRITERS

JAY PARINI
Editor

SUPPLEMENT XIX

CHARLES SCRIBNER'S SONS
A part of Gale, Cengage Learning

GALE
CENGAGE Learning

Detroit • New York • San Francisco • New Haven, Conn • Waterville, Maine • London

GALE
CENGAGE Learning®

British Writers Supplement XIX

Editor in Chief: Jay Parini

Project Editor: Lisa Kumar

Permissions: Christine Myaskovsky

Composition Specialist: Gary Leach

Buyer: Cynde Lentz

Publisher: Jim Draper

Product Manager: Philip J. Virta

For product information and technology assistance, contact us at
Gale Customer Support, 1-800-877-4253.
For permission to use material from this text or product,
submit all requests online at **www.cengage.com/permissions**
Further permissions questions can be emailed to
permissionrequest@cengage.com

LIBRARY OF CONGRESS CATALOGING-IN-PUBLICATION DATA

British Writers. Supplement XIX / Jay Parini, editor.
　p. cm.
　Includes bibliographical references and index.
　ISBN-13: 978-1-4144-8027-5 (hardcover : alk. paper)
　ISBN-10: 1-4144-8027-X (hardcover : alk. paper)
　1. English literature--20th century--History and criticism. 2. English literature--20th century--Bio-bibliography. 3. Commonwealth literature (English)--20th century x History and criticism. 4. Commonwealth literature (English)--20th century--Bio-bibliography. 5. Authors, English--20th century--Biography. 6. Authors, Commonwealth--20th century--Biography. I. Parini, Jay.

PR85.B688 Suppl. 19
820.9--dc23
[B]　　　　　　　　　　　　　　　　　　2012018246

Charles Scribner's Sons an imprint of Gale, Cengage Learning
27500 Drake Rd.
Farmington Hills, MI, 48331-3535

ISBN-13: 978-1-4144-8027-5
ISBN-10: 1-4144-8027-X

Printed in Mexico
1 2 3 4 5 6 7 16 15 14 13 12

Acknowledgments

The editors wish to thank the copyright holders of the excerpted criticism included in this volume and the permissions managers of many book and magazine publishing companies for assisting us in securing reproduction rights. We are also grateful to the staffs of the Detroit Public Library, the Library of Congress, the University of Detroit Mercy Library, Wayne State University Purdy/Kresge Library Complex, and the University of Michigan Libraries for making their resources available to us. Following is a list of the copyright holders who have granted us permission to reproduce material in this volume of *British Writers*. Every effort has been made to trace copyright, but if omissions have been made, please let us know.

COPYRIGHTED EXCERPTS IN *BRITISH WRITERS*, VOLUME 19, WERE REPRODUCED FROM THE FOLLOWING BOOKS:

ABBS, PETER. From *Icons of Time: An Experiment in Autobiography*. Gryphon Press, 1991. Copyright © Peter Abbs, 2001. Reproduced by permission of the author. / From *Personae*. Skoob Books Publishing, 1995. Copyright © Peter Abbs, 1995. Reproduced by permission of the author. / From *Angelic Imagination: New Poems 1994-1996*. Gryphon Press, 1997. Copyright © Peter Abbs, 1997. Reproduced by permission of the author. / From *Love After Sappho*. Halfacrown, 1999. Copyright © Peter Abbs, 1999. Reproduced by permission of the author. / From *Viva La Vida*. Salt Publishing, 2005. Copyright © Peter Abbs, 2005. Reproduced by permission of the author. / From *The Flowering of Flint: New and Selected Poems*. Salt Publishing, 2007. Copyright © Peter Abbs, 2007. Reproduced by permission of the author. / From *Voyaging Out*. Salt Publishing, 2009. Copyright © Peter Abbs, 2009. Reproduced by permission of the author. Gioia, Dana. / From *Voyaging Out*. Salt Publishing, 2009. Copyright © Dana Gioia, 2009. Reproduced by permission of the author. / Budy, Andrea Hollander. "Interview with Peter Abbs." Copyright © Peter Abbs. Reproduced by permission of the author. / Seiferle, Rebecca. From *TheDrukenBoat.com*. TheDrukenBoat.com, 2000. Copyright © Rebecca Seiferle, 2000. Reproduced by permission of the publisher. / *Urthona Magazine*, v. 27.48, summer 2010.

Copyright © 2010 by Craig Jordan-Baker. Reproduced by permission of the author.

ALDISS, BRIAN. From *Galaxies Like Grains of Sand*. Signet, 1960. Copyright © Penguin Putnam Inc., 1960. Reproduced by permission of the publisher. / From *Helliconia Spring*. Atheneum, 1982. Copyright © Simon & Schuster, Inc., 1982. Reproduced by permission of the publisher. / *Literature/Film Quarterly*, v. 32.4, October 2004. Copyright © 2004 by Literature/Film Quarterly. Reproduced by permission of the publisher.

CARTWRIGHT, JUSTIN. From *In Every Face I Meet*. Hodder & Stoughton Limited, 1995. Copyright © Hodder & Stoughton Limited, 1995. Reproduced by permission of the publisher.

DONAGHY, MICHAEL. From *Collected Poems*. Pan Macmillan Ltd., 2009. Copyright © Pan Macmillan Ltd., 2009. Reproduced by permission of the publisher. / Keats, John. From *The Poems of John Keats*. Pearson Education Limited, 1970. Copyright © Pearson Education Limited, 1970. Reproduced by permission of the publisher. Pan Macmillan Ltd., 2009. Copyright © Pan Macmillan Ltd., 2009. Reproduced by permission of the publisher. / *Guard-*

ACKNOWLEDGEMENTS

ian Book Review, October 2011. Copyright © 2011 by Guardian Media. Reproduced by permission of the publisher. / Poetry, v. 196.4, July/August 2010. Copyright © 2010 by Poetry Foundation. Reproduced by permission of the publisher.

HANLEY, JAMES. "Review of Another World." From Times Literary Supplement. The Times Literary Supplement, 1972. Copyright © The Times Literary Supplement, 1972. Reproduced by permission of the publisher.

HARSENT, DAVID. From A Violent Country. Oxford University Press, 1969. Copyright © David Harsent, 1969. Reproduced by permission of United Agents. / From Selected Poems. Oxford University Press, 1989. Copyright © David Harsent, 1989. Reproduced by permission of United Agents. / From Mister Punch. Oxford University Press, 1984. Copyright © David Harsent, 1984. Reproduced by permission of United Agents. / From News from the Front. Oxford University Press, 1993. Copyright © David Harsent. Reproduced by permission of United Agents. / From A Bird's Idea of Flight. Faber & Faber Limited, 1998. Copyright © Faber & Faber Limited, 1998. Reproduced by permission of the publisher and author. / From Marriage. Faber & Faber Limited, 2002. Copyright © Faber & Faber Limited, 2002. Reproduced by permission of the publisher. / From Legion. Faber & Faber Limited, 2005. Copyright © Faber & Faber Limited, 2005. Reproduced by permission of the publisher. / From Night. Faber & Faber Limited, 2011. Copyright © Faber & Faber Limited, 2011. Reproduced by permission of the publisher.

MACLEAN, SORLEY. From From Wood to Ridge: Collected Poems in Gaelic and In English Translation. Carcanet Press Limited/Birlnn Ltd., 1999. Copyright © Carcanet Press Limited/Birlinn Ltd., 1999. Reproduced by permission of the publisher.

PEARCE, PHILIPPA. From Minnow on the Say. HarperCollins Children's Books, 2000. Copyright © HarperCollins Children's Books, 2000. Reproduced by permission of the publisher. /

New York Times, November 1968. Copyright © 1968 by The New York Times Company. Reproduced by permission of the publisher. / The Guardian, November 2008. Copyright © 2008 by Guardian News Service Ltd. Reproduced by permission of the publisher.

PHILLIPS, ADAM. New Statesman, April 2001. Copyright © 2001 by New Statesman. Reproduced by permission of the publisher.

ROBERTSON, JAMES. From Fae the Flouers o Evil. Kettillonia, 2001. Copyright © James Robertson, 2001. Reproduced by permission of the author. / From I Dream of Alfred Hitchcock. Kettillonia, 1999. Copyright © James Robertson, 1999. Reproduced by permission of the author. / From Sound Shadow. Black & White Publishing, 1995. Copyright © Black & White Publishing, 1995. Reproduced by permission of the publisher. / From Stirling Sonnets. Kettillonia, 1999. Copyright © James Robertson, 1999. Reproduced by permission of the author. / From Voyage of Intent: Sonnets and Essays from the Scottish Parliament. James Robertson and Luath Press Ltd., 2004. Copyright © James Robertson and Luath Press Ltd., 2004. Reproduced by permission of the publisher and author. / From Hem and Heid. Kettillonia, 2009. Copyright © James Robertson, 2009. Reproduced by permission of the author. / From Kettillonia, n.d. Copyright © James Robertson. Reproduced by permission of the author. / Okri, Ben. From Joseph Knight. HarperCollins Publishers Ltd. (London) and Phoenix Publishing House, Inc., 2003. Copyright © HarperCollins Publishers Ltd. (London) and Phoenix Publishing House, Inc., 2003. Reproduced by permission of the publishers.

SMITH, CHARLOTTE TURNER. From The Poems of Charlotte Smith. Edited by Stuart Curran. Oxford University Press, 1993. Copyright © Oxford University Press, 1993. Reproduced by permission of the publisher.

SYAL, MEERA. The Guardian, November 1999. Copyright © 1999 by Guardian News Service Ltd. Reproduced by permission of the

ACKNOWLEDGEMENTS

List of Subjects

Introduction

W. Somerset Maugham, one of the most gifted of modern British novelists and storywriters, once said: "To acquire the habit of reading is to construct for yourself a refuge from almost all of the miseries of life." Maugham was, apart from being a prolific author, a prolific reader. As he knew, good writing begins with good reading. And this reading provides a refuge, a place where you can settle and think, find warmth, find courage, even directions for living. One of the purposes of *British Writers* has always been to examine the work of significant writers in a variety of genres, taking into account their daily lives and their work, seeking the points of contact between these often separate streams. Over many years, in the volumes published in this series, we have tried to show how the individual writer's reading may have figured in the creation of her or his own literary imagination. And we have tried to open the work of these writers to a general audience.

The series brings together a range of articles on authors who have a substantial reputation. As in previous volumes, the subjects have been chosen for their contribution to the traditions of British, Irish, or Anglophone literature (being texts written in English, indebted to the British tradition to some extent, often written by authors from former colonial states. Such a definition includes, for example, Canadian, Australian, New Zealand, and South African writers). We hope readers will find these articles entertaining as well as informative, and that they will prove worthwhile for those with a considerable knowledge of a given author but also form a useful introduction for those only beginning to grow familiar with this author. A good part of each article is, in fact, biographical and historical as well as critical.

British Writers started life as an offshoot of a series of monographs that appeared between 1959 and 1972, the *Minnesota Pamphlets on American Writers*. These pamphlets were popular at the time. They were well written and informative, taking into account the work of ninety-seven American writers in a format and style that attracted a devoted following. The series proved invaluable to a generation of students and teachers, who could depend on these reliable and interesting critiques of major figures. The idea of reprinting these essays occurred to Charles Scribner, Jr., an innovative publisher during the middle decades of the twentieth century. The series appeared in four volumes entitled *American Writers: A Collection of Literary Biographies* (1974). *British Writers* followed, gathering a series of essays originally published by the British Council. These proved popular as well, and nineteen supplements (including this one) have followed, extending and amplifying the series. The goal of the supplements has been consistent with the original idea: to provide clear, detailed essays aimed at the general reader. We try to take into account the latest critical thinking on each author.

The authors of the essays in Supplement XIX are mostly teachers and scholars. Many have published books and articles in their field. As anyone looking through these articles will see, all of our critics have been held to the highest standards of clear writing and sound scholarship. Jargon and theoretical musings have been discouraged, except when strictly relevant. Each of the essays concludes with a select bibliography of works by the author under discussion and secondary works that might be useful to those wishing to pursue the subject further. In this supplement, the nineteenth in the series, we

INTRODUCTION

treat three classic authors from previous centuries—Sheridan Le Fanu, Charlotte Turner Smith, and Richard Chenevix Trench. For various reasons, these have yet to be considered in this series. For the most part, this supplement centers on modern and contemporary writers from various genres and traditions, most of whom have had little sustained attention from critics, although they are well known. Peter Abbs, Brian Aldiss, Justin Cartwright, Michael Donaghy, James Hanley, David Harsent, Shirley Hazzard Elspeth Huxley, Mary Lavin, Patrick Leigh Fermor, Sorley MacLean, Nuala O'Faolain, Philippa Pearce, Adam Phillips, James Robertson, and Meera Syal have all been written about in the review pages, often discussed at considerable length, and their work has in each instance found an audience of devoted readers, and yet their careers–perhaps Leigh Fermor is an exception here–have yet to attract sustained scholarly attention. That will follow, but the articles included in this supplement form a beginning of sorts, an attempt to survey the unique universe of each writer.

As ever, our goal in putting forward these biographical articles is to draw readers back to the poems, plays, stories, novels, travel books, memoirs, or essays—to help them in their journeys toward these writers who have made a deep impression on the English-speaking world. These articles should enable students and general readers to enter into the work of these writers with a fresh eye, helping them to understand how in each case the writer summoned a particular vision, moving from page to page, creating a singular and coherent universe or–as Maugham said–a place of refuge—in language.

—JAY PARINI

List of Contributors

Nicholas Birns. Nicholas Birns is Associate Teaching Professor at Eugene Lang College, the New School University. He is the author of *Understanding Anthony Powell* (University of South Carolina Press, 2004), and the co-editor of *A Companion to Australian Literature Since 1900* (Camden House, 2007), which was named a CHOICE Outstanding Academic Book of the Year for 2008 and of *Vargas Llosa and Latin American Politics* (Palgrave. 2010). His book *Theory After Theory: An Intellectual History of Literary Theory From 1950 to the Early 21st Century* was published by Broadview in 2010. SHIRLEY HAZZARD

J. C. Bittenbender. J. C. Bittenbender, Ph.D., is a professor of English at Eastern University in St. Davids, Pennsylvania where he teaches twentieth-century British literature. He specializes in modern Scottish and Irish literature and has published articles on Robert Burns, James Kelman, Alasdair Gray and other Scottish writers. His other areas of academic interest include James Joyce, Bakhtinian theory and censorship studies. SORLEY MACLEAN

Andrea Hollander Budy. Andrea Hollander Budy (pronounced BEW-dee) is the author of three poetry collections: *Woman in the Painting* (Autumn House Press, 2006), *The Other Life* (Story Line Press, 2001), and *House Without a Dreamer* (Story Line Press, 1993), which won the Nicholas Roerich Poetry Prize. Other honors include the D. H. Lawrence Fellowship, a Pushcart Prize for memoir, and two poetry fellowships from the National Endowment for the Arts. She is the Writer-in-Residence at Lyon College, which awarded her the Lamar Williamson Prize for Excellence in Teaching. She lives in Portland, Oregon. PETER ABBS

Susan Butterworth. Susan Butterworth is a freelance writer who specializes in literary biography and criticism, especially of nonfiction writers. She has contributed articles on Vera Brittain, Kate Thompson, and Malcolm Bradbury to the *British Writers* series, as well as articles on Gay Talese, M. F. K. Fisher and Jon Krakauer to the *American Writers* series. She has published travel essays in newspapers and *The Best Women's Travel Writing* anthologies published by Travelers' Tales. She teaches college composition and literature courses at Salem State University and has taught eighth-grade English in her hometown of Marblehead, Massachusetts. PATRICK LEIGH FERMOR

Frances A. Chiu. Frances A. Chiu is an Assistant Professor at the New School University. She received her Ph.D. from Oxford University. She has presented papers at the ASECs, BSECs, DeBartolo, and Eighteenth- and Nineteenth-century British Women Writers conferences. Publications include (as editor) Ann Radcliffe's *Gaston de Blondeville* and Sheridan Le Fanu's *The Rose and the Key;* as well as contributions to *Eighteenth-century Life, Le Fanu Studies, Notes and Queries, Romanticism on the Net,* and Scribner's *British Writers* Retrospective Supplement III. She was recently nominated for a Distinguished University Teaching Award. SHERIDAN LE FANU

Julie Ellam. Julie Ellam is a postdoctoral research assistant at the University of Hull, working on the eight volumes of the edited collection of Ellen Terry letters (Pickering and Chatto). She is also the author of three books, including *Love in Jeanette Winterson's Novels* (Rodopi 2010). ADAM PHILLIPS

INTRODUCTION

Jonathan Ellis. Jonathan Ellis is Senior Lecturer in American Literature at the University of Sheffield (UK). He is the author of *Art and Memory in the Work of Elizabeth Bishop* (2006), as well as articles and essays on Samuel Beckett, Paul Muldoon and Sylvia Plath. He is currently co-editing *The Cambridge Companion to Elizabeth Bishop* and completing a study of twentieth-century letter writing. He has been the recipient of a Leverhulme Early Career Fellowship, and more recently, a British Academy Research Development Award. MICHAEL DONAGHY

Angela M. Garcia. Angela M. Garcia lives and works in Corvallis, Oregon with her husband and two children. She teaches English as a Second Language to adults at Linn-Benton Community College as well as to elementary and middle schoolers within the public school system. Her critical commentary has focused on writers from Louisa May Alcott and Edith Wharton to Anna Quindlen to Billy Collins. NUALA O'FAOLAIN

Joshua Grasso. Joshua Grasso is an Assistant Professor in English at East Central University (Oklahoma). He has a Ph.D. from Miami University and specializes in the long eighteenth century and postcolonial studies. Recent articles have appeared in *Digital Defoe 2.0, The CEA Critic,* and *The Explicator.* He is currently working on a project exploring art and travel in the eighteenth century. ELSPETH HUXLEY

Maureen Manier. Maureen Manier studied in Dublin during her junior year at the University of Notre Dame. She completed an independent study project on Mary Lavin that included several interviews with the author conducted at Bewley's Café on Grafton Street. Manier is the vice president of marketing and communications for Riley Children's Foundation in Indianapolis. MARY LAVIN

Robert McKay. Robert McKay teaches English Literature at the University of Sheffield (UK). His research focuses on the literary representa-tion of animals and he is currently completing a book on the ethics of species in contemporary fiction. JUSTIN CARTWRIGHT

Abby Mims. Abby Mims' stories and essays have been published in several literary magazines and anthologies, including *The Santa Monica Review, Swink, The Normal School* and *Woman's Best Friend: Women Writers on the Dogs in Their Lives.* She has an MFA in Creative Writing from University of California, Irvine and is at work on a collection of essays. PHILIPPA PEARCE

Niall Munro. Niall Munro works primarily in the field of American literature in the areas of poetry and drama. His Ph.D. examined the queer modernist aesthetic of the poet Hart Crane, and he is currently at work on a study of the Federal Theatre Project. He has taught at Oxford Brookes University and Goldsmiths College, University of London. DAVID HARSENT

Helena Nelson. Helena Nelson is a lecturer in English and Communication at Adam Smith College, Fife. She is the originator and editor of the independent poetry imprint HappenStance Press, and a poetry reviewer for a number of UK magazines, as well as a practising poet. Her own poetry collections include *Starlight on Water* (Rialto, 2003) and *Plot and Counter-Plot* (Shoestring Press, 2010.) JAMES ROBERTSON

James Purdon. James Purdon is a Fellow of Jesus College, Cambridge. He has published on seventeenth-century biography and material culture, and is currently researching the relation-ship between early twentieth-century British fiction and technologies of information management. JAMES HANLEY

A. M. Sánchez-Arce. Dr. A. M. Sánchez-Arce is a Senior Lecturer in twentieth and twenty-first-century literature at Sheffield Hallam University (UK). She has written numerous es-says and articles on contemporary British and American writers and has edited *European In-tertexts: Women's Writing in English in a*

INTRODUCTION

European Context (Peter Lang, 2005) with Patsy Stoneman and Angela Leighton. She is currently finishing a book on the filmmaker Pedro Almodóvar for Manchester University Press and editing a collection of essays on identity and form. MEERA SYAL

Patrick A. Smith. Patrick A. Smith is the author of *"The true bones of my life": Essays on the Fiction of Jim Harrison and Tim O'Brien: A Critical Companion,* among other books, interviews, articles, and reviews. Smith is associate professor of English at Bainbridge College (GA). BRIAN ALDISS

Matthew Sperling. Matthew Sperling is Fellow by Special Election at Keble College, Oxford. He studied there and at Corpus Christi College, Oxford, the Scuola Normale Superiore in Pisa, and Gravesend Grammar School. He is co-editor of a book of essays, *Geoffrey Hill and his Contexts,* published by Peter Lang in 2011, and has written on numerous topics in modern poetry. Thanks are due to Thomas Williams for his assistance with this article. RICHARD CHENE-VIX TRENCH

Marianne Szlyk. Marianne Szlyk is an Associate Professor of English at Montgomery College's Rockville Campus (Maryland). Her review essay on Elizabeth Inchbald appeared in *British Writers* Supplement XV. She has published an article on Restoration satire in the *Sun Yat-Sen Journal of Humanities* as well as book reviews in various journals including *1650-1850: Ideas, Aesthetics, and Inquiries in the Early Modern Era, The Journal for Early Modern Cultural Studies,* and *Nineteenth-Century Gender Studies.* She earned her Ph.D. in Restoration and Eighteenth-Century British Literature from Purdue University in December 2004. CHARLOTTE TURNER SMITH

BRITISH WRITERS

PETER ABBS

(1942—)

Andrea Hollander Budy

On the dust jacket of Peter Abbs's 2009 poetry collection, *Voyaging Out*, the American poet and critic Dana Gioia states: "Peter Abbs is the rarest of writers—a philosophical poet with a genuine lyric gift. His poems are equally arresting for their substance as their style." Abbs has been compared with a cadre of diverse writers including Seamus Heaney, Tony Harrison, and James Joyce, and like each of them, he has created a highly distinguished and compelling body of work, although he is less well known than many of his contemporaries.

Throughout his works, Abbs draws on autobiography, biography, and mythology in the context of philosophical exploration. His poetic style is consistently lyrical—he's a poet of the ear as well as the mind—its foundation of traditional verse apparent in all his books.

Peter Francis Abbs was born on February 22, 1942, at Cromer in Norfolk on the east coast of England. His parents, Eric Charles Abbs, a bus driver, and Mary Bertha Bullock, a shop assistant, already had one son, Paul. The new child's emergency cesarean birth nearly three months prior to his expected arrival was traumatic not only for his mother, but, as evidenced in the sonnet "Premature Birth" in his third poetry collection, *Icons of Time*, part of the poet's "slow impeded waking into life" (p. 15) involved his mother taking him to convalesce at the Oak Woods, where her father was head gardener for Upper Sheringham Hall in the eponymous park. Here in a secluded house adjoining a large walled kitchen garden the infant began to make some progress, although the doctor had predicted that his chances of survival were slim.

After five months, Abbs did improve, and the family moved to Sheringham. However, until the mid-1950s when his grandfather retired from being head gardener, Abbs spent most holidays and most Sundays in the Oak Woods, which became very important to his imaginative life. The walled garden, shaped in a kind of mandala where all paths led to a central pond, appears—along with the woods that lay to the north—in a number of Abbs's poems, especially in *Icons of Time* and *Viva la Vida*. The young Abbs spent many days wandering alone at the Oak Woods, meandering in the kitchen garden, and dawdling under the trees. Solitude there was a kind of paradise for the future poet.

In Sheringham, Abbs attended Saint Joseph's Catholic School. His mother was a pious Catholic, and his father's conversion to the faith before their marriage (and in order for the marriage to take place at all) very much angered Eric Abbs's Methodist parents. Peter Abbs's father's side of the family was rural, working-class, puritanical, and strongly Nonconformist. The poet remembers his paternal grandfather saying in his broad Norfolk accent such phrases as "Read between the lines" and "I do not believe in any God you dress up for" (unpublished personal interview by Andrea Hollander Budy, to be noted henceforth as simply "personal interview"). This Methodist inheritance is described in the poems "Myrtle Cottage at West Runton" and "Grandmother Reading at Myrtle Cottage." They were poor, but they possessed a certain dignity and pride. The mapping of their world ended at Norwich, the main cathedral town about twenty-five miles away. Beyond Norwich stretched the abyss.

Abbs's mother's family was also rural, but more open to education and training, more entrepreneurial, and strongly Roman Catholic, though his grandfather Bullock was deeply patriotic and always stood to attention when the National Anthem played. He had been sent to

Siberia in 1917 to put down the Bolsheviks. Every morning thereafter, he woke early from terrible rheumatic pains resulting from exposure to the bitter climate.

Abbs absorbed his mother's Catholic faith but was never convinced by his father's Catholicism. On certain unpredictable Sundays he would return from morning Mass to savage the priest's sermon, leaving Abbs's mother furious with an impotent rage as she tried to shield her children from both his crude swear words and his heretical sentiments. Hating what she saw as his coarse language and low background, "Eric," she would expostulate (personal interview), "How could you—in front of the boys!" These conflicts echo in subliminal and refracted ways throughout Abbs's writing (for example, "Other Gifts" in *Viva la Vida*, p. 15).

The Catholic school Abbs attended until he was eleven is evoked in "The Other Child" and "A Catholic Childhood." After a few rather unproductive years at school—the only thing Abbs can remember learning efficiently was the little red catechism—he decided (perhaps at the suggestion of the parish priest) to train for the priesthood. He longed to see the statue of the Sacred Heart move so he could claim to have been called by God. This period in his life is captured in the writer's autobiographical prose story "The Vocation" (*Autobiography in Education*, pp. 149–167).

In 1954 he entered a seminary outside Liverpool to prepare to become a Mill Hill missionary father, a vocation that would require twelve years of training. But Abbs was unhappy at the seminary, missing the security of home and much intimidated by the missionary fathers who ran the college. He cried himself to sleep for the first few nights in the long junior dormitory where each boy had a small wooden cell. The days were long. They began with early morning meditation and Mass, and continued with manual labor and then conventional lessons. Most meals were taken in absolute silence or with evangelical texts being read from the rostrum, some of them in Latin. Abbs catches something of this experience in "The White Gull's Beatitude" and the autobiographical "Saint Peter's College for Catholic

Vocations: 1954." When he left a few years later he felt the door of the seminary finally shutting him out forever. Recalling this feeling, he says (personal interview), "I experienced a sense of shame and a deep sense of uncertainty. Who was I without that supporting routine, without the ritual of bells, the daily pattern of prayer?"

Perhaps it is this act—the severing from the fruition of what seemed early to be a religious calling—that spawned Abbs's desire to become a poet. And not just a poet, but a deeply spiritual one. In *Against the Flow*, his 2003 prose work about education, the arts, and postmodern culture, Abbs speaks of this dissolution, wherein the priest, after learning that Abbs has decided to leave the seminary, ushers him out of the building without allowing him to take leave of his classmates. He is not even allowed to tell them he is leaving.

At this time his father made a decision that from Abbs's point of view was the best act in his father's otherwise uneventful life. "He saved me from oblivion," Abbs says (personal interview). His father contacted the principal at what was then called Norwich Technical College, so that his son could continue his studies rather than be confined to the local secondary school at Sheringham. Says Abbs of his father, "It must have taken him considerable courage to make this arrangement, for 'education' was a domain outside of his experience and he was, at root, a shy and uneasy man. It was an act of love for which I never thanked him. But, without doubt, he had secured an exit for me out of what could well have become a dark and repetitive labyrinth for the rest of my life" (personal interview).

After his rather impoverished seminary education—all memorized doctrine without intellectual or imaginative substance—Abbs traveled each day to Norwich, where at sixteen he embarked on his A-levels and discovered for the first time the world of speculative ideas and what he terms the "cosmos of poetry." Inwardly, it was a seismic event, expanding the contours of his world. (Abbs has written about this in "Born Rural Working Class" in his 1996 prose volume, *The Polemics of Imagination.*) Here he discovered with high intoxication some of the poets who were to influence him for the rest of his life: Gerard Manley Hopkins, D. H. Lawrence, Wilfred Owen, and Walt Whitman. Not surprisingly, he also began in a kind of creative fury to write, not only poetry, but also two novels, which he later destroyed. And he read, without any guidance, whatever philosophy he could find, including the *Communist Manifesto.*

It was a heady time. Ignited by the electricity of ideas, theories, and imaginings, he soon came to doubt all the Catholic beliefs with which he had until then completely and passionately identified. This period of mixed emotions—tension, elation, insecurity, self-consciousness, sexual frustration, and inner transformation—is caught in the sonnet "The Loss of Faith."

In 1961 Abbs went to the University of Bristol to study English and philosophy. Here he started a poetry magazine called, significantly, *Vision*, and at the same time he managed to alienate the university's philosophy department by insisting on the supreme value of existentialism. He did not do well academically because he "arrogantly and childishly attacked logical positivism, the orthodoxy of the time, in every question on every written paper" (personal interview).

In 1963 he married Barbara Ann Beazeley. The following year their daughter Annabel was born, and in 1966 they had a second daughter, Miranda. (The marriage would dissolve three decades later, in 2002.) At about this time, Abbs completed a one-year teacher-training course, soon afterward began teaching English, and quickly became excited by the idea of a creative and authentic education. The result, written in two angry weeks, was Abbs's first book, *English for Diversity* (1969), a youthful reaction against the stultifying dullness of the grammar school in which he taught. It was to be the first of a number of books written over the next twenty years, all of them devoted to establishing a poetics of English teaching, wherein the study of literature and the discipline of creative writing were seen as vital interactive forces predicated on the cognitive power of the imagination. The manuals *The Forms of Narrative* and *The Forms of Poetry* (both 1990), which Abbs coauthored with John Richardson, were the practical summation of this

work. All these books were very much part of a general movement to make education more copious and more creative. Abbs was greatly influenced by the work of Marjorie Hourd, Sybil Marshall, and David Holbrook, at the time dominant figures in the field of literary and expressive education.

After teaching for three years in Bristol, Abbs and his family (a son, Theodore, was born in 1973) moved to Wales, where he struggled to become a freelance writer. He also worked as a research fellow at the University of Wales in Aberystwith. The experience of living in a small Welsh village is captured in Abbs's first published volume of poetry, *For Man and Islands*, an uneven collection of poems showing the influences of Ted Hughes, Seamus Heaney, and R. S. Thomas, which came out in 1978. Later he would write an evaluation of the work of Hughes and Thomas, who wrote with an intoxicating and inspiring urgency (see "The Revival of the Mythopoeic" in *The Polemics of Imagination*, pp. 154–166). "I wanted to emulate their sweep, their mythic perception, their dissidence," he says. "I also loved the muscular musicality of their best work, the Anglo-Saxon cadence and alliterative linguistic congestion. All poetry, I thought, had to have this musical element to qualify; without the mesmerizing patterning of sound, it descended to some form of prose, whatever typographical shape it took on the white page" (personal interview).

While living in Wales, Abbs founded *Tract*, an independent journal whose aim was to generate a debate about the state of culture and to promote a fuller recognition of the importance of the arts in education. He wrote the entire first issue himself and called it *The Politics of Imagination.* The title announced the intention of the whole series. He ran the journal single-handedly most of the time, addressing by hand and sticking stamps to a few hundred envelopes each quarter. Although continually running out of money, in the name of freedom he turned down the offer of an Arts Council grant. During its ten-year life, *Tract* ran for thirty issues, each consisting of a monograph, followed often by some poems by such writers as R. S. Thomas and Kathleen Raine, and some trenchant reviews of recent work. While the journal had only questionable influence, it provided a necessary matrix for Abbs's own developing thinking.

In 1977, after five years in the heart of Wales, Abbs left to become lecturer in education at the University of Sussex, England. There he continued to work on the poetics of English and began to extend the work to include the broader concept of aesthetic education. This culminated in his editing the Falmer Press Library of Aesthetic Education, a sequence of books covering each major art form guided by a common coherent philosophy. Derived largely from the philosophical work of Ernst Cassirer and Susanne Langer, the volumes were pitted against many of the practices deriving either from progressivism or a kind of modernism that dismissed the importance of skills and all the artistic works provided by an inherited culture. Key concepts were "expression of" and "initiation into." Also vital to the program of publications was the crucial idea that "some forms of knowing are nonpropositional in nature." Put more positively, the arts were seen as inherently cognitive. According to Abbs, "They mattered because they revealed certain vivifying truths about being human. At their best and most characteristic, they were lanterns to illumine the dark flux of our experience. They were the kinesthetic nonpropositional agents of evolving consciousness" (personal interview).

At the same time as Abbs was working on the poetics of English and the primary value of a broad aesthetic education, he was also writing his own poems. The two activities seemed complementary and one and the same in spirit. *Icons of Time* was an attempt to write an autobiography entirely in sonnets. Seamus Heaney saw the manuscript and suggested various revisions to sharpen the narrative and to make more dramatic the underlying threads. This was followed in 1995 by *Personae*—a determined attempt to move out into the broader culture for connection and inspiration—and in 1997, *Angelic Imagination*. These volumes were followed by *Love After Sappho* (1999), a book once again employing the sonnet form but with the theme confined to love as set by the earliest love poet in Western

culture, and *Viva la Vida* (2005), a volume ranging widely from more intimate autobiographical poems to a long sequence evoking the last years and breakdown of the philosopher Friedrich Nietzsche. The broad aim was to marry, once again, the philosophical and lyrical impulses, and to keep the concerns of poetry open and ambitious. For those who read Abbs's educational work, the connections were no doubt clear and obvious.

But it was the writing of poems that Abbs believed (and still believes) most important. At the age of sixteen it had come upon him as an inner vocation, and that perception never changed. "I was not a priest of the church, but more truly the votary of words," he says (personal interview). "If I felt a poem coming into existence I would drop all other commitments and give myself over to the patient arts of midwifery. Even in committee meetings I would often have the rough lines of a poem attached by a paperclip to the sober agenda."

Since the 1990s, Abbs's concerns have moved from education to take on the work of what is termed New Metaphysical Art. (See "Art Against the Zeitgeist" in *Against the Flow*, pp. 130–152.) At the heart of this movement was the feeling that art had lost its way in a materialist civilization driven by money and technology and that it had to reclaim its former metaphysical role. The movement's manifesto, authored by Abbs, claimed, "Art must begin again the broken conversation with eternity."

Part of this more-encompassing view of art had to "integrate the place of ecology in our understanding of our now perilously insecure planet" (personal interview). With this in mind, in 2002 Abbs edited an international poetry anthology titled *Earth Songs*, which attempted to bring together the contemporary poets in America and Britain who were most sensitive to these pressing matters. As poetry editor of the journal *Resurgence*, a position he has held since 2004, he likewise aims to represent the best new eco-poetry being written. Abbs's preface to *Earth Songs* further outlines the case for a remarriage of consciousness and nature.

During the poet's early years teaching in Wales he had often used autobiography as a learning tool, and it became an important element in his notion of creative pedagogy. If we do not bring our deepest selves to our learning, Abbs believes, nothing can happen. All knowledge carries an unconscious autobiographical charge.

Over the years, this perspective led Abbs to one further pursuit: a kind of archaeology of the self, a study still in progress. The first sign of its existence can be seen in his 1974 prose work, *Autobiography in Education*, while its latest expression appears in a series of articles on the history of the self in the *London Magazine*. The prose has an obvious connection with much of Abbs's poetry. In both he emphasizes continuity and unity, as well as an overarching concern with the symbolization of our lives: the persistent articulation of our elusive humanity. He sees creative life, at its highest, as an Orphic and Socratic conversation down the ages.

ICONS OF TIME

While *Icons of Time* (1991) is Peter Abbs's third poetry collection, the first two—*For Man and Islands* (1978), published when Abbs was twenty-six, and *Songs of a New Taliesin* (1981), when the writer was twenty-nine—are, like the early works of many other prominent writers, derivative. With the appearance of *Icons of Time,* when the poet was forty-nine years old, however, the poems are unmistakably Abbs's own in voice, style, and focus. Subtitled *An Experiment in Autobiography*, the book investigates in a series of sonnets the poet's life story. Abbs's use of the sonnet form is masterful; he compresses ardently felt emotion into a language rich in texture and substance. And while the poems are autobiographical, they are never confessional. Nor does a poem merely reveal an anecdote or memory; the poems are vehicles of discovery wherein Abbs looks at particular details from his life in order to learn who he is, why he has struggled, and what he has struggled with and sometimes been defeated by.

The sonnets are sometimes written in first person, sometimes in third. Often he addresses himself, but in the sections on his father and his marriage, he may directly address the person with whom he is concerned, his father or his spouse. In the sections on his loss of faith, he sometimes addresses God.

Abbs's experiment in autobiography, which persists throughout his oeuvre and quickly becomes no longer an experiment but a proven way of seeing, is exceptionally successful for at least a couple of reasons demonstrated in *Icons of Time*. First, his focus on autobiography is never solipsistic. No other means, Abbs seems to imply, will render discovered truths about human existence. (He writes of this in numerous prose treatises on the necessity of using autobiography and creative writing in education.)

His autobiographical poems are also successful in their ability to simultaneously probe the poet's life and ruffle readers' perception of their own lives in the significant way that learning someone else's story often impacts our own through its parallels, reversals, and omissions.

Finally—and perhaps because of Abbs's deep interest in and knowledge of philosophy—the autobiographical poems suggest and sometimes take on the power of morality tales. Thus, it is the very combination of a focus on the self along with the magnification of the details of a life rendered through the lens of philosophy that contribute to these poems' significance.

The volume is divided into five parts, the first, "Prologue," a kind of philosophical introduction to the rest. Here the poet, a grown man, returns to his childhood landscape to answer one of the big questions: how did I become who I am? As he begins to glimpse the place where he spent his childhood, he feels like a familiar stranger. One is reminded of the close of Thornton Wilder's *Our Town* (1938), when the now-dead Emily, after being allowed to visit scenes of her previous life, can neither resist nor, finally, sustain her scrutiny. "Do any human beings ever realize life while they live it?—every, every minute?" she asks. In his prologue, Abbs announces that he aims through his own scrutiny to do just this.

The book proceeds chronologically, and the reader learns about the poet's premature birth, his first school, and what he remembers of it: "Was I ever here?" he asks rhetorically (p. 21), "Learning God by rote?" Later sent away to St. Peter's College for Catholic Vocations, Abbs describes the loneliness of being away from home: "The blocked homesickness streamed down my face" (p. 23).

Amid the loneliness, however, here Abbs also first tasted the power of language. In "An Undelivered Letter" he writes,

> And I, ham actor, sick to please
> Tried to outstrip the illustrious saints for years,
> Addicted to the dark, violet, heart-shaped words.
>
> (p. 24)

Was the future poet addicted at the time to prayer, or to saying the rosary, or to language itself? If the last, of course, then the addiction was to something living, symbolized not by a bead or pebble, but a seed.

"The Loss of Faith" opens with an epigraph from Nietzsche, whose life and philosophical works Abbs would honor in later poems in later books. The epigraph focuses on the "infinite nothing" of the universe, and the poem itself addresses Abbs's realization that perhaps there is no God after all—or if there is, "God created the world *ex nihilo*. And withdrew. / Then, one day, the nothingness seeped through" (p. 27). These last lines follow Abbs's claim that he has examined the living world, asking of each thing its goal or purpose. His discovery: "The ornate dome of faith cracks and splits" (p. 27).

In these ways, the book's journey continues as one of questioning religious faith and discovering philosophical truths. As Abbs's subsequent work reveals, it's clearly the important journey of his life and work. As if to underscore this point, the book's third section, "Father and Son," begins with an epigraph from G. W. F. Hegel (that a philosopher is quoted is significant in that Abbs has established his movement from a reliance on religious tenets to philosophical ones): "Spirit gains its truth only by finding itself in absolute dismemberment" (p. 29).

The fifteen poems in this section are stunning sonnets. In the first, "Tongue-Tied," the poet addresses his father directly, admonishing whatever invisible law it was ("suicidal note passed down to us") that forced silence between father and son. Was it only the "Numbing contract" of their "rural class" or something about their personalities that necessitated that they "dam" their thoughts and feelings? Perhaps both. But the cause is only part of the equation. In the poem Abbs describes the poisonous atmosphere of their relationship:

> The anger mounting in the throat was swallowed back;
> And swallowed back it became all hell to know
> What the dumb thing was which choked us so.
>
> (p. 31)

Silence and the inability to speak one's heart and mind become paramount in the poems about Abbs's relationship with his father. In "Generations of Farm Hands" he wonders if perhaps the silence, resentment, and anger within his family rose from "being born rural working-class" (p. 34). He sometimes implicates himself, as in "Predicament":

> Whatever truth stirred
> In our shallow lives we hammered down.
> Daily, we slew our aspiring selves and deemed
> It wise.
>
> (p. 35)

But in "Written in Guilt" he admonishes his father for refusing to wholly partake of life: "You looked on, spectral, awkward, half-ashamed, / And craved extinction years before it came" (p. 36).

Section 4 of *Icons of Time* is titled "Affairs of the Heart." Here poems directly address or focus on his wife, and it is clear throughout this section that the relationship between the spouses is turbulent. But Abbs does not simply offer up poems of complaint. Instead, as with the poems about his father, he questions action and motivation. Never welcome is a particularly easy answer; marriage is complicated. In "Ungratified Desire" (p. 50) the speaker complains that his infant child interrupts conjugal consummation.

"Estranged" closes this way: "We argue. We touch. Refrain. Argue again. / Turn to sleep. Toss restlessly. Back to back" (p. 55).

While the speaker and his wife endure a troubled relationship, compared with friends whose "marriages fray and break" (p. 61), they are "Too far gone to see the hell we're in" (p. 57). "Love's Battleground" spells out the specifics of what a failed marriage looks like. "Nothing grafts or roots or grows between us," Abbs writes. "Your eyes open like blades. They're quick to cut. / My mouth is loaded with words. They aim to kill" (p. 58). Yet at the end of the poem the couple kiss "like adolescent kids" in a gesture meant to help balance the pain.

The final section of the book is "Moving Out." Here Abbs retraces his early relationship with God:

> I would
> Preserve the taste of Him until the end
> Of time!

he says of his younger self, a "gawky teenager, … / a cauldron of overheated / Appetites, desirous of martyrdom" (p. 67).

The book's aptly named closing sonnet is "Epilogue Poem: The Apple." Its third stanza reaffirms a key kernel: "I am what I apprehend. / What I have struggled with is who I am" (p. 72). This last sentence is a word-for-word repeat of the last line in the final poem from the opening prologue, "Who I am." Although Abbs has taken us through an essential examination of his life, this repetition implies that he doesn't yet know enough. Here is the concluding tercet:

> The cooling air eddies at my finger tips.
> The apple on this branch is not yet picked,
> Touched by moonlight, before perception split.

PERSONAE AND OTHER SELECTED POEMS

In his preface to *Personae and Other Selected Poems* (1995), Peter Abbs states, "I believe the function of poetry is essentially mythic and healing" (p. xiii). He also says, "Certainly the poems are attempts … to place the truths of the heart in the house of imagination" (p. xiii). And he recognizes, when examining the arc of the poems in the collection, which include selections from his previous three books, that there is

> a recurring movement from autobiography to myth, from the concern with place and identity in *From Man and Islands* to a preoccupation with persona and myth in *Songs of a New Taliesin*, to be repeated a second time in the subsequent movement from *Icons of Time* to *Personae*. There is a distinct pattern here, a movement from the heart to the imagination back to the heart and so on.
>
> (p. xiii)

Here and in other prose acclamations, Abbs's claim is for a poetry that is "closer to our common lives," that is existential in import, while at the same time deeply committed to the importance of skill and artistic form.

The forty-three poems that constitute the entire section of "new" poems in *Personae* are either in the voices of or center upon such well-known figures as the philosophers Peter Abelard, Heraclitus, Socrates, René Descartes, Friedrich Nietzsche, Simone Weil, Ludwig Wittgenstein; the artists Albrecht Dürer, Rembrandt, Artemisia Gentileschi, Vincent Van Gogh, Egon Schiele, Stanley Spencer, Edward Hopper; the writers Catullus, Dante, Emily Dickinson, D. H. Lawrence, Sappho, George Seferis, Rainer Maria Rilke, Virginia Woolf; and biblical and mythical figures such as Orpheus, Medusa, Persephone, Isaac, Icarus, Noah, Ophelia. This section of the book is divided into subsections: (1) It Begins, (2) The Philosopher Investigates, (3) The Painter's Testimony, (4) The Poet Speaks, (5) Of Love and Sexuality, (6) Of Depression, Estrangement, and Death, (7) Of Transformation and Renewal, and (8) Coda.

In a review of *Personae*, the American poet and critic Rebecca Seiferle notes that Abbs's interest is the intersection of the personal with both the historical and the mythic. Seiferle sees Abbs as a poet of "the new paradigm," one who uses myth "not merely as a postmodernist twitch or to give weight to personal trivia but as an awakening to a new view of reality and to the earth itself" (online). Unlike the poets Eleanor Wilner and Sylvia Plath, both of whom, according to Seiferle, use myth in their work to house personal feeling, Abbs uses it as a trajectory to move from the personal or mythic outward into the world. Such a trajectory is a healing motion of the self, and the poems are vehicles in which an essential depth of being is examined and becomes a means for the psyche—through altered perception grounded in imagination—to reenter the world anew.

Seiferle's admiration for Abbs is profound: "Abbs shoulders the weight of our culture as if it were a marble head unearthed in an ancient ruin." Poetry is not a hobby; it's a powerful means through which human beings can heal. "Abbs is a poet of hope," Seiferle claims, "of hope cast in the form of uncertainty."

Kathleen Raine, in her review of the collection, calls Abbs "a poet of the raven" (p. 52). She means to differentiate the raven in the story of Noah from the dove, which brings back a literal sign that land is nearby. The dove is the dove of comfort. But before Noah sent out the dove, he sent a raven, whose experience Abbs renders in his poem "In Defence of the Raven." In the poem, Abbs reminds us that while we should "cherish the dove" (p. 172), we must also remember the raven, symbol of "Far horizons, black holes, exploded nova stars; / [...] the curved edge of God's / Incommensurable mind" (p. 172). Thus, in seeing Abbs as a poet of the raven, Raine understands the poet's existentialist view, a man who turned away from formal religion to adopt the Socratic spirit, turning the unanswered question into the very means of questing.

Raine praises Peter Abbs for his powerful facility with language, the culturally rich context within which he sets his poems, and "his commitment to the most courageous and exacting human values" (p. 53). Claiming Abbs's poems in *Personae* as "some of the finest poems written by any poet of [his] generation" (p. 52), Raine concludes her review by remarking that Abbs is "one of the few poets whose work is not 'promise' but hard-won, well-earned maturity" (p. 53).

Many of the new poems of *Personae* are in the voices of such figures as Descartes, Heraclitus, Van Gogh, and the like—individuals who were singularly *alone* in their genius. "Artists are the broken vessels of their age" (p. 128), Abbs has Vincent Van Gogh say in "Letter to Theo from His Brother: June 1889." The utterance is hallmark Abbs. Artists and philosophers are distinct personages in that they remain observers of their experiences and are thereby separate from other people. Hence, there is always an element of existential loneliness within them. We see this in another poem about a painter, "The Loneliness of Edward Hopper." In his own voice rather than Hopper's, Abbs examines one after another of the artist's works, searching for the man within the images. At the close of the poem he imagines the painter executing a 1915 painting of the sea: "I sense the artist / In that cliff face of 1915, gaunt and arrogant—." The sea cannot be captured on canvas, acknowledges the poet, not truly.

It surges over the shingle bank, to sob
In seaweed in the dripping dark. Unseen.
Almost ungrasped. Paint substantiates the loss.

(p. 130)

Always the artist "substantiates the loss." And Abbs, himself an artist of language, reminds us of this, substantiating losses through language.

The poems in section 5, "Of Love and Sexuality," demonstrate Abbs's ability to write poems of great sensuality. He may be a poet of the raven, but there is a calming gentleness in his poems about love and sex. One of the most sensual is the sonnet "Stanley Spencer's Beatitude," in which Abbs describes an elderly couple making love.

The final poem in the collection, "New Constellations" (p. 174), another sonnet, is a reminder of Abbs's reverence for autobiography as a way of releasing and realizing the self. We are creatures of story, Abbs implies, and the more closely we examine our own histories, as well as those of others (hence, all those persona poems), the deeper we will evolve and integrate. The poem opens: "You do not begin alone; rather, you extend / A narrative" (p. 174). And closes: "The past, which never truly was, returns again" (p. 174). Why wasn't the past ever truly the past, one wonders. Is it because the past always integrates itself within the present? It is never a separate conveyance. Nor is it able to be distinguished from one's memories and perceptions.

ANGELIC IMAGINATION

Abbs selects as the epigraph to *Angelic Imagination: New Poems 1994–1996* (1997) a quotation from Ernst Cassirer, the German philosopher responsible for introducing during the first half of the twentieth century the idea of philosophical idealism: "The highest objective truth that is accessible to the spirit is ultimately the form of its own activity" (p. 3).

It is indeed fitting that sixteen of the book's mere twenty-three poems—in other words, the bulk of the collection, all of those poems in the main section of poems in *Angelic Imagination*—are collected under the heading "New Constellations," which is the title of the final poem in Abbs's previous poetry collection, *Personae*.

In his preface to *Angelic Imagination*, Abbs says, "The aim of a poem is to define our predicament and, beyond that, to find sources of hope, creativity, and consolation" (p. 7). The collection is divided into two sections. The first, "New Constellations," includes poems that attempt to "create anew" various artistic endeavors by others—poems, paintings, and sculpture. The second part, "In Memoriam," is more personal, and, Abbs says in the preface, he hopes these poems will help "to release energies … which bear upon our common … humanity" (p. 7).

Bookending the collection are a prologue and an epilogue, both of which center upon the definition of the Word, used in the biblical sense. This is fitting, considering this poet's continual celebration of and concentration on the importance of the authentic use of language, as well as his own transformation from a boy enthused by the possibilities of religion into a man anointed by the intensely spiritual force inherent in a primacy of words.

The poems in section 1, "New Constellations," focus on the mythical Prometheus, the painters Edvard Munch, Pierre Bonnard, and Jan Vermeer, and the philosophers Wittgenstein and Nietzsche. Additionally, he transforms poems (as opposed to creating straightforward translations) by Paul Celan, Sappho, and Rilke.

"Artist's Manifesto," an ars poetica, implies that in order to set the imagination free the artist must "[detonate] his mind to let in God's" (p. 23). This necessity of letting go of control is paramount in Abbs's philosophy of creativity. The very brief poem closes this way:

Oh!—to set the imagination free

In the hard crucible of nature, to begin
To murder fate, to let the incandescent angel in!

(p. 23)

The first poem in the book's second section, "In Memoriam: A Poem in Five Movements," is also the title poem of the entire volume. Dedicated to a nine-year-old child, Kate Cooper, whose death from cancer is mourned, the poem praises the girl's courage to create music (she plays original compositions on a recorder) as if to ward off death. Throughout the five "movements" of the poem, Abbs evokes the mythical Orpheus. Like him, this girl is transcendent: "she is Orpheus whose change / of key is magical / and constant" (p. 34).

Other poems in this section are also elegiac. In "Intimations of Mortality" (p. 37), Abbs imagines himself no longer alive in a late November landscape in which "the first frosts are cleansing" the earth. The "frosted lawn is a beautiful / Altar cloth" not intended for a god. Instead there is the poignant clarity of nature alone: "The pond is a sheet of glass; / It returns the sky. Immaculate. Blue. Silent. Vast" (p. 37).

LOVE AFTER SAPPHO

Love After Sappho (1999), whose eight sections include a prologue and a coda, examines the many kinds and manifestations of love. Here are poems that take into account the earth and the damage human beings have done to it—"A Violent Cleansing" (p. 12), for example—but also the damage we humans do to ourselves by turning our backs on the natural world and polluting it, even with the noises that betray silence (for example, "At Cuckmere Estuary," p. 13). What does love mean in its most spiritual sense? We cannot explain away what we have done and continue to do. "There are no reasons left" (p. 13).

But it is not only subject matter that makes this book so powerful. Apparent too is Abbs's skill at traditional form: all the poems in the book are either full-fledged sonnets or they use this traditional form as their structural base, metrically and emotively, as well as intellectually. Even the book's structure is itself built like a sonnet, its opening sections introducing the complications of love, its middle sections intensifying such complication until a turn is introduced, leading to a closing section that has the feel of resolution, although not solution (for love, after all, is not a commodity that can be solved or even put to rest).

Abbs's paramount belief that the power of poetry pivots and relies upon autobiography is obvious throughout his work. And although an expert craftsman of the poetic arts, he never sacrifices message for music, but neither does he value the former over the latter. Instead, he waits until there is a powerful melding of the two before allowing a poem to be published.

One of the strongest sequences in the volume is contained in "Last Rites," a series of poems about Abbs's mother's dying. He proves here, as he did in his third poetry collection, *Icons of Time*, that poetry's purpose is in part to speak the difficult, sometimes unspeakable, emotions. As in "Requiescat in Pace," his elegy for his father in *Icons of Time*, in which he claims poetry as the means to "break and bear the silence" (p. 43) between son and father, so too the present sequence reveals the unpleasant yet important feelings of an adult child shouldering the close presence of a dying parent. In such poems Abbs is able to face the depths of what it means to be both an individual and a member of a family. He refuses to look away and instead stays by his dying mother's bedside, both as mourning son and poet of witness.

Not only a series of sonnet-like elegies to his mother, the poems in this section of the book demonstrate again Abbs's reliance on poetry to speak for the man who, in the case of his relationship with his parents, was unable to speak in situ those thoughts he felt an urgency to deliver.

Other sections of the book examine love in a variety of manifestations—especially between spouses or lovers—but no easy summation is presented. Throughout Abbs demonstrates a willingness to expose details of his own life in order to bring forth possible metaphysical truths.

Along with love poems written for his life partner (*Love After Sappho* is the first of Abbs's volumes to be dedicated to "D"), the book contains poems that acknowledge the pain associated with the end of marriage. The section "Post-Modern Love" describes the splitting apart of a couple. "Nothing's secure," Abbs writes in "A Bleeding Wreath," whose final couplet reads "And there are no gods left to lay a bleeding wreath / For the sundering of marriage—suddenness of death" (p. 6).

The fourth section of the collection is titled "Love's Labor," and its eleven poems illuminate the power of romantic love. "Who said there could be no more love poetry?" Abbs asks rhetorically in "Incomparable Beauty."

> For each day some-one, somewhere,
> Falls into love's vortex. Is half dismembered,
>
> Half encompassed there.
>
> (p. 25)

In "Let Us Live and Love," which is written in the spirit of and after a poem by the Latin poet Catullus, Abbs demonstrates his ability to write with humor. Here are the poem's last seven lines:

> Then let us mock tomorrow's pen-pushers,
>
> Academics, smart-arse critics
> Who'll freeze our lust in lists and figures.
> How the ticker tape reels from their lips!
> Jargon. Acronyms. Facts. Classificatory lists:
>
> *Catullus, Gaius, Valerius. Etcetera. Circa. Idem.*
> *Master of iambics.* Fuck the lot of them!
>
> (p. 27)

The book's fifth and sixth sections, "The Dance of Syllables" and "Coda," celebrate once again the exaltation of language.

Today I hear of a living language
where *poem* and *breath*
are one and the same.

(p. 66)

Such a declaration epitomizes Abbs's earnest belief regarding the link between life and the language of poetry.

Here once again we observe a poet whose lyric gifts match his philosophical beliefs about the importance of creativity and the nature of humanity. So many of us never consider what it means to be human, nor do we take responsibility for our relationships. Although not a manifesto, *Love After Sappho* calls us to do both.

VIVA LA VIDA

Like Abbs's previous work, the poems in *Viva la Vida* (2005) are masterful in style and substance, their subjects autobiographical or biographical. An entire section is devoted to Nietzsche, and there are individual poems in the second section of the book, "Ancestor Worship," that explore the lives of mythical figures, artists, and philosophers.

In "Child of Pisces," the book's first section, we again encounter the poet-speaker preoccupied with the issues, raised in Abbs's earlier collections, of the difficulties of his childhood: his father's silence, the narrow confines of his Catholic schooling. But these confinements are balanced against his present understanding of the power of beauty and truth in their ability to transcend suffering.

While the book's second section, "Ancestral Worship," honors the art and philosophy found in the works or life of such figures as Odysseus, Minerva, Prometheus, Sappho, Saint Augustine, Rumi, Dante, William Turner, Gerard Manley Hopkins, Franz Kafka, Frida Kahlo, Bonnard, and others, its third section, "Viva la Vida," is made up entirely of love poems. Among these palpably powerful pieces is the opening poem of the section, "Blowing Dandelion Clocks at Seaford Head." Here "at / The high white edge, precarious" as new love, the speaker and his lover "[puff] ephemeral seeds, black // Specks of hope

into the amorphous blue" (p. 49). In this poem, as in much of Abbs's work, the metrically sound, rhyming tercets are handled with such skill as to be only secondarily noticed. Evidenced throughout the collection, the music of language—as demonstrated in diction and syntax—is an important condition of Abbs's art.

All eleven poems in the fourth section, "Ecce Homo: On Nietzsche's Madness," concern the final years and growing madness and anguish of the philosopher. The sequence opens with a sonnet describing Nietzsche's self-imposed hermitage and closes with a description of his funeral. This is not the first time that Abbs has used this philosopher in his poetry. There are important parallels between the two men. Both experienced a loss of faith. For Abbs, poetry became the healthful passage into self and spirit. Religion brought forth "Dead words / In the throat" ("Child of Pisces," p. 4), while language in its purest means had the power to change not only the poet but also the world, which it "Raised up, articulate, edged, / Sheer" ("Child of Pisces," p. 5).

It is the fifth and final section, "Ars Poetica," that reveals as it illustrates through example Abbs's treatise on the purpose of poetry. In evidence again is the poet's skill at using economy of form to contain powerful emotion. Built with the anaphora "It will," the sixteen-line poem accumulates power as it lists those tasks the undefined "it" of the poem will accomplish. Moving from the external world that includes whales, gulls, skylarks, and frogs, to the human-made one where dictionaries exist alongside the "spontaneous ramblings of children," Abbs inserts into the poem more abstract phenomena such as silence and even death. But the poem closes with an insistence that even as it is "born in blood, [rises] in estrangement, [and climaxes] in breath," whatever the "it" is "will remain in quest" (p. 93).

Throughout this seventh volume of poetry Abbs moves, section by section, as if through the movements of a symphony beginning with the trauma of existence and intensifying toward the affirmation of love. Even in the poems about suffering, Abbs finds *le mot juste* with which to describe experience so that we may join him in intimate understanding of the possibilities of transformation. For example, in "The White Gull's Beatitude," a poem about Abbs's life as one of the "pale seminary boys" at St. Peter's School for Catholic Vocations, the young Abbs spots a white gull "wheeling above … yelping his beatitude // In the terror of his freedom" (p. 12), and Abbs longs to be like the creature. "Yet I lacked his impetuosity," Abbs says.

> I stayed on
>
> Aping the mumbling priests, a poor ventriloquist trying to conform.
> Daily I mouthed the pallid prayers, lisped the theology by rote,
> The bleached abstractions sticking like fish-bones in my throat.
>
> (p. 12)

Notice the assonance in "poor," "rote," and "bones" in the above lines, as well as the precise, image-bearing diction in the following: the gulls "wheel" and "yelp," the young Abbs "apes" the priests who "mumble" only himself to become "a poor ventriloquist" who "lisps pallid" prayers that are nothing more than "bleached" abstractions that "stick" in the "throat" of the struggling boy like "fish-bones." The language here is clear and mostly single-syllabled, a kind of Anglo-Saxon outburst, authentic and blunt.

Another of Abbs's talents in evidence in the volume, as in all his collections, is the ability to successfully mix abstract language with concrete image. Perhaps this is the gift of the philosopher in him, the wish to explain the unexplainable in whatever language he can find. But image alone cannot suffice; he must bring the philosophical world with its abstract intellectual expressions together with the emotional world and its detailed narratives—a mind-body phenomenon. A good example of this mixing is demonstrated in "Other Gifts," in its entirety below:

> From my father the pang of existence.
> Habitual unease. Guilt before appetite.
> The long silence.
>
> From my mother the iron junta of appearance.

> The will to advance. Obsequious
> Desire to please.
>
> From the North Sea the weather of possibility.
> Clear horizons. The imperative of poetry.
> A salt asperity.
>
> From the Oak Woods the press and curve
> Of things. Incomparable whiteness of water lily.
> The perfect globe of figs.
>
> From the Catholic Church the acid of doubt.
> Magic of incantation. Anodyne of prayer.
> The terrible seeking out.
>
> (p. 15)

Besides this mixing of abstract and concrete diction, here too is evidence of Abbs's allegiance to traditional verse and his understanding of its aural power: the stanzas' anaphoric opening stanza gestures ("From … / From … / From …") combined with the final stanza's pure rhymes of "doubt" with "out," which pull the poem's disparate visual images together through the interplay of sound repetitions.

In *Viva la Vida*, as in other volumes, Abbs demonstrates his skill at combing the depths of autobiography and coming forth with wisdom useful not only to the poet himself but to all of us. Similarly, he is able to inhabit the spirit of other personae and locate truths applicable to our lives and times, continually confronting our existential predicament.

In all Abbs's work, the poet seems to have adopted Robert Frost's notion that in a well-organized book of, say, twenty-four poems, the twenty-fifth is the book itself. Thus, the order of poems is as significant as the order of lines within a poem. Assuming we read the book from first poem to last, we are taken on a journey. And, in Abbs's case, that journey is often from confinement toward release.

THE FLOWERING OF FLINT

In his foreword to this eighth collection, *The Flowering of Flint: Selected Poems* (2007), Abbs claims that the primary task of poetry is "to break, blow, burn and make us new," as well as "to perplex and unsettle, to keep us somewhat unstable and open to change" (p. xiii). For this 2007 volume, Abbs not only selected poems from his previous books, but he removed those poems he no longer believed successful. Because the new poems at the end of the retrospective number only seven, the poet's progress on his aesthetic journey cannot be altogether appreciated. He says of these poems that he hopes they demonstrate that he is "not settling down, but keeping faith with the ineffable spirit of life itself" (p. xiii).

It is interesting to note that in the "selected" part of the book, Abbs chose to include only five poems from his first collection, *For Man and Islands* (1978), and from his second, *Songs of a New Taliesin* (1981), only two. The selections from later books are, understandably, in greater numbers, although from *Viva la Vida* (2005), Abbs chose poems from only two of the five sections, "Child of Pisces" and "Ecce Homo: On Nietzsche's Madness," along with the single poem "Ars Poetica" from the volume's final section, "The Living Word."

Of the new poems, perhaps most exciting is the poet's exultation of language itself, that very savior of the man whose spirit was quashed by religion and borne up by words in their essential and relevant power. In "Learning How Not to Live," for example, he asks, "What did I learn at school but the grammar of schism?" (p. 165). He and his fellow students

sat with our eyes down and learnt the sentence of stasis—
As though the querulous

Questions of life had to be always excised.

(p. 165)

Abbs has long insisted that his early education was a hindrance to substantial learning, because it was devoid of an awareness of self. (For much of his adult life Abbs would write about the nature and importance of the study of the self: the crucial significance of the examined life, the need for a reflective existence.)

Beginning in the mid-2000s, Abbs and his life partner, Lisa Dart, began spending part of each year on Paros, a Greek island, where they became affiliated with the Aegean Center for the Fine Arts, directed by John Pack, the director of the Aegean Center and a photographer with whom Abbs collaborated for the book *The Greater Journey* (2008), which features Pack's photographs and Abbs's poems. Among the new poems in *The Flowering of Flint* is a poem written for John Pack; at the close of "Witnessing," Abbs speaks of the way in which a man can leave his own country and find a deeper sense of belonging by connecting to a much older and more encompassing tradition. Characteristically, the emphasis is on each person's being part of a vast symbolic continuum:

It's why I left my home

And came to this ancient burial ground, seeking what I didn't know:
Christos Anestis! A myth for being here; the words for saying so.

(p. 166)

The discovery of Greece has added a further dimension to Peter Abbs's later poetry. He has written a number of creative versions— "transformations"—from modern Greek poets such as Constantine Cavafy, Angelos Sikelianos, George Seferis, and Nikos Gatsos.

In one way or another all these new poems in the book celebrate an earnest joy in the power of language: "Listen to the way words fall" (p. 170), Abbs writes in "The Way." And the title of the section's final poem is "Finding Words" (pp. 171–172).

Nor is it unusual for a book of Peter Abbs's poetry to pay close attention to the natural world. Thus, in *The Flowering of Flint* the landscape is prominent: the Norfolk coast of his childhood, the chalk hills of Sussex, the Aegean Sea of Paros. Just before the book's publication, Abbs edited *Earth Songs,* an anthology of eco-poetry, not a surprising undertaking for a man who has written extensively in prose on ecological issues. Such prose aside, it is clear throughout his poetry that the undisturbed natural world is honored and cherished by this poet. One need only look at the table of contents of this and others of his books to note the prominence of landscape.

VOYAGING OUT

All but the first two previous collections of poetry by Abbs had been divided into five sections; neither the first, *For Man and Islands*, nor the second, *Songs of a New Taliesin*, a chapbook, is divided at all. Thus, *Voyaging Out* (2009), which is divided into only two sections, suggests thereby a significant change for the poet. Of the thirty-six poems in the volume, thirty-three comprise the book's first section, "Peregrinations"; the other three, which Abbs calls "transformations" (rather than translations) after his eponymous section title, actually consist of twenty-one individual poems collected under three distinct titles, the first written "after" Rumi; the second, Dante; and the third, Rilke.

Abbs's concerns in the volume remain unchanged from those apparent in previous books: troubling childhood experiences, the nature of love and spirit, aesthetic appreciation, and the power of authentic language. As before, he achieves these thematic explorations both directly in autobiographical poems and less directly in poems about the lives of others, especially visual artists and philosophers.

The volume's revealing title, *Voyaging Out*, suggests the nature of the explorations: journeys both into the outer landscapes of place and the inner landscapes of the human, including that most inward investigation into the poet's own heart and mind. The book's opening poem, "Self Portrait," evidences this voyage wherein "endings / are beginnings, where the country of despair / borders the frontier of possibility" (p. 3).

As obviously and strongly in this book as anywhere in his previous collections, Abbs shows himself as a spiritually invested writer. His quest remains ultimately the same one voiced in his earliest poems, as expressed in these lines that first appeared in *For Man and Islands* and were reprinted in *The Flowering of Flint*:

> Where would you lead
> me, and what
> would you have of
> me, restless

and enigmatic
spirit?

(p. 3)

In the present volume, his struggle to live a spiritually authentic life is no less obvious. But it is perhaps the emphasis on the uplifting power of the spirit that permeates *Voyaging Out*. Taking himself to task, as it were, Abbs writes in one of his "transformations" of a poem by Rumi,

> Today you wake anxious, vexed by small things;
> even so, do not go upstairs to your study
> to shuffle your papers—
>
> or to make notes from someone else's notes
> from someone else's … One thing we know:
> this morning will not return—
>
> so why not take down the lute from the wall,
> open the window
> and pluck some new chords.
>
> There are a thousand ways of kissing the ground.

(p. 43)

Exemplary of the volume, this poem delineates the spiritual place Abbs has reached by the time of the book's publication. The poems no longer wallow in struggle to understand the past, but neither do they exude estrangement from the life of the spirit. As Abbs has traversed the often difficult terrain of the examined life, he has found himself as if on a pinnacle. The climb was sometimes treacherous, but he kept on, never turning away from the darkness but instead embracing the mystery even when that mystery proved painful and unfulfilling. And it is no mistake that Abbs makes this epiphanic journey in poetry. "I want my words to emulate the thing itself" (p. 29), he writes in "A Brief Lesson on Poetry"—evidence that this poet never relaxes his scrutiny of all aspects of his vocation.

The reviewer Jeremy Hooker points out that Abbs's "other" life as a polemicist (he has been a prolific prose writer on issues of culture and education and the importance of autobiography) sometimes shows itself in his poetry. Perhaps this is understandable for a man who seemingly never finishes his searing search for answers to the largest metaphysical questions. The reviewer Craig Jordan-Baker sums up Peter Abbs's work as "part pastoral, part bardic, thoughtfully sculpted, vitally felt" (p. 48). Jordan-Baker also—and rightly— suggests that Abbs's style is "direct, declarative and weighed toward the bold existential significance of its images and themes" (p. 48). This reviewer's witty summation of the book may be seen as true for this poet's entire poetic legacy thus far: "Overall, this is a volume both exciting and contemplative, forward-looking and backward-nodding, peregrinating and transforming" (p. 48).

Perhaps the best way to get a sense of the kerneled essence of the intense and intentional work of Peter Abbs is to hear from the poet himself, in an interview with Robert Graham:

> My hope is that we may be able to house ourselves more fully in our imagination so that we can relate creatively to the historical continuum and that we feel a sense of solidarity with that, not alienation. Then we can find our own story within that larger collection of stories. In a similar way, I would hope that we can place ourselves imaginatively inside Nature and see it as part of us and us as part of it, reflecting it back at a higher level. I'm talking about the deep reclamation of historical and ecological dimensions in the arts, in education and in society at large.
>
> *(The Polemics of Imagination, p. 114)*

Selected Bibliography

WORKS OF PETER ABBS

Poetry

For Man and Islands. Shropshire, U.K.: Tern Press, 1978.

Songs of a New Taliesin. Shropshire, U.K.: Tern Press, 1981.

Icons of Time: An Experiment in Autobiography. Lewes, U.K.: Gryphon Press, 1991.

Personae and Other Selected Poems. London: Skoob Books, 1995.

Angelic Imagination: New Poems 1994–1996. Lewes, U.K.: Gryphon Press, 1997.

Love After Sappho. London: Halfacrown Books, 1999.

Selected Poems. London: Halfacrown Books, 2002.

Viva la Vida. Cambridge, U.K.: Salt Publishing, 2005.

The Flowering of Flint: Selected Poems. Cambridge, U.K.: Salt Publishing, 2007.

The Greater Journey. With the photographer John Pack. Paros: Aegean Center, 2008. (The entire book is available online at http://www.greaterjourney.org/the_journey.html.)

Voyaging Out. Cambridge, U.K.: Salt Publishing, 2009.

Guides and Anthology

The Forms of Poetry: A Practical Guide. With John Richardson. Cambridge, U.K.: Cambridge University Press, 1990.

The Forms of Narrative: A Practical Guide. With John Richardson. Cambridge, U.K.: Cambridge University Press, 1990.

Earth Songs: A "Resurgence" Anthology of Contemporary Eco-Poetry. Dartington, U.K.: Green Books, 2002.

Prose Books on the Theory of English

English for Diversity. London: Heinemann, 1969.

Root and Blossom: The Philosophy, Practice, and Politics of English Teaching. London: Heinemann, 1976.

English within the Arts. London: Hodder & Stoughton, 1982.

Prose Works on Culture, the Arts, and Education

Autobiography in Education. London: Heinemann, 1974.

Proposal for a New College. With Graham Carey. London: Heinemann, 1972.

Reclamations: Essays on Culture, Mass-Culture, and the Curriculum. London: Heinemann, 1979.

A Is for Aesthetic: Essays on Creative and Aesthetic Education. London: Falmer Press, 1988.

The Educational Imperative: A Defence of Socratic and Aesthetic Learning. London: Falmer Press, 1994.

The Polemics of Imagination: Selected Essays on Art, Culture, and Society. London: Skoob Books, 1996.

Against the Flow: Education, the Arts, and Postmodern Culture. London: RoutledgeFalmer, 2003.

Edited Symposia on the Arts

The Black Rainbow: Essays on the Present Breakdown of Culture. London: Heinemann, 1975.

Living Powers: The Arts in Education. London: Falmer Press, 1987.

The Symbolic Order: A Contemporary Reader on the Arts Debate. London: Falmer Press, 1989.

BIOGRAPHICAL AND CRITICAL STUDIES

Adams, Anna. "*Viva la Vida* by Peter Abbs." *Temenos Review,* no. 10:233–238 (2007). (Review.)

Buckner, Adrian. "Jewels of Consciousness." *London Magazine,* October–November 2002, p. 114. (Review of *Selected Poems.*)

Burns, Richard. "Love and Guilt Tracked Through Snow." *Independent*, April 3, 1991. (Review of *Icons of Time*.)

Graham, Robert. http://www.peterabbs.co.uk/about.shtml.

Hooker, Jeremy. "Song at the Hazardous Edge." *Resurgence,* no. 257:68 (November–December 2009). (Review of *Voyaging Out*.)

Jordan-Baker, Craig. "A Feverish Call to Arms." *Urthona*, no. 27:48 (summer 2010). (Review of *Voyaging Out*.)

McCarthy, Patricia. "Navigating Darkness." *Agenda* 37, no. 4:91–94 (spring–summer 2000). (Review of *Love After Sappho*.)

Oxley, William. "*Viva la Vida*." *Sofia* 76:21 (March 2006). (Review.)

Padmacandra. "*Viva la Vida*." *Urthona,* no 25:46 (summer 2008). (Review.)

Peschiera, Raul. "In Case You Missed It: *Love After Sappho* by Peter Abbs." *Resurgence,* no. 202:61 (September–October 2000). (Review.)

Raine, Kathleen. "'Your clumsy silent hands seem almost eloquent.'" *Resurgence,* no. 171:52–53 (July–August 1995). (Review of *Personae and Other Selected Poems*.)

Rice, Nicky. "What I Have Struggled with Is Who I Am." *Resurgence*, no. 150:53 (March-April 1992). (Review of *Icons of Time*.)

Seiferle, Rebecca. "*Personae and Other Selected Poems* by Peter Abbs." *Drunken Boat* (summer 2000), http://www.thedrunkenboat.com/abbs.htm. (Review.)

Tredell, Nicolas. "Voicing the Silence." *PN Review150* 29, no. 4:76 (March–April 2003). (Review of *Selected Poems*.)

BRIAN ALDISS

(1925—)

Patrick A. Smith

BY THE EARLY 1940s, Brian Aldiss had been transformed from a mischievous boy in northern England's boarding schools to a seasoned soldier in World War II. "Give a young man a gun, train him to shoot, dress him in whatever uniform, put him among similar young men, and he becomes that archetypal figure, *the soldier*," Aldiss writes with more than a little cynical detachment in his 1998 memoir *The Twinkling of an Eye* (p. 147). Still, his childhood provided enough magic, wonder, and turmoil to fuel a career as a writer and editor (many of the volumes published with his friend and fellow science fiction writer Harry Harrison) spanning roughly six decades and nearly one hundred books. Aldiss' reputation in America has been made more from word-of-mouth recommendations of science fiction aficionados than from the attention of casual readers, but the wide-ranging author has earned mention in his native Britain alongside Isaac Asimov, Ray Bradbury, and Arthur C. Clarke as the standard-bearers for twentieth-century science fiction.

BIOGRAPHY OF A BIBLIOPHILE

Brian Wilson Aldiss was born in 1925 in East Dereham, England, to Stanley Aldiss, a manager in the family business, and Elizabeth May Wilson Aldiss. Young Brian would be joined six years later by a sister, Elizabeth. The family lived above H. H. Aldiss and Sons, a department store founded by Brian's grandfather, Harry Hilyard. The first few years of Brian's life framed the sort of childhood that Americans often associate with late-Victorian English towns: long days at the town's fair, organ music drifting through the windows of the upstairs apartment, languid days playing in the streets during a time of relative peace after the grim specter of World War I (in which his father had fought) just a decade before. That pastoral existence would be all too brief for the boy, who would be sent to various of the region's boarding schools and learn early the importance of independence and imagination.

Indeed, beneath the tidy Norfolk exterior lay a disquieting reality that Brian Aldiss would carry with him throughout his adult life, including the guilt that his mother felt at having lost a daughter before Brian's birth and his mother's subsequent smothering attention, as well as the creeping imminence of a war that he would be charged to fight before his eighteenth birthday. Perhaps most unsettling to the boy, though, was the distance and stubborn silence of a father who would never support Brian's dreams of becoming a writer, wishing instead for him to come along in the family business. "When I told my father that I was thinking of throwing up my job and becoming a writer, he was horrified. His life experience had taught him to cling to what was," Aldiss writes. "Whereas my life experience had taught me that better things were round the corner" (*Hell's Cartographers,* p. 182).

Early separation from the family would affect Aldiss a great deal, and the author recalls those years with a mixture of nostalgia and dismay, likening the experience to that of Pip in Charles Dickens' *Great Expectations*: "I was sent ... to be educated and to become a little gentleman. ... Thousands of English boys endured and still endure the public school system; most of them survive in some way or other" (*Hell's Cartographers,* p. 185). In 1933, Stanley Aldiss sold his share of the business to a brother and moved the family to the seaside town of Gorleston-on-Sea, one of the last idyllic memories for Aldiss; after another move in 1939, this time to Devon, Aldiss would enroll in the West Buckland School, which provided a welcome respite from his burgeoning teen angst.

The budding artist became popular with his peers for his outgoing personality and his story-telling antics. Along with an active social life, Aldiss began to grow intellectually, reading the work that would inspire him later: the French novelist Émile Zola, whose naturalist fiction of the French working classes influenced both British and American writers for a period of twenty or so years at the end of the nineteenth century; the British science fiction deity H. G. Wells, whose *Time Machine* (1895) and *The War of the Worlds* (1898) were staples among young men of the time; and the stories published by John W. Campbell, the vaunted editor of *Astounding* magazine who discovered many of the great science fiction writers of the first half of the twentieth century. The stories Aldiss wrote in secret and later told to his classmates reflect his burgeoning sexuality—likely the salacious concerns of adolescence that any reader would recognize in the juvenilia of a favorite writer—and his keeping those works from the prying eyes of the headmaster while entertaining his peers no doubt cultivated the playfulness and inventiveness that later came to characterize Aldiss' science fiction.

In 1943, Aldiss and countless other young men would be conscripted into the British Army to fight the ongoing war. For the next four years, he would serve with the Royal Signals regiment in the Far East, entranced by the beauty and exoticism of India, Burma, Sumatra, and Hong Kong and content with the departure from daily life in England. At the same time, Aldiss was displeased at keeping in abeyance his passion for reading and writing. "Happily, the whole family drama, the mysteries and unspoken things, were left behind while I was in India," Aldiss recalls in *The Twinkling of an Eye*. "There we could stand up and be men. We said goodbye not only to England and family, but—it proved almost the harder thing—to books, which are practically another life" (p. 146). Aldiss looks back on his service with the same sort of nostalgia and a strong sense of place that prompted his fellow science fiction writer Arthur C. Clarke to spend his last half century in Sri Lanka. (Those war experiences are related later in Aldiss' mainstream fiction, as well, particularly in the semiautobiographical efforts in the Horatio Stubbs trilogy—*The Hand-Reared Boy* [1970], *A Soldier Erect* [1971], and *A Rude Awakening* [1978], which became causes célèbres in Britain for their frank sexuality.)

During an especially bleak time in his service in Burma, Aldiss discovered the British science fiction writer Olaf Stapledon's *Last and First Men*, a novel published in 1931 and still read today, along with its companion piece, *Star Maker* (1937), as cornerstones of modern science fiction in Britain. Those novels would influence all of Aldiss' own early work in the genre. After leaving the army, Aldiss found himself at loose ends; in the short term a bothersome prospect, though in hindsight a break from the drudgery of the workaday world was the best thing that could have happened to a young veteran—he had not yet turned twenty-one—looking to make his mark in the world. "When I came back from the Far East after four years, I was no longer an adolescent, but a seasoned man," Aldiss recalled in a 2004 interview with John C. Tibbetts. "I didn't fit into anything. ... I was broke and life was awful. I felt very estranged from it all" (p. 249). Aldiss eventually found work in Sanders & Co., an Oxford bookstore; around the same time, he married Olive Fortescue.

His proximity to books allowed Aldiss to immerse himself even further in the life of the mind (he tells the story with great relish in the 1990 memoir *Bury My Heart at W. H. Smith's*). An autodidact with an insatiable intellect, Aldiss read widely outside fiction, particularly in the sciences and philosophy; for the first time, he took seriously the idea of one day becoming a professional writer. The tranquil lifestyle in the bookstore agreed with him, and in 1954, he began writing autobiographical pieces for the *Bookseller*, a trade magazine. That same year, he made his first science fiction sale, a short story titled "Criminal Record," published in the magazine *Science Fantasy*. Finally, Aldiss was being paid to write the kinds of stories that he would tell his classmates and, more importantly, to develop the straightforward, "readerly" style that became his trademark when he turned his attention to science fiction.

The *Bookseller* pieces were collected as *The Brightfount Diaries* in 1955, the same year as the birth of his first child, Clive (Wendy would follow, and later Timothy Nicholas and Charlotte May from a second marriage). That first book signaled the beginning of a long, distinguished, and eclectic career as a novelist and essayist. Success with prose also ended Aldiss' brief flirtation with the notion of writing poetry full-time. Although he would consistently produce verse and publish several collections of poetry over the years, the fiction always paid the bills. Within two years of the appearance of *The Brightfount Diaries*, a collection of science fiction titled *Space, Time, and Nathaniel* (1957) would appear (the stories "Dumb Show" and "The Failed Men" are the book's lasting contributions), cementing his reputation.

Those two much different books would only hint at Aldiss' far-reaching diversity as a writer in the coming decades. Far from squelching what would become a unique voice in the science fiction wilderness, Aldiss' relatively staid middle-class upbringing forced him to craft his own identity as a writer and to plumb the depths of imagination and his own experiences in the war for source material. In addition to his fiction, Aldiss also wrote a regular science fiction review column for the *Oxford Mail* from 1954 to 1967, and he would continue that trend of close examination of important issues in science fiction throughout his career as one of the most astute and prolific commentators on the state of the profession, putting his interest in the connection between the two succinctly in his contribution to *Hell's Cartographers*: "Criticism and creation always went hand-in-hand as far as I was concerned" (p. 189).

In 1957, Aldiss bested many of Britain's top science fiction writers to win a short-story competition in the *Observer*, a London newspaper, for a piece set in the future year 2500 titled "Not for an Age." The story's publication brought him his first fans, as well as his first editor, E. J.

Carnell. (The two remained friends and colleagues until Carnell's death in 1972.) Beginning in 1958 with the publication of *Non-Stop*, Aldiss, who was named "Most Promising Author" at that year's World Science Fiction Convention, became a fixture in the science fiction world. He would also eventually become a de facto spokesperson for the keepers of the science fiction flame. In 1960, along with the Oxford icon C. S. Lewis, Aldiss founded the Oxford University Speculative Fiction Group; in 1969, the British Science Fiction Association christened him the "Most Popular British Science Fiction Writer."

In 1973, he established himself as one of the preeminent critics in the field with the appearance of *Billion Year Spree* (the recipient of both Hugo and Special British Science Fiction Associate Awards), a volume of important and enlightening essays on the history of science fiction that draw on Aldiss' capacious intellectual curiosity in science, history, and philosophy. The follow-up volume, *Trillion Year Spree* (1986; Hugo Award winner), revised and updated to reflect more than a decade's progress both in the genre and in science and technology, offers ingress into the author's mind, providing a comprehensive historical and social context for twentieth-century science fiction. The epigraph to *Trillion Year Spree*, taken from Kurt Vonnegut's 1985 novel *Galápagos*, also hints at the author's wry sense of humor and the influence of his early family life as a motivating force in his writing career: "Someday my father would stop writing science fiction, and write something a whole lot of people wanted to read instead." Those lines reflect, some fifty years on, Aldiss' own experiences as a boy, when Stanley Aldiss ignored his son's interest in writing, pushing him in directions that, even then, young Brian knew he could never go. If there is a lesson to be learned from that simple epigraph, it might be that all of Aldiss' fiction contains comedy of a sort, whether it be the visual comedy of some of his early novels—the interior spaces of the starship in *Non-Stop* and the vegetative dystopia of *Hothouse* (1962) both convey an unexpected, if dark, humor—or the trippy, experimental *Barefoot in the Head* (1969), which skewers more than a few counterculture clichés and illustrates an ongoing passion for the intricacies of language.

After parting ways with his first wife, Aldiss married Margaret Manson in 1965, a union that the author has written about with great tenderness and that seems to have set him on a good path creatively. The two spent six months traveling together in Yugoslavia the year before they married. The country captivated the author and provided engaging material for his single travel narrative, *Cities and Stones* (1966); the extended adventure was also a much-needed break from the personal and professional pressures that had accumulated over the better part of a decade, since the publication of *The Brightfount Diaries* and a steady rise to success.

Aldiss continued to publish widely, from the success of the epic *Helliconia* trilogy (in the early 1980s) to the conclusion of the Squire Quartet (in 1994) to memoir in *Bury My Heart at W. H. Smith's: A Writing Life* (1990) to further criticism in *The Detached Retina: Aspects of SF and Fantasy* (1995). When Margaret died in 1998, a lengthy process remembered poignantly in the memoir *When the Feast Is Finished*, Aldiss found himself alone for the first time in his adult life. By the turn of the century, he had become one of the most prolific authors and editors of the century, publishing across the spectrum of genres, including novels, short story collections, nonfiction, drama, poetry, and anthologies. "That younger me, that boy who insisted on telling stories in the dormitory, is still around, I suppose." Aldiss says of the extraordinary longevity fueled, still, by a boyish wonder. "There are always those larger things that I think about more and more—the origins of mankind, the planet, the universe: how does it all happen and how does it all work out? So, the writing goes on" (Tibbetts, p. 254).

INFLUENCES AND THE EARLY SCIENCE FICTION

"My intention was partly to write social novels," Aldiss recalls of the thematic concerns of his early science fiction (*Hell's Cartographers*, p. 189). In his autobiographical essays, Aldiss repeatedly credits his reading of the British science fiction writer Olaf Stapledon's work as a cornerstone of his development. "While great things went forward into the world—destruction and victory—Stapledon's voice proved to be what was needed, in marked contrast to the pedestrian chat of soldiers," Aldiss writes about his awakening literary sensibility. "His daring time-scale in particular corresponded to something felt in the bloodstream. ... For the last and first time in my life, I deliberately stole a book. I could not bear to be parted from it" (*The Pale Shadow of Science,* 1985, p. 53). Stapledon's expansive, catalogic history of the world, covering two billion years and introducing distinct phases in human evolution, also manages to take into consideration the individual. Stapledon continues to be regarded by practitioners as one of the most influential science fiction writers to come out of the generation following the ascendency of fellow Briton H. G. Wells to the science fiction godhead. In that sense, Stapledon's influence seems to be more of a logical confluence for Aldiss than a serendipitous meeting of two like minds across generations. Timing and circumstance, of course, influenced a young man who savored Stapledon's richly detailed world and the ersatz (although by no means slapdash) history, turning his back for a moment on the destruction and chaos of World War II.

The shape of the narrative left its mark on Aldiss, who would play with vast expanses of time (his own second novel, *Hothouse*, takes place more than two billion years in a dying Earth's future) and still maintain a humanist perspective, "one individual soul ... confronted with the necessity of comprehending the cosmic process of which it is part: a noble and ever-contemporary quest" (*The Pale Shadow of Science,* p. 54). Later, Aldiss would return to the roots of science fiction, immersing himself in Wells's work with a critic's eye, admiring the master's fertile imagination and command of language, both necessities for the genre's continued evolution. "Within his own domain, Wells is *sui generis*," Aldiss writes with obvious admiration in *Trillion Year Spree*. "Wells is the Prospero of all the brave new worlds of the mind, and the

Shakespeare of science fiction" (p. 133). Even cutting-edge science fiction weathers under the critical eye, although Wells's lasting legacy cannot be overstated.

Aldiss' own early short stories look back to science fiction's Golden Age, the period from the late 1930s to the mid-1950s, drawing not only on Stapledon's work but on that of E. E. Smith, Isaac Asimov, Frederik Pohl, and James Blish, among many others, writers who published speculative stories in immensely popular magazines such as *Modern Boy*, *Marvel*, *Amazing*, and *Astounding*. Also, along with a host of British writers coming of age in the middle of the last century, Aldiss was greatly influenced by American cinema and music, particularly jazz and blues. Those broad interests in the arts fueled Aldiss' eclecticism and his later experimentation with language and its limits.

Not surprisingly, Aldiss' earliest fiction took the short form, an expedient way for the author to find his voice and construct a coherent vision before rocketing off into longer, more ambitious projects. (That early work also shows a fascination with human psychology that would manifest itself fully in the late 1960s with the rise of the "New Wave" in science fiction.) In the introduction to *Space, Time, and Nathaniel*, Aldiss compares short fiction to poetry, the goals of each to engage with its internal rhythms, a compression of meaning and language, and to delight with rigorous attention to form and structure that carries great weight with the attentive reader. Although Aldiss navigates the pitfalls of high-wire science fiction with a casual mastery, the depth of which becomes apparent only in multiple readings, he revels in the *process* of writing, his stories and novels conveying an attractive and ingenuous sense of discovery.

On the strength of the critical success of *Space, Time, and Nathaniel*, Aldiss published his first novel, *Non-Stop*, in 1958. (The novel was subsequently published in America under the title *Starship*, perhaps an unintentional spoiler.) A "generational" story, the subgenre of science fiction explored in the long form by Robert Heinlein, whose *Orphans of the Sky* (1963) influenced Aldiss and others, the novel follows a tribe who have unknowingly lived for more than twenty generations aboard a spaceship. That lengthy isolation has allowed the ship's inhabitants to create their own mythology and rituals for the world as they know it: the Dizzies, a tribe of humans who, through mutation, have hyperactive metabolisms and truncated lives, inhabit the Quarters with no knowledge of the outside world. The Dizzies possess rudimentary technology, though the tribal structure indicates a return to a preindustrial social organization, with a chieftain and a code of conduct based on superstition and legend.

Although the tribe could go on in this way indefinitely—Aldiss' fascination with stasis comes to the fore for the first time in *Non-Stop*—the action moves toward its inevitable conclusion when the wife of a hunter, Roy Complain, a member of the Dizzies, disappears. With little to lose, Complain joins Marapper—a priest with a map of their world, and the only member of their tribe to have any inkling of the truth that awaits them—and three other passengers on a quest through the ship's unexplored regions to meet their fate. At first, Complain is little moved by Marapper's contention that their world is something other than it seems: "'That theory again!' Complain said sullenly. 'What if the world is called Ship, or Ship the world, it makes no difference to us'" (p. 23). When confronted with the truth of their confinement—that their genetics have been compromised by contaminated water from Procyon, a distant planet where the ship had ferried colonists centuries before, and they have been under observation from untainted humans for generations—Complain's worldview changes, and with it his motivation.

The labyrinthine world inhabited by Complain and his companions serves the story well, placing the characters in perilous situations meant to extrude their essential humanity, even if the battle scenes, a bit of romance, a hero more prone to decisive (if questionable) action than contemplation, and an explosive ending suggest that Aldiss cannot quite cut ties with the Golden Age plot devices so familiar to him. Importantly, *Non-Stop*'s world-within-a-world frame would drive much of the later narrative in his fiction, the plights of his flesh-and-blood characters microcosms of the larger issues facing humanity in the space age. The dystopian theme developed in *Non-Stop* would appear in various forms over the next decade as Aldiss explored means of isolating his characters in order to observe and catalog their all-too-human responses.

Non-Stop was followed two years later by *Galaxies Like Grains of Sand* (1960), a short-story cycle spanning one hundred million years in the evolution of mankind and the habitation of the galaxy. *Galaxies* signals the first appearance of the overview-synopsis, brief summaries introducing vignettes that reveal, in a process of gradual discovery, the history of human galactic expansion. The preface to the volume offers a note whose sentiment will be repeated in the collection's short stories, as well as many of Aldiss' novels: "Of the laws we can deduce from the external world, one stands above all: the Law of Transience. Nothing is intended to last. ... The long mirror of the past is shattered. Its shards lie trampled underfoot. Once it covered all the walls of all the palaces; now only a few fragments are left, and these you hold in your hand" (p. vii). In each of the collection's eight entries, the synopsis contextualizes the galaxy's history at the time the story takes place, so that the stories themselves can develop individual characters.

That continuous shifting narrative focus, from the complex logistics of world- (and galaxy-) building to scenes of individuals in extraordinary circumstances, the "fragments" referred to in the preface, drives *Hothouse*, a dystopic vision of Earth's descent into climatic hell. One of Aldiss' several major achievements in science fiction, *Hothouse* won the Hugo Award in 1962 as the year's best novel. The prescient message in *Hothouse* deals with issues of death, environmental apocalypse (a recurring theme that prefigures the author's attention to the Gaia hypothesis in his later masterwork, the *Helliconia* trilogy), and human nature. Two billion years in the future, Earth no longer rotates; the sun is about to go nova. Vegetation has overtaken the planet, leaving the few remaining humans to live in the branches of the world-tree, just above the lush—and dangerous—plant life evolving on the forest floor and

growing from Earth to the moon, the site of an afterlife of sorts to which humans "go up" as a literal and symbolic gesture of transfiguration after their time on Earth has passed. Gren, banished from his tribe, falls in love with Poyly. A sentient morel mushroom takes over Gren's mind, jeopardizing the couple's future and the fate of the planet.

With a matter-of-factness that prevents the novel from slipping into abjection, Gren considers his own fate:

> Dimly he knew that [the world] would all be there when he was dead—that it would even be a little richer for his death, as the phosphates of his body were reabsorbed by other things: for it seemed unlikely he would Go Up in the manner approved and practised by his ancestors; he had no one to look after his soul. Life was short, and after all, what was he? Nothing!
>
> (p. 86)

Later, Aldiss briefly characterizes the human capacity for hope: "Life on the big slope was endurable, and sometimes more than just endurable, for the human spirit has a genius for making mountains out of molehills of happiness" (p. 193). Taken in the abstract, the novel might fit as well in the "New Wave" a decade later as it does in Aldiss' early phase, focused as it is on the struggle of individuals to survive in a surrealistic landscape that, regardless of the characters' actions, will inevitably be destroyed by a dying sun (a naturalist component to Aldiss' fiction here and elsewhere should not be ignored). Science underpins the story, though the novel's fantasy elements compel readers to suspend disbelief and suggest the author's continued narrative and stylistic innovation.

Aldiss' first true postapocalyptic vision comes in *Greybeard* (1964), a novel that, Aldiss writes, "grew partly out of my longing for the children and partly out of a splendid literary image Mike [the science fiction writer Michael Moorcock] had of people travelling down a river" (*The Shape of Further Things*, p. 110). Driven in part by a painful transition in his personal life—his first marriage broken, he would marry again the following year—the book also bridges the author's early period and a burgeoning "New Wave" in science fiction. In 2029, "The Accident," a nuclear holocaust that destroys most of mankind, renders humans incapable of procreating (in that sense, the novel prefigures P. D. James's 1992 dystopian tale, *Children of Men*). Ravenous stoats threaten to overrun what remains of the village of Sparcot, and the leader of a small tribe, Algernon Timberlane, the "Greybeard" of the title, leads his people out of harm's way. The novel tracks the progress of Greybeard, his wife, Martha, and others down the Thames toward Oxford and, finally, through London to the sea.

For years, the tribe has endured a sort of entropic nightmare, its energy winding down as its inhabitants age without hope of replacement: "Sparcot was a citadel for the ailments: arthritis, lumbago, rheumatism, cataract, pneumonia, influenza, sciatica, dizziness. Chests, livers, backs, heads, caused much complaint, and the talk in an evening was mostly of the weather and toothache" (p. 21). One of the novel's overarching ironies is that Greybeard's father was once a successful toy maker. With children absent from society, the man's skills and passion became useless; disconsolate, he commits suicide. Greybeard, now past middle age, seeks solace in the act of survival, if not redemption for mankind's foolhardiness. Both a veiled commentary on the cold war and a proto-ecological statement, the novel calls into question mankind's specious claims on nature. A glimmer of hope at the novel's end leaves any absolute interpretation in doubt, even if Aldiss slyly sides with nature.

Aldiss' first science fiction novels and stories were nothing if not close examinations of the big ideas popular with writers of the period. In the manner of Stapledon, he introduced a secular humanist perspective absent in much of the formulaic fiction of the Golden Age. From the outset, Aldiss' fiction hinted at something working beneath the surface, a sensibility owing much to the author's broader interests in the sciences and psychology. Those characteristics would find voice in the New Wave.

THE NEW WAVE

"Briefly, since Moorcock took over, this country's sf has become lively as never before. Moorcock was the Prophet. Ballard was his Saint. When Judy Merrill arrived from America, she turned into Jehovah and pronounced the whole thing to be the New Wave," Aldiss writes with some ambivalence toward arguably the first major movement in science fiction since the advent of the Golden Age more than three decades before. "However, the others involved in this spectacle have suffered by it," he continues (*The Shape of Further Things*, p. 115). Science fiction has always reflected broader historical, scientific, and social trends, and the lush tumult of the 1960s counterculture provided an outlet for stories that opened eyes in a genre that had—according to many of its leading practitioners—become tired, if not moribund.

By the middle of the decade, the covers on science fiction novels mirrored their content: psychedelic patterns, anthropomorphized creatures and shape-shifting humans, colors straight from a Jimi Hendrix black-light poster. Popular science fiction films such as *Planet of the Apes* (1968), *2001: A Space Odyssey* (1968), and *Fantastic Voyage* (1966) focused attention on the outward-inward dichotomy that would define the New Wave. Still, Colin Greenland writes in his critical study of the movement, "While the romantic heritage of fantastic fiction, temporarily enhanced by the ambiguous glamour of psychedelic drugs, caused some to write of the beauties of dream-worlds, the general tone was of disenchantment, depression and doom" (p. 66). Greenland's characterization of the New Wave takes into account its connection with a society's increasingly disaffected young people, not incidentally science fiction's largest audience. Michael Moorcock (who would edit the influential journal *New Worlds* and publish regularly himself), J. G. Ballard, Charles Platt, and Aldiss (whose own connection to the group was unwitting, at times, it seems) are the British writers most often associated with the New Wave. (The American writers Judith Merrill, John Sladek, Samuel R. Delaney, Thomas Disch, Harlan Ellison, Roger Zelazny, Pamela Zoline, and Kit Reed, as well as the British and American poets D. M. Thomas, George Macbeth, Bill Butler, and

Peter Redgrove, are also generally included in such discussions).

Aldiss' claims for the perceived sea change in science fiction during the period were never quite as grand as some critics have suggested. In fact, Aldiss has much in common with Ballard, a rough contemporary who died in 2009. Both writers followed similar career paths, building reputations as keen social commentators more interested in storytelling than hewing to the tenets of any necessarily proscriptive literary movement. Although primarily remembered for his science fiction novels and short fiction (*The Drowned World* [1962], *Concrete Island* [1974], *The Atrocity Exhibition* [1970]), Ballard, toward the end of his career, experimented with more "mainstream" forms (much as Aldiss has since the outset), even if he never strayed far from the dystopian abyss into which he frequently peered.

For his part, Aldiss always had an uneasy relationship with the notion of a "New Wave" in science fiction. Perhaps that ambivalence can be explained, in part, by his continued production through most of the century's major movements in science fiction, a career whose longevity makes the short-lived New Wave a blip on the science fiction radar (although Michael Moorcock has produced consistently over the decades, only Ballard could claim to have kept up with Aldiss in terms of output and diversity of forms and styles). Even for Aldiss, though, the movement was a symptom, if not an overt catalyst, of the sweeping transformation in science fiction brought about by a break from traditional narrative structures and settings and a more rigorous psychological examination of its characters.

No doubt one of the reasons that Aldiss came through the New Wave with his reputation intact was a matter of timing, his bridging the gap between more traditional forms (Aldiss and Ballard were half a generation older than most of the writers associated with the movement) and the socially and psychologically progressive experiments of the 1960s and early 1970s. "Unlike his predecessors, he will not subscribe to a convenient materialism; unlike his contemporaries, he will not allow his imagination to disdain matter, or ignore its claims," Greenland writes.

"Yet nor will he reject any ideas and techniques of either party, if he feels they may be useful to him. He does not submit to conventions just because they are conventional; nor does he avoid them for the same reason" (pp. 79–80). In the New Wave, fresh voices were encouraged, plot-lines and characters previously thought of as *outré* instead welcomed and evaluated.

According to Aldiss in *The Shape of Further Things*, the shift—in hindsight more incremental than revolutionary—was "precisely in [science fiction's] taking itself more seriously: not as prediction: not as Practical Mechanics: not as private pabulum for those who loved Edgar Rice Burroughs as boys and have never outgrown him; not even as satire: but as science fiction. As one of the (minor) arts" (p. 106). Any worthwhile concern is suspicious of dilettantes. But even Aldiss, who by the mid-1960s could be seen as a solidly "establishment" writer, recognized that H. G. Wells and the Golden Age writers were, to a crop of young guns born in the 1940s, ancient history. The New Wave aspired to be different, with mixed results.

Lasting roughly from the publication of *The Dark Light Years* in 1964 (again, *Greybeard* might be considered a transitional book when considering Aldiss' various "periods") to the psychedelic and unrepentantly counterculture *Barefoot in the Head* in 1969, the New Wave years were some of the richest for Aldiss in terms of the movement's influence on the later fiction, with particular attention to meaning-making, identity, and isolation, though the novels coming out of the period were neither his most critically acclaimed nor the most popular.

The Dark Light Years (1964) and *Earthworks* (1965), two relatively minor efforts, are rehearsals for the more introspective and psychologically rigorous novels to come out of the later part of the decade. If, as Greenland suggests of the New Wave generally, the most visionary work deals in "disenchantment, depression and doom," then Aldiss' work certainly fits that category. *Earthworks* was followed by the award-winning *Saliva Tree*, a novella originally published in 1966 in *The Saliva Tree, and Other Strange Growths* and subsequently in *Best SF Stories of*

Brian W. Aldiss (1988), featuring H. G. Wells and a Cook's tour of nineteenth-century Britain intellectual thought through the lens of a counter-culture ethos.

Three novels that articulated the New Wave ethos were serialized in *New Worlds* under Moorcock's auspices and appeared in print at the end of the decade: *An Age* (1967; published in the United States as *Cryptozoic!*), *Report on Probability A* (1968), and *Barefoot in the Head* (1969). All three novels contain dystopian elements, though the brief anti-novel *Report* less so (perhaps because it had been written several years before the others and initially turned down by Aldiss' publisher), describing as it does so little forward movement. Reference is made to Holman Hunt's 1851 painting *The Hireling Shepherd*, though even that familiar pastoral image of young love seems to have little impact on the novel. Instead, Aldiss revels in the idea that *nothing really happens.*

A passage toward the end of the *Report*—a narrative so spare that even the observers are known only by the initials S, G, and C, and their primary observation targets as the generic Mr. and Mrs. Mary—hints at the Möbius strip of reality into which the players have been drawn: "Turning to Congressman Sadlier, he said, 'Well, that's how it seems to be. Our robot fly has materialized into a world where it so happens that the first group of inhabitants we come across is studying another world they have discovered—a world in which the inhabitants they watch are studying a report they have obtained from another world'" (p. 96). An extended science fiction take on Abbot and Costello's "Who's on First?" routine, the novel posits a reality defined by the complete absence of meaningful human interaction, a theme dominant in the author's earlier fiction, though never presented with such deadening repetition (the notion of stasis would come to fruition much more successfully a decade later in *The Malacia Tapestry*).

Directly influenced by the French *nouveau roman*, a turning away from traditional narrative, the novel challenged readers as post–Golden Age (read: backward-looking) science fiction had not for some time. "From these exemplars I took

courage," Aldiss writes of his reading of the *nouveau roman*. "I would cleanse my prose of its antiquities. So I developed the central situation in *Report*, a situation charged with a drama which is never resolved. Moreover, I withhold the emotion involved, so that a reader must put in emotion for himself" (*Hell's Cartographers,* p. 199). Alain Robbe-Grillet (*The Erasers, The Voyeur, Jealousy*), the style's most renowned practitioner, earned his reputation in the 1950s. Less than two decades after Robbe-Grillet sought new ways to develop recurring, recursive narratives, Aldiss' novel responds to the pulps and their more traditional—and, to Aldiss' mind, stagnant—forms.

Report was followed a year later by *Barefoot in the Head* (1969), which explored and exploded counterculture tropes using a pastiche of the stream-of-consciousness narrative popularized by James Joyce in his dense, highly stylized novels *Ulysses* (1922) and *Finnegan's Wake* (1939). *Barefoot* opens with an apocalyptic scene straight from the palette of the sixteenth-century Dutch painter Hieronymus Bosch, a Europe under siege from bombs full of hallucinogens in the "acid head" war (an obvious play on the phrase "dropping acid" still amuses). The narrative and its rambling, dissociative protagonist, Colin Charteris, are predictably surreal, even if the chaotic goings-on make ironic sense when read in the context of a 1960s Europe in the throes of cultural revolution. "Then stand there half-inspecting each other in the semi-dark you do not see me I do not see you: you see your interpretation of me I see my interpretation of you" (p. 58), Charteris observes in the Gordian knot of his own surely coherent mind. Charteris, self-appointed messiah, drives across Europe gaining popularity for his views. After the failure of a biopic of his life (an image that prefigures the observation station Avernus in the *Helliconia* trilogy), Charteris is declared mentally incompetent. Nothing is more *real* than reality, Aldiss suggests, and Charteris' downfall is a disquieting failure of communication that begins with language's inability to make meaning when distanced from positivistic input.

The disconnect between a recognizable Britain—the technology culture underpinning the novel's events recalls the work of Ballard and Philip K. Dick—and the cognitive dissonance created in readers by the protagonist's disjointed words and actions relegates plot to a secondary role, emphasizing the process of meaning-making; or, as Tom Henighan writes, "Communication has degenerated into the equality and incomprehension of Babel: art, religion, politics, economics, and popular culture jostle together in the ironic Utopia ('nowhere') of mass society" (p. 71). Language, which Aldiss has always wielded as a powerful mediating force—particularly in the early fiction where clear, declarative sentences accrete one to the next to create compelling fiction—disappears in the unfiltered hiss of white noise, meaningless blather that, one might easily think after reading even brief passages in *Barefoot*, Aldiss views with more than a little contempt.

"THE ANCIENT ART OF STORY-TELLING": WAYS OF KNOWING, INERTIA, AND HELLICONIA

Always seeking fresh vistas from which to write his novels and short fiction—and perhaps, in part, to put the perceived excesses of the New Wave behind him—Aldiss hit upon the idea of refashioning the classic novels that he considered to be the roots of science fiction, including Mary Shelley's *Frankenstein; or, The Modern Prometheus* (1818), H. G. Wells's *The Island of Dr. Moreau* (1896), and Bram Stoker's *Dracula* (1897). That examination, which begins with *Frankenstein Unbound* (1973), falls along epistemological lines as Aldiss' protagonists seek knowledge on their way, finally, to understanding. "The impulse behind my writing *Frankenstein Unbound* was, in a way, exegetical," Aldiss recalls. "I hoped to explain to people what Shelley's story was really about" (Tibbetts, p. 250). Aldiss' quest for the origins of occult knowledge—immortality, shifting identity, man's symbiotic and arrogant relationship to nature—drives the author's quest for a philosophy that would attempt to explain mankind's raison d'être. That quest is a crucial step in Aldiss' evolution

as a writer, and the first on a path that would culminate, nearly a decade later, in the *Helliconia* trilogy.

In *Frankenstein Unbound*, Aldiss introduces Joseph Bodenland, a former secretary of state in a near-future that undergoes periodic "timeslips," tossing characters back and forth on the sea of time without warning. The victim of one such timeslip, Bodenland arrives in nineteenth-century Switzerland, where he meets the poets Lord Byron and Percy Bysshe Shelley at the Villa Diodati and falls in love with Mary Wollstonecraft, Shelley's lover (and eventual wife) and the author two years later of the groundbreaking *Frankenstein*. The Romantic impulse appeals to the entranced Bodenland. Contemplating the outwardly pastoral towns in the distance, Bodenland evokes "the paintings of a German Romantic artist, Caspar David Friedrich, with his embodiments of all that was gloomy and meager about Nature in the north. I could imagine myself in the still world of his art" (p. 196). After a brief, ill-fated affair between Bodenland and Mary and an attempt at solving the mystery of the untimely death of Dr. Frankenstein's young brother, the time traveler sets his sights on destroying Frankenstein's monster, who, with his new bride, lights out for the frozen lands that have sprung up around Geneva in the increasingly unstable conditions. Time passes at first in increments of weeks and months and then, eventually, after Bodenland escapes a prison in Geneva, by what the narrator surmises to be centuries or eons, literally reshaping the world before his eyes. At last, Bodenland arrives in a city so foreign that he has difficulty making sense of anything he sees.

Importantly for Aldiss, Mary Shelley's forward-looking novel, the true focus of *Frankenstein Unbound*, departed from the linearity of "rational" thinking that had held sway up to the early nineteenth century, characterized by the Enlightenment in Europe and called into question by the rise of the Romantic after the French Revolution in 1789. Even though his motivation for writing the novel is primarily academic, and the quest for knowledge key, Aldiss concedes that "knowledge brings no guarantee of happiness" (*Trillion Year Spree*, p. 51).

The two volumes that complete the gothic trilogy, *Moreau's Other Island* (1980) and *Dracula Unbound* (1991), both deal with similar issues as *Frankenstein Unbound*, though neither matches the philosophical rigor of the first novel, an unfortunate symptom of Aldiss' wide-ranging sensibility and his insistence on seeing the vision of the loose trilogy come to fruition, despite a number of competing writing interests in the nearly two decades from conception of the gothic project to its completion. The second installment, an homage to and contemporary update of H. G. Wells, "implicitly condemns the injustices wrought by western science in league with political exploitation of both nature and of the less-developed societies that remain close to nature," according to Tom Henighan (p. 83), and the concluding volume, prompted by a conversation between Aldiss and the film director Roger Corman, with whom the author had worked to adapt *Frankenstein Unbound* to the big screen in 1990, returns Joe Bodenland to Dallas at the turn of the twenty-first century with an idea for unlimited waste disposal that hinges on man's mastery of time. When Bodenland's paleontologist friend, Bernard Clift, discovers impossibly ancient human remains, the two are destined to meet the *Dracula* author Bram Stoker and to deal with the global vampire uprising of the twenty-sixth century. Of the three gothic novels, only *Frankenstein Unbound* is considered one of the author's first-rank efforts—the books suffer not from a failure of imagination but from an abundance of ambition.

In the late 1970s, after the publication of *Frankenstein Unbound*, Aldiss retreated into more conventional narrative, including the mainstream Horatio Stubbs books and the straightforward fantasy *The Malacia Tapestry* (1976). As Aldiss writes in *The Pale Shadow of Science*,

> Now the massif central of science fiction was crumbling. Sf which adhere to rational posits was becoming rarer. Younger writers, particularly in my own country, were hedging their bets by writing a form of science fiction which might, with luck, pass

for ordinary fiction, or by creating texts which lodge themselves comfortably in a nostalgic past rather than the future. Everywhere, everyone was writing fantasy; novels abounded in which the hero—or the hero with his miscellaneous gang—is impossibly heroic, where what prevails is an air of general implausibility or, to give implausibility its euphemistic name, magic. In short, it seemed as if the rational was out of favor, along with the ancient art of story-telling.

(pp. 122–123)

That return to "the ancient art of story-telling" motivated Aldiss to create the *Helliconia* trilogy—*Helliconia Spring*, *Helliconia Summer*, and *Helliconia Winter*—three books published in the early 1980s that, in a career spanning more than half a century and millions of words on the page, will likely be considered Aldiss' masterwork. Inspired by a conversation with his fellow writer Bob Shaw in the late 1970s, Aldiss began writing in earnest three years later, developing each volume quickly. Discovering early in the process that the idea deserved a more thorough treatment, he made the difficult—in hindsight, logical—decision to publish three volumes. At the same time, Aldiss continued his other mainstream projects, including *Life in the West* (1980), the first volume in the Squire Quartet (so named for the series' protagonist, Tom Squire).

Always drawing on his roots in "traditional" science fiction, despite his insistence on making those efforts new, Aldiss recalls that, in the case of *Helliconia*, "ambition grew in me to construct a great story, a new kind of scientific romance which would look substantial even when set beside the epics of the science fiction writer I admire most, Olaf Stapledon" (*The Pale Shadow of Science*, p. 122). The author borrows the phrase "scientific romance" from Wells, contending that his own rational approach to evolution and its consequences—the verifiable location of Helliconia in the constellation of Ophiucus, for instance—grounds the trilogy in a scientific context lacking in most fantasy. In fact, the fantastic elements that pervade the *Helliconia* trilogy find voice in the earlier novel *The Malacia Tapestry* (1976), which has proven to be the single effort from Aldiss to be rooted solely in the fantastic.

Any historical context—in this case, a vaguely familiar central European Renaissance society—offers the reader signposts to interpretation of the novel's (admittedly few) events. In Malacia, law dictates that nothing changes. Stasis rules, the absence of change is strictly enforced by law, entropy grudgingly accepted; the countryside's native animals are dying out, and even the artists whose lives are the narrative's focus, including the unemployed actor Perian de Chirolo, are helpless to affect positive change. The novel's chapter titles hint at a sort of superficial, timeless beauty at the same time evoking inertia through the use of set pieces with titles reminiscent of Old Masters paintings: "Woman with Mandoline in Sunlight" (p. 146), "The Ancestral Hunt" (p. 208), "Castle Interior with Penitents" (p. 257). The Original Curse of Malacia—that, in part, knowledge "'will gain you no wisdom—it will only make more painful what you hitherto enjoyed through ignorance'" (p. 246)—defines the society's intellectual and artistic stagnation, the accepted price of peace in a world where "war is the common instrument of change" (p. 310).

The art of the fantastic informs the *Helliconia* trilogy, as well. A message in a note to his son Clive at the beginning of *Helliconia Spring* confirms Aldiss' intentions: "All art is metaphor, but some art forms are more metaphorical than others; perhaps, I thought, I would do better with a more oblique approach. … It was to be a stage for the kind of drama in which we are embroiled in our century." That context threads its way through the trilogy. Replacing an ostensible Renaissance setting in *The Malacia Tapestry* for Helliconia, Aldiss handles the world-building details by placing the planet a thousand light years from Earth, caught in the dual orbits of a binary-star system: Helliconia by its primary sun, Batalix, and the two in a highly elliptical path by the larger Freyr. The three bodies move in harmony to a three-thousand-year-long symphony. Seasons come and go, slowly and inexorably, as Batalix and Freyr comingle; or, as Aldiss describes in *Helliconia Spring* by way of describing society's ebbs and flows, "another year … finished, and another. A generation grew up,

another grew old. Slowly numbers increased under Dresyl's peaceful rule, while the suns performed their sentry duties overhead" (p. 133). That clever bit of physics allows Aldiss to tie the work directly to a contemporary context engendered not by geopolitical expedience (he wrote all three novels even as the Soviet Union, in danger of "going nova" itself, still held the undivided attention of the West), but by hard astronomical certainties.

In *Helliconia Spring* (1982), which won the John W. Campbell Memorial Award and the British Science Fiction Association Award, Aldiss uses to good effect the overview-synopsis, a narrative device that first appeared in the early short-story cycle *Galaxies Like Grains of Sand*, ending the novel's opening section with a brief passage introducing the space station Avernus—"Kaidaw" to the Helliconians, who have no idea what the object might be as they watch it skim across the night sky in regular intervals—and its role as a silent sentinel observing daily life on the planet's surface. Relative to Helliconia's benighted inhabitants, the Avernus is a marvel of technology, even if the several thousand Avernians aboard struggle to make sense of their own lives. The space station bridges events between Helliconia and Earth, revealing both the living history of Helliconia (Aldiss' fellow science fiction writer Robert Charles Wilson uses a similar device two decades later in his 2003 novel *Blind Lake*) and parallel occurrences on Earth, which will undergo profound change of its own, a crisis brought about by a nuclear war that destroys most of the planet's population.

The first novel takes its power both from the development of Helliconia and the observational (and later, voyeuristic) relationship that entertains and instructs the watchers on Earth, who will never be able to experience Helliconia, despite witnessing the goings-on there through the Avernus' unblinking eye. Paradoxically, the Avernians cannot return to Earth and neither, because of a lethal virus endemic to the planet's people, can they travel to Helliconia without sacrificing their own lives (a key plot point in the later *Helliconia Summer*). Stuck in orbit around the planet, they suffer isolation similar to that experienced by Complain and the Dizzies in *Non-Stop*. The Avernians, fully aware of their own limited options, come to see their technology and their knowledge of Helliconian societies as a mocking insult to their inability to *act*.

The novel's hero on Helliconia is Yuli, a figure seemingly plucked out of Virgil's *Aeneid*, whose people have escaped the hardscrabble existence and centuries-long torpor of another winter. Yuli shuns the religion of Wutra, god of the skies, and founds the thriving city of Oldorando. Early in the novel, in a long, atmospheric prelude that sets the tone for the novel's action, Yuli recalls how the "elders had spoken of the two sentinels in the sky, and of how the men on earth had once offended the God of the Skies, whose name was Wutra. So that Wutra had banished the earth from his warmth" (p. 39). If Wutra found the people deserving of his attention, Yuli was taught, "then he would remove the frosts" (p. 39). In *Spring*, as in the trilogy's subsequent installments, religion explains the world's profound seasonal changes to the satisfaction of the Helliconians, at least initially. Far from bringing peace and prosperity to the land, however, the changing climate throws society into chaos and uncertainty, eventually calling into question religion's efficacy and forcing a reevaluation of society and its goals. Uncertain of their own destiny and always subject to the whims of nature, the people unwittingly open themselves to phagor attack.

The goatish phagors, like nightmarish apparitions, reign in winter, and the Helliconians have evolved to better compete with them when the weather warms. A phagor captured in battle forces the gawkers to see their own misgivings reflected in the demonic phantasm before them: "Everyone fell silent as the monster stood among them, glaring at them with his large scarlet eyes. His arms were lashed behind his back with leather rope. His horned feet pawed restlessly at the ground. In the gathering dark, he seemed immense, the bogeyman of all their nocturnal dreams, a creature from uneasy dimday sleeps" (p. 130). Physiologically and intellectually foreign to the humans, the phagors move on oddly jointed limbs so as "to strike terror into small boys' hearts," and "though these monstrous creatures could master the Olonets tongue, they were far from human. The thoughts in the harneys of their heads ran aslant" (p. 131). The last sentence of that Joycean description has echoes of the surreality of the earlier *Barefoot in the Head* and prefigures the essential failure of communication and lack of understanding that characterizes much of the trilogy.

The lacunae between the Helliconians and their enemies, the Avernians and the humans to whom they continue to send images, and the humans who—predictably—destroy themselves, refashion the curse (as Aldiss put it in *The Malacia Tapestry*) of knowledge acquisition and the necessary, messy byproduct of entropy (as in *Greybeard*). The scope of the first novel—and the same would be true for *Summer* and *Winter*—again mirrors the epic sweep of Stapledon's *Last and First Men*, reflecting Aldiss' mature concern for the incorporation of larger, in some ways riskier, issues drawn from nearly all of the earlier science fiction, producing a back-and-forth effect through scrupulous attention to issues great and small. Aldiss' novels work on the horizontal, of course, the movement of plot from point A to point B. The fullness of the author's vision only manifests, however, in the literature's vertical components—characterization, setting, emphasis on thematic and stylistic concerns—which offer readers a dialectic that encourages the interplay of ideas and transcends mere story.

A major work from an established writer, *Helliconia Spring* gave way a year later to *Helliconia Summer*, perhaps the greater accomplishment, according to critics and the author himself. Aldiss claims the middle volume "as the richest prose [in the trilogy]. Among other things, I read and attended performances of Shakespeare's *A Midsummer Night's Dream* to prepare myself for its writing" (*The Pale Shadow of Science*, p. 126). Gerald Jonas, who would review Aldiss' work as often as any critic, succinctly articulates the novel's achievement: "[Aldiss] writes of cultures, of entire species, of the ever-changing physical environment that shapes and is itself shaped by the forces of life. Yet he does not forget—what true Darwinian could?—that the key unit of evolutionary change is the individual, struggling, sometimes blindly and sometimes with hard-earned foresight, to survive and multiply" (p. 31).

In *Summer*, the Helliconians are less fearful of phagor attack (humans outnumber phagors three to one in the seasonal transition), though the unforeseen cultural and social shifts brought about by climate change and the relative comfort that simple technological advances make possible undermine the inhabitants' efforts toward progress. King JandolAnganol of Borlien, a man still bound to religion, has forsaken Queen Myr-demInggala to pursue personal and political ends, as in the unconscionable decision to dismiss his queen and to associate with the hated phagors. As Aldiss has made clear before, increases in knowledge and technology are useful only when wielded responsibly, and even the leaders of such great movements as the earlier exodus from the winter darkness of caves into the brilliant light of another spring have no frame of reference for their efforts and little sense of what that future might hold. Caught in time and held captive by the seasons, society adapts, to some extent, though any society's highest achievements are built upon its predecessor's foundation. In Aldiss' earlier fantasy *The Malacia Tapestry*, peace comes only with the sacrifice of change; on Helliconia, stasis foments unrest and war.

Earth's inhabitants, at first interested in the goings-on but investing little empathy in the plight of the Helliconians, begin to view the evolving culture and its struggle for survival in a much different light once mankind becomes threatened itself, destroyed by its own hand: "Over the centuries, as Great Spring on Helliconia turned to Summer, matters were changing. Observation was developing into commitment. The watchers were being changed by what they watched; despite the fact that Present and Past on the two planets could never coincide, an empathetic link was now being forged" (p. 34). Humans watch the Helliconians with an increased understanding of the interconnectedness of events, their consequences rippling into the future immeasurably as humans turn to "eductainment" and the inhabitants of Helliconia, who have no

knowledge of Earth, for solace and instruction. Of course, the irony of that attitude toward space travel, which mankind has ceased since putting the Avernus in orbit around Helliconia, is that Earth itself has become desolate, the result of humans' inability to see beyond simple political and economic expediencies. The humans watch the slowly unfolding drama of JandolAnganol with interest and trepidation, understanding that "strands of the web—the religious strand not the least—had been woven long ago which now entangled the king of Borlien" (p. 35).

For the inhabitants of the Avernus, life continues in its maddening, devilishly glacial pace. Harsh as life on the surface of Helliconia can be—and the Avernians have cataloged the many ways to perish on the planet—the isolation of the space station demands that the inhabitants play out their lives caught always just short of Helliconia and still impossibly far from Earth. Life on the Avernus, although "utopian—that is to say, pleasant, equable, and dull" (p. 77)—suffers from a lack of the very thing that its inhabitants had hoped to avoid: change. Even religion holds little sway; as an organizing principle, it would have had little effect, as the limitations imposed by life on the Avernus already preclude many of the actions proscribed by religions. Only in the Helliconia Holiday Lottery—in which once every decade during the long summer, when one "lucky" passenger on the Avernus wins a trip to Helliconia—will an inhabitant of the Avernus be assured of both the experience of a lifetime and certain death once infected with a fatal virus shortly after arriving on the planet's surface.

In a chapter aptly titled "In the Presence of Mythology," Billy Xiao Pin, the scion of a family whose task on the Avernus is to chronicle the lives of Helliconians, ruminates on the disparity between the illusory life that he must live on the Avernus and the "real," if potentially more dangerous, lives that he watches unfolding daily from the surface. The Avernus has been in orbit around Helliconia for more than three thousand years, and virtual reality programs form the sole boundary between sanity and space madness for the station's inhabitants. Billy takes in some of

Helliconia's most famous sights through "VR." Still, he cannot help but think that, "pleasing though such excitements were, the mind was always aware that every danger, each remote vista, was imprisoned in a mirrored room no more than eighteen feet long by twelve feet wide" (p. 123). Seemingly against reason, then, Billy and his family (although not his Advisor, who, significantly, "feared any dynamism" [p. 123]) are delighted when Billy wins the Helliconian lottery. He will leave the Avernus, descend to Helliconia's surface, and die within a number of days. The scene is broadcast to anyone who wishes to witness Billy's predictable death. After all, "privacy encouraged dissidence" (p. 124).

Billy's brief time on Helliconia, where he is an outsider and hardly to be believed for his outlandish story of having come from the stars, ends with his inevitable death, occasion for Aldiss to interject a statement that coalesces the essence of his science fiction:

> Every living being is created from dead star-matter. Every living being must make its solitary journey upward from the molecular level towards the autonomy of birth, a journey which in the case of humans takes three-quarters of a year. The complex degree of organisation involved in being a higher life-form cannot be forever sustained. Eventually, there is a return to the inorganic. Chemical bonds dissolve.
>
> (p. 280)

With Billy's death now legend on Helliconia, King JandolAngonol's power play pales by comparison.

In the same way that the numbers of characters bringing their chaotic energy to the mix indicate a world in transition in *Spring* and *Summer*, Helliconia's desolate winterscape—characterized most pointedly by Sibornal, the planet's northernmost continent—provides the backdrop for *Helliconia Winter* (1985). The capstone novel to Aldiss' ambitious and, with the hindsight of nearly three decades, largely successful effort, "as in the previous books, the impact of climate on behavior is dramatized in a way that does full justice to the maddening unpredictability of individuals who remain free to resist the environmental imperatives they cannot

escape" (p. 7), Jonas writes. In *Helliconia Winter*, the trilogy's dominant ethos, that of the Helliconians' resiliency and man's ongoing struggle for progress, even with full understanding of the futility of such an endeavor, comes full circle.

Brought on by Helliconia's inexorable movement away from Freyr and the promise of another long winter—the true beginning of which will be marked on the Day of Myrkwyr, Freyr's last appearance for hundreds of years—the story focuses on Luterin Shokerandit, who journeys to the farthest poles of Helliconia and braves the Great Wheel of Kharnabhar (his father has been its Keeper), an isolated monastery that rotates once every ten years, in the process becoming a virtual prison. The Wheel, Helliconians believe, holds the secret to the coming of spring after another eternal winter.

As in the earlier work, larger issues prevail in *Winter*, Aldiss' fascination with the Gaia hypothesis taking precedence over the novel's plot and tying the three installments together. In a passage early in the novel, Shokerandit leads his men into battle. Even intense fighting on both sides cannot match the power of the two stars that determine the arc of civilization: "When Batalix sank once more, the fight was still undecided. Freyr was below the horizon, and three hours of darkness ensued. Despite attempts by officers of both camps to continue the fighting, the soldiery sank to the ground and slept where they were, sometimes no more than a spear's throw from their opponents" (p. 34). Powerless to act even against hated enemies, the Helliconians suffer a fate described by the literary naturalism that peaked in the two decades around the turn of the twentieth century and was characterized in the United States by the work of Stephen Crane, Frank Norris, and others who had read the work of the French novelist Émile Zola (*Germinal* [1885], *Therese Raquin* [1867]). Nature is flatly indifferent to the plight of man, Crane bemoaned in his story "The Open Boat"; similarly, Aldiss' characters succumb to the fates of their predecessors in the last Great Year and untold winters before.

That naturalistic outlook has much in common with James Lovelock's Gaia hypothesis, itself intertwined with the loosely constructed religions—Wutra (Spring), Akha (Summer), and Azoiaxic (Winter)—that serve as organizing principles for each of the three distinct societies arising from the Helliconian seasons (in *Helliconia Spring*, Gaia is represented by "The Original Boulder," a bastardization of the phrase "The Original Beholder"), offering a context against which the novels' events take place. Aldiss discusses his views on Lovelock's work briefly in *Bury My Heart at W. H. Smith's*:

> Jim Lovelock's Gaia hypothesis proposes that all life in Earth's biosphere is an organism formed by a single evolutionary process...

> The stars in the case of our earthly drama are human men and women—at least according to human men and women. No doubt elephants, dolphins and cats think differently. But the fact of the matter is that all visible life forms could disappear from the stage and the show would still go on. Invisible life, microbes, bacteria, etc., far outweigh the visible. *The importance of mankind lies mainly in its own eyes, for all that anthropic cosmology argues to the contrary.*

> (p. 176; emphasis added)

The proclamation can be read as an expanding of the idea Aldiss first set out in *Greybeard* concerning man's competition with Earth rather than an existence in a symbiotic relationship that might be beneficial to both. One of the most telling passages in any of the Helliconia novels comes near the end of *Winter*, when Shoyshal, a minor character "in the northern hemisphere of Earth in a year that would once have been called 7583," articulates the essence of Aldiss' philosophy:

> We're here because of astonishing luck. Forget about the Hand of God, about which the Helliconians are always agonizing. There's just luck. I don't mean only luck that a few humans survived the nuclear winter—though that's a part of it ... Think of the bombardment which altered conditions so sharply that the dinosaurs failed, to give mammals their chance. I could go on.

> (p. 248)

SHORT FICTION, MAINSTREAM FICTION, AND A LEGACY IN LETTERS

Aldiss has become one of the most prolific literary writers of the last century, and any essay of this scope risks giving short shrift to one or the other of the author's strengths, the science fiction or the mainstream novels nearly equally popular in Britain. After the publication of *The Brightfount Diaries* in 1955, Aldiss focused most of his attention until the late 1980s on his science fiction, although he has never lost sight of the diversity of genres, publishing over the decades more than two dozen mainstream and experimental novels ranging from war stories to social commentary to quirky crossovers to pastoral romance, including *The Primal Urge* (1961), *Brothers of the Head* (1977), *Sanity and the Lady* (2005), and *Walcot* (2009). "A writer reinforces the discontinuities of his or her personality by writing different books. Novels can be a kind of forcing houses. They seal off old experience, and lead on to new perceptions. Experienced in this light, they generate tides of excitement in a writer's life," Aldiss explains. "Writing, being in some aspect a form of self-analysis, allows us a chance to create ourselves. In infancy, chance shapes character; in full adulthood, characters shapes the chances" (*The Detached Retina*, p. 195).

Beginning in 1970 with *The Hand-Reared Boy*, the first in the Horry Stubbs trilogy of semi-autobiographical novels that limns a young soldier's experience in World War II (*A Soldier Erect* and *A Rude Awakening* would follow), Aldiss' mainstream fiction appeared consistently alongside his science fiction. Over a period of more than a decade beginning around the time that *Helliconia* began to take shape, Aldiss published the Squire Quartet, four novels—*Life in the West* (1980), *Forgotten Life* (1988), *Remembrance Day* (1993), and *Somewhere East of Life* (1994)—of British middle-class society, from the economic and political uncertainty of the early 1980s to a near-future that threatens to explode in the sort of dystopia readers of Aldiss' fiction had come to expect.

Even in his mainstream fiction, which situates the author in a literary context, Aldiss still returns to the science fiction tropes that inform nearly all of his writing, including isolation, change (or stasis), discovery, language, religion, and science. In the foreword to his definitive short-fiction collection, *Best SF Stories of Brian W. Aldiss* (1988), published in the United States as *Man in His Time* (1989)—which distills more than three hundred stories published over half a century into twenty-two pieces—Aldiss expresses his admiration for the nineteenth-century American writer Washington Irving and for William Shakespeare, whose spirit pervades Aldiss' work in all forms: "My delight in a sense of mystery has called forth most of these stories; very rarely were they written to order. The commercialization of the science fiction field has led to much writing to order, with the result that a New Brutalism prevails" (p. x). The short fiction, compressed and necessarily focused on what Edgar Allan Poe called the "single effect," becomes a testing ground for the larger ideas that later make their way into the novels, both science fiction and mainstream, dealing as they do primarily with social issues such as war, economies and politics, and strained interpersonal relationships.

The accessible *Man in His Time*, a primer for Aldiss' longer work, includes the eponymous title story, as well as frequently anthologized works such as "All the World's Tears," "Who Can Replace a Man?" "The Girl and the Robot with Flowers," *The Saliva Tree* (the Nebula Award–winning novella written on the centenary of H. G. Wells), "Last Orders," and "The Gods in Flight." The story "Super-Toys Last All Summer Long," which was eventually adapted as the feature film *A.I.: Artificial Intelligence* in 2001 by Steven Spielberg, is by far Aldiss' best-known work for Americans; ironically, few could name the story's author. The piece is indicative of Aldiss' broad appeal—many of the collection's pieces might be considered "crossovers," or "social science fiction"—yet the author remains relatively anonymous with popular audiences. Many of the mainstream novels that should be better known in the United States are, sadly, difficult to find in domestic editions.

The story of the long road to the big screen for "Super-Toys" is worth retelling, for what it says about how even popular science fiction can be ghettoized (or, worse yet, ignored), as well as for Aldiss' ambivalent response to working with the renowned filmmaker Stanley Kubrick in the late 1970s. Aldiss admired the prickly Kubrick's work a great deal, particularly the films *Dr. Strangelove* (1964), *A Clockwork Orange* (1971), and *2001: A Space Odyssey* (1968). Having recently published *The Malacia Tapestry* (1976), Aldiss sent Kubrick samples of his work, and the director settled on an adaptation of the 1969 short story "Super-Toys Last All Summer Long" as a long-term project. "Super-Toys" examines a post-scarcity world in which technology has eliminated obesity, tamed the overcrowded and bleak cityscape with nearly perfect Whologram representations of calming vistas, and provided robotic children—temporary stand-ins—for couples hoping one day to have their own, if only they can win the parenthood lottery. When their surrogate son, David, falls in love with his parents, the couple consider sending him back to the factory to be reprogrammed, having no need for him anymore.

The story caught Kubrick's eye. Intense and aloof in his relationship with Aldiss, Kubrick invited him to work at his mansion, "Castle Kubrick," a short drive from Aldiss' home in Boar's Hill. The two put in long days and, despite Aldiss' concern for some of Kubrick's suggestions as to how they might handle the story, Aldiss went along with the director's vision, learning a valuable lesson about crafting screenplays in discrete, "non-submersible units" that would later guide his own writing. Inevitably, it seems, the collaboration never took flight. "I'll never forget the day when he suddenly said, 'It's not working, Brian. We'd better part company.' He was very blunt about it," Aldiss recalls. "He just lit a cigarette and turned his back on me. He didn't even say goodbye. The limo was waiting" (Tibbetts, p. 253). One wonders if Kubrick lost interest in the project or discovered, along the way, that Aldiss' short fiction contains an elemental quality that defies interpretation, except through the words on the page.

Another of the anthology's stories asks perhaps the two most important questions in the Aldiss canon. First published in 1965, "The Girl and the Robot with Flowers" is a frame story in which the relationship between a science fiction writer and his wife is as important as the apocalyptic tale he tells of a machine society preparing to return to Earth to destroy their makers. The story melds the intimate—a simple, loving relationship between a man and a woman—and the impossibly large—the destruction of planets—to make a profound statement on perception. When robots are sent from Earth to destroy the inhabitants of the planet Iksnivarts, observers on Earth view an iconic image, broadcast around the world as a sign of technological progress, of a robot picking flowers. If what viewers saw was real, the scene would indicate evolving personality traits in the robots and an evolution in the relationship between man and machine. The reality, not surprisingly, is something much more sinister. "I was chary about telling [my wife] that in my present mood of happiness I felt only contempt for my robot story, and would do however skillfully I wrote it," the writer muses at story's end. "There was no war in my heart; how could I begin to believe in an interplanetary war with all its imponderables and impossibilities? When I was lapped by such a soft and gentle person as Marion, why this wish to traffic in emotionless metal mockeries of human beings?" (p. 79). Those questions resonate with any reader familiar with the body of Aldiss' work. Over more than sixty novels and collections, Aldiss often feels the temptation to destroy humanity out of spite for its brutishness and short-sightedness. Rarely, though, is mankind not given a chance at rebirth.

The author's remarkably broad vision leaves little room for a discussion of his poetry (of which he has published a handful of volumes, including *At the Caligula Hotel* [1995], *Songs from the Steppes of Central Asia* [1995], *A Prehistory of Mind* [2008], and *Mortal Morning* [2011]) or any speculation as to what his legacy might be in letters over the next fifty years. Perhaps his reputation will be built, ultimately, on the quality of the work (the quantity cannot be questioned), though as Tom Henighan astutely points out, "Aldiss is nearly unique among creative artists in that the nature of his produc-

tion has almost hopelessly fractured his potential audience" (p. 124).

No matter. The writing, Aldiss would say, goes on. In 2000, the author, who still lives in Oxford, was named Grand Master by the Science Fiction Writers of America; in 2005, he was awarded the Order of the British Empire for his profound and continuing contribution to letters in Britain. Aldiss, who over the first decade of the 2000s also established himself as a serious painter (his first solo exhibition was in Oxford in 2010), seems little inclined to slow. In 2007, at the age of eighty-two, he published *Harm*, a near-future tale of society's response to terrorism, real and imagined, and an alternate universe in which humans struggle to start anew. True to form, Aldiss himself seems less concerned with his reputation than with his ongoing, lifelong engagement in the process of creation. In his perceptive 2004 interview, John Tibbetts defines a prolific and astonishingly versatile literary writer:

> [Aldiss] writes and speaks with equal authority on the works of Sophocles, the aforementioned Bishop Berkeley, William Godwin, G. K. Chesteron, Aldous Huxley, and Philip K. Dick. And threading through most of his works is the scarlet thread of an irrepressible, picaresque humor, placing him in a tradition extending from Rabelais to his late friend, Kingsley Amis. ... In short, Brian Aldiss is an outstanding example of that vanishing breed, the Man of Letters.
>
> (p. 247)

Selected Bibliography

WORKS OF BRIAN W. ALDISS

Fiction (Novels and Collections)
The Brightfount Diaries. London: Faber and Faber, 1955.

Space, Time, and Nathaniel. London: Faber and Faber, 1957.

Non-Stop. London: Faber and Faber, 1958. Published in the United States as *Starship*. New York: Criterion, 1959.

Galaxies Like Grains of Sand. London: Granada, 1960; Boston: Gregg, 1977.

The Primal Urge. New York: Ballantine, 1961.

Hothouse. London: Faber and Faber, 1962. Published in the

United States as *The Long Afternoon of Earth*. New York: American Library, 1962.

The Dark Light Years. London: Faber and Faber, 1964; New York: New American Library, 1964.

Greybeard. London: Faber and Faber, 1964; New York: Harcourt, Brace and World, 1964.

Earthworks. London: Faber and Faber, 1965.

The Saliva Tree, and Other Strange Growths. London: Faber and Faber, 1966; Boston: Gregg, 1981.

An Age. London: Faber and Faber, 1967. Published in the United States as *Cryptozoic!* Garden City, N.Y.: Doubleday, 1968.

Report on Probability A. London: Faber and Faber, 1968; Garden City, N.Y.: Doubleday, 1969.

Barefoot in the Head: A European Fantasia. London: Faber and Faber, 1969; Garden City, N.Y.: Doubleday, 1970.

The Hand-Reared Boy. London: Weidenfeld & Nicolson, 1970; New York: McCall, 1970.

A Soldier Erect. London: Weidenfeld & Nicolson, 1971; New York: Coward, McCann, and Geoghegan, 1971.

Frankenstein Unbound. London: Jonathan Cape, 1973; New York: Random House, 1974.

The Malacia Tapestry. London: Jonathan Cape, 1976; New York: Harper & Row, 1977.

Brothers of the Head. London and New York: Pierrot, 1977.

Last Orders, and Other Stories. London: Jonathan Cape, 1977.

A Rude Awakening. London: Weidenfeld & Nicolson, 1978; New York: Random House, 1979.

Enemies of the System: A Tale of Homo Uniformis. London: Jonathan Cape, 1978; New York: Harper & Row, 1978.

New Arrivals, Old Encounters: Twelve Stories. London: Jonathan Cape, 1979; New York: Harper & Row, 1979.

Life in the West. London: Weidenfeld & Nicolson, 1980.

Moreau's Other Island. London: Jonathan Cape, 1980. Published in the United States as *An Island Called Moreau*. New York: Simon & Schuster, 1981.

Helliconia Spring. London: Jonathan Cape, 1982; New York: Atheneum, 1982.

Helliconia Summer. London: Jonathan Cape, 1983; New York: Atheneum, 1983.

Seasons in Flight. London: Jonathan Cape, 1984.

Helliconia Winter. London: Jonathan Cape, 1985; New York: Atheneum, 1985.

Best SF Stories of Brian W. Aldiss. London: Gollancz, 1988. Published in the United States as *Man in His Time*. New York: Atheneum, 1989.

Forgotten Life. London: Gollancz, 1988; New York: Atheneum, 1989.

Dracula Unbound. London: Grafton, 1991; New York: HarperCollins, 1991.

Remembrance Day. London: HarperCollins, 1993.

Somewhere East of Life: Another European Fantasia. London: Flamingo, 1994; New York: HarperCollins, 1994.

Super-State: A Novel of a Future Europe. London: Orbit, 2002; New York: Little, Brown, 2002.

Affairs at Hampden Ferrers. London: Little, Brown, 2004.

Sanity and the Lady. Hornsea, U.K.: PS, 2005.

Harm. London: Gerald Duckworth, 2007; New York: Del Rey, 2007.

Walcot. Uppingham, U.K.: Goldmark, 2009.

Nonfiction

Cities and Stones: A Traveller's Jugoslavia. London: Faber and Faber, 1966.

The Shape of Further Things: Speculations on Change. London: Faber and Faber, 1970; Garden City, N.Y.: Doubleday, 1971.

Billion Year Spree: The History of Science Fiction. London: Weidenfeld & Nicolson, 1973; Garden City, N.Y.: Doubleday, 1973.

Hell's Cartographers. London: Weidenfeld & Nicolson, 1975.

The Pale Shadow of Science. Seattle, Wash.: Serconia Press, 1985.

Trillion Year Spree: The History of Science Fiction. With David Wingrove. London: Gollancz, 1986; New York: Atheneum, 1986.

Bury My Heart at W. H. Smith's: A Writing Life. London: Hodder & Stoughton, 1990.

The Detached Retina: Aspects of SF and Fantasy. Liverpool: Liverpool University Press, 1995; Syracuse, N.Y.: Syracuse University Press, 1995.

The Twinkling of an Eye; or, My Life as an Englishman. New York: Little, Brown, 1998.

When the Feast Is Finished. With Margaret Aldiss. New York: Little, Brown, 1999.

Poetry

At the Caligula Hotel. London: Sinclair-Stevenson, 1995.

Songs from the Steppes of Central Asia: The Collected Poems of Makhtumkuli: Eighteenth Century Poet-Hero of Turkmenistan. Caversham, U.K.: Society of Friends of Makhtumkuli, 1995. (Versification of the poems of Magtymguly, based on translations by Youssef Azemoun.)

A Prehistory of Mind. Bay City, Mich.: Mayapple Press, 2008.

Mortal Morning. Newcastle upon Tyne, U.K.: Flambard Press, 2011.

Film Adaptations

Frankenstein Unbound. Directed by Roger Corman. Twentieth Century Fox (United States) and Blue Dolphin (United Kingdom), 1990.

A.I: Artificial Intelligence. Directed by Steven Spielberg. Warner Bros., 2001. (Based on the short story "Super-Toys Last All Summer Long.")

PAPERS

Collections of Aldiss' papers reside in the Bodleian Library at Oxford, the Special Collections and Archives at the University of Liverpool, and the Special Collections at Reading University, Reading, England.

BIOGRAPHICAL AND CRITICAL STUDIES

Collings, Michael R. *Brian Aldiss.* San Bernardino, Calif.: Borgo Press, 1986.

———, ed. *Reflections on the Fantastic: Selected Essays from the Fourth International Conference on the Fantastic in the Arts.* Westport, Conn.: Greenwood, 1983.

Greenland, Colin. *The Entropy Exhibition: Michael Moorock and the British "New Wave" in Science Fiction.* London: Routledge and Kegan Paul, 1983.

Griffin, Brian, and David Wingrove. *Apertures: A Study of the Writings of Brian W. Aldiss.* Westport, Conn.: Greenwood, 1984.

Henighan, Tom. *Brian W. Aldiss.* New York: Twayne, 1999.

Jonas, Gerald. "Science Fiction." *New York Times Book Review,* February 26, 1984, p. 31. (Review of *Helliconia Summer.*)

———. "Science Fiction." *New York Times Book Review,* April 28, 1985, p. 20. (Review of *Helliconia Summer.*)

Mathews, Richard. *Aldiss Unbound: The Science Fiction of Brian W. Aldiss.* San Bernardino, Calif.: Borgo Press, 1977.

Randall, Neil. Review of *Dracula Unbound. Globe and Mail* (Canada), May 18, 1991.

Tibbetts, John C. "Brian Aldiss' Billion Year Spree: An Interview." *Literature/Film Quarterly* 32, no. 4:246–254 (2004).

JUSTIN CARTWRIGHT

(1945—)

Robert McKay

JUSTIN CARTWRIGHT IS fond of relating a joke told by his father, the respected journalist and writer Alan P. Cartwright: a journalist says to his son, "Don't tell your mother where I work; she thinks I'm a piano player in a brothel." The humorous touch on what from a different point of view might be an unpleasant human story is an instructive moment, catching an important tone of Cartwright's fictional universe. He enjoys bathetic wit pointed at hypocrisy and delusion, especially when they are invested in an arena of commercially driven creativity. Working against these, his literary world is darkly realistic if not pessimistic, insisting again and again on the baser physical realities. His often dislocated central male figures are usually engaged in at least potentially grand projects; but these only encourage a blindness to what is, in the end, their fundamental obsessiveness about sex and mortality. Despite or perhaps because of this, Cartwright's men relate to women from a position of no more than detachment and distrust and, if they have children, parenting is a secondary concern at best. The biographical irony is that Cartwright has been long deeply rooted in London, a fixture of its literary life—living in the same house for over twenty years with his wife, Penny Smalley, a retired teacher of disabled students; they have two children. This stability in Cartwright's adulthood followed a youth marked by the conventional education of the South African establishment. He was born in Cape Town on April 20, 1945, to Alan P. and Nancy McAllister Cartwright, and he has one brother, Tim. Later, after the family moved to Johannesburg, where his father was editor of the liberal *Rand Daily Mail* newspaper, Cartwright boarded at the prestigious Bishop's School, a thousand miles away in Cape Town. After this, a high school exchange to Michigan was followed by the universities of Johannesburg and Trinity College, Oxford; it is a postcolonial itinerary often similar to his characters' lives. But the final irony behind Cartwright's fun at his father's joke, which is certainly at the expense of many of those very characters, is that he has himself written prolifically for the newspapers since the turn to literary writing in his late thirties, after a varied career writing a pulp novel and two thrillers, in advertising, making films, and producing political election broadcasts.

COLONIAL ADVENTURES IN IRONY: THE CURTIZ NOVELS

After his first, now effectively disowned, literary work, *Freedom for the Wolves* (1983), a pensive story of nineteenth-century colonialism that becomes a pointed attack on 1960s apartheid and its roots, the major early phase of Cartwright's career as a literary novelist begins properly in 1988 with *Interior*, the first of three novels appearing consecutively over the next five years that are narrated by the same character—Timothy Curtiz. By the time Cartwright published the last book in the suite he had been nominated for one of the United Kingdom's major literary prizes, the Whitbread Book Award (for the second in the sequence, *Look at It This Way,* in 1990), won one of South Africa's most important book prizes (the M-Net award, for *Masai Dreaming,* 1993), and had reached a crucial point in the establishment of a literary career in the United Kingdom, being reviewed consistently (and indeed broadly with praise) in the major broadsheet newspapers. Indeed, many of Cartwright's major preoccupations as a novelist and the stylistic features that recur throughout his later work were already visible in this early sequence.

Cartwright's novels explore the never-simple relationship between characters' ideals, their ideologies, and the quotidian detail of their lived experience. Whatever their actual ages, his central figures (who are always male) tend to display the ambivalent characteristics one might associate with a stereotype of the middle-aged intellectual middle class, and Curtiz is a quintessential Cartwright character-narrator in this regard. He is a witty and mostly engaging, occasionally self-conscious, but also too comfortably opinionated man, given to sententious pronouncements like "I find this one of the ironies of Israel: in a nation of Jews, all the Jewish roles have been allotted" (*Interior*, p. 103) and "I see women as closer to the tragic than men because of the frailty of their expectations which have no solid foundation in the world" (*Masai Dreaming*, p. 102). He is old enough to feel the need to look back on his youth but young enough to feel acutely the sense of loss and nostalgia that accompanies his compulsion to do so. And his life has lost focus because a particular phase of activity in both romance and employment has come to a troublesome end. Such a narrator is ideal for Cartwright to explore that point where an apparently secure life, and crucially the personal myths that support it, disintegrate to reveal a more tentative, tenuous, and ironic relation to the world.

The very title of *Interior* (1988) neatly suggests two closely related themes that Cartwright explores in the story. "The Interior" is an outmoded colonial term for central Africa, so the word signals the persistence of colonial attitudes long after independence in Banguniland, the fictional country in which the action is set. The title also foregrounds individual perception and internal psychology. As such it is clear from the outset that the novel intends to rework Joseph Conrad's *Heart of Darkness* (1903), a novel whose broad shape it directly echoes—a narrating character tells the story of his search for a colonial adventurer whose loss and psychological collapse in Africa is shrouded in myth. Conrad distinguishes his metropolitan narrator Marlow fully enough from Kurtz, the colonialist subject of his story, to allow only for ironic allusions to the affinities between them. Cartwright, on the other hand, multiplies and intensifies this complicity, not least because both his narrator, Timothy Curtiz, and the adventurer he is looking for, his father, Lance P. Curtiz, clearly take their name from Conrad's enigmatic colonialist.

A jobbing journalist and documentarian without a project, Curtiz finds himself in Banguniland because it takes him away from Magda, the impulsive and sexually energetic wife from whom he has recently separated (Cartwright peppers the narrative with Curtiz' sexual reminiscences). Before long he has a vague plan to unpick the mystery that surrounds the death of his father in 1959: "the truth was the reasons I had come to Banguniland did not bear explanation," he says (p. 45). Lance P. Curtiz was apparently lost overboard on an expedition when researching a story for *National Geographic* about a remote Israelite tribe, something of an indigenous spiritual aristocracy in Banguniland, named the Orefeo. A characteristic of the novel's rather deliberate strategy of mysteriousness is the machinery Cartwright mobilizes to place a certain absence at the heart of Tim Curtiz' character. The paternal Curtiz name is only the last in a series of noms-de-plume for Lance Curtiz' own work as a trade journalist, and indeed his (and thus Tim's) authentic identity is never clarified. It is a mark of Cartwright's confidence with fictional tone—though this owes much to the Graham Greene of *The Quiet American* (1955)—that he extends such mysterious moments into a manic and often darkly comic narrative in which Tim is repeatedly embroiled in Banguni political events, with a quick-changing cast of well-sketched cameos, and the profound mixes freely with the surreal. A local taxi driver who claims Timothy's father is still alive is, we find out, both the star player on the national soccer team and the brother of an important Banguni chief. He in turn is the leader of a political resistance movement that overthrows the country's dictator who, it transpires, had ordered the massacre of the Orefeo in the early 1980s, with some survivors rescued in secret by the Israelis.

As this plot unfolds, Tim's inquiries take an astonishing turn, not with any successful and life-affirming denouement such as the discovery of the living father but rather of his embalmed remains. Cartwright's broad point, much like Greene's, is that the meaning of the individual life can be separated neither from its self-serving and mercenary motives nor from historical and political truths. As such, *Interior* is a novel that pulls in contradictory directions. By aligning Curtiz' quest to attain knowledge about a traumatic moment in his personal history with the grander project to discover hidden colonial histories in Africa, the novel's narrative momentum invokes and then surges toward revelatory knowledge. But the realities and disappointments of Curtiz' experience in the novel act as a brake, demanding a more tentative and pessimistic view of the world it portrays.

It is ironic that the backdrop for Curtiz' next appearance, in *Look at It This Way* (1990), should be the London of the late 1980s, portrayed as a glamorous-turned-tawdry world in which the rich are trapped by rapidly falling house prices, journalists are little more than hacks, finance is corrupted by insider-trading, and advertising is controlled by modish style-gurus. For the novel is itself a good example of an aggressively market-conscious literary culture, in that the manuscript was the subject of a feverish competition among several major publishers, with its relatively novice author leaving the editor who had nurtured his shift from writing minor thrillers and television tie-in books to literary novels. "I still don't completely understand publishing and agents," Cartwright admitted to Nigel Fountain of the *Guardian* (p. 23), but he moved to a publisher that would orchestrate the kind of publicity campaign necessary to secure both television rights (Cartwright himself scripted the BBC's production) and the recognition of major prize committees.

The novel's ambivalent London scene is ironic, too, because its main idea picks up from the guiding quest for paternal knowledge in *Interior* to explore the contradiction between Curtiz' ongoing search for some grand meaning in life and his craven attitude about what he might achieve as a writer. It is hard not to detect a hint of shame in Cartwright's picture of the hack, which recurs many times in his work, given his ongoing work for the broadsheets (he wrote 221 features and reviews between 1995 and 2011). And yet, it is by exploring such attitudes that *Look at It This Way* continues Cartwright's interest in the question of how, why, and whether people should strive for a sense of meaningfulness in life—and, in the end, the necessarily unresolved nature of such striving.

The novel is only loosely related to *Interior*. The scene and characters are now thoroughly metropolitan and the mode has shifted to one of broad social satire, but some important elements are retained and developed. Curtiz remains, but a signal of the slippery nature of reality in the book is that seemingly salient character details are altered. He has separated from Magda, but, whereas his willingness at the end of *Interior* to parent the offspring of her affair was tentative evidence of his acceptance of human vulnerability, the girl, Gemma, is now unequivocally his own daughter. Curtiz' presence in London is financed by a huge fee earned impersonating a rich globe-trotter for a credit card commercial and a job writing ersatz sociological sketches for the fictional magazine *Manhattan*. "A poor man's Gore Vidal" (p. 36) is the general opinion cited by Victoria, Tim's contact in advertising and soon to be his lover, after she has left her philandering and corrupt city trader boyfriend Miles. Curtiz' drive to discover something more profound, some meaning that subtends human existence, insistently punctuates the novel, however, to fill the vacuum left in a London where the city has fragmented along economic, social, cultural, and even linguistic lines. This point is insisted upon when spelling that aims to capture working-class Londoners' accent appears in parentheses after their speech is reported in Curtiz' Standard English, "think" becoming "(fink)," for example. Critics rightly and often praise Cartwright's ease with literary technique, if sometimes only like James Saynor to damn him with faint praise as a "nifty stylist" (p. 49); and this unusually awkward effect is an example of his occasional tendency to overwork theme into style.

Against this, several different themes seem to offer unifying potential as the narrative progresses. Symbols of nationhood, separating history from myth, shared bonds of social taste, the pull of romantic love, sexual desire as a natural imperative, financial success, erudition and scholarship, and embracing one's cultural roots all feature as ideals at some point. Clearly some are more nostalgic and sentimental than others, but there is little sense that any has lasting value; where we think we see pattern and significance the world is a chaos of meanings. The most complex working out of this point involves the first key instance in Cartwright's work of an oft-repeated fictional gesture: drawing on the peculiar power that the presence of animals has in the human world and, beyond this, on the rich resonance of animal imagery.

Early on, Curtiz writes up a vignette about an aging cockney who, as a public functionary in 1930s South Africa, had killed a lion that attacked him. Seeking local color for the article, and recognizing the rich symbolic resonance the lion has in England, Curtiz hopes to interview "Simba" Cochrane in front of a lion at the London Zoo. But soon each element of this story escapes Curtiz' pragmatic use of it, spreading virally through the novel, accruing more and more significance as it does so. Cochrane's illegitimate Nigerian child contacts Curtiz, who sponsors a reunion, which fails because Cochrane is senile; Curtiz develops an obsession with lion lore and feline natural history; this bonds him to Victoria, who is studying George Stubbs's animal paintings; the lion is stolen from the zoo by an animal rights group and only eventually released outside it, just in time to be wrongly suspected of killing Miles, who is wandering there. A facsimile newspaper report of this supposed event opens the book, but Curtiz' lion-knowledge suggests that Miles was in fact killed by a London ne'er-do-well whom he had wronged, himself (just to confuse matters) associated with animal activists. Among all of this, the book's structural irony is that the development and denouement of this plot are consummately well-made, just as its internal confusions and contradictions serve perfectly to undermine any hope Curtiz might have of a meaningful resolution to the ontological emptiness the novel neatly diagnoses.

Securing this point, *Look at It This Way* keeps with the strategy of unexpected and telling changes in narrative perspective that became something of a Cartwright trademark beginning with his *Freedom for the Wolves* (which went out of print after its initial softcover edition). By bluntly juxtaposing narratives in two distinct parts that focus the perspectives of a grandfather and grandson living a century apart, that book first captured the sense, which colors all of Cartwright's writing about Africa, that the social present is always deeply if imperceptibly shaped by the colonial past. And the most astonishing stylistic moment in *Interior* comes when the narration unexpectedly switches, after 175 pages of Tim's tale of the ongoing search for his father, to an account of the father's survival from his own perspective. This happens with no apparent explanation whatsoever in the plot structure and is barely justified when Tim eventually discovers his father's rambling journal with his remains in Orefeo territory. But in *Look at It This Way* the implication that the narrative should not be trusted is given to the reader more clearly. The third-person omniscient narrator, which for most of the book appears to complement the first-person account with the other characters' stories, is suddenly revealed in a parenthetical aside, a few pages from the end of the book, to have been Curtiz all along. The disorienting effect casts a belated shadow of doubt over every aspect of the book; this is good preparation for the final novel in the Curtiz series, which is a rich exercise in disillusionment.

With a complex narrative set mostly in modern Swaziland and Tanzania, *Masai Dreaming* (1993) has the flavor of a second attempt at the basic material of *Interior*, but it is more tonally complex and structurally coherent; it is certainly the most originally imagined of the Curtiz books. The central theme is the clash between the grand narratives we use to bring coherence to our world and our inherently contradictory and, as the novel shows, properly multiple sense of human life and history.

Again Curtiz is seeking to discover some fundamentally important piece of "truth," in the context of a failed relationship (now, Victoria is left behind in London) and in the context of a much-debased creative project. The moral stakes are considerably raised from those of the preceding books: finding a missing father and searching for unity in a fractured urban society; for in this case, Cartwright's focus links the Holocaust and the twentieth-century legacy of colonialism. The biography of a Jewish anthropologist of the Masai, Claudia Cohn-Casson, forms the basis for Curtiz' research as the scriptwriter of the film *Masai Dreams*, which will become (as we know from the novel's opening pages) a formulaic Hollywood romance starring Mel Gibson and Julia Roberts. His film aims to capture a "universal human spirit" in the guise of the mythically doomed love between Cohn-Casson and a Masai tribesman called Tepilit. In yet another example of his mercenary streak, Curtiz knows that this is what he ought to deliver: "the wider audience wants this story to flatter them, by presenting them with a simple conflict of love and duty, good and evil. They don't want some morbid exploration of the inexplicable" (p. 220). Doing so, he makes great play of the human tragedy of Cohn-Casson's supposed death at Auschwitz and how this transcends the awkward ironies of her position between the first and third worlds. But the case is not quite so simple, as Curtiz elsewhere diagnoses the universal human spirit that gives power to such tragedy as precisely the kind of idealism espoused by the early anthropologists who shaped Cohn-Casson's career (the phase "universal human spirit," in fact, is from Émile Durkheim).

The book has another complex plot, which is gradually worked out across short, sometimes synoptic and allusive chapters that interweave several different time frames and narrative layers. The often speculative facts of Curtiz' African adventure and his romantic past rub up against the details of Cohn-Casson's life in the 1930s and 1940s, various more or less trustworthy versions of them are freely intermixed both with other characters' recollections and with Curtiz' imagined re-creations for the script. The story is based on the unraveling of three narrative knots, each of which involves a traumatic event, and together they ruthlessly expose the universalizing

worldview as no more than self-delusion. In the first, the intercultural anthropological encounter is a scene for the tragedy of colonial (and neocolonial) power. In part to finance her research, Cohn-Casson had acted as the intermediary to the Masai for an early Hollywood filmmaker named Waindell. But the farcical result of his attempt to stage a lion hunt is the death of two Masai and Tepilit's killing of a colonial district officer, a crime for which he is hanged.

This dark history is replayed in the examination of the traumatic moments of both Curtiz' and Cohn-Casson's romantic pasts. When Claudia's English lover Fairfax confesses to Curtiz that he had accused her of catching syphilis from Tepilit, an event that presaged her return to Europe and her deportation to the camp, there is a direct echo of Curtiz' own story (not to mention Curtiz' earlier inclusion of this development into his script). Curtiz had left England for Africa, hurt by Victoria's sexual indiscretion with a character known only as "Steve," demanding that she be tested for HIV-AIDS. The details of these encounters, erotic and otherwise, obsess Curtiz' imagination throughout the book (as in *Interior*, Curtiz is also full of opinion about sexual proclivities and mores and their meanings). But when Steve turns out to be the very S. O. Letterman who is producing Curtiz' script, that revelation is the only unearned and histrionic twist in a novel that is an otherwise richly textured portrayal of character and action, with subtle correspondences and meaningful echoes throughout.

As if to drive home that a key point of the Curtiz sequence is that any, but especially a writers', supposedly coherent account of reality is not to be trusted, Cartwright revisits Curtiz' apparent if dubious omniscience. In one lengthy sequence, for example, Curtiz narrates Letterman's ruthless casting-couch seduction of a French actress angling to play Claudia; that this takes on an element of surreal fantasy (the actress, it transpires, is a transsexual) only redoubles the effect that any reality we see is inseparable from Curtiz' (self-deluding) perception. Here, though, the duplicity of the excursions into others' minds and life stories is much more successfully integrated into the fabric of the novel, with its slipping between layers of reality all the way through. Curtiz' complicity with Letterman, the very man responsible for his unhappiness, shows up that Cohn-Casson's original complicity with the neocolonial charlatan Waindell had already undermined any hope of her anthropological work transcending cultural difference.

Cartwright can develop such ideas equally well by quiet realist effect. As Curtiz details a lengthy picture of cattle trucks transporting Cohn-Casson and other French Jews to Auschwitz, the moral impact of Jews being treated like animals is complicated by echoes of carefully realized scenes in the book of the functional butchery of cattle in the land of the Masai, for whom cattle are actually deities. Moral outrage based on universal human empathy seems too trite a sentiment to cope with an irredeemably conflicted human world in which violence spreads in all directions. It remains a point of contention whether the "quiet verities" attested to here, as through the book's narratological trickery, outweigh the perhaps unintentional bathos and disparity of tone in a novel that mixes tragic history with personal obsession so freely. Cartwright "is really too good at old fashioned things like character and setting," for Hugo Barnacle, "to serve himself best by post-modern mucking about" (p. 27). But the risk of imbalance is perhaps simply the effect of Cartwright's faith in one of the fundamentals of literary realism—that historical truth can only be realized in the context of an individual life in the world. Having explored the ironic duplicities of narrative address as far as he can with Curtiz, he would test out this faith all the more fully in the next phase of his career.

EXPLORATIONS OF THE MORAL SELF: THE MIDDLE-PHASE NOVELS

William Blake's poem "London," a quotation from which gives *In Every Face I Meet* (1995) its title, begins with "I" and ends with the word "hearse"; it is a poem that imagines the moralizing urban self experiencing a death of the human spirit delivered by the corruption of city life. Cartwright transplants these themes to a glum 1990s London with the story of a day in the life of Anthony Northleach, and as his Dickensian name suggests, any worth the southern capital city has (moral or otherwise) certainly lies elsewhere. Influenced by the work of John Updike, a writer Cartwright much admires, the portrait of Northleach is a difficult one to make fictionally successful. He is a ponderous if rather vacuous man whose life for most of the novel seems to be in perpetual denouement. The waning kudos from his time as a rugby player just about helps him to succeed in his job. When he unexpectedly finds himself promoted to company director, despite his contempt for the new corporate ethos and language (Cartwright's short career in advertising allows for the leaden tone of manager-speak to be well-pastiched), it is only to help the others spread their debts. Against this deflated scenario Cartwright documents the disparate ways in which Northleach, whether in meetings or wandering in the seedier streets of London, vaguely imagines a more transcendent and meaningful life.

He alights on three flawed ideals, tried out often but with little conviction: a version of the sublime offered by rugby prowess; the possibility of political renewal with the release of Nelson Mandela; and the transcendentalism of Emmanuel Swedenborg:

> He feels heavy. Geraldine [his wife] has theories about blood sugar levels. He is inclined to believe them because he usually feels tired in the middle of the day. … *Lunch, lunch, lunch.* To get away from this nonsense. To leave this pastel, creepy meeting room. To be running with the ball under his arm leaving Lagisquet, the Bayonne express, clutching at the air made turbulent by his passing. To be flying over the turf. To be on the launch from Robben Island with Nelson Mandela. To be conversing with the angels in Stockholm. He screams at the managing director: *Time, ref, time. Blow the fucking whistle.*
>
> (p. 52)

This is a major shift in technique from the Curtiz novels, proceeding by way of interior monologue and a narration firmly focalized through characters' minds; it is a style ideal for portraying the city as the conflation of a multiplicity of individuals, as Cartwright has perhaps learned from Virginia Woolf's *Mrs Dalloway* (1925). Nevertheless, it does have the effect of underwriting a certain solipsism, with the book's omniscient narrator granting authority to each character's perception of the world. This allows Northleach to seem very much like the opinionated Curtiz at times; it is never Cartwright's style to shy away from his central characters' unpleasantness, but it can also lead to a certain moral queasiness, as when Northleach's casually offensive opinions (for instance about women or homosexuality) strike the tone of general social commentary.

In a rare moment of exuberance, Northleach buys tickets for himself and his dissolute rugby buddy Mike to witness Mandela's release, thinking that through Mandela's persistence he captures the realistic meaning of life: "Nelson is going to reveal that human striving—*My life is the struggle*—is the human condition. He sees now that to be human is to seek the ideal, without any expectation of achieving it" (p. 165). But precisely as Northleach realizes this, the novel plots toward a culmination that powerfully confirms it, through urgent scenes that put Cartwright's literary apprenticeship writing thrillers to good use. Mike rescues Northleach from a random street attack by Jason, the pimp of Chanelle, a prostitute who is the novel's main subsidiary character. He does so by rugby-tackling Jason, but he is killed in the process. Jason's own lionizing of Mandela, by falsely imagining him as a Rastafarian leader, symbolizes a black urban underclass expressing itself by commodifying its heroes. This, Cartwright suggests, is of a piece with his mugging someone in the street to pay for a new BMW: a point that reiterates Cartwright's ongoing distrust of that idealism which for Northleach motivates human life.

Cartwright anticipates some readers' critique of the bluntness of this portrayal of the urban underclass by framing the novel with the court case that prosecutes Northleach for allegedly murdering Jason after his fatal scuffle with Mike. These scenes are delivered via the perceptions of Julian Crapper, another self-serving freelance journalist, whose self-righteous and politically correct opinions allow him to be taken in by the prosecution's slender case. In a neat twist on the darkest moment of Blake's poem, the "harlot's curse," Chanelle's evidence leads to Northleach's acquittal, but, as is usual for Cartwright, the truth of the fatal events is never revealed. His point is that life offers us no indubitable evidence of its meaning; and yet we are compelled to make sense of it through always flawed methods, whether moral theorizing, legal decision-making, fetishizing sports heroes, or chasing fantastic political ideals. Such moral realism must, nevertheless, accept the irony that sometimes such empty ideals can inspire authentic action: as Mike's tragically heroic rugby tackle proves.

Imagining the story of contemporary London as such an ambivalent moral tale won Cartwright the Commonwealth Writer's Prize and a place on the short list of the Booker Prize; and making sense of London is a topic he returned to in his 2011 book, *Other People's Money*, a state of the (post–Lehman Brothers) nation novel. But Cartwright won Britain's second-most-prestigious fiction award, the Whitbread, for *Leading the Cheers* (1999), a more expansive work in which he revisits the short period of his adolescence spent at high school in Fenton, Michigan. In a short biographical essay about the events that shape the novel, "Another Country," Cartwright grants that the writer of fiction no more than "implies the events of his life" (p. 103), and *Leading the Cheers* is a deeply felt exploration of the troubling but inevitable power of the imagination over reality. Through it, we shape and reshape our past in order to maintain a needed coherent sense of self, even as this remains "a sort of tyranny, the burden of being human" (p. 151).

Dan Silas, the book's central figure, is an interesting development of the Cartwright type, and this leads to a marked lightening of mood. The story spends much less time on the familiar crisis that precedes the events of the story (Dan's broken marriage, duplicitous wife, and failed career), because Dan is psychologically exhausted by the preening self-assurance that had apparently seen him good in life. "Since I had been dismissed I was contemplating a more open and receptive relationship with life," he says (p. 21), and so the focus of the novel is his rapprochement with the friends of his youth on a trip back to the United States to speak at their high-school reunion. Here, his openness takes the form of "a compulsion to allow my past some air and light, as though it could quickly develop in different ways" (p. 142).

The central case for revision is his history with Gloria, a woman with whom he had what he thinks was a brief but exciting teenage fling, culminating in a stolen moment of lovemaking on Thomas Jefferson's bed on a class trip to Monticello. (The book explores various symbolically American places, including the remnants of Ford motor factories.) Yet for Gloria, Dan discovers, it was a distressing event: she is convinced it was Dan (not the other boyfriend she kept hidden from him) who left her pregnant with a daughter who was later violently murdered. This is a recognizable narrative design for Cartwright, as the central character visits the country of his past to seek the truth about some traumatic moment that occurred there. But despite the distressing tone of the subject matter, Dan's pleasure in "being wised up to the fragility of [his] assumptions" (p. 205), and his concomitant desire to act responsibly toward those whose sense of their lives does not match his own, marks a remarkable shift in novelistic atmosphere from the relentlessly ironized self-obsession of the earlier books. This is ensured by a change to an open and clearly expressive technique, Dan's first-person present-tense delivery, with little narrative chicanery or opaque interiority.

A slide toward morally ambivalent relativism is, however, the major risk opened up by Dan's newfound interest in others' competing versions of the shared past and his desire to expand his own accordingly. After Dan meets the killer of Gloria's daughter in prison, an oblique way of making reparations and acknowledging Gloria's alternative version of the past he had taken so happily for granted, he tells her what she wants to hear: that her daughter did not suffer. The book's horrible irony is that Dan's pragmatic but humane abandonment of the truth aligns as neatly with Gloria's self-help book attitude to life, "You must only accept that which is true to your inner self"(p. 218), as it does with the true message from the killer, an abject and murderous individualism: "Everyone is a god who has the freedom to create his own truth" (p. 164).

Cartwright offers no solution to this conundrum, instead developing it by aligning the personal story with a broader social one. For Gary, Dan's erstwhile best friend, believes himself (by way of a nervous breakdown when at Harvard) to be a member of the Ojibway Native American people. When Dan goes along with Gary's spiritualist belief and participates in his rituals the scenes could appear ridiculous, but Cartwright plays them delicately and straight. For although Dan always retains a connection to the rational, to respect Gary's world, even though it is imaginary, is another aspect of the reparations he is making. This is a genuine enough sense of responsibility, even though Dan is aware it smacks of atonement for his liberal guilt. The successful unfolding of this story involves Dan illegally returning native artifacts to Gary and his Ojibway friends and in turn researching the information required for the repatriation of the remains of a tribal ancestor. In Cartwright's moral universe, we see, it does not matter whether or not Gary is fantasizing his Native American ancestry, given that his relationship with the tribe is accepted by and meaningful to both him and them. Equally, returning the stolen artifacts and remains must be morally right, even if the primary inspiration to do so is apparently inauthentic. If this ends-justifying-means consequentialism comes dangerously close to confirming Dan's observation that "everyone, even serial killers, can take refuge in claptrap" (p. 169), it is a risk that is taken in the book to help effect the crucial if "small migration" in Dan's morality from self-centeredness to ethical responsibility (p. 272).

Because the novel takes as its narrative focus the developing effect that this corrective shift has on Dan's relationships with others—indeed it is really more the result of Dan's experiences in the novel than indicative of a noticeable flourishing of his own character during it—there is little opportunity in *Leading the Cheers* to do more than suggest the person that Dan will become. Exploring the new modality of experience—in this case, romantic love—that can open up after a central character develops self-understanding through the acceptance of moral complicity is instead the subject of Cartwright's next novel, *Half in Love* (2001), which is dedicated to his mother.

It is his least critically acclaimed book, not perhaps because this is at root only a subtle change in direction from the world of *Leading the Cheers*; critics were not wholly convinced by the novel's portrayal of the turn-of-the-millennium political class, with some figures who have recognizable analogues in key figures in the New Labour government of Tony Blair. This shortfall is surprising, given Cartwright's long experience in politics: he was awarded the MBE (Member of the Most Excellent Order of the British Empire) for his work in the 1980s producing election broadcasts for the Liberal Party and the Liberal-SDP Alliance, the ever permanent bridesmaids of the British electoral system. Yet, an accurate portrait of a particular group of politicians and their period is not the principal intent of *Half in Love*, as much as is a more general romantic novel of social ideas (and ideals). Its focus is on the tribulations in the relationship—an affair presented as a grand love—of the two central characters, Richard McAllister, an intellectual brought into government by his friend the prime minister to "introduce some idealism into the manifesto" (p. 72), and Joanna Jermyn, an "English rose" actress who has starred in a massively successful romantic film. In Richard and Joanna's orbit is a set of character types that are further exercises from Cartwright's sketchbook: the Hollywood lothario, the self-aggrandizing leftist playwright, the lovable-but-plain stable-girl, the dubious new-age psychotherapist. But the novel's presiding questions are whether Richard and Joanna's relationship will survive the series of disillusionments and corruptions they suffer, whether political, familial, sexual, or artistic, and whether by doing so it can redeem them. In turn, with the love of Richard and Joanna, Cartwright tests out the ideal of romantic love as a possible source of broader social renewal.

The novel begins by describing the tingling of a scar on Richard's skin, the result of his being stabbed at an English soccer match after he has dismissively insulted a loutish supporter. It becomes clear that the man, Carl Panky, is a neo-Nazi who holds a grudge against Richard for testifying in the past against his cousin. In contrast to his generally warm feeling for rugby, touched on in a number of books and explored at length in his memoir of postapartheid South Africa, *Not Yet Home* (1996), this is an instance of Cartwright's profound suspicion of organized national sport, seeing in it the potential for a quasi-fascist atmosphere and a pretence of community. Richard's scar forms a recurrent motif in the book: his wound and the attack it remembers symbolically remind the reader of the inevitable social antagonism in the society that Richard's idealistic political peers dream of perfecting. Beyond this, too, the intimate sensation of the healed scar on Richard's flesh indicates his persistent social guilt and sense of moral complicity. We see these in action when Richard fails to give clear evidence against Panky in his trial for attempted murder; it is an ironic moment, quintessential of Cartwright's literary method. Richard has lost faith in the legal system, in part because it seems too keen to deliver the current political will of his friends in government (a crackdown on inner-city racism). The principal reason, however, is that his relationship with Joanna has faltered under the pressure of the tabloid gaze and its potential political impact (she sleeps with a costar). This has shattered any conviction and sense of faith that he had, and exacerbated the nihilist sense of the irrationality and meaninglessness of the world that was brought on by the stabbing in the first place. The irony, however, is that while it seems clear that Panky is guilty, Richard's own evidence is no less than honest (he did not see his attacker). Political and moral pragmatism, as well as the broader factual truth of the incident, are given over to the personal truth of Richard's experience.

The result is that Richard comes to his fullest recognition of the pragmatic basis and concomitant false idealism of politics: "democracy by its very nature is not a great endeavour: ... it is a compromise that must be dressed up in the language of idealism in order to make people believe" (p. 273). Richard accepts that he should have no part in this less-than-honest politics, but a similar idealism has been powerfully present in his virtual worship of Joanna and of their relationship. Love brings with it a certain enchantment and a surfeit of utopianism, an obsessive irrationality and an imagined sense of perfection. But these fantastic intensities of love are destructive because actual human beings necessarily fail to live up to them. The eventual purpose of the novel, then, is to explore, through his reconciliation with Joanna, Richard's other key realization: "You were said to get over love, to see that in some way you had been deceived, and to return to the real world. But the truth is that love gives the illusion—if it is an illusion—that there is a more real world. That was surely why love corresponded so exactly to human longings" (p. 296).

This is the ironic position (which the novel effectively endorses) of being "half in love": recognizing in love its necessary utopian energy but avoiding the dangerous fantasies of authenticity and wholeness that one associates with the grand romance, with "being in love." Cartwright ends the book by significantly swapping a biological metaphor for an artificial one: whereas Richard and Joanna once longed to become of one skin, something that might be thought to graft away Richard's scar and hide the traumatic truths it symbolizes, now they lie together "so close, you couldn't fit a single piece of paper between them" (p. 309). This detail, which simultaneously invokes a potential separation of Richard and Joanna as it denies it, gestures toward the complex potential of human love that the novel seeks to convey.

Through *Half in Love*'s African subplot, Cartwright reinforces the novel's broader critique of idealism by revisiting another of his key themes: the relationship between humans and animals. Both Richard and Joanna achieve a certain transcendence of their worldly woes through horse riding. But researching the history of his great-uncle, an expert horseman who fought at Mafeking in the Boer War, Richard comes to understand that if the persistence of the human-horse bond might seem to be "a romance written in the margins of history" (p. 287), the actuality is more tragic. The horses his great-uncle looked after at the insistence of his superior, Robert Baden-Powell, were ill-suited to the African terrain and so their main use was as food. Richard, in turn, finds himself selling his own beloved horse to pay the debts of his philandering father. This realism about human-horse relations is an important and pessimistic corrective to the escapism offered by the human dream of complete immersion in the other-than-human world. Such misconceived escapism is the guiding theme of Cartwright's next novel, short-listed for the Whitbread prize, *White Lightning* (2002).

In addition to drawing most powerfully on Cartwright's biography (many details of the novel's characterization and setting, as well as its overall mood, reenvision aspects of his life), *White Lightning* is the novel that most successfully integrates the theme of moral self-exploration into a novelistic whole and in doing so combines each of the major elements of Cartwright's narrative world thus far. These are the presence of animals, especially with the animal world casting a symbolic and ironic light on the human world; the experience of exile, the trauma of the past (particularly in colonial Africa), and how these shape the moral challenges of building a contemporary community; the difficult legacy of fathers replayed in a son's troubled middle-aged masculinity (often expressed in the form of a very energetic libido); the danger of allowing social myth to shape belief and action; and an inquiry into the dubious ethical potential of literature when considered against this latter process.

The narrator-protagonist is James Kronk, a failed film director who returns from London to his native Cape Town, where his mother is dying. With his opening line, "I was waiting for my mother to die" (p. 1), Cartwright revises the finality of the first words of *White Lightning*'s most notable precursor, Albert Camus's *The Outsider* (1942): "Mother died today. Or maybe yesterday,

I don't know" (p. 9). With this and other allusions, Cartwright is nodding heavily to the reader that his is a novel of contemporary existence, though perhaps one that expects of its characters resignation rather than blank indifference. Certainly, Kronk's dead father, an entomologist turned popular natural historian, will eventually be found to be a plagiarist (one successful work, *Animal Chatter*, is named after a Kiplingesque book of stories by the novelist's own father). Kronk's young son has died while he was in bed with a Swedish actress; this destroys both his staid married life and the affair that enlivened it. Similarly, his dreams of becoming a film auteur have not materialized; he only got so far as to make one salacious film, which, as we find out in a number of flashbacks, is based closely on Cartwright's only foray into feature directing, *Rosie Dixon, Night Nurse* (1978). The film offers an effective development of the novel's general atmosphere, in which abject failure attends upon already outmoded ambition, and *White Lightning* nicely extends this by featuring, in the actress Irene Ball, a well-drawn cameo clearly modeled on one important actor who worked with Cartwright: Beryl Reid. Ball, now embalmed in alcohol, is a dispiriting shadow of the exuberant postwar era of British comedy. Kronk's filmmaking dreams have degenerated into commissions from dubious companies and even shadier neoconservative politicians (Cartwright here very freely reimagines the 1990s political career of Sir James Goldsmith).

Kronk becomes gradually embroiled in life on the Cape peninsula. In what he characterizes as "an act of atonement … for the past, and for the lies and the deceit" (p. 47)—he is referring to his relationship with his mother as well as to the broader colonial history—he assumes responsibility for what he finds there. He not only takes over his mother's cottage and buys the surrounding farmstead, but he becomes the protector of Zwelakhe, a local Xhosa boy with HIV, and the boy's family. In a related endeavor, he also adopts a baboon (which he names Piet), an erstwhile children's attraction at the farm. These relationships guide the central plot and form the conceptual heart of the book, which works relentlessly to short-circuit Kronk's various routes to personal renewal. By looking after Zwelakhe, he appears to be aiming to expiate the guilt of his culture's ignorance of black South Africa (remarked figuratively by his mother's excision from his childhood photographs images of the son of a cook who drowned after Kronk invited him into the swimming pool). A very similar unconscious mechanism seems to be at work with Piet, as Kronk repeatedly refers to him as "my boy," the colloquial colonial epithet used to refer to black servants. And yet there are some genuinely thoughtful and moving scenes as he convinces himself that he is genuine in this "friendship," hoping to understand the human-animal relationship to help him publish his father's final manuscript (even if it also helps him work up a film script not unlike *Every Which Way but Loose*). But this all only intensifies the irony that Kronk's every act of paternalistic care for Piet and Zwelakhe seems to mourn his own lost, indeed abandoned, paternity. When Zwelakhe is killed, apparently by Piet but (it is hinted) more likely by a local man disgusted by his illness, Kronk releases Piet into the wild, only for him to be attacked by wild baboons; this leaves Kronk with no option but to shoot him. It is quite clear that friendship across species (like the whale-loving environmentalism of one of Kronk's brief lovers) is never more than a romantic dream.

As that dream collapses, Cartwright infects the entire textual world with the darkest postcolonial irony. Even the farmstead he has tried to renovate must be handed over on a legal technicality to a multinational mining company. There can be no escape, whether personal or social, from the traumas of the past, nor from the horrible moral exigencies of the present. So what is doubtless Cartwright's most pessimistic novel ends with a powerfully symbolic scene of moral and personal blankness. An omniscient narrator reports that Kronk is back in London, the removal of narrative control reinforcing that experience has shorn him of both his ideals and his sense of worldly value. His job as a motorbike courier allows him only to pick out "themes" (p. 246) from fortuitous coincidences in the origin and destination of the parcels he shuttles from place to place, and these grant no more than illusory coherence to his life: a feeble end to his search for atonement in the novel. Cartwright's last word, then, after his exploration of the moral self in the middle phase of his career, is to write it out of his work.

CONSOLATIONS OF FAMILY AND FRIENDSHIP: THE LATE-PHASE NOVELS

From this deracinated moment, Cartwright begins the late phase of his work: a series of three novels that proceed, a little more optimistically, to atomize the values, complexities, troubles, and restorative possibilities of two institutions almost entirely absent as subjects of concern in his earlier work—the middle-class English family and male heterosexual friendship. These are not, perhaps, of obvious centrality to the concerns of twenty-first-century English literature; even those quintessentially metropolitan English novelists of his generation, with whom Cartwright is often compared, Martin Amis and Ian McEwan, looked outward in the years after September 11th toward more urgent political questions. Nonetheless, the first of these late novels, *The Promise of Happiness* (2004), combined for Cartwright the recognition of the prestigious Hawthornden Prize and the popular circulation that comes with induction into the world of the television book club (on the U.K. talk show *Richard and Judy*).

The organizing narrative event of the book is the fencing of an ornate Louis Tiffany mausoleum window by Ju-Ju (Juliet), the golden child and sister of the comfortably middle-class Judd family, on behalf of her Upper East Side art-dealer boyfriend. Being starved of their idolatry after her imprisonment causes the family to implode: her father, Charles, is aimless and her mother, Daphne, bereft and confused; her brother Charlie is disaffected; and her younger sister Sophie is locked in a phase of adolescent acting out. Only Ju-Ju's eventual release is cast as the family's possible resurrection (it is a plot marked by several not noticeably ironic allusions to its Christian rhetoric: the window, for instance, depicts the resurrection and was stolen by one Larry Agnello). What marks out Cartwright's care

as a novelist, though, is that he fills out his characters with just enough realistic detail to show that such idolatry is not simply illogical fantasy. Rather, it emerges in response to the reality of lived experience. Daphne and Charles had a stillborn daughter before Ju-Ju was born; we also see just enough misogyny in Charles's reported affair with a lonely coworker, and in his tetchy frustration with his wife's quasi-maternal dedication to his well-being, to allow us to believe he would idealize his daughter because she places no such demands on him.

Cartwright has always been fascinated by solipsism, but Charlie's reflections on Ju-Ju's imprisonment display a new intensity of self-absorption that infects several of the characters in *The Promise of Happiness*: "When the judge, that sneering bitch, said that Ju-Ju would have to learn that nobody was above the law, what she failed to observe was that to take Ju-Ju from her lover and her father and from art and beauty was cruel and unnatural punishment" (p. 134). It is a genuine enough white-collar crime, however, even if a familiar late-narrative flourish informs the reader that the window was not in fact stolen, strictly speaking obviating Ju-Ju's offense. It is thus something of a struggle to take such pronouncements as Charlie's seriously (particularly, in the age of Guantanamo, its shaky Bill of Rights rhetoric, and its willful aestheticism in that context). And yet, Cartwright's portrayal of these characters is more than usually generous (revising the technique of *In Every Face I Meet* and *Half In Love*, chapters are given over to the thoughts of each character in turn); the effect of irony in the book is as a consequence considerably less biting. It is, therefore, a novel that firmly requires of its reader an acceptance of the inherent value of its topic—the tribulations of the bourgeois offered as emblematic of society more broadly—if it is not to come close to camp: taking too seriously what is essentially frivolous.

From such a vantage point, it is clear that whereas *White Lightening* detailed a failed search for selfhood in the absence of family, *The Promise of Happiness* is interested to fill out the ways that idealism might thread through a family's interpersonal life and to explore the strategies that a family forges to retain its sense of hope. In the end, the novel indicts the middle-class aspirational worldview for just this project of finding the perfect family, home, retirement, friends, even pet dog—it is an only nominally coherent group of ideals that turns dangerous when expected to function as a full guarantor of valuable existence. Cartwright suggests that in notions of family we find an irrepressible desire to seek more and more elaborate symbols of a secure identity, or perhaps, in this case, of homeliness. We hyperinvest in others, turning people into a form of fetish that obscures the complex human reality. The heavy melodrama of Ju-Ju's long-awaited return, an elaborate set-piece of Englishness played (where else?) at a provincial train station, encapsulates this point as her father, Charles, simply does not recognize her:

> She sees them, standing quite close together, under the bridge that crosses the platform. He's wearing a dark-blue fleece and a cap, and she, a head lower, is in a green puffa jacket.
>
> … Mum runs and hops forward to embrace her. Dad waits. She looks towards him. He comes forward. She is still in her mother's arms; her mother is crying.
>
> "Who are you?" he says.
>
> "No, Dad, no," says Sophie, "don't say that, Dad, please."
>
> "It's OK, Sophie. Dad, it's me. It's Ju-Ju."
>
> "He hasn't got over the pneumonia. Charles!"
>
> "It's Ju-Ju, Dad."
>
> "Ju-Ju? You have ruined our fucking lives."
>
> (pp. 289–290)

As that doubting last question mark makes clear, the real woman before him can never be "Ju-Ju," as the cloying diminutive will forever name Charles's imagined perfect daughter. This climactic scene casts a pall over the apparently upbeat denouement of the book, Charlie's wedding: the most classic of romantic-comedic closures, it is a symbol of family coherence and renewal. And

yet, if the Judd family's process of idealizing and idolizing is indeed irrepressible, as the novel suggests, such rituals will—indeed should, for Cartwright—continue for the simple reason that they exercise "the promise of happiness," rather than delivering a sense of plenitude, the desire for which his novels consistently encourage us to outgrow.

That said, *The Song Before It Is Sung* (2007), Cartwright's thirteenth and most intently philosophical novel, finally grants more worth to a sense of the ideal than any of his other works. This is because it takes as its broad subject the conflict between romantic nationalism and liberal pluralism, tested in the crucible of 1930s Nazism and against a quintessential moment of moral action: the Valkyrie plot to assassinate Hitler in July 1944. These competing views are embodied in the complex friendship between a Jewish intellectual, Elya Mendel, and a German aristocrat, Axel von Gottberg. These are Cartwright's avatars for the Oxford political philosopher Isaiah Berlin (1909–1997) and his friend Adam von Trott (1909–1944), from whom Berlin was estranged after von Trott wrote a letter to the *Manchester Guardian* repudiating the newspaper's claim that there was anti-Semitism in the German courts in the 1930s. It is Cartwright's first foray into fiction based on extensive historiography, and if some (such as John Gray and Adam Mars-Jones) have expressed concern at the book's factual and character inaccuracies, rising to genuine disquiet about Cartwright's entry into this morally fraught terrain, Berlin himself is certainly an understandable subject. Cartwright had been an admirer since reading him as an undergraduate at Johannesburg University, and he saw Berlin speak when studying politics himself at Oxford. Cartwright fleshes out his appreciation of Berlin in his ruminative book-length memoir of the university, *This Secret Garden* (2008). But in an essay titled "Berlin, My Hero," Cartwright calls him "the greatest exponent of a broadly liberal, pluralist politics there has ever been" (*Jewish Quarterly*). The somewhat proprietorial remarks about Jewishness in the same piece also cast a light on the otherwise surprising recurrence of reflections on and imaginings of

Jewish identity throughout his work: "I can sum it up simply by calling myself a wannabe Jew. From my earliest days I have had the sense that Jews embody the distillation of what it is to be human. As if being Jewish were somehow a more extreme version of being human" (*Jewish Quarterly*). But in *The Song Before It Is Sung*, Jewishness is less at the forefront of Cartwright's attention than is the exploration of Berlin's ideas through a rich human drama.

The crux of the novel is a complex dilemma of political philosophy: the character Axel von Gottberg was motivated by "an idea of an alternative Germany of spiritually conscious people, enlightened Germany, which would inherit when Hitler was gone"; but "[his] friends in England did not understand; they wished to crush Nazi Germany into the dust. But they didn't realise that by saying this they were offering the German people no option but to stick with Hitler" (pp. 164–165). Inspired by the romantic notion of a pure German spirit, von Gottberg believes himself, thinks Elya Mendel, to be "an agent of history"; but "the idea that history has agents is deeply repugnant to Mendel. It runs contrary to everything he believes about personal responsibility. It lies at the heart of fascism." The irony, of course, is that it is precisely his spiritually informed agency that gives von Gottberg the courage to attempt Hitler's assassination.

The story that is shaped around this moral-philosophical paradox emerges via a recognizable Cartwright narratorial figure, Conrad Senior, befriended by the late Mendel when Senior was a student and bequeathed, along with Mendel's letters, the task of cohering them into the story of his friendship with von Gottberg. Conrad is dissolute, however, and his practical and upwardly mobile wife, Francine, is on the way to leaving him, exasperated by his ponderous failure to achieve anything with this last in a succession of abortive creative projects. Cartwright captures this all well against the resonant details of a dissolving marriage: Conrad's ignorant comfort among the mess of documents balanced by Francine's efficient but sanguine list dividing their possessions; hopeless reconciliations; jealous demands and recriminations. But the reason

Conrad struggles to get anywhere with the project is that its demands are clearly impossible. Looking beyond the personalities in the letters to his enigmatic father (an apartheid-appeasing newspaperman), "it is his task to give a coherent account of these lives, and so perhaps of his own" (p. 120). Conrad's lesson in the novel is to abandon this principle of coherence, with its logical affinity in the novel to the book's other grand project: von Gottberg's ideal of a spiritually unified Germany. He learns, certainly, that such coherence will not reside in an all-explaining "truth"; the novel's ultimate example of this brute reality is a film of von Gottberg's hanging. Watching it is a moment of abject, chaotic horror that utterly traumatizes Conrad, disabuses him of his fondness for Mendel's philosophical prevarications about von Gottberg's ideology, and returns him to his original writer's block.

The novel offers only the subtlest resolution to this dilemma, one that insists on the entry of literature into the book's philosophical conundrums. Its title derives from a quotation of Alexander Herzen, favored by Berlin: "what is the song before it is sung?" It alludes to the necessarily human-given basis of every ideal and, equally, insists that such ideals can only take their value from that very basis, just as a song's beauty only emerges in the singing. This is, fittingly, the ethos of the novel as a whole. The book ends with Conrad re-creating von Gottberg's final swim in the lake on his beloved German estate, an emotive narrative closure that endorses his tragic heroism. But this is importantly balanced by the novel's very deliberate—human-given—construction. It has become gradually clear that the novel we are reading—a relatively disjointed compendium of Conrad's bathetic story; sections imagining the lives of von Gottberg, Mendel, their friends and lovers; and the interpolated letters and memoirs of some of these people—is Conrad's own tentative, flawed, and determinedly not idealistic attempt to give sense to the tragic event that corrupted Mendel and von Gottberg's friendship.

The last novel to be covered in this essay, *To Heaven by Water* (2009), begins with its central character listening to his brother declaiming "The

Windhover" by Gerard Manley Hopkins; it ends with David Cross reciting the sonnet himself. That Cartwright on both occasions fully transcribes the poem (unsurprisingly without its dedication, "to Christ our Lord") makes clear that its meaning is central to the novel's. Hopkins's poem is a series of stunning images in which the speaker is enthralled to watch a hawk soar in flight and then, even more beautiful, flip upside down when it buckles in the wind. The poem celebrates a beauty that is all the more intense because it emerges, exceeding perfection and transcendence, from the natural, mortal reality—a reality of imperfection that resides everywhere. Picking up this theme, Cartwright revisits the social world of *The Promise of Happiness*, the troubled middle-class family and its aging paterfamilias. But whereas in that novel the epitomizing note of imperfection was the black moment of Juliet's crime, here the disruptive taint of trauma, corruption, and tragedy spreads to each major character.

It is true that there is a certain recursiveness to Cartwright's imagination that takes effect visibly in *To Heaven by Water*, spreading from narrative organization and technique to almost insignificant detail: this is one of at least seven novels, for example, in which a woman is carefully described with a crease between her thighs and hips that carries an erotic charge for a man. As one of his early champions, the novelist and critic D. J. Taylor, puts it, "The result is not so much a series of novels as a single text, whose separate compartments leach endlessly into each other." But this allows the book, and the Hopkins-inspired consolations it offers, to be read in conclusion as an apt summation of Cartwright's work to this point.

Building the atmosphere of the book by revealing one by one how its characters' ideal lives are besmirched by worldly reality, the book displays all of Cartwright's efficiency in the organization of plot and his narrative accomplishment. If a whole family has been affected by the death to cancer of the mother, Nancy, each member of the family has his or her individual dark moments. David is a relaxed if aimless retired television news anchor, but his apparent social smoothness masks deep unease and troubling memories (a girlfriend in his youth abandoned to drown, the repeated sight of brutal violence when reporting from Afghanistan and elsewhere). A depressive boyfriend stalks David's twenty-something daughter, Lucy, until his eventual feigned suicide attempt. His puerile son, Ed, is unsatisfied by the life that has been handed to him on a plate, so he drifts into and out of an affair with his legal trainee. Perfect though Ed's wife, Rosalie, appears to be, the spiritual emptiness brought on by their childlessness and her discovery of Ed's affair causes her to drunkenly seduce her father-in-law, who promptly retreats to his native South Africa to visit his dying brother, Guy. Guy, in turn, has in effect abandoned his family in search of spiritual affinity with nature in the Kalahari and what he sees as the primitive wisdom of the Bushmen. But the transcendence this offers is elusive at best: in scenes reminiscent of his early novels, and sharing with them some of his most richly evocative and convincing writing, Cartwright first shows this pastoralism in action as the characters appreciate the beauty of the African landscape; he then casts a heavy shadow of irony over it by way of the brutal reality of colonial violence portrayed in the cave paintings Guy reveres and the more mundane destruction of Guy's phobic need to kill snakes.

It is a fictional atmosphere in which every character is like Lucy: "I am not immune in any way to life's realities" (p. 262). This is an example of the unexpected interruptions of the first person that pepper the narrative and have a peculiarly arresting effect: acting to remind the reader of how tenuous and momentary is the coherence, honesty, or lucidity of individual experience when set against the weight of social expectation and code. And yet, at end of the novel, all the characters (except Guy, who commits suicide-by-trampling with his beloved elephants in the desert) are carefully avoiding, hiding, or just plain ignorant of the realities, celebrating the baptism of the mixed-generation child. This moment embodies an ideal of the future lived in acceptance, if not denial, of the "usual hypocrisies," of what one character calls "the necessary fictions" (p. 290), pointedly quoting a phrase used by a friend of Friedrich Engels to describe his theory about the unreality of value in a capitalist world: "I have beliefs but I don't believe in them," is David's succinct, paradoxical summation (p. 292). *To Heaven by Water* portrays a world that is to be valued all the more acutely because of its exposure both to life's destructiveness and to the impossibility of moral redemption. And this, for Cartwright, is our only world: perhaps the object lesson of his late phase, as of his work as a whole.

Selected Bibliography

WORKS OF JUSTIN CARTWRIGHT

NOVELS

The New Avengers 4: Fighting Men. London: Futura, 1977. (A taut but relatively formulaic adventure thriller, written for a series of novels tied in to the eponymous 1970s television series.)

The Revenge. Chicago: Contemporary Books, 1978. (An unusual if occasionally crass post-Watergate conspiracy thriller focused on the assassination of an Irish American candidate for the US presidency.)

The Horse of Darius. London: Hamish Hamilton, 1980. (The most stylistically accomplished of Cartwright's thrillers is set in the Middle East; the plot addresses various attempts to assassinate the Shah of Iran.)

Freedom for the Wolves. Harmondsworth, U.K.: Penguin, 1983.

Interior. London: Hamish Hamilton, 1988.

Look at It This Way. London: Picador, 1990.

Masai Dreaming. London: Macmillan, 1993.

In Every Face I Meet. London: Sceptre, 1995.

Leading the Cheers. London: Sceptre, 1999.

Half in Love. London: Hodder & Stoughton, 2001.

White Lightning. London: Sceptre, 2002.

The Promise of Happiness. London: Bloomsbury, 2004.

The Song Before It Is Sung. London: Bloomsbury, 2007.

To Heaven by Water. London: Bloomsbury, 2009.

Other People's Money. London: Bloomsbury, 2011.

MEMOIR

Not Yet Home: A South African Journey. London: Fourth Estate, 1996.

This Secret Garden: Oxford Revisited. London: Bloomsbury, 2008.

FILM AND TELEVISION BASED ON THE WORKS OF CARTWRIGHT

Look at It This Way. Screenplay by Justin Cartwright. Directed by Gavin Millar. BBC Films, 1992.

Daisy. Screenplay Justin Cartwright. Directed by Peter Duffell. BBC Films, 1980. (A screen adaptation of Cartwright's *Freedom for the Wolves*.)

FILM AND TELEVISION DIRECTED BY CARTWRIGHT

Rosie Dixon, Night Nurse. Columbia Pictures. 1978. (The making of this film is fictionalized in *White Lightning*.)

The World About Us: The Lion of Swaziland–King Scbhusa II. BBC Films, 1980. (A fictionalization of this subject appears in *In Every Face I Meet*.)

Q.E.D.: The Long Night of the Lion. BBC Films, 1983.

Dispatches: Beyond the Rubicon. Cartwright and Associates, 1990. (A documentary about academic discussions of apartheid.)

Omnibus: Mayibuye I Afrika: Let Africa Come Home. BBC Films, 1997. (Details of the making of this film appear in *Not Yet Home*.)

The Secrets of the Dead Sea Scrolls. Orion Foundation, 1999. (Cartwright's interest in this topic appears in a number of his books.)

Witness: The Quest for the True Cross. Icon Films, 2001.

SELECTED JOURNALISM

"Walking in the Shadow of God." *Financial Times*, March 16, 1996.

"Wasps in the Sandwiches." *Financial Times*, August 17, 1996, p. 1.

"Perspectives: The Lessons and Bruises of Life's Great Scrum." *Financial Times*, July 5, 1997, p. 3.

"Unspeakable Fear." *Guardian*, August 20, 1998.

"Another Country: Life Stories." *Times Magazine*, October 3, 1998, p. 103.

"The Indestructible Power of Belief." *Guardian* (http://www.guardian.co.uk/books/2000/may/27/historybooks.books), May 26, 2000.

"The End of the Pier Show and the Cult of Celebrity." *Guardian*, July 28, 2001.

"Familiar Ground." *Guardian*, November 3, 2001.

"Berlin, My Hero." *Jewish Quarterly* (http://www.jewishquarterly.org/issuearchive/article8255.html?articleid=451), winter 2008.

"Now South Africa Must Stay True to Mandela's Vision." *London Evening Standard*, January 8, 2010.

"Once upon a Life: Justin Cartwright." *Observer Magazine* (http://www.guardian.co.uk/lifeandstyle/2010/aug/22/justin-cartwright-once-upon-life), August 21, 2010, p. 5.

JUSTIN CARTWRIGHT

BIOGRAPHICAL AND CRITICAL STUDIES

SELECTED INTERVIEWS

Brown, Mick. "A Writer's Life: Justin Cartwright." *Daily Telegraph* (http://www.telegraph.co.uk/culture/books/3622212/A-writers-life-Justin-Cartwright.html), August 15, 2004.

Fitzherbert, Claudia. "Animal Attractions." *Daily Telegraph* (http://www.telegraph.co.uk/culture/books/fictionreviews/3580918/Animal-attractions.html), August 3, 2002.

Fountain, Nigel. "The Lion, the Pitch, and the Whitbread." *Guardian*, October 29, 1990, p. 23.

Rabinovitch, Dina. "Justin Cartwright: The Cheerleader Who Broke Ranks." *Independent,* January 13, 2001.

Robinson, David. "Just Cartwright Interview: Out of the Ordinary." *Scotsman* (http://living.scotsman.com/books/Justin-Cartwright-interview-Out-of.5397582.jp), June 24, 2009.

Wroe, Nicholas. "How to Get Ahead in Novelising." *Guardian* (http://www.guardian.co.uk/books/2000/sep/09/fiction.whitbreadbookawards2002), September 9, 2000.

——. "This Stuff Matters." *Guardian* (http://www.guardian.co.uk/books/2007/feb/17/fiction.featuresreviews4), February 17, 2007.

SELECTED REVIEWS AND CRITICISM

Adams, Tim. "Ingerland, Their Ingerland." *Observer*, January 14, 2001, p. D16. (Review of *Half in Love.*)

——. "In Pursuit of Happiness." *Observer Review* (http://www.guardian.co.uk/books/2009/jun/21/to-heaven-by-water-justin-cartwright), June 21, 2009, p. 20. (Review of *Masai Dreaming.*)

Baker, Phil. "A Master of How We Live." *Sunday Times Book Review*, September 13, 1998, p. 13. (Review of *Leading the Cheers.*)

Barnacle, Hugo. "A Panadol Box Behind the Ear." *Independent*, September 4, 1993, p. 27. (Review of *Masai Dreaming.*)

Bray, Christopher. "Dark Continent of the Mind." *Independent on Sunday*, August 22, 1993, p. 29. (Review of *Masai Dreaming.*)

Brownjohn, Alan. "A Last Redoubt of Englishness." *Times Literary Supplement*, August 20, 2004, p. 21. (Review of *The Promise of Happiness.*)

Eder, Richard. "*Interior* Is Waylaid by Ghosts." *Los Angeles Times* (http://articles.latimes.com/1989-05-11/news/vw-3253_1_justin-cartwright-ghost-quest-into-deep-africa), May 11, 1989. (Review of *Interior.*)

Ferraro, Julian. "Finding Oneself in Hollybush." *Times Literary Supplement*, September 11, 1998, p. 22. (Review of *Leading the Cheers.*)

Gates, David. "Sinsemilla and Sensibility." *New York Times Book Review* (http://www.nytimes.com/2009/08/16/books/review/Gates-t.html), August 13, 2009. (Review of *To Heaven by Water.*)

Glazebrook, Olivia. "The Return of the Native." *Spectator* (http://www.spectator.co.uk/books/21023/part_2/the-return-of-the-native.thtml), August 14, 2004. (Review of *The Promise of Happiness.*)

Gray, John. "Freedom Fighter." *New Statesman* (http://www.newstatesman.com/books/2007/03/von-trott-hitler-berlin), March 12, 2007. (Review of *The Song Before It Is Sung.*)

Lezard, Nicholas. "Marks of Weakness, Marks of Woe." *Independent*, September 30, 1995. (Review of *In Every Face I Meet.*)

Marais, Mike. "Reading Against Race: J. M. Coetzee's *Disgrace*, Justin Cartwright's *White Lightning,* and Ivan Vladivasic's *The Restless Supermarket.*" *Journal of Literary Studies* 19, nos. 3–4:271–289 (2003).

——. "'We Know Bugger-All About Baboons': Nature and Exile in Justin Cartwright's *White Lightning.*" *English Academy Review* 20, no. 1:69–87 (2003).

Mars-Jones, Adam. "Enough of This Nazi Martyrdom." *Observer Review* (http://www.guardian.co.uk/books/2007/feb/04/fiction.features3), February 3, 2007, p. 24. (Review of *The Song Before It Is Sung.*)

Papineau, David. "A Bloke's View." *Times Literary Supplement*, September 15, 1995, p. 22. (Review of *In Every Face I Meet.*)

Saynor, James. "Mr Curtis, He Dead." *Independent on Sunday*, August 22, 1993, p. 49. (Review of *Masai Dreaming.*)

Stead, Margaret. "Manifesto Minister." *Times Literary Supplement*, January 19, 2001, p. 22. (Review of *Half in Love.*)

Taylor, D. J. "*To Heaven by Water,* by Justin Cartwright." *Independent on Sunday* (http://www.independent.co.uk/arts-entertainment/books/reviews/to-heaven-by-water-by-justin-cartwright-1739631.html), July 10, 2009.

OTHER WORKS CITED

Camus, Albert. *The Outsider.* Translated by Joseph Laredo. London: Penguin Classics, 2000. Originally published 1942.

MICHAEL DONAGHY

(1954—2004)

Jonathan Ellis

MICHAEL DONAGHY WAS one of the most innovative and influential contemporary poets of the late twentieth century. Born in the United States to Irish Catholic parents, Donaghy spent the final two decades of his life in London, where he worked as a freelance writer, a talented musician, and an inspiring teacher. In his lifetime, Donaghy published three full-length collections of poetry—*Shibboleth* (1988), *Errata* (1993), and *Conjure* (2000)—together with a much-admired short prose work, *Wallflowers: A Lecture on Poetry with Misplaced Notes and Additional Heckling* (1999). In 2005 a fourth volume of poetry titled *Safest* was published posthumously. It took its name from the computer file in which Donaghy had been storing poems for his next collection. In 2009 his *Collected Poems* and an edition of his prose, *The Shape of the Dance: Essays, Interviews and Digressions*, appeared with introductions by Sean O'Brien and Clive James respectively. In addition to reprinting Donaghy's four collections of poetry, the *Collected Poems* also includes fourteen previously unpublished poems. *The Shape of the Dance* begins with *Wallflowers*. The book also brings together a number of important essays, introductions, and reviews. In the final section, five interviews with the author provide crucial biographical information.

At the time of his death at the age of fifty, Donaghy's reputation among British and Irish poets was extremely high. Each of his three poetry collections attracted the attention of both critics and prize committees. He received the Geoffrey Faber Memorial Prize and the Whitbread Poetry Prize for his first collection, *Shibboleth*. After the publication of his second volume, *Errata*, he was given generous grants from the Arts Council of England and the Ingram-Merrill Foundation in America, and in 1994 he was among twenty poets under forty years old selected for the controversial "New Generation Poets" promotion (other poets included were Simon Armitage, Carol Ann Duffy, Lavinia Greenlaw, Mick Imlah, Kathleen Jamie, and Don Paterson). His third collection, *Conjure*, won the Forward Poetry Prize, Britain's biggest contemporary poetry award, as well as being short-listed for both the 2000 T. S. Eliot Award and the Whitbread Poetry Award.

In America, where his books were not available and relatively few of his poems were published, he was hardly known at all, a situation that has not changed much since his death. Catherine Tufariello, in an essay published the year before he died, called him "the best-kept secret in American poetry" (p. 67). In an obituary for the American journal *Poetry*, Jon Mooallem admitted that "we could never quite call him one of ours, and yet he was precisely the sort of artist American poetry so desperately needed" (p. 237). Like other poet-exiles, Donaghy remains better known in the country he died in rather than the country in which he was born. He was England's most beloved American contemporary poet, his poems arguably more popular than work by John Ashbery, Jorie Graham, or Sharon Olds.

When asked by John Wall whether he wanted to be classified as "British, Irish, or American," Donaghy gave the following reply: "My heritage is Irish, Catholic and proletarian. You can't shake any of those things, no matter how hard you try. But I can't locate in myself any trace of nationalism or patriotism or class allegiance, which is to say I feel a bit of a trespasser everywhere" (*The Shape of the Dance* [hereafter referred to as *Dance*], p. 141). This trespassing spirit extends to the character of the poems as well. While Donaghy had favorite poets—John Keats, W. H. Auden, Robert Frost, Elizabeth Bishop, Louis MacNeice, and Derek Mahon, among them—he never belonged to any movement or school of poets. "Movements," he once said, "are dreamt up by publicists to help us sell poetry or by journalists and academic bores to help us misunderstand it" (*Dance*, p. 99). "No room for membership cards in my wallet" (*Dance*, p. 144), he warned another interviewer.

Nationality is too simple a descriptive straitjacket for Donaghy's poetry. As he said elsewhere, "I have no interest in promoting a particular national identity for myself as a poet. ... When I sit down to breakfast, however, I'm an imperfect Irish-American longtime resident of the cosmopolitan North London Borough of Haringey" (*Dance*, p. 178). Donaghy occupies all of these locations in his writing, sometimes simultaneously. He can be as American as Robert Frost or Wallace Stevens, as English as Ted Hughes or Philip Larkin, as Irish as Seamus Heaney or Derek Mahon. Like Paul Muldoon, who made the opposite transatlantic journey, he also speaks in a hyphenated "Irish-American" voice. Attempting to read his poetry in relation to individual literary movements creates, as Donaghy cautions, more misunderstandings. He has love poems like John Donne, conversation poems like Samuel Taylor Coleridge and William Wordsworth, dramatic monologues like Robert Browning, and travel poems like Elizabeth Bishop. Perhaps this range and variety is Donaghy's most characteristic feature. "I'm afraid I'm more a Zelig than a Pessoa" (*Dance*, p. 187), he replied when asked why he had made up a fictional Welsh poet in his first book, *Shibboleth*.

FOUR REASONS TO DISTRUST BIOGRAPHY

In an interview with John Stammers in 2003, Donaghy expressed surprise that an author of "three skinny little books should be the subject of so many 'profiles'" (*Dance*, p. 169). Donaghy was ambivalent about providing biographical material for "four reasons":

First, I'm not the definitive authority on my work. In fact, I'm not at all sure I write my books. I feel it's more that my books get written through me. Second, I wind up making insufferably pretentious statements like that last one. Third, I like to think my work is still developing and I suspect that any attempt to "explain" myself interferes with or limits that development. And finally, I'd like to be remembered for my poems, not my charming personality. I say this not because I'm an especially reticent or private individual—but because my work has a life of its own and if it works, it's as much "about" the reader's life as about mine.

(*Dance*, p. 169)

The latter belief was an important one for Donaghy who felt that poems should be as much "about" other people as himself. In *Wallflowers,* Donaghy celebrates experiences such as "bedtime stories and ritual dramas like *Oedipus Rex* or the Mass" in which "the audience are participants in total immersion, surrendering consciousness and voice to the story. But to read critically, as poetry readers do, alone in bed, or at their desks, or huddled together around the workshop table—wallflowers—is to scribble in the margin" (*Dance*, p. 10).

Anything that comes in the way of such an intimate encounter, the encounter between poem and reader, was, in Donaghy's opinion, an unnecessary distraction. Biography, as can be seen in all of his interview replies, was top of his list of reader distractions. He thought that it clogged up the margin for readers, taking away the metaphorical white space around a poem whereby readers' own lives and thoughts might finish the poem. Readers in agreement with Donaghy's philosophy might obviously skip the next section.

Those still here might like to bear in mind another of Donaghy's statements about the relationship between art and life:

I'm warning the reader not to expect "the real Michael Donaghy" in any documentary sense. I'm not sure I'm a reliable narrator of events even to myself. Just as poets' ideal readers are always ghostly composites of themselves, their contemporaries, deceased influences, their family and friends, so readers must realize that poets, too, are ghostly compounds of fact and invention. So a story I write from the point of view of a Japanese courtesan or an early Christian saint may be as or more autobiographical than a poem about the death of my father.

(*Dance*, p. 198)

"The real Michael Donaghy" cannot be found in the poems. If there are autobiographical elements to them (Donaghy implies that there may be), they are likely to occur in poems that appear to have nothing to do with the life story. Here, with all these caveats, is Donaghy's biography.

THE "REAL" MICHAEL DONAGHY

Michael John Donaghy was born in the Bronx, New York, on May 24, 1954. Donaghy's Irish parents, Patrick and Evelyn Donaghy, immigrated to America sometime between 1949 and 1950. His father was from Belfast, his mother from Tralee. Both parents worked at the Statler Hilton hotel in Manhattan, his father in the boiler room, his mother as a hotel maid. Around the time Donaghy was four years old, the family moved back to Ireland for a year and lived briefly in both his parents' hometowns. His father had hopes of finding work back in Belfast. According to Donaghy: "They always regarded themselves as Irish-in-exile so this was to be their triumphant return home. But the work never materialized, so we returned, broke, to the Bronx, where my father eventually got work in a factory that made printing presses" (*Dance*, pp. 169–170). The Donaghy family settled in the South Bronx, an area that had once been predominantly Irish. Indeed, in the 1920s and 1930s it was briefly celebrated for the concentration of Irish musicians who lived and recorded music in the area, a history Donaghy looks back on nostalgically in several poems, particularly the "O'Ryan's Belt" section of *Errata*.

Certainly growing up in the South Bronx had a profound effect on Donaghy's development as both a young man and a poet. It was, he frequently admitted, "a dangerous place to live even in the sixties. ... I wasn't tough and I attribute my survival to the fact that I kept off the streets" (*Dance*, p. 141). Maddy Paxman, Donaghy's widow, remembers Donaghy saying that as a child his parents would send him to play and that he would often take refuge in the public library, getting himself a very broad education in the process. Donaghy is self-conscious about how he presents such experiences: "I want to avoid overdramatizing this" (*Dance*, p. 141), he informed John Wall in a 1996 interview. "I don't want to over-dramatize the South Bronx" (*Dance*, p. 148), he told Conor O'Callaghan the year after. "I could say it was a hard life, and perhaps I should," he mused aloud in 2003. "But my childhood friends would laugh to hear me putting on 'the poor mouth.' After relating these details in several interviews my story is beginning to sound like an over-dramatized application for marginality status, the cliché sob-story of the working-class writer" (*Dance*, p. 170). Dramatic or not, he was still reflecting on his experiences in the Bronx a full two decades after leaving home in the 1970s. "I still dream about the Bronx," he admitted in 1996. "I suppose it's like an experience of war. Except in my case I spent the war hiding in a foxhole. The Bronx is important to me because of the genii of the place, its local gods" (*Dance*, p. 142). By the time he was thirty, Donaghy had lost both parents—his mother at the age of forty-nine when he was still a teenager, and his father in 1983, in his early sixties.

Life in the "foxhole" included exposure to Irish music and poetry. Donaghy's mother sang traditional songs to him and his father played the harmonica. There was also an uncle who had an accordion. However, it was not until much later, when Donaghy was in college, that he took up the tin whistle and bodhran. Although his father left school at fourteen, he had a broad range of passions which he shared with his son, including machinery and mysticism. The first poem in Donaghy's debut collection, *Shibboleth*, is called, not incidentally, "Machines," and is in many ways a tribute to his father's "gadgetry of love" (*Collected Poems*, p. 5). Donaghy's interest in poetry undoubtedly came from his father, who always kept books in the house. It was there as a boy that he became "intoxicated by the music in Hopkins and Dylan Thomas" (*Dance*, p. 172). Donaghy's literary education was furthered by a lucky encounter as a teenager. From 1972 to 1977, he worked as doorman on an apartment block on Fifth Avenue, where the family now lived in the basement behind the boiler (his father was the building superintendent). Reading on the job was forbidden, but during the summer doormen were allowed to hold rather than wear their hats, so Donaghy kept a book hidden inside the crown. One day one of the residents noticed he was reading Gerard Manley Hopkins. She turned out to be the treasurer of the famous poetry reading series at the 92nd Street Y. As his punishment for reading at work she gave him a free subscription to the Poetry Centre. Donaghy had never been to a poetry reading before, but within a month he had seen both the Argentine author Jorge Borges and English poet Basil Bunting. He later described attending the poetry reading series as "my conversion" (*Dance*, p. 190).

A second "conversion," this time to Irish poetry, occurred during Donaghy's time as an undergraduate at Fordham University. Around 1974, he enrolled in a course on twentieth-century Anglo-Irish literature taught by a young teacher named Mary Fitzgerald. The course concentrated on James Joyce and Samuel Beckett, but Fitzgerald also introduced students to the burgeoning contemporary Irish poetry scene. She invited Seamus Heaney to do a poetry reading on campus and took students to hear Robert Lowell read in Manhattan. More important for Donaghy's particular development as a poet, she encouraged him to read the work of Derek Mahon. The young writer found Mahon's poetry immediately "seductive. It was a revelation to encounter this singing line, this wit, this panache, this performed personality, after the vast solemn impersonal footnoted systems of the Modernist long poem" (*Dance*, p. 173).

In 1977 Donaghy went west to the University of Chicago to begin but ultimately never finish a PhD on the Italian philosopher Giordano Bruno. He was introduced to the poems of Elizabeth Bishop and James Merrill but became increasingly critical of the academic study of literature, in particular the rise of theory. In the acknowledgments to *Wallflowers*, for example, Donaghy mocks the "modern pedagogues" who "want to be the main event." "If poetry depended on intellectuals for its survival," he felt, "it would be about as current as hieroglyphics" (*Dance*, p. 40). "I thought I'd do a degree in literature because I loved literature," he later said. "Then I realized that my colleagues hated literature. It's

like saying that I decided to do vivisection because I loved animals. It's not the same thing, is it?" (*Dance*, p. 150). In interviews, Donaghy liked to tell the story of being asked to leave the room by Paul de Man. In the poem "No" (which was unpublished during Donaghy's lifetime), he dreams of wearing the same suit for six years, developing an amphetamine psychosis, and in a final flourish, sitting before de Man "with two ideas / inked on my knuckles" (*Collected Poems*, p. 223). Donaghy does not, unfortunately, divulge what these "two ideas" might be. Instead of finishing his PhD, he began to spend time playing flute with a traditional Irish band and working as poetry editor of the *Chicago Review*. He went through a John Ashbery phase, completed what "amounted to a book-length collection of sub-Ashbery smartass surrealist verse" (*Dance*, p. 173), abandoned that, and eventually finished a chapbook called *Slivers* (1985), which formed the basis of his first full-length collection of poems, *Shibboleth*. He also fell in love, and when Maddy Paxman returned to England in 1985, he followed her. They married in 2003. Their son, Ruairi, to whom Donaghy dedicated his third book *Conjure*, was born in 1996.

The move to Britain was both a personal and a professional success. Donaghy received a contract for *Shibboleth* from Oxford University Press the year of his arrival, and the title poem, "Shibboleth," came second in the National Poetry Competition. Donaghy continued to play music on a professional basis. He recorded a CD with the jazz band Lammas and another with the composer John Wall. In collaboration with the director Miranda Pennel and the distinguished Beckett actress Fiona Shaw, he also made a short film, *Habit*, the text of which is included in the *Collected Poems*. It was awarded first prize at an international cinema festival in Valencia, Spain. Following the success of *Shibboleth*, Donaghy was invited to review poetry for a range of British newspapers and periodicals. He also appeared on BBC Radio and as a guest on television programs such as the BBC arts series *The Late Show*. In 1999 he was made a fellow of the Royal Society of Literature.

Donaghy was particularly influential both as a performer of his own work and as a teacher of poetry. He was famous for reciting his poems from memory. Indeed, he thought being able to memorize a poem an important test of a poem's success. "I'm striving for a memorizable form," he once explained, "and reading from memory tests the poem" (*Dance*, p. 145). In *Wallflowers*, he expanded on the importance of "memorizable form." It is one of his most important statements on poetry:

> When we learn a dance step, a part in a play, a song, or a poem by heart, we give it a body to live in. We own a poem, or at least our expression of it, in a profoundly deeper way than is possible if it's stored away on a page. … If its words are ingrained in our memories they're constantly available to our unconscious, like a computer program running in the background. If its words are inscribed on our hearts, they can guide us out of our emptiness.
>
> (*Dance*, p. 38)

From 1988 Donaghy held various part-time positions at Birkbeck College and City University. In his role as Creative Reader-in-Residence for the Poetry Society in 1998–1999 he organized discussions of poetry to revive its appeal for readers who had been put off by the overly cerebral approach taken in schools. Donaghy frequently railed against the proliferation of creative writing programs in America. "A typical assignment in these classes is a poem a week," he reported, "whether or not one has anything to say—and after graduation one is expected to publish a collection and go on to teach … creative writing. This bizarre inbreeding has produced a new kind of academic verse, not the bookish stuff literary critics do for a hobby, but the unique idiom of full-time writer-teachers" (*Dance*, pp. 95–96). On other occasions, however, Donaghy was quite prepared to defend the usefulness of workshops. "Naturally, you can't make people rigorous, sensitive, or witty. But you can finesse them out of cul de sacs or suggest poems they might want to read or train them in habits of reading. … And yes, the attention I give to student work might be more profitably spent on my own poetry. But it's still the best job I've ever had" (*Dance*, p. 200). In his introduction to *The Shape of the Dance*, Clive James identifies at least a dozen gifted young poets who "benefited from his combination of a wide-ranging sympathy and a tight focus on language. If they are now a school without a name, it was because he taught them the merits of unbelonging" (p. viii). They include poets such as Paul Farley, Annie Freud, John Stammers, and Greta Stoddart.

Donaghy died suddenly of a brain hemorrhage on September 16, 2004. As David Wheatley observed in a 2009 review of Donaghy's *Collected Poems*: "The death of Michael Donaghy in 2004 at the age of 50 has been one of the most deeply felt losses to the poetry world in recent years. Not since Sylvia Plath almost half a century ago had an American poet living in Britain so decisively entered the bloodstream of his times" (p. 14). The consequences of Donaghy's legacy, both as friend, mentor, teacher, and writer, are, in other words, still being felt.

SHIBBOLETH

Donaghy's first book, *Shibboleth* (1988), focuses on the relationship between language and power. Its title poem alludes to a famous story in the Bible. When the Israelites suspect a soldier of being an enemy Ephraimite in disguise, sent across the Jordan as a spy, they test him by making him say the code word, "shibboleth," which the Ephraimites cannot pronounce correctly. In Donaghy's contemporary version of the story, probably set during the Second World War, the test of belonging is based not on linguistic proficiency but on popular knowledge such as baseball statistics and the name of Tarzan's monkey. "By the second week of battle," the speaker informs us, "We'd become obsessed with trivia" (*Collected Poems*, p. 21; all page citations for poems from *Shibboleth* refer to this volume). The poem concludes with the following defiantly unheroic epiphany:

> The morning of the first snowfall, I was shaving,
> Staring into a mirror nailed to a tree,
> Intoning the Christian names of the Andrews Sisters.
> "Maxine, Laverne, Patty."
>
> (p. 21)

On first reading, Donaghy's twentieth-century "Shibboleth" is as trivial as the knowledge it records. What does the poem have to say about the experience of war? How can remembering these things matter? Yet to Donaghy "such minutiae" count. For instance, like an archaeologist, he is fascinated by what remains of physical bodies after we have died. In "Touch," for example, he marvels at the "shards" of hip and skull that suggest a newly found skeleton was "young, thirteen perhaps" (p. 13). In "Pornography," while the rest of the audience is mesmerised by Leni Riefenstahl's infamous propaganda film *The Triumph of the Will*, the speaker's gaze is on the projector beam and what "the smoke and dust revolve in and reveal" (p. 28). What "Shibboleth" and other poems suggest, in other words, is that apparent trivia is significant, not just as a way of detecting infiltrators but as a way of remaining human and of humanizing otherwise frightening or unnatural situations. "Staring into a mirror nailed to a tree," the speaker contemplates a modern crucifixion, his own just as much as other people's. What distracts him from this, transforming the mirror from an object of narcissism and probable tragedy to an object of surprise and potential beauty, is the memory of saying things well, in this case the childlike poetry of the three Andrews sisters' Christian names: "Maxine, Laverne, Patty."

For Donaghy, knowledge like this can offer a much more revealing insight into character than conventional tests of citizenship and identity. As Sean O'Brien observes in his introduction to the *Collected Poems*: "He didn't simply have opinions: he *knew* things—about literature, history, music, science, anthropology, non-Western cultures" (p. vii). The title poem, like the collection as a whole, is unembarrassed about knowing things and the magic of sharing that knowledge with other people. Knowledge also allows us to fit in, to pass. Passing is undoubtedly a key theme in Donaghy's poetry. As Maddy Paxman pointed out in personal e-mail correspondence about the poem: "My reading of this poem is that it's about someone trying to 'pass' or fit in, without knowing the precise rules of the game, which Michael

never felt he did, either as a son of Irish immigrants in America, or an American in London." For Donaghy, the "shibboleth" test was not an exceptional event but an everyday occurrence. We all know something someone else doesn't. The art of his poetry is the art both of passing this knowledge on and passing it on in a way that we can remember. An art too that asks about the consequences of not knowing the rules.

Almost every poem in the collection focuses on the activity of remembering. Donaghy is not above detailing history that one might prefer to forget. In "Auto da Fé," for example, the poem's speaker attempts to explain why his uncle fought in the Spanish Civil War on General Franco's side. Although nephew and uncle pass the night "in heated argument," no real explanation is ever given. What we have in its place is a gesture that, like the information gathered in "Shibboleth," looks at first glance relatively trivial:

> And as he spoke he rolled a cigarette
> And picked a straw and held it to an ember.
> The shape his hand made sheltering the flame
> Was itself a kind of understanding.

> (p. 23)

The speaker stops short of elaborating what this gesture might mean. In "sheltering the flame," an image of light and in the Catholic tradition, of the Holy Spirit, might the uncle be aligning the fight in Spain with a fight for religion? Is this why he went to Spain with the Irish volunteers? The poem's title, "Auto da Fé," refers to the ritual of public penance, or "act of faith," of condemned heretics that took place when the Spanish Inquisition had decided a person's punishment. The act of burning at the stake for heresy eventually became the primary meaning of the phrase *auto da fé*, even though it was not the original meaning. In choosing to name the poem after such a controversial religious ritual, Donaghy invokes a history of penance and punishment that goes back centuries. In this way, he contextualizes the Spanish Civil War in a way few English-speaking poets do, relating the conflict to medieval and Renaissance history. General Franco's forces famously fought against the Spanish Republic "For Christ, for the Caudillo, for the

King." Indeed, this is the very last line of Donaghy's poem. The speaker's dead uncle never shares his thoughts with us, however. If he remains on Franco's side fifty years later, he never says. If he regrets what he has done, he is not about to tell us about it. Donaghy significantly casts this blocked investigation into the past as a sonnet. Poetic form may not help the poet to tell the truth, but it can at the very least help him to order his thoughts. A dream in sonnet form is, one might argue, an act of faith, too, faith in poetry's ability to imagine "a kind of understanding" that straightforward memoir-writing often misses.

At least one other poem in *Shibboleth* is explicitly about the Spanish Civil War: a rich and suggestive narrative poem called "Ramon Fernandez?" Other poems also invoke that war's contentious legacy, particularly three short poems in the middle of the collection ("Partisans," "Majority," and "News Item"). Donaghy draws inspiration from other iconic events, too, including the sinking of the Titanic, seen not from the Titanic itself but from one of the many ships sailing nearby who mistook her rockets for fireworks. "Our radio was out," the poem's speaker admits, "and we didn't know / The band was only playing to calm the passengers" (p. 33).

Donaghy liked to say his three main subjects were "Music and Sex and Drinking," the title of another poem in *Shibboleth*. Music certainly comes first in such a list, even when sex is present. In "Cadenza," a piece of music by Mozart variously evokes a golden morning in Alexandria during which the poem's lovers kiss and presumably sleep together, a night in London a few months later when a woman calls the poem's speaker to tell him she's miscarried their child, and a Christmas outside the resonantly titled St. Michael's Church on Highgate Hill, where the speaker wonders: "How did I get here?" (p. 18). Remembering a cadenza by Mozart does not make sense of any of these bewildering series of events, though the speaker does make a point of identifying it accurately: "And there it was, / The end of K285a, / Dubbed like a budget soundtrack on our big scene" (p. 17). Remembering Mozart gives form to

experience. In *Wallflowers*, Donaghy reflects on the function of form in poetry by talking about its function in music. "For the poet," he argued, "form functions as a kind of 'frame' or 'scaffold' from which the poem can be constructed. Stravinsky maintained that only in art could one be freed by the imposition of more rules, perhaps because these rules limit the field of possibilities and escort us beyond the selection of tools and media to laying the first stone of the work itself" (*Dance*, p. 12). In "Cadenza," accurately describing Mozart's music is the main rule of the poem. It is the frame from which the speaker can approach the great moments of life that in this poem include not just sex, new life, and death but perhaps also infidelity:

I heard it again in London a few months later,
The night she called me from the hospital.
"I've lost it," she said, "it happens …" and as she spoke
Those days in Egypt and other days returned,
Unsummoned, a tide of musics, cities, voices,
In which I drifted, helpless, disconsolate.
What did I mourn. It had no name, no sex,
"It might not even have been yours," she said,
Or do I just imagine that she said that?

(p. 17)

In *The Oxford Companion to Twentieth-Century Poetry*, Neil Powell suggests that Donaghy's love of allusiveness "can become overburdened, as when his precise reference to a cadenza in Mozart (K.258a) is called upon to support an entire poem" (p. 131). Donaghy's point is not that one needs to know this particular cadenza to understand the speaker's experiences, but that musical forms, like poetic forms, can be the means to summon various states of being, including love, mourning, and remembrance.

Other notable poems about music include "Remembering Steps to Dances Learned Last Night" in which an anonymous goatherd-turned-musician reminisces about his time on the island of Ithaca and his less-than-heroic exit when Odysseus arrives home to slay his wife's suitors, and "The Tuning," in which a lute player is led to his death by an ambiguous angel. In both these poems, Donaghy speculates on the function of the artist. What should the artist do when he hears the screams of his friend or the siren call of immortality? Is he right to remember the dance over the dancer? This is the conclusion of the first poem:

> What would you have done?
> I staggered home in the dawn rain, still half drunk,
> Forgetting one by one the names of my dead friends,
> Remembering steps to dances learned that night,
> that very night,
> Back to my goats, goat stink, goat cheese, the governing of goats.
>
> (p. 39)

As in "Auto da Fé," Donaghy does not take sides. If the man is at fault for abandoning and then forgetting the names of his dead friends, we are not allowed to feel morally superior to him. Donaghy borrows the atmosphere of the poem from various sources, mostly medieval. The poem it most closely resembles, however, is arguably Samuel Taylor Coleridge's "The Rime of the Ancient Mariner." In both poems, a solitary man asks the reader what we would have done. It is difficult to give a reply.

The book is full of awkward encounters like this, when the listener is brought into the poem not to make us feel welcome but to share in the speaker's disquiet. At times, silence is created by cultural distance. What do we make of the dance in "The Toast" that "some scholars say" is "only a code for the steps of another dance, long since forgotten" (p. 47)? How can the American tourist make sense of the folk music in "The Natural and Social Sciences"? Donaghy is also interested in the permanent silence created between two people that is caused by death: certainly, *Shibboleth* has its fair share of elegiac poems in which the speaker is talking to a ghost who cannot reply or in which he may be a ghost himself. In one extraordinary poem, the simple-seeming "The Present," both speaker and listener appear to exist outside of time. "Forget the here-and-now," the speaker suggests. "Make me this present then: your hand in mine, / and we'll live out our lives in it" (p. 12). "Tell me about touch," the speaker asks the dead bones of an early female ancestor

in a poem called "Touch." "Did the caress shape your hand or your hand the caress?" (p. 13).

The most affecting of these elegiac poems is an autobiographical-sounding poem, "Letter," in which the speaker recalls his father's funeral and the difficult days and weeks afterward. The speaker attempts, in an echo of T. S. Eliot's poem "The Waste Land," to put his father's papers "in order" (p. 19). Apart from drawer after drawer of signatures, nothing remains in his father's hand. "No diaries, no labelled photographs, no lists." "Maybe writing frightened you," the son speculates as if talking aloud to a person who might still hear him. "Maybe ink and graphite made / Too rough a map of your fine love" (p. 19). The speaker refuses to put words into his father's mouth both because his father can no longer speak for himself and because he never trusted words in the first place. In commemorating his father's "fine love," then, he has to employ a form of communication, "ink and graphite," that left his father silent. Or so it seems halfway through the poem. For it is at this point that the speaker remembers an experience from the past that is both a memory of his father's love and a memory of his father reciting poetry:

> But remember one August night
> When I was weak with fever and you held my head
> And reeled off "The Charge of The Light Brigade"
> (Of all things) to calm me. You had it by heart;
> By breath. I'd hear that breath when you talked to yourself
> Spitting tiny curses, or muttered in your sleep,
> Or read, as monks and rabbis do, aloud, soft.
> Breath that would hardly steam a mirror,
> Whispering like gaslight. Day after year
> After night I missed the words.
>
> (p. 19)

Even though the father himself never wrote, he did love the writing of others. He simply could not express that love in his own words. In writing a poem to the father after his death, a kind of verse-letter, the son is continuing their epistolary relationship. When his father was alive, the only letter he ever received from his father was an empty one with his name "scratched carefully in onionskin." Now that he is dead, he will not even receive this, though in a sense nothing has changed between them. He still hears his father's breath in other poets' words.

ERRATA

Donaghy's second collection, *Errata* (1993), is in many ways a continuation of ideas and themes pursued in *Shibboleth*. Its title, *Errata*, referring to an error in writing or printing, alerts us to the importance of language again, particularly to those everyday moments when we misinterpret signs, whether reading a book, a person, or a situation. "L" begins with the familiar command to "Switch off the engine and secure the car" (*Collected Poems*, p. 76; all page citations for poems from *Errata* refer to this volume). It is the end of a driving test. "I'm going to approve your licence," we are relieved to hear in the final stanza, even though the examiner does not care much for the speaker's "*interpretation* of the Highway Code" (p. 76).

A narrative summary of the poem might suggest that "L" stands only for "Learner." The learner in this reading of the poem is both the speaker learning to drive and the examiner learning about the speaker's work as a poet. This is not necessarily an error in reading what literally happens in the poem, but it is an error in understanding the range of tensions set in play by the speaker and examiner's brief conversation. In response to the latter's question about "your line of work," the speaker tells him "the truth." "The truth" is never spoken aloud, or at least never spoken in the poem. "Driving and writing have a lot in common," the examiner replies in response to this "truth," although he takes almost the entire length of the poem to expand on what he actually means.

Donaghy is perhaps following the examiner in linking the act of driving with the act of writing poetry. A poet's line of work is, after all, the work of adding lines to paper (another meaning of "L"?), just as driving a car successfully requires the ability to follow lines or markings in the road. In what other ways might writing be like driving? Well, a poem, like a car, can be described as a form of mechanical object. One

might note one of Donaghy's signature poems, "Machines," in which he marvels at the "machinery of grace" (*Collected Poems*, p. 5) visible in bicycles, music, and, by extension, poetry, or recall his comment in an interview about being interested in "linguistic engineering" (*Dance*, p. 182). Poems, like cars, can also be described as homes in motion, transporting us from place to place. The original meaning of *stanza* is, of course, room. In the context of a driving test, it is difficult to forget the importance of rules. Just as one must follow the rules of the road to acquire a license, so must one follow the rules of poetic form and poetic tradition to be considered a poet. To pass the unofficial test of being a poet is thus in many ways similar to passing a driving test. Lines and stopping distances matter, whether bringing a car or a poem to a halt. Knowing how the machine works is essential as well, whether one is talking about the mechanics of gears or the mechanics of meter. "It's all a matter of giving—proper—signals" (*Collected Poems*, p. 76) is the examiner's final advice, the conversational pauses performing both like the dashes of an Emily Dickinson poem and like the lights on a car's indicator. Who commits the greatest error in the poem, then? The speaker or the examiner? Arguably, it is the poet-speaker for underestimating the examiner's understanding of signals. As his answer suggests, he does not in fact need any lessons in understanding poetry. He might look like the learner to begin with, but he is in reality anything but. He is the nonpoet, the ideal reader, who instinctively knows what poetry is all about.

Donaghy loves to turn first impressions on their head, even if it runs the risk, as here, of making himself look foolish. In "Liverpool," the poem's startling opening question—"Ever been tattooed?" (p. 75)—turns out to be as much about religious scars as the art of writing on the body. Everybody is tattooed in some place, Donaghy suggests, even, or perhaps particularly, if one is a saint. A colloquial introduction thus hides a deeply important theme, the daily harm we encounter in loving others, whether that love is directed earthward or heavenward. Donaghy's poems frequently begin in medias res like this. They are the verbal equivalent of Renaissance paintings by an artist like Caravaggio, who often depicted human beings reaching out from within the canvas to pull the spectator in. Donaghy catches our attention with a seemingly artless observation or question, before leading us, like Alice, down a series of increasingly surreal rabbit holes (there is a prose poem in *Errata* called "Alas, Alice").

In "The Brother," even the poem's title is misleading. The speaker doesn't actually have a brother but is nevertheless drawn to imagining him at various family gatherings: "The only man at my wedding not wearing a tie; / Avuncular, swaddling my nephew over the font" (p. 109). As in "Liverpool," Donaghy's Catholic heritage is clearly to the fore. The poem ends with the speaker imagining meeting his fictional brother for real. "I must break bread with my own flesh and blood" (p. 109), he declares. The poem's final line alludes both to the Catholic sacrament of Communion and to the specific biblical accounts of Christ breaking bread with his disciples at the Last Supper and after his crucifixion, when he met two of the disciples on the road to Emmaus and was invited to have supper with them. The disciples famously only recognized Christ when he broke the bread before them. A poem that begins like a comic sketch—"Dropping a canapé in my Beaujolais / At some reception, opening or launch" (p. 109)—has, over the course of fourteen lines, suddenly transformed into the description of a miracle. One is perhaps equally surprised to discover that Donaghy has written another sonnet. If the imaginary brother with whom he breaks bread can be identified as Christ, it is perhaps also John Donne or Gerard Manley Hopkins, both poets famous for wrestling with God in sonnet form.

Donaghy is a master at narrative reversals. In "The Incense Contest," a story of infidelity unfolds only gradually to the smell of "clove and cinnamon and sandalwood" (p. 65). The reader is fooled as the speaker once was into thinking the eponymous incense contest is a trivial affair. It is only toward the very end of the poem that we become attuned to other smells, too, including not just the Prince's eventual death but to his smell on every woman there, including the speaker's cousin and sister. "Signifyin' Monkey" is another astonishing verse narrative that turns on a misreading, this time of a sign. A Chicago security guard stops for lunch at what he thinks is a Chinese restaurant called "Fighter Monkey." "Looking back," as so many of Donaghy's speakers do, he wonders why he did not simply catch the train home. Fighter Monkey is not a restaurant at all, but a place where Barbary apes are trained using sign language. The trainer, it quickly turns out, has a grudge against the security firm where the speaker works. Instead of providing him with lunch, he decides to treat his guest as lunch, inviting the monkey to attack. Donaghy leaves out much of what happens next, though we know that the speaker gets out of it alive by the fact that he is telling us the story:

> I remember he laughed as he made the sign.
> The asshole. Lost a thumb to his own monkey.
>
> It's easy. Look, he'd been her only trainer.
> Guard or no guard, he'd signed "I'm lunch."
> The blood! Of course they had to shoot the monkey.
>
> (p. 100)

The error here, in contrast to "L," is in reading signs too imaginatively. The security guard, who makes his living observing others, fails at the simple task of reading a fluorescent sign in the street. He thinks every business in Chinatown must be a restaurant, every DayGlo sign an invitation to lunch.

The error of judgment is clearly prepared by Donaghy in the poem's title, which alludes to a famous work of literary criticism by Henry Louis Gates, Jr., called *Signifying Monkey* (1988). Gates's study explores the relationship between African and African American oral traditions and black literature. It remains a seminal work of literary criticism, particularly in his discussion of the Signifying Monkey, one of the most popular figures in African American folklore, music, and popular culture. In Donaghy's "Signifyin' Monkey," racial tension is, perhaps not surprisingly, one of the main subjects of the poem. While the speaker's race is unspoken, for example, the trainer's is not. He is introduced theateningly as "this white guy built like a bodyguard / wearing a T-shirt showing a shrieking monkey" (p. 99). In drawing attention to the man's whiteness, does the speaker identify his color as different? Is this argument about lunch really an argument about race? In a provocative gesture, Donaghy also makes his signifying monkey real in the poem. In contrast to Gates's book, his monkey isn't a folklore figure or method of speech, but "a kind of Rottweiler monkey / that took her orders and talked back in Sign." She weighs, the speaker guesses, "forty pounds easy. / And teeth! She could have had me for lunch." It is worth noting the monkey's female sex here, too, adding gender to an already explosive mix involving linguistic, racial, and species conflict. In Donaghy's contemporary version of the Western shoot-out, we discover at least three living beings at risk as a result of the speaker's original error: the ambiguous speaker who may be African American but is probably not white, the trainer who is identified as white but could of course be from anywhere, and the Barbary ape, who is not properly an ape at all but a monkey and who comes not from America but from Europe and North Africa. The female animal gets shot. The two men escape. A comic poem is suddenly deadly serious.

The heart of *Errata*, both emotionally and structurally, is a sequence of poems called "O'Ryan's Belt." The name, O'Ryan, is another of Donaghy's inventions. No such name exists in Irish. It refers to what Donaghy always called "the Irish constellation," Orion's belt. According to "The Hunter's Purse," the first poem in the sequence, O'Ryan was a "Sligo fiddler," a record of whose fiddle playing is a prized object among Irish people:

A legend, he played Manhattan's ceilidhs,
fell asleep drunk one snowy Christmas
on a Central Park bench and froze solid.
They shipped his corpse home, like his records.

(p. 83)

The poem's speaker owns his own version of the record. Unfortunately, it now skips. But rather than mourn the loss of O'Ryan's music and the very different Manhattan it evokes, the speaker instead reflects upon the record's repetition, the way it "hiccoughs / back to this" as a memory of O'Ryan's own last moments alive: "a napping snowman with a fiddlecase; / a flask of bootleg under his belt" (p. 83). The poem is part anecdote, part record, too. It commemorates O'Ryan's life and death and gives us a version of the records that remain of his playing, through a poem that both moves forward in time and is frozen in the past.

The second poem in the sequence, "A Repertoire," is equally moving. Set in the Bronx in 1971, it tells the story of "an old guy in our neighborhood" who would regularly play songs that the young people had never heard. One Easter day, the man "sat us down / and made us tape as much as he could play" (p. 84). The old man, it later becomes clear, is living on borrowed time. He has cancer in his blood and is "childless and afraid" (p. 84). The choice of Easter day, the most significant date in the Christian calendar, is obviously important. The speaker of the poem and his unnamed friends play the role of disciples to the old man's Christ. Their job, like that of the disciples, is at least in part to record as much of his musical wisdom as they can remember. The job of the recorder has its trials too. In "A Reprieve," Donaghy looks at Police Chief Francis O'Neill's decision to pardon a well-known criminal "if he agrees to play three jigs / slowly, so O'Neill can take them down" (p. 85). Chief O'Neill is famous among Irish musicians for his *O'Neill's Music of Ireland* (1903), the so-called bible of Irish music, a collection of over eighteen hundred tunes that he wrote down over the years; he had been one of the first people to do so, since most Irish music is transmitted orally. The poem imagines the events behind one such transcription. Donaghy was fascinated by O'Neill's life and intended to write a longer poem about him (see "Fragment" in *Safest*). As elsewhere in Donaghy's poetry, there is a remarkable attention to the details of the human body, in this case to the hands of both criminal and police chief. Nolan's hands "are brown with a Chinaman's blood" that leaves "coppery stains" on the keys of his blackwood flute (p. 85). Artistic genius is also capable of brutal violence. O'Neill is marked in his own way as well. Donaghy depicts him "scratching in his manuscript like a monk / at his illuminations" (p. 85). The fate of medieval monks was often to die young as a result of working with materials that today are known to be highly toxic. The act of "scratching" does not sound very healthy either, as much an act of self-punishment as an act of writing. While musical achievement brings Nolan a reprieve for his sins, it does not grant him atonement or forgiveness. Perhaps the same is true of O'Neill "scratching" out the jigs. Donaghy does not end the poem on a moral note, however. Like O'Neill, he is more than happy to sacrifice morality for music. The songs, too, have also been given a reprieve.

CONJURE

Conjure is Donaghy's most autobiographical-sounding collection. In an article for the Poetry Book Society, Donaghy both encourages and warns against biographical readings but without the same vehemence against biography as in earlier interviews. The word, "conjure," he explains,

> derives from Latin *conjurare*, to swear together, suggesting a ritual performed by two or more celebrants, not a solitary act. I tried to avoid talking to myself in the reader's presence because it's rude. But I invite my readers to play the role of eavesdroppers and hope they won't insist on knowing precisely who I'm taking to (even if it's them). I fancy I'm bound by the sanctity of the *confessional*—not as in "confessional poetry," mind, but the box where the sacrament is conducted. It's pointless to speculate, and I'm not about to say, whether any given poem in this collection is a fable or an indiscreet disclosure slipped in to satisfy readers' appetite for "intensity."

> (*Dance*, p. 102)

Sean O'Brien comments on the fact that the book opens with "three poems dealing with near misses and attempted encounters with fathers. The poems share a certain hermeticism in that while the author's 'actual circumstances' (he spoke at times of his father) are somewhere in the offing, the poems take place in an apparently fictionalized context and are all in some way concerned with lies and illusions and attempts to invoke what is not there" (*Collected Poems*, p. xv; all

page citations for poems from *Conjure* refer to this volume).

This is familiar territory for Donaghy. Certainly, *Conjure* contains several poems that would not appear out of place in *Shibboleth* or *Errata*. "Annie," a poem to "my never-daughter" probably influenced by Wordsworth's "Lucy" poems, employs a similar conceit to "The Brother." In both poems, Donaghy makes us believe in and care for a person that the poet admits is entirely fictional. To pull off this trick once is audacious. To repeat it is the sign of real genius. Donaghy, as in earlier collections, also remembers growing up in the Bronx. In "My Flu," the speaker recalls being "eight and in bed with my flu" (p. 131). The child's illness inside the house is accentuated by the rising political temperature outside: "Oswald's back from Minsk. U2s glide over Cuba. / My cousin's in Saigon" (p. 131). Donaghy isn't interested in the complex political history of June 1962, however. What he remembers most about this time is the details of his bedroom, in particular his father's sudden presence there, "his hand beneath my head / until one world rings truer than the other" (p. 131). "Local 32B" takes place a decade later, this time in the Upper East Side apartment in Manhattan where Donaghy worked as a doorman in the 1970s. Amid various allusions to several other poems, including W. B. Yeats's "An Irish Airman Foresees His Death," there is a miraculous appearance by the Italian tenor Luciano Pavarotti:

> Once I got a cab for Pavarotti. No kidding.
> No tip either. I stared after him down Fifth
> and caught him looking after me, then through me,
> like Samson, eyeless, at the Philistine chorus—
> Yessir, I put the tenor in the vehicle.
> And a mighty tight squeeze it was.

> (p. 147)

The poem looks and sounds like it ought to be a sonnet until you count the lines. There are fifteen, not fourteen. The fifteenth line, "And a mighty tight squeeze it was," suggests Pavarotti's bulk causes not only the cab driver problems of space, but also the poet. While the cab driver just about fits him in to his vehicle, the poet has to give him an extra line.

Where *Conjure* arguably departs from Donaghy's earlier poems is in its handling of emotion. As O'Brien points out, the three poems that open the collection, an unofficial triptych on the subject of fatherhood, each engage with Donaghy's own personal history, in particular the early death of his father. The first poem in the book, "The Excuse," is a response to of one of the twentieth century's most famous poems on fatherhood, Sylvia Plath's "Daddy." In Plath's poem, the speaker stages a conversation with a father figure who exists in a liminal state between life and death. At different times in the poem, he is identified as both a devil and vampire. The speaker repeatedly expresses a desire to talk to this figure, a desire represented in the colloquial phrase to get "through" to him as if talking on the phone. At the end of the poem, the speaker announces to the father that she is "through" with him (Plath, *Collected Poems*, p. 224). Yet to be "through" is to be both connected to the father but also to end their relationship. The daughter-speaker makes the connection, as it were, only to slam the phone down.

Donaghy invokes this now-mythic poetic conversation to create something altogether more comical and whimsical than Plath's poem but with a similar emotional charge. In his poem, as in hers, the father figure is as much imaginary as real. In fact, Donaghy admits to having made up the father's "sudden death" in the opening lines of the poem. What he presumably does not make up is his memories of his father and the effect of his loss, whether "sudden" or not, on his present-day existence. The change of tone in the poem, from the humor of its first stanza to the sorrow of its conclusion, is one of Donaghy's most striking poetic achievements. "My people were magicians," he declares, before relating the story of his father rigging up a wire beneath the table to a doorbell. In Donaghy's poem, unlike in Plath's, we hear the father's explanation. *"Son, when your uncle gets me on the phone / He won't let go. I had to rig up something"* (*Collected Poems*, p. 121). The humor of this deliberately interrupted conversation, the father cutting short his brother on the phone by means of a home-installed wire, make the sadness of the permanently interrupted

conversation, that between father and son, even more poignant.

> Midnight. I pick up and there's no one there,
> No one, invoked, beyond that drone. But if
> I had to rig up something, and I do,
> Let my excuse be this, and this is true:
> I fear for him and grieve him more than any,
> This most deceiving and deceived of men …
> *Please hang up and try again.*
>
> (p. 121)

The ellipsis in the penultimate line is perhaps the poem's most eloquent moment. In attempting to pay tribute to his father, "This most deceiving and deceived of men," the line goes dead and the voice breaks down. It is difficult to imagine the emotion both lost and remembered in those three dots on the page.

Talking, or rather not talking, to his father is the subject of the next poem in the sequence, "Not Knowing the Words." In this poem, the speaker describes his father's habit of apparently talking to himself when alone. "Walk in, he'd pretend to be humming softly." Has he, the poet wonders, been "talking to her"? We never find out. "Her" is presumably the father's wife, who is of course also the speaker's mother. Yet the words *father*, *mother*, and *son* are never used in the poem. The reader has to make an educated guess from the poems that come before and after this one, to infer that the same people are involved. In the second half of the poem, the speaker recalls the last time he saw his father alive and the coat he wore as he was hugging him. The coat is preserved in a sack in the attic.

> Am I talking to him now, as I get it out
> and pull its damp night down about my shoulders?
> Shall I take up the task, and fill its tweedy skin?
> Do I stand here not knowing the words
> when someone walks in?
>
> (p. 122)

"Caliban's Books" completes the sequence. Here, Donaghy asks the reader to "Bear with me. I'm trying to conjure my father, / age fourteen, as Caliban" (p. 123). In this poem, as in "Not Knowing the Words," the speaker attempts to resurrect his father's ghost through his belong-ings, in this case his paperbacks "scribbled on, underlined, memorized." Unfortunately, the results are disappointing. As in both previous poems, the son's conjuring acts do not conceal the fact that he is alone.

Conjure has other highlights, too, not least the long narrative poem "Black Ice and Rain," a virtuoso poem about sexual desire that reads like a Hitchcock thriller. The last poem in the book, "Haunts," brings the story of fathers and sons to a fitting close. It is already one of Donaghy's most admired poems, written in a single long sentence of fifteen lines. It begins and ends with the same phrase, "Don't be afraid," first spoken by a father to his son, later by a son to his father. The father figures shift imperceptibly through the poem as the sons becomes fathers, these younger fathers still sons. The first voice in the poem may be Donaghy's own father, for example, or Donaghy himself. Michael Dirda favors the latter reading:

> Donaghy pictures his grown-up son detecting his father's spectral presence everywhere in later years—in the name he scribbles, in a book he's inherited, in the reflection of his own face in a window. ... Yet right now, in the moment of writing, the son is still just a toddler, asleep upstairs. The father has simply conjured up in his mind the boy's future self, and yet finds himself surprised at hearing a voice unlike that of the child he knows. ... So the comforting phrase—spoken by Donaghy in the poem's opening and by his son at the end—echoes back and forth in time, like an outgoing and returning radar blip. In essense, the imagined future son takes on the grown-up's role, giving solace to his dad.
>
> ("The Singing Line," p. 367)

SAFEST

Donaghy's final collection, *Safest*, was published posthumously in 2005. Maddy Paxman provided the following note on its title and content:

> "Safest" is the name of the computer file in which Michael had stored the poems towards his next collection. On the day he was taken into hospital, although we had very little time before he lost consciousness, he told me that these were the poems he wanted published. I don't know whether he had

intended this as the book's title (previous folders were called "Safe" and "Safer"), or if it was simply a way of keeping track. But "Safest" seemed somehow appropriate, and as near as we could get to a title he'd chosen himself.

> As to the manuscript, we used only the poems he had selected, resisting the temptation to put back in those he had previously rejected, or include material not yet finished. The exception to this is the fragment of a longer poem about Chief Francis O'Neill, which would I know have been in the book had he lived to complete it—it was a project dear to his heart.
>
> (*Collected Poems*, p. 169)

Safest is certainly a fitting title for a collection structured around images of safe passage, between consciousness and sleep, youth and age, life and death. Sean O'Brien suggests that a further stage of poetic development was in progress in these poems, "albeit inescapably shadowed by the intensifying awareness of mortality which he experienced after his health grew fragile in the last few years of his life" (*Collected Poems*, p. vii). This may be the case, but it is worth remembering the preoccupation with elegy and self-elegy in all of Donaghy's work, right back to his first collection. *Safest* feels like a quickening of pace rather than a change in direction. As Don Paterson argued in a short piece in the *Guardian*: "Donaghy was a slow worker, and really only wrote one book, which was published in instalments. There were no particularly noticeable developments of either technique or subject matter; the former had always been seamless enough to be largely invisible and his interests were so eclectic, nothing so base as a 'theme' would ever emerge anyway" (p. 3).

In the much anthologized early poem, "Smith," for example, Donaghy celebrates the "forger's nerve" in lying about his own name not just in a hotel guestbook but from the time he was a child. "Every signature's / A trick we learn to do," the speaker suggests, "Like Queequeg's cross, or Whistler's butterfly" (*Collected Poems*, p. 15). "Disquietude," from *Safest*, continues the theme. "Our names have sounds besides the ones we hear," the speaker warns.

Sometimes, when I wake beside you in the night
and the door of sleep slams shut and locks beside
   me,
I hear it creep up out of silence, a brash hush,
a crowded emptiness, the static of the spheres.

It's like a tap left on. But it's my own warm blood,
the flood that's washing all the names away,
of schoolmates, kings, the principal export of
   somewhere,
and all the sounds as well—a lullaby, a child's
   voice—
my own warm blood that must be blessed.

(Collected Poems, p. 190)

It is difficult to offer a commentary on such lines without simplifying them. This is a poem about both the loss of identity at night and the intensification of self-knowledge that happens at the same time. At such moments we encounter "a crowded emptiness" that is a gathering of the names and sounds that make us who we are and a washing away of memory and experience. In the acknowledgments to *Wallflowers*, Donaghy thanks a professor named James K. Chandler who once read "Coleridge's 'Frost at Midnight' aloud, all 567 words of it, paused, and asked us if we thought it was beautiful" (*Dance*, p. 41). "Disquietude," and countless other poems in *Safest*, deserve similar treatment.

THE CONDITION OF REMEMBRANCE

In an important short essay on John Keats's poetry, Donaghy reflects on what he calls the "condition of remembrance" (*Dance*, p. 79). "Poetry isn't just the oldest form of literature," he argues. "It precedes literature. Imagine a society before the invention of writing: the *only* way of preserving important information. Methods of hunting and navigation, the history of the tribe and its place in the cosmos all have to be cast into a rhythmic pattern and rendered memorizable" (*Dance*, p. 79). Donaghy once recalled being awoken from a terrible depression by a poem by Keats. He met a woman in a bar who recited "Ode to Melancholy" from memory. His astonishment at the beauty of the poem jolted him out his own melancholy. He went as far as

to say "it saved my soul" (*Dance*, p. 80). If "Ode to Melancholy" saved Donaghy's soul, another of Keats's poems, "This Living Hand," appears to have inspired some of his best poetry. The later poem is akin to a magic trick. A speaker encourages us to imagine a "living hand" right before us:

This living hand, now warm and capable
Of earnest grasping, would, if it were cold
And in the icy silence of the tomb,
So haunt thy days and chill thy dreaming nights
That thou wouldst wish thine own heart dry of
   blood
So in my veins red life might stream again,
And thou be conscience-calmed. See here it is—
I hold it towards you.

(Keats, The Complete Poems,
New York: Longman, 1970, p. 701)

Donaghy admitted that on one level "the poem is just Keats emotionally blackmailing the object of his desire." At the same time, he loved its "extraordinary ending, in which the most immediate gestural challenge coincides with the closure that contains the poem, poses the problem of what the aesthetic object wants of us. In any act of reading, the reader attempts to restore the words to a source, a human situation involving speech, character, personality. We read a poem to verify the axiom of presence: we read to meet the other" (*Dance*, p. 81).

This is a remarkable statement for a contemporary poet to write, particularly one brought up in a confessional age of writing in which poets were frequently encouraged to write in order to know oneself better rather than anybody else. Donaghy was attracted to poems rather than poets. He believed the poem to be a two-way mirror. "By an accident of typography," he once wrote, "the printed poem is traditionally laid out as a block of text in the centre of the page." It has the shape of "a mirror or a window."

Windows show us the world outside our rooms, but when night falls and we switch on the lights we see only ourselves reflected in the dark glass, and sometimes, briefly, we mistake our own image for a presence outside. Mirrors, on the other hand, show us ourselves, but years on when the silver backing wears away we see past ourselves to whatever lies beyond.

(Dance, p. 25)

Donaghy does a lot of deliberate and inadvertent mistaking in his poetry. If we go looking for the poet's presence, we may find the occasional reflection, ours just as much as his. But if we pay attention to what is actually there, as he so often encourages us, we may see past what we were originally looking for "to whatever lies beyond."

Selected Bibliography

WORKS OF MICHAEL DONAGHY

POETRY

Slivers. Chicago: Thomson Hill, 1985.

Machines: A Poem. Guildford, U.K.: Circle Press, 1986.

Shibboleth. Oxford and New York: Oxford University Press, 1988.

O'Ryan's Belt. Madison, Wis.: Silver Buckle Press, 1991.

Errata. Oxford and New York: Oxford University Press, 1993.

Conjure. London: Picador, 2000.

Dances Learned Last Night: Poems 1975–1995. London: Picador, 2000.

Safest. London: Picador, 2005.

OTHER WORK

The Poetry Quartets: 6. British Council/Bloodaxe, 2000. (Recording. Includes poems by Donaghy.)

Wallflowers: A Lecture on Poetry with Misplaced Notes and Additional Heckling. London: Poetry Society, 1999. (Prose.)

COLLECTED WORKS

Collected Poems. With an introduction by Sean O'Brien. London: Picador, 2009. (Contains the full texts of his four published volumes, *Shibboleth, Errata, Conjure,* and *Safest,* together with a number of uncollected poems.)

The Shape of the Dance: Essays, Interviews, and Digressions. Edited by Adam O'Riordan and Maddy Paxman, with an introduction by Clive James. London: Picador, 2009. (Contains a number of essays, introductions, reviews, and miscellaneous prose works, as well as five interviews. It also reprints his contemporary classic, *Wallflowers.*)

CRITICAL AND BIOGRAPHICAL STUDIES

Bate, Jonathan. "The Green Line in Contemporary Poetry: The Michael Donaghy Lecture 2006." *British and Irish Contemporary Poetry* 1, no. 1:1–18 (spring 2008).

Dirda, Michael. "The Singing Line." *Poetry* 196, no. 4:360–368 (July–August 2010). (Review of *Collected Poems* and *The Shape of the Dance.*)

Mooallem, Jan. "My People Were Magicians." *Poetry* 185, no. 3:237–240 (December 2004).

Padel, Ruth. "Michael Donaghy." In *52 Ways of Looking at a Poem.* London: Vintage, 2004. pp. 197–200.

Paterson, Don. "On *Conjure* by Michael Donaghy." *Guardian Book Review,* October 8, 2011, p. 3.

Powell, Neil. "Michael Donaghy." In *The Oxford Companion to Twentieth-Century Poetry.* Edited by Ian Hamilton. Oxford and New York: Oxford University Press, 1996. P. 131.

Tufariello, Catherine. "Michael Donaghy." In *New Formalist Poets.* Edited by Jonathan N. Barron and Bruce Meyer. Vol. 282 of *Dictionary of Literary Biography.* Detroit: Gale, 2003. Pp. 67–77.

Wheatley, David. "Between the Flash and the Report." *Guardian Book Review,* April 4, 2009, p. 14. (Review of *Collected Poems.*)

JAMES HANLEY

(1897—1985)

James Purdon

IT IS OFTEN said of an author who escapes wide public notice that he or she is "a writer's writer." Rarely is that judgment confirmed by so distinguished and varied a group of admirers as in the case of the novelist James Hanley, whose prolific half-century of writing earned him the highest acclaim of his peers, though only a modest degree of commercial success. "A novelist of distinction and originality," in the words of E. M. Forster, Hanley began his literary career with sea stories drawing on his service in merchant ships before and during the First World War. Hanley would go on to produce almost thirty novels—some set at sea, others in wartime England or the Welsh hill country—as well as numerous works of short fiction, two memoirs, an early book of reportage, and several plays for stage, radio, and television. His work explores the lives of working men and the marginal poor in a style influenced by the realism of Émile Zola and by American naturalism, by high modernist stylistic experiment, and by nineteenth-century French and Russian fiction. Nor was high regard for his achievement confined to English literary circles. In a preface written for *No Directions* (1943), Hanley's novel of the London Blitz, the expatriate American author Henry Miller lauded its "savage and explosive" comedy (*No Directions* [1990]), p. v), while William Faulkner (who later slipped a Royal Air Force officer named "Hanley" into his 1954 novel, *A Fable*) praised Hanley for using language "like a good clean cyclone" (*Boy* [2007], p. i). A few years after Hanley's death, Anthony Burgess assessed him as "the kind of novelist whose eligibility for the Nobel Prize has become clear only posthumously" (*Boy*, p. vi).

The strange disparity between Hanley's high reputation and his later obscurity puzzled admirers of his novels even before his death, though it may be explained in part by an unevenness born of prolificacy and also by the extended hiatus he took from prose fiction in order to concentrate on dramatic writing. As early as 1971, he was the subject of an anonymous *Times Literary Supplement* profile titled, "A Novelist in Neglect: The Case for James Hanley," whose author complained that, with one exception, "none of his twenty and more works of full-length fiction is in print." Though his novels are intensely political, and his politics, broadly speaking, those of the socialist left, Hanley was never a natural party member. Nor was he always in political agreement with acquaintances in left-wing literary circles who encouraged his early work. Readers of Hanley are likely to agree with the assessment of Ralph Wright, who wrote in the *Daily Worker* that "he allows not one scrap of direct propaganda to enter his novels" (December 4, 1935). Never naturally gregarious or attention-seeking, Hanley enjoyed close relations and warm correspondence with a small circle of friends, and spent his most productive years living with his wife, Timmy, in a small village in rural Wales.

BIOGRAPHY

James Hanley was born in England on September 3, 1897, in Kirkdale, a working-class district near the Liverpool docks, into a family of working-class Irish Catholic immigrants. Even these most basic facts are a matter of some controversy, for Hanley always claimed to have been born in Dublin, and in 1901, but more recent genealogical research suggests otherwise. His grandfather, Edward Hanley, had been a printer and typesetter, and served for a time as secretary of the Dublin Typographical Society. James's own father, also named Edward, was in training with a Dublin solicitors' office before going to sea. According to Chris Gostick—whose invaluable research into Hanley's life is appended to the 2007 edition of *Boy* (originally published in 1931)—Edward Hanley met James's mother, Bridget Roache, in Liverpool, and the couple were married on June 10, 1891. Bridget's own family, from Queenstown, County Cork, had served as ships' pilots and sailing boat captains, meaning that James had strong links to the sea through both his mother and his father, as well as an inherited connection with the printed word from his grandfather. The Hanley family were members of Liverpool's large community of Roman Catholic Irish migrants, and James and his siblings were baptized at the local church, Saint Alexander's. Six children in all survived into adulthood, including James's brother Gerald Hanley (1916–1992), who later gained a reputation as a novelist in his own right, chronicling the decline of the British Empire in East Africa. The Hanleys attended the church school, which James seems to have left in 1910 at the statutory age of thirteen. The most complete account written by Hanley about his early life is *Broken Water: An Autobiographical Excursion* (1937), although the reader in search of authoritative information should bear in mind that the memoir is a patchwork of real and imagined experiences, often of the same events he had fictionalized in early novels.

In 1933, Hanley told Henry Green that his memory of his youth before he went to sea was all but nonexistent. "I cannot remember a single day of my boyhood—or youth," he wrote to Green, "When I went away to sea at the age of 13 I in fact became a man" (quoted in Fordham, p. 24). Hanley's misrememberings cloud the water somewhat even in this private correspondence. In fact, he seems to have worked ashore in a clerical job until 1915, when, at the age of seventeen, not thirteen—and not twelve, as stated in the *Oxford Dictionary of National Biography*—he signed on to the SS *Nitonian* as an ordinary seaman for his first transatlantic voyage.

For the next two years, Hanley would serve aboard ships carrying supplies and Canadian troops across the North Atlantic, and taking soldiers to the Middle Eastern and Mediterranean theaters of war. These years were particularly rich ones for Hanley's later imagination: though he had not yet begun to write in earnest, he listened carefully to the rhythms and inflections of shipboard speech and became an astute observer of the eccentricities and habits of his crewmates. Many of Hanley's most memorable seafaring characters, especially in later short stories, are distillations or combinations of men he met while aboard ship, and a heavily mythologized version of some can be found in Hanley's second autobiographical book, *Don Quixote Drowned* (1953). In the title piece of that collection of sketches, Hanley writes about the accidental drowning of the sailor Crawley, in a scene that clearly repeats and refines the drowning of a quartermaster in *Broken Water*: "And then that sudden and horrible shout, half scream, half swear, and Crawley, groping about on that midships island in pursuit of, of all things, a chicken, as I later learned; Crawley, clinging anywhere in between each savage roll, must have suddenly slipped and been flung over" (p. 36).

In *Broken Water*, Hanley finds the man hanging from a rail and tries to help him in the seconds before he slips away into the ocean. The older Hanley of *Don Quixote Drowned* is less close, yet he too draws out those last seconds—in which the inevitable is recognized but has not yet arrived—by deferring the verb almost to the end of a sentence that would prefer not to end. The attitude, too, has changed: where the Hanley of *Broken Water* needed to explain this absurd death as "comical … but alas tragic" (p. 123), the older man shifts the emphasis: "Then I saw it all as tragic. Today it seems like a fiendish joke" (p. 37). His desire to rewrite the moment after fifteen years, however, suggests something more than quiescent acceptance. It is clearly an important moment for Hanley's writing, and one to which he frequently returns: the instant of recognition between two human beings in the face of an unforgiving world, against which the redeeming elevation of tragic struggle seems itself to diminish to a fiendish cosmic joke.

In 1917 Hanley jumped ship to join the Canadian Expeditionary Force. He fought at

Amiens in August 1918 and was invalided out with chest pains, possibly as a result of contact with poison gas. He was still only twenty-one years old. When the war ended in November, he returned home to Liverpool, where he worked as a railway porter and spent his free time on an impressively autodidactic regime of musical and literary studies. It was at this period that Hanley formed some of his lifelong cultural attachments: to Nikolay Gogol and Fyodor Dostoevsky and Theodore Dreiser; to Henrik Ibsen and August Strindberg; to Modest Mussorgsky and Beethoven and Bach. He also began to write in earnest, having published some short stories during his time at sea. His first efforts, which met with rejection, included a "Soldier's Journal of the War," which was returned by a London publisher with the advice that the author should burn it, "not as rubbish [...] but because he thought it went a bit too far as a picture of the war" (*Broken Water,* p. 248). At last, the novel *Drift* was picked up for a pittance by Scholartis press, a small publishing house founded by the lexicographer Eric Partridge. Hanley gratefully accepted. Having packed a bag and sold his books, he traveled to London, where *Drift* was published in the spring of 1930.

Arriving in London alone, Hanley stayed for a time at the home of Charles Lahr, whose Progressive Bookshop in Holborn was the center of a left-leaning group of writers including H. E. Bates and D. H. Lawrence. During this time, he worked on several writing projects, including the important early stories "A Passion Before Death"—hand-printed in 1930 by C. J. Greenwood—and "The German Prisoner," which drew on his experiences in the trenches of Amiens and was published in a small edition (also in 1930) from Lahr's home in Muswell Hill. Hanley also had a brief affair with Lahr's wife, Esther. In October, he left London for Wales, where he would meet his future wife, Dorothy Enid Thomas, known as Timmy. The couple began to live together the following year at Ty Nant, near Corwen in Merionethshire, though they would not marry until 1947. They returned briefly to London where Liam, their only child, was born on April 4, 1933. Meanwhile Hanley's second

novel, *Boy* (1931), had been published by C. J. Greenwood's small firm, Boriswood.

In light of Hanley's mature work, *Boy* appears as the apprentice piece that it is. Nonetheless, it was well-received, and should have been the making of his career. Instead, the novel became the center of a censorship scandal when, late in 1934, a complaint was brought against it, and Boriswood—which had issued a new edition in a foolishly risqué dust jacket—was convicted for publishing an obscene libel. All copies of *Boy* were destroyed. It was a setback that Hanley felt deeply. Disillusioned by what he saw as the publisher's cupidity, he refused to contemplate the publication of a new edition of the novel until the very end of his life.

Hanley was prolific throughout the 1930s. In 1934, he helped to set up the British section of the Writers International organization, and the following year he was appointed as a delegate to the International Congress of Writers for the Defence of Culture in Paris. He continued to work on novels, as well as contributing shorter work to publications as varied as *Lilliput*, the *Spectator*, the *London Mercury, New Writing, Left Review,* T. S. Eliot's *Criterion,* and the left-leaning documentary journal *Fact.* Hanley's literary ambitions and modernist influences appealed no doubt to the mandarin Eliot, while his working-class background and subject matter certainly appealed to the editors of *Left Review* and of *Fact.* In July 1937, the latter, though primarily a magazine of nonfiction, devoted its fourth number to "theory and examples" of drama, poetry, "documentary," and fiction, for which an extract from Hanley's *The Furys* (1935) served as the exemplary text. The publication of drafts and off-cuts as short stories came to be a favorite working method: other extracts from the same novel had appeared in *Left Review* in the year of its publication. This practice did not always endear Hanley to critics, one of whom complained, in a belated review of the small volume *Quartermaster Clausen* (1934), that the story "The Return" was substantially identical to an episode from *The Furys.* "Some of the detail is different," the anonymous reviewer pointed out in the *Times Literary Supplement,* "but except for the last two pages it is essentially the same incident" ("Other New Books," p. 161). As Valentine Cunningham astutely notes in a retrospective review-essay for the same newspaper in 1978, Hanley liked to emphasize the "apocalyptic, ending-obsessed" (p. 1302) form of the short story in ways that cast into relief the slow grind of endurance that constitutes proletarian experience in his longer fiction.

In 1937, Hanley wrote and published his only book of nonfiction about that proletarian world. *Grey Children: A Study in Humbug and Misery* appeared in the autumn, overshadowed somewhat by George Orwell's *The Road to Wigan Pier*, which had been published in the spring. In fact, Hanley had read a proof of Orwell's book and had learned from it. Where the structural bifurcation of *Wigan Pier* into documentary and theory marks most fully the emergence of Orwell as a sifting and judging commentator, in *Grey Children,* Hanley transcribes and transmits above all the voices of the miners of South Wales. The book begins with a collection of statements by members of the mining community whose daily life and economic situation the book investigates. The form recalls, at first glance, the set of epigraphs prefixed to Hanley's beloved *Moby-Dick.* But the polyphonic voices Hanley presents here have more to do with a constellation of contemporary developments in the invention of documentary writing as a genre central to the literary culture of the late 1930s. One can hear similar polyphonies presented in the work of the Mass Observation movement, whose *First Year's Work, 1937–1938* was being researched and compiled as Hanley's book was published, and in the films produced by John Grierson and his colleagues for the Empire Marketing Board and the GPO Film Unit. It was in 1937, too, in the same issue of *Fact* that had extracted from *The Furys*, that Storm Jameson first theorized "documentary" as a crucial tool of the progressive literary left.

Toward the end of the decade, as war began to appear inevitable, Hanley kept up a rigorous writing regime, publishing several further volumes of short stories and working on plays for radio. In 1939 the Hanley family moved back to London temporarily, renting for short periods or staying at the homes of friends, including that of the novelist V. S. Pritchett. In the short story "It Has Never Ended," a bombed-out elderly couple find themselves forced to move between rooming houses and rely on the hospitality of friends, much as the Hanleys had done. At this time, Hanley was attempting to establish himself as a writer of radio plays for the BBC. His first success in this endeavor was *Convoy*, broadcast in June 1941. It was arranged that Hanley, as a writer doing work for the nation's broadcaster, should be exempted from military service, yet he seems to have been temperamentally unsuited to producing the kind of propaganda required by the authorities. Hanley's bleak vision was unlikely to provide the kind of morale boost hoped for by the Ministry of Information.

At the beginning of 1941, the Hanleys returned to Wales, this time to Llanfechain in Montgomeryshire (now part of Powys), where, apart from James's short stints in London writing for the BBC, they would remain for the next two decades. It was the community of Llanfechain that Hanley would transmute into the fictional Llangyllwch of his later fiction. "I have lived with the Welsh for twenty years," he wrote in *Don Quixote Drowned*: "Now I would not live with anybody else. I like them. I like them because they are courteous and cunning, eccentric, provincial, artistic, insular, poetic, dramatic, fierce, and sometimes mad. ... In this land nobody is odd who gives himself to imaginative expression; he is not looked on as different, he is just one of them" (pp. 113–114).

The place itself he described as "an island surrounded by mountains" (p. 101), and noted with approval that "on this island ... nobody sits below the salt, it is just a free-for-all" (p. 75). Among Hanley's friends in Wales was the poet R. S. Thomas, whose father had worked, like Hanley, in the merchant navy and who served as rector at Manafon between 1942 and 1954. From his home in Wales, Hanley would write and publish his finest mature work, beginning with *The Ocean* in April 1941, and including *No Directions* and *Sailor's Song* (both 1943), *The Welsh Sonata* (1954). and *Levine* (1956). He would also complete *The Furys* cycle with a final novel, *An End and a Beginning* (1958).

The 1960s were a difficult decade, as Hanley began to concentrate on dramatic works. In 1963, he moved back to London with Timmy and wrote more frequently for BBC television. John Fordham, in his useful and thorough study of Hanley's life and work, suggests that the move may have been prompted not only by James's desire to be closer to the theatrical world but also, perhaps, by the increasing unhappiness of Timmy, who may have been suffering from depression.

Disappointed by his lack of dramatic success, in the 1970s Hanley returned to novel writing with a series of late works in which dialogue, honed by his dramatic writing, took on new importance. These were *Another World* (1972), *A Woman in the Sky* (1973), *A Dream Journey* (1976)—which returned to characters from *No Directions*, interpolating that novel almost unaltered—and *A Kingdom* (1978). Reviewing *A Woman in the Sky*, the novelist Paul Scott, who in 1970 had helped to secure for Hanley an Arts Council of Great Britain grant of £1,000, wrote that it was "a variation on what seems to have become the author's favorite theme: the importance attached by the lonely to the lives they have made for themselves." The anonymous reviewer of *Another World* in the *Times Literary Supplement* had put it in more elaborate terms:

> Wherever they may be, in foc's'les, tight houses in tight streets, Hanley people have always from the outsider's view moaned and suffered, mocked each other's misfortunes, committed crimes, squabbled, been utterly obsessed by trivia: but below the surface there can be detected the light of human satisfaction, and the deeper you go into a Hanley novel the more radiant it becomes.
>
> ("The Satisfactions of Hell," p. 649).

After the publication of *A Kingdom*, Hanley continued to write, but he published no more novels. In 1980, shortly after Timmy's death, he moved to a small flat in Lissenden Gardens, Highgate, near the home of his son Liam. He died on November 11, 1985—Armistice Day—at the age of eighty-eight.

SEA STORIES, WAR STORIES

Hanley's first novel, *Drift* (1930), tells the story of the Rourke family, and especially that of Joe Rourke, a working-class boy whose intellectual aspirations are frustrated by his strict Roman Catholic parents. "He's reading bad books," Joe's father tells the local priest: "One of them filthy books by a scoundrel named Zola" and "a book called 'Ulysses' by a dirty renegade Irishman named Joyce. I tore it up" (pp. 18, 103). Following the teachings of the church, they destroy Joe's borrowed novels, frustrating his creative ambitions. Joe takes up with a young prostitute, and later with a group of bourgeois revolutionaries; ultimately his wish to be free of his family leads him to renounce his mother, inadvertently hastening her death, and to be renounced in turn by his dying father. The novel ends with Joe walking into the countryside and into a storm, raging against a God from whom he cannot escape but in whom he no longer places his faith.

An apprentice work, *Drift* never approaches the achievement of those works of Zola and Joyce—particularly *A Portrait of the Artist as a Young Man* (1916)—that are its models. In its inconsistencies, however, one can see the seeds of the later Hanley's linguistic experiment and lyricism. The greatest intensity of language is concentrated at the novel's points of highest emotion, as at the funeral of Joe's mother: "No more excitement until the bell tolled again. Hubbub of voices talking about the poor. Hubbub of voices criticizing Mick's shabby black coat and vest. Woman wearing a green shawl blowing her nose with great energy" (p. 178). This telegraphic prose can be heard, too, in early short stories such as "The Last Voyage," published in the same year as *Drift*, in which Reilly, a superannuated seaman, faces the indignity of forced retirement and a meager pension and at last commits a symbolic suicide by jumping into a ship's furnace. Looking at his sleeping children, Reilly thinks of his failure: "Was nothing now, he felt. Nuisance. And young men coming along all the time. Young men from same street. Street that was narrow, and at the back, high walls so that sun could not come in" (*The Last Voyage and Other Stories*, p. 18). Shorn of articles, Hanley's

JAMES HANLEY

style here resembles that of his friend Henry Green, who in an interview with Terry Southern explained the contrivance as a way of making his prose "as taut and spare as possible, to fit the proletarian life I was then leading" (*Paris Review* 19, summer 1958, p. 73). Like Green, who confessed that in retrospect he found the style affected, Hanley would in later novels seek more subtle ways of introducing unfamiliarity into his prose, tempering its proletarian tautness with the flexions of natural speech.

In his early fiction, Hanley was working to master and to use the tools provided not only by Joyce and Zola but also by the idiosyncratic and cosmopolitan pantheon of English, American, European, and Russian writers he had assembled during his years as a merchant seaman and his later period of self-education. Given the opprobrium in which those advanced writers are held by Joe Rourke's parents in *Drift*, it is the great irony of Hanley's long and exceptional career that he should still be best known for his second novel, *Boy* (1931), which four years after its publication was successfully suppressed on charges of obscenity. Its protagonist, Arthur Fearon, is another of Hanley's oppressed youths. Talented, bright, and ambitious to become a chemist, Fearon is forced to leave school by his poor parents, who put him to work at the docks. Beaten by his father, and subjected to a humiliating initiation ritual by the other working boys, Fearon stows away in the coal bunker of a merchant ship. After his discovery, he works as the ship's boy, enduring the pederastic advances of the mate and the cook, before catching syphilis from a prostitute in an Alexandria brothel and being euthanized in his delirium by the ship's drunken captain.

Although Hanley had expurgated the novel's most objectionable words and scenes before the publication of the first edition by Boriswood, the publisher was successfully prosecuted four years later after releasing a new edition adorned with a suggestive cover image. The suppression of *Boy* damaged Hanley, who for many years, even after the ban had been rescinded, refused to allow the novel to be reissued. It may also have damaged Hanley's reputation: rallying to the defense of

Boy, his supporters, from E. M. Forster to Anthony Burgess, have been obliged to overstate its achievement in order to justify its publication. Yet it remains an uneven and unstructured early work, containing hints of its author's talent rather than a forceful statement of his literary gift. In fact, Hanley's best writing of this period is to be found in short stories such as "The German Prisoner" (1930), in which two lost English soldiers, caught in an abandoned trench, torture, abuse, and kill a young German soldier in a horrifying excess of sexual sadism, before turning on each other. The soldiers, isolated and confused by the fall of a thick fog, descend into an orgy of madness that compresses into a single incident the wider madness of organized violence occurring all around them in the fields of France. At the end of the story, by the time the fog rises, the English soldiers have beaten the German boy's face to a pulp, raped him with a bayonet, and trampled his body down into the mud, which at last consumes them all.

At the end of "Narrative" (1931), too, fog clears on a scene of death after the crew of a torpedoed merchant ship, adrift in a leaking boat, recognize the futility of their struggle against the force of the sea: "It was inevitable surrender, without protest, to a force that overwhelms and drags down all life" (*The Last Voyage*, p. 268). Here Hanley returns to that scene of his youth: the doomed seaman slipping away into the vast and lonely death-giving ocean. Hanley's fog is not the sort of fog that Joseph Conrad's Marlow encounters in *Heart of Darkness* (1902), where savagery lurks outside its "white shutter"; rather, what is implicit in Conrad is made explicit in Hanley: violence is what the fog cloaks within its opacity. Yet these soldiers have none of the self-possession of a Marlow, nor any rational self-understanding before the realization of their culpability drives them to frenzy. Lifting, the fog leaves only a moment's clarity: no Joycean epiphany, but rather a washed-out illumination in which, as in Samuel Beckett, human failure becomes the transcendent certainty of the ongoing tragedy of living.

That expansiveness—"*all* life"—is important, for Hanley is not a writer to whom it is easy to attribute a clear position in the ideological disputations of the 1930s. He put his case succinctly in a letter to his friend Tom Jones, in 1935: "The more I study the people of today, the more I like the people of yesterday, and this isn't being old fashioned, but strikes at the core of one of the deepest instincts of humans. Lots of people think a pile about instigators and all the amorphous mass of modern isms, but I prefer vegetating with nature" (Fordham, p. 143).

In the white space that decouples a period from a movement—"modern isms"—Hanley neatly summarizes the difficulty of placement that later critics have attempted to overcome in order either to integrate his work into the tradition of high modernist experiment or to offer a critique of that tradition's elitism. It is an eloquent gap: one that reminds us of the value of the particular amid the amorphous and of the problematic relationship between individual humans and the mass of humanity that still drives debates about literature and political commitment.

In *Don Quixote Drowned* (1953), Hanley published what is perhaps his most revealing statement about aesthetics and politics. It is typically oblique, appearing in "A Writer's Day," a sketch that begins teasingly as a breezy report on the daily routine ("My first thought on waking is generally, Is the pump working?" (p. 57) before expanding into a meditation on the literary and political movements that have come and gone during his writing life. Here the bourgeois members of the thirties literary left appear as "a certain flight of proletarian duck" (p. 75): "There was Bill's first novel about a ravished laundrymaid, and Ted's brilliant long-short story about his mother, dying so cruelly of cancer. … Then there was Mary's revelation about her stepmother who worked in a northern factory, under grey skies, where everybody sweated unduly between the thighs" (p. 80). The disgust here is real, but quite different in kind from the disgust felt by an Orwell, say, at the presence of the chamberpot under the breakfast table. One feels that the degree of disgust registered in undue sweat is in part a displacement of Hanley's disgust for the unfeeling deployment of these worn tropes of working-class experience: of factory and illness,

of gray skies and domestic servants. The milieu takes in "Jack Chubb, a promising documentary writer, [who] had for some time been rather worried by a rude word that Marx had called him" (p. 80) and includes, too, "the poets and the Mass Observers," class tourists "standing astonished at factory benches, crawling about in coal mines, […] and writing loud sonnets about the margarine queues" (pp. 80–81). "Just look at them," writes Hanley. "Carrying with them a world bellyache and leaving nothing behind them but their caps, and a literary bogeyman standing on Wigan Pier, since duly canonised" (p. 79). The multiple levels of irony resolve into a clear sense that Hanley's distaste is directed not at the efforts of the bourgeois left to comprehend and stand in political solidarity with the working classes but rather at their abject failure to cultivate any real *human* solidarity or empathy. Without that, and in the face of a revolution repeatedly postponed, the desire for the improvement of the conditions of the working classes would remain a mere velleity, and the only possibility would be to move on to other projects. Again, like Beckett, Hanley knew that tragedy for ordinary men and women was now a matter of perseverance in the conditions of everyday life; this in contrast to many more idealistic writers of the interwar left, for whom, as Valentine Cunningham neatly puts it, "the notion of the proletarian world enduring was unendurable" (p. 1302). Artistic and cultural life, for Hanley, were neither idle distractions from the truth of material conditions nor mere tools for the prosecution of political programs; rather, as his fiction forcefully shows, art itself could aim to redeem and resolve the suffering of individual human beings under conditions of industrial impoverishment. Art, Hanley believed, could bring individuals together in acknowledgment of each other's full interiority and humanity, offering a form of redemption that would be the very condition, and not merely the servant, of political transformation.

But the snipe at the "literary bogeyman," Orwell, is not the most direct attack to be found in "A Writer's Day." For Hanley's reverie on his flight of proletarian duck is prompted by discovering an old collection of socialist and communist books while searching for something to read among his copies of Thomas Hardy and James Cook's *Voyages*. This search leads him to the subject of Conrad, who appears in Hanley's imagination as an ancestor of those thirties class tourists.

> Conrad, a rather self-conscious man, who sometimes tripped over his own vanity, happened one day to trip over a stone in the for'ard quarters ... and drew back somewhat shocked, for he had turned up a nest of ants. He was fascinated yet repelled. How extraordinary! Did such things exist for'ard of the bridge? He must have a look aft some time. Also he must get back on the bridge, have a chat with Marlow about it. That is, if Marlow wasn't too busy himself airing his precious views and philosophising by the yard.
>
> (*Don Quixote Drowned*, p. 78)

There is something of the anxiety of influence in this delation: Hanley, writing in the early 1950s, registers his disagreement with Conrad, the author with whose writing his earliest work had frequently been compared and the marks of whose influence it clearly bears. Increasingly popular in nineteenth-century England, with its global dominance of oceanic trade and its sense of naval superiority, the sea story had been transformed during the age of steam. To Conrad, England was the maritime nation par excellence, "where men and sea interpenetrate, so to speak" ("Youth," p. 3). By the time Hanley went to sea, England was embroiled in a war with the ascendant industrial power of Germany, and no longer so assured of its mastery of the seas. Hanley's sea was not Conrad's sea, and his view from the furnace and the forecastle was not Conrad's view from the bridge. The interpenetration of man and sea was for him not a matter of symbolic symbiosis but instead was a bodily immersion in a dirty and recalcitrant element that could at any moment exact revenge on mariners for its subjugation by the forces of capital and industry.

For Conrad—whose impressionist inclinations, famously summarized in the preface to *The Nigger of the "Narcissus"* (1897), were "before all, to make you *see*"—the ocean, placid or rough, remained principally an optical phenomenon. It was, as the title of his memoir *The Mirror of the Sea* (1906) suggests, a specular surface, performing its enigmatic work of reflecting the unfathomable depths of the human mind by its visible characteristics. By contrast, Hanley's sea is, as one of his own titles puts it, a *Hollow Sea* (1938); it gapes as a material correlative of the "gulf of desire," the "abyss" into which Joe Rourke repeatedly stares in *Drift* (p. 11). If Conrad's sea is apprehended by looking, Hanley's tends to affect a different sense altogether. Before all, it makes you *smell*. It smells in the bilges, where the young Arthur Fearon in *Boy* (1931) stands knee deep bailing out "stinking water" and "green slime" (p. 35). It smells in *The Ocean* (1941), where a delirious, dehydrated shipwreck survivor hallucinates a giant cockroach as a familiar phobia taking him away from the real, unbearable horror of immediate circumstances: "like shrimps he once picked on the shore; it had a sea smell" (p. 95). "Nine at the time, smelt it off my father," says Manion in *Sailor's Song* (p. 13), while in *Broken Water* it is the young Hanley himself who takes in "that curious smell of the sea, that deep, impenetrable, unmistakable smell of the sea which is like no other smell on earth" (p. 67).

Smell, in these contexts, is the most unmistakably proletarian sense: smells tend to intensify the closer one gets to the bottom of the supply chain. It is the sense that most reliably unsettles the bourgeois observers of working-class life in the 1930s. But if smell bears these associations with the work of production, it also comes into play in Hanley's thinking about *reproduction*, and in the relations between mothers and sons. It is smell that disgusts Joe Rourke in his final altercation with his overbearing mother: "He felt the smell of her body and recoiled. He was conscious of a physical disgust descending on him like a blanket ... He could feel the huge breasts rising and falling as if a sea were near to him" (*Drift*, p. 168). If for Buck Mulligan, in *Ulysses* (1922), channeling Swinburne, the sea is a "grey sweet mother," for Hanley the maternal relation is fraught with a disgust that pushes his characters from the maternal home toward the ocean, and toward other women, who, to Denny Fury, are "insatiable. Give her a single opening and you were overwhelmed at once. You were caught up in the tidal flow, a flow that carried in its wake regrets, protests, insinuations, hints" (*The Furys*, p. 43). Throughout these webs of significance—which bind the maternal, the sexual, and the oceanic—weaves a thread spun from that initial moment of horror at the death of Crawley, the man overboard, who, as he vanishes, utters "but a single word, 'Mother,' as though she were somewhere near, ready to save him, to lift him up out of the torrents of water" (*Don Quixote Drowned*, p. 37).

While disparaging Conrad, Hanley expressed his affiliation to another great sea writer, Herman Melville, whose influence is increasingly visible in his fiction from *Captain Bottell* (1933) onward. Later in life, Hanley would dedicate a short critical appreciation to that author's work, *Herman Melville: A Man in the Customs House* (1971), which celebrates Melville's tragic vision. It is a lyrical essay, beginning with *Moby-Dick*, both novel and whale, rising out of the depths of the ocean: "Breaking surface, it appeared as a black cloud, and hung heavy and burdensome, confounding and frightening men. But later it was landmark and light, forever shored up against all land-locked literature" (pp. 1–2).

Melville's whale is the forerunner of the menagerie of symbolic animals that appear at key moments in Hanley's novels, harbingers that offer humanity a more hopeful place in the natural world than that implied by the inorganic and deadly industrial sea. In *Broken Water*, Hanley recalls the moment when he first decided to go to sea. Like all of Hanley's early memories, it is a moment rewritten through the lens of his later symbolic understanding of nature. He describes a family visit to Howth Head, near Dublin, where, having wandered off on his own, he sees a solitary seabird perching on a rock. The bird becomes a sort of shamanic familiar:

> Suddenly I shut my eyes and said to myself, "If the bird flies east I'll go to sea, if it flies to any other point of the compass I won't." ... And in a second it had happened, my fate was sealed, it was all over. I would never mention the sea again to a soul, but I would keep the vow I made. The bird flapped its wings, suddenly soared into the air, my eyes following it with the greatest excitement, and it flew off to the east.

(pp. 24–25)

This symbolic gull is the first in a line of nature spirits that signal moments of decisive change, usually in the final moments of Hanley's novels. In *The Ocean* (1941), it is a whale, more comforting than Melville's, that plays around the shipwrecked sailors' lifeboat "like a light come into a dark room, a world looming up, peopling the sea, sending out warmth to them in their little boat" (p. 97). Reading across the whole body of work, this engagement of animal life serves to mark the persistence of an older manner of relation to the natural world in a time of industrial power, and helps to explain what might otherwise seem to be excesses or oddities in Hanley's work, such as the white horse that plunges through the burning city at the end of the air raid in *No Directions* (1943).

Written at the height of anti-German sentiment, and including the widely believed libel that German U-boat captains liked to spray machine-gun fire on escaping lifeboats, *The Ocean* is something of a propaganda piece based on Hanley's experiences and knowledge of convoy service during the First World War. But it is also a tight and subtle examination of a group of men—a sailor, an elderly priest, a teacher, a petit-bourgeois businessman, and a delirious, injured man—in the confined space of a lifeboat adrift in the wide ocean. John Fordham finds its precursors in Stephen Crane's short story "The Open Boat" (1897) and in Hanley's own early story, "Narrative," but one might also think of a wider wartime context of stories in which the lifeboat becomes, like Conrad's ships, a microcosm of a world that throws together different classes or nationalities, as in Alfred Hitchcock's film of 1944, *Lifeboat*.

In 1943, Hanley published his two great wartime novels. *Sailor's Song* was his last novel of the sea, in the sense that the sailors who appear in his subsequent books tend to find themselves shipwrecked, in a double sense, either by psychological traumas (often acquired in the course of wartime service) or by their own shortcomings, as with Captain Marius in *The Closed Harbour* (1952). Again in *Sailor's Song*, the human effort of a small group to overcome inevitable dissolution into death is organized around a shipwreck; the novel's wrought prose develops the earlier telegraphic style, with its proletarian associations, but also anticipates the lyrical style that Hanley would develop to accommodate the more sedate yet no less intense rhythms of his later rural novels. In *No Directions*, set on a single night of the London Blitz, a Chelsea tenement house provides the micro-society, disrupted in this case by German air raids and by class conflict. Perspectives shift in the bombed-out fragmentation of an oneiric narrative that fluctuates between documentary realism and expressionist distortion until the painter Clem, running in delirium from the air-raid shelter for a view of the destruction, discovers an impossibly terrifying vision of beauty that equates the unfathomable horror of technological warfare with that of the implacable ocean of Hanley's memory:

> He stood entranced at the blazing sky. All that light, a sea, an ocean of light, from what vast reservoir had it flooded up, this drenching light, blazing red, and suddenly to his left a falling green, cataracts of light, red, and yellow and green, this riot of colour shouted at you.
>
> "God!" he said, "it's magnificent, it's—"
>
> (p. 135)

Running on, Clem finds, of all things, an escaped white stallion. Mounting the horse, he manages to guide it—or does it guide him?—out of the blaze. Clem's actions, in part delirious, in part driven by his empathy for another living creature, offer him the opportunity to turn his terror into art: "he suddenly loved this beast, a giant trust lay between them, first demented and now calm, it would go where he went" (p. 138).

Those are the words of a writer who was beginning to feel in control of his chosen medium. Years later, in an appreciation of the work of his friend John Cowper Powys, Hanley would praise Powys's "sense of inner order." "Writing," he continued, "whatever may be said to the contrary, is a continuous battleground. Without this order and discipline there are no directions" (*John Cowper Powys*, p. 4). It is

significant that Hanley, in writing about the battleground London had become, reached the pinnacle of his achievement in a novel that struggles so powerfully to make aesthetic order out of its acknowledgement of the shattering destruction brought about by bombing. If, in its final moments, *No Directions* asks too much of art, one can only respond that here, as in his earlier stories of shipwreck and warfare, Hanley sees an irreducible value in the courage of a fragile and isolated humanity forced to recognize its insignificance alongside the inevitability of its own annihilation.

THE FURYS *CYCLE AND POSTWAR FICTION*

In 1935, Chatto & Windus had published *The Furys*, the first volume of Hanley's long family saga of the same name. Read alongside the earlier novels, it represents a widening and deepening of the channel cut by *Drift* (1930), reworking the concerns of that novel into the beginning of a far more complex and satisfying exploration of the life of a working-class family. The *Furys* sequence was conceived as a trilogy—*The Furys* (1935), *The Secret Journey* (1936), and *Our Time Is Gone* (1940)—and later expanded with two novels, *Winter Song* (1950) and *An End and a Beginning* (1958). It can be thought of as an attempt to do for the working class what John Galsworthy's *The Forsyte Saga* (1906–1921) had done for the wealthy middle class, but the more apt comparison is perhaps to the French romans-fleuves of the nineteenth century, and in particular to Zola's chronicle of *Les Rougon-Macquart*. As the title and family name suggests, however, Hanley also set out to write a novel of mythic resonance, drawing on the example of Joyce's *Ulysses* in order to juxtapose the industrial decay of twentieth-century Liverpool not, as Joyce had done for Dublin, with the epic matter of *The Odyssey*, but with the tragic drama of Aeschylus's *Oresteia*.

The first volume, *The Furys*, can be regarded as the first novel of Hanley's mature period, integrating the expressionist, naturalist, and experimental tendencies that had jostled uneasily in *Drift* and *Boy*. It begins the story of an Irish Catholic family of economic migrants living in the dockland area of Gelton, Hanley's version of Liverpool. Early in the novel, Peter, the youngest son of the family, returns home having been dismissed from the Dublin seminary where, in deference to his mother Fanny's wishes, he has been training for the priesthood. Like *Drift*, the novel is set during the period of industrial unrest that wracked Liverpool in the summer of 1911, after striking seamen were joined by dockers and transport workers in their fight for improved pay and working conditions. While the threat of industrial action grows, Peter resolves to go to sea as his father did before him. Meanwhile, Peter's brother Anthony lies in a New York hospital, having fallen from a ship's mast after volunteering for a dangerous job in stormy weather. At home, their mother struggles to extract Anthony's wages and compensation money from the convoluted bureaucracy of the shipping company.

At the center of the novel is a long set-piece in which strike action at last boils over into a violent struggle in the central square of Gelton between police and striking workers. Peter and his father watch in horror as mounted police charge the crowd: "A baton was something more than a piece of weighted wood. It was the symbol of authority, it had no respect for neutrality. The very hand that wielded it succumbed to its power. Its sickening hum, as it swung to and fro in the air, had taken the place of the indistinct hum. Its song has assumed control" (pp. 201–202).

Hanley is interested here in the kind of power that Michel Foucault would later describe: a power that circulates through the discursive structures of society, eddying around "symbols of authority" rather than flowing from a single point of origin. As the police baton charge concentrates at a single point the power of state violence, so too the crowd threatens to break toward destruction rather than channeling the power of resistance. Separated from his father, Peter falls in with a strange character, Professor Titmouse, a professor of anthropology who is an effete combination of shabby academic, seedy philosopher, and Mass Observer (before that movement

existed). Professor Titmouse becomes, briefly, Peter's cicerone in the swirling force that surges through the crowd like the sea currents of maritime fiction and allows Hanley to voice the contradictions of violence in mass struggle. Hauling Peter up on to the back of a stone lion—another symbolic animal that offers a perspective on the concerns of the surrounding novel—he quizzes Peter as they watch looters break into a tailor's shop:

> That action was backed up by the moral force of the crowd. No. Immoral force. But is it fair? Is it honest? Is this a peaceful gathering? Is it a fair protest against brutality? You are laughing at me. … I shall not disturb your enjoyment of the fun. But the man's action is a bad one. It harbours frightful possibilities.
>
> (p. 245)

The professor is a shady character, who in the end attempts a fumbling molestation of Peter; but his overblown crowd psychology nonetheless speaks to real concerns that run not only through Hanley's fiction about the 1911 Liverpool strikes but also through other novels that reflect the class struggle of the 1930s: from the striking Clydesiders of James Barke's *Major Operation* (1936) to the proletarian crowd that ransacks the railway hotel in Henry Green's *Party Going* (1945). One can see, here, part of what troubled even Hanley's admirers on the left: a sort of heteroglossia in the presentation of the novel that is never content to argue the case without emphasizing the human context of all political understanding and action.

The tragic model of Hanley's sequence becomes clearer with the second Furys novel, *The Secret Journey*. This book centers on the story of the loan taken out by Fanny Fury from a private moneylender named Anna Ragner in order to pay the outstanding expenses of Peter's abandoned seminary education. It ends with Peter stabbing Ragner before symbolically choking her with the outward signs of her wealth: "He lifted the ringed fingers of her right hand, bunched them together and forced them brutally into the dead woman's mouth. The features seemed to distend, the mouth beneath the glaring eyes seemed to be devouring the jewelled hand" (p. 564). It is a scene of penetrative violence that calls to mind the shocking sadism of "The German Prisoner." Yet here the gendered violence is symbolic as well as purely corporeal. We have already seen the connections, in Hanley's treatment of women, between illicit sexual desire, disgust for the maternal body, and the fierce natural power that links women and the sea as two parts of the dangerous and desired other. By choking the moneylender with her own ringed fingers, Peter enacts a matricidal silencing that is the displaced fulfillment of his own feelings toward his overbearing mother.

The *Furys* cycle was a hugely ambitious work, yet the effect of its extraordinary length—well over two thousand pages—was to dilute the local intensities that Hanley had begun to master. The later volumes continue the story through Peter's time in prison, Denny Fury's return to seafaring, the First World War, and Peter's efforts after his release to start a new life in Ireland. There can be little doubt that Hanley succeeded in producing the minutely detailed and sympathetic tragic work he set out to write, but the sequence, taken as a whole, lacks the more satisfyingly condensed effects of the stand-alone novels on which Hanley worked during the 1940s and 1950s.

After two relatively unsuccessful postwar works—*What Farrar Saw* (1946), a short, monitory fantasy of a nationwide traffic jam, and *Emily* (1948), the story of a damaged soldier's return from action in Burma—Hanley revisited the Fury family with *Winter Song* (1950), which concentrates on the later life of the Fury parents after Denny Fury's return from the sea. There followed, under the pseudonym "Patric Shone," the uneven and rather sentimental *The House in the Valley* (1951, reprinted as *Against the Stream*, 1981). Hanley's pseudonymous attempt at reinvention suggests his growing frustration with the lukewarm critical and commercial reception of his most recent books. Wisely abandoning "Patric Shone," he found a different kind of reinvention by concentrating once again on the subject that had gained him an audience. *The Closed Harbour* (1952), widely regarded as a return to form, charted the decline of Marius, a former captain who, having lost his ship at sea under mysterious circumstances, finds himself ma-

rooned and disgraced in the port of Marseilles. The influence of Conrad, and especially of *Lord Jim* (1900), is unmistakable; yet for Marius, unlike Jim, there is no act of reinvention or sacrifice. Hanley's bleak vision is that of an author who, having made increasingly desperate attempts to renew his own career, thought perhaps that a hoped-for renewal was beyond his powers. With *The Closed Harbour*, however, he regained a degree of critical and commercial approbation.

The following book, *The Welsh Sonata* (1954), consolidated that achievement. Told in part by an omniscient narrator and in part by "Goronwy Jones," a "policeman and retired bard" (p. 7) of the small Welsh town of Cilgyn, it is a powerfully original work, as though Dylan Thomas, in writing the radio drama *Under Milk Wood* (1954), had set out to map the inner life of a place not through a series of sketches and dreams, but in the form of a mystery novel. The prose—prose poetry, perhaps, is the more fitting term—was Hanley's best since *No Directions*, catching the cadences and accelerations of Welsh English with none of the infelicities of register or tone that occasionally mar the dialogue in earlier books. The story concerns the disappearance of a local tramp, known as Rhys the Wound. As Hanley circles around this mythical, mystical figure, he also limns the landscape and the inhabitants of a Welsh community. They are farmers and shopkeepers, publicans and shepherds and farriers. Despite the novel's lyrical style and hints of allegory, Hanley's folk are living figures with their own habits and difficulties, drawn from his own community in rural Wales. Structurally, the novel resembles the sonata form from which it takes its title, building a series of thematic developments and recapitulations in tribute to Hanley's own love of classical music. It is a novel whose texture is woven of time and community and landscape, and one that confidently intensifies its language to celebrate those interweaving threads. Of particular density are the moments at which the mysterious, semimythical tramp appears:

How he will look to others.
A tall man with a cloud of silver upon his head.

No man's shirt ever graced his breast.
And just any old sack flung cape-like about his shoulders that some farmer does not want, or any old rag fallen from a tree.
Warrior's trousers from old wars and never was any different except once when Pugh Williams's black ones were too short for his long legs.
Wears any old boots at all, and on a summer's day, nothing.
Can be seen at a distance by the living cloud of his hair, and by glimpses under a moving sack of the shining gold of his chest.

(p. 17)

The Welsh Sonata shows Hanley more fully committed to the sound of language itself than he had been at any time in the ten years since *Sailor's Song*, yet here that commitment produces a prose that draws both on the scissile poetics of modernist experiment and on the more fluid and familiar rhythms of common speech.

In *Levine* (1956), that formal experiment is replaced by an increasing interest in dialogue. Since his self-administered cultural education of the 1930s, Hanley had been an admirer of Ibsen and Strindberg, and *Levine* marks the moment when dialogue takes shape as a formal principle in his prose style. The novel itself is perhaps Hanley's final attempt to work through the themes that had become recognizably his own, in settings and with characters who are comfortably Hanleyan. It deals with a Polish sailor, Felix Levine, who, having been shipwrecked, and having washed up as a refugee in a northern English town, becomes locked into an unhappy relationship with an older woman. Hanley runs through the familiar tropes of femininity and masculinity, domineering families, and the fine line between support and dependence; and while Levine is one of his most accomplished works in this vein, one can also hear the strain of a restless writer seeking a new form, a way to renew his craft once again. He found it by turning away from the novel and toward dramatic writing.

Hanley spent most of the 1960s honing his craft as a playwright, producing work mainly for radio and television (though a short-lived stage production of *Say Nothing*—produced as a radio play in 1961 and released as a novel in 1962—

appeared at the Stratford East Theatre in August 1962). Working across these different media allowed Hanley to write as he had in the 1930s: a radio play could be revised for television with comparative ease, and existing short stories could be combined or adapted. He returned to novel writing in the early 1970s, bringing an ear attuned to speech rhythms and giving greater prominence, in his later work, to exchanges of dialogue. *A Woman in the Sky* (1973), for instance, takes place almost entirely as a series of conversations, with narrative interpolations restricted to transitions and brief expository remarks. In the book's opening lines, Hanley deftly brings the reader into the middle of an uncomfortable conversation between a suspicious tower block resident and an inquisitive priest:

"Yes," she said, "yes."

"And then?"

"She went on up."

"Who went on up?" he asked, groping.

"Who'd you think?"

"That's what I'm asking you," he said.

"Ask decent then, and keep your voice down," Lil said.

"I presume you're referring to the unfortunate lady?"

"You presume correctly," Lil replied.

"Ah!" he said, and "Oh dear!"

"Here long?"

"Her? 'Bout three years, I think. Get them out of the way these days, push them up, under their feet, they say. How it is."

(p. 1)

Hanley, who had begun his writing life in the shadow of Stephen Dedalus, here begins a novel about a broken-down, itinerant, elderly woman with the word that marks Joyce's hopeful conclusion to *Ulysses*. Not surprising, perhaps, that such a beginning should segue so quickly into the resignedly Beckettian "How it is" that sounds in the voice of different characters throughout *A Woman in the Sky*.

In his last published work, *A Kingdom* (1978), Hanley returned to his earlier themes of rootedness and escape, and of obligation and conflict within families. The book takes place in a remote part of Wales, where Cadi Evans is preparing to bury her dead father. Her sister Lucy, now settled elsewhere with her husband, David, returns for the funeral, and the novel explores the relationship between the sisters as well as the events that have led up to their estrangement from one another. In a nuancing of the familial theme in *The Furys*, we find here a woman who, though in many ways constrained by her sense of familial duty, nonetheless finds a powerful sense of independence in her rootedness that is quite distinct from her sister's dependence upon her husband. If these late novels are less sure of the redemptive possibilities of art, they are nonetheless faithful to the artist's obligation to his own vision of the gulf between the vulnerability and insignificance of human life on the cosmic scale, and the vastness of the interiority of individual human beings.

CONCLUSION

Toward the end of the first *Furys* novel, Fanny Fury receives a visit from her son-in-law, Joe Kilkey. Mrs. Fury looks down on Joe, but Joe—knowing that she has recently had difficulties with money, with the dockers' strike, and with the disintegration of her hopes for her son Peter's entry into the priesthood—has brought her a gift, a ticket for a weeklong retreat in a country convent. The gift touches Fanny so deeply that, when Joe leaves, she has to sit down, laying her head on the arm of the rocking chair in which her aged and crippled father spends his days. It is a moment of peace in a novel of turmoil. Suddenly: "A series of sharp coughs from the occupant of the high-backed chair reminded her that she must be up and doing. Reality was pressing in, breaking down the texture of her dreams" (p. 382).

This is the constant note in Hanley's fiction. Everywhere, human hope and kindness labor against a reality of poverty, of work, of dissolution, that presses in. Yet these qualities, if transitory, are nonetheless the common thread in the texture of human experience, and for Hanley it is art that retains the power to reveal and reknit these strands of feeling. It is art that holds out the hope of a future of diminished suffering, for any such future must be predicated upon the full understanding of the interiority and self-sufficiency of other beings that art, above all, has the power to instill.

As well as the novels mentioned here, Hanley published short stories too numerous to discuss in detail, many of which deal with similar themes, and some of which continue or expand the story of *The Furys*. Hanley had been a sailor, and he retained in his prose not only a liking for maritime turns of phrase but also the sailor's tale-telling habit, repeating the same stories in different books with different shadings and emphases. Indeed, Hanley's life and work may remind us of the passage in Walter Benjamin's essay *Der Erzähler* (1936–1937), in which Benjamin identifies two archetypal storytellers in, on the one hand, the far-ranging traveler and, on the other, the man of the local landscape. The one, he writes, "is embodied in the resident tiller of the soil, and the other in the trading seaman" (*Illuminations*, 2007 edition). Hanley never tilled soil, but his trajectory took him through a series of self-reinventions from the vast sea to the quiet fields of a rural community.

Yet Hanley's large body of told and retold tales is perhaps partly responsible for the neglect into which his work has fallen. With no independent means, he wrote fast in order to live. If that is not always a practice conducive to consistency or quality, it should be remembered that Hanley's vast output includes some of the finest short stories of World War I and one of the defining novels of World War II, as well as a series of extremely accomplished and compact fictions stretching from the mid 1930s to the late 1970s. His work raises significant questions about the place of working-class writers in English literary studies, about the enduring though neglected legacy of modernism in British fiction after the Second World War, and about the important role such now-marginal writers can play in forcing us to reconsider our Auden- and London-centric histories of 1930s left-wing thought and writing.

Selected Bibliography

WORKS OF JAMES HANLEY

SHORT FICTION

The German Prisoner. London: privately printed, 1930.

A Passion Before Death. London: privately printed, 1930.

Men in Darkness: Five Stories. London: John Lane, 1931.

Half an Eye: Sea Stories. London: John Lane, 1937.

People Are Curious. London: John Lane, 1938.

Between the Tides. London: Methuen, 1939.

At Bay and Other Stories. London: Faber and Faber, 1944.

Crilley and Other Stories. London: Nicholson & Watson, 1945.

The Last Voyage and Other Stories. London: Harvill, 1997.

NOVELS

Drift. London: Eric Partridge (Scholartis Press), 1930. Reprint. London: Nicholson & Watson, 1944.

Boy. London: Boriswood, 1931. Reprint. Richmond, U.K.: Oneworld Classics, 2007.

Ebb and Flood. London: John Lane, 1932.

Captain Bottell. London: Boriswood, 1933.

Quartermaster Clausen. London : Arlan at the White Owl Press, 1934.

Resurrexit Dominus. London: privately printed, 1934.

The Furys. London: Chatto & Windus, 1935.

Stoker Bush. London: Chatto & Windus, 1935.

The Secret Journey. London: Chatto & Windus, 1936. Reprint. London: Faber Finds, 2009.

Hollow Sea. London: John Lane, 1938.

Our Time Is Gone. London: John Lane, 1940. Reprint. London: Faber Finds, 2009.

The Ocean. London: Faber and Faber, 1941.

No Directions. London: André Deutsch, 1943. Reprint, with preface by Henry Miller. 1990.

Sailor's Song. London: Nicholson & Watson, 1943.

What Farrar Saw. London: Nicholson & Watson, 1946.

Emily. London: Nicholson & Watson, 1948.

A Walk in the Wilderness. London: Phoenix House, 1950.

Winter Song. London: Phoenix House, 1950. Reprint. London: Faber Finds, 2009.

The House in the Valley [as Patric Shone]. London: Jonathan Cape, 1951. Reprinted as *Against the Stream.* New York: Horizon Press, 1981.

The Closed Harbour. London: Macdonald, 1952.

The Welsh Sonata. London: Derek Verschoyle, 1954.

Levine. London: Macdonald, 1956.

An End and a Beginning. London: Macdonald, 1958. Reprint. London: Faber Finds, 2009.

Another World. London: André Deutsch, 1972.

A Woman in the Sky. London: André Deutsch, 1973.

A Dream Journey. London: André Deutsch, 1976.

A Kingdom. London: André Deutsch, 1978.

WORKS FOR RADIO, TELEVISION, AND STAGE

Convoy. BBC Radio, May 30, 1941.

Return to Danger. BBC Radio, January 15, 1942.

Shadows before Sunrise. BBC Radio, Home Service, December 6, 1942.

Winter's Journey. CBC Radio (Canada), January 29, 1957.

Gobbet. BBC Radio, Third Programme, October 6, 1959.

Say Nothing. BBC Radio, Third Programme, April 25, 1961.

The Furys. BBC Radio North (Northern Ireland), September 21 to November 26, 1961.

Say Nothing. BBC Television, February 19, 1964; CBC TV (Canada), May 5, 1965.

Inner World of Miss Vaughn. BBC Television, April 1, 1964.

Another Port, Another Town. Granada Television, May 4, 1964.

One Way Only. BBC Radio, Third Programme, December 10, 1967.

Plays One. London: Kaye & Ward, 1968.

It Wasn't Me. BBC Television, December 17, 1969.

The Furys. BBC Radio, February–March 2001.

NONFICTION

Broken Water: An Autobiographical Excursion. London: Chatto & Windus, 1937. (Autobiography.)

Grey Children: A Study in Humbug and Misery. London: Methuen, 1937.

Don Quixote Drowned. London: Macdonald, 1953. (Autobiographical sketches.)

John Cowper Powys: A Man in the Corner. Loughton: K.A. Ward, 1969.

Herman Melville: A Man in the Customs House. Loughton, U.K.: Dud Noman Press, 1971.

ARCHIVES

The BBC Written Archives Centre in Reading, U.K., holds a collection of James Hanley's unpublished radio scripts and screenplays.

JAMES HANLEY

BIOGRAPHICAL AND CRITICAL STUDIES

Cunningham, Valentine. "The Voice of the Voiceless." *Times Literary Supplement,* November 10, 1978, p. 1302.

Fordham, John. *James Hanley: Modernism and the Working Class*. Cardiff: University of Wales Press, 2002.

Gibbs, Linnea. *James Hanley: A Bibliography*. Vancouver: William Hoffer, 1980.

Gostick, Chris. "Extra Material on James Hanley's *Boy*." In *Boy*. By James Hanley. Richmond, U.K.: Oneworld Classics, 2007.

"A Novelist in Neglect: The Case for James Hanley." *Times Literary Supplement*, June 11, 1971, p. 675.

"Other New Books." *Times Literary Supplement*, March 14, 1935, p. 161.

Scott, Paul. "Up and Out." *Times Literary Supplement*, October 5, 1973, p. 1157.

Stokes, Edward. *The Novels of James Hanley*. Melbourne: Cheshire, 1964.

"The Satisfactions of Hell." *Times Literary Supplement*, June 9, 1972, p. 649.

Wright, Ralph. "There Is Greatness in James Hanley." *Daily Worker*, December 4, 1935.

OTHER WORKS CITED

Benjamin, Walter. *Illuminations*. Translated by Harry Zohn. Edited by Hannah Arendt. New York: Schocken, 2007.

Conrad, Joseph. *"Youth" and Two Other Stories*. New York: Doubleday, Page, 1924.

DAVID HARSENT

(1942—)

Niall Munro

DAVID HARSENT IS one of poetry's finest modern ventriloquists. As his work has evolved, one constant has been the desire to intensely inhabit the voices of others, whether these characters might be a traditional English puppet, a hare, a sniper staring down at his targets, or a painter—to mention only a few of Harsent's subjects. His characters are no dummies, however, for they frequently exhibit a fluent command of rhythm and diction that places them convincingly within their contexts, and reveals their passions, motivations, and inner thoughts. In order to give these voices full throat, Harsent realized quite early on that he needed to sustain them through a series of poems, and he has become a master of the dramatic sequence, constructing complex narratives that have density, referring back to themselves in the repetition of phrases and imagery.

As befits an author of many voices, Harsent also inhabits a number of different worlds as a writer, and he has used four different pseudonyms. Under these names and his own he has written opera libretti, a play, a literary novel, crime thrillers, and television comedy and drama series, but it is poetry that he regards as his main employment and responsibility. Poetry is essential to him and a means by which he might make sense of the world. It is quite simply a way of life.

David Harsent was born on December 9, 1942, in Bovey Tracey in Devon, a town that lies northwest of Newton Abbot and on the outskirts of Dartmoor National Park. Harsent's family background was working-class and his father was employed as a bricklayer, but at the time of Harsent's birth he was fighting with the British army in the Western Desert Campaign in North Africa, and Harsent did not meet him until he was six years old. By that time he and his mother had escaped German bombing raids to settle in Princes Risborough in Buckinghamshire to live with Harsent's aunt, grandmother, and great-grandmother in a flat above a post office. In an interview, he recalled that as a seven-year-old in this matriarchal setting, he knew "far more about the rhythms of menstruation than I did about the male camaraderie of football terraces" (Nicholas Wroe interview).

Harsent dates his sense of himself as a writer to when he wrote a story at school, explaining that he felt the story was merely "on loan" to the teacher to whom he submitted it. But Harsent has identified three crucial events in his life that determined his course as a poet. The first of these occurred when he was ten. On his way to Sunday school, the young Harsent tripped and fell down a steep stairwell, landing on a concrete floor. Forced to convalesce in bed, Harsent was provided with library books to read, including a collection of "boy's own" adventures. Between the stories, Harsent discovered poems that he later learned were border ballads, narrative poems derived from the lives of people living along the border between England and Scotland in the sixteenth and seventeenth centuries. They depicted relationships between men and women, were frequently violent and dealt with the supernatural, used regular rhymes and rhythms, were written in dialect and often included lively dialogue. Bewitched by these pieces, Harsent asked his grandmother to go back to the library and bring back a whole book containing the poems. She returned with Sir Arthur Quiller-Couch's *The Oxford Book of Ballads*, and the subject matter and style of those ballads have continued to be an influence on Harsent's work ever since. His 2011 collection, *Night*, even includes an original ballad of his own.

DAVID HARSENT

Harsent's accident meant that he missed the exam he should have taken at the end of his primary education, but he nonetheless went on to attend Aylesbury Technical College (now Sir Henry Floyd Grammar School) near his home. Harsent hated the school and the teachers, whom he regarded as underqualified and physically confrontational, and he left at age sixteen with only three qualifications, including one in metalwork. He was discouraged from pursuing his studies at a sixth-form college or university by his father, but because he enjoyed reading and the family needed the money, he was instead sent to work in a bookshop in Aylesbury. Harsent had published his first poem the previous year, and in the shop he continued to read widely, albeit in an undirected way, helping himself to copies of books in which he had a particular interest. His reading became more focused when he met another bookshop employee, Henry de Beaufort Saunders, who is commemorated in *A Bird's Idea of Flight* (1998). A keen poet himself, Saunders was in the process of translating Charles Baudelaire's *Les Fleurs du mal* into English. Harsent identifies this meeting, and Saunders' mentoring of him, to be the second of the key influences upon his writing career. He was encouraged by the older man to read poets such as Baudelaire, Arthur Rimbaud, and Paul Verlaine, and the dangerous lifestyles of these poets appealed to the teenage Harsent as much as their work.

During his time at the bookshop, Harsent, at age nineteen, married his first wife. Over the next few years the couple had three children and the family occupied a small house with the only toilets located in an outbuilding, but Harsent continued to write there and send his poems out to journals and periodicals. (One of these children, Simon Harsent, has become a well-known photographer, and father and son collaborated in 2010 on an advertising campaign for the World Wildlife Fund titled *Fragile Beauty*, in which three of Simon Harsent's photographs, "Ocean," "Rainforest," and "Icefield," were combined with three poems by David Harsent on the same subject.)

The third key moment in Harsent's writing career took place at this point when he met the poet and publisher Ian Hamilton. Harsent had been sending his poems out to a number of publications, among them the *Times Literary Supplement* (*TLS*) and the *Review*, and when a poem was rejected from one periodical he would send it to the other. It was only later that Harsent realized that Hamilton oversaw the submissions to both publications, so he had been sending his work to the same person twice. Hamilton, however, was interested in Harsent's poems and published his short collection *Tonight's Lover* as one of the pamphlet supplements to issue 19 of the *Review* in 1968. Hamilton also passed Harsent's work on to the poet and editor Jon Stallworthy, who had founded the Oxford University Press's modern poetry list in 1959 and who published Harsent's first collection, *A Violent Country*, in 1969.

Harsent was now becoming better known and his poetry recognized: he won an Eric Gregory Award in 1967 and the Cheltenham Festival Prize in 1968, and he was part of the group of writers around Hamilton and the *Review*, meeting other authors such as Martin Amis, Julian Barnes, Christopher Hitchens, Hugo Williams, Al Alvarez, and John Fuller, the latter two of whom formed the triptych of poets with Harsent published by Hamilton in the *Review* pamphlets of 1968. In poetry, Ian Hamilton's preference was for the short, intense lyric poem, and although Harsent wrote in a similar form in pieces like "Poem" or "Rouault," he became increasingly interested in how these short poems could represent—as he has put it—beads on a necklace. Even in *Tonight's Lover*, there is evidence of Harsent experimenting with a sequence of short poems in "The Woman and the Roses," a form he would develop in *A Violent Country* with a series of seven separate poems titled "The Woman ..." and continue in *Dreams of the Dead* (1977). The poetic sequence has since become Harsent's hallmark.

Harsent was still working in the bookshop in Aylesbury at this time, but he also began doing freelance writing. Ian Hamilton gave him a job as fiction critic for the *TLS* in 1965, a position he held until 1973, and he also worked as poetry critic for the *Spectator* during the period 1970–1973. As Harsent explains, a change in his financial circumstances was at first beneficial for his writing:

> I was in my early twenties and married with two children when I got an Arts Council bursary for my first book. […] I'd been working in a bookshop for ten years. The bursary enabled me to leave the shop and take some time out before getting another job—in publishing, as it happened.
>
> (James Byrne interview)

Harsent worked first with ABP Publishing (which accepted his poetry volumes as his qualifications), and then as editorial director at Arrow Books in London from 1977 to 1979, where he published writers such as Angela Carter and Ruth Rendell. Although Harsent also worked as a successful editor-in-chief and director of André Deutsch (1979–1983), and then ran his own imprint, Severn House, he disliked the work, not least because he realized that he was writing and publishing very little of his own poetry. He left publishing and decided to try another way of making money: writing a crime thriller of the type he had been used to editing. *Crows' Parliament* (1987) was written under the name "Jack Curtis" (Harsent's grandfather), auctioned off to a high bidder at the Frankfurt Book Fair, and well received upon its publication. Harsent subsequently published several more books under the names of "Jack Curtis" and "David Pascoe," and also a series as "David Lawrence," featuring Detective Sergeant Stella Mooney. It is the success of these books, Harsent says (they have been translated into fifteen languages), that allows him to continue to write poetry, and he aims to write one crime novel a year.

The Stella Mooney stories are police procedurals, and Harsent sets the books in an area of northwest London that includes some of the wealthiest and most deprived parts of the capital. As critics have noted, Harsent pays particular attention to the bodies which DS Mooney has to examine, frequently opening novels with the discovery of corpses—often in various stages of decomposition—and the same is true in his 2007 novel, *Down into Darkness*, the title a line from

Harsent's libretto *The Minotaur* (2008), referring to the Cretan labyrinth. This time the discovery is made by a young couple in the midst of an erotically charged embrace, exemplifying the connection which Harsent frequently makes between sexuality and death.

As a result of his success in crime fiction, Harsent has also had a successful screenwriting career as "Sam Lawrence" and "David Pascoe," writing for a number of BBC television series, such as the comedies *Love Hurts* (ten episodes in 1992–1994), *Class Act* (three episodes in 1995), *Goodnight Sweetheart* (nine episodes in 1997–1999), *Birds of a Feather* (two episodes in 1998), and more recently *Twisted Tales* (one episode in 2005), the hospital drama *Holby City* (eleven episodes in 2008–2010), and the BBC soap opera Eastenders (two episodes in 2011). He has also written several episodes of the long-running ITV police dramas *Midsomer Murders* (five episodes in 2006–2011) and *The Bill* (five episodes in 2010), for which Harsent wrote the final two episodes to be transmitted in 2010. He also contributed one episode to a court drama, *Garrow's Law*, broadcast on the BBC in 2011. Harsent has had links to television and the theater for some time, since his second wife, Julia Watson, is an actress who has worked extensively in both mediums.

Harsent is also known for his opera libretti, and particularly for his collaborations with the British composer Sir Harrison Birtwistle, with whom he began work in the 1980s, writing the libretto for *Gawain* (1991). It was the first of Harsent's several collaborations with Birtwistle, and Harsent has also written texts or libretti for other composers, including an opera designed for television about the death of Diana, Princess of Wales. That piece, *When She Died*, with music by Jonathan Dove, linked the stories of three people on the day of Diana's funeral, and was broadcast on Channel 4 in the United Kingdom in 2002. It reached an audience of nearly a million viewers, but received much adverse tabloid press publicity for a scene in which one character hires a prostitute to dress up as the princess, then removes her clothes and performs a ritual over her body. The opera was later staged at the Vienna Kammeroper in March 2007.

Harsent has also worked to produce English versions of poetry in other languages, working from literal translations. He worked on the poetry of the Somali poet Maxamed Xaashi Dhamac (known as "Gaariye") for the School of Oriental Studies in London's World Poets's Tour in 2005, and in 2011 he was translating the work of the Greek poet Yannis Ritsos. Harsent's best-known translations, however, are those he did of the Bosnian Goran Simić, working from literal versions of the poems created by Simić's wife, Amela. Some of these were published in a limited edition entitled *The Sorrow of Sarajevo* (1996), followed by the volume titled *Sprinting from the Graveyard* in 1997. Harsent's connection with Serbia began in the 1980s, when he visited the country at the invitation of the British Council, and in 1988 he coedited a collection of contemporary British poetry with Mario Suško. During a reading in Sarajevo, Harsent had a brief exchange with the former Bosnian Serb leader Radovan Karadžić. Harsent, though, had no idea who the man was at the time, leading him to remark later that he "could have killed the son of a bitch there and then and saved everyone a lot of trouble" (Nicholas Wroe interview). *Sprinting from the Graveyard* features poems that Goran Simić wrote while Sarajevo was under siege between 1992 and 1995, when he was able to escape and settle in Canada. Harsent's versions of Simić's poems were also included in *Sarajevo*, a 1994 opera by Nigel Osborne.

Harsent, who lives with his wife and daughter in Barnes, in southwest London, was appointed distinguished writing fellow at Sheffield Hallam University in 2008, is an honorary research fellow at Royal Holloway University, and is a fellow of the Royal Society of Literature. He won a Cholmondeley Award from the Society of Authors in 2008. As well as translations, his work in progress in 2011 included an unfinished novel; a staged version of his "Legion" sequence (from *Legion*, 2005) titled "Psychodrama," and several new opera projects, including a "green" opera, "The Hoop of the World," with music by Alan Lawrence, "The Locked Room", a libretto to ac-

company music by Huw Watkins, scheduled for performance at the Edinburgh International Festival in 2012, and a concert version of Charlotte Perkins Gilman's short story "The Yellow Wallpaper," with a score by Simon Holt.

"THERE'S NO WAY BACK / THROUGH ALL THAT VIOLENCE": DECAY AND DREAM

Harsent's early poems, published in the *Review* pamphlet *Tonight's Lover* in 1968 and subsequently collected into his first collection, *A Violent Country*, suggest some of the preoccupations that have continued to concern him to the present: an engagement with the natural world, particularly its inhuman, elemental forces; the dissection of the sexual attraction between men and women; and how an individual makes sense of the world around them and their place within it.

"Legendry," the poem that opens *A Violent Country*, suggests an interest in mythology and folklore that would resurface in Harsent's opera libretti (*Gawain* and *The Minotaur*, for instance) and is in part derived from his early reading of the border ballads. The poem does not locate the action, but it does suggest parallels between the human violence and violence in the natural world. At the same time, the voice of the poem does not enter fully into the kinds of adventures that Harsent found in the book that first exposed him to poetry. On the contrary it adopts an ironic, even humorous tone—a tone that reoccurs constantly in later work—and strives to undercut the genre without parodying it.

In the poem, the romantic notion of the quest is dismissed in paradoxical imagery and curt sentence length. Those features and the banal repetition of "he" suggests a blank incomprehension that the ideal could be so crudely shattered. "Legendry," questions whether it is possible for such romanticism to survive in the modern world, at a time when American troops were using napalm and chemical warfare, killing North Vietnamese civilians and Vietcong troops, and destroying the natural environment.

In the poems that follow "Legendry," Harsent continues to dispel illusions in an attempt to strip back what is inessential and get to the elemental force within a human being. Frequently this shows up how close the human is to the animal world. In "Simeon Stylites," Harsent continues an exploration of the asceticism that he had begun with "The Ascetics," speaking in the voice of Simeon, the Christian saint who is said to have lived for more than thirty years on top of a pillar. Harsent's Simeon dismisses those who come to worship or celebrate him. Characteristically, Harsent focuses upon the intense solitariness of the figure, and his reduction. Simeon's example may have inspired many in their spiritual lives, but there is nothing fertile or living here except the creatures that thrive on decay. This Simeon is a secular saint, whose religion is negation. In equating the unadorned natural world with the human, Harsent suggests a possibility for poetic description to get at essential truths about our lives.

In the seven poems that conclude *A Violent Country*, each one featuring "The Woman," Harsent posits a close interaction between an unnamed female figure and the natural world. The poems deal with issues of fertility, death, and forms of self-analysis, especially in the eight-part final poem, "The Woman's Soliloquies," in which a combination of an omniscient voice and the voice of the Woman suggest a desperate kind of solipsism, in which she can only rely upon herself, since the world outside is often incomprehensible.

After this first collection, Harsent published two further books: *Ashridge*, in a 1970 limited edition, and *After Dark* in 1973. *After Dark* features a number of short lyrics inspired perhaps by the influence of Ian Hamilton and certainly by Harsent's own circumstances. With its description of the difficulties faced by a man coming back from war to his family, "Two Postscripts to My Father" looks ahead to *News from the Front* (1993) and concludes sadly.

With *Dreams of the Dead* (1977), Harsent began working seriously and extensively with the sequence form, and that collection featured three sequences: *Truce*, which was first published in a limited edition by Sycamore Press in 1973; "Dreams of the Dead," which first appeared in its entirety in the *New Review* in April 1976; and "Moments in the Life of Milady." *Dreams of the Dead* also contained three poems about Mr. Punch, which gestured toward Harsent's next book, a book-length series of poems about the puppet. *Truce* and "Dreams of the Dead" are both early sequences that exemplify Harsent's attempt to create "a partially obfuscated narrative of which the reader gets the most intense moments and infers the rest" (Nicholas Wroe interview). Like the final soliloquies of *A Violent Country*, *Truce* features a woman who is confined: physically in her home, perhaps because of war, and mentally within her memories, and the speaker describes how she uses these memories to imagine places beyond her confinement. The twenty-seven short poems that make up the significant sequence "Dreams of the Dead" are each dated with months and days, running nonconsecutively from April 30 to August 23. Each poem, spoken by an omniscient voice, describes or reflects upon a dream that the male subject has had, and as the sequence progresses, dreams overlap into daytime reality so that it is sometimes difficult for the dreamer, or for the reader, to tell one from the other, providing a dramatic conflict with the exactness of each poem's dating. Harsent also provides motifs that allow the poems to connect or comment upon one another, involving imagery of birds, the sun, mirrors, unnamed women in the background, the sea.

"[AN] INNER LIFE SO KEEN": TWO SEQUENCES, AN OPERA, AND A NOVEL

Mister Punch (1984) is generally regarded as Harsent's breakthrough volume, since it demonstrated a significant departure from his previous work. The sustaining of a dramatic voice through these poems is a considerable achievement, and Harsent by turns reinforces and undercuts the typical assumptions about the character of Mister Punch. The voice that he creates, and the various situations in which he places that character, are reminiscent of John Berryman's Henry poems, or Ted Hughes's collection *Crow* (1970).

Originally Pulcinella from the Commedia dell'Arte, the Punch figure gradually evolved from the Italian marionette seen by Samuel Pepys in London into his present form as a puppet, commonly found in shows presented to children from traveling booths, especially at the English seaside. He is a hunchback, with a hooked nose and chin, a painted face fixed permanently in a smile, and scarlet clothing. He frequently wields a slapstick, with which he beats—and even murders—his wife, Judy, and their child. He is lusty and can be obscene, and has frequent altercations with authority. Always playing to the audience, his aim in life is to raise laughs by whatever means necessary.

Harsent employs all of these features in his characterization of Punch, but adds depths to his psychology and his environment. In the opening poem, "Mr Punch," Harsent uses the violence inherent in the Punch and Judy show to suggest a threatening scene, despite appearances. In this poem, the ribbons and flags might suggest the booth where Punch and Judy perform, but "belladonna" hints at the poisonous actions of Punch, who leaves his wife and children to picnic while he satisfies his lust elsewhere. Harsent's adeptness with lineation, especially with the line breaks at "child" and stanza break at "dance" successfully challenge the reader's expectations: the threat is not to the child, as the lineation might suggest, but neither does the dance result in joy—except for Punch. The sound of the glass, which later is made to sing and break, is an eerie and disturbing counterpoint to the children's dance. The juxtaposition of their innocence and Punch's illicit desire illustrates the conflict between the original, bawdy background for Mister Punch and the way he is often seen today.

From this beginning, which offers a recognizable, if disconcerting view of Punch, Harsent proceeds to challenge traditional views. He finds Punch in the ancient world, in Samos, Patmos, and Athens, and offers poems about a series of paintings that suggest features of Punch's character, such as Alberto Giacometti's *Woman with Her Throat Cut* and *Masks Confronting Death* by James Ensor. Harsent sees the conflict between Punch and Judy or the man and the woman as central to Punch's identity, but rather than rehearse the violence that is perpetrated by Punch

on Judy, he suggests rather that she has a certain power over him that makes him act irrationally. As a reader moves through the book they encounter Punch worshipping the female, being manipulated by her, even deriving strength from her words and image when he is sick. In the seven of "Punch's Nightmares," she is always a presence, even in the powerful fifth dream, which depicts Punch's retreat from an apparent scene of war with his child and its nurse. This child, which he is famous for beating and killing in his show, is here the key focus of the poem, his terrible wound, perhaps inflicted by Punch, perhaps by fighting, prominent. The child serves to remind Punch of a wife he has lost, and of his own inadequacies. Punch's nightmares are recognizable ones, but because of the violence of the tradition that he inhabits, the nightmares are truly terrifying.

Punch sometimes seems on the very edge of sanity. In "Punch at His Devotions," he confesses and prays to the Virgin Mary for forgiveness. Trapped in his persona, Punch struggles to find the language necessary to speak properly to Our Lady, for every time he attempts to prove his devotion and his penitence, his comic self intervenes with nonsense words, catchphrases from his show, and merely serve, as "*la*" becomes "Lady" or "*Lamb*," to make him seem ridiculous, even blasphemous.

Before his success with *Crows' Parliament*, Harsent wrote a literary novel, *From an Inland Sea*, which was published in 1985. The narrative comprises fourteen chapters and explores the relationship between a couple who live together but are not married. Each part is dated according to the length of time the lovers have cohabited, but rather than beginning with the start of their relationship, the novel begins with "The Second Year. May," and makes short references to earlier stages in their life together. The novel concludes ambiguously, with the date "The Fifth Year. 16 October—." The final three chapters are titled with specific dates in September and October, as if Harsent suggests readers should pay particular attention to them, for they are critical in understanding the relationship he is describing. However, like one of the earlier poetic sequences, he leaves the reader free to infer details and incidents. Both the characters are unnamed, though other named characters do appear in the book, and locations are generally recognizable. Despite his protestations to the contrary, Harsent clearly has put something of himself into this novel, particularly in the second section, where the male character's reference to his upbringing in a house full of women, and his attraction to Alfred Noyes's ballad poem "The Highwayman," are clearly drawn from Harsent's own experiences.

In its episodic structure—no chapter is more than eighteen pages long—the novel is based around intense descriptions of intense, physical experiences. A number of the sections describe European holidays that the lovers take, often to Mediterranean locations, and the sun is a significant feature. In the opening section of the book, the male character is badly sunburned: "In the mirror, dimly lit, he was almost luminous. His skin twitched. There were strong, intermittent pains and it burned. He felt as if he were standing too close to an immense electric fire. His teeth chattered" (*From an Inland Sea*, p. 7).

Shortly after this description, the man and woman have sex, and the experience described is characteristic of the way that pleasure and pain are in close proximity in this novel. Although the narratorial voice is in the third person, the story is largely focalized through the male character, and so the intense experiences, which frequently also disorient, are often seen through his eyes: various sexual experiences, drunkenness, sickness, even disease are all incidents repeated in the course of the narrative.

Such experiences are also tied to Harsent's fascination with primitive instincts and emotions, which are described here in typically acute detail. Frequently these primitive outbursts go far beyond what might be considered ordinary behavior: confronted by a dog that had been bothering him, the man stones it to death; during a particularly vicious argument with the woman, the man seizes a broken whisky glass and quite deliberately cuts the woman's thumb. Sexual lust and blood lust frequently meet in the novel: on a shooting weekend with wealthy friends in the country, he becomes convinced that the woman who has been appointed to bag the game birds he has been shooting would welcome his advances, and he seeks to take advantage of her by visiting her room late at night. Hunting reoccurs in another part of the book where he spends a holiday in a remote part of the country shooting and then gutting rabbits and pheasants. Another chapter, set in France, combines these lusts with a disturbing incident in which the couple, getting out of their car to have sex in a wood, encounter two gypsy men who threaten to rape the woman, only for the man to attack one of the men with a craft knife, severely wounding him.

This incident, however, is complicated by Harsent's narrative technique. The following section of the chapter suggests that the woman had been asleep in the car all along, and although the man mentions a gypsy encampment, there is no indication that the incident in the wood actually occurred. This episode, and the disturbing questions it raises (if the incident did not occur, was he responsible for its creation, or did she dream it?), suggest something of the endemic conflict between truth and falsehood in the novel, exposed in the lovers' lies and infidelities, which are laid bare to the reader. It also encourages the reader to question the reliability of the narrative as a whole. Such ambiguity indicates the presence of another of Harsent's themes that was particularly prominent in "Dreams of the Dead": the blurring of dreams and reality. Early on in the book, the male character considers a scene in which his lover is having sex with another man, and it is not clear whether this is a scene that may have happened in reality or a way he has of torturing himself. Later in the novel, the woman wakes from a nightmare that she understands is partly the result of a tale he had told to her about the death of a knight. Apart from contributing to the unsettling tone of the narrative, these events also serve to question the strength of the couple's bond: is it strong because of the damage they do to each other, or does it represent a perverse relationship that can only ever do harm?

The title of the novel suggests not just the stretch of water that the couple visit on one of their holidays but also intimates the way in which

Harsent tries to represent the interiority of these characters in unusual ways. In one of the last sections, the male character begins giving himself stage directions which he subsequently acts out. In doing so he acknowledges that "[i]t was as if life was towing him in its wake" (*From an Inland Sea*, p. 146), suggesting something of the lack of certainty and lack of control that are features of the novel.

The title is also a metaphor for the contradictory nature of the relationship. They are a couple, but also very separate individuals: whereas she thrives on a business trip in the metropolitan bustle of New York City, he selects a remote rural location in which to hunt with his dog; he appears to have no real sense of direction, whereas she is obsessed with maps; in new places she advocates walking ahead of him so that they would have slightly different memories of the places they visited. Yet she often believes that he knows her well because of the way that he studies her so closely. This compulsion to observe her seems also to be a desire to possess her, an idea to which Harsent will return in his sequence "Marriage." On different occasions, he seeks to preserve her presence or create mementoes. But his regard of her is often unhealthy, and such obsessions reach their limit in the penultimate chapter of the book, in which he takes photograph after photograph of her—to her amusement and for which she poses to begin with, but finally to her outrage when he follows her to a restaurant and photographs her eating lunch with a colleague. The novel ends with the man taking a holiday by himself that seems to mark a departure: he is unable to picture her face any longer, and he is suffering with an ailment that may be disease contracted from his visit to a prostitute. Her absence means he is alone in a country where he does not speak the language, visiting churches where he prays, meaninglessly, for relief, and inhabiting a kind of purgatory from which there is no escape.

In 1989, Harsent published his first *Selected Poems*, which became a Poetry Book Society Recommendation. Apart from selections from his earlier books it also closed with three new poems: "The Analysand," which featured one of the first appearances of the hare, a key Harsent character; "Playback," which originally appeared as a poster-poem for Greenpeace illustrated by Ralph Steadman; and "The Windhound," an anthropomorphic sequence that Harsent says was important in his writing of the *Gawain* libretto that premiered in 1991.

In the mid-1980s, Harsent was contacted for the first time by the composer Sir Harrison Birtwistle, who asked him whether he might be interested in collaborating on a new opera. Birtwistle had read a review of Harsent's collection *Mister Punch,* which drew parallels between the poems and Birtwistle's 1967 opera *Punch and Judy.* Harsent began work on the libretto, which became *Gawain*, based on the anonymous, fourteenth-century English poem *Sir Gawain and the Green Knight.* Commissioned by the Royal Opera House, the opera was first performed in May 1991 and had revivals in 1994 and 2000.

In *Gawain*, Harsent altered the focus of the poem to place much greater emphasis upon the female characters, especially Morgan Le Fay, the sorceress and Arthur's half-sister. She has a limited role in the poem, but in Harsent's libretto, although she is often unseen, she is always in the background physically and vocally, acting as a trickster or antagonist.

The poem also allows Harsent to develop his interest in the friction between the human and natural worlds, and as in his previous collections, this conflict is often seen as a violent, sexual relationship. Harsent sets up a parallel view on stage of Gawain's host, Bertilak de Hautdesert, out hunting, and Bertilik's wife, Lady de Hautdesert, trying to seduce Gawain. In offering visions of inner and outer worlds, the libretto also explores typical Harsent territory such as the dream worlds of "Dreams of the Dead" or the different forms of interiority in *From an Inland Sea.*

In Morgan Le Fay's attempts to compromise Arthur's self-aggrandizing, self-satisfied court, the libretto also recalls Harsent's poem "Legendry" and his interest in undermining traditions, in this case the heroic tradition. The Green Knight who invades the court scorns the notion of courtly heroism that the knights maintain, and when Gawain returns there after his final encounter with the Green Knight and his own humbling, he does so full of self-knowledge and lamenting his own greed, self-love, and cowardice. The charting and struggle toward this realization, whether intended or not, is characteristic of Harsent's other characters such as Mister Punch and the protagonist in *A Bird's Idea of Flight*. The libretto form itself with its use of repetition and rhyme also suits Harsent, not just as a poet but also because of his tendency to write in sequences and encourage a reader or audience member to infer details of emotion, character, and motivation from the words and phrases that are sung in repetition.

Harsent's concern with the sequence form continued in his next book, *News from the Front* (1993). The whole collection is based around the relationship between a man who has gone to war; his common-law wife, who remains at their Devonshire home; and their son, who is born shortly after he leaves. The book contains writing that the man composes while he is away, including a bestiary for his son that uses animals like hares, rats, and stoats to reflect both on his life at home and at war. The poems also include the early ideas of the son (captured in the sequence "Storybook Hero," which was originally published in a limited edition in 1992), and the notions of the wife, whose thoughts, Harsent says, "are so strong, her inner life so keen, that the man appears to be brought almost within reach" (*News from the Front*, p. 9).

Harsent gives a strong sense of community life continuing in the man's absence: the mother and son look after the local church and go carol singing, and the poet offers a picture of the wild landscape of Dartmoor, close to where they live. That location is bleak and pitiless: one poem, "Childe," describes the death of a Dartmoor man many years before in a blizzard; the man had tried to save himself by killing and cutting open his horse and climbing inside the corpse. The scene is juxtaposed with the contemporary scene of the boy, disturbed by the sight of soldiers near his home, and his desire to climb under the skirt of his mother, who is described in the violent but

practiced act of plucking the feathers from a goose.

"Elsewhere" shows how the wife tries to bring a sense of her husband's experience closer to her by having her house in a regimented order, while "Foxtor Mire" suggests that the death of horses, sucked down into the quicksand-like marshes of Dartmoor's dangerous places, could have parallels with the deaths of men at war. Such correspondences encourage the reader to reflect on where the conflict and the "front" really were: at the battles abroad, or at home.

The penultimate poem, "The Church Ale," offers an unusual and sophisticated view of the return from war, and in its rhythms, colloquialisms and wordplay, unexpected diction, and technique of listing, this poem marks a shift in Harsent's poetics that would be fully realized in *A Bird's Idea of Flight*. In the conclusion to the poem Harsent suggests the distressing disorientation of the return: the men seem utterly unknown to those at home, since it is impossible for those on the home front to understand the wartime experiences. Each man still relies heavily upon his comrade, for only the other man in front can comprehend what it was like to have "left" so many friends and parts of themselves upon the battlefields.

A BIRD'S IDEA OF FLIGHT *AND* MARRIAGE: *A DIFFERENT KIND OF SEQUENCE*

Harsent himself has suggested that *A Bird's Idea of Flight* marked a significant departure from his previous work. The preoccupation of the volume, death, may not be such a shift, especially since by now the poet had written a number of grisly crime novels, and the book also finds Harsent working in a sequence again (as he did in his 1997 limited edition book, *The Potted Priest*), but there is a difference in the actual form of the individual poems. Harsent puts the change down to a conversation with Ian Hamilton, who had read *News from the Front* and suggested that Harsent might try lengthening the lines of his poems. Rather than appearing as a collection of lyric poems, *A Bird's Idea of Flight* has the look and feel of a form somewhere between poetry and prose, a form that has the density and detail of a prose narrative but that also features the rhythms and rhymes or half-rhymes of poetry. It is a form of dramatic sequence that particularly suits Harsent's blend in the book of morbid humor and restless movement, heightening the peculiar situations into which his protagonist stumbles.

That speaker is on a thanatological journey, seeking knowledge about his own death, and each one of the twenty-five poems describes a visit he makes to places more or less associated with death. He is frequently accompanied by the figure of Death himself, who takes on various disguises and roles. The journey is circular, with twelve poems signifying the journey out, a pivotal poem, and then twelve to represent the journey back, out of the realm of death. The sequence opens and closes with a visit to "The Archivist," who advised him in the first place not to undertake the journey, telling him that he would learn little of use. Among his visits, the speaker sees catacombs, where Death acts as a guide, leading the speaker in a dance with the dead bodies from the vaults; he sees a garotte demonstrated in "The Black Museum"; recalls a drunken night out with friends; and in the tenth poem, "Coverack," is led—by a swimming hare—to view a shipwreck off the Cornish coast, where he meets Death once again.

Of course in seeking something like "a bird's idea of flight," the speaker is seeking the impossible, and many of the voices and even the glances of those he meets warn him off his Icarus-like pursuit. He leaves himself open to ridicule—from the hare, from Death, from the other characters—and the drama of the sequence is to be found in Harsent's creation of atmosphere, especially through startling juxtapositions, rather than in any revelations about death itself. In the thirteenth poem, "The Turning Point," the speaker hears a sound that he gradually recognizes as himself. Paradoxically, Harsent presents the journey as one of cowardice: instead of facing life itself and coming to terms with the despair that can be faced by us all, the speaker

seeks refuge in what may or may not be to come. Rather than being a dead end, the lesson of the journey should lead the protagonist to a reaffirmation of his life and its value.

Harsent's 2002 collection, *Marriage*, shortlisted for both the Forward Poetry Prize (Best Poetry Collection of the Year) and the T. S. Eliot Prize, continues to develop the formal features of *A Bird's Idea of Flight*. If not as formally experimental, *Marriage*, which consists of two contrasting dramatic sequences, retains the long lines that Harsent had used previously, and it continues to deploy subtle full and slant rhymes. It also significantly extends the poet's interest in the visual arts.

The first of the sequences, titled "Marriage," is based—Harsent warns very loosely—on the relationship and then marriage of the painter Pierre Bonnard (1867–1947) and Marthe de Méligny (1869–1942). The speaker of the poems is a fictional character whom Harsent sees as a painter-husband whose subject—and addressee—is always his model-wife (or "Ur-wife" as she is described in one poem). Certainly the twenty-seven-poem sequence features a number of Bonnard's signature objects and scenes—the bath, the red-checkered tablecloth, the breakfast things, the bedroom, the nude female—but it goes far beyond just a mechanical representation of these in language. After thirty years of living together, Bonnard and Marthe de Méligny married, only for Marthe to reveal in the wedding ceremony that her true name was actually Maria Boursin. Without explicit reference to it, Harsent places this uncertainty in the background of his work, as well as presenting the overlaps and conflicts that exist in the relationship between a man who is an artist and a woman who is his muse, his lover, and then his wife. In the universalizing title of his collection and in the fact that he does not name his characters, Harsent also suggests that these domestic scenes can be read more generally. The dedication of the collection to his second wife, Julia Watson, also suggests the collection might be partly read as autobiography, though as with his previous work, Harsent would distance himself from any readings that suggest close relationships between himself and his characters.

The sequence makes powerful use of the overlap that existed in the Bonnard–de Méligny relationship between art and life, frequently suggesting ways in which the painter might find art in the domestic, and such observation blurs the line between husband and painter. In poem XV, the speaker watches carefully as his wife steps from the bath. In this scene, the professional artist who observes the movements and colors is also the husband who uses colloquialisms to give a sense of his own eroticized desire for this woman. Later in the same poem, the speaker describes how he made love to this woman against the kitchen table, which she would later set for breakfast with the red-checkered cloth.

Yet for all the moments of keen observation, one of the key themes in the sequence, stemming from Marthe's false identity, is the extent to which the speaker can ever really know his wife. Poem V is replete with references to knowledge and mystery—before dinner she puts on makeup and colors her hair, and while he notices this, he also understands that it means he does not quite recognize her.

In poem V, the imagery of the noose suggests the speaker's desire to capture his model-wife both artistically and personally. The difficulty of doing so is constantly there in the sequence. Underlying this is the uncomfortable possessiveness of the painter-husband who sometimes idealizes and sometimes objectifies her. He suggests that she is putting on makeup just to help his depiction of her, and he contemplates her as *The Biddable / Spouse* (p. 26), at once pliant to his touch and the subject of his paintings to be bid for and sold. Yet in the last few poems of the sequence, which register the fact that Marthe/the model-wife has died and that the incessant bathing did nothing to help cure her suspected tuberculosis, the acute glare of the painter can be turned only onto himself, and make him his only subject. Nevertheless, in the final poem Harsent shows how this man cannot comprehend life without his wife. The idea that he cannot place her—in the house, in his painting—makes him convinced that she must be just

out of view and that it will be possible for her to reenter the door, or the canvas, at any moment. The fact that he cannot call her back to life suggests that perhaps he never knew and never painted her properly at all.

As its Latin title suggests, the second of the sequences in the book, "Lepus," features the hare, a character which has appeared frequently in Harsent's work. Harsent's early life in Devonshire, followed by his childhood in rural Buckinghamshire, began his interest in brown hares, and this was significantly deepened by his reading of a book by the British anthropologist and psychologist John Layard, *The Lady of the Hare* (1944). One half of Layard's book recounts his Jungian psychoanalysis of a woman who dreamed of sacrificing a hare, while the second half offers an intercultural history of the hare. In 1999, Harsent collaborated with Harrison Birtwistle on a fifteen-minute song cycle titled *The Woman and the Hare,* commissioned by the Nash Ensemble of London. The piece features Harsent's text (later published in his 2005 collection *Legion*) being both sung and spoken, the vocals of a soprano interweaving with the speech of a reciter (Harsent's wife Julia Watson in the premiere) and the accompanying instrumental ensemble. First performed in March 1999, the piece was repeated in 2000, and subsequently performed at the Megaron in Athens in 2002, with the American premiere taking place at Carnegie Hall in 2005.

For Harsent, the hare is associated with witchcraft, is a figure of misrule and a trickster, and these elements appear throughout the poems of "Lepus," the titles of which are drawn or adapted from section headings in Layard's book. Sometimes the poem is in the voice of the hare herself, and sometimes in the voice of a human speaking about the hare and reflecting on its place in mythology and folklore. Harsent presents the hare as being in continual conflict with the human world, and more often than not she wins in the struggles. The hare is always feminine, and frequently that femininity is associated with sexuality. She appears in "Lepus" as a seductress in a bar, as an erotic dancer, and, in "The hare enjoys being hunted," as a tease, drawing on the hunting pack of dogs and humans comfortable in the knowledge that she will always escape.

The hare herself imagines and revels in the erotic charge that she sees generated by her own pursuit, suggesting once again the proximity of sexual activity and primitive violence, but the style of her disappearance tells of her sexual inaccessibility. With the surefooted instinct of a performer, the moment of "*hoopla!*" celebrates not only the excitement of the moment in which she might be seized, but also an older definition, that of obscurity, for throughout the chase the hare dodges in and out of view, leaves "tags" of scent like graffiti, and pretends to be weak.

The chase is presented as a gender struggle, and elsewhere in the sequence the hare favors the female and fools the male. In "The hare as fecundatrix," a giant chalk engraving of a hare on a hillside serves as a space to which women from ancient times seeking help with their fertility come, leading their men up the hill and having sex with them there on the chalk replica. In "The hare pounds the herb of immortality in the moon," the hare provides a potion to aid wives who commit suicide. The hare's link with ancient civilizations is also a link with such rituals, and in "The hare as willing sacrifice" the animal herself describes how the various parts of her anatomy are valued by different cultures.

The final poem in the sequence, "The hare used as a hieroglyph for the auxiliary verb 'to be,'" imagines the hare as a slippery character, as difficult to run to ground in language as she is in the field. The title suggests both her obscurity and her necessity for civilizations as something that allows us to represent ourselves. Harsent presents her as a necessary challenge for humanity, a protean figure who is reliable in her unpredictability. Without her, language and art would be limited to only what can be seen, not what can be imagined. The way in which she seems unfathomable offers a link between "Marriage" and "Lepus," speaking to the sometimes glorious, sometimes bitter relationship between men and women, and the magical and mundane means by which we seek to understand it.

"THAT SMELL I COULDN'T PLACE? IT'S BLOOD AND SORROW": WAR, MYTH, AND DARKNESS

The genesis of Harsent's next collection, *Legion*, was unexpected and twofold. In the back of his mind, Harsent retained the subject matter and emotional charge of the versions of Goran Simić's poems that he had completed. Then he was given a 2002 commission from the British poet Jo Shapcott, who was writer in residence at the Royal Institution of Great Britain, a charity that promotes science to the general public. Shapcott asked a number of fellow poets to write a poem based upon one of the lectures that were being given at the Royal Institution. Rather than making the subject matter his source, Harsent mistakenly wrote a poem inspired by the title of one of the lectures: "From metals with a memory to brilliant light-emitting solids." Looking back on his writing of the poem, Harsent has said that he must have been very conscious of the world outside: the United States and Britain had been bombing Afghanistan, and the invasion of Iraq was about to begin. As a result of this, he explains, the poem "changed under my hand. The 'metals with a memory' became smart bombs, the 'brilliant light-emitting solids' became what they hit, i.e., people. I absolutely didn't see it coming" (Nicholas Wroe interview).

The collection is not exclusively a sequence of war poems. The third section collects a number of unrelated poems, including translations of poems by Yannis Ritsos, and "The Woman and the Hare (I)," mentioned above, which was set to music by Harrison Birtwistle. The second section, "Stelae," comprises eight poems that return Harsent to his early childhood, since each is named after a "tor," or granite rock formation, from Dartmoor. The poems, which also take the shape of columns of rock on the page, interweave factual information about the history of the tors with more personal, idiosyncratic detail, such as the way in which a drunk man might navigate on a foggy night by determining which side of the tor is more weathered. The effect of the poems is to question the telling of history and fact, leaving the reader to size up the relative worth of something like academic history as opposed to folklore.

The collection is best remembered, however, for the opening sequence, "Legion," thirty poems that give voice to both the oppressors and the oppressed in various anonymous wartime situations. In leaving the locations unnamed, Harsent does not suggest obvious sympathy for one side or the other; indeed, his point is that war can never be a straightforward matter, and he has been quick to point out that he has never been a public poet, since poetry with a cause sounds to him much like propaganda. (Harsent once wrote an article that decried the idea of a poet laureate, affirming once again that for him poetry is a way of life rather than an occupation, and that to write "occasional" verse is to trivialize the art.) Through these voices the sequence touches on many aspects and individuals involved in conflict: a troop on patrol, civilians in hiding, women driven to commit suicide in fear of what might come, a sniper, a village in the midst of a religious ritual surprised by invading soldiers. Running through the sequence are "Despatches," five poems that provide a common thread, even if they themselves—as if acknowledging the impossibility of remaining whole in such conflict—are fragmented. Often these despatches are missing sections as if they have been censored, but whether for security reasons or because the events are just too awful to be recorded is left for the reader to judge and, even unwillingly, to fill in the blanks.

Harsent is particularly good at presenting the senselessness of war. He often places the quotidian—objects, rituals—at the forefront of the poem, which makes the destruction and disruption of these things all the more poignant. In a number of poems he also shows how language is rendered meaningless. "Snapshots (I)," a title that might suggest photographs taken on vacation, presents instead a stream of images of the dead. The absurd title is complemented by the absurdity of the collective nouns that Harsent uses, as if to suggest that such things should not be possible, or that if they do occur, language is insufficient to describe them. While a sequence like "News from the Front" owed much to Harsent's previous dreamlike sequences, "Legion" is unflinching and raw in the way that it describes how the mind

and body in conflict become detached from the normal sense of things, whether in killing or in contemplating the possibility of being killed. In "Chinese Whispers," a boy goes missing as a convoy passes through a village, and his death is described with the language of euphemism, of "collateral damage" and "ethnic cleansing." It is this kind of restrained, inappropriately detached voice, combined with Harsent's usual black humor and his willingness to enter into the kinds of voices and minds that inhabit conflict, that make *Legion* a successful collection, and one that convinced many of his readers (incorrectly) that Harsent himself must have had experience in a war zone.

Between *Legion* and his 2011 collection, *Night*, Harsent published two libretti and *Selected Poems, 1969–2005* (2007). Both the libretti were collaborations with Harrison Birtwistle, and both dealt with Greek myth. *The Corridor* (2009) was a short scena for soprano, tenor, and six instruments, comprising nine sections, each one featuring a man (Orpheus), a woman (Eurydice), and five shades (musicians). Each part reflects upon only one element of the story of Orpheus and Eurydice: the moment when, as he emerged from the Underworld, he turned back to see her following him, only for him to realize he had looked back too soon, that she was still in the darkness, and that she would now be lost to him forever.

The Minotaur (2008) explored the relationship between Theseus, Ariadne, and the Minotaur himself. Whereas the traditional version of the myth tells how the Minotaur is the illegitimate offspring of Pasiphae, the queen of Crete, Harsent deftly combines versions of the narrative so that the white bull that emerges from the sea to couple with Pasiphae is actually Poseidon. Adopting the story that Theseus too was the son of Poseidon, Harsent creates a blood triangle between Theseus, Ariadne (Pasiphae's daughter by her husband, Minos, the Cretan king), and Asterios, her half-brother and the human part of the Minotaur, an arrangement that allows Harsent to construct poignant mirror images—rather like those in *Gawain* between Gawain and the Green Knight—between Theseus and Asterios. Emphasizing the complex human side of the Asterios-

Minotaur character, Harsent gives the monster an inner life and describes how he is compelled to act in the way that he does, even despite himself. He is a victim: Ariadne desires her half-brother's death as much as she desires Theseus and an escape from Crete, and Asterios is goaded by the "Innocents," the human sacrifices thrown into the labyrinth, into raping and killing them. In Harsent's libretto it is in his final confrontation with Theseus that Asterios gains a command of language and, as he sees it, his humanity. Theseus' subsequent slaying of him therefore makes the justified death of this "monster" far more ambiguous than it might be in the usual telling of the story.

That tendency for Harsent's work to disquiet is also evident in *Night*, the poet's 2011 collection, which was short-listed for both the Forward Prize (for Best Collection) and the T. S. Eliot Prize. The book is remarkable for its thematic consistency: virtually every poem, including the long concluding sequence, reflects upon the liminal period of night and how a lack of light disturbs sense and understanding. The untitled opening poem works rather like an epigraph to set the tone, suggesting a cast of characters that are indicative of the fantastical ones that will be met later in the collection. At the same time, Harsent acknowledges the concrete reality of night, its anarchy and dangers. Indeed, despite the evanescence described in so many poems, Harsent also drips through a series of poems about blood, as if they were beats of a pulse.

Most of all, he points to the way in which night obscures, rendering our perceptions untrustworthy, as in "The Hut in Question," a poem written for an anthology about the poet Edward Thomas, and which was short-listed for the Forward Prize (Best Single Poem) in 2007. It is this doubt that appears repeatedly: in the powerful one-sentence poem "Ghosts," where ghosts hope but fail to recognize the living; in "Vanitas" (another Harsent poem set to music by Harrison Birtwistle), where a woman is watched in taut silence; or in "Scene One: A Beach," which puts the speaker in a physical and emotional place where any kind of progress is in question. Such a place is also evident in the sequence of seven poems in the book that explore the garden, a liminal space that sometimes suggests cultivation, sometimes wildness and the unexpected. It is on the edge of things, like so much of *Night*.

The torments of insomnia that are detailed in the ten-part poem "Night" are more fully developed in the long sequence "Elsewhere," which closes the collection. A phantasmagoric journey spoken by a man who seems to have rid himself of all attachments, it is reminiscent of *A Bird's Idea of Flight*. Like that book-long sequence it is a circular journey, with the end of the poem describing the protagonist as gaining some self-knowledge, that the past is untouchable and that he must have "no thought beyond the next step" (p. 95).

David Harsent's poetry is frequently described as difficult and well-crafted, which has led some critics—and even the poet himself—to suggest that his work has a modernist aesthetic. There is little doubt that he has a command of rhyme, lineation, and, in his later collections, rhythm, that is the equal of any other poet now writing in Britain, but he also has a tone of playfulness to his work that consciously undercuts any attempt to place him. It is a tone that also enables him, sometimes brutally, to pull apart traditions and well-established figures, such as those of myth or folklore, and remake them. With the considerable influence of Ian Hamilton in the background, Harsent cannot be said to have modernized himself all on his own, but the visceral power of his imagery and his inventive use of language mark him out as a writer of independence and great elemental force.

Selected Bibliography

WORKS OF DAVID HARSENT

POETRY

Tonight's Lover. London: Review, 1968. (This was the second of three poetry supplements that accompanied issue 19 of the *Review*.)

A Violent Country. London: Oxford University Press, 1969.

(Harsent was awarded an Arts Council grant after publishing this collection. The book was also a Poetry Book Society Recommendation.)

Ashridge. Oxford: Sycamore Press, 1970. (Limited edition.)

After Dark. London: Oxford University Press, 1973.

Truce. Oxford: Sycamore Press, 1973. (Limited edition.)

Dreams of the Dead. Oxford: Oxford University Press, 1977. (Winner of the Geoffrey Faber Memorial Prize, 1977. Harsent was awarded a second Arts Council grant after publishing this collection.)

New Poetry 7. (As editor.) London: Hutchinson, 1981.

Mister Punch. Oxford: Oxford University Press, 1984.

Savremena Britanska Poezije [Contemporary British Poetry]. (As editor, with Mario Suško.) Sarajevo: Writers' Union, 1988.

Selected Poems. Oxford: Oxford University Press, 1989. (A Poetry Book Society Recommendation.)

Storybook Hero. Oxford: Sycamore Press, 1992. (Limited edition.)

News from the Front. Oxford: Oxford University Press, 1993.

The Potted Priest. Hereford, U.K.: Five Seasons Press/ Snickersnee, 1997. (Limited edition.)

A Bird's Idea of Flight. London: Faber and Faber, 1998. (Short-listed for the T. S. Eliot and Forward Poetry Prizes, 1998. The book was also a Poetry Book Society Choice.)

Marriage. London: Faber and Faber, 2002. (Short-listed for the T. S. Eliot and Forward Poetry Prizes, 2002. A Poetry Book Society Choice.)

Legion. London: Faber and Faber, 2005. (Winner of the Forward Prize, 2005. Short-listed for the T. S. Eliot Prize and Whitbread Poetry Award, 2005. A Poetry Book Society Recommendation.)

Selected Poems, 1969–2005. London: Faber and Faber, 2007. (Short-listed for the Griffin Poetry Prize. A Poetry Book Society Recommendation.)

Night. London: Faber and Faber, 2011. (Short-listed for the T. S. Eliot Prize. Short-listed for the Forward Prize (Best Collection). A Poetry Book Society Choice. A poem from this collection, "The Hut in Question," was short-listed for the Forward Poetry Prize (Best Single Poem) in 2007.)

TRANSLATIONS (POEMS OF GORAN SIMIĆ)

The Sorrow of Sarajevo: Poems. Cornwall, U.K.: Cargo, 1996.

Sprinting from the Graveyard. Oxford: Oxford University Press, 1997. (A Poetry Book Society Recommended Translation.)

LIBRETTI

Gawain. Words by David Harsent, music by Harrison Birtwistle. London: Universal Edition, 1991. Commissioned by the Royal Opera House. First performance: Royal Opera House, 1991.

"Serenade the Silkie." Words by David Harsent, music by Julian Grant. Commission for the Prussia Cove Festival, 1994.

"The Woman and the Hare." Words by David Harsent, music by Harrison Birtwistle. Commissioned by the Nash Ensemble. First performance: Purcell Room, Southbank Centre, London, 1999. U.S. premiere: Carnegie Hall, New York, 2005. (Nominated for a Grammy Award. The words to the piece appear in *Legion*, pp. 53–54.)

"When She Died." Words by David Harsent, music by Jonathan Dove. Commissioned by BBC Channel 4 Television and broadcast in the United Kingdom in 2002. Staged production: Kammeroper, Vienna, 2007.

"The Ring Dance of the Nazarene." Words by David Harsent, music by Harrison Birtwistle. Commissioned by BBC Radio and VARA (Holland). First performance: Concertgebouw Promenade Concert, Amsterdam, 2004.

The Minotaur. Words by David Harsent, music by Harrison Birtwistle. London: Boosey & Hawkes, 2008. Commissioned by the Royal Opera House. First performance: Royal Opera House, April 2008.

The Corridor. Words by David Harsent, music by Harrison Birtwistle. London: Boosey & Hawkes, 2010. First production: Aldeburgh, U.K., June 2009.

"Crime Fiction." Words by David Harsent, music by Huw Watkins. First production: Music Theatre Wales, March 2010.

"The Yellow Wallpaper." Words by David Harsent, music by Simon Holt.

"The Locked Room." Words by David Harsent, music by Huw Watkins. First production scheduled for the Edinburgh International Festival, August 30, 2012.

CRIME FICTION

Crows' Parliament [Jack Curtis, pseud.]. London: Corgi, 1987.

Glory [Jack Curtis, pseud.]. London: Penguin, 1988.

Sons of the Morning [Jack Curtis, pseud.]. London: Bantam, 1991. (Published in the United States as *Point of Impact*.)

Conjure Me [Jack Curtis, pseud.]. London: Corgi, 1993.

Mirrors Kill [Jack Curtis, pseud.]. London: Bantam, 1994.

The Confessor [Jack Curtis, pseud.]. London: Orion, 1997.

DETECTIVE STELLA MOONEY NOVELS

The Dead Sit Round in a Ring [David Lawrence, pseud.]. London: Michael Joseph, 2002. (Published in the United States as *Circle of the Dead*.)

Nothing Like the Night [David Lawrence, pseud.]. London: Michael Joseph, 2003.

Cold Kill [David Lawrence, pseud.]. London: Michael Joseph, 2005.

Down into Darkness [David Lawrence, pseud.]. London: Michael Joseph, 2007.

OTHER WORK

From an Inland Sea. London: Viking, 1985. (Novel.)

Another Round at the Pillars: Essays, Poems, and Reflections on Ian Hamilton. (As editor.) Cornwall, U.K.: Cargo, 1999. (Festschrift. Limited edition.)

CRITICAL AND BIOGRAPHICAL STUDIES

Byrne, James. "Interview: David Harsent." *Wolf,* no. 11:30–36 (November 2005). (Also available online: http://www.wolfmagazine.co.uk/11_interview_dh.php.)

Harsent, David. "Interview: David Harsent." *Guardian,* October 6, 2005 (http://www.guardian.co.uk/books/2005/oct/06/forwardprizeforpoetry2005.forwardprizeforpoetry1).

Harsent, David. "There's Nothing Poetic About the Poet Laureate." *Guardian,* May 5, 2009 (http://www.guardian.co.uk/books/booksblog/2009/may/05/poet-laureate-poetry).

Miller, George. "David Harsent on *Night.*" *Thought Fox: The Faber Blog* (http://www.thethoughtfox.co.uk/?p=3781 includes a link to an audio interview with Harsent by George Miller on the Faber Poetry Podcast).

Morra, Irene. *Twentieth-Century British Authors and the Rise of Opera in Britain.* Aldershot, U.K.: Ashgate, 2007 (Chapter 2 of this study, "Nation, Modernity, and the Operatic Stage," pp. 45–53, examines *Gawain.*)

Patterson, Christina. "David Harsent: The Pity, and Poetry, of War." *Independent,* January 13, 2006 (http://www.independent.co.uk/arts-entertainment/books/features/david-harsent-the-pity-and-poetry-of-war-522695.html).

Smith, Jules. "David Harsent: Critical Perspective." British Council Literature (http://literature.britishcouncil.org/david-harsent#criticalperspective).

Vianu, Lidia. "Postmodernism Has Proved Such a Muddle and Mess." *Desperado Essay-Interviews.* Bucharest: Editura Universitatii din Bucuresti, 2006. (Also available online: http://lidiavianu.mttlc.ro/David%20Harsent.htm.)

"Writers' Rooms: David Harsent." *Guardian,* March 28, 2008 (http://www.guardian.co.uk/books/2008/mar/28/writers.rooms.david.harsent).

Wroe, Nicholas. "David Harsent: A Life in Writing." *Guardian,* February 18, 2011, p. 12 (http://www.guardian.co.uk/culture/2011/feb/21/david-harsent-life-writing-poetry).

SHIRLEY HAZZARD

(1931—)

Nicholas Birns

SHIRLEY HAZZARD IS a novelist who has lived out globalization in the sinews of her life and in her writing. An Australian by birth, she has traveled and lived far from Australia for most of her life, yet over her career she has been increasingly regarded by Australian critics as a vital part of the national literary heritage. Part of her deeply Australian quality, paradoxically, is her internationalism. Australians have historically been great travelers and many of Australia's greatest creative thinkers have lived as expatriates. Hazzard's fiction not only includes significant action on four continents—North America, Europe, Asia, and Australia—but also displays issues of travel and migration as they impact on the concrete lives of individuals. The title of Hazzard's 2003 novel, *The Great Fire*, directly cites the cataclysms—of the world wars, the atomic bomb, the Holocaust, colonization, and deconsolidation—that inform even the most private moments of her narratives. Hazzard was no bystander to these events. She worked at the United Nations for ten crucial years in the 1950s and early 1960s and was thus present at the creation of the postwar international order, a subject she has addressed in both her fiction and nonfiction. Her early exposure to postwar Japan, and her later residence in an Italy not far removed from the era of Benito Mussolini, further enriched the weft of her writing. Yet Hazzard does not use her proximity to momentous doings as a crutch. Her fiction pulsates with the autonomous life of character and experience. In perhaps her most famous novel, *The Transit of Venus* (1980), the loves and losses of her chief character, Caro Bell, are felt as keenly by the reader as in any instance of modern fiction. Hazzard's fiction does not, though, just concern discrete lives, but has powerfully general implications. As Geoff Dyer, commenting on his rereading of *The Transit of Venus* in the June 28, 2004, issue of the *New Statesman*, commented, "Destiny—the way that people kept apart by circumstances are drawn together or, conversely, the way that people thrown together by circumstance are yet condemned to mutual isolation—is one of the themes to which Hazzard obsessively returns" (p. 54). Hazzard traces her characters' trajectories on the world map, not in the spirit of anecdotal gleaning but to limn longer perspectives that beckon well after the literal action of the plot has been absorbed. Although Hazzard is not overtly encyclopedic in her work in the style of a James Joyce or Thomas Pynchon, her work is informed by an extraordinary amount of reading and allusions, both overt and covert, to the European literature, art, and music of the past four centuries. Hazzard's gripping plots and the plangent way she chronicles love and loss may entice the reader in, but on further exploration the books reveal a mission that is as much cultural as emotional: to live a life among artistic masterpieces, to take their measure, and to try to live as seriously as these artistic works mandate.

Shirley Hazzard was born January 30, 1931, in Sydney. Both her parents were born in the United Kingdom. Her father, Reginald Hazzard, an engineer and, later, a trade representative, was Welsh, while her mother, Catherine Stein Hazzard, was Scottish. The Hazzard parents had met in Sydney while both were working for Dorman Long, the British firm that was building the Sydney Harbour Bridge. The Hazzards had an elder daughter, Valerie, born in 1928, who spent a good portion of her adult life in Queensland. Shirley Hazzard grew up in Mosman, an eastern suburb of Sydney linked to the city by ferry, and attended the prestigious Queenwood College (a girls' high school) there. Hazzard's parents, who according to her daughter had very different temperaments, ended up separating in 1951, with Catherine Hazzard moving to London and Reginald Hazzard, after diplomatic service in New York City (anticipating his daughter's work for the United Nations), retiring to Sydney.

In her Boyer Lectures for 1984, delivered on Australian Radio National and published the next year as *Coming of Age in Australia,* Hazzard gives a sense of the atmosphere of her upbringing: correct, British, to a degree sheltered, but also full of exposure to the Australian landscape, character, and experience, so different from that of the society that had colonized it. The Sydney in which Hazzard grew up was, as she remembered it, a distinctly provincial place, far removed from wherever in the world events were occurring and great art was being made and discussed. In a 2005 Australian Broadcasting Corporation television interview with Kerry O'Brien, Hazzard describes the Australia of her youth as "male-dominated" and "philistine." The British background of Hazzard's parents and the generally British and colonial tone of Australian education—especially that in private schools largely for the upper classes—augured perhaps that Hazzard would grow up feeling only a lukewarm connection with Australia. But Hazzard's seventeen years of living in Sydney remained etched into the grain of her imaginative vision, as her moving citation of the nineteenth-century Australian poet Henry Kendall's "Bell-Birds" in her *Transit of Venus* indicates. In a 2005 *Paris Review* interview with the poet J. D. McClatchy, Hazzard spoke of the role played by "Australians such as Banjo Paterson and Henry Lawson and Henry Kendall," in the poetry element of her school curriculum, and that these poets were read side by side with balladeers of the British empire and staples of the English lyric canon. Despite the regimentation and traditional curriculum of the Queenwood School, its literary offerings helped Hazzard forge the distinct mix of influences and orientations that were to characterize her adult fiction. During those years Hazzard also read modern British novelists such as Joseph Conrad, whose themes of corruption amid cultural encounter were to resonate in her own later work.

Like many Australians of her generation, Hazzard's pivotal experiences of growing up occurred abroad, the great world outside what then seemed a sleepy southern continent. In her case, this occurred early, on a visit with her father—who after the war had moved from the business world to bureaucratic service as trade commissioner in Hong Kong and later, after he moved to New Zealand, as a formal diplomat—to Japan in 1947. This visit dropped her suddenly into the cauldron of a land in the first stages of recovery from the devastation of war—both from its own aggression and from the Allied bombings, including the atomic attacks on Hiroshima and Nagasaki. The Japan experience, which was to achieve artistic fruition half a century later in *The Great Fire* (2003), opened Hazzard's eyes to a part of the world, East Asia, that few Australians had yet seen. Even though Hazzard was to spend much of her life in the more traditional Australian expatriate destinations of Western Europe and the United States, that her first international exposure was to Japan gave her an angle on the world, a scope, that rendered her work not only unprovincial but, despite its frequent setting in Europe, not Eurocentric. In 1948, she went to Hong Kong, where she held her first job, working for British Combined Services Intelligence. This interval produced Hazzard's first romance, which she has frequently mentioned in interviews, to an older man who has never been named.

Hazzard then moved briefly to New Zealand, where her father was involved in refugee processing and where she herself worked in an administrative position for the British high commissioner (the equivalent of ambassador) during parts of 1949 and 1950. This experience, though short, gave her another look at an English-speaking settler society so similar to, yet different from, her own, and also afforded her exposure to the problem of "displaced persons" in the wake of wartime disruption that resonated, both literally and metaphorically, in her later work. Taking on these responsibilities early in life, when she was still navigating the shoals of adult emotion, gave Hazzard a presciently mature sense of the analogies between diplomacy and emotional contact. Hong Kong and New Zealand also provided the background for some of the reading that was to inform Hazzard's later work. In the *Paris Review* interview, Hazzard related, "Hardy was a mighty discovery, and I read a great deal of Hardy when I was in Hong Kong and deeply in love." She also read T. S. Eliot and the poetry of Giacomo Leopardi, which she learned Italian (in New Zealand) in order to read after encountering the John Heath-Stubbs translation of the great Romantic-period Italian poet. Even before she approached Europe, she was immersed in its literatures and languages.

Her parents' separation in 1951 effectively ended Hazzard's enmeshment in her family of origin, and she was free to seek new agendas. She did so by moving to New York and, from 1952, working for the fledgling United Nations organization, at a time when, despite the stresses of the Korean war and the "iron curtain" of a divided postwar Europe, it was still hoped that an international organization including nearly all nations could effectively promote world peace and concord Hazzard's experiences, both with the immediate bureaucratic circumstances of her employment and the gaps between the proclaimed ideals of the organization's mission and its often petty and self-interested institutional practices. During these years, Hazzard traveled widely in England and Italy (she spent 1956–1957 in Naples supporting a UN mission dealing with the aftermath of the 1956 Suez Crisis in which Britain, France, and Israel had invaded Egypt). Her Naples sojourn helped inspire *The Bay of Noon* (1970); she also visited the northern city of Siena to stay with the Vivante family, whose beautiful house, the Villa Solaia, inspired *The Evening of the Holiday* (1966). But Hazzard did not begin to think of herself as a writer until the end of her twenties. In April 1961, she published her first short story, "Woollahra Road," in the *New Yorker*. This story, set in 1930s Australia and centering around a mother-child relationship, was never collected by Hazzard, but it led to an astonishingly prolific period in which she was to write four major works of fiction—two story collections, one novella, and one full-length novel—in less than a decade. Her editor at the *New Yorker*, the distinguished novelist and short-

story writer William Maxwell, was struck by the accomplishment and poise the work displayed, and rapidly accepted a series of stories, which ended up comprising Hazzard's first book, *Cliffs of Fall* (1963).

The period 1962–1963 was somewhat of an *annus mirabilis* for Hazzard. In 1962, she left United Nations employ and dedicated herself full-time to the writer's life. The year 1963 saw not only her first book but, in January, her meeting of (introduced by the novelist Muriel Spark) and, in December, her marriage to Francis Steegmuller, a well-known New York literary figure renowned as a translator of Gustave Flaubert and an editor of his letters. Steegmuller also wrote some popular genre novels, mostly under pseudonyms, but was more known as a nonfiction than a fiction writer. Steegmuller in many ways put Flaubert on the American literary map, influencing scores of writers who would otherwise not have encountered him so directly. He also helped make people aware of Flaubert (in his correspondence) as one of the modern age's great literary critics as well as a writer of unmatched style, irony, and reserve. Steegmuller's wide reading in French literature combined with Hazzard's being steeped in Italian writing and culture to give her immediate literary milieu an anchor in continental Europe beyond the mere polish normally acquired by the sophisticated Anglo-American. Steegmuller and Hazzard had a harmonious and intellectually companionable marriage, in which their overlapping circles of friends provided ample stimulation for their diverse interests. Steegmuller also offered Hazzard greater access to an older generation of literati—he was a Columbia classmate of Jacques Barzun and Lionel Trilling—than someone her age would have normally obtained, situating her in a very deep way in a New York literary scene in which, when considering the depth of her *New Yorker* ties, she was hardly an interloper or a newcomer. This world, although not large in the number of constituents and rather cohesive in its contours—touching such New York institutions as the *New Yorker* the Century Association, Columbia University, and the group of critics and academics loosely known as "the New York Intellectuals"—was also enormously influential and erudite, and provided intellectual nurture for Hazzard during the major phase of her career. Other contexts, such as Naples and the island of Capri in Italy, provided a similarly defined yet culturally rich milieu where Hazzard wrote and discussed literature with like-minded friends; Hazzard and Steegmuller owned houses in both places and spent much time in Italy. Steegmuller, whose first wife, the painter Beatrice Stein, had died two years before he married Hazzard, had formerly been a professor at the University of Wisconsin. By the time Steegmuller married Hazzard—when he was fifty-seven—he had settled down to the life of an independent man of letters in New York, living in a rented apartment in Manhattan's East Sixties in a famous, Gordon Bunshaft–designed building that epitomized a certain late-modernist style, where Hazzard was to continue to reside after she was widowed in 1994. Hazzard sold their home on Capri in the mid-2000s.

CLIFFS OF FALL

Cliffs of Fall takes its title from Gerard Manley Hopkins' "O the mind, mind has mountains; cliffs of fall / Frightful, sheer, no-man-fathomed. Hold them cheap / May who ne'er dwelled there." These lines from the nineteenth-century British Jesuit poet's "Terrible Sonnets" reflect common mid-twentieth-century practice of taking a novel (or short story collection) title from a famous line from poetry, Shakespeare, or the Bible, and it also registered Hopkins' tremendous popularity and canonicity in an era where he was championed by such influential critics as F. R. Leavis. The title, though, had a denotative as well as connotative component. The characters in these stories often are people well situated in life who are suddenly confronted by inadequacies or gaps they had not previously envisioned. "Harold" is a story from the collection that Hazzard, when interviewed by Richard Ford at the Ninety-Second Street Y for the PEN World Voices Festival in April 2010, particularly commended. Set at a villa near Siena it features a number of prosperous and cultivated guests who, if anything, are too much so: "The only criticism that might have been made of them was that their background and prospects had been provided so amply as to encroach a little on the scope of the present; nothing had been left to chance—perhaps on the assumption that chance is a detrimental element" (*Cliffs of Fall,* p. 145). But then a middle-aged Englishwoman arrives with a late-adolescent son, Harold, who does not appear to fit in, is awkward and ungracious compared to the other gilded youth. Harold's evident difference from the rest leads to questioning from the other guests, elucidating the fact that he is a poet. When he begins to read from his poems, he recites "distinctly but without emotion" (p. 153), not intending to please the audience, and in fact "no longer intensely aware of them, or, indeed, of himself." Though Harold's mother soon bids him to stop and go to sleep, his recitation has unquestionably broken the complacency of the house party, has shown them something wholly other, that cannot be accommodated within the other guests' bourgeois self-satisfaction. That "Harold" as a name is associated with the Romantic bravado of Lord Byron also indicates a certain skepticism toward polished, modern surfaces and a longing for a wilder art; thus the story, itself so well-crafted, has a complex relationship to its own style. "Vittorio" similarly ends in a spirit of astonishment. A British couple, Jonathan and Isabel Murray, are renting rooms from Vittorio, a classical scholar. Jonathan notices a certain flirtation between his wife and Vittorio, and Vittorio suspects Isabel has a crush on him. But what astonishes Vittorio is when he finds at the end that Isabel has bought one of his works—a difficult work of classical scholarship, written in Italian, a language she does not know well at all. This gesture, going well beyond flirtatious interest to something profound and intrinsic, flabbergasts him. It also turns the story from a conventional exploration of Aeolus temptation for an Englishwoman abroad to a conjecture that the ultimate daring, or even trespass, of love is to become interested in art and learning for their own sake. This kind of epiphany-centered story is not the only sort Hazzard assayed. "The

Picnic" concerns a woman, Nettie, who has had an affair with a man named Clem who is now married to May. The reader expects that Nettie, whom May, in a "magnanimous" spirit (p. 164) leaves alone with Clem, will feel the pangs of an old flame. Instead, though, she reflects that she had little in common with Clem and that their liaison was somewhat of a fluke, and that the permanent, if limited, pattern he now has left on her life belies what a bore she fundamentally thinks he is. In "Harold" and "Vittorio," the breakthrough at the end has to do with unexpected ardor; in "The Picnic," it pertains to unexpected banality. Not all the stories in *Cliffs of Fall* rely on unexpected endings. In "Villa Adriana" the young man and woman who feature in the story are dissatisfied with their relationship at the beginning, and in the end they are still dissatisfied, but their conversation and musing as they amble their way through the alleged former villa of the Roman emperor Hadrian make for an incisive, evocative character study. "In One's Own House" is a more ambitious story along similar lines. Russell and Miranda have been married for some years and are staying with Russell's mother, Constance, in Italy. Constance more or less ignores Russell in favor of her younger son, James, whom she had raised virtually on her own after her husband had died. James nurtures a hidden passion for Miranda, which he decides to avow to her, only heightening the hurt she already feels. The common situations in these stories—the sufferings and injuries of love, Anglo-Italian cultural interactions—are less important than Hazzard's nimble capacity to twist the contraptions of narrative so that at any instance they are apt to capture different emotional states: exaltation, loyalty, anguish, and resignation. Thus the differences between the stories are as important as their similarities.

The title story, set in Switzerland near Geneva, concerns a couple, the Britishers Cyril and Greta Strickland. The Stricklands are visiting Elizabeth, whose husband has just been killed in an accident, early on in their marriage. Though there is a mild romantic incident in the story—when Elizabeth fends off the semiamorous attentions of a French visitor, Étienne Maillard—most of the story has to do with Elizabeth's bereavement, and with her decision to move to America both as a way of getting over her loss and of acknowledging that it has happened, as an act of deliberate mourning. By the early 1960s the sexual situations that Hazzard concentrates on in most of the other satires in the book were becoming more common subject matters for literature, but death and loss remained greater taboos: Elizabeth's desperate struggle to feel her loss, yet to go on in life, visibly renders the gap between her own sense of devastation and the ability of others to lead a normal life. Yet Hazzard indicates that Elizabeth's departure from Geneva is not a flight, but a step forward.

Cliffs of Fall earned respectful reviews, though given that it was Hazzard's first book, and that it was a story collection rather than a novel, it did not reap the widespread attention that subsequent books did. Reviewing the 2004 reissue of the collection, the *New York Times Book Review* contributor Scott Veale quoted critic Stanley Kauffmann, who in a 1963 review stated that Hazzard "plunges bravely up to her ankles in ... little currents of domestic crisis" (p. 20).

THE EVENING OF THE HOLIDAY

The Evening of the Holiday (1966) seems at first to merely be an extended version of the stories in *Cliffs of Fall,* and indeed it was originally published, self-contained, in an issue of the *New Yorker.* Like most of the stories the novella is set in Italy and concerns the bittersweet ending of a romantic liaison. Yet if the narrative arc is similar, the feel of the text is very different. The fuller length allows Hazzard to introduce minor characters and wry aphorisms that do not advance the plot but provide atmosphere and depth over and above any necessary background. Even more noticeably, Hazzard gives freer vein to extensive nature descriptions, which is one of the most resonant aspects of the novel, especially as summer turns into autumn and then winter. The mood of the story is one of cyclical, seasonal change. But this cyclical trajectory is darkened for the point-of-view character, a young Englishwoman of Italian background named Sophie, by her breakup with the separated but not divorced Tancredi and the death of her aunt Luisa. The description of the cleanup after a storm in rural Tuscany is particularly fine:

> They all set to work—raking up the rubbish from the grass, staking and tying up the larger plants and building up earth around the small ones. To Luisa this activity was instantly comforting. Why do we make such an issue of everything, she wondered, putting in order a row of zinnias, pressing the wet soil so firmly into place that her fingerprints remained around each plant. It was all in the course of events—things blowing apart, being set to rights, flowering again.
>
> (p. 78)

It is this meditative and introspective spirit that distinguishes the book, more than the rather frail narrative strand. Yet it could be argued that Hazzard's interest even when she is not describing scenery or people's responses to it is less in what happens than in the differences of attitudes displayed between characters. Since Sophie is herself partially Italian, this is not simply the stereotyped encounter of a buttoned-up Englishwoman with a more sensuous Italian. These character prototypes, descended ultimately from Henry James, are of course there, but Hazzard plays with them not just by tweaking Sophie's decent but by making her an individual beyond her culture. Tancredi remarks that her name is Greek (meaning "wisdom"), and indeed, Sophie is not just different in culture but is deeper and more thoughtful than anyone else in the novel. The title suggests an elegy, leaving behind a time of play and leisure, somewhat like the return from Arden of the Duke and his retinue at the end of Shakespeare's *As You Like it*. For Sophie, though, it is not the relationship with Tancredi or even being in Italy herself that is ultimately what must end. Sophie must confront her own moral and psychological seriousness. For Tancredi, there is only the surface. He can feel and care, but he cannot take life seriously. He cannot ask searching questions of it beyond his own comfort. Hazzard's attentive mastery of the setting—her description of the Sienese Palio suggests a more severe version of a roughly contemporaneous book like Elizabeth Spencer's *The Light in the*

Piazza (1960)—belies the major stake of this book being in the study of character and morality. Sophie cannot have Tancredi because he is married, albeit separated. Even in a more liberal postwar Italy, marriage matters, notwithstanding the actual relationship is long since consigned to history. But on a deeper level, Sophie and Tancredi cannot end up together because life means different things for each of them. Despite their affinity for and caring about each other, Sophie will always be questioning the given while Tancredi will more reflexively affirm it, and thus they are incompatible. A secondary triumph of the book is the dying aunt Lucia, who summons up not just the wisdom of age but also its practical recognition of just what are the possibilities and impossibilities of a given set of human relationships.

PEOPLE IN GLASS HOUSES

Concurrently with her early fiction set in Italy, Hazzard was publishing short stories against the background of the United Nations. These stories, which appeared in *People in Glass Houses* (1967), presented just as unusual a tableau as the trope of the English person in Italy presented an accustomed one. Other than journalism or popular spy fiction, very little literary writing had taken on the United Nations. The idea of an international organization, a bureaucracy serving the entire world and not just one national conception or ideology, was something novel, and Hazzard's seeing it as the subject for fiction was an innovative move. There had been little comparable fiction, for instance about the United Nations's predecessor body, the League of Nations in Geneva (although Frank Moorhouse was later to write two remarkable novels on the subject). In turning from Italy to the United Nations, Hazzard was vaulting from a traditional vein in which she worked with craft and innovation to a genre of writing that had virtually not yet been invented. That as late as 2011 David Foster Wallace's posthumously published novel *The Pale King* was being hailed for dealing with the working of a large, anonymous organization, bringing the systemic aspect of this material to fiction, shows what an early glimpse of a literary take on this sort of material *People in Glass Houses* constituted. In the collection's first story, "Nothing in Excess," it is made clear by the title alone that, despite the internationalism of the organizations' personnel and milieu, like so many private corporations it encourages mediocrity and slights truly inventive minds like Algie, a man who is let go basically because he is too original. The aim "of the Organization was such as to attract people of character; having attracted them, it found it could not afford them, that there was no room for personalities, and that its hope for survival lay … in the subordination of individual gifts to general procedures" (p. 16). In the second story, "The Sorrow of Flowers," the poignant, lofty rhetoric of a guest speaker is mocked in juxtaposition to the routine administrative language of daily business; Hazzard makes clear that one of the problems of the organization is a problem of language. In operating within the contours of truth-functional, emotionally neutral language, the organization has clipped the broad human palette of expression down to a narrow, anodyne strand that restrains its employees even while its ideals speak of international outreach and mutual understanding.

Conversely, there are times when words like "devotion" are used of diplomatic interests in magniloquent ways that would no longer apply to personal relationships; even when emotive language is maintained, therefore, it is fustian, ossified, orotund. The mockery here, though, is not savage. In this world, people cannot sustain relationships, cannot have meaningful emotional rendezvous; a potential romantic liaison is stanched. But the very bureaucratic tidiness also allows men and women to relate to each other professionally without the ultimately standardizing intrusion of sex. As the beginning of "The Meeting" indicates, this anodyne neutrality can sometimes appear as a kind of pastoral, a separate world hedged off from the bustle and malice of the great city, which encloses it. But a lack of purpose vitiates such potential; meaningless meetings consume the time of the employees, and creativity becomes curtailed into meaningless doodles made to pass the time. If the stories

in *People in Glass Houses* remain in this comic-anthropological vein, there are some moments of greater depths. Clelia Kinglake, who appears in several of the stories and is somewhat of a point-of-view character, manages in "A Sense of Mission" (whose Italian setting is reminiscent of Hazzard's other set of stories) to put her stamp on her work. Yet overall, as in the final story, "The Separation of Dinah Delbanco," *People in Glass Houses* paints a picture of futility and waste, where the most international and diverse institution in history becomes, in practice, utterly banal and monochrome. The book was well reviewed, with commentators commending its satiric incisiveness and dry wit. The Australian critic R. G. Geering, a friend and supporter of the previous Australian novelist perhaps most comparable to Hazzard, Christina Stead, commended the volume for its artistic achievement.

THE BAY OF NOON

After experimenting with two very different veins of short fiction, Hazzard was ready for her first full-length novels. Though set in the south of Italy around Naples, with its lazy summer days and NATO military installations (where the penultimate story in *People in Glass Houses* had been set), rather than the Tuscan setting of *The Evening of the Holiday*, *The Bay of Noon* (1970) is as recognizable a development out of the novella as the novella was with respect to the stories contained in *Cliffs of Fall*. One notable difference, however, is that the narrator, Jenny, speaks throughout in a confident first-person voice. When Hazzard was first starting out as a writer, the critical insistence—prescribed by Henry James and etched into dogma by Percy Lubbock in *The Craft of Fiction* (1921)—was that fiction should be written from the limited, third-person point of view. Hazzard was too talented to have to adopt these limits. Jenny's presentation of the material in the first person allows the character to muse about the difference between past and present, memory and experience, in ways that a third-person reflector simply cannot do. The narration conveys the convoluted and often subtle turns of love and friendship between Jenny, her Italian friend Gioconda, Gioconda's romantic interest, Gianni, and the mysterious British scientist, Justin P. Tulloch: who these characters are, what their affinities, aspirations, sexualities consist of, are at the simmering heart of the book, verging on a revelation that the book delivers only tacitly. If Hazzard incarnated the Victorian novel's emotional amplitude, she did not embrace its easy emotional revolution, what Giaconda describes as "the demand for comprehension" (p. 89) with its potential to simplify and vulgarize human relationships.

The implicitness of this emotional subtlety is balanced by the visible specificity of Hazzard's detailed knowledge of the topography of Naples. This is not pertinent so much in terms of mere accuracy but for the sense that pervades the novel of a thoroughly rendered background, of a composition accountable to the preconditions of how the author conceived it. Indeed, without this tangible setting, the books would be a series of suggestions. The local habitation Hazzard so skillfully sculpts gives it heft and anchor. *The Bay of Noon* is a novel in which the awareness of time, of change and retrospection, is rendered so magisterially, so authoritatively, as to evoke—despite the book's far more realist surface—writers such as Virginia Woolf and Marcel Proust. This, though, does not render the novel's incidents exclusively somber or profound; a sense of comic ruefulness, of the absurdity of life's chances, pervades the book. For all its eloquence and its sense of gravity, *The Bay of Noon* contains considerable humor. Indeed, the immediate grain of its sentences present a fiercer and more barbed texture than a boiled-down account of its romantic plot would augur; Hazzard here succeeded in taking the novel of amorous voyage as far away from conventionality as possible, to braid in new perspectives while remaining within a taut, quasi-lyrical frame. As Tulloch says, "true love is the cultivation of forgetfulness" (p. 46). What can and cannot be told is key to this book. The inarticulate, or the unarticulable, is almost a character in itself.

The novel did not receive as wide a response as did Hazzard's subsequent books; for instance, apparently it was not reviewed in the *New York Times Book Review*. It was, however, in 2010 nominated for the "lost" Booker Prize for 1970, a retrospective honor conceived because there was no official winner of the prize in that year, as the award's announcement time was readjusted. Hazzard had distinguished company in this battle, including her compatriot Patrick White, for *The Vivisector*—though ultimately losing to the late Anglo-Irish writer (and already established Booker winner) J. G. Farrell, for his historical novel *Troubles*. Her nomination, though, signaled how far her reputation had risen since the novel's release forty years before.

DEFEAT OF AN IDEAL *AND* COUNTENANCE OF TRUTH

Defeat of an Ideal: A Study of the Self-Destruction of the United Nations (1973) was a serious nonfiction look at the institution examined satirically in *People in Glass Houses*, namely the United Nations. It is completely different, though, in tone. The implications are also slightly different. Whereas the short story collection pictured the organization collapsing under its own bureaucratic contradictions, *Defeat of an Ideal* specifically blames the United States and the legacy of the anti-Communist McCarthy era in the early 1950s for diminishing both American fiscal contributions to the United Nations and any moral sustenance of it. In a sense Hazzard was arguing that the United States had repeated its behavior of 1919–1920, when it refused to enter the League of Nations, which it had originally proposed—only in the case of the United Nations, the United States had entered and was wielding power in the organization but was fundamentally refraining from the encouragement of any supra-sovereign role for it. Hazzard's slightly younger fellow Australian, Frank Moorhouse, also tacitly made this point in his League of Nations diptych of novels, *Grand Days* (1993) and *Dark Palace* (2001), and Hazzard's sense of a supranational mission that extends beyond a multilateral American one surely proceeds from her Australian status. Though Hazzard's critique was contemporaneous with those of the U.S.

ambassador to the United Nations, Daniel Patrick Moynihan, and others in the United Nations' who frequently expressed an anti-Israel and pro–third world tone, Hazzard did not sympathize with Moynihan and those who agreed with him. The torque of her critique is fundamentally different. For Hazzard, the climate within the country that hosted the body, the United States, was what prohibited the deal from taking any realized form. Hazzard, though, also faulted the almost inherent bureaucratic interstices of the United Nations itself, and indicated that weaknesses in personnel and administrative vision had brought the organization down. Hazzard's disappointment gained its wounded edge precisely because it was the result of a real hope left disappointed and unfulfilled.

The period of *Defeat of an Ideal* was a particularly political one for Hazzard. In the 1970s, Hazzard frequently reviewed books for the *New York Times Book Review,* such as *The Eye of the Storm* by her fellow Australian Patrick White, who won the Nobel Prize in 1973. She also wrote letters to the *Times* on such subjects as the U.S. role in Cambodia in the early 1970s and the United Nations refusal to heed the moral witness of the Soviet dissident and novelist Aleksandr I. Solzhenitsyn, showing both her ethical concern and her political unpredictability.

It is precisely because Hazzard was not a prolific journalist—that she saw her calling as above all that of an imaginative writer—that these nonfiction works were so painstakingly and deliberately written, as they involved a conscious asceticism, a disciplining of the muse to testify to a truth perhaps less exalted than the delights of fiction but which at instances was necessitated by the pressure of events. In Hazzard's second book on the United Nations, *Countenance of Truth: The United Nations and the Waldheim Case* (1990), the mendacity of the former UN secretary-general Kurt Waldheim about his Nazi past made an uncompromising truthfulness—the book takes its title from a line of John Milton, one of the first crusaders for conscience and freedom of speech—imperative. Hazzard had first mentioned her suspicions about Waldheim's Nazi past in an article in the *New Republic* in January

1980, but it was only six years later that the scandal of his wartime activities came to full international light. Although ruthless in her exposure of Waldheim's prevarication and hypocrisy, there is less a vindictive than an elegiac tone to the book, as if the author realizes that the Waldheim scandal was not just the defeat of an ideal but its entire erosion. Buried within the stern witness of Hazzard's prose is a mourning for a time that idealists like the younger version of the author herself thought a new order of global cooperation could be built, outside of national power-structures and structurally unencumbered by personal taint. But Hazzard is nonetheless scalding in her portrait of the United Nations, particularly so when she notes that Waldheim was elected as a neutral figure who would not offend either side in the cold war—despite suspicions of his Nazi ties—whereas the superb Finnish diplomat Max Jakobson was rejected because he was Jewish. It is an index of how smoldering Hazzard's rigorous indignation was that Christopher Lehmann-Haupt, the normally unflappable daily book reviewer for the *New York Times*, averred that Hazzard's tone of "outraged disillusionment with the tattered history of the United Nations" was untoward. Soon after, such a tone of skepticism became the norm in public discourse, even after the United Nations became less fettered by the end of the cold war.

THE TRANSIT OF VENUS

The Transit of Venus (1980) could well be mistaken for an autobiographical bildungsroman. Its heroine, Caro (Caroline) Bell, is roughly Hazzard's age and shares, in broad measure, the circumstance of her life. But to see the book as direct autobiography would be a mistake, as, whatever its inspiration, incidents and sequences are so rearranged as to make any reduction to biographical experience impossible. What is true, though, about Hazzard is that, though not confessional, she is also not reticent, and the reader comes to know the author well through the work, although not in the sense of any direct revelation. Moreover, there is no question about the novel being concerned with only private experience; from the first sentence, the book unfolds against the continual "devastation" (p. 3) wrought within the twentieth century.

The Transit of Venus is fundamentally about two sisters: Caro and Grace Bell (Caro is a few years older). Grace is fair in complexion, and correspondingly lighter in treatment; Caro is darker both in looks and soul. Hazzard uses the convention of the dark-fair female split from the nineteenth-century novel (for instance, Rowena and Rebecca in Sir Walter Scott's 1819 novel, *Ivanhoe*; alternately a dichotomy like Becky Sharp and Amelia Sedley in William Makepeace Thackeray's 1848 novel, *Vanity Fair*) in sharply altered, unromantic circumstances. But *Transit*—though it was often perceived through a feminist frame when first issued—is not merely about women. Edmund "Ted" Tice, the astronomer who falls in love with Caro and—we are told early on in the book—is doomed to an anticlimactic death, has been seen by many as one of the great male characters in twentieth-century fiction. Ted first enters Caro's life as a protégé of the astronomer Sefton Thrale, whose son Christian ends up marrying Grace. Carol and Ted first meet in the early 1950s, when the Bell sisters are in Britain, having virtually sundered their ties with Australia after both their parents died in boating accident and their elder sister, Dora, had proven an overly sober termagant. (Caro is nonetheless financially generous to Dora, even while others with more money are not.) The expendability, the nonpresence, of parents is a repeated theme in Hazzard's oeuvre and may be an indicator of what is, after a point, the absence of the overt Australian theme in her narrative, as if the memory of her parents were tantamount to the residue of her Australian upbringing. Yet the descriptions of the sisters' Australian girlhood in chapter 5, "Something You'll Remember Always," are among the finest passages in the novel:

> Now Caro and Grace Bell did not go home at once after the lessons but walked along the beach below the school, getting sand in their shoes and stockings, picking up chipped shells and flinging them away. Seaweed sworled in dark, beady tangles, swallowed up by the tides, bleared by an occasional medusa. A boy or pair of boys would speak to them,

boys in grey knickerbockers and striped ties. The uniforms were a guarantee: schools recognized each other like regiments.

> Grace was a flower.

> Caro's hair hung heavy on her shoulders, as no child's will do.

> (p. 48)

These passages, though, are only the prelude to adult love in the Northern Hemisphere, its splendors and miseries. Ted and Caro feel an insensate pull to each other, but fate intervenes, leaving Caro to be involved with, first, the charming but capricious playwright Paul Ivory, then with the man she ultimately marries—the philanthropic, conscientious political activist Adam Vail, who dies tragically young. By having Ivory be the son of a prominent poet, Rex Ivory, who dies in the Changi prison camp in Japanese-occupied Singapore, Hazzard depicts these young people as living under the ominous shadow of war and suffering. Poetry, though, is also, as a genre and a mode, an insensate force in the novel. Hazzard's own style is not poetic—indeed it is thoroughly novelistic and prosaic—but the awareness of poetry as a verbal level hovering over the book's discourse gives a sense of intricacy and texture in verbal expression far exceeding the average realistic novel.

The book's plot evades convenient summary, yet it can be said that two revelations—one of Ted's having helped a German prisoner of war escape (against all obligations of his as a soldier) and the other of a lurid episode involving Paul and a youthful homosexual lover—provide the bookended emotional releases of the book. That Ted witnessed Paul's crime and has not told Caro—as Paul finds to his surprise—conclusively establishes his extraordinary moral sensitivity and probity. As Hazzard shuffles the three men in the deck of Caro's love life—Ted, Adam, and Paul—it is only fitting that the strongest of them, Ted, proves his valor by his discretion with respect to the sins of the weakest of them, Paul. In Hazzard's reckoning of love, we have passed beyond rivalry or competition to a deep sense of the stakes of love and the necessity of the lover to have an emotional respect for them, whatever the outcome.

The sense of there always being one more person in the love equation than the exclusivity of erotic claims would warrant is one application of the title: a "transit of Venus" occurs when Venus passes between the sun and the earth, just as Adam and Paul often obscure Ted and Caro's view of each other. But the title also has another implication: one of the spurs of the southward voyage of Captain James Cook, the first Englishman to land in Australia, was to see the 1769 transit of Venus. Thus a transit of Venus occasioned the European exploration of Australia, and then almost two centuries later it serves as a metaphor for Australia's exploration of Europe: that is, of Caro's progress "back" to the metropolitan world, with the added inflection of Caro, as a woman, being more naturally under the sphere of Venus than was the exploring Captain Cook. The titles of the book's four sections— "The New World," "Contacts," "The Old World," and "Culmination"—also support this sense of Caro's odyssey as an inversion of Cook's voyage, an exploration launched from Australia back into the centers of civilization and within the heart, toward the contradictions of love.

The novel revolves around erotic, romantic passion. But what matters is less the mechanics of who loves who than the willingness of men and women to open themselves fully to each other and take each other's love seriously, as a sentimental affirmation, whether or not that love is practical for them. Hazzard's characters are not romantic in the sense of being love-besotted or thinking love will provide easy answers to life. But they do use love as a way of taking the highest estimate of other human beings. Nor does love exclude society. Bliss and heartbreak are always mixed with the news headlines and with the idiosyncrasies and contrasts of place and context.

The end of *The Transit of Venus* is structurally complicated. Though we have been told previously that Ted Tice is dead, our last sight of him in the novel, technically speaking, is of his departure from Caro. Yet we know that Ted will die as a result of that departure, and the poignancy of the novel's end with him still living is all the more sharp as the reader's last sight of him is in

motion. Moreover, the twist at the end—the revelation about Paul's past—makes us reevaluate the entire narrative. Though Hazzard rightly disavows any deliberate inspiration from Henry James—she is far less confirmed a maker of narrative mysteries, far less coy about her object of meaning—the emotional impact of the sudden, postponed revelation makes the reader mentally rework what they had just traversed, the way one might do when reading one of James's most curiously wrought fictions.

The Transit of Venus is a retrospective account of the previous forty years, but it was also a book of its own time, the late 1970s and early 1980s. With regard to the other sorts of novels being written in the decades after World War II, Hazzard's book was not only more ambitious but less hemmed-in than a book such as Kathrin Perutz's *A House on the Sound* (1965), an accomplished performance within the Lubbockian paradigm, which left its author no assured way of stepping beyond it. Hazzard, on the other hand, was able to broaden her palette and reach back into history and memory without yielding her sense of form and of a consciously sculpted stance. Hazzard is attuned to history, but she is neither its prisoner nor its publicist. As an inheritor of the modernist legacy of a world for whom history was a nightmare from which it was trying to awake, she looks at historical background through a lens of disconsolation, which makes her different from later novelists concerned with twentieth-century history, such as Nicole Krauss and Julie Orringer, who concentrated more on the positive remains of tragedy—that is, what could be recouped from the historical morass. Hazzard, no total pessimist, is not incognizant of the remains, but for her the emphasis is always on the disconsolations of the morass. This lends the book an air of being replete with substance, moored down by the discipline of an ascetic alertness to limitation.

Also relevant here is *Transit*'s genre-sampling; there is romantic elegance, of the sort that Oliver Leith in Hazzard's later novel *The Great Fire* might have conceived; there is limpid purity, of the sort perhaps practiced by the poet-character Rex Ivory in this novel; but there is also satire, with such nonnaturalistic names such as "Sefton Thrale," "Dr. Angus Dance," and "Tertia Drage" being reminiscent of Charles Dickens or even Thomas Love Peacock. If one critical reaction to the work were that it presumed too much on the emotional situations contained therein for significance, a riposte might be that this ballast of sentiment is needed to provide torsion to a book that is so self-conscious of its multigeneric, frequently allusive nature. The heft and reference of *The Transit of Venus* was at a total opposite from the manic innovation of such "metafictive" writers as John Barth and Thomas Pynchon—both born in the same decade as Hazzard. Yet she was similar to these writers—as well as to more comparable contemporaries such as Joyce Carol Oates, John Updike, and Philip Roth—in using her work to make sense of the tumultuous and often calamitous twentieth century; it could be argued, though, that Hazzard's work made a more conscious commitment to personal relationships than did any of the above-named writers.

Hazzard's ability to put the breath of a triple-decker novel into the crafted frame of a more sculpted medium length has entranced and, occasionally, distanced readers, who see the result as haughty and tedious. This might be so if the unfolding of plot was the point, but Hazzard requires we play close attention to every sentence, every form of reference, and not merely turn the page on to the next enticement.

The Transit of Venus did extraordinarily well, making most top-ten lists for books of the year and being selected as the Quality Paperback Book Club's award winner for fiction as well as winning the National Book Critics Circle Award in the United States. Writing in the May 15, 1980, *New York Review of Books*, Robert Towers observed: "*The Transit of Venus* affords many pleasures, chief among which is the brilliantly metaphorical style," though he also criticized the book for a "cultural knowingness" that becomes "mannered" (p. 33). Writing in the *New Republic* for January 26, 1980, Anne Tyler called the book "wonderfully mysterious" (p. 29) and praised the book's endowment of routine life-moments with resonant meaning. In 1982, the *New York Times*

reported that Gillian Armstrong, a director who had earlier adapted the Australian classic *My Brilliant Career* by Miles Franklin, was filming *The Transit of Venus*, but the film was never made.

The Transit of Venus made Hazzard a household name among readers of American fiction, and it was especially admired for its combination of domestic experience against a broader, often quite meditative, historical canvas. Hazzard became an honored member of the New York literary world. In 1982, she received the supreme accolade of being elected to the American Academy of Arts and letters. Throughout her career, she continued to receive these sorts of honors, for instance in 2003 being named one of the New York Public Library's Library Lions and being honored at a special dinner.

Not only did *The Transit of Venus* do well in bookstore sales after its appearance, garnering broad acclaim, but it stayed with readers in the decades afterward, being constantly treasured and rediscovered. This was all the more remarkable in that, though Hazzard published essays, reviews, and nonfiction books, she did not publish another novel for twenty-three years, and thus *Transit* was not supported by a constant stream of new novels that would have automatically kept their author's name in the literary conversation.

COMING OF AGE IN AUSTRALIA AND "BREAD AND CIRCUSES"

Hazzard periodically returned to Australia, with visits occurring in 1976 (which she wrote about for the *New Yorker*) as well as in 1984 and 1997, which produced substantial writing. Her 1977 "Letter from Australia" in the *New Yorker* is a far-too-little-examined document that gives the lie to any assertion that Hazzard disowned or distanced herself from Australia. Written just after the sacking of the Gough Whitlam–led Australian Labor Party government by Governor-General Sir John Kerr (a controversial decision of dubious constitutional legitimacy), Hazzard vigorously defends Whitlam's record and castigates his right-wing critics, putting herself demonstrably on the Australian left, as her 1970s book reviews put her on its American equivalent. Hazzard also is enthusiastic about both the younger generation of Australian writers—she hails the "new Australians" of refugee origin as a breath of fresh air in the nation's culture—and older contemporaries like Patrick White and the poet Judith Wright, as well as, startlingly, classic Australian writers of the nineteenth and early twentieth centuries such as Marcus Clarke (1846–1881) and William Gosse Hay (1875–1945), both of whom never before had been, and likely will not be again, mentioned in the *New Yorker*. Much like her quotation of the Henry Kendall line from the iconic 1869 poem "Bell-Birds," written in the Australian bush, "When fiery December sets foot in the forest" (*The Transit of Venus*, p. 55), Hazzard clearly sees it as her mission to promote and preserve awareness of these writers, against a stereotype of Australia as the "amorphous nadir" ("Letter," p. 32) of the world. In other words, she is not dismissing all that came before her as inadequate, or congratulating herself on her escape to a literary culture of greater pedigree and plenitude.

Hazzard also speaks to Australian achievement in the visual arts. The *New Yorker* letter thwarted American stereotypes of Australia as a place of cultural quietude and derivativeness, and it heralded an era of greater attention to Australia that would be manifested in the early 1980s Australian film boom and the growing visibility of Australian literature in American culture.

Hazzard's 1984 visit yielded more controversy. The Boyer Lectures she gave on ABC radio, published in 1985 as *Coming of Age in Australia*, seemed to many Australian critics, including the redoubtable and irreverent cultural nationalist Don Anderson, to fall back into the errors of what A. A. Phillips had labeled the "cultural cringe," criticizing Australia for being provincial and philistine. What these observers missed is that Hazzard was not discussing the Australia of the present but the past, and why she left it. Necessarily, Hazzard could only testify to her own experience (upper-middle-class, living in Sydney) of the country, but however offended some Australians might have been, no one could say this experience was not her own and that she

was not speaking to it faithfully. Moreover, it must be considered that, for Hazzard's generation, a world had been opened up to them beyond being reabsorbed into Britain or going to European countries where they could not speak the language. In the aftermath of the Pearl Harbor attack, the Australian prime minister John Curtin had said that Australia looked to America, without any inhibition from its longtime ties to Britain, to defend it. Australians of Hazzard's generation could also look to America as a place to make their careers, and they inevitably found it a wider venue than their own country could at that time possibly provide. Whereas other writers of Hazzard's generation, such as her stylistic peer David Malouf, lived much of the time outside Sydney and did not suffer for it, Hazzard's disinclination to touch base with Australia more regularly, her lack (as compared to a writer like Peter Carey) of strong Australian publishing ties, and her very residence in the United States made her a more marginal figure on the Australian scene than her work deserved. This changed, though, in the 2000s with a more transnational vision of Australian literature gaining favor even within Australia.

Although she was a global writer in subject and scope, Shirley Hazzard made her literary career in the United States, and the key publishing and editorial figures in her career have been in the U.S. spheres of those industries. But she did have an important editor in Britain—Carmen Callil of the Virago Press—and her Australian identity made her eligible to be seen in British publishing terms as a semi-native, as when she was included in the 2010 short list for the 1970 "lost" Booker Prize.

In 1997, Hazzard made an important contribution to Australian national debates by commenting in regard to the planned push for Australia to sever its ties with the crown; in giving the Sydney Institute's 1997 Larry Adler Lecture, titled "Bread and Circuses: Thought and Language in Decline," Hazzard said that the "excitement of making a republic seems almost a thing from the past" (p. 27). Echoing a theme in "Letter from Australia," Hazzard also expressed criticism toward the contemporary emphasis on technology and expressed regret that Australia had fallen prey to this as much as had its longer-established Northern Hemisphere counterparts.

At a reading and reception at the Australian consulate on Forty-Second Street in New York City, for the *Macquarie PEN Anthology of Australian Literature* in September 2009, Hazzard spoke of herself as "definitely an Australian writer" and praised the works of Patrick White, especially *The Tree of Man* (1955). She also reminisced about her days at the United Nations to the current Australian delegation, some of whom were fifty years her junior.

When the present writer had tea with Hazzard at her New York apartment on April 10, 2011, she was absorbed in an article by Andrew Quilty in the *New York Times* travel section on the Great Ocean Road between Adelaide and Melbourne. She had never before, she said, heard of this road, but was fascinated by the beauty of the photographs supplied with the article. Though she lived her life outside Australia, and though Australia was not the main focus of her work, Hazzard's temperament remained resolutely Australian.

GREENE ON CAPRI

In 2000, Hazzard published *Greene on Capri*, a short memoir of her friendship with the British writer Graham Greene (1904–1991). The book is not a eulogy of Greene nor a discussion of his achievement as a writer, but instead depicts both admirable and exasperating traits about his personality. The narrative grapples with Greene as an astonishing, endlessly provocative figure, who fascinates Hazzard precisely by his difference from her. From the happenstance of their meeting—that both remember Robert Browning's 1845 poem "The Lost Mistress,"a poem of lost love and a savored touchstone for Hazzard from her Sydney childhood—to the vicissitudes of the often stormy friendship Greene had with Hazzard and Steegmuller—Greene is presented as an obstreperous, publicity-seeking (and publicity-garnering) figure. Hazzard, nonetheless, sees Greene as estimable in his love of literature, his

concern with the fate of the world, and the dedication and gusto with which he pursues life. Again, Hazzard, through her marriage to Steegmuller, gained access to a sense of the generation before her, giving her a cultural reach that, for instance, enabled her to write the introduction to *The Portrait of Zélide,* an ingenious work of creative nonfiction originally published in 1927 by the American aesthete Geoffrey Scott (1884–1929), noted among other things for being a friend of Edith Wharton. This affinity for the proximate one or two preceding generations enabled Hazzard to view Greene as a sort of equal in a way for which otherwise her relative youth would have disqualified her. There were also, though, experiential affinities between Hazzard and Greene. Both had matured in the aftermath of a great war they had been too young to experience as adults but which they witnessed as self-aware adolescents. Both had a sense of the disposability of parental and contextual backgrounds in making their careers and a certain vision of worldliness as a generative background to their fictions—despite their very different fictional terrain.

Importantly, Greene is only one part of the title. Capri, a venue Hazzard knew as well as anyone, an island of appeal for the psychologically damaged power elite since the time of the emperor Tiberius, is a coprotagonist of the book. At times it seems as if "the oddity of that winter meeting" (p. 8) with Greene is just the premise, what Henry James would have called the *donnée,* for a reflection on the many years Hazzard and Steegmuller spent living on Capri. It is also, necessarily, a reflection on expatriation as such—a crucial subject for Hazzard—and on what it means to be lovingly and keenly attached to a place that one knows intimately but that can never be, fundamentally, one's own.

Greene on Capri was well reviewed, although critics tended not to place it within Hazzard's oeuvre but instead saw it as a simple tribute to Greene as literary lion. But, importantly, it kept Hazzard's name before the reading public shortly before her next major work was to appear. In that the memoir was Hazzard's first book since Steegmuller's death in 1994, *Greene on Capri* was also a commemoration of this all-important partnership, whose living memory never left Hazzard's work. It also marked Hazzard's move to a new publisher, Farrar, Straus and Giroux, arguably New York's most prestigious literary firm.

THE GREAT FIRE

Hazzard's novel *The Great Fire* appeared in 2003, although an excerpt had appeared in the *New Yorker* as early as June 1987 (the Peter Exley–Rita Xavier strand of the story) and June 1990 (with the character who eventually became "Helen Driscoll" named "Julia Bogle"), suggesting the work's long gestation. Aldred Leith is the son of Oliver Leith, a renowned novelist who had started out as a geologist, written a short account of his work in that field, and eventually became a writer of a romantic vision sufficiently self-aware to survive in an anti-romantic modernist age. Despite Oliver Leith's artistic achievement and his genuine generosity and empathy, his son mistrusts him for his cold, detached, emotionally predatory nature, and his death is greeted by Aldred as at once a loss and liberation. Leith, at thirty-three, is a major in the British army, and he arrives in Japan to continue his work, commissioned by the U.K. military, on societies in the aftermath of war (he had previously visited still smoldering China). Stationed at a military base near Hiroshima, Leith is ideally placed to record the face of society in the aftermath of devastation.

In Japan, Aldred Leith meets the Driscoll family, who seem in some ways another version of the Bell family in *The Transit of Venus*: provincial, Australian, stretching their tendrils out into the greater world, which will provide either stage or foil for them, by which they will either become accommodated or regurgitated. Importantly, Aldred becomes friendly with both Benedict and his seventeen-year-old sister, Helen, and Benedict's early death from cancer is one of the bonds that tie Aldred and Helen together. Just as Aldred had met one of his early flames, Aurora, through the death of her son Jason, the

linkage between a male friend and female lover is psychologically important here. After meeting Helen, Aldred goes on a journey to Hong Kong and then Europe, his extended absence enabling him to write Helen detailed letters that make up a good deal of the novel (and provide its most overtly discursive, descriptive passages), as well as to reflect on his own past.

If Helen is Aldred's second happiness, Italy is his first happiness, and Gigliola and Raimonda, two young women he had met there, will always be a kind of ideal for him. But Aldred is able to use the strengths of his lost past to rebuild a future for himself, transcending the sadness and inertia of the interim. In a sense, Australian identity stands for the unproven entering the world of experience; in another, it stands for global interconnection itself, lived out on a personal scale and as a result of consequential, sometimes desperate, personal choices.

Aldred's life is not just in the present of its novel but in its past. His Australian friend Peter Exley is an important barometer for him, recalling him to a mission of altruism and sacrifice for the good of others when Aldred threatens to become lost in a potential morass of desire and career ambition. As Robert Dixon puts it, "Leith's work is facilitated by the American military occupation of Japan but fundamentally at odds with it, and potentially subversive of US authority" (p. 274). The search for a moral compass that is outside the confines of institutional power and is premised upon more personal values is at the heart of the book. The Frys, mother and daughter, are crucial characters in the last section, set in Wellington, New Zealand, who help both frame and cement Aldred's and Helen's love. The daughter, Elinor, named after Florence Nightingale (whose true first name was Elinor), had lost her fiancé in the First World War. Cut off by this loss from experiencing love herself, Elinor urges the younger generation to seek it; rather than being bitter, she urges younger people to explore their most emotionally ample horizons.

The Fry and Exley narratives function virtually as inset stories, not extensively interlocking with the Leith-Driscoll narrative. But their prudence adds to the gravity of the book, indicating that the story Hazzard is telling is one of an entire society yet also insisting that this society can only be composed by accumulated minutiae of individual circumstance. The familiar reader of Hazzard will greet certain elements—Italy, Australia, global conflict, love, and loss—less in narrative terms than as part of a compositional syntax that any Hazzard novel must, formally, have. Hazzard is (to employ John Stuart Mill's famous dichotomy) a "made" not a "born" writer—someone who came to writing relatively late and for whom it is a vocation of dedicated craft, not a hydraulic irruption of imaginative prowess. Thus the experienced Hazzard reader, reacting to the novel in terms of composition rather than plot or even mood, can even more appreciate the arduous labor that must have been required for these syntactic elements to tally meaningfully in an absorbing narrative without any overt sign of forcing or ornamentalism. *The Great Fire* also possesses minor characters of a nuance and global thrust usually to be found in a far longer novel. Tad, the generous American who cedes his place in Helen's life to Aldred, demonstrates one aspect of globalization; Rita Xavier, the Portuguese-Chinese woman whom Peter Exley is dissuaded from taking home by the White Australia policy (which sharply discouraged Asian migration to Australia), represents another. Though Peter invokes his homeland's intolerance (along with its suburban boredom and inertia) as a reason—perhaps an excuse—for his not marrying Rita (and there is a sense that multiracialism is in the novel's tomorrow not its today), the novel thoroughly bans any sense that the European sensibility can be intact or prevalent after the disruptions of the war and the violence that Europe-derived culture showed it could unleash, in using the atomic bomb. That this admission comes from Hazzard, a Europhile if there ever was one—someone who knows Capri and Naples as well as she knows the triumphs of modern European culture in literature, art, and music—makes the point unusually worth heeding. That the period of the early 2000s in which the novel was published was seeing a recrudescence of Eurocentrism in the context of what the political scientist Samuel P. Huntington called "the clash of civilizations" made Hazzard's implicit but eloquent assertion not just a retrospective conservation but a tract for the times.

Throughout the novel, Australians are augurs of this post-European world: at one point, Peter, an Australian, is the only "European" present in the room at a Roman Catholic wedding; at another the inevitability of racial mixing is demonstrated by Hendriks, a Dutchman, revealing that, although he still identifies as Dutch, he has partially Javanese ancestry. Even Antarctica (mentioned as source of the cold winds blowing into Wellington) and Africa (where Aurora goes to begin a new life after the loss of Jason) are mentioned. (Latin America is not mentioned much, but it did play a considerable role in *The Transit of Venus*, in that Adam Vail's philanthropic work was largely directed toward that region.) A thorough sense of Britain (including the postwar Labour government) and of America (especially its popular music and slang) is also provided. Without any grandiose sense of panorama or sweep, intricately patterned rather than encyclopedic, the novel is global in its bones. Hazzard does not lecture the reader about the places she mentions, but she lets the reader feel the presence of what Brigitta Olubas calls their "cosmopolitan modernity" (2010, p. 4) in the lived force of their enunciation in dialogue. Her sense of the global is not descriptive but dramatic, an aspect heightened all the more by the intense, if restrained, sense of elegy that suffuses the book: of a time long ago when fateful steps were taken. At the same time, Hazzard's avoidance of a large-scale perspective means that *The Great Fire* does not look back in retrospect, and thus it avoids the over-the-shoulder perspective of such nearly contemporaneous works as Ian McEwan's *Atonement* (2002) or Les Murray's verse novel *Fredy Neptune* (1999).

For how few people is individual choice truly indicative of a moral option or a conscious avowal of principles? Even less than with *The Transit of Venus* could *The Great Fire* be directly linked to Hazzard's biography, as she includes elements germane to her own life but reshuffles them in such a way as they can never be identifiable in one-to-one terms. Milieu and values matter more than events; it is the tone, the mood, the meaning of the novel that resonates above all.

The ending of *The Great Fire* depicts a generation still young in years, with many decades ahead of them, but scarred and traumatized for life by the proximity of death: "Many had died. But not she; not he. Not yet" (p. 278). The illusion of youthful permanence afforded to those who matured in peacetime is unavailable for them; these are not young adults, but old souls. In this way, *The Great Fire* not only augurs aspects of the collective history between its time of setting and date of composition (decolonization, the growing role of Asia in world affairs, nuclear-induced fear) but also the private lives of the people alive at the time, which will always be tinged with a sense of loss and a bearing of gravity from the events they had witnessed (at first- or secondhand) in the 1940s. This Janus-faced sense, though only made explicit at the novel's end, suffuses it from the beginning, as seen in the dual valence of the novel's opening sentences: "Now they were starting. Finality ran through the train, an exhalation" (p. 3). Aldred and Helen have a shared experience of survival to bolster their relationship; even at the beginning, their love is not stereotypical young love, but love that has traversed discord and sustained itself through a catastrophe.

The pent-up demand for a new Hazzard novel combined with the perceived excellence of the book to garner overwhelmingly positive reviews on its appearance in 2003. One of the few exceptions was John Banville in the *New York Times Book Review,* who accused the book of "mannered haughtiness" (p. 7). In the *Atlantic,* the distinguished novelist Thomas Mallon praised Hazzard's "precise lyricism and emotional microscopy" yet stressed that Hazzard's vision was "global and historical" (p. 156). Similarly appreciative of Hazzard's skill on both the tactical and strategic level, an anonymous reviewer for the *Economist* observed that Hazzard's "descriptive powers are as muscular when depicting characters as they are with this uniquely shell-shocked era" (p. 7). Hazzard won the National Book Award in the United States in 2003, picked by a jury that included the novelists Jay Parini,

Antonya Nelson, Alice Elliot Dark, Peter Cameron, and Jean Thompson. The book also won, in 2004, Australia's most prestigious literary prize, the Miles Franklin Award, demonstrating not only an expanded definition of what Australian literature was but Hazzard's renewed acceptance from a homeland that a few years before had seemed to spurn her.

In interviews done around the time of the release of *The Great Fire*, Hazzard mentioned that she was working on another novel, but this had not appeared as of 2011. Hazzard continued to flourish as a staple of the New York literary scene, a figure who was common reference point for a broad sector of the literary and social world of the city. Her friends included (until her death in 2002) the writer and editor Anne Fremantle, her fellow expatriate the Australian novelist Kate Jennings, the Irish novelist Annabel Davis-Goff (who read from Hazzard's work at the Ninety-Second Street Y in April 2010), the poet and educator Ned O'Gorman, and the Georgetown University special collections librarian Nicholas Scheetz. She was widely admired by readers of many stripes—by academics and belletrists; by literary people and by readers in other disciplines; by audiences in America, Australia, and Britain. An international conference to be held in New York in fall 2012 and cosponsored by Columbia University and the New York Society Library was planned to demonstrate this respect proceeding from so many different quarters. Hazzard's sober regard for the world combined with her refusal to relinquish the claims of art to make her a writer of care and trenchancy matchless in her time. Though her work lacked the sheer length, and perhaps persistence, of a John Updike or a Philip Roth, in regard and influence she was their equal. As Jonathan Galassi, long associated with the publishing firm Farrar, Straus and Giroux and a noted translator, said for a 2010 catalog of the New York Society Library exhibition mounted to honor the literary work of Hazzard and Steegmuller:

> First, there is the utter beauty of her sentences, which carry within them an awareness of, an absorption in, the literary traditions that they honor and bring so vividly into the present. Then there is

the roundedness, the surprising presence, of her characters. She is an observer of preternatural acuteness, on whom nothing has been lost. What one feels always operating in Shirley's work is a distillation—of time and history, knowledge and experience—in the service of a vision that is redemptively tragic. Not only is she among the most intelligent of contemporary writers; she is also among the most humane, the most loving toward her characters and hence toward us, her readers.

(p. 8)

Selected Bibliography

WORKS OF SHIRLEY HAZZARD

NOVELS

The Evening of the Holiday. London: Macmillan, 1966; New York: Knopf, 1966.

The Bay of Noon. London: Macmillan, 1970; Boston: Little, Brown, 1970.

The Transit of Venus. London: Macmillan, 1980.

The Great Fire. New York: Farrar, Straus and Giroux, 2003; London: Virago, 2003.

SHORT STORY COLLECTIONS

Cliffs of Fall. New York: Knopf, 1963; London: Macmillan, 1963.

People in Glass Houses: Portraits from Organization Life. New York: Knopf, 1967; London and Melbourne: Macmillan, 1967.

NONFICTION

Defeat of an Ideal: A Study of the Self-Destruction of the United Nations. Boston: Little, Brown, 1973; London: Macmillan, 1973.

"We Need Silence to Find Out What We Think." *New York Times Book Review*, November 14, 1982, pp. 11, 28.

"Papyrology at Naples." *New Yorker*, August 29, 1983, pp. 79–83.

Coming of Age in Australia: 1984 Boyer Lectures. Sydney: ABC Enterprises for the Australian Broadcasting Corporation, 1985.

Countenance of Truth: The United Nations and the Waldheim Case. New York: Viking, 1990; London: Chatto & Windus, 1991.

The Ancient Shore: Dispatches from Naples. With Francis Steegmuller. Chicago: University of Chicago Press, 2008.

UNCOLLECTED STORIES

"Woollahra Road." *New Yorker*, April 8, 1961, pp. 58–62.

"Sir Cecil's Ride." *New Yorker*, June 17, 1974, pp. 28–35.

OTHER WORK

"Letter from Australia." *New Yorker*, January 3, 1977, p. 32–59.

"Bread and Circuses: Thought and Language in Decline." *Sydney Papers* 9, no. 4:28–35 (1997). (Speech delivered to the Sydney Institute, August 13, 1997.)

Introduction. In *The Portrait of Zélide.* By Geoffrey Scott. Reprint. London: Constable Press, 1997.

Greene on Capri: A Memoir. London: Virago, 2000; New York: Farrar, Straus and Giroux, 2000.

BIOGRAPHICAL AND CRITICAL STUDIES

BIBLIOGRAPHIES AND CONCORDANCES

Beston, John B. "A Bibliography of Shirley Hazzard." *World Literature Written in English* 20:236–254 (1981).

Scheick, William J. "A Bibliography of Writings by Shirley Hazzard." *Texas Studies in Literature and Language* 25:249–253 (1983).

STUDIES AND REVIEWS

Banville, John. "Venus in Transit." *New York Times Book Review,* October 12, 2003, p. 7.

Baym, Nina. "Artifice and Romance in Shirley Hazzard's Fiction." *Texas Studies in Literature and Language* 25:222–248 (1983).

Bird, Delys. "Text Production and Reception: Shirley Hazzard's *The Transit of Venus.*" *Westerly* 1:39–51 (March 1985).

Capone, Giovanna. "Shirley Hazzard: *Transit* and *The Bay of Noon.*" *Australian Literary Studies* 13, no. 2:172–183 (1987).

Colmer, John. "Patterns and Preoccupations of Love: The Novels of Shirley Hazzard." *Meanjin* 29:461–467 (1970).

———. "Shirley Hazzard's *The Transit of Venus.*" *Journal of Commonwealth Literature* 19, no. 1:10–21 (1984).

Dixon, Robert. "'Turning a Place into a Field': Shirley Hazzard's *The Great Fire* and Cold War Area Studies." In *Reading Across the Pacific: Australia–United States Intellectual Histories.* Edited by Nicholas Birns and Robert Dixon. Sydney: University of Sydney Press, 2010. Pp. 265–280.

Dyer, Geoff. "Written in the Stars." *New Statesman,* June 28, 2004, p. 54 (http://www.newstatesman.com/200406280046). (Review of *The Transit of Venus.*)

Evans, Trish. "Shirley's *Transit* Is a Rare Event." *Weekend Australian,* November 29–30, 1980, p. 13.

Galassi, Jonathan. "In Praise of Shirley Hazzard." In *Literary Lives: Shirley Hazzard and Francis Steegmuller.* Edited by Harriet Shapiro. New York: New York Society Library, 2010.

Garrett, Jan. "The Transits of Hazzard." *Look and Listen* 1, no. 4:36–39, 96 (November 1984).

Lehmann, Geoffrey. "The Novels of Shirley Hazzard: An Affirmation of Venus." *Quadrant* 25, no. 3:33–36 (March 1981).

Lehmann-Haupt, Christopher. "Books of *The Times*: Waldheim as a Symbol of the Flaws of the U.N." *New York Times*, April 19, 1990.

Mallon, Thomas. "Princess of Discrimination." *Atlantic,* November 2003, p. 156.

McClatchy, J. D. "Shirley Hazzard: The Art of Fiction No. 185." *Paris Review,* no. 173 (spring 2005). (Online at http://www.theparisreview.org/interviews/5505/the-art-of-fiction-no-185-shirley-hazzard.)

McDougall, Russell. "Beyond Humanism? The Black Drop of Shirley Hazzard's *The Transit of Venus.*" *Journal of Commonwealth Literature* 30, no. 2:119–133 (1995).

Moon, E. B. "Fate, Individual Action, and the Shape of Life in Shirley Hazzard's *The Transit of Venus.*" *Southerly* 43:332–344 (1983).

Moore, Susan. "Meaning and Value in Shirley Hazzard's *Transit of Venus.*" *Quadrant* 28, no. 5:75–79 (May 1984).

O'Brien, Kerry. "Shirley Hazzard's Rich and Varied Career." *The 7:30 Report,* Australian Broadcasting Corporation, June 23, 2005 (http://www.abc.net.au/7.30/content/2005/s1399427.htm). (Interview transcript.)

Olubas, Brigitta. "Rewriting the Past: Exploration and Discovery in *The Transit of Venus.*" *Australian Literary Studies* 15, no. 3:155–164 (May 1992).

———. "Anachronism, Ekphrasis, and the 'Shape of Time' in *The Great Fire.*" *Australian Literary Studies* 23, no. 3:279–289 (2008).

———. "Visual Art and Bourgeois Forms in Shirley Hazzard's Fiction." *Southerly* 68, no. 1:13–23 (2008).

———. "Shirley Hazzard's Australia: Belated Reading and Cultural Mobility." *Journal of the Association for the Study of Australian Literature.* 2010 Special Issue (http://www.nla.gov.au/openpublish/index.php/jasal/article/viewArticle/1509).

Pierce, Peter. "Conventions of Presence." *Meanjin* 40, no. 1:106–113 (1981).

Rutherford, Anna. "Mars Versus Venus: The Dialectics of Power in Shirley Hazzard's *The Transit of Venus.*" *Kunapipi* 18, nos. 2–3:309–327 (1996).

Sellick, Robert. "'Some Godlike Grammar': The Narrator in *The Transit of Venus.*" In *Aspects of Australian Fiction: Essays Presented to John Colmer.* Edited by Alan Brissenden. Nedlands, Australia: University of Western Australia Press, 1990. Pp. 87–96.

Shapiro, Harriet. *Literary Lives: Shirley Hazzard and Francis Steegmuller.* New York: New York Society Library, 2010.

Towers, Robert. "Period Fiction." *New York Review of Books,* May 15, 1980, pp. 32–36. (Review of *The Transit of Venus.*)

Twidale, K. M. "Discontinuous Narrative and Aspects of Love in Shirley Hazzard's Short Stories." *Journal of Commonwealth Literature* 26, no. 1:101–116 (1991).

Tyler, Anne. Review of *The Transit of Venus. New Republic,* January 26, 1980, pp. 29–30.

Veale, Scott. "New and Noteworthy Paperbacks." *New York Times Book Review,* July 4, 2004, p. 20.

Wieland, James. "'Antipodean Eyes': Ways of Seeing in Shirley Hazzard's *The Transit of Venus.*" *Kunapipi* 5, no. 2:36–49 (1983).

"Words of Love and War.&sdquo; *Economist,* October 30, 2003, p. 7.

Wyndham, Susan. "Hazzard Ahead." *Weekend Australian,* July 17–18, 1993, pp. 26–32.

ELSPETH HUXLEY

(1907—1997)

Joshua Grasso

THE STORY OF Elspeth Huxley's life runs parallel to the decline of British colonialism and the rise of a "postcolonial" society throughout many regions of the former empire. That she chose this very transformation as the subject for her greatest writing is no coincidence; having spent her formative years in Kenya, she was uniquely qualified to see both sides of the colonial struggle. Like many writers of colonial fiction, such as Rudyard Kipling, she was a woman of two worlds, able to think and speak indigenously. However, quite unlike these writers, she became less "English" as time went on, slowly distancing herself from official party lines or British snobbery. She was an enormously prolific writer; it is almost impossible to make a true assessment of her complete opus. However, a few works remain in print and give a fair approximation of the whole, works that stand out by their poetic insight and a clear, unsentimental view of African life. Any student of twentieth-century literature or postcolonial studies must inevitably come to grips with *The Flame Trees of Thika* (1959), which despite the vagaries of political fashion remains a vital document of colonial Africa. Through it we are able to understand the fragile balance of power that created castles out of sand, importing British culture to Kenya and ports beyond. As Huxley writes in *The Flame Trees of Thika*, "respect was the only protection available to Europeans who lived singly, or in scattered families, among thousands of Africans accustomed to constant warfare and armed with spears and poisoned arrows ... [once] challenged, it could be brushed aside like a spider's web" (p. 16).

LIFE AND WORKS

Elspeth Josceline Grant was born July 23, 1907, to Jos and Nellie Grant, who would soon be among the forefront of immigrants to settle British East Africa. Jos, more formally known as Josceline Charles Henry Grant, was a Scotsman of a somewhat quixotic nature, eternally chasing the next "get rich quick" scheme. After fighting in the Boer War, he invested in a diamond mine in Portuguese East Africa; the mine failed and his partner, one Lord ffrench (with two lowercase *f*s) absconded without paying his debt. According to family history, the mine only produced one "gem"—the wedding ring with which he proposed to Nellie. Nellie Grosvenor, from a well-established family (boasting many dukes of Westminster), was perhaps an unusual match for Jos: to his dreaminess, she brought level-headedness and a shrewd business sense. However, she complemented his ambition and wanderlust, and was more than willing to accompany him to Africa in the hopes of starting a lucrative coffee farm. Fearing the effects of the African wilderness on a young child, the parents traveled there alone, leaving young Elspeth in the care of family friends. The reality of turn-of-the-century Kenya is much as Huxley documented in her famous fictional memoir, *The Flame Trees of Thika* (1959): railways and settlements were scarce, and a famine had decimated many Kikuyu villages, making native labor difficult to find. After numerous delays the couple managed to begin laying the groundwork of the farm in May 1913. As C. S. Nicholls describes in her biography of Huxley,

> The temporary grass structure they lived in while the stone house went up was built in one block, with two bedrooms twelve feet by ten feet, a small bathroom between them and a sitting room of fourteen feet by ten feet ... The square outside walls were of papyrus lined with local grass. There was a steep pitched roof of Ithanga or swamp grass, real wooden doors and windows painted green, and a

stone-paved verandah ... The horses occupied grander quarters than did their human owners.

(p. 21)

Whether or not this was the career Nellie Grant bargained for, she made it her life's work and slowly, over the following years, established a working farm. She would remain here until 1965, when, along with many white settlers, she made the difficult journey back home.

In late December 1913, plans were made to bring six-year-old Elspeth to British East Africa. However much they longed for a reunion, the decision was fraught with peril; plague, malaria, smallpox, typhus, and scores of other diseases, many of them fatal, awaited the would-be settler. Nevertheless, Elspeth arrived on December 29 with her guardian, Daisy Learmonth; her governess; and a maid. Something of her first impressions can be gleaned from the opening of *The Flame Trees of Thika*, when the young narrator arrives in Thika with her mother: "I cannot characterize this [smell], nor compare it with any other, but it was the smell of travel in those days, in fact the smell of Africa—dry, peppery, rich and deep, with an undertone of native body smeared with fat and red ochre and giving out a ripe, partly rancid odour which nauseated some Europeans when they first encountered it but which I, for one, grew to enjoy" (p. 10). The welcome party must have been short, as the young couple was far too busy planting coffee bushes and learning to communicate with their Kikuyu servants. By Huxley's own admission, their family life was never close. Jos Grant, though always affectionate to his daughter, was often rambling on some business scheme or other, while Nellie remained on guard against sentimentalism and other forms of weakness. This left Elspeth on her own to amuse and educate herself; not surprisingly, she attached herself to many of the Kikuyu servants, such as Njombo, who exposed her to a uniquely African outlook. In particular, the stories and folklore captivated the youngster's imagination, offering her explanations of good and evil, life and death, and the balance between man and nature that were vastly different from those of the English.

Before Elspeth could receive a proper "English" education, preferably at a colonial boarding school, rumors of World War I emerged. As British East Africa was particularly vulnerable to German attack, nearly every male settler joined a local squadron and marched off to war. Jos was among these, joining the Fourth Battalion of the King's African Rifles, leaving Nellie, Elspeth, and a few neighboring farmers completely alone. The stress of this situation must have been telling on Nellie, who suddenly found herself acting the diverse roles of farmer, father, mother, and businesswoman. Elspeth was spared much of the confusion by short stays with family friends like John and Gertrude Hill-Williams in neighboring Molo. Elspeth was to remember this time fondly, fictionalizing the Hill-Williamses as the Crawfurds (in *Flame Trees*) and writing much of the family and the surrounding area. When she returned home with her mother a few months later, the domestic scene was busier—and perhaps more precarious—than ever. Servants were hard to find during the war, and matters of discipline harder to enforce without the presence of men about. Elspeth was sent off to a boarding school in Nairobi, while Nellie struggled in desperate isolation. Nothing of her boarding school experience is mentioned in *The Flame Trees of Thika,* which breaks off with mother and daughter returning resolutely to England.

With the war threatening to continue for some years, Nellie Grant did indeed decide to return to England, if only to further Elspeth's much-neglected education. Passage home was not easy to obtain, but last-minute luck seems to have decided their fate. As Nicholls writes, "One day in June [Nellie] got a wire to say that an insane woman who had been intended to go home ... had grown too mad to go, and she could have the two berths. The ship was leaving in two days. She dashed into Nairobi to arrange finance and tell Miss Seccombe [the director of Elspeth's school], then drove back to Chania Bridge so fast that the car shed both second gear and reverse" (p. 46). After a difficult voyage home beset with plague outbreaks they disembarked in England: Elspeth went to a respectable school (much to Nellie's relief) and Nellie threw herself headlong into the war effort. Shortly thereafter, Jos was wounded by an accidental grenade explosion and released from service, where he became a military attaché in Madrid. Nellie hastily moved there to be with Jos, leaving Elspeth behind yet again, where she witnessed Zeppelin raids by the Germans. Unbeknownst to Elspeth, her father had an affair in Madrid that further strained relations between Nellie and Jos (Nicholls, pp. 48–49). When the family reunited, even Elspeth could sense the growing distance, which is dutifully recorded in her sequel to *The Flame Trees of Thika, The Mottled Lizard* (1962).

Once the war ended in 1918, her parents were eager to return to Thika to see if anything of their farm remained (it had been entrusted to the care of Sammy, their Masai servant). Jos went first, soon writing home (if we can trust the opening pages of *The Mottled Lizard*) with the request: "Please bring shaving brush and windmill" (p. 1). Nellie left soon after, with Elspeth safely (or so they thought) enrolled at school in London. While the farm proved virtually intact, an unexpected piece of bad news came when Elspeth was expelled for betting on horses. The parents had to frantically hire a governess to escort her on the long voyage back to British East Africa. When this governess proved unacceptable, Nellie decided to take over her daughter's education herself, teaching her scraps of Latin, history, and Victorian literature. However, Elspeth's own interests ran more to contemporary poetry, as she recalls in *The Mottled Lizard*:

> I liked war poems the best, the more savage the better, and knew by heart most of Siegfried Sassoon's and many of Wilfrid Owen's and Robert Nichols'; and the gentle magic of Walter de la Mare worked as powerfully in the glare of the African bush as among the haunted shadows, moonlit orchards, and crepuscular churchyards that inspired his muse.
>
> (p. 99)

Not surprisingly, her first forays into writing occurred around this time—a journalistic account of a local hunt, an assignment that was originally intended for Nellie. Her mother casually offered it to Elspeth, who undertook it with great enthusiasm. The piece was soon published in the *East African Standard* under her pen name, "Bamboo." A version of this story appears in *The Mottled Lizard,* when she discovers her name and story in print: "The world changed immediately; the sun was generous but not unkind, the flies bearable … the black clouds that had gathered over the Aberdares magnificent and awe-inspiring rather than an indication that I should get soaked on the way home" (p. 109).

Another coming-of-age moment occurring behind the scenes was the transformation of British East Africa into Kenya. This officially occurred on June 11, 1920, immediately transforming the colonial outpost into a political hotbed. The white settlers felt hemmed in by increasing numbers of Indian immigrants, as well as by the Africans themselves, who began to mobilize for greater representation. This caused numerous problems for the family, which Jos tried to settle in various ways: by entering local politics, trying to buy lucrative land in ever-more-remote regions, or gambling on new technology such as a recently invented coffee-drying machine. In the end none of this panned out, and the Grant marriage was strained to the breaking point. Nellie decided to establish her own farm and in deed, if not in word, affected a formal break with her husband. Though Huxley's African novels do not mention this as such, it is telling how little time "Robin" and "Tilly" spend together in *The Mottled Lizard*, and how often their plans and schemes contradict one another. As a teenager, of course, Elspeth had her own concerns, particularly her budding career as a writer. She was not only winning awards, but experimenting in tone and style; no longer content to mimic polo accounts she had read elsewhere, she was now diving into the history of the sport and showing a marked interest in the relationship of past and present. Though most of the newspapers preferred that she stick to the subject, her journalism is a tempting first glimpse of the novelist to come, perhaps the very reason she immortalizes it in *The Mottled Lizard.*

In 1924, when Elspeth was seventeen, Nellie enrolled her in Nairobi High School to enable her application to Cambridge. Nellie now lived entirely at her new farm in Njoro (far northwest of Thika), while Elspeth divided her time between school and helping her father. With Jos often absent or trying to sell the farm (which he, too, had lost interest in), Elspeth was forced to become much more self-dependent than the average seventeen-year-old. Besides spending time among her Kikuyu acquaintances, she also met Karen Blixen, the author of *Out of Africa* (1937, written under the pen name Isak Dinesen), whose own fiction would mirror many of the same themes and locales as Elspeth's. Though this life would offer her an endless store of anecdotes and impressions, her schoolwork was less inspirational; she failed her Latin exams and was not accepted at Cambridge. Setting her sights somewhat lower, she got into Reading College's agriculture program. As C. S. Nicholls remarks, "Although Elspeth would be best known for her writings on Africa, as a young woman she was excessively impatient to get away. The world beckoned, she answered the call, and she never returned to live permanently in the continent of her childhood" (p. 81). Despite the need for all young people to see the world, Huxley's decision may have also been prompted by her instincts as a writer. Like Kipling, who wrote the majority of his Indian works (including the 1901 novel *Kim*) only after leaving India, Huxley needed physical and emotional distance to truly "see" the world of her past.

As might have been expected, Huxley soon found both Reading College and her course of study disappointing. She did manage to gain a diploma in 1926, though, as Nicholls points out, only "on condition that she completed her fieldwork. The university's archives are silent as to whether she fulfilled this obligation" (p. 83). Instead of returning home to apply her degree, Huxley made the astonishing decision to go to the United States to study at Cornell (a trip funded by her aunt, much to her mother's chagrin). Her experience at Cornell was much the same as at Reading and her studies ultimately floundered. That said, she made friends easily and had an active social life, a life documented in some detail in her third fictionalized "memoir," *Love Among the Daughters* (1968). Apparently

she still had no interest in returning to Kenya, perhaps sensing the proximity of her future career—though writing as such was not foremost on her thoughts.

With her student visa expired and extremely short of money, Elspeth Grant returned to England in 1928 fully intending to regroup and make another go at America. Having been raised in a British colony, she never became entirely comfortable with life in the mother country, particularly the stuffy traditions and lack of opportunity; America, in the midst of the Jazz Age, seemed like the proper milieu for an artist. She ultimately found work with the Empire Marketing Board, an advertising company that specialized in Commonwealth products. She began writing pamphlets for the company, which spurred her on to more ambitious articles for local and international papers. However, the most notable occurrence for her in this period was meeting her future spouse, Gervas Huxley, head of the company's publicity committee. Gervas, whose cousin was the more famous Aldous Huxley, had recently fought in World War I, and the experience so traumatized him that he abandoned his studies at Oxford (which had been interrupted in 1914). Recently divorced, Gervas was a perfect match for Elspeth: urbane, good-looking, and, like her father, an active man anxious to see the world. After a brief courtship they married on December 31, 1931, and honeymooned in Cornwall. As they worked in the same department, it was understood that one of them would have to abandon their duties at the Empire Marketing Board. Gervas used his connections to find work at the Ceylon Tea Board, a lucrative post that allowed Elspeth to quit Empire to pursue writing in earnest.

Her first project was a peculiar one for a writer wishing to establish herself: she asked to write the biography of the recently deceased Hugh Cholmondeley, Baron Delamere (1870–1931), the de facto leader of the European settlers in Kenya and an old family friend. Her wish granted, she traveled home to begin her research, staying away from Gervas for long periods of time (as she frequently would whenever she researched a book—often to his annoyance). Her first book is a touchstone to the woman she was and to the writer she would soon become. Titled *White Man's Country: Lord Delamere and the Making of Kenya* (1935), the work extensively maps out not only Delamere's character but the political and social realities of Kenya, both of which she knew firsthand. At this time Huxley was very procolonialist and believed that Africa could never be ruled without English guidance. This stance attracted many negative reviews from more progressive critics, yet the general consensus was positive; she had not only produced a well-written book but had offered a complex—if ultimately, sympathetic—portrait of the colonial world. In later years Huxley would retract many of the sentiments expressed in *White Man's Country*; in a 1968 reprint of the book, she felt she needed to remind readers of the beliefs of that earlier time, in which "the land to which Delamere came was, by European standards, wholly primitive … Europeans were civilised, Africans were not; *ergo*, the European incursion that carried with it Christianity, literacy, the *pax Britannica* and an end to famines and epidemics could be nothing but a boon to Africans" (Nicholls, p. 112). It is apparent that the more she lived and wrote through her memories of Africa, the less she saw Africa as "primitive" and the promise of colonialism as a "boon." Indeed, with every new book the destructive power of colonialism increased for her, further affecting the way she remembered her childhood environment.

Committed to the world of letters, Huxley traveled the world looking for new ideas and subjects. In the 1930s she toured throughout America (both with and without Gervas), in particular studying the Dust Bowl conditions of the Great Plains. A series of articles resulted from this trip, but nothing as substantial as a book. Perhaps sensing where her true interests lie, she spent time with her parents in Kenya and renewed her link with the Kikuyu. The initial result of these visits was two mystery novels set among the lands and people she knew: *Murder at Government House* (1937) and *Murder on Safari* (1938). These books are her first attempt to fictionalize the world of her childhood, and they

proved successful enough to launch her career. Following close on their heels was a more ambitious work that provides the greatest link to her more mature, lasting fiction: *Red Strangers* (1939) would be her first book about the Kikuyu, ambitiously written from their point of view. The book follows three brothers whose lives are the lives of all Africans confronting the transforming and destructive powers of colonialism. Surprisingly for such an early book, Huxley is critical of Christianity and sympathetic to the language, customs, and ceremonies of the Kikuyu, even devoting a famous passage to female circumcision (which her publisher demanded be removed for squeamish readers; she refused, prompting a change of publisher). Writing from the Kikuyu perspective was a tremendous artistic challenge, and to prepare for it, she took a course in anthropology taught by the celebrated professor Bronislaw Malinowski at the London School of Economics. Coincidentally, one of her classmates was the future president of Kenya himself, Jomo Kenyatta, a member of the Kikuyu tribe. The pressure of writing the work expressed itself in her private letters, notably one to Gervas where she admits, "I believe there *is* a really good book there—I am still in a complete fog as to how it is to be handled, but a lot of nebulous ideas are beginning to float about … I can't hope to get a real insight into the native mind" (Nicholls, p. 127). As with all her novels, Huxley worked largely by intuition and inspiration, refusing to make a detailed plan and revising substantially as she went along.

Despite her fear, *Red Strangers* found almost universal approval from critics, not the least for its novel subject matter. Clearly Huxley had found her voice as a writer as well as her lifelong subject. For the next fifty years, with minor variations, all of her books would embellish these familiar themes of African life. As she established herself as a writer, so, too, did she settle down to middle-class respectability. The couple purchased Woodfolds, a seventeenth-century farmhouse not far from London, and began to concentrate on farming and domestic pursuits—chief among these the birth of her only son, Charles, on February 13, 1944. Huxley also found an outlet for her talents with the British Broadcasting Corporation, which engaged her for broadcasts as diverse as "Mud and Flood: The Mississippi, Friend or Enemy?" (1938) to "A Boy's Life in Kenya" (1939). To many listeners, Huxley was becoming the voice of the colonial world, though she was still thought to represent the more conservative, pre–World War II point of view.

In the 1950s Huxley wrote less and less fiction, becoming increasingly interested in the fate of Kenya, which was experiencing severe growing pains. In the late 1940s, a movement among the Kikuyu terrorized the white settlers throughout Kenya; this movement, called the "Mau Mau" (the true origin and meaning of the name is unknown) was formed to put a violent end to the European presence in Kenya. The Mau Mau organized themselves into loose gangs that pillaged farms and executed both whites and Kikuyu alike (chiefly those Kikuyu who refused to take the Mau Mau oath of allegiance). Huxley followed this rebellion from England with extreme interest and fear, especially since Nellie was hemmed in by insurgents on every side. In her nonfiction of the period, consisting of *Four Guineas* (1954), *Kenya Today* (1954), and *What Are Trustee Nations?* (1955), she predicted a grim fate for the Africa envisioned by Mau Mau supporters such as Kenyatta, whom she considered more or less responsible for the movement. While she believed Europeans often destroyed the very paradise they hoped to inhabit, she also thought it unlikely that Africans, once given back their homeland, would restore it to its pristine glory. Such views made her seem even more reactionary to liberal and postcolonial critics, yet she spoke from no political or theoretical cul de sac. In her view, as Nicholls explains, "If the white farmers, with capital and access to modern knowledge and techniques, had failed to farm profitably in places like Kenya, black farmers would be no different" (p. 257).

Huxley's trips to Africa reminded her how quickly the old world was passing away. Her father, Jos, died on April 12, 1949, after years of deteriorating health and mental abilities. Her mother, too, felt less in control of her farm, especially as many of the workers were secretly Mau Mau. Nevertheless, Nellie Grant remained committed to living in Kenya, despite Huxley's desperate pleas for her mother to move closer to the family in England. Yet this stubbornness proved fortuitous, since Nellie remained a living link to Huxley's childhood home. She and Nellie had often discussed Karen Blixen's *Out of Africa,* which discussed people and situations that Nellie knew firsthand. Both were dissatisfied with the novel and had often discussed writing their own collaborative work on the area. Though this never came to pass, it undoubtedly led Huxley to contemplate a book on her childhood that could resurrect the people and landscape of that seemingly distant time. The book, written at the very end of the 1950s, became her greatest success, garnering praise from both England and America, with immediate talk of a sequel. Paradoxically, Nellie was somewhat lukewarm about the book, possibly for the same reasons she disliked *Out of Africa.* C. S. Nicholls records Nellie's response upon reading the manuscript, which centered on the exclamation that "I am NOT like Tilly" (p. 310). Despite fears by American publishers that the readership of the book—which centers on the colonial life in distant Africa—would be too provincial, it sold extremely well and made Huxley financially comfortable for the first time (all the more important as Gervas had lost his job with the Tea Board in 1952).

Her increased stature soon attracted the attention of heads of state, who invited her to become a member of a commission to decide the ultimate fate of Northern Rhodesia (which threatened to divide into three separate states: Zambia, Zimbabwe, and Malawi). She took this role quite seriously, and though the proceedings were mired with the expected posturing and red tape, her views on Africa's future benefited from the exercise. The result of the commission, the Monckton Report of 1960, was not wholly satisfactory for anyone involved, and it convinced her that "the British had to leave Africa, and that this had better happen sooner than later, to avoid black uprisings" (Nicholls, p. 325). The commission also inspired one of her most satirical novels, *The Merry Hippo* (1963), which gleefully mocked the colonial power dynamic with thinly veiled portraits of her peers.

The 1960s proved a traumatic time for Huxley personally, despite a number of important and innovative publications. Gervas' health steadily declined, making it difficult for her to travel or research new books. Nellie, too, was forced to confront the inevitable: Kenya was no longer a place for white landowners. A mass exodus of white farmers left for England, Australia, South Africa, and, strangely, Portugal, where Nellie decided to go (much to Huxley's dismay). Nellie left Kenya for good in 1965, losing a great deal of her former spirit and self-sufficiency. Huxley tried to assist her as well as she could, though she was also dealing with her son's teenage ennui; he had disappointed the family by not getting into Rugby, his father's school. Of course, none of this personal turmoil shows up in her fiction, particularly the follow-up to *The Flame Trees of Thika*, the remarkable, witty novel *The Mottled Lizard* (1962). This, along with two other African works, *Forks and Hope* (1964) and *A Man from Nowhere* (1964), prefaced a temporary break from her African obsession. Growing older, and perhaps feeling more distant from Africa than ever, she sought new projects in unfamiliar themes and locales.

A profound social conscience dominates her next books, which looked first in her own "backyard" for inspiration. A timely work, *Back Street New Worlds: A Look at Immigrants in Britain,* which appeared in 1964, sought to capture the stories and the feeling of being immigrants in a strange, new land (which was not so dissimilar to the experience of her own parents in Africa). As with her African fictions, the book stressed the difficulty of assimilating cultural viewpoints in such a small space; London might as well be Kenya in this instance. The same sentiments colored her next book, something of a departure for her, titled *Brave New Victuals* (1965). As the title suggests, she examined the means of modern food production—an inquiry that led her to become even more pessimistic about the fate of mankind. Having grown up in Africa and seen how everything feeds and is food for another, she continued to see mankind as

playing a mere part—and not the dominant one—on the world stage. As she remarked at the time, "Our earth is like an apple being eaten by maggots. The maggots increase by devouring the apple which then falls to pieces, hollow and empty. The maggots then die for lack of sustenance. The sun sees to the remains" (Nicholls, p. 369). Needless to say, these works enjoyed little popular success, though they added valuably to the critical debate on immigration and food production. As the 1960s continued, relations with her longtime publisher, Chatto & Windus, soured. Her chief editor there, Norah Smallwood, was herself losing ground in the company, and the young Turks at the firm understandably turned a skeptical view upon Huxley's social agenda.

In an attempt to make money and revitalize her career, Huxley traveled to Australia to write a work firmly in the travel-writing tradition. The result, *Their Shining Eldorado* (1967), was a commercial and critical disappointment, largely owing to Huxley's lack of interest in the subject. Perhaps as an antidote she returned to her own life to write the final installment of her memoir "trilogy," the sparkling novel *Love Among the Daughters* (1968), which fictionalizes her Jazz Age experiences in England and America. As if to show there was still some fight in the old dog yet, she horrified her publishers by suggesting the book be called "All Bitches Fight" (Nicholls, p. 390). The ultimate title was coined by her publishers and she accepted it, however much the original captures the true spirit of the work (and the woman herself). In some ways, this book was her last hurrah; she wrote no more important fiction after *Love Among the Daughters*, and turned increasingly to work that was ready-made: biographies, letters, and journals.

In 1971 Gervas, after a long illness, felt that his time had come. He asked his wife to help end his suffering, which is less shocking than it might seem, given that Huxley was a member of the Voluntary Euthanasia Society. He died on April 2, and even though she was well prepared for the blow, it took a tremendous toll. Within a few years Nellie showed signs of the end as well. Though she doggedly refused to leave Portugal, she could no longer walk or take care of herself. Huxley went to Portugal herself to arrange long-term care for her mother. Before she could leave her mother fell into a coma and died in Lisbon on August 21, 1977. Needless to say, this double tragedy impaired Huxley's creative faculties and left her casting for subjects to engage her—no doubt simply to occupy her mind. This may be why her next projects are all biographies of legendary figures: *Florence Nightingale* (1975), *Scott of the Antarctic* (1977), and *Livingstone and His African Journeys* (1974). A more personal touch came when she went through Nellie's letters and saw in them a narrative not dissimilar to her own African fictions. In 1979 she published a work that must have renewed her spirit, *Nellie: Letters from Africa*. This laid the groundwork for her final works on Africa, most notably the travel-memoir *Out in the Midday Sun* (1985), which was a final, glorious return to the world of the "flame trees."

Huxley wrote to the very end of her life, which astonishingly came only in 1997. Toward the end she toyed with putting writing aside, even in 1992 writing to her publisher point-blank: "I don't think I'll try any more scribbles" (Nicholls, p. 451). However, a final trip to Kenya in 1995 may have inspired her creative juices, because in 1996 she was busy writing a new crime story to be called "The Black Prince Murders." However, a diagnosis of terminal liver cancer intervened; Huxley was confined to a hospital and a daily round of pain medication, and the book remained unfinished. She died on January 10, 1997. Her obituary notices singled her out chiefly as the writer of *The Flame Trees of Thika*, which perhaps more than any other book she wrote encapsulates the power of her writing and the range of her astonishing life.

TWO AFRICAN "MEMOIRS": THE FLAME TREES OF THIKA AND THE MOTTLED LIZARD

Written when Huxley had already established a prolific career as a writer, *The Flame Trees of Thika* (1959) was her first truly autobiographical novel. However, one can easily make too much of the work's subtitle, *Memories of an African*

Childhood. The work is not a memoir per se, nor did she intend it as such. The idea of calling the work a memoir came from her publisher, Norah Smallwood, who upon reading the manuscript immediately referred to it as an autobiography. Huxley objected that the work only covered a very short span of her life, and even though she was the ostensible narrator, much had been invented in the interest of fiction. Smallwood persuaded her to at least accept the subtitle, which placed it in the realm of autobiography without giving up its status as a novel. Huxley reluctantly agreed, and thus the work, originally titled "The Vertical Rays of the Sun," became *The Flame Trees of Thika* (thought to be a more evocative title). The published work quickly became Huxley's most successful book, winning praise in both Britain and America, which led to numerous editions and a six-part miniseries by the BBC in 1981. In 2011 the book remained in print as part of the Penguin Classics series. It seems in this case her publisher was right: the public clearly responded to a beautifully written, nostalgic yet realistic memoir of a young girl's coming-of-age in colonial Africa.

Anyone remotely familiar with Huxley's life will notice some small variations in character and chronology, most notably in the names of her parents, which appear in the book as Robin and Tilly. Though all the main points of her early biography are signposted, the work is primarily impressionistic rather than plot-driven. Specific dates fall away, and a clear transition between this and that event is not attempted. Also fictional is the novel's point of view: that of young Elspeth herself, a proverbial fly on the wall, narrating colonial Africa through the fragmented perspective of childhood. Huxley plays fast and loose with these memories, often reconstructing adult conversations on extramarital affairs and colonial politics, which the future writer could have scarcely overheard. As C. S. Nicholls writes, the author wanted a book about Africa "without too much fact intruding, as real life all too often lacks narrative drive, proceeding as it does in inconsequent fits and starts between periods of monotony. But to establish a believable fiction, certain incidents would have to have a little of the truth in them" (p. 304). Clearly, *The Flame Trees of Thika* is a not a modernist experiment in voice, but an adult's nuanced reflection of the joys, pains, and confusions of growing up between two worlds, especially as both worlds were rapidly disappearing.

In other works, Huxley had attempted to answer the question of "what now?" with Kenya and colonial Africa in general. Perhaps her most definitive answer is to be found in this novel, which had come a long way from her first work, *White Man's Country*, in defending the claims of Anglo-Africans. Yet even here, Huxley focuses on the inner lives of the settlers, allowing her readers to sympathize with their daily struggles in a beautiful but unforgiving environment. One of the primary themes of the work is the Englishman and -woman's faith in the power of work and civilization. Even Thika, a middle-of-nowhere wilderness miles from the nearest railway, is envisioned as a prosperous future suburb of Nairobi. The narrator's father is more or less swindled into buying unpromising land in the hopes of starting a lucrative coffee farm. While both he and his wife quickly learn the reality of their situation, neither is willing to admit defeat. With a little work, they assure themselves, civilization will take its course. Robin's first act is, quite sensibly, to build a house; but the workers are puzzled by Robin's plans, as they disregard every common-sense notion of African house-building. Njombo, who becomes their most faithful servant, trembles at the thought of building a rectangular house, since "goodness knows how many evil spirits would not find shelter in a house with corners. He had been as far as Thika and had therefore seen the Indians' houses, which were rectangular ... but he had never been asked to take part in the actual building of such a monstrosity" (p. 36). He ultimately decides to humor the Englishman, although he stops short at building with nails, which seem wasteful and extravagant. The compromise proves a sound one: the house is still standing when the family abandons the farm fifteen years later.

Throughout the novel, the narrator slyly captures the colonists' inability to see Africa in its native light. Having created the abstract no-tion of "Kenya," the English insist on seeing its native population as "Kenyans," rather than as Kikuyu, or Masai, or Dorobo. Even worse, they expect the Africans to conform to their own notions of discipline, time, and property—again, all abstract notions that mean little to nothing to the average Kikuyu. As the narrator learns, the native tribes abide by their own laws and moral codes, but they feel the Europeans are another species entirely; therefore, European property is viewed as "exempt from ordinary laws; it sprang up like grass after rain, and for a Kikuyu to help himself was no more robbery than to take the honey from wild bees" (p. 83). While Robin and Tilly struggle to understand the natives' behavior, Elspeth is transformed by her surroundings, identifying more and more with Njombo and his magical stories. Indeed, the Kikuyu are reluctant to share their stories or magic with Europeans, yet Njombo (among others) takes the child under his wing. Before long, she begins to question the reality of English order, fascinated by the possibility of

a third world [which] lay beyond, inside and intermingled with the two worlds I already knew of, those of ourselves and of the Kiyuku: a world of snakes and rainbows, of ghosts and spirits, of monster and charms, a world that had its own laws and for the most part led its own life, but now and again, like a rock jutting up through earth and vegetation, protruded into ours, and was there all the time under the surface. It was a world in which I was a foreigner, but the Kiyuku were at home.

(pp. 191–192)

As she grows older, she finds herself increasingly aware of this "third world," a reality her parents cannot see even though they are unwittingly ruled by it.

Despite the colonists' notions of cultural superiority, the old African ways remain and prove surprisingly resistant to "civilization." This is clearly revealed when Njombo falls sick as a result of a "spell" cast by another worker, Sammy. Though Njombo has no clear illness and is given every possible medication, he declines day by day until it seems death is inevitable. This is a terrible blow to the family, as it threatens to take away not only their most valuable servant but "their faith in European medicine, which they had believed fully a match for heathen superstition or toxicology" (pp. 140–141). The world of "monsters and charms," however ludicrous to Robin and Tilly, cannot be reasoned away or inoculated against. The spirits and magic of the Kikuyu are real and present in Thika and must be dealt with on their own terms. They finally arrange to have Sammy remove the spell (which takes a fair bit of negotiation, as magic is a taboo subject among Europeans), at which point Njombo miraculously recovers. Increasingly from this point on, the narrator's parents—and Tilly, especially—attempt to master the language, customs, and common sense of their adopted land. This is understandably rare among their fellow settlers, who have come to Kenya to teach—not to be taught superstition or native witchcraft.

The question as to why they *are* here is dramatically (and perhaps, somewhat fictionally) caught by the young Elspeth as she listens to her parents in a lazy afternoon conversation with their neighbors, the Palmers, and another young farmer, Alec Wilson. The Palmers form the most interesting counterpoint to Robin and Tilly, as Hereward is a by-the-numbers military man, while his young wife, Lettice, is a divorced Romantic indifferent to colonial society. While discussing whether or not Lettice is quite suited for a prolonged safari, Tilly observes that all women, even the most delicate, must adapt themselves to the demands of Africa. Her husband is taken aback by this statement, remarking, "I have no wish for my wife to be a savage ... There is no need for the womenfolk to concern themselves with such things" (p. 119). For most settlers, their wives are to be museum pieces from England, carefully preserving the social niceties that distinguish English womanliness. Even Lettice mocks this paternal attitude, asking if one day African women will be expected to practice "water-colour sketches and German *Lieder*?" (p. 120). Robin, with more than a touch of misogyny, claims African women are unsuited for the refinements of civilization. Indeed, while many Kikuyu men are brought into the familial fold, women remain a complete blank, noted only when they

are married or deceased. His response upsets Tilly (hinting at a marital discord that mirrors the true nature of their relationship), prompting her to make a grand, almost Kiplingesque, statement:

"Surely that's the whole point of our being here ... We may have a sticky passage ourselves, but when we've knocked a bit of civilization into them, all this dirt and disease and superstition will go and they'll live like decent people for the first time in their history." Tilly looked quite flushed and excited when she said this, as if it was something dear to her heart.

(p. 120)

That this is "dear to her heart" reveals the journey Tilly has taken in her relatively short time in Thika. Initially disappointed by Robin's business blunder, she has become a true exponent of colonization as a grand project of human evolution. Her bitter disappointment has been replaced by her faith in her work, which allows her to escape the drudgeries of her sex for a truly "masculine" ideal. In Africa, she seems to say, women can work and change the world alongside men, doing the same jobs and enduring the same difficulties. This certainly echoes the career of Nellie, who almost single-handedly ran the farm once Robin lost interest and became embroiled in ill-fated business ventures. Naturally, the men do not share her idealism, with Alec Wilson responding, "That is not the point of *my* being here ... I came to escape the slavery one has at home if one doesn't inherit anything. I mean to make a fortune if I can. If that helps to civilize anyone I shall be delighted, but surprised" (p. 120). The natives are there, certainly, but only as a means to an end—that end being the true business of colonization, to make money. However, Alec touches on a crucial similarity with Tilly: he means to escape from the "slavery" of home. Everyone here is either poor, restless, Romantic, ambitious, disgraced, or otherwise unsuited to a "proper" English existence. Though all look at Africa through English spectacles, none of them have a return ticket home. They are here to find a new life and hide in the most exotic locale an Englishman or woman could think of. Africa loomed large in the cultural psyche, either in Rider Haggard's cartoonish exploits or in the more realistic journeys of Mary Kingsley. They came to the last place they hoped to find English civilization (as Africa was, in their minds, the antithesis of English order and commercialism); however, colonialism always followed one step behind them, destroying what made Africa "exotic."

The Flame Trees of Thika also separates itself from other colonial fictions by focusing almost exclusively on the story's wives and daughters. The men frequently disappear in the narrative, as they are out on safari, following up on business leads, or fighting in wars. Ultimately the business of making it in Africa falls to the women, under whose guidance the family farm stands or falls. This is certainly the case with Tilly, who emerges as the work's true hero. It is Tilly who nurses the sick, maintains order, oversees the crops, and educates her daughter. This is also the most biographical aspect of the book, since Tilly is an affectionate portrait of Nellie, who becomes more or less abandoned by her husband's caprices. Perhaps one of the most telling points is in how the narrator describes her mother's disgust with "emotional" women, such as Lettice. As she writes, emotion

> was a word of condemnation, because Tilly was a devotee of reason; she came of a Liberal family and believed that powers of intellect should prevail. In fact, no one was a greater victim of emotions, at least of the more generous kind, but she felt that to give way to them was rather disgraceful, and hoped by frowning upon them ... to drive them away.
>
> (p. 71)

Tilly instinctively realized that in Africa a woman was either forging a new life or pining for home. Unwilling to fall prey to regret or homesickness, she decided to become the "man" her husband could not, and in a sense, both father and mother to Elspeth. This sets her apart from most of the other wives in the book, as she was becoming Kenya's version of the new woman; indeed, in real life, Nellie Grant was often addressed by the Kikuyu as "Bwana Memsahib" or "sir madam" for her audacious authority (Nicholls, p. 23).

While Tilly finds meaning in her work, other wives, such as Lettice Palmer, are not so fortunate. Lettice has no illusions about a new world or the triumph of reason. Her relationship with Hereward fading, she seeks another man to rescue her from this colonial backwater. However, Lettice is another remarkable creation, in her own way bold and unconventional. She does not share her husband's haughty colonialism and delights in provoking him, particularly in matters of race. In one instance, when Hereward wants to shield the "ladies" from a crowd of seminaked Kikuyu, she remarks, "Nakedness doesn't seem to matter when people are black or brown ... White bodies look like clay waiting to go into a kiln. Natives look as if they've been fired and finished; perhaps that's why they don't strike one as indecent" (p. 117). Though she can never be Tilly, she also isn't terribly interested in being the dutiful colonial wife, the role expected of her by Hereward and Thika society.

Lettice begins an ardent flirtation with Ian Crawfurd, a local farmer, and she notes to Tilly that "when other people commit [sins], you are startled, but when you commit them yourself, they seem quite natural" (p. 123). However, as a woman who has already fled from society, she realizes she has nowhere else to go. Either because she wishes to protect Hereward from scandal, or because war overtakes Africa as it does the rest of Europe, she decides against "sinning." Ian later dies in the war, and Lettice, brokenhearted, resigns herself to her fate. However, on the eve of Lettice's departure from Kenya, she tells Elspeth, "I don't belong here, it is a cruel country that will take the heart out of your breast and grind it into powder, powdered stone. And no one will mind, that is the worst of it. No one will mind" (p. 264). Progress is made, the land is tamed, but women like Lettice are left behind, unknown even to their own husbands. Sadly, she can only confide in a young girl who is only beginning to understand the incredible longing and loneliness of the colonial housewife.

By 1959, when the book was published, Huxley's views on Africa and colonization had matured dramatically. Where once she had defended the colonists' right to be part of a modern Africa, she now demurred, feeling that Africa was best left to Africans. Without making a grand show of this, the novel allows us to see the essential harmony of the African world and the inability of colonists to modernize it in any practical way. A beautiful explanation of this occurs as Tilly is attempting to see Kupanya, the village chief, to force Sammy to remove Njombo's spell. The servants keep delaying her, making it quite clear that this is not her business; nevertheless, she insists and grudgingly sets the wheels in motion. She remarks that getting anything done here is "like walking on ice" (p. 154). The narrator takes this simile a step further:

> Sometimes, when Tilly made a cake, she let me use the beater, which had a red handle that you turned. The two arms of the beater whirled round independently and never touched, so that perhaps one arm never knew the other was there; yet they were there together, turned by the same handle, and the cake was mixed by both. I did not think of it at the time, but afterwards it struck me that this was rather how our two worlds revolved side by side.
>
> (p. 154)

Though both "arms" are turned by the same wheel (God, life, fate), they live in two different worlds, unable to truly meet or appreciate one another's work. Both could do good work in Africa, Huxley suggests, but there would never be a meeting of the minds as she once hoped, or which many of the colonists claimed was inevitable. The religion and customs of Africa were far older than the European culture, older than Christianity. For a handful of colonists to hope to uproot it within a few generations speaks to the hubris of colonization, as well as the tragic blindness of Western civilization.

As a child, the narrator is more at home in Africa than in England, which at this point is evoked chiefly through schoolbooks and lessons. While her parents struggle to translate the foreign culture around her, she grows up fluent in its language, customs, and ideas. Her depiction of Africa, while grounded in no comprehensive anthropological study, is therefore distinctive and authoritative (as much as a child can be authoritative). Thus, while young Elspeth can scarcely understand the reality of World War I, she can understand why the Kikuyu are so anxious to fight. It is not, as most assume, out of loyalty or identification with the British, but rather

the prospect of law and order being removed … All the men in their thirties are pulling their spears out of the thatch where they've been hidden, and telling frightful whoppers to the newly-circumcised about the Masai, who in fact always beat them, while the young lads are saying "Those old has-beens had no more fight in them than a chicken. But *now* you'll see something!"

(p. 255)

The narrator remarks several times how the warriors are desperate to take out their spears and be themselves again, a self that the colonists are all too keen to keep locked away in the shadows of history. Yet the Kikuyu (and other tribes) can only be Kikuyu, just as the English can never be truly African. The two arms churn the same flour but will never change places or become one nation.

We also glimpse Huxley's change of heart (or perhaps, reclarification of her views) when she reflects on the legacy of colonialism. This is all the more poignant as many settlers were leaving Africa in the 1950s and the way of life recorded in *The Flame Trees of Thika* would vanish entirely. However, the question remained: was the legacy of the settlers worthy of the incredible struggle and sacrifices made over successive generations? Though Huxley could write fondly of her childhood in Kenya, she could not ignore the impact on the people and the environment, both of which were casually exploited for short-term gain. Unlike the Kikuyu, the colonists never left the world as they found it; lands were torn up, animals were hunted into extinction, and Africans were indoctrinated with European ideas and culture. Toward the end of the book, Huxley recalls a painting of the Garden of Eden, showing man and nature living in perfect harmony. How different it was in Africa (particularly among the Dutch settlers, in this case), where a companion painting might have shown "Adam setting a trap, and Eve chewing a morsel of liver. The Dutch, of course, had rifles, and fingers that itched to press the triggers. This they did as soon as they had recovered from their astonishment. They shot a kongoni, and had a good meal" (p. 239). So many settlers came to Africa for its beauty and freedom; sadly, these qualities were vanishing generation by generation, until all that could be found was a dim reflection of Europe, which neither colonists nor Africans could enjoy.

Of course, in an age that no longer needs Englishmen and -women to speak for Africa, *The Flame Trees of Thika* might seem an anachronism. Huxley's colonial critiques are on target, but they are hardly sufficient compared to the works of Chinua Achebe or Ngugi wa Thiong'o. Perhaps this is exactly the point and, to some extent, the appeal of the work. Huxley was a writer with the talent and compassion to avoid propaganda. Whatever her views, they lie hidden in the fabric of the work itself. Readers could accuse her of being equally anticolonial and unfashionably English. Indeed, Smallwood initially found the work unsympathetic to the Kikuyu and urged Huxley to "highlight their endearing qualities—their gaiety, childishness, crinkly smiling faces, and their occasional flashes of simple wisdom" (Nicholls, p. 307). The quaint racism of this request must have amused Huxley, who wanted no such thing. The narrator understands and loves both sides of the cultural divide of colonial Africa, but at times can understand neither. She privately questions whether the Kikuyu really love her animals, and she laments the savage tortures they inflicts upon goats and cattle in the name of magic. At the same time, she paints the endless safaris and sport hunting of the colonists as a "civilized" form of torture, which more often than not ends up destroying the delicate balance of nature.

In a haunting passage, the narrator innocently asks Hereward Palmer why an animal needs to be moving to shoot it. Hereward gruffly tells her that she does not understand "the meaning of the word sport" (p. 124). This meaning is laid clear when, in the next paragraph, Hereward shoots a "running" duiker, which turns out to be pregnant. The young girl is forced to watch the Kikuyu skin the animal, removing "a perfect little baby duiker, its fur already on it, waiting to be born. Even its tiny feet, no larger than a finger nail, were perfectly formed … It lay there half-entangled in a slimy sac of tissue that the beater had torn aside, and looked so tragic that I burst into tears" (p. 125). Whether or not this is true autobiography, the memory haunts the adult nar-

rator so much that "every fleck of colour in that tremendous sky [was] branded on my mind so as to become as much a part of my existence as an eye or hand" (p. 128).

After the great success of *The Flame Trees of Thika*, many readers—and indeed, her publishers—expected a sequel. *The Mottled Lizard* followed only a few years later, in 1962, but quite unlike the previous volume, it covered a larger span of time and relied more on autobiography (understandably so, as the narrator is at a more critically aware age). The title is from Kipling's poem "The Watcher," whose message (that the "mottled lizard" knows more of the world than we do) provides a fitting commentary on colonial hubris in Africa. Unfortunately, Huxley's American publishers vetoed the title and allowed her to suggest an alternative one; in this case, she offered *On the Edge of the Rift*, which Nicholls suggests "had a triple meaning: it contained the name of the Rift Valley, where the book was set; it indicated the change from colonialism to nationalism; and denoted her own break from her African home" (p. 337). The book proved only a modest commercial success though it won extraordinary critical praise—this time even from Nellie, who is reported to have "howled" throughout (Nicholls, p. 337).

Perhaps what most separates *The Mottled Lizard* from its predecessor is the narrator's growing awareness as a character and a woman. Though she still remains largely behind the scenes, her presence affects the story more than in *The Flame Trees of Thika*. While there Huxley had to reconstruct her memories of childhood, filtering them through adult sensibilities; here the narrator is, practically speaking, an adult. As a young woman she was beginning to make the connections that would come to fruition in her later writings. Perhaps for this reason, *The Mottled Lizard* reads more autobiographically, as if certain passages were copied from a yellowed teenage notebook. This is most palpably felt at the beginning of the novel, when the narrator awakens to her first morning in Kenya:

> I think that if one lived to be a hundred, and watched the dawn break and the sun rise over the highveld of Africa every morning, one would never

tire of it, just as a sailor will always find delight in watching the sea. And indeed there is the same play of light, the same endless changing, forming and reforming of cloud and shadow, the same sense of the creation of the world before one's eyes.

(p. 8)

Having been away for so long, she can more clearly see the beauty and sublimity of the landscape. Yet this experience of beauty is tempered by an increasing awareness of the landscape's fragility. While talking with the wilderness-seeker Henry Oram, Robin remarks that he is the means of destroying the very wilderness he adores. Henry acknowledges this but responds, "One's got to civilize the country, and make a living for one's family ... Civilization's what we're here for—to tame the country, bring the natives up, build a new colony like they've done down south and in African. There's no finer thing" (pp. 56–57). These words ring curiously hollow considering that Henry—like so many settlers in Kenya—has fled from civilization like the plague. Henry ultimately consoles himself that "the last native [won't have] his pair of trousers" for another hundred years or more (p. 56). Yet the teenage narrator sees a different reality. Every animal of the field is the farmer's curse, every natural wonder is an impediment to civilization. As the narrator remarks, in less than forty years, "scarcely any [animals] would be left and ... like grain between grindstones, they would find no salvation" (p. 212).

Yet it is not just the natural world that excites her pity and admiration; the local tribes, still dismissed as so many "niggers" to the settlers, become her true mentors in the novel. As a child she glimpsed a strange, invisible world that lay between the night and day; upon her return, she continues to discern its existence in the tribes' language and customs. The English world she was born into is one of division: night and day, good and evil, breakfast, lunch, and supper. For the Kikuyu, she notes, "no one thread was isolated or finite. Everything flowed from something else, just as all springs and streamlets ultimately join a single river, and nothing was ever concluded ... There was no beginning and no end" (p. 193). Here is the dilemma of colonial Africa in a nutshell; how can a circle have

corners, or an entire land be owned by one person or nation? Of course, the Kikuyu perspective had no validity for the English, since they were not recognized as a legitimate culture; even Tilly felt that educating them was her pious duty, the infamous "white man's burden." Yet what would this education erase from the African soul? What visions and poetry would be lost forever, vanishing into the darkness? The title of the work, *The Mottled Lizard*, suggests that even the lizard beneath a rock sees a world far more mysterious than the collected wisdom of England. The narrator experiences this in the wilderness of Nyeri, where she feels completely out of her depth: "the tiny dikik, the prowling Dorobo, knew the meaning of each rustle, saw the cocoon under the leaf, but I, with my supposedly superior intelligence, blundered dully forward, blind and dumb" (p. 44).

This awareness allows her occasionally to mock the pretentions of English civilization as it attempts to "preserve" itself among the wilds of Kenya. When the local government passes decency laws to ensure that the less "civilized" tribes cover up properly, the result is straight farce: "the Kavirondo ... responded by wrapping the blankets around their heads, revealing to all that they were not circumcised" (p. 35). Another comedy of translation occurs when the Oram family stages a performance of *The Tempest* for the locals. Unfortunately, the Meru people had no word for shipwreck—much less for ship!— and the family's attempts to explain this concept betray the profound cultural divide:

the best that could be done to describe a ship was "a thing like a cart that travels on top of a great deal of water." Even then, for cart you had to use the Indian word *ghari*. If you stuck strictly to Meru, for cart you would have to say "a thing made of wood on top of things that are round like pots and roll like stones" ... The simple word shipwreck would then become something like: "the thing that travels on top of the water like the thing that made of wood on top of things that roll like stones broke, and the people inside it fell into the water," so it was probably that the Meru would gather only a hazy idea of the story.

(p. 63)

The Oram family understandably clings to the "bow" of civilization, which the ritual of

Shakespeare's poetry enacts. However, as Huxley suggests, this heritage is seen as a universal performance written in the very language of man. That Shakespeare's art might defy the linguistic and philosophical lens of another civilization is not seriously considered. Thus the Meru look on, puzzled and perhaps amused, but without the expected awareness of European superiority and knowledge.

Equally ridiculous are the newcomers to Kenya, such as the narrator's Cousin Hillary, an effete, fin-de-siécle type who sees the African climate as an embodiment of savage darkness. Inspecting Tilly and her daughter, he can only lament, "your mind has already retreated perhaps beyond recall, into a visceral abyss … And to think of this unfortunate, doomed child, condemned forever to the pit from which a few Greeks once clawed their way into the first pale sunlight of the intellect" (p. 126). Like many Europeans, Hillary is enchanted by the landscape and its people, making many forays to photograph crocodiles and village ceremonies; unfortunately, this is all done in the interest of African "Orientalism," which regards its subjects the way one might a rare species from the ocean's depths. As the narrator observes, "Europeans rarely questioned their own customs: what they did was right and civilized, what others did was savage and stupid. No doubt all people think like this about their own habits" (p. 135). What the "child" understands instinctively the educated scholar cannot. Hillary sees crudity where he might discern sophistication, exoticism instead of an epiphany of cultural awareness. He leaves Africa with his many suitcases full of pictures to publish and study, but without having seen anything of the actuality of Africa or its cultural richness. These he casually dismisses as barbarisms fit only to poison the wells of Athenian thought.

The attentive reader leaves *The Mottled Lizard* humbled by the beauty, richness, complexity, and ambiguity of Kenya. Though nostalgic, the portrait is not sentimental, nor is it "*Dances with Wolves*" in Kenya. The natives, though full of compassion and humor, are also (to the narrator) occasionally heartless and inscrutable. Yet she also realizes that to call a native anything—

whether kind, cruel, wise, despicable—is to do so in *English*. It is almost impossible for a Western observer to see Kenya as the Kikuyu, or the Meru, or the Dorobo do. We are not them, nor they us, and her novel can only reiterate the point through Huxley's unique poetry. When Tilly asks why the Kikuyu will not buy oranges (which grow abundantly in the area), she is given the response, "Why should we pay for these fruits which grow on trees, when we can send a boy to steal them at night?" (p. 27). When Tilly counters that the oranges have not been stolen, the speaker says that they only steal what has value. If the oranges were sold, they would suddenly be desirable, and instead of buying them, the Kikuyu would steal them. Tilly dismisses this as utterly ridiculous, which it is—from a European-colonial point of view. The narrator, of course, loves this anecdote for what it reveals of the mistranslation of African life. How can Tilly own the oranges that she grows and sells? Why should the Kikuyu pay for what nature offers in abundance, a gift that the Europeans, by their very presence, call possession, and the act of taking, stealing. Neither the terms nor the concepts translate; what passes for the "truth" exists as a fleeting observation caught in the shadows and smells of Huxley's Africa.

CRITICAL RESPONSES

Elspeth Huxley's works have shared the fate of many "colonial" artists as varied as Rudyard Kipling and Edward Elgar, whose achievements have been reduced to coarse jingoism or a nostalgic yearning for empire. Her most important books appeared at a critical time in British literature, when native voices were separating themselves from the colonial umbrella and loudly—often, violently—demanding independence. Despite the general commercial success that was enjoyed by books like *The Flame Trees of Thika* and *The Mottled Lizard*, a sense of disapproval hung over these works from the margins. In Joseph Muwanga's review of *The Mottled Lizard* in the journal *Transition*, he writes, "Mrs. Huxley knows what she is writing about. The only unfortunate thing is she gives the impression of being an enemy of change. She is not pleased with 20ᵗʰ century in Africa and with all that goes with it. She is more at home with the Empire Age" (pp. 52–53). This type of response to Huxley was increasingly typical in the late twentieth and early twenty-first centuries, though such a reading seems to be founded on nothing more than her perspective: a young girl (and then teenager) looking at these "changes" without political dogma. While the writer certainly had views on Africa's future, as an artist she was careful to distance these from the views of the narrator, whose experience of Africa was shaped by her surroundings, both colonial and indigenous alike. However, as African literature came into its own, questioning whether or not the English language could accurately represent African life, a work such as *The Flame Trees of Thika* could easily seem like the grossest anachronism.

Perhaps more harm than good came of the 1981 BBC production of *The Flame Trees of Thika*, which put Huxley back in the spotlight and won new fans to her somewhat-forgotten books. As a series the work is more or less faithful to the original, though the ambiguity of Huxley's text is softened, and certain characters, such as Tilly (played by Hayley Mills), become friendlier and less arch. Huxley personally visited the set and gave the production her blessing, though she was no doubt aware of the horrors of adapting a novel for the small screen. Though the series enjoyed great success in Britain and America, some read it as a blatant attempt to kindle nostalgia for the old empire. Indeed, the series followed close on the heels of the director's (John Hawkesworth) wildly successful BBC series *Upstairs, Downstairs,* which also evoked turn-of-the-century England with meticulous period detail. In Africa, such lavish attention to England's colonial past could only rankle. In 1990, the African writer Wole Soyinka published an article in *PMLA* that slighted both the series and Huxley's achievement:

> the government actually purchased the television version of Elspeth Huxley's *Flame Trees of Thika,* a beautifully written work by the way but one that even a school pupil will recognize as a sundowner

piece of colonial nostalgia, much in the current fashion of the film *Out of Africa,* on which so many millions of dollars were lavished to relieve the decadent, patronizing caress of Africa and Africans.

(p. 116)

Clearly, a modern Africa had no need to be reminded of colonial decadence, much less to celebrate a fashionable nostalgia for the "old days."

Only since very late in the twentieth century have critics returned to Huxley's work, slowly unearthing hearsay and propaganda from the actual tenor of the books. Only *The Flame Trees of Thika* remains in print, though other books, such as *Red Strangers, The Mottled Lizard,* and the mystery novels are widely available in various used editions. This lack of available texts makes it difficult to reevaluate Huxley's achievement and appreciate her alongside more available "African" texts such as *Out of Africa* or James Fox's *White Mischief* (1988). Thomas R. Knipp's 1990 essay, "Kenya's Literary Ladies and the Mythologizing of the White Highlands" is a thought-provoking assessment of Huxley's art. Knipp claims that *Flame Trees* is more realistic than works like *Out of Africa* because of Huxley's satire, which prevents the work from becoming too nostalgic or romantic. While he still finds a "white princess" (p. 4) enshrined at the heart of the book (the narrator herself), the essay forces us to reread the work in light of postcolonial scholarship and the history of modern Africa. Perhaps the greatest triumph for Huxley scholarship is C. S. Nicholl's magnificent biography of Elspeth Huxley, which explores the intricate relationships of her life, chiefly with her mother, Nellie; with her husband, Gervas; and with her longtime publisher, Norah Smallwood. Nicholl's biography is also the most comprehensive study of Huxley's writing, as everything from fiction, nonfiction, biography, and other occasional pieces are represented and discussed at length. Published in 2002, the biography forces those who have never (or would never) read Huxley to read against the grain of political correctness. If we judge an author for the sins of her culture, then what work or author or body of literature can we rescue from the ovens of critical disapproval?

Selected Bibliography

WORKS OF ELSPETH HUXLEY

NOVELS

Murder at Government House. London: Methuen, 1937.

Murder on Safari. London: Methuen, 1938.

Death of an Aryan. London: Methuen, 1939. Reprinted as *The African Poison Murders.* London: Dent, 1986.

Red Strangers. London: Chatto & Windus, 1939.

The Walled City. London: Chatto & Windus, 1948.

I Don't Mind if I Do. London: Chatto & Windus, 1950.

A Thing to Love. London: Chatto & Windus, 1954.

The Flame Trees of Thika. London: Chatto & Windus, 1959. Reprint. London: Penguin, 2000. (Quotations in text are from this Penguin Modern Classics edition.)

The Mottled Lizard. London: Chatto & Windus, 1962. U.S. edition published as *On the Edge of the Rift: Memories of Kenya.* New York: Morrow, 1962. (Quotations in text are from the Morrow edition.)

The Merry Hippo. London: Chatto & Windus, 1963.

A Man from Nowhere. London: Chatto & Windus, 1964.

Love Among the Daughters. London: Chatto & Windus, 1968.

NONFICTION AND BIOGRAPHY

White Man's Country: Lord Delamere and the Making of Kenya. 2 vols. London: Macmillan, 1935.

East Africa. London: Penns in the Rocks Press and William Collins, 1941.

Race and Politics in Kenya. With Margery Perham. London: Faber and Faber, 1944.

The Walled City. London: Chatto & Windus, 1948.

The Sorcerer's Apprentice. London: Chatto & Windus, 1948.

Four Guineas. London: Chatto & Windus, 1954.

Kenya Today. London: Lutterworth Press, 1954.

What Are Trustee Nations? London: Batchworth Press, 1955.

A New Earth. London: Chatto & Windus, 1960.

Back Street New Worlds: A Look at Immigrants in Britain. London: Chatto & Windus, 1964.

Forks and Hope. London: Chatto & Windus, 1964.

Brave New Victuals. London: Chatto & Windus, 1965.

Their Shining Eldorado. London: Chatto & Windus, 1967.

The Challenge of Africa. London: Aldus Books, 1971.

The Kingsleys: A Biographical Anthology. London: George Allen & Unwin, 1973.

Livingstone and His African Journeys. London: Weidenfeld & Nicolson, 1974.

Florence Nightingale. London: Weidenfeld & Nicolson, 1975.

Gallipot Eyes: A Wiltshire Diary. London: Weidenfeld & Nicolson, 1976.

Scott of the Antarctic. London: Weidenfeld & Nicolson, 1977.

Nellie: Letters from Africa. London: Weidenfeld & Nicolson, 1979.

Out in the Midday Sun. London: Chatto & Windus, 1985.

Nine Faces of Kenya. London: Collins Harvill, 1990.

Peter Scott: Painter and Naturalist. London: Faber and Faber, 1993.

MANUSCRIPTS AND CORRESPONDENCE

Huxley's manuscripts, correspondence, transcripts of interviews, and other personal documents are held at the Bodleian Library's Library of Commonwealth & African Studies at Rhodes House at the University of Oxford.

BIOGRAPHICAL AND CRITICAL STUDIES

BIOGRAPHY AND BIBLIOGRAPHY

Cross, Robert, and Michael Perkin. *Elspeth Huxley: A Bibliography.* Winchester, U.K.: St. Paul's Bibliographies, 1996.

Nicholls, C. S. *Elspeth Huxley.* New York: Thomas Dunne, 2003.

CRITICAL STUDIES AND REVIEWS

Blood, Hillary. "The Flame Trees of Thika." *African Affairs* 58, no. 232:260–261 (July 1959). (Review.)

Duder, C. J. D. "Love and the Lions: The Image of White Settlement in Kenya in Popular Fiction, 1919–1939." *African Affairs* 90, no. 360:427–438 (July 1991).

Knipp, Thomas R. "Kenya's Literary Ladies and the Mythologizing of the White Highlands." *South Atlantic Review* 55, no. 1:1–16 (January 1990).

Lassner, Phyllis. *Colonial Strangers: Women Writing the End of the British Empire.* New Brunswick, N.J.: Rutgers University Press, 2004.

Muwanga, Joseph. "A Point of View." *Transition*, nos. 6–7:52–53 (October 1962).

Shaw, Martin. *Colonial Inscriptions: Race, Sex, and Class in Kenya.* Minneapolis and London: University of Minnesota Press, 1995.

Soyinka, Wole. "Twice Bitten: The Fate of Africa's Culture Producers." *PMLA* 105, no.1:110–120 (January 1990). (Special issue: African and African American Literature.)

MARY LAVIN

(1912—1996)

Maureen Manier

EFFECTIVE SHORT STORIES re-create life's moments; they flash intense emotion, wrangle with strangling cultural mores, and pose lingering, sometimes haunting questions. The Irish short story writer Mary Lavin achieves this and much more in a canon that spans fifty years and provides vivid, powerful glimpses into the minds and hearts of her characters. Unlike many writers of her generation, her stories do not plunge into the stormy waters of Irish national identity. Her stories live in a world that is externally Irish but transcends time and place as they seek to reveal an understanding of what is universally human. Unlike many of her Irish contemporaries, her writing more closely resembles the Chekhovian model, in which, as the critic Richard Peterson writes, "nothing seems to happen but everything is revealed" (p. 387).

To reach that simple, often stunning message, Lavin would write hundreds of pages that included long, descriptive backstories for her characters. Then she would attack those pages with a kind of analytical intensity, until she had stripped the story to its most essential moments and words. Janet Dunleavy describes this approach as "economic, disciplined, compressed" (p. 149). Or, as V. S. Pritchett described Lavin, she was an artist "with the power to present the surface of life rapidly, but as a covering for something else" (quoted in Dunleavy, p. 147).

That "something else" is found in an array of deceptively familiar characters—mothers, daughters, sons, widows, and priests—living in predictable surroundings of Irish small towns or crowded Dublin row houses. Lavin never typed her manuscripts and suggested in an interview with the Irish poet Eavan Boland that her physical connection with writing impacted the final product: "The advantage was that, after a few drafts, I knew my characters with an incredible intimacy" (p. 143). Lavin told Boland that her characters, who might originally have autobiographical roots, grew during this process until, "they had, as it were, assumed a new life. They were newly born people" (p. 143).

As deceptively simple as the settings and circumstances of Lavin's stories and two novels might appear, there is nothing simple about the emotions stirring within her characters. Grieving widows contend with stark futures only occasionally lit with glimmers of possibilities. Young women and men strain against the restraints of family and social status to find their voice. Mothers who have devoted their lives and subsumed their own dreams toward raising their children deal with the reality of rejection, real or imagined, by those children. It is into these worlds that Lavin invites her readers.

MARY LAVIN'S PERSONAL JOURNEY

Mary Lavin's autobiographical footprints and influences are easily perceived in her stories and novels. Mary Josephine Lavin was born in Walpole, Massachusetts, on June 12, 1912, the only daughter of Tom and Nora Lavin, who were both natives of Ireland. Tom Lavin had left his home in Roscommon, Ireland, to work in Massachusetts for a wealthy American family. It was during a voyage back to visit Ireland that he met his future wife, Nora Mahon, who was returning from visiting an uncle who was a priest in the United States.

Nora Mahon Lavin's own circumstances would play a major role in Mary's developing worldview as well as in the perspectives of many of her characters. Nora's father was a middle-class merchant. As one of twelve children her own financial circumstances were not strong, but her attitude remained that of a member of the middle class. Her own experience in America left her anxious to return home. But having fallen in love with Tom Lavin on the boat returning to Ireland, she reluctantly returned to America three years later to marry him and live the next decade in a place she openly despised.

One of the aspects of her life in America that Nora most disliked repeatedly resurfaces as a theme in Mary Lavin's stories. Nora's own middle-class standing in Ireland made her contemptuous of the work her husband did as a horse groom, chauffer, and general caretaker of a wealthy American family's property. She undoubtedly discussed her feelings with her one and only child, with whom she forged a close if complicated bond during their time in America and the year they spent in Ireland living in the small Irish village of Athenry with Nora's parents before Tom's return. Although she was just ten when she moved to Ireland, Mary Lavin told Zack Bowen in an interview that "for years whenever I wrote a story, no matter what gave me the idea, I had to recast it in terms of that town" (p. 18).

Beset by her concern for outward appearances, Nora Lavin pressured Tom to send her the money to purchase a small home in Dublin. Soon after, Tom returned to his family in Ireland. But he was soon commuting between managing the country estate purchased by his American employer and spending time in Dublin with his wife and daughter. Despite their prolonged separation, it is clear that Tom and Mary shared a relationship that produced its share of stress with both of their relationships with Nora. They might not have been together often, but when they were their arguments often overwhelmed their daughter.

Living in Dublin meant that Lavin enrolled in the Loreto Convent school and began a more serious period in her education. She excelled in her studies and was captain of the debating team. At University College Dublin, she won first honors as an undergraduate and stayed to write a master's thesis on Jane Austen, which was accepted with honors in 1937. Lavin seemed destined to pursue a career in academics. She returned to her former school to teach French while working on a doctoral dissertation on Virginia Woolf. But while there she reconnected with her former classmate, William Walsh, a Dublin attorney, and they married in 1942.

During this period, as she moved from UCD to teaching French to marrying Walsh, Lavin also began to reconsider her academic pursuits. Her first short story, "Miss Holland," was published in 1938 in *Dublin Magazine*. Lavin later explained that as she was working on her dissertation on Woolf she began to wonder what Woolf might be doing or thinking at that very moment. And as she began to wonder, Lavin literally took the pages of her dissertation, turned them over, and began to write her own first short story about the internal longings and imaginings of Agnes Holland.

During her twelve-year marriage to Walsh, Lavin continued to write and be published; her three daughters were born between work on stories and novels. In 1943, the year that Lavin was awarded the James Trait Memorial Prize, her first daughter, Valentine, was born. Elizabeth was born in 1945, the same year as Lavin's first novel, *The House in Clewe Street*, was published. Lavin published the collections *The Becker Wives and Other Stories* in 1946 and *At Sallygap and Other Stories* in 1947. In 1950, her second novel, *Mary O'Grady*, was published. Her third daughter, Caroline, was born in 1953. With growing success as a writer and happy being a mother and wife living in the Abbey, a farm in County Meath that the couple had purchased with an inheritance left by Lavin's father, Lavin was devastated by the death of her husband in 1954.

The years that followed were challenging and overwhelming. Lavin had three children to raise and pressing financial issues, about which she worried her entire life. For the first five years, her productivity was significantly impaired. She received Guggenheim awards in 1959 and in 1960. The first fellowship inspired her to travel to Italy to work. But with three children running around hotels and pensions, she found she had little time to write. The next year she stayed in Ireland and finished the stories in *The Great Wave*

(1961) and *In the Middle of the Fields* (1967). These awards helped her to resume her career with the energy and determination she had lost in the wake of her husband's sudden death. In the decades after 1954, Lavin was awarded the Katherine Mansfield Prize (1961), the Ella Lynam Cabot Award (1971), the Eire Society of Boston Gold Medal (1974), the Gregory Medal (1975), and the Irish Foundation Literature Prize (1979).

As a first-year student at UCD, Lavin had befriended a young Australian student right off the boat who was studying to be a Jesuit priest. Michael Scott and Lavin became good friends during those years, but they had agreed his duty was to his religious order, and he returned to Australia to become ordained. After William Walsh's death, Scott was concerned about Mary Lavin's well-being and stayed in closer contact with her in the fifteen years that followed. In 1969, he applied for release from his vows. When it was granted, six months later, Scott and Lavin were married.

Scott and Lavin spent the next twenty-three years together, commuting between their home in Dublin and the Abby farm that Lavin had purchased so many years before. During these years, Lavin was awarded an honorary doctorate from University College Dublin and was elected Saoi by the members of Aosdana, an affiliation of creative artists in Ireland, for achieving singular and sustained distinction in literature. Scott died in 1991. Lavin died in a Dublin nursing home on March 25, 1996.

Lavin's personal journey is frequently reflected in the plots of her stories: young widowhood, conflict between city and country life, class struggles, financial woes, and even lingering ambivalence about priests and religion. But what unravels in these stories are also the universal quests that unite us beyond our circumstances with their "untidy powerful emotion," says Lavin (*Collected Stories*, p. xiii). What is happiness, and can it be found and kept? How do we define freedom, and how do we respond to lives dominated and constrained by circumstances and people? V. S. Pritchett compares Lavin's skill to that of Russian novelists and short story writers, saying, "She has the same animal eye for every-

day life, the same gift for immersing herself in people and not sacrificing the formlessness of their lives to the cleverness of a formal art. She feels too much to be adroit, anecdotal or outside" (in Mary Lavin, *Collected Stories*, p. xii).

LAVIN'S NOVELS

Lavin told Eavan Boland that in her early years of writing, "There just didn't seem to be any difference between cooking a dinner or writing a story" (*Writing Lives*, p. 142). For Lavin, the short story format often fit better with a busy life raising her daughters, first as a housewife and then as a young widow. But she did foray twice into the genre of novels, both times before the death of her first husband. Never happy with the product, Lavin later commented she thought the novels, *The House in Clewe Street* (1945) and *Mary O'Grady* (1950), were more like a group of short stories strung together, and she wished she had perfected each of those stories rather than place them in the longer format. What the novels do accomplish is exploring in more depth and detail two of the major themes that resound in so many Lavin stories: the social class system and the maternal search for familial happiness.

From the opening pages of *The House in Clewe Street* it is clear this novel will focus on the impact of social class clashes on the main characters. Theodore Coniffe, the family patriarch, expresses that impact in a tirade about ivy—a thinly cloaked metaphor for what might best be described as "class creep":

> Ivy! Ivy! The enemy of civilization! It should be uprooted and destroyed every time it ventures to show its head … I never pass a house upon which ivy has taken its grip without shuddering to think of the way that it is pushing its way between mortar and brick, penetrating every crevice, dislodging the very cornerstones of the house.
>
> (p. 13)

Theodore and his wife Katherine believe they represent those cornerstones in their small town—Katherine's own sense of status stemming from personal vanity, as conveyed succinctly early in the novel: "There are some women, and

Katherine Coniffe was one of them, in whom vanity is so great that it cannot be altogether condemned, since it is the pivot upon which their whole life turns" (p. 22). It is upon these perceptions of status and self-importance that a family tragedy that spans generations is built. "The sense of rigid social order is augmented by an intense awareness of social class as an irrevocable factor shaping the events of the novel," suggests Zack Bowen in his study of Lavin for the Bucknell University Irish Writers series (p. 64).

Early in the novel Katherine fears she is losing her youthful beauty only to discover she is pregnant at what she views as an embarrassingly late age. She is immediately more concerned about appearances than about her child's or her own health. When his wife dies in childbirth Theodore immediately decides to bring home his two older daughters, Theresa and Sara, from boarding school to care for their new baby sister, Lily, "thrusting them at once into the stiff costumes of adult responsibility" (*The House in Clewe Street*, p. 39).

When he meets Cornelius Galloway, Theodore decides that this young solicitor is an ideal suitor for one of his older daughters. He invites him to his home to meet Theresa and Sara and wages a campaign to close the deal. Unbeknownst to Theodore, Cornelius is completely acquiescent with his plan as he tries to discern what the status of a son-in-law would be in the Coniffe family. "Now Theodore, in resolving to throw all his weight into the task of obtaining Cornelius as a son-in-law, was like a man who, wishing to break his way through a door, musters all his strength together, laces his muscles, clenches his fists, tightens his lips, rises from the floor upon the balls of his feet, and, fixing his eyes upon the panels of the door, throws himself upon it with gigantic force, only to find that the door which he believed to be bolted had not been bolted at all" (p. 51).

The surprise to all concerned, however, is that Cornelius bursts through that door and proposes to Lily rather than her sisters. He had been prepared to sacrifice love for his ambitions by proposing to one of the older Coniffe women. But, as he observes, "it had been revealed to him

in a single moment that there were no sacrifices to make" (*The House in Clewe Street*, p. 69) Cornelius had been lightly flirting with the youngest sister when he realized that although young she was old enough to be the recipient of his more serious attentions. In that same moment her sister Sara also sees it, "Sara … seemed yet to see into the very heart of the change that had come over Lily" (p. 69).

Tragedy soon ensues, however, when, to Theodore's embarrassment, Cornelius is killed in a hunting accident, confirming, as one of the gentry says, that "a man must be bred to horses" (p. 99) In the span of a few short months, Lily finds and loses love—and more significantly for her family, she loses love in a humiliating way that questions their status. "The radiance that shone over Lily was gone. Indeed, it had shone about her so short a time it was almost as if it had never been" (p. 99). Lily gives birth to Cornelius's son, Gabriel. But even with the innocence and joy that Gabriel brings into his mother's and grandfather's lives, now only misery, disappointment, and a vague sense of humiliation pervade the Coniffe home. When Theodore dies, Theresa's reaction shows the exact depth of her own misery: "Father is much better off where he is, than ever he was in this life. Indeed we will all be better off when we are laid in our coffins. What is this world? Nothing!" (p. 146).

Gabriel eventually emerges in this novel as someone who questions the social standing that was so important to the Coniffes. In viewing a disfigured homeless woman, he speaks with a level of sympathy and even empathy unknown to his birth family. "To think of creatures like that cut off from birth from every phase of human happiness, doomed to spend the whole of their lives under conditions of miserable pain and humiliation. And yet they have done nothing, absolutely nothing to inherit such a fate" (p. 238).

When Lily dies, Gabriel feels "an incalculable change" come over his life (p. 249). Before his mother's death it was unlikely that he would have done anything to cause any kind of unrest in the Coniffe household for fear of its negative impact on his mother. But with her gone he suddenly feels the first hint of a freedom he has never felt before. He no longer views his future as inevitable. That freedom leads him to Omny, the young servant girl whom his aunt Theresa brings into the house to replace Mary Ellen, the family housekeeper and Gabriel's surrogate mother. Omny also represents something Gabriel had never experienced: she is carefree and, although close to her family, completely unfettered by their expectations. The two escape Clewe Street to Dublin.

The critic Marianne Koenig describes Omny as one of the book's achievements, in "her animal vitality, her spiritual crudeness, her cunning, her sure sense of her own identity" (p. 255). In contrast, Koenig finds Gabriel's attitude toward Omny as pathetic and absurd. Regardless of interpretation, however, the couple's departure provides the book's most crucial dramatic act.

Soon this impetuous romantic flight becomes mired in a new reality. Gabriel feels compelled to marry Omny, find a job, and settle down, while Omny is energized by her surroundings. She immerses herself in her new life, takes up with other men, and, when she discovers she is pregnant, is resolute that she will not have the child. Gabriel tries to convince her that they should marry, return home, claim money from his grandfather's estate, and work to give this child a life of contentment that they never had. They argue, and Omny rushes out of the house. A few days later her body is found after she dies from an abortion.

At this moment in the novel, it seems that Gabriel might accept that all the venomous opinions his aunt Theresa ever spouted to him are true. Omny's behavior was to be expected. He doesn't belong in this place with these people. He should immediately return to Clewe Street, to his proper place in the world. But instead Gabriel demonstrates that he has learned from this experience. He is not solely the product of his upbringing. He recognizes the mistakes and the tragic part he played in Omny's death. He decides to stay in Dublin, to testify at Omny's inquest and accept whatever responsibility he bears. In realizing how much he does not know, a moment of true hope for his future is born: "Of this city he knew nothing; he had never seen it, never for

one hour been a part of it ... hope rose in his heart, a faint ray perhaps, wan and pale, but as pure and true as the first white javelin of light that pierces the darks of morning. He held up his head, and strode forward" (p. 530).

Zack Bowen approved of this characterization of the novel's end, calling it an "important final insight for a *Bildungsroman* protagonist" (p. 70). However, Koenig argues that Gabriel's recognition does not necessarily translate into acceptance, instead finding him to be priggish and condescending. Both interpretations have some validity—the final scene of the book does hinge on the melodramatic. Gabriel still speaks of Omny more in terms of his own feelings about her than about her personal tragedy. But his moment of clarity is also hard-won. Gabriel has grown from his experiences; and, ultimately, he does represent a break if not the end to the cycle begun by Theodore and Katherine.

In contrast, Lavin's second novel, *Mary O'Grady*, does not deal with the main character's growth. Rather, this is a family epic that follows Mary through the birth of five children, the death of her husband and two of her daughters, the madness of her eldest son, the missionary exile of her youngest son to Africa, and the difficult marriage of her surviving daughter. As Zack Bowen says, "Her poverty, her pride, and her seemingly unerring sense of what is right save neither herself nor her children from a variety of domestic calamities" (p. 60). Whatever meaning exists in this book lives in the Grady family— outside of time and to some extent place. Tellingly, the time period of the book appears to cover the period of Irish civil unrest with no mention or interest.

From her earliest days as a mother Mary O'Grady lives in fear of losing what she has. She worries about her children falling from her arms. Later she worries about them leaving and what that might mean. Her thoughts haunt her and yet she knows there is nothing she can do to stop time or fate from progressing. One day as her whole family is gathered in a happy scene, Mary's mind wanders to the future and her son Patrick catches the look on her face. "What's the matter, Mother? You look as if you'd buried your whole family" (*Mary O'Grady*, 1986 ed., p. 71).

Sadly, Mary's worries start to come true: first, with the sudden death of her husband, Tom. Her eldest son, Patrick, leaves soon after for America, where at first his experiences are extremely successful. He writes frequently and sends money home. But the stock market crash of 1929 devastates him and he returns home seriously depressed, needing long-term institutionalization. Mary's daughters, Ellie and Angie, and their boyfriends die in a plane crash at a local fair. Her youngest son, Larry, is determined to provide solace and support to his mother: "I'll never leave you, Mother," he tells her. "Nor," we are told, "could he see any earthly reason why his vow should ever be broken" (p. 183).

A priest's urging that Larry enter the seminary, however, takes him away from his mother. As concerned as Larry is about his mother's response, the priest reassures him with what might be the most pivotal line of the novel: "How wonderful they are; our Irish mothers" (p. 188). Larry, more than any of her children, apprehends how difficult his decision will be for his mother, and in response to the priest, he thinks to himself: "The priest was so detached, so impersonal, and, not only that, but he seemed to attribute the same detachment to him—Larry" (p. 189).

When the priest visits Mary, she, for perhaps the first time, allows herself to feel anger toward one of her children. And, as she feels anger toward Larry, she lets the anger flow toward Patrick for his decision to go to America, "and perhaps her heart hardened a little" (p. 196). But her sorrow abates when she realizes Larry's own genuine regret. "In a moment her arms were around him, and they were both crying, and after a few minutes they could not say if they were tears of sorrow or tears of joy" (p. 199).

Mary's remaining daughter, Rosie, is dumbfounded by this scene and remains relatively clueless about her mother's emotional needs in the years that follow. Mary herself only begins to be aware of her feelings as she watches Larry leave and she finally admits the bitterness:

> There now! She had satisfied it; the spleen that had been rising in her for a long time and which, like

the twilight of smokiness and drabness that had settled upon the walls of the house, was settling inside her heart … She had spared neither toil nor sweat nor sacrifice, and yet life, that had been as sweet as milk and honey, was souring, hour by hour.

(p. 203)

Mary does, as all "wonderful Irish mothers" would, have pride in Larry's entrance into the seminary. And so it is another stinging blow for her when Larry is turned out of the seminary because of Patrick's mental-health issues. The priest decides that because of Patrick's mental weakness, Larry might not be able to bear the strain of the priesthood. In what Mary regards as an act of selfless kindness, meant to save her from embarrassment, Larry decides to go to Africa as a missionary and become ordained while there. "She had looked into his heart, and what she had seen there had filled her with love and compassion, and a feeling of awe" (p. 333).

In what seems to be Mary's last chance at familial happiness, she looks to her daughter Rosie's marriage to Frank, hoping they are happy despite not yet having children together. But on the night of their eighth anniversary Rosie comes to Mary having decided to leave her husband. At first, Mary tries to dissuade her daughter, but as she listens to Rosie explain her marriage's difficulties she becomes increasingly sympathetic, especially when Rosie talks about the emptiness of not having had a child. "Oh Mother! If you knew the feeling of loneliness; of emptiness— she pressed her hand, not to her heart, but spread wide upon her bosom, as if the feeling she sought to describe was felt by her whole body, her whole being" (p. 371).

Of course, Mary had never known that emptiness, because throughout all life's challenges she had always felt the fullness of being a mother and the love she felt for her children. As she talks to her daughter, she suggests that perhaps this feeling of loneliness and the aching in Rose's heart were placed there by God because she is now expecting a child. Rosie soon realizes that this is true, and she begins to reconsider her decision to leave Frank. The last few pages of the novel—in which Mary still does not know what the future will hold for her daughter but nonetheless feels an important corner has been turned—detail Mary's slow release of the life onto which she has held so tightly through so much. She gives Rose the money she had saved since Patrick had returned (money she had given to him for his trip to America). She had planned to use the money for Ellie's wedding and then for Larry's ordination. Now, she feels confident it will be used by her daughter as she prepares for her first grandchild. She passingly even hopes that Rosie will decide to return to Mary's home village of Tullamore—something Mary was never able to do and that she knows even in death she will not do, when she is buried next to her husband and daughters.

As Mary slowly lets go of that last hope, she makes the statement that tells her daughter what has always been at the core of her life, all that has ever mattered to her. "Didn't I have all of you children? Didn't I have your father? And didn't we all have our love and affection for each other? What more could we have had than that?" (p. 380). All that Mary wants as she reflects on her life and on her death is to be fully reunited. "That's all I'd ask of God for all Eternity, just to see you all again, and look at your faces for ever and ever" (p. 380).

In the moment of her mother's death, Rosie feels the deepest love possible for her. She understands her as she has never understood her before, both because of their conversation and also because of the child she is carrying. She knows that for her the future will hold, as it did for her mother, exquisite love and anguish.

Mary O'Grady is not a typical heroine or protagonist. She is not introspective and there are many questions about her choices left unanswered. She loves Tullamore and her mother—why then doesn't she ever return to her or to her home village, even after Tom dies? Why doesn't she challenge Larry about going to the seminary when she can see it is breaking his heart? Why doesn't she try to convince Patrick to reenter the world after he has recovered? But the book is not about answering these questions or exploring Mary's motivations. Instead, there is a simplicity about Mary wherein lies the book's central message.

As Augustine Martin writes in the book's Virago Modern Classics edition, Mary knows that life holds "no guarantee of happiness, nor, in fairness, any promise of misery" (1986 ed., p. 387). The "Irish mother" to which the priest refers is not some paragon of perfection who survives the word as a veil of tears. Rather, she is more like Mary O'Grady. She faces the joy, love, pain, disappointment, grief, and laughter of life and grabs on to each moment, because in each of those moments what endures is the love she feels as a mother. And the greatest hope she has from the first day each child enters the world is to be with them again in the hereafter. Martin calls what greets Mary in death as "consummated motherhood" (p. 383).

As with *The House in Clewe Street*, *Mary O'Grady* has not stood most critics' test of time. Marianne Koenig's strongest criticism is that the character of Mary O'Grady fills the book so completely that there is no room "to stand back from her and decide which attitude to take towards her" (p. 258). Koenig wonders whether Lavin's motivation was to show the "obsessive singlemindedness" of Mary's motherhood, but, if it is, then not providing a frame of reference has rendered it "almost meaningless as a whole" (p. 259).

It is hard, nonetheless, to walk away from *Mary O'Grady* believing it be meaningless. Mary might not be complexly depicted, but she is still a character whom readers are challenged to understand. Early in the novel she is a loving wife and adoring mother who enjoys bringing lunch to her husband each day and taking her children for long walks. That love for her family defines her in this world and the next. Following Mary through her life's ups and downs, the reader expects her to rage at God for her family's challenges. But that never happens. It is not that she does not suffer through the losses. She is literally unconscious for days after hearing of her daughters' and their boyfriends' deaths. But her love as a mother provides her with strength and determination to endure this world and to enter the next with radiant hope.

Similarly, it seems that writing *The House on Clewe Street* and *Mary O'Grady* armed Lavin in her unfolding career as a short story writer. The themes, the characters, and the questions contained within her novels provided the fodder for the shorter, more intense snapshots created by her short stories.

MARY LAVIN'S SHORT STORIES

Within the snapshots of Mary Lavin's short stories readers find her testing a series of universal truths. Familiar characters recur in her stories—mothers, widows, unhappy married couples, dominant siblings, and priests—demonstrating distinctly varied responses to similar circumstances. Zack Bowen describes Lavin's "vision of reality" as harsh: "In the tightly controlled, sometimes fatalistic sphere in which her characters live, many of them succumb to a life of quiet frustration or desperation, while others try to escape, to rationalize, to hide, or to seek freedom through love, nature, insanity, or death" (p. 23).

The "fatalistic sphere" of Lavin's stories is tightly controlled, so tightly controlled that "an envelope of silence" surrounds many of her stories, providing both "distance and resonance," says Marianne Koenig (p. 247). Plot lines are not surprising. With few exceptions the turns of fate are even somewhat predictable: death, disaffection, loss. But the ache in Lavin's characters' hearts calls out to readers with a clear and distinct voice, leaving them to ponder such daunting questions as what is true and what is false? what is love and happiness? what is freedom? and what survives when all else is gone?

"Miss Holland" was Mary Lavin's first published story and tells the tale of a lonely woman trying to adjust to her life and her new surroundings. In many ways her first story sets the tone for those that follow, as Lavin creates a character who symbolizes social differences that are hard to bridge. The reader never knows exactly what has led Agatha Holland to make this move from her former life of wealth to this boarding house in Dublin—although there are references to her education and to her past life of luxury lived with her father. But now her circumstances have changed. Rather than to the spas of Europe, she is having a taxi deliver her trunks to a home where she will occupy one room. Miss Holland initially tries to feel positive about her new home. She is appalled by the ugly mantelpiece in her room, but she tells herself, "I must not look at it. I must not admit that it is ugly" (*Tales from Bective Bridge,* p. 185). She tries to bring the beauty from her previous life into her new life; she hopes that the other boarders will like her as if it is the first day at a new school. She wants to fit in and make this very unfamiliar place her home. But each day she feels more and more isolated and eventually is living a life completely in her own mind: "Miss Holland spoke to herself silently … as clearly and coherently as if she were speaking out loud to another person: I must define their ugliness, their commonness, their bad taste" (p. 198). Only in defining her life in these terms does Miss Holland survive, even though hers is an existence of intense loneliness and isolation. "She went out of the dining room. The doorknob clattered to the floor. No one noticed her going. No one picked up the knob" (p. 199).

Perhaps what is most shocking in Lavin's stories is the discovery of who is able to find contentment despite their harsh realities. In "Frail Vessel," for instance, Liddy marries a man she deeply loves—a union that contrasts with her sister Bedelia's marriage of convenience. Ultimately, a combination of Bedelia's lack of support and Liddy's husband's own character failures lead him to commit a crime that he must leave town to escape. Liddy loves her husband to that last moment of his departure, even deciding not to tell him she is pregnant, because she knows that will make leaving even harder on him. Bedelia is disgusted by Liddy's behavior and furious about a future in which she and her husband must now take responsibility for Liddy and her unborn child. But Liddy sees her reality quite differently: "Her body, beautiful, frail even in its fertility, was still a vessel for some secret happiness Bedelia never knew" (*The Stories of Mary Lavin,* vol. 1, p. 19). Even knowing, as Bedelia emphasizes to her, that her husband will likely never return, Liddy says, "Even so!" (p. 19).

Liddy has known a great love that Bedelia will never know. That experience, as fleeting as it was, has given her something that intensifies her internal and external beauty. Her child might be fatherless, but he is the symbol of a love that Liddy treasures even in sadness. Liddy's future is uncertain. But the love she experienced will always give her something that will enrage and confuse Bedelia.

Lally in "The Will" also chooses love over her family and evokes a rage that travels through years, miles, and even eternity. The story opens after the mother's funeral with the reading of her will, in which she leaves nothing to Lally. Her siblings apologize for the grudge their mother expressed by not including Lally, even as Lally assures them the only thing she regrets is not seeing her mother before she died. At first, it appears her siblings want to right their mother's wrong and provide Lally, now a widow who runs a boarding house, and her children with financial support. But it soon becomes apparent that they share their mother's grudge. They say they resent Lally because she has embarrassed them by keeping a boarding house and by letting herself go, with rotten teeth and dirty clothes. But it eventually becomes obvious that their grudge is actually about Lally escaping what they never did: the tight control their mother exerted over all of them: "A grudge against her gnawed at them" (*The Long Ago*, p. 14).

Meanwhile, Lally rises above the pettiness of her siblings' concerns, as she runs to speak to the priest before she catches her train. "She was very bitter against me all the time, and died without forgiving me. I'm afraid for her soul," says Lally (p. 20), and she asks the priest to say masses for her mother, promising to send him the money. She is besieged by thoughts of how many masses she can have said for her mother with the little money she has. Lally left her family for love, and that love has brought her a contentment and peace that no other member of her family has or will ever know.

Knowing happiness, a happiness that she explains is not the same as pleasure, is also something that Vera in "Happiness" experiences. Vera has dealt with difficult realities, including

becoming a widow with young children. But she asserts that those experiences have not colored her worldview. "Just remember that I had a happy life—and that if I had to choose my kind of heaven I'd take it on this earth with you again, no matter how much you might annoy me!" she tells her children (*Happiness and Other Stories*, p. 11). Vera talks to Father Hugh of "onslaughts" made on her happiness after her husband's death, when others tried to convince her that "life is a vale of tears" and told her, "You are privileged to find it out so young!" (p. 24).

And yet for all her talk of happiness, Vera does waver slightly as she faces her own death and worries about memories from her past. Finally, reassured by her daughter and accepting that her happiness is still with her in her final moments, Vera dies with the deepest sense of peace: "Her head sank so deep into the pillow that it would have been dented had it been a pillow of stone" (p. 33). Vera's happiness was real and, ultimately, helps her leave this world for the next.

A widow's story is also the focus of "The Cuckoo Spit." In this story, another Vera loses her husband and talks of a peace built from acceptance, "I was thinking that, there is, after all, a kind of peace at last when you face up to life's defeats … there is a strange peace in knowing that the best in life is gone forever" (*Collected Stories*, p. 377). At the point she meets Fergus, Vera has decided that she has lost the ability to experience the kind of happiness only known to the young and in love. Soon, however, she feels that rush and expectation as she is attracted to this younger man. Although their love remains unconsummated, the depth of her emotions revives Vera: "'But isn't it strange that a love that was unrealized should have'—'Given such joy?' he said quietly. 'Yes, yes,' she said gratefully, then she closed the door behind them. 'And such pain'" (p. 379).

In feeling great love and great pain, Vera feels more alive than she's been in the four years since her husband's death and, says Catherine A. Murphy, she develops an "awareness of the ambivalent effect of this force on the human heart" (p. 72). Still, Lavin leaves no doubt that

Vera would prefer to have had these moments with Fergus than to have continued believing that part of her life had died with her husband.

Lavin's story "The Widow's Son" most directly asks the question that plagues the human condition: do our actions even matter? The story offers two possible endings to what happens to the widow's son—one where he dies, the other where he moves away. Both endings, however, leave the widow alone and questioning her choice and leaving readers to ask that same question. "Perhaps all our actions have this double quality about them; this possibility of alternative, and that it is only by careful watching, and absolute sincerity, that we follow the path that is destined for us, and, no matter how tragic that may be, it is better than the tragedy we bring upon ourselves" (*The Stories of Mary Lavin*, vol. 1, p. 113).

Just as "The Will," "Frail Vessel," "Happiness" and other Lavin stories explore the surprising forms that happiness and peace can assume, so do stories such as "A Gentle Soul," "Sarah," "A Cup of Tea," "A Happy Death," and "The Becker Wives" explore the contrasting emotions of its characters: bitterness, isolation and loneliness. In "A Gentle Soul," Lavin portrays a character consumed by bitterness: "No blacker, nor colder, no more close, no more silent than her own black heart" (*The Stories of Mary Lavin*, vol. 1, p. 40). Agatha possesses her father's preoccupation with social status, looking down her nose at Jamey Morrow, who helps with their family's farm. Her sister Rose is more like their mother, a kinder and gentler soul. Rose longs to respond to Jamey's interest in her, but she knows she can't stand up to her father's and sister's scorn, "That is all there is between us, I thought, or ever like to be: looks of love, and looks of accusation" (p. 48). When Jamey dies in an accident at their home, Rose's father reveals the true darkness of his beliefs: "'It's easily seen you know little about the Morrows or their class,' he said. 'They're always looking out for a chance to put down their betters'" (p. 52). Rose longs to stand up for Jamey, but instead she betrays him in death by suggesting he had caused his own accident to prevent the Morrow family from col-

lecting money from her father. From that moment, even though Rose hates her sister, she is also forever bound to her—and will be even in death. "And to think that when my last hour comes that it will be her side that I will be laid in the earth, and with her dust that mine will mingle!" (p. 54).

In "Sarah," the title character is known in the town to have a "bit of a bad name" because she is a single mother with children of unknown paternity. And while there is grudging regard for her work ethic and her faithfulness to the church, the town and her own brothers look down upon Sarah and essentially treat her as an outcast living in their midst. Sarah shows no interest in naming her three sons' fathers, but as she prepares to give birth to her fourth child, she decides to write a letter to the wife of her child's father, a woman for whom she worked and who is pregnant herself. It's unclear why Sarah makes this decision; it seems likely that she is tired of being the only one scorned by the town and wants others to recognize the father's transgression.

Her decision has entirely unanticipated consequences. Without the slightest regard for his sister or her unborn child, Sarah's brother Pat throws her into the rainy night after learning about the letter from the man's wife. Pat explains that he could tolerate the other pregnancies, because he thought the fathers were lowlifes. But having learned that this child's father is a prominent citizen, he can no longer look away. The cruelty of his action is only fully realized the next morning. When Oliver, the father of Sarah's child, is talking to his wife, Kathleen, he learns Sarah's fate: "That's where they found her in the morning, dead as a rat. And the child dead beside her!" (*The Stories of Mary Lavin*, vol. 2, p. 23). Although Sarah has done no harm to her brother and is only as guilty as Oliver, her isolation is complete when her life and that of her child are thrown away like garbage. And Oliver, who learns the news the next day from his wife—who has decided to protest that she doesn't believe the contents of the letter—is left to continue living the privileged life into which he was born.

A very different kind of isolation and exclusion, but just as personally devastating, is experienced by the mother in "A Cup of Tea." The subject of the story is, as Richard Peterson suggests, "deliberately and deceptively simple and insignificant" (p. 293). The mother looks forward to her daughter's visit from college, preparing for and anticipating it for days beforehand. But her excitement is quickly extinguished, as she is reminded that the bond she wishes to have with her daughter is instead shared by her daughter and her husband—someone working behind a closed door whom we never meet. Unable to speak of her pain, the mother instead boils the milk for her daughter's tea, ostensibly to prevent it from spoiling. When her daughter complains of the taste, the mother replies, "Perhaps if you hadn't stayed so long upstairs I might not have had time to boil it ... The evening was spoiled anyways. The whole week of work and preparation was spoiled. Everything was spoiled" (*The Long Ago*, p. 34).

Such deep irony is expressed in that cup of tea. Nothing could be less at the center of this mother-daughter relationship, yet it is all they seem able to discuss. The daughter, Sophie, is caught in the middle of her parents' unhappy marriage. She revels in talking to her father, only to have that pleasure cause pain to her mother. She longs to connect with her mother but is unable to do so because of their differences and her mother's jealous resentment. In the end, Sophie finds comfort in one impossible yet overriding wish for a world in which "people would all have to become alike. They would have to look alike and speak alike and feel and talk and think alike. What a wonderful place the world would become!" (*The Long Ago*, p. 37).

Irony is again expressed in the title of the story "A Happy Death." In this story, often thought to be one of Lavin's best, the wife is preoccupied with outward appearances. She takes in boarders so that she can provide new clothes for her husband. When he is demoted to a janitorial position, she strives to keep him hidden in their damp kitchen so that no one knows of the indignity. Even when he is in the hospital dying, the wife seeks to provide him what she thinks of as "a happy death" by buying sweets and decorative fruit so that others can see he is well cared for and loved. A nun tries to encourage her to worry about her husband's soul, instead, but it is too late. As the wife urges her husband to recite the act of contrition, he instead professes his love for her, and he dies happy, feeling that in his final moments they are finally alone together. But the wife screams as she protests that "God has not heard her prayers, and had not vouchsafed her husband the grace of a happy death" (*The Stories of Mary Lavin*, vol. 2, p. 240).

The couple in this story has spent their lives failing to understand each other or finding happiness. And, so, ironically, as Zack Bowen writes, there is happiness in death for the "husband's emancipation from the social and religious tyrannies imposed by his wife ... also in his ultimate freedom from ever having to understand her" (p. 37). But the wife is not freed by death or by the "happiness" of her husband's death. Instead, she will spend the rest of her time on earth overwrought by her self-imposed torments.

The perception of reality is skewed in "A Happy Death." The couple could live a quiet life of happiness together. But instead the wife is preoccupied with appearances and the husband is miserable because their home is overrun by strangers. In "The Becker Wives," reality is again distorted, both by Theobald's desperate need to marry someone extraordinary as well as by the madness of his wife, Flora.

Theobald is disturbed by his father's entreaty to him and his brothers to marry women like his mother. As he looks at his two older brothers' wives he even says to his unmarried brother, Samuel, "I hope you'll have some aspiration towards a better social level" (*The Becker Wives*, p. 18). Samuel doesn't share Theobald's biases and instead points to the happiness of his brothers' marriages. Still, when he chooses a wife, Honoria, who comes from a family of great means, Samuel hopes that will quiet Theobald's concerns. Instead, Theobald expresses frustration that his brother has failed to marry someone who raises the family's social status. Honoria's family might have money, but they do not possess the social stature Theobald covets. With this in mind, Theobald brings Flora into the Becker family.

Flora carries the distinctions Theobald hoped his brothers' marriages would possess. Theobald explains that Flora comes from a very old family, but, more importantly, he explains that she is amazing and accomplished, exclaiming, "Oh, there's no end to her gifts" (p. 51). What she lacks in wealth Theobald believes she makes up for in "worldly wisdom." Immediately, she impresses the family with her skills as a mimic, actually pretending to be a camera documenting her family introductions. The family's reaction is just as Theobald hoped, "It was side-splitting. Never in their lives had the Beckers met anyone remotely like this" (p. 51). The Beckers are quickly enthralled, and Theobald takes tremendous pleasure in their reactions and soon marries Flora.

After they return from their honeymoon, however, Theobald begins to realize the challenges of being married to someone like Flora. He describes her impact on the people at a gathering at their apartment: "She was like a flame playing over them incessantly, withering the life out of them" (p. 63). To which Flora responds, much to Theobald's irritation, by trying to mimic a flame. What begins as irresistible charm soon causes concern as the Beckers begin to see that Flora's impersonations are beyond her control—something she does when alone as well as in a crowd. The family learns this when they see her impersonating Honoria when she is by herself one evening. Eventually, they realize Flora has crossed the line from captivating eccentricity to madness.

Flora's descent is particularly painful for Samuel, who had formed a bond with his brother's wife and believes, perhaps, that in assuming his wife's identity she shares his feelings. He hushes her, even calling her Honoria. And, as they wait for the doctor, he reflects on what the family has lost. "It was all over; the fun and the gaiety. Their brief journey into another world had been rudely cut short ... And the bright enchanting creature that had opened that vista to them had been but a flitting spirit never meant to mix with the likes of them" (p. 96).

Theobald, who only sought to raise the social status of his family, had done something far more extraordinary. He had introduced vibrancy to his family that they had never experienced. In losing Flora they have lost that glimmer, even as she almost physically seemed to disappear: "it was as if she had begun to dissolve into the wraith-like creature of light that first flashed on them all in its airy brilliance" (p. 97).

Loss of identity is another recurring theme in Lavin's work. While this struggle is usually told through her female characters, it is vividly embodied in the character of Manny in "At Sallygap." Manny is leaving for Paris with his band when he is suddenly swayed by his feelings for his girlfriend, Annie. He impulsively leaves the boat, and when his friends throw him his violin, it smashes into pieces. Manny's future dreams are left on that pier. He and Annie, who leave that day with so much love and promise, revert to a life Manny never expected to live— running a shop and living in an apartment above it. Reminiscing about the changes in his life from that day when he left the boat to this day, Manny makes what is a stunning decision for him.

Once he was a man who would sail to Paris; now he miserably lives an existence that is slowly suffocating him, controlled by Annie's "whipping tongue." And so, to Manny's own surprise, he chooses not to take the bus and instead he walks back to Dublin, full knowing the rage that he will encounter at his late return. "A rare recklessness possessed him, and when shortly after night came down this feeling of recklessness strengthened" (*The Stories of Mary Lavin,* vol. 2, p. 33). During this walk Manny finds a peace that has eluded him since that fateful decision on the pier: "Things always turned out for the best in the end. If he had gone away, he might never have come up to Sallygap, and then he would never have found out that peace was not a matter of one city or another, but a matter of hedges and fields and waddling ducks and a handful of stars" (p. 34).

However, the beauty of his walk disappears as he returns to Annie and realizes, perhaps for the first time, just how much of himself he gave away by getting off the boat for Paris. Beauty exists outside the ugliness of his life with Annie, but it is nothing he can recapture. "For there was no sanctuary from hatred such as he saw in Annie's eyes … She had him imprisoned for ever in her hatred" (p. 42).

Manny lost his identity the day he decided to give up his dream and stay in Dublin with Annie. And, in many ways, Annie lost respect for Manny on that day. Their future was built on a foundation of expectations that neither fulfilled. And, as Thomas Murray describes it, "The shuttered and darkened shop which awaits Manny on his return to Dublin is a symbol of the closed-heart Annie has nurtured ever since the day of her first victory over him" (p. 125).

In many cases, Lavin's protagonists are widows who feel the loss of their identities after they lose their husbands. In the story "In a Café," two widows meet in a Dublin café. Mary has been widowed for two years; Maudie widowed after less than a year of marriage. It becomes quickly obvious that although they share the title of "widow" they reside in two very different emotional places. Already Maudie assumes and is expecting that she will remarry. She is still the person she was before her husband died. But Mary is less certain that she will or wants to remarry. She is struggling to know who she is and what she wants. She finds herself drawn to the artist she meets in the café where she and Maudie meet. However, when she arrives at his house she realizes that only one emotion has brought her to this place and she only has one thought she wants to share: "I'm lonely. That was all she could have said," she thinks to herself. "I'm lonely. Are you?" (*In a Café: Selected Stories*, p. 201).

Mary realizes that what she wants that day is her husband. And in emotionally accepting his loss, she is able to envisage her husband for the first time since his death and begin the journey of finding herself again. "Not till she had taken out the key of the car, and gone straight around to the driver's side, not stupidly, as so often, to the passenger seat, not till then did she realize what she had achieved" (p. 202).

Being a nun's mother is certainly an identity in itself in Catholic Ireland. But Mrs. Latimer in

"The Nun's Mother" is surprisingly troubled by this new moniker. She knows she should feel comforted that now she has a nun to pray for her, but instead she feels confused about her daughter Angela's motivation. What had caused Angela to make this decision, to leave behind a comfortable life with the promise of a husband and children? Mrs. Latimer can't help but wonder about this mystery and also can't help but wonder if Angela's decision says more about Mrs. Latimer as a mother than about Angela's faith and commitment to the church. Her husband urges her to speak to Angela in more depth about her decision, and Mrs. Latimer plays out many such conversations in her head. But she never initiates those discussions with her daughter. Ultimately, no matter how many questions and doubts she has about Angela's decision, she is most concerned with herself and what this new identity means to her. She cannot bear to find out something that changes her self-image or how she appears to others: "It was hard to be a mother. Hard to be vigilant night and day and at the end of it not to know whether you had failed or triumphed" (*The Long Ago*, p. 212). And so Mrs. Latimer decides to accept her new identity with great if false pride and bury every question and doubt she had considered because, after all, "Everyone would be kind to her now, and treat her with high respect as well. For she had proven herself. She was the mother of a nun" (p. 212).

Although she was American born and retained her American citizenship, Lavin's own identity endures as one of the twentieth century's most prominent Irish short story writers. And yet, in contrast to her contemporaries, the "Irishness" of her stories is found more in settings and familiar characters than in plots or themes. Lavin deals with the Irish experience personally rather than politically—particularly with her women characters. Her focus on identity is particularly relevant to modern Irish women whose identity was often oversimplified in twentieth-century Ireland. Mothers and widows are well-drawn characters in Lavin's novels, with feelings and motivations that are brought into sharper focus.

Only a few of her stories even reference what the Irish referred to as the "troubles." And although a story such as "The Patriot Son," for instance, occurs with the backdrop of the Irish-British conflict, the story focus is still more on the emasculating effect of his dominant mother on the story's protagonist, Matty. Matty has let his mother prevent him from connecting with his childhood friend, Sean, whom she knows has rebellious leanings. But when Sean tells Mattie of plans to set fire to the British barracks across from his family's shop, Matty feels temporarily emboldened. He even convinces himself that he has been shot by the soldiers, as he allows his friend to escape. Instead, he quickly learns that his mother's dominance, and his loss of masculinity, is complete, when instead of being shot he has only cut his leg. And, as his friend Sean lies dead from a gunshot wound from the soldiers he has led to him, his loss of dignity is complete as his mother yells, "He's up there on the top of the pig-shed! She cried … He must have been frightened out of his wits!" (*The Stories of Mary Lavin,* vol. 1, p. 255). In trying to assist his friend, Matty's actions have instead led to Sean's death and to what will surely be his lifelong, life-altering remorse.

In talking about her career, Mary Lavin told Bonnie Kime Scott, "I am a one-armed writer … I am interrupted 50 times an hour. I am disorganised, all held together by safety pins … I live a life of the mind. That is where it is together" (p. 263). This description also holds true for Lavin's stories. Common themes and familiar characters dominate, but each story also occupies its own distinct space, a space in which readers gain insight and understanding for that "something else" that lies just below the surface we all occupy.

Selected Bibliography

WORKS OF MARY LAVIN

NOVELS

The House in Clewe Street. Boston: Little, Brown, 1945.

Mary O'Grady. London: Michael Joseph, 1950. Reprint. London and New York: Virago, 1986.

SHORT STORIES

Tales from Bective Bridge. Boston: Little, Brown, 1942.

The Long Ago. London: Michael Joseph, 1944.

The Becker Wives. London: Michael Joseph, 1946; New York: New American Library, 1946.

At Sallygap and Other Stories. Boston: Little, Brown, 1947.

The Great Wave and Other Stories. London: Macmillan, 1961.

In the Middle of the Fields and Other Stories. London: Constable, 1967; New York: Macmillan, 1969.

Happiness and Other Stories. Boston: Houghton Mifflin, 1970.

A Family Likeness. London: Constable, 1985.

COLLECTED WORKS

The Stories of Mary Lavin. Vol. 1. London: Constable, 1964.

Collected Stories. Boston: Houghton Mifflin, 1971.

The Stories of Mary Lavin. Vol. 2. London: Constable, 1974.

The Stories of Mary Lavin. Vol. 3. London: Constable, 1985.

In a Café: Selected Stories. London and New York: Penguin, 1999.

PAPERS

A collection of Lavin's papers resides in the Morris Library at the Southern Illinois University Special Collections Research Center.

CRITICAL AND BIOGRAPHICAL STUDIES

Boland, Eavan. *Writing Lives: Conversations Between Women Writers.* Edited by Mary Chamberlain. London: Virago, 1988. Pp. 138–145. (Interview.)

Bowen, Zack. *Mary Lavin.* Lewisburg, Pa: Bucknell University Press, 1975.

Dunleavy, Janet Egleson. "Mary Lavin, Elizabeth Bowen, and a New Generation: The Irish Short Story at Midcentury." In *The Irish Story: A Critical History.* Edited by James F. Kilroy. Boston: Twayne, 1984. Pp. 145–168.

Koenig, Marianne. "Mary Lavin: The Novels and the Stories." *Irish University Review* 9, no. 2:244–261 (autumn 1979).

Mahlke, Regina. "Mary Lavin's 'The Patriot Son' and 'The Face of Hate.'" *Studies in Anglo-Irish Literature.* Edited by Heinz Kosok. Bonn, Germany: Bouvier Verlag Herbert Grundmann, 1982. Pp. 333–337.

Murphy, Catherine A. "The Ironic Vision of Mary Lavin." *Mosaic* 12, no. 3:69–79 (1979).

Murray, Thomas J. "Mary Lavin's World: Lovers and Strangers." *Eire-Ireland* 7, no. 2:122–131 (1972).

Neary, Mary. "Flora's Answer to the Irish Question: A Study

of Mary Lavin's 'The Becker Wives.'" *Twentieth Century Literature* 42, no. 4:516–526 (winter 1996).

Peterson, Richard F. "The Circle of Truth: The Stories of Katherine Mansfield and Mary Lavin." *Modern Fiction Studies* 24, no. 3:383–394 (1978).

Scott, Bonnie Kime. "Mary Lavin and the Life of the Mind." *Irish University Review* 9, no. 2:262–278 (autumn 1979).

Shumaker, Jeanette Roberts. "Sacrificial Women in Short Stories by Mary Lavin and Edna O'Brien." *Studies in Short Fiction* 32, no. 2:185–197 (spring 1995).

SHERIDAN LE FANU

(1814—1873)

Frances A. Chiu

THE SCHOLAR M. R. James, himself a writer of ghost stories, did not claim a "very exalted place" ("Lecture,") in the overall literary canon for Joseph Sheridan Le Fanu. But he did repeatedly acknowledge that the author of *In a Glass Darkly* (1872) and *Uncle Silas* (1864) stood "absolutely in the first rank as a writer of ghost stories," adding, in a preface to Le Fanu's posthumous collection *Madam Crowl's Ghost* (1923), "That is my deliberate verdict, after reading all the supernatural tales I have been able to get hold of" ("Introduction"). Even the seemingly faint praise accorded to Le Fanu's novels by Henry James as "just the book to read at midnight in an English country house" (*Munsey's Magazine*) suggests the popularity his works enjoyed at the turn of the century. Certainly, some seventy years after the publication of Le Fanu's mystery novel *Wylder's Hand* (1864), Dorothy L. Sayers would channel it in her own mystery, *The Nine Tailors* (1934), while mentioning him in *Gaudy Night* (1935) and her unfinished *Thrones, Dominations*. Le Fanu, in short, has enjoyed a strong following among some of the best writers of mysteries, supernatural fiction, and thrillers even if his works are not as widely read as those of Wilkie Collins. Only since the late 1980s, with the resurgence of critical interest in the gothic, have scholars begun to reexamine his short stories and novels more thoroughly

BIOGRAPHY AND SOCIAL CONTEXT

On August 28, 1814, Joseph Sheridan Le Fanu was born to the Reverend Thomas and Emma Dobbin Le Fanu, at 34 Lower Dominick Street, Dublin. Both sides of the family belonged to the margins of the Anglo-Irish gentry as members of the clergy. The Le Fanus were proud of their ancestry; descended from a Huguenot soldier, Charles de Cresseron, who fought for William III during the Battle of the Boyne, they were also allied to the Sheridan family. Alicia Le Fanu, the author's grandmother, was a sister of the playwright Richard Brinsley Sheridan (1751–1816) and the great-aunt of the novelist and feminist Caroline Norton (1808–1877). But if the Le Fanus and Dobbinses were predominantly Tory and genteel, there were also a few members with more radical leanings. Apart from the Whiggish Sheridan, who famously supported the French Revolution and opposed the Act of Union between Britain and Ireland, Emma Dobbins' father sympathized with John and Henry Sheares, both of whom played leading roles the Rebellion of 1798: Emma herself was later to confess how she admired the memory of Edward Fitzgerald sufficiently to steal his dagger from Major Swan before hiding it "among the feathers of my bed" (quoted in Le Fanu's memoir *Seventy Years of Irish Life*, p. 17). Over time, these radical nationalist sentiments would periodically surface in the fiction of Sheridan Le Fanu, both overtly and covertly.

Until 1826, the Le Fanus resided at Phoenix Park, an area that bordered the village of Chapelizod, which provided the setting for his novel *The House by the Churchyard* (1863) as well as for James Joyce's *Finnegan's Wake* (1939). With Thomas Le Fanu's acceptance of a deanery at Emly, a position that offered an additional source of income to his absentee rectorships at Abington and Ardnageehy, the family of five moved to Abington (County Limerick). It was here that the Le Fanus witnessed faction fights and sectarian violence, as the Tithe Wars erupted in the wake of Catholic emancipation, when Catholics began to protest the payment of tithes to the Protestant,

Anglican clergy of the Church of Ireland (the Irish counterpart to the Church of England). The Le Fanus themselves—particularly Sheridan, his older sister Catherine, and his younger brother William—also experienced physical threats and violence after one of their relations, the Reverend Charles Coote, demanded payment of a tithe from Father Hickey. Nor was this the family's only misfortune. Since Thomas Le Fanu was reluctant to claim arrears in the wake of the Tithe Wars, his income further dwindled after the passing of the Church Temporalities Act, which eliminated two archbishoprics and eight bishoprics. The fact that the family was intent on keeping up appearances made matters more difficult: such may explain the considerable presence of genteel men frustrated by impending poverty in Le Fanu's novels.

The future novelist entered Trinity College, Dublin, in 1832 as a Tory conservative, remaining so for much of his life: even if he agreed on higher taxes for absentees and was later to endorse Catholics in positions of authority. Here, he studied law while joining the College Historical Society and befriending the cofounder of the *Dublin University Magazine*, Isaac Butt (1813–1879), a staunch Tory conservative who became a proponent of land reform and a leader of the Home Rule movement during the 1860s. Le Fanu, however, ultimately abandoned law after being called to the bar in 1839; it was then that he decided to become a proprietor and editor of several Dublin newspapers, including the *Dublin Evening Mail* and the *Warder*. More importantly, he would also embark on a literary career, writing verse, short stories, and novels. By the time of his marriage to Susanna Bennett in 1844 (for which Butt served as witness), he had published a number of stories that would eventually comprise the *Purcell Papers* (1871), as well as two novels in the vein of Sir Walter Scott: *The Cock and Anchor* (1845) and *The Fortunes of Colonel Torlogh O'Brien* (1847). It is worth noting that the majority of these early works were set in Ireland—perhaps reflecting Le Fanu's fledgling involvement with the Young Ireland movement from its inception through 1848.

With the death of Susanna in 1858, Le Fanu withdrew from society to the point that he earned the moniker of "the Invisible Prince." This new-found seclusion at 10 Merrion Square spurred him on to renew his efforts at novel writing until his death in 1873, as his proprietorship of the *Dublin University Magazine* between 1861 and 1868 allowed him to serialize *The House by the Churchyard* in 1863, *Wylder's Hand* and *Uncle Silas* in 1864, *Guy Deverell* in 1865, *Tenants of Malory* in 1866, *Haunted Lives* in 1867, and *The Wyvern Mystery* in 1868, all on a monthly basis. Along with *A Lost Name,* which was published in *Temple Bar* in 1867–1868; *Checkmate,* in *Cassell's Magazine* in 1870–1871; and *The Rose and the Key* and *Willing to Die* in *All the Year Round* in 1871 and 1872, respectively, all were subsequently issued as full triple-decker novels by either Richard Bentley or Tinsley in London. In addition, Le Fanu would also produce two collections of shorter fiction, *Chronicles of Golden Friars* (1871) and *In a Glass Darkly* (1872), while continuing to publish a number of short stories including "Sir Dominic's Bargain," "Laura Silver Bell," and "Dickon the Devil," all in 1872. When Le Fanu was not writing or editing, he would stalk bookstores for fiction and nonfiction on the supernatural, inquiring with a smile, "Any more ghost stories for me?"

In his final years, Le Fanu suffered from heart disease. Perhaps the sense of suffocation contributed to an oddly fitting recurring nightmare which he recounted to his physician—that he was about to be crushed alive in a crumbling old mansion. His death on February 10, 1873, led the physician to declare, "At last, the house has fallen."

In order to understand some of the central themes and tropes in the fiction of Le Fanu, it is also important to have a grasp of contemporary national issues, particularly given his career in political and literary journalism. Even though the Act of Union in 1800 was intended to quell all conflict between Britain and Ireland, many problems continued to fester. After all, Roman Catholics, who comprised the bulk of the Irish population, still endured a minority status after Oliver Cromwell's invasion in 1652 and the Williamite wars of 1688–1691, since the repeal of the most punitive penal laws (which had disinherited and disenfranchised them toward the close of the preceding century) did little to redress longstanding inequalities and inequities. By contrast, Protestants, particularly those belonging to the state-sanctioned Church of Ireland, represented only 10 to 15 percent of the population but constituted 50 to 60 percent of the landowning class. Nor did the passing of the Catholic Emancipation Act in 1829 resolve conflicts, as the Le Fanus were themselves to experience in the crossfires of the Tithe Wars. This sense of grievance was stoked no less by reports of widespread evictions, especially those instigated by the third Earl of Leitrim and the Marquis of Conyngham; even magazines generally conservative on Irish issues, such as Charles Dickens' *All the Year Round*, animadverted on "gross outrages and flagrant invasions of the tenants' rights and prerogatives" (p. 374). Not least, the emergence of the Young Ireland movement during the late 1830s unleashed a fresh appreciation of Irish art, poetry, and music while also encouraging nonsectarian Irish patriotism, in spite of the fact that most of its leading members were Protestant.

It was the famine of 1845–1848, however, that served as an impetus for widespread nationalist consciousness, with Catholics and Protestants alike decrying the ostensibly lackadaisical attempts by the British government to distribute food and other provisions. The fact that Ireland lost nearly a quarter of its population through disease, starvation, and emigration led some nationalists to accuse the British government of practicing genocide. Nationalists were also to criticize the Encumbered Estates Act of 1849, enacted to facilitate the sale of debt-ridden estates. Many regarded it as a means of selling even more land to the English and Scottish; in his *History of Ireland*, the Young Irelander and future Fenian John Mitchel repeatedly execrated the measure for allowing "London Jews, money brokers and insurance officers" to hasten the sale of Irish properties to the British (vol. 2, p. 240). Not surprisingly, the events of the famine and its aftermath convinced many of the necessity of radical reform. If the Tenant Right League sought to establish the three Fs—fair rent, fixity of tenure, and free sale of land—by constitutional means during the 1850s, radical Fenians began organizing in 1858 for an armed revolution aimed at the immediate dissolution of the Union. These ideas eventually encouraged Isaac Butt, who had already drifted away from Tory politics in 1849, to propose what he referred to as "Home Rule," a federalist arrangement that would enable Ireland to legislate for herself domestically while remaining a part of the Union. The debate on federalism would in turn generate subsequent movements for independence, culminating in the founding of the Irish republic in 1916.

What is arguably even more important than the events themselves are the themes and tropes that materialized in political discourse of the day. A fundamental sense of alienation and disaffection in discussions of sectarian prejudice and land ownership, was frequently articulated in highly dramatic terms. If Ireland was personified as a languishing damsel in distress, Britain was viewed as her persistent, centuries-long aggressor—and most strikingly, as an "alien" and "vampire." In his pamphlet *Irish Grievances* (1868), James Morison blamed not only an "alien Church" for scorning "the religion of the people" but also an "alien proprietary" for expelling the original owners: an act that was accomplished by a "foreign power" with "the intensest forms of hatred and cruelty" (pp. 69–71). Not least, Butt himself had recourse to the word "alien" for spectacular effect in his writings on land reform, claiming that "deep and dark in the … inner life of the peasant, lies the ever-present remembrance that whole soil of Ireland was wrested from its rightful possessors, and given by force and fraud to be the inheritance of aliens" (1866, p. 42); indeed, the former Tory Protestant Unionist deprecated the landlord class as "the most vicious creation of the most vicious set of circumstances that ever degraded a nation." If Britain was an "alien" state, it was equally branded a "vampire." Just as Sydney Owenson (Lady Morgan) deplored British government in Ireland as a "species of political vampyrism [sic]" in her *Patriotic Sketches of Ireland* (p. 85), the anonymous pamphleteer "FTCD" (Fellow of Trinity College Dublin) of *The Ireland of To-day* referred to Protestant bishops as a class that "vampire-like, have drank in the blood of Ireland to satiety" (note, p. 30). Moreover, the writer of *The Irish Land Question Impartially Considered* (1870) fulminated at the "vampire plagues" (p. 8) of landlords, likening the periodic waves of confiscation to a "slow poison" that paralyzed all trade, commerce, and agriculture; "avarice, intrigues, and rapacity of man" had destroyed a land otherwise "so favoured by the dispensations of Providence" (p. 30). It is perhaps not altogether surprising that conservatives would complain that "no attempt was made to curb the license of the Fenian press" where "every extravagance of language was indulged in." Sensational times, it would appear, demanded a sensational rhetoric.

Much of this animus was intensified by popular views of racial difference, particularly during a period when evolution was hotly debated. If the Irish were derided as "white chimpanzees," they were also stereotyped as having "something feminine in them" (Matthew Arnold, 1867, p. 108); by contrast, the English were presented as the more stereotypically masculine of the two, being characterized by a "combination of hardness, narrowness," and "want of consideration for other people's feelings" (Arnold, 1882, p. 67). This animus was further deepened by a new interest in national history, recently revived by the Young Irelanders. Thomas Davis declared that Ireland

> is beginning to make up a record of English crime and Irish suffering, in order to explain the past, justify the present, and caution the future. She begins to study the past—not to acquire a beggar's eloquence in petition, but a hero's wrath in strife ... (If we attempt to govern ourselves without statesmanship—to be a nation without a knowledge of the country's history ... we will fail in policy, society, and war.)
>
> (p. 28)

Butt would likewise dwell upon the importance of history in his writings, pointing out recurring ills that varied only slightly through the ages; he was keen to note that there was little difference between conservative and liberal governments in Britain since the latter ruled Ireland "by enactments more arbitrary than any previous ministry

ever ventured to propose," going to "distant ages and foreign countries to revive and import and to combine the rudest and most refined modes of trampling down liberty" (1871, p. 72). History repeated itself, as one conquest assumed yet another form in a different century.

It is thus hardly surprising then that few nationalist historians applauded the passing of the Union in 1800, regarded by Richard Brinsley Sheridan himself as an act of "fraud" and "force" when he compared it to those "Irish marriages which commenced in fraud and were consummated by force," advising, "Let us not commit a brutal rape on the independence of Ireland" (quoted in Mitchel, vol. 2, p. 56). Indeed, nineteenth-century nationalists were apt to imagine Ireland and Britain respectively as the young virgin and her loathsome suitor, with the Irish Parliament, described by contemporary historians W. J. O'Neill Daunt and Goldwin Smith as some of the most "reckless" and "extravagant" members of the Ascendancy, assuming the role of Ireland's avaricious guardian, one eager to sell his ward off for financial gain. Viewed in such a light, the marriage between Ireland and Britain proved a tragic sham engineered to oppress and plunder the Irish people, marked not only by numerous insurrection acts, coercion bills, and arms bills but also the rapid disappearance of trade and displacement of political power from Dublin to London.

Ultimately, there was no other choice than to declare legislative independence, as the Union proved to be anything but a union. It was high time for Ireland to retrieve her lost name and inheritance. If Daniel O'Connell (the "Liberator") and his fellow nationalist James Fintan Lalor had severally vowed the necessity of "checkmat[ing] the government of England," Butt and his fellow federalists came to view independence as a means of driving England into a corner "to checkmate her—to silence her ... for the honour of Ireland, for the good even of England herself" Grattan, p. 34).

Even though Le Fanu ridiculed the "cock-a-doodle-do of Meagher, Mitchel, and other stage rebels" some twenty years after his involvement with the Young Ireland movement, it is nonetheless hasty to assume that he embraced Unionism thoroughly. After all, as Butt explained, "No mistake could be greater than to suppose that all even of those who are determinedly opposed to Fenianism are, therefore, well affected to the government under which they live" (1866, p. xvii). It is significant that the *Dublin University Magazine*, while under Le Fanu's editorship, published an essay on Lord Plunket that addressed the flaws of the eighteenth-century Irish Parliament while regretting its extermination under the Union and referring to the Union itself as an "enslavement." The *Dublin University Magazine*'s admiration for those who resisted its enactment would also emerge in an article, "Notes on Eloquence," that praised the famously nationalistic Henry Grattan as "the most imaginative of orators, ancient or modern" while citing an anti-Unionist speech as "a more eloquent peroration than can be found in the oratory of any other nation or age" (September 1863, pp. 296–309). At best, then, Le Fanu's marked silence on the disestablishment of the Irish Church and the promotion of the Home Rule movement may imply ambivalence rather than outright opposition.

THE EARLY YEARS: IRISH FICTION AND VERSE

Given the heightened interest in Irish lore and history during the late 1830s, it is not simply fortuitous that Le Fanu focused on Irish subjects for at least two and a half decades—until his London publisher, Richard Bentley, demanded that he set his future novels in England. Some of the central themes and tropes associated with his novels, particularly forced marriages, family feuds, and disputed inheritances, are already present in his early work, beginning with his ballad "Phaudhrig Crohoore" (1839). As William Le Fanu later recounted in his memoir *Seventy Years of Irish Life* (1893), "Phaudhrig" was drafted as a response to his own request for an Irish "Lochinvar," a popular poem of Sir Walter Scott. What is distinctive in Sheridan Le Fanu's variation, however, is a stronger emphasis on the idea of the forced union and the avarice of the bride's father as he pressures her to wed a wealthy man.

The poem concludes with a reference to the Rebellion of '98:

> As he lived a brave boy, he resolved so to fall.
> And he took a good pike—for Phaudhrig was great—
> And he fought, and he died in the year ninety-eight.
> An' the day that Crohoore in the green field was killed,
> A sthrong boy was sthretched, and a sthrong heart was stilled.
>
> (*Poems*, p. 134)

As such, it is not difficult to read "Phaudhrig" as a covert critique of the Union: the man who is loved by the bride and challenges a marriage of convenience is naturally one who fights for Irish independence. If "Phaudhrig" references the rising of '98 only cursorily, Le Fanu's poem "Shamus O'Brien" focuses squarely on his stand at the dock when he is waiting to be hanged—before being released in the nick of time by a sympathetic priest. Having "fought for ould Ireland from the first to the close," Shamus has few regrets:

> Though I stand here to perish, it's my glory that then
> In her cause I was willing my veins should run dry
> An that now for her sake I am ready to die.
>
> (*Poems*, p. 120)

When he is freed, he cheerily thumbs his nose at the powers that be (i.e., the British governing forces):

> Your swords they may glitter; your carbines go bang,
> But if you want hanging; it's yourselves you must hang.
>
> (*Poems*, p. 125)

Although "Shamus" was popularized by Samuel Lover in America, Le Fanu did not have it published until a few years after its composition because the Young Irelander William Smith O'Brien, ironically enough, had just been sentenced for high treason in 1848.

While "Phaudrig Crohoore" and "Shamus O'Brien" can be said to celebrate Irish patriotism in their tributes to the Rebellion of '98, their radical overtones are considerably diminished by the use of comic mimicry, according to Le Fanu's biographer W. J. McCormack. The theme of rebellion is instead replaced by that of national unity in some of his shorter fiction and novels. Like "Phaudhrig," the plot of "Bridal of Carrigvarah" centers on the idea of a forced marriage. Here, the young Richard O'Mara falls in love with the simple Irish girl, Ellen Heathcote—although his wealthy father insists that he marry Lady Emily, an English aristocrat; the reader is pointedly informed that Richard dismisses this prospective marriage as "nothing more than a kind of understood stipulation, entered into by their parents," a sordid sort of affair deemed "a matter of business and calculation than as involving anything of mutual inclination on the part of the parties most nearly interested in the matter" (*Purcell Papers,* p. 161). Trouble ensues when the treacherous servant of the O'Maras, Dwyer (who is already bent on acquiring the lease of the Heathcotes), slyly discloses Richard's secret marriage to the brother of Lady Emily. Richard dies when he is slain by Emily's brother in a duel. If the stalwart Phaudrig supports the rebellion of '98, it is not surprising either that the treacherous Dwyer turns informer: the man guilty of betraying a kind master and his lover is also responsible for betraying his nation. Other stories, such as "Ultor de Lacy" (1861) disseminate a somewhat different but related message in its implicit criticism of those supporting the English establishment. Here, the daughter of a Jacobite falls in love fatally with the ghost of a rebel kinsman once imprisoned and brutally executed by a Protestant ancestor during Elizabeth's reign.

In turn, Le Fanu's earliest novels, written during the height of the Young Ireland movement and the devastating years of the famine, can be read as parallel reinterpretations of Irish Jacobite history. *The Cock and Anchor* (1845) sets forth a promising yet fleeting vision of Protestant and Catholic union, even if the Protestant Mary Ashwoode expires before she is able to wed her Jacobite lover, Edmond O'Connor. However, the relationship is doomed from the start as the male Ashwoodes, father and son, are not only "unboundedly luxurious" and "prodigal to reckless-

ness" (1895, p. 76) but unprincipled enough to sacrifice Mary for the purposes of recovering their squandered resources. Mary is initially urged by her father to marry the decrepit aristocrat Aspenly, before her brother's losses through gaming subsequently lead him to force the detested Nicholas Blarden upon her. Indeed, Richard and Henry Ashwoode would appear to embody the general moral degradation of the Whigs, particularly when Henry betrays Edmond despite being rescued by him, and in Aspenly we are introduced to a man of "violently Whig politics and connections" (p. 90). But the association with Whiggishness and immorality is perhaps best summed up in the character of the Lord Lieutenant, Wharton, an "unscrupulous and daring political intriguer" as well as a "sensualist and an infidel" (p. 102) openly disdained by one of the foremost Irish patriots of the eighteenth century, Jonathan Swift. By contrast, the Tories Oliver French and O'Connor's benefactor, Audley, are blunt, forthright, and compassionate; French is able to overlook his long-running feud with the Ashwoodes by protecting Mary. It is this marked sympathy for Tory Jacobitism that distinguishes the novel from those of Sir Walter Scott's, as Victor Sage has observed. What is more difficult to ascertain in Le Fanu's apparent Jacobite and Tory sympathy, however, is whether it leans toward a tacit defense of contemporary Tory, Unionist politics or an anti-Unionist and anti-Whiggish Young Irelander bent. Framed as such, the question remains uanswerable: nonetheless, the coercion urged by Blarden (including the changing of locks, servants, and guards) with the cooperation of Henry implicitly invokes the contemporary nationalist allegation that the Union served only to usher in British-imposed martial law. According to Jason King, it is probable that Le Fanu's literary revisualization of Jacobite Catholic history, one instrumental for constructing a narrative of "political dispossession" (p. 71), was additionally impacted by a popular discourse fixated on Catholic disinheritance and the displacement of the native Irish. It is significant too that O'Connor's friend Captain O'Hanlon, makes use of nationalist tropes of lost birthright and inheritance:

Is it a common thing, think you, that all the gentle-
men, all the chivalry of a whole country—the
natural leaders and protectors of the people—should
be stripped of their birthright, ay, even of the poor
privilege of seeing in this their native country,
strangers possessing the inheritances which are in
all right their own; cast abroad upon the world;
soldiers of fortune, selling their blood for a bare
subsistence ...

(p. 8)

The sense of a lost birthright and inheritance is
again underscored at the very ending of the novel.
As Mary eventually falls ill and dies, Henry is
hanged, and O'Connor slain in the wars, Blarden
lives a long life of luxury.

If *The Cock and Anchor* offers a tragic
interpretation of Jacobite losses, *The Fortunes of
Colonel Torlogh O'Brien* (1847) presents a more
optimistic one of national reconciliation. Published in the same year as William Thackeray's
Vanity Fair, this panoramic novel of the Williamite wars features dizzying shifts of scenes
encompassing castles, courts, battlefields, and
inns as well as an array of characters ranging
from lowly time servers to James II himself. A
sense of balance is already present in the opening
chapters with Le Fanu's evenhanded criticism of
Irish mobs and his mockery of English prejudice
against the Irish, such as displayed by Dick Gos-
lin, one of (Protestant) Percy Neville's men, when
he initially derides Ireland as a "nest of land sav-
ages" (p. 13) all while complaining about the
lack of "gentlemanlike amusements" like bear-
fighting. As in *The Cock and Anchor*, there is an
alliance between Catholic and Protestant when
the Catholic Torlogh falls in love with the
Protestant Grace Willoughby, the daughter of Sir
Hugh Willoughby: coincidentally, the present
owner of Glindarragh, a castle that once belonged
to the O'Briens. It is Torlogh—a man distinguished by a shamrock on his forehead (caused
by a bullet) and feared by Grace's elderly nurse
as "a terrible man of war and blood" (p. 18)—
who not only rescues Grace from the clutches of
the ruffian Hogan but also narrowly saves her
father from the gallows when the latter is wrongly
betrayed by his kinsman Miles Garrett, a Protestant turned Catholic. But unlike *The Cock and
Anchor*, virtue is determined not by creed or even

politics but by individual morality, as "apostacies
were confined to men of second-rate importance
and ability" (p. 270). If Hugh bravely resists oppression in stereotypically Whiggish fashion
while Torlogh displays compassion and bravery,
Garrett is the amoral opportunist, Jeremiah Tisdal
a cowardly perjurer, and Garvey the servile fol-
lower who ends up despised by all and subjected
to the horrors of the strappado. As such, when
Grace attempts to dissuade Torlogh from fighting
in the Battle of the Boyne, Hugh champions his
decision, deeming it honorable. Appropriately
enough, the novel closes with scenes of concilia-
tion, first as Hugh forgives Tisdal, granting him
money to sail to America, and finally as many of
the characters return to Glindarragh. It is here
that Grace's nurse, once fearful of Torlogh,
celebrates his accomplishments, "for there is not
a handsomer or a cleverer gentleman in Ireland's
grounds" (p. 339). At last, the young couple, "the
breathing representative of that new alliance"
will finally bury "all the feuds and discords of
the past" (p. 339).

In a tale that shifts away from these politicized romances, *The House by the Churchyard*
(1863) represents a convergence of sorts between
the wide-ranging tableau of characters in *Torlogh*
and his future thrillers, with an underlying plot
that delves into the story of a murder committed
some decades earlier. There are also elements of
comedy reminiscent of Charles Lever's picar-
esque sketches involving the lisping Lieutenant
Puddock, the helpful and active Father Roach,
the flighty Mrs. Macnamara and her boisterous
daughter, Mag, as well as romance, of which the
tragic one between Captain Devereux and the
frail, soon-to-die Lilias Walsingham is
predominant. Not least, there are a few scattered
gothic touches, including an inset story centered
on the Tiled House where the equally mysterious
son and heir to Lord Dunoran secludes himself: a
house supposedly haunted by a ghostly disembodied hand. The actual murder plot, however, does
not actually insinuate itself until some ways into
the novel, when the financially strapped physician Sturk gradually recognizes Dangerfield as
the perpetrator of a murder that he witnessed two
decades earlier—a murder for which Lord Duno-

ran had been falsely arraigned. Sturk's attempts to blackmail the natty, polished, and ambitious Dangerfield backfire when the latter attacks him before having him trepanned. Sturk, however, is still able to testify against him in a trial, where the fact of Dangerfield's crimes are revealed and that of the deceased Lord Dunoran's cleared, so that his son can finally inherit his title and property. Although the murder plot is relatively attenuated within the general context of the novel, particularly when compared to his other mysteries, it reveals Le Fanu's developing interest in the sly, polished, and sinister gentlemanly criminal, particularly a returning criminal whose iniquities must be finally confronted and punished. That Le Fanu may have felt dissatisfied with the preparation and resolution of the plot may explain why he refashioned this trope of the returning murderer eight years later in *Checkmate* (1871), bringing sharper focus to the villain and his motivations.

GHOST STORIES AND OTHER SHORTER FICTION

Le Fanu is probably best remembered for his supernatural tales and novellas. A reading of such stories as "Schalken the Painter," "Disturbances on Aungier Street," "Squire Toby's Will," "Madam Crowl's Ghost," and the stories that comprise *In a Glass Darkly* easily attests to the substance of V. S. Pritchett's claim that Le Fanu possessed "the gift of brevity, the talent for the poetic sharpness and discipline of the short tale" as well as "an infallible eye for the essential thing, the power of unimpeachable definition" (p. 9). Equally distinctive is his eye for visual detail, or nascent cinematic appeal as astutely noted by Ivan Melada: for instance, a spectral form that expands dramatically from a snuffer ("Wicked Captain Walshawe, of Wauling," *Dublin University Magazine,* April 1864), a mysterious, muffled-up man wearing green goggles and a respirator ("The Mysterious Lodger," *Dublin University Magazine*, January and February 1850), and a ghostly army whose torsos and legs fade in and out ("Ghost Stories of Chapelizod," *Dublin University Magazine*, January 1851). But perhaps most remarkable is his ability to create a

lingering sense of fear and foreboding, one enhanced by a strategic dropping of clues that gradually confirm the reader's fears, leaving little room for skepticism. This impression of terror is made especially compelling in stories that depict the workings of a guilty conscience—whether the crime is an abuse of authority, murder, the filching of an inheritance, or an engagement in an unholy compact for gain. Indeed, this fascination with fear from an internal source—fear triggered by conscience—rather than an external (e.g., supernatural) source can properly be said to pave the way for modern psychological horror.

One of his earliest stories, "Schalken the Painter," reveals Le Fanu's skill at building suspense. The idea of the forced marriage is further gothicized in this story as the young woman, Rose Velderkaust, is sold in marriage by her uncle, Gerard Douw, to a wealthy man, Vanderhausen of Rotterdam—who is gradually revealed to be a corpse. The action of the story opens, appropriately enough, with the strange suitor suddenly materializing as Schalken struggles with his rendering of devils and saints in his new painting of Saint Anthony's temptations. That there is something slightly disturbing about Vanderhausen is suggested not only by his equally unfathomable vanishing, but his preternatural appearance when he pays another visit to Douw's apartments. His eyes reveal "a certain indefinable character of insanity," while his lips are "nearly black" (p. 190). But even more disquieting are his odd movements, "as if the limbs were guided and directed by a spirit unused to the management of bodily machinery" (p. 191). None of this, however, quite deters Douw in spite of his initial disgust and recurring misgivings. This impression of uncanniness is strengthened by details on the curious nighttime arrival of the man and his bride at Rotterdam, during which the driver of the coach notices "strange men" bearing a "large litter, of an antique shape" (p. 194)—as the tearful Rose wrings her hands; the fact that Douw begins a fruitless search for his niece and son-in-law months later proves equally alarming. But Le Fanu does not ease the pressure just yet. As the reader's suspicions that the groom is in fact a living corpse are confirmed when Rose bursts into Douw's residence, crying out for a priest because "the dead and the living can never be one," the scene grows even more frightening when Schalken detects a "shadowy and ill-defined form" (p. 196) gliding into the room, one which eventually snatches up Rose again. It is not until the end of the tale, however, that Le Fanu finally reveals Rose's corpse husband in "livid and demoniac form" sitting "bold upright" (p. 201) in a bed found among the vaults of the church.

If "Schalken the Painter" unfolds quickly, "An Account of Some Strange Disturbances in Aungier Street" (which appeared in *Dublin University Magazine* in December 1853) displays Le Fanu's skill at rendering a convincing impression of dark premonition while playing with the reader's sense of objectivity. This preternatural eeriness begins with the mansion itself, an ancient structure that is equally evocative of living death and decay; the very walls and ceilings are "queer and bygone" while the age of the woodwork cannot be disguised by any degree of "modern finery and varnish" (*Madam Crowl's Ghost*, p. 69). Especially disconcerting is the structure of the back bedroom, with its "two queerly-placed melancholy windows" and the "shadowy recess," that bears a "specially sinister and suggestive character" at night: one betraying "latent discord—a certain mysterious and indescribable relation, which jarred indistinctly upon some secret sense of the fitting and the safe" while "rais[ing] indefinable suspicions and apprehensions of the imagination" (p. 70). In short, the mansion is uncanny—or *unheimlich*, to use a word coined by Freud decades later.

The reader's apprehensions are further raised by the layering of events as Le Fanu segues three different accounts in an overarching first-person narrative such that characters interrupt each other, comparing and confirming their experiences. Here, Dick, the more impressionable of the two medical students renting the mansion, begins his narrative with a description of his dreams, in which he sees the portrait of Judge Horrocks, the hanging judge: given his general susceptibility and his subsequent use of tonic and liquor ("kept my spirits up by pouring spirits down," p. 73),

the reader remains somewhat doubtful of his experiences. Nonetheless, Dick's terror is rendered highly convincing, particularly as he hears the grotesque sound of an "unearthly tread" descending the stairs:

> I screwed up my courage to a decisive experiment—opened my door, and in a stentorian voice bawled over the banisters, "Who's there?" There was no answer but the ringing of my own voice through the empty old house,—no renewal of the movement; nothing, in short, to give my unpleasant sensations a definite direction. There is, I think, something most disagreeably disenchanting in the sound of one's own voice under such circumstances, exerted in solitude, and in vain. It redoubled my sense of isolation, and my misgivings increased on perceiving that the door, which I certainly thought I had left open, was closed behind me; in a vague alarm, lest my retreat should be cut off, I got again into my room as quickly as I could, where I remained in a state of imaginary blockade, and very uncomfortable indeed, till morning.
>
> (p. 74)

There is a brief moment of humor when the source of the sound is discovered to be a "monstrous grey rat"—albeit a rat bearing the "infernal gaze" of the portrait: a comic respite redolent of some of Le Fanu's comic tales where supposed ghosts are revealed to be living beings presumed to have been dead (e.g., "Jim Sulivan's Adventures in the Great Snow" and "Billy Malowney's Taste of Love and Glory" in *The Purcell Papers*).

But the relief is short-lived, lasting only until the other student, Tom, recounts his experiences to Dick. If the corroborations in their vision of an old man clothed in a red dressing gown and black cap begins to suggest a supernatural agency at work, Tom's narration heightens the sensation of eeriness as he recalls the ominous sound of a cord being drawn slowly along the floor, lifted and falling down again in coils. In all of this, Le Fanu makes the terror all the more plausible with Tom's persistent attempts to be skeptical:

> I now began to recover a little. I was fagged and exhausted, and at last, overpowered by a feverish sleep. I came down late; and finding you out of spirits, on account of your dreams about the portrait, whose *original* I am now certain disclosed himself to me, I did not care to talk about the infernal

vision. In fact, I was trying to persuade myself that the whole thing was an illusion, and I did not like to revive in their intensity the hated impressions of the past night—or to risk the constancy of my scepticism, by recounting the tale of my sufferings.

(p. 78)

The story is drawn to a chilling climax when the housekeeper, who has been listening to the two students, explains not only that his room was once the bedroom of Horrocks, "the hanging'est judge that was known in Ireland's ground" (p. 83), but that the "shadowy recess" that so un-nerved Dick was the very site where the judge prepared the ropes for his suicide prior to hang-ing himself from the banisters: in short, she confirms their suspicion that the house is indeed haunted by an unhappy spirit. Le Fanu continues the hair-raising thrills to the very conclusion of the story by providing the housekeeper's brief accounts of other "quare stories" in the house: the death of the judge's natural daughter result-ing from her fright at the judge's ghost, as well as other "cross accidents, sudden deaths, and short times in it" (p. 84). Despite the possibility of natural causes for these tragedies, Le Fanu succeeds at creating the impression that all are effected by the malevolent spirit of the judge—particularly as he mentions but does not explain the case of Nicholas Spaight, "a very strange story" with "many very curious particulars" (p. 84). In short, even if there is "wriggle room" left for a rational explanation for their visions—the men are either drunk or exhausted—Le Fanu cleverly manages to convey that the "wriggle room" is miniscule.

Particularly masterful is Le Fanu's portrait of a fear borne from guilt. It is not so much the "headless coachman of the legendary heiress griz-zling her way through the centuries that frighten us the most," as brilliantly put by Pritchett, but rather our minds as guilt "patters two-legged behind its victims" and "retribution sits adding up its account night after night, the secret doubt scratches away with malignant patience in the guarded mind" (p. 10); in other words, "we haunt ourselves" (p. 7). Indeed, given Pritchett's claim that "Anglo-Irish society … was a guilty society," one haunted by "insecurity and bad memories" (p. 9), is it entirely accidental that Le Fanu's

stories are also racked by guilt—especially when the fictional criminals are later revealed to have wrongly disinherited and deprived others of their property or abused their authority? To some extent, there are already hints of this guilt in "Aungier Street," with the madness of the "hanging'est judge that was known in Ireland's ground," one most likely hastened by his blood-thirsty executions. A comparable idea of a haunter plagued by guilt surfaces in "Madam Crowl's Ghost" as the eponymous widow is prone to bouts of insanity—insinuated not only by the straitjacket hanging in her closet but by her ghostly visit to the secret room where she once murdered a stepchild for his inheritance. In "The Familiar" (originally "The Watcher" before its publication in *In a Glass Darkly*), a man who once abused his authority by a merciless flogging of an underling is subjected to the stalking of a man who resembles that underling exactly: except for the uncanny fact that the victim has been dead for years. The fears and anxieties ac-companying guilt are even more deftly handled in such stories as "Green Tea," "Squire Toby's Will," and "Justice Harbottle." If the ghostly monkey imagined by the clergyman in "Green Tea" (from *In a Glass Darkly*) can be interpreted as a manifestation of his guilty curiosity in pagan religion, "Squire" and "Harbottle" (*In a Glass Darkly*) offer discerning treatments of the haunted conscience, fusing together internalized and externalized horror seamlessly.

In "Squire Toby's Will" (published in *Temple Bar*, January 1868), a black-headed, white-bodied bulldog appears during a period when the two sons of the squire are quarreling over his will, with Scroope determined to claim the estate as the elder brother, even though the will designates Charles as the heir. Although Charles is initially amused by the dog—to the consternation of his servant, Cooper—he begins to grow more uncom-fortable, particularly as the dog bears a curious resemblance to his pug-faced father. In his nightmares, Charles dreams of the dog assuming the form of his father while urging him to restore some of the inheritance to Scroope:

Among these was the now not unfrequent troubling of his sleep with dreams and nightmares. In these his canine favourite invariably had a part and was generally a central, and sometimes a solitary figure. In these visions the dog seemed to stretch himself up the side of the Squire's bed ... with a horrible likeness to the pug features of old Squire Toby ... and then he would talk to him about Scroope, and tell him "all wasn't straight," and that he "must make it up wi' Scroope," that he, the old Squire, had "served him an ill turn" ... Then in his dream this semi-human brute would approach his face to his ... till the face of the beast was laid on his, with the same odious caresses and stretchings and writhings which he had seen over the old Squire's grave. Then Charlie would wake up ... fancy he saw something white sliding off the foot of the bed ... and always when he had been visited by such dreams the dog next morning was more than usually caressing and servile, as if to obliterate, by a more than ordinary welcome, the sentiment of disgust which the horror of the night had left behind it.

(*Madam Crowl's Ghost*, p. 24)

Although Le Fanu leaves some room for a rational explanation—after all, Charles has suffered a severe injury that prevents him from exercising and keeping mentally fit—natural and supernatural increasingly begin to merge. Is it purely a coincidence that the dog appears to behave threateningly whenever Charles dreams about his father, and especially when he finally decides against restoring all of the property to his brother after his discovery of the deed? Or that it screeches strangely like a human when it is shot? The blend of supernatural and natural comes across powerfully after the death of the hump-backed, long-necked, and sharp-nosed Scroope. Not only do mysterious howls and wails begin to resound through the hallways, but his apparition also gradually materializes: first as a distinct silhouette against the wall, and more impressive still, in an engraving of a wolf, as it begins to assume his features.

It is in "Justice Harbottle" that Le Fanu revisits "Aungier Street," re-creating and transforming it into a grand tale of guilt: one that is no less filled with sublime phantasmagoria. The English counterpart of Horrocks, Harbottle is the "wickedest man in England" as well as a "dangerous and unscrupulous judge," prone to handling "cases his own way in spite of counsel, authorities, and even of juries, by a sort of cajolery,

violence and bamboozling" (*In a Glass Darkly*, 1993 ed., p. 88); One night, as Harbottle is returning from a play with two men after having unjustly executed Lewis Pynebeck, he sees—or imagines—a giant set of gallows with "skeletons swinging lightly by their chains" in a "black moor stretching lifelessly from right to left, with rotting trees, pointing fantastic branches in the air." He is next taken to the High Court of Appeals, presided over by a "Justice Twofold," an exaggerated version of Harbottle himself, "at least double his size, and with all his fierce colouring, and his ferocity of eye and visage" (p.108); like Harbottle, he "seemed to feel his power over the jury, and to exult and riot in the display of it" (p. 109). Frightened by the verdict—that he is to be sentenced to death on the tenth of the following month—he roars, shocking others in the coach. That the dream is more than a dream but rather a premonition of sorts is soon evinced by the presence of ghostly figures in the house, especially as his mistress' daughter sees the silhouette of Pynebeck. Even more potent is the image witnessed by a maid of a "monstrous figure" in the back kitchen beating "a mighty hammer the rings and rivets of a chain" (p. 116) while pointing to a dead body. It is discovered almost immediately afterward that Harbottle has hanged himself from the banister at the top of the great staircase.

Not least, Le Fanu is remembered for one of the most compelling pieces of vampire literature ever written, "Carmilla," the concluding tale of *In a Glass Darkly*. Here, Le Fanu weaves in the idea of a returning evil where the vampire Carmilla attacks the protagonist Laura twice: once when she is a young child and again in her teens. Although Laura finds herself alternatively attracted to and repulsed by Carmilla's attentions, she falls ill. A visit from her father's friend General Spielsdorf, however, reveals that Carmilla is a vampire who must be destroyed, particularly as she has already killed his own daughter. It is perhaps here that we can detect further resonances from contemporary nationalist discourse. While some have assumed the character of Carmilla as a personification of the native Irish given Le Fanu's Tory Protestant upbringing, it is as plausible to assume otherwise, given Le

Fanu's sheer exposure to a broad range of political discourse—not to mention his involvement with the Young Ireland movement. Not altogether accidentally, the story is set in rural Styria, the border between Austria and Hungary: two nations that shared an alliance comparable to that of England and Ireland until 1867. The colonial framework is laid in place when we see a "hideous black woman" with her "teeth set as if in rage" (p. 257), whom critics have read as a colonial counterpart of a native Irish Carmilla: or could the angry woman be manifesting her repressed rage at the powerful Carmilla? The likelihood of the latter possibility increases as Carmilla is frequently identified by others as "noble" and "aristocratic": traits that would have much more readily attributed to a Protestant Ascendancy by a late-nineteenth-century readership. Her attacks on the peasants invoke the nationalist claim that the propertied classes were "vampire plagues." Even more significantly, her contempt toward the peasantry corresponds to contemporary stereotypes of the Anglo-Irish landlord, while her furious reaction to the hymns sung at the funeral for a dead peasant girl can be said to evoke not only Protestant disdain for so-called Catholic superstition but also the growing strain of English skepticism that Isaac Butt distrusted in his writings on education: a skepticism reinforced in her dismissive reaction to Laura's father's professions of God's omniscience—"And this disease that invades the country is natural. Nature. All things proceed from nature" (p. 270).

At the same time, Carmilla's control over Laura is also not dissimilar from the British "policy of compulsion" in Ireland, particularly when Carmilla tells Laura, "You are mine, you shall be mine, you and I are one for ever" (p. 264) and "You will think me cruel, very selfish, the more ardent, the more selfish." The very fact that Carmilla is compared to a "boyish lover" further links her with the popular notion of a masculine Anglo-Saxon. Perhaps there is also an implication that the relationship between Britain and Ireland is not unlike a perverse homoerotic relationship? Nor is it entirely coincidental that the portrait of Mircalla (Carmilla in another

incarnation) is dated 1698—three years following the enactment of the penal code in 1695. In short, the Carmilla that bleeds Laura is the same Carmilla who bled her during her childhood—not unlike the Ireland imagined by James Morison in *Irish Grievances*, who imagined her as "bitter, moody, and wretched now" not because she was conquered "two centuries ago," but because "the sharp and cruel effects of that conquest are cutting and maiming her still" (p. 74). Finally, the collected historical accounts of her various incarnations and crimes provided by the General, the woodman, and Baron Vorderberg broadly replicate nationalist narratives on English oppression in Ireland. The General's explanation of his reluctant belief in the existence of vampires, as if revisiting Lady Morgan's claim that the British government in Ireland was a "species of political vampirism," is not without political overtones. Accusing Laura's father of believing in nothing "but what consists with your own prejudices and illusions" and that he himself "remembers when I was like you, but I have learned better" (p. 293), Vorderberg explains that "I have been forced by extraordinary evidence to credit that which ran counter, diametrically, to all my theories. I have been made the dupe of a preternatural conspiracy" (p. 294). Old prejudices must be reexamined; what once appeared outlandish may not be so after all. His newfound credence in the existence of vampires might be said to correspond to a growing consensus in the perception of English oppression in Ireland, just as Isaac Butt himself was to abandon Protestant Tory Unionism for Home Rule. After all, if the Styrians are proven correct in their suspicions of a vampire at work, who is to say that the Irish are not also correct in their own suspicions of English and the Anglo-Irish Tory Ascendancy?

THE NOVELS

In her preface to a 1947 edition of *Uncle Silas*, Elizabeth Bowen claimed that she had always imagined the 1864 novel as "an Irish story transposed to an English setting," with its "hermetic solitude and the autocracy of the great country house, the demonic power of the family myth, fatalism, feudalism, and the 'ascendency' outlook" (p. 8). Indeed, much the same can be said for nearly all of Le Fanu's other novels with English settings. One might even venture beyond to claim that they refract, as if in a glass darkly, some of the central issues that haunted contemporary nationalist discourse. Not unlike his Young Irelander peers who dwelled on the idea of an Ireland deprived of her just inheritance, Le Fanu dwells on the analogous idea of a disputed family inheritance. And not unlike nationalists who regarded the friction between Ireland and Britain as a feud between two sisters, Le Fanu was also to focus on interfamilial feuds, whether distant relations, cousins, siblings, or even mother and daughter to a greater extent than other contemporary writers of supernatural fiction such as Louisa Baldwin, Charles Dickens, Lettice Galbraith, and J. H. Riddell. Similarly striking is Le Fanu's preoccupation with the idea of a persisting or returning evil, as identified by M. R. James, whether in the form of a returning villain, the repetition of a crime, or a recurring ill: an idea not altogether dissimilar from nationalist impressions of an Ireland repeatedly oppressed and plundered by Britain. Although some of these ideas are already evident in his shorter fiction, the novels can be said to develop them further. While it would require a stretch of the imagination to assume that Le Fanu was bent on promoting a nationalist agenda or crafting national allegories, such a proposition becomes somewhat less absurd when we consider that nationalists considered the history of Ireland a romance: after all, Thomas D'Arcy McGee's *Popular History of Ireland* (1863) was advertised as a work that demonstrated how "truth is often stranger than fiction" with Irish history being "more romantic than romance." Could it be that Le Fanu was conversely inspired by such a view, penning his novels as imaginative alternative histories of a haunted nation?

As if combining the separate tropes of the irresponsible father-guardian and the longstanding family feud in *Torlogh O'Brien* with that of the returning murderer from *House by the Churchyard*, *Uncle Silas* shifts away stylistically from Le Fanu's sprawling narratives to produce a slower, more brooding work, revisiting a relatively simple plot from his short story "Passage in the Secret History of an Irish Countess" (*Purcell Papers*). Here, the dying Austin Ruthyn assigns the guardianship of his daughter to his disreputable younger brother, Silas, in an effort to vindicate the family name; the latter was once alleged—and later proven—to have murdered a man. But as the daughter, Maud, slowly discovers, Silas is still anything but virtuous; he endeavors to force her into marrying his son, Dudley, before making an attempt on her life. If there is something to be said for an economical treatment of a plot, the opposite could be said for *Uncle Silas* since it is precisely the rich atmosphere and description that does full justice to it.

Certainly, the isolation of the protagonist is underscored, beginning with her relatively happier years at Knowle. It is not only physically isolated—a place full of "funereal but glorious woods" where "fancies and regrets float mistily in the dream" (p. 11) but emotionally isolated as well. Despite her father's apparent benevolence, there is already a hint of paternal remoteness, implied not only by his willingness to sacrifice her for the protection of the family name but also in his retention of Madame de la Rougierre against the desires of Maud and Cousin Monica: even with Maud's belief that "I am sure my father loved me, and I know I loved him" (p. 1). This sense of remoteness is redoubled at Bartram Haugh, where Austin's mysteriousness is magnified in his brother's near preternatural aspect, with its "fearful monumental look" and "singularly vivid eyes" (p. 189). The house itself, with its "forlorn character of desertion and decay" is similarly a more formidable counterpart of the Knowle estate, particularly since it is "condemned and avoided, and the very name of its inmates tabooed" (p. 161). The impression of danger is no less conveyed by fears of the unknown and the uncertain, for instance, the "unknown danger" about Madame de la Rougierre.

Indeed, the addition of Rougierre herself is one that lends a disturbing uncanniness to the work. If she is physically grotesque, with her "bleached and sallow skin, her hollow jaws" (p. 18), her actions prove even more unsettling to

Maud, as is colorfully displayed in her morbid humor:

> "Come now," cried Madame ... "I am Madame la Morgue—Mrs. Deadhouse! I will present you my friends, Monsieur Cadavre and Monsieur Squelette. Come, come, leetle mortal let us play. Ouaah!" And she uttered a horrid yell from her enormous mouth, and pushing her wig and bonnet back, so as to show her great, bald head.

(p. 32)

The comparisons to the wolf in Little Red Riding Hood and the strange pig-lady, with "a mongrel body and demon soul" (p. 31), lend her a macabre aspect with its implied return to childhood fears. But her most startling appearance occurs as Maud explores the upper floor of Bartram Haugh. Roaming the hallways like the "conscientious heroine of Mrs. Ann Radcliffe," and half expecting to find a "strangely furnished suite of apartments," Maud enters several rooms, including one where "the great bony figure of Madame de la Rougierre was before me." Bursting into "a loud screeching laugh," she "danced some fantastic steps in her bare wet feet" with her characteristic "old Walpurgis gaiety" (p. 352). Appropriately enough, the cause of Madame's death is grotesquely humorous; her sleeping figure is mistaken for Maud's when Dudley reenacts his father's murder of Charke years ago in the same room.

The sense of eerie premonition is likewise heightened to effect in *A Lost Name* (1868), a rewriting of "Some Account of the Latter Days of the Hon. Richard Marston, of Dunoran," a short story that was serialized in *Dublin University Magazine* from April through June 1848 before being published as a novella in 1851. If the plot of *Uncle Silas* involves the reenactment of a murder in the same room, *A Lost Name* accentuates the idea of a recurring evil and repeated history. Unlike the original version, a concise detective mystery centered on the murder of a guest to the family estate, the novel offers deeper reflections on the various motives of the murderer, particularly his feelings for the beautiful governess. But even more distinctive is a new emphasis on a cyclical family curse—along with an emphasis on a lost name and inheritance. The

contemporary world, as the narrator states, is one where "the present is the inheritance of evil" (p. 126). This sentiment is enhanced by the addition of a gothic family curse: the Raby estate, of which the Shadwell family is its soon-to-be last owners, is doomed to suffer a tragedy every 110 years, since it was cursed by a Lady Mildred, the "gaze-lady" who committed suicide after her husband proved unfaithful to her. That history repeats itself is borne out when the brooding and frustrated Mark Shadwell falls in love with his daughter's governess, Agnes, before murdering his cousin Roke Wycherly out of jealous rivalry for her attentions during Roke's visit. As if further highlighting this sense of historic inevitability, Le Fanu's characters repeatedly mention the legend of the "gaze-lady." Mark's visionary servant, Carmel Sherlock, informs him that the supposedly haunted site is "mixed with my fate, sir, and yours,—and has blighted your house—and I feel the presence of the spirit" (p. 78), just as Agnes herself explains that the gaze-lady "comes like a beautiful woman, and very plausibly—more as if a chance had brought her, than by design—and so she grows into an influence which she uses, with the wisdom, to entangle and beguile, and draw them into those dangerous currents of life which are strewn with dead men and shipwreck" (p. 134). Bearing a star in the palm of her hand like the supposed "gaze-lady," and variously compared to a "tigress" and "pythoness," the femme-fatale Agnes becomes the latest incarnation to wreck the family. Since she partly witnesses Mark's murder of Roke, she is able to blackmail him (which the reader does not see) and thereby lure him away from his wife and daughter before embarking on an affair with another man: Mark's accidental sight of their kiss brings the family history to a full circle as he proceeds to commit suicide—like the "gaze-lady" herself—after removing Agnes from his will and settling the property on his daughter. As the narrator informs us at the end, the name of "Shadwell of Wynderfel, or of Raby, a title which we meet with often in old county chronicles, and which mingles historically with others in the lists of splendour and of war, will turn up no more. It is 'A Lost Name'" (p. 465). Not least, unlike the earlier version, the novel reinforces this sense of loss with ample allusions to earlier literature and history. Although many of Le Fanu's works cite classic and contemporary literature, *A Lost Name* is arguably the most self-consciously literary: just as the names of Shadwell and Wycherly allude fittingly to the libertine dramatists of the Restoration, the narrator and characters make ample references to the Bible and works of Dante, Chaucer, Cervantes, George Herbert, Richard Sheridan, Samuel Taylor Coleridge, and William Makepeace Thackeray (with the ambitious Agnes not unlike a gothicized Becky Sharp), as if suggesting the values of literature and history to the interpretation of life—a lesson disastrously disregarded by Shadwell.

That Le Fanu was also preoccupied with the idea of a returning evil in the shape of a returning villain or source of trouble is amply demonstrated in two tightly structured thrillers, *The Wyvern Mystery* (1869) and *Checkmate* (1871), with the former itself an expansion of "A Chapter in the History of a Tyrone Family" (if not a variation of Charlotte Brontë's *Jane Eyre* from 1847, which was itself possibly influenced by "Tyrone Family") and the latter a variation on *The Cock and Anchor*. If the original plot, not unlike that of *Uncle Silas*, already implies a returning evil—namely, in the shape of the husband's first wife, who is blind and half-mad, confronting the husband and his second wife—the novel emphasizes this return all the more. The "mystery" here is the subject of Charles' and Henry's discussion after Charles, the older brother, marries Alice: what will Charles do about that "old soger" who threatens to reveal the truth about their marriage years ago? The "old soger" turns out to be the half-blind and mad Dutchwoman, Bertha Velderkaust, who has caught wind of the marriage and returns to Charles' estate in order to kill Alice. But Bertha is not the only returning evil. Henry, the younger brother, returns to the estate after Charles' illness and death, this time to abduct their child, also named Henry, in order to deprive him of his inheritance. During all of this, Alice is subjected to anxieties, if not fears, of repeating the unhappy lives of previous generations of Fairfield wives. The fact that *The Wyvern Mystery* alludes to famous fairy tales directly and indirectly (as noted by Sally Harris) bolsters the impression of history retracing itself—not unlike the referencing of works of literature in *A Lost Name*. Similarly, *Checkmate* addresses the idea of history repeating itself, not only in its very rewriting of *Cock and Anchor* but also with its focus on a villain who returns to the same family estate where he once fatally attacked the heir. What renders the novel especially uncanny, however, is an elderly servant's sense of familiarity about Longcluse; the servant associates his voice with the night when Henry Arden was murdered some twenty years earlier. Experiencing a "vague and terrible recognition" (p. 6) reminiscent of Sturk's in *House by the Churchyard*, she tells David, the brother of Henry, that "it must be something that's no' canny, as you used to say" (p. 87). In fact, the novel might even be said to approximate a history itself as it seeks to discover the true identity of the murderer. David's investigations eventually lead him to Paris, where he meets Baron Vanboeren in order to discover the truth of Longcluse's persona. It is fitting that the discovery takes place in a chapter titled "Resurrections," where Le Fanu declares that "history repeats itself," sometimes "in literal sobriety, sometimes in derisive travesty [sic], sometimes in tragic aggravation" (p. 286). Here, David learns that Longcluse is the second incarnation of the villain Yelland Mace, who attacked his brother before having his face remolded by Vanboeren. By the end of the novel, a trial and letter reveal that Longcluse/Mace was not only responsible for the murder of Henry but also for that of Lebas at the beginning of the novel—and that he is none other than Edwin Raikes, a long-lost relation of the Ardens. Not least, Longcluse's interest in tales and ballads of demonic and spectral lovers considerably strengthens not only the impression of the uncanny but also the uncanny return.

If Le Fanu is chiefly admired for some of his better plots and brooding atmosphere, he is undeservedly less so for his characterization, despite his vivid, Austenian sketches of minor characters and portraits of villains that go beyond the stock renderings generally found in sensation novels and mysteries. The guests at Marlowe Hall in *Guy Deverell* (1865), a mystery that centers on a hidden deed and a subsequent wrongful disinheritance, are crisply delineated, from the frostily aristocratic yet passionate Lady Alice, the blustering and slow-witted General Lennox, the perverse Miss Blunkett, to the General's wife, Lady Jane, a woman who is seemingly blasé and uncaring yet frustrated in her love for Marlowe: nearly all have their distinctive behaviors and speech patterns. The same may be said for the characters at Lady Vernon's estate in *The Rose and the Key* (1871): the obsequious Dr. Malkin, the haughty and self-entitled vicar Foljambe, his slightly deaf wife, the pretentious yet awkward Zachary Smelt, and the blustering Irishman Revd Doody, who winds up helping to rescue the protagonist. Even more striking are Le Fanu's sketches of semi-comic villains such as Josiah Larkin, the attorney and religious hypocrite who appears in *Wylder's Hand* (1864), *The Tenants of Malory* (1867), and *Haunted Lives* (1868). If *Wylder's Hand* reveals him at his canniest in his consummately polite yet devious gulling of the naive Reverend Wylder (the younger brother of the slain heir), *Malory* provides a portrait of an affected man endeavoring to impress his social superiors but somehow missing the mark. For instance, while visiting Cleve Verney, Larkin enters with "a stride that was meant to be perfectly easy and gentleman-like" yet ruins the effect not only with clothes that are always "new" and uniformly "lavender," but a lengthy, unctuous, name-dropping drawl to which Cleve barely attends:

> "My occupations, and I may say my habits, call me a good deal among the residences of our aristocracy," he continued with a careless grandeur and a slight wave of his hand, throwing himself a little more back, "and I have seen nothing, I assure you, Mr. Verney, more luxurious and architectural than this patrician house of Ware, with its colonnade, and pilastered front … nothing certainly lends a more dignified charm to the scene, Mr. Verney, than a distant view of family property, where, as in this instance, it is palpably accidental—where it is at all forced, as in the otherwise highly magnificent seat of my friend Sir Thomas Oldbull, baronet; so far from elevating, it pains one, it hurts one's taste" and Mr. Jos. Larkin shrugged and winced a little, and shook his head—"Do you know Sir Tho-

mas?"—"no—I dare say—he's quite a new man, Sir Thomas—we all look on him in that light in our part of the word—a—in fact, a *parvenu,*" which word Mr. Larkin pronounced as it if were spelled *pair vennew* …

"Have you had had breakfast, Mr. Larkin," inquired Cleve, in answer to all this.

(vol. 1, pp. 142–143)

It is a pretentious style that in turn distinguishes Larkin from that of his client, the ambitious but vacuous Kiffyn Fulke, whose sentences are confused and meandering—and prone to conclude with a verbal tic, "about it."

No less distinctive are Le Fanu's portraits of his more complex villains, who are flawed but not entirely unsympathetic. Again, *A Lost Name* serves as an illuminating example. In many ways, it is as much a character study of the tortured protagonist, Mark Shadwell, as a murder mystery. Although ambitious, Mark does little to accomplish his aims (i.e., become an MP); instead, he takes little responsibility for his actions, preferring to distrust or blame others, such as his neighbors or Amy, his suffering wife, for his lack of worldly success. Given his morbidity, passivity, and overweening sense of self-pity and pique, it is not surprising that he assumes that the only options left to him are desperate ones. As such, he fails to dismiss Agnes even after having received warnings from others, including the well-intentioned vicar, Stour Temple. Similarly, unable to control his impulses despite his better instincts, he murders Roke and abandons Amy.

Quite the opposite of Mark is the enterprising Guy de Beaumirail of the novel *Haunted Lives* (1867), which invokes the relatively new use of a double identity in a novel. Languishing in jail after crimes of fraud committed on members of the family of Laura Challys Gray, a distant relation, de Beaumirail assumes a new identity as "Alfred Dacre" and woos Laura in order to marry her and gain her property: a plan partly hatched by the conniving attorney Larkin, the Scottish capitalist Gillespie, and moneylender Levi. It is strangely fitting that her cousin Lord Ardenbroke—who is unaware of De Beaumirail's disguise—warns her that Dacre "is a 'double'—a

Doppelganger" and thereby "unearthly" (vol. 1, p. 179). Things do not go as planned, however, when de Beaumirail falls unexpectedly in love with Laura. If he regards himself as "sometimes legion—ever so many spirits in the same person" (vol. 2, p. 211), he also wishes he were "altogether a devil" since he is "perplexed and made inefficient by stupid yearnings after Eden"; but more to the point, he is aware that "a divided being is self torture, not a grain of conscience or all conscience" (vol. 2, p. 176). Ironically, then, the use of a feigned self leads de Beaumirail/Dacre to acquire not only self-knowledge but also conscience, which deters him from pursuing the plot any further as he confesses toward the conclusion of the novel, "a crisis within me is at hand … the somnambulist you have known so long is waked at last" (vol. 3, p. 150). Even if the element of disguise is somewhat overplayed, the fact of a "double" expressing himself can be said to pave the way to the development of supernatural fiction like Robert Louis Stevenson's Dr. Jekyll while anticipating the broader literary fascination with the unconscious.

But perhaps one of Le Fanu's most gripping villains is Barbara Vernon of *The Rose and the Key,* with her paradoxical combination of "fire and ice" that is at once fantastic yet credible. An accomplished woman who might easily serve as a prototype of sorts for the so-called New Woman at the turn of the century, she is a multifaceted character, even if the events in the novel are seen less from her perspective than is the case of Shadwell. Being "very clever," not unlike "one of the best lawyers," she is treated "with great deference," such that "whenever they had anything to ask or to say, they looked to her, and she seemed to understand everything about it, better than anyone else in the room" (2007 ed., p. 84). Tragically, her considerable "talent of command" and "so much administrative ability" (p. 71) are combined with a near irrational willfulness as other characters comment on her "self delusion" and an "inflexibility" founded on "irresistible impulses" (p. 114). Certainly, her behavior toward Maud is mixed, as she alternates between sheer coldness and rage—even as she shows emotion for others, especially for a deceased lover and her son by him, Captain Vivian. Her legal talents and her irrational hatred of her daughter—a relationship that might be said to mirror nationalist perceptions of hatred between Britain and Ireland—paradoxically become the rationale for an attempt to disinherit her by consigning her to an insane asylum, Glarewoods.

ASSESSMENT AND LEGACY

Given Le Fanu's apparent obsession with a tight cluster of themes revolving around abused authority, disputed inheritances, family conflict, a sense of recurring ills (either in the form of a returning villain or recurring crime), we are naturally led to consider the influence of nationalist thought, especially in the works he (re)wrote in the late 1860s, when the Home Rule movement began to take shape. Was Le Fanu in fact convinced by these arguments? Is it coincidental, for instance, that machinations over inheritance or other property are waged between siblings (e. g., "Squire Toby's Will," *Wyvern Mystery*), relations (e.g., *Uncle Silas, Torlogh O'Brien, A Lost Name, Checkmate,* "Carmilla," *Willing to Die*), parent and child (e.g., "Madam Crowl's Ghost," *The Rose and the Key*)—reminding us of the dispute between Ireland and Britain, variously referred to as "sister islands" and "Mother Britain"? Certainly, the very titles of *A Lost Name* and *Checkmate* invoke Young Irelander and Home Rule anxieties that Ireland was in danger of losing its "name" and "inheritance" while being "checkmated" by Britain.

The possibilities become stronger when other seemingly incidental details are weighed. In *Wyvern,* Charles' supposed wife is Dutch and constantly referred to as the "old soger": could this be inflected by anti-Whiggish sentiment toward William III, particularly as a renowned military leader of a nation that once sought the guardianship of Elizabethan England? Similarly, could the unholy alliance between Larkin, the Jews Levi and Goldshed, and the Scottish capitalist, Gillespie, have been inspired by contemporary allegations that the sale of Irish land to Britain was hastened by a combination of attorneys,

Jews, money brokers, and capitalists? It is perhaps telling too that *Wyvern, Checkmate*, and *Rose and the Key* all invoke the theme of coercion, as if affirming John Mitchel's claim that "the Coercion act was always ready in the [Dublin] Castle. … to keep the people for ever helpless in the hands of their mortal enemies" (*History of Ireland,* vol. 2, p. 473). Alice's son is "stolen" from her by Henry and placed under the rigorous and violent guardianship of Archdale. Richard, under the direction of Longcluse, brings his sister Alice under house arrest, making sure to procure new servants who will be unlikely to help her. Barbara Vernon dispatches a spy to report on Maud before attempting to have her institutionalized at Glarewoods, where she is carefully disarmed of her scissors and writing instruments. Finally, is it significant that his heroines—Laura of *Haunted Lives*, Alice of *Checkmate,* and Maud of *Rose*—all long for independence, steadfastly denying any desire to marry through much of their respective narratives?

Perhaps for Le Fanu, Ireland was a haunted nation after all. Indeed many of these themes so beloved by Le Fanu would continue to haunt future generations of Irish writers, including Bram Stoker, W. B. Yeats, Elizabeth Bowen, and Iris Murdoch. And perhaps to a greater extent than Le Fanu himself, they too would question, challenge, and probe the Ascendancy as they adapted the very tropes of abusive power, recurring evils, and family conflicts.

Selected Bibliography

WORKS OF SHERIDAN LE FANU

NOVELS: FIRST EDITIONS

The Cock and Anchor: Being a Chronicle of Old Dublin City. 3 vols. Dublin: W. Curry, 1845.

The Fortunes of Colonel Torlogh O'Brien: A Tale of the Wars of King James. Dublin: J. McGlashan, 1847.

The House by the Churchyard. 3 vols. London: Tinsley, 1863.

Uncle Silas. 3 vols. London: R. Bentley, 1864.

Wylder's Hand. 3 vols. London: R. Bentley, 1864.

Guy Deverell. 3 vols. London: R. Bentley, 1865.

All in the Dark. 2 vols. London: R. Bentley, 1866.

Tenants of Malory. 3 vols. London: Tinsley, 1867.

Haunted Lives. 3 vols. London: Tinsley, 1868.

A Lost Name. 3 vols. London: R. Bentley, 1868.

The Wyvern Mystery. 3 vols. London: Tinsley, 1869.

Checkmate. 3 vols. London: Hurst and Blackett, 1871.

The Rose and the Key. 3 vols. London: Chapman and Hall, 1871.

Willing to Die. London: Hurst and Blackett, 1873.

Seventy Years of Irish Life. New York: Macmillan, 1893.

SHORT STORIES

"Spalatro, from the Notes of Fra Giacomo." *Dublin University Magazine,* March 1843, pp. 338–351, and April 1843, pp. 446–458.

"The Fatal Bride." *Dublin University Magazine*, January 1848, pp. 15–44.

"Some Account of the Latter Days of the Hon. Richard Marson of Dunoran." *Dublin University Magazine*, April 1848, pp. 473–497; May 1848, pp. 585–607;and June 1848, pp. 728–756.

"The Mysterious Lodger." *Dublin University Magazine,* January 1850, pp.54–71, and February 1850, pp. 225–235.

"Ghost Stories of Chapelizod." *Dublin University Magazine*, January 1851, pp. 85–98.

"An Account of Some Strange Disturbances in Aungier Street." *Dublin University Magazine*, December 1853, pp. 721–731.

"Ultor de Lacy: A Legend of Cappercullen." *Dublin University Magazine*, December 1861, pp. 694–707.

"Borrhomeo the Astrologer: A Monkish Tale." *Dublin University Magazine,* January 1862, pp. 55–61.

"An Authentic Narrative of a Haunted House." *Dublin University Magazine,* October 1862, pp. 476–483.

"Wicked Captain Walshawe, of Wauling." *Dublin University Magazine*, April 1864, pp. 449–456.

Beatrice: A Verse Drama in Two Acts. Dublin University Magazine, November 1865, pp. 533–544;, and December 1865, pp. 671–683.

"Squire Toby's Will." *Temple Bar*, January 1868, pp. 212–236.

"Loved and Lost." *Dublin University Magazine,* September 1868, pp. 254–267; October 1868, pp. 381–394; November 1868, pp. 500–518; December 1868, pp. 617–632; January 1869, pp. 19–33; February 1869, pp. 142–154; March 1869, pp. 381–395; and April 1869, pp. 505–511.

"The Child That Went with the Fairies." *All the Year Round,* February 5, 1870, pp. 228–233.

"The White Cat of Drumgunniol." *All the Year Round,* April 2, 1870, pp. 420–425.

"Stories of Lough Guir." *All the Year Round,* April 23, 1870, pp. 493–498.

"The Vision of Tom Chuff." *All the Year Round,* October 8, 1870, pp. 450–456.

"The Dead Sexton." *Once a Week.* Christmas issue, 1871, pp. 10–18.

"Sir Dominic's Bargain." *All the Year Round,* July 6, 1872, pp. 186–192.

"Laura Silver Bell." *Belgravia Annual,* 1872, pp. 33–40.

"Dickon the Devil." *London Society.* Christmas issue, 1872.

"Hyacinth O'Toole." *Temple Bar,* August 1884, pp. 483–501.

SHORT STORY COLLECTIONS AND POEMS

Chronicles of Golden Friars. 3 vols. London: R. Bentley, 1871.

The Purcell Papers. 3 vols. London: R. Bentley, 1871.

In a Glass Darkly. London: R. Bentley, 1872.

The Watcher and Other Weird Stories. London: Downey, 1894.

The Poems of J. S. Le Fanu. Edited by A. P. Graves. London: Downey, 1896.

Madam Crowl's Ghost and Other Tales of Mystery. Edited by M. R. James. London: G. Bell, 1923.

REVIEWS BY LE FANU

"*The Leadbeater Papers* by Mary Shackleton Leadbeater." *Dublin University Magazine,* August 1862, pp. 236–246. (History of Quaker colony in County Kildare.)

"Two Gossiping-books of Travel." *Dublin University Magazine,* September 1862, pp. 346–358. (Review of Arthur Brinkman, *The Rifle in Cashmere,* and Arthur Pole Hampton, *Kangaroo Land.*)

"Cyrus Redding's New Novel." *Dublin University Magazine,* October 1862, pp. 483–492. (Review of *All's Well that Ends Well.*)

"*Mildrington the Barrister.*" *Dublin University Magazine,* June 1863, pp. 703–706. (Review of novel by P. H. Fitzgerald.)

"*Lispings from Low Latitudes.*" *Dublin University Magazine,* July 1863, pp. 65–66. (Review of a drawing room book by Lady Gifford.)

"*Their Majesty's Servants.*" *Dublin University Magazine,* February 1864, pp. 155–160. (Review of *Their Majesty's Servants: Annals of the English Stage, from Thomas Betteron to Edmund Kean* by Dr. Doran.)

"Fitzgerald's Life of Sterne." *Dublin University Magazine,* March 1864, pp. 328–338.

"Felon Biography." *Dublin University Magazine,* April 1864, pp. 440–448.(Review of *Memoirs of Jane Cameron, Female Convict.*)

POLITICAL WRITING AND JOURNALISM FOR *DUBLIN UNIVERSITY MAGAZINE*

"Original Letters (No. 1): Swift," September 1838, pp. 269–272.

"Original Letters (No. 11): Political," April 1839, pp. 431–438 [misnumbered 338].

"Pawn-Broking in Ireland: Mr. Barrington's Suggestion—Charitable Institutions of Limerick," December 1839, pp. 675–682.

"The State Prosecutions," June 1848, pp. 785–788.

"The Irish League," July 1848, pp. 115–118.

"Lord Palmerston," November 1865, pp. 598–600.

"The Opening Session," February 1866, pp. 235–240.

"The Reform Bill of 1866," May 1866, pp. 597–600.

MODERN EDITIONS

The Cock and Anchor. London: Downey and Co, 1895.

Wylder's Hand. New York: Dover, 1978.

Guy Deverell. New York: Dover, 1984.

In a Glass Darkly. Edited by Robert Tracy. Oxford: Oxford University Press, 1993.

Uncle Silas. Edited by W. J. McCormack. Oxford: Oxford University Press, 1993.

The Wyvern Mystery. Edited by Julian Cowley. Phoenix Mill, U.K.: Sutton, 1994.

Checkmate. Edited by Jessica De Mellow. Phoenix Mill, U.K.: Sutton, 1997.

Madam Crowl's Ghost. Edited by M. R. James. London: Wordsworth, 1999.

The Complete Purcell Papers. Philadelphia: Xlibris, 2001.

The Rose and the Key. Edited by Frances Chiu. Kansas City, Mo.: Valancourt, 2007.

MANUSCRIPT SOURCES

King's College Archive Centre, Cambridge, U.K.: King's/PP/LEF/1/3. Papers of the Le Fanu family.

National Library of Ireland, Dublin: n. 2976, p. 2597. Letters and an unfinished story.

BIOGRAPHICAL AND CRITICAL STUDIES

Backus, Margot. *The Gothic Family Romance: Heterosexuality, Child Sacrifice, and the Anglo-Irish Colonial Order.* Durham, N.C.: Duke University Press, 1999.

Bowen, Elizabeth. "Introduction to *Uncle Silas.*" London: Cresset Press, 1947. Pp. 7–23.

Browne, Nelson. *Sheridan Le Fanu.* London: Arthur Barker, 1951.

Chiu, Frances. Introduction to *The Rose and the Key*. Kansas City, Mo.: Valancourt, 2007. Pp. i–xlvii.

———. "'History Repeats Itself': *Checkmate* and the Rewriting of the Union." *Le Fanu Studies* 5, no. 1 (2010). (http://www.lefanustudies.com/checkmate.html).

Crawford, Gary William, and Brian J. Showers. *Joseph Sheridan Le Fanu: A Concise Bibliography*. Dublin: Swan River Press, 2011.

Hall, Wayne E. *Dialogues in the Margin: A Study of the Dublin University Magazine*. Washington, D.C.: Catholic University of America Press, 1999.

Harris, Sally C. "A Realistic Fairy Tale: The *Wyvern Mystery*." *Le Fanu Studies* 3, no. 1 (2008). (http://www.lefanustudies.com/wyvern.html).

Howes, Marjorie. "Misalliance and Anglo-Irish Traditions in Le Fanu's *Uncle Silas*." *Nineteenth-Century Literature* 47, no. 2:164–186 (September 1992).

James, M. R. "Introduction." *Madam Crowl's Ghost*. London: Wordsworth, 1999.

———."Lecture on Le Fanu." Delivered March 16, 1923, to the Royal Institution of Great Britain. (http://www.users.globalnet.co.uk/~pardos/ArchiveLeFanu.html).

King, Jason. "'Rapparees' or 'Refugees'? The Normative Image of Involuntary Displacement in Nineteenth century Irish Literature," *Ireland and Europe,* ed. Leon Litvack and Colin Graham (Dublin: Four Courts Press, 2006), pp. 61–76.

"Literary Chat." *Munsey's Magazine*, October, 1893, p. 108.

McCormack, W. J. *Sheridan Le Fanu*. Oxford: Oxford University Press, 1997. (Biography.)

Melada, Ivan. *Sheridan Le Fanu*. Boston: Twayne, 1987.

Pritchett, V. S. Introduction to *In a Glass Darkly*. London: John Lehmann, 1947. Pp.7–11.

Sage, Victor. *Le Fanu's Gothic*. London: Macmillan Palgrave, 2004.

Walton, James. *Vision and Vacancy: The Fictions of J. S. Le Fanu*. Dublin: Dublin University College, 2007.

OTHER WORKS CITED

Arnold, Matthew. *On the Study of Celtic Literature*. London: Smith, Elder, 1867.

———. "The Incompatibles." *Irish Essays*. London: Smith, Elder, 1882, pp. 1–81.

Butt, Isaac. *Land Tenure in Ireland: A Plea for the Celtic Race*. Dublin: John Falconer, 1866.

———. *Irish Federalism: Its Meaning, Its Objects, and Its Hopes*. 3rd ed. London: W. Ridgway, 1871.

Davis, Thomas. "The History of Ireland." In *Literary and Historical Essays*. Dublin: James Duffy, 1846. Pp. 28–38.

Dickens, Charles. "Thugee in Ireland." *All the Year Round*, June 28, 1862, pp. 374–378.

FRGS. *The Irish Land Question Impartially Considered*. London: Chapman & Hall, 1870.

FTCD. *The Ireland of To-day*. Dublin, 1868.

Grattan, Richard. *Vox Hiberniae*. London: Trubner, 1870.

McGee, Thomas D'Arcy. *Popular History of Ireland*. New York: Sadlier, 1863.

Meagher, Thomas Francis, ed. *Speeches on the Legislative Independence of Ireland*. New York: Redfield, 1853.

Mitchel, John. *The History of Ireland*. 2 vols. Glasgow: Cameron, Ferguson, 1869.

Morison, James. *Irish Grievances Shortly Stated*. London: Longmans, Green, Reader, and Dyer, 1868.

Owenson, Sydney (Lady Morgan). *Patriotic Sketches of Ireland, Written in Connaught*. Baltimore: Dobbin & Murphy, 1809.

PATRICK LEIGH FERMOR

(1915—2011)

Susan Butterworth

SIR PATRICK LEIGH Fermor has been described by more than one admirer as sui generis: one of a kind. He is known primarily as a travel writer, especially for his account of a walk across Europe undertaken in 1934 when he was nineteen years old. But the accomplishment of Patrick Leigh Fermor, known as Paddy to his many friends, or known more formally as Sir Patrick, goes far beyond travel narration. His work encompasses a diverse array of nonfiction categories as varied as his interests: memoir, adventure, bildungsroman, history, literature, anthropology, geography, religion, architecture, language, and culture. His oeuvre—seven books of nonfiction, a novel, scores of magazine articles, introductions, and translations—contains threads of a life well-lived and well-considered. While Leigh Fermor's themes are diverse, many of them are recurring: from visiting, writing in and about monasteries, the dying and decaying of old ways both aristocratic and nomadic, the enduring connection between past and present to hospitality, Lord Byron, and swimming. In the end, as a youth between the wars, a war hero, a wandering scholar of civilization, a convivial guest and host, Patrick Leigh Fermor's life and work exemplifies a rich way of living and being that is passing from this world. He was one of the last of a generation.

AN UNCONVENTIONAL UPBRINGING

Patrick Michael Leigh Fermor was born February 11, 1915, in London, England, the son of Lewis Leigh Fermor (1880–1954) and Muriel Eileen Taaffe Ambler (1890–1977). His father was a distinguished geologist who spent most of his working life as the director of the Geological Survey of India. His mother came from a family with links to India. The two were married in 1909, and had a daughter, Vanessa, four years before Patrick was born.

Not unusual for children born of colonial civil servants during the First World War, young Patrick Leigh Fermor was left behind when his mother and sister sailed back to India soon after his birth, meaning to bring the infant son to India when the oceans were safer or the war ended. For four years he was left in foster care with a farmer's family in Northamptonshire. When his mother and sister returned and took him to London, all attempts at school ended in disaster. Eventually a psychiatrist recommended Salsham Hall, a coeducational school for "difficult" children near Bury Saint Edmunds in Suffolk. This was what today would be called an "alternative school," with an eccentric staff and clientele, and there he enjoyed considerable freedom. His mother was rather unconventional as well, writing plays and learning to fly a Moth biplane. When this school closed, young Paddy Leigh Fermor attended a series of preparatory schools, always breaking rules and being sent home.

In the author's introduction to the 1977 volume *A Time of Gifts*, he writes of one of these expulsions: "But this particular disaster happened to coincide with one of my father's rare leaves from directing the Geological Survey of India. He and my mother had parted by then, and since these furloughs only came round every three years, we scarcely knew each other" (p. 10). His father, a naturalist, took him along on a collecting trip to northern Italy, and his love for travel and art was born.

Patrick Leigh Fermor spent the next three years living with a family in Surrey, studying with a few other boys, preparing for exams. There he received a good education in classics, literature, poetry, and painting. He passed the entrance exams to King's School, Canterbury, where he wrote, read, sang, acted, and painted. He continued to break rules, however, and in his third year was expelled for breaking the town-gown taboo: he was caught holding hands with the grocer's daughter in the back room of the shop—and his schooldays were over.

At seventeen, he began to prepare for the Royal Military Academy Sandhurst and an army career. He spent the next two years in London reading and studying with tutors. However he was beginning to move in more bohemian circles, and also beginning to realize how unsuitable he was for the life of an upper-class English soldier in peacetime. Because he had published a couple of poems, Paddy Leigh Fermor decided to write. By late summer 1933 he had moved out of his tutor's and into his own rooms, intending to work, but found himself in an environment of parties and late nights instead. His money was running out, and he wasn't writing. By early winter he had made the decision to leave London and travel through Europe on foot.

A WALK ACROSS EUROPE

In early December 1933, not yet nineteen years old, Patrick Leigh Fermor set off from London by steamer to the Hook of Holland and began the walk down the Rhine and Danube rivers through Holland, Germany, Austria, Slovakia, Hungary, Romania, and Bulgaria to Constantinople (the city had been renamed Istanbul in 1930, but he continued to use the name Constantinople), a journey that is described in *A Time of Gifts* (1977) and *Between the Woods and the Water* (1986). The twelve-hundred-mile journey took a little more than a year and changed his life. In *A Time of Gifts* he writes of a personal landmark, a coming-of-age epiphany, that occurred in Slovakia as "a change which had been taking place ever since my departure from England. In the past, I had always arrived on any new scene trailing a long history of misdeeds and disasters ... for a quarter of a year there had been no rules to break except ones I had chosen" (p. 283).

Leigh Fermor's education had been classical, if a bit erratic. In his nineteenth year, his outlook

was immeasurably broadened. He learned firsthand the languages, history, religion, and culture of a dozen civilizations and ethnicities. He was infinitely resourceful. Once he was safely on his way, he wrote home and informed his parents of his plans. They agreed to send him a modest allowance. He started out sleeping in seaman's inns, bargeman's hostels, and barns, but in spite of setbacks such as having his passport, bag, and money stolen from a youth hostel, he prospered. Several days spent with a baron in Munich resulted in some letters of introduction that proved useful down the road. As a wandering student he encountered a marvelous custom of hospitality to travelers: the village mayor would give him a voucher for bed and board at the local inn, paid for by the parish. "I wonder how many times I took advantage of this generous and, apparently, very old custom?" he muses in *A Time of Gifts*. "It prevailed all through Germany and Austria, a survival perhaps, of some ancient charity to wandering students and pilgrims, extended now to all poor travellers" (p. 115).

Leigh Fermor describes himself as apolitical, but walking across Germany and Austria in 1934, he could not help but notice the signs of gathering war. In the towns, politics and the presence of Hitler's National Socialism were visible, but Leigh Fermor describes himself as "ill-prepared ... for any form of political argument. In this respect, I might have been sleep-walking" (p. 130).

The scholar-traveler did have a gift for friendship. He was welcomed, first in inns and hostels and student rooms, later by landed gentry he met through his letters of introduction. He was passed from manor house to manor house by these hospitable members of a breed that would essentially vanish after the Second World War. In an article for the *Daily Telegraph* weekend magazine (May 12, 1990) called "Rumania— Travels in a Land before Darkness Fell," Leigh Fermor wrote: "by the time I got to Transylvania ... the Spartan trudge had turned into a stroll from one schloss to another" (quoted in *Words of Mercury*, p. 40). As his journey advanced at a leisurely pace, he passed days and weeks with Hungarian and Romanian aristocracy, many impoverished, but all gracious and well-versed in the arts of civilization and all delighted to entertain their engaging young English guest. "I was passed on from house to house like a bad penny," he wrote (*Words of Mercury,* p. 41). He was observing and participating in a way of life that had remained static for centuries, and while he was "absorbed in everything but politics" (p. 40), he could not help but notice the "elegant decay" (p. 42) of the gentry's way of life.

Leigh Fermor arrived in Constantinople on New Year's Day 1935. The planned journey complete, he continued to live and travel in the Greek archipelago and the Balkans. His first weeks in Greece, and his twentieth birthday, were spent learning the language at the Eastern Orthodox monastery on Mount Athos, the first of many monastery stays. From Mount Athos he moved on to the Monastery of Saint Barlaam, one of a group of isolated monasteries in the mountains of Thessaly known as the Meteora. March 1935 found him riding with the victorious royalist army, which had successfully suppressed the recent coup d'état, though he did not actually participate in any fighting.

ROMANCE IN ROMANIA

Working his way westward across Macedonia and then southward through northern Greece, he had reached Athens by the summer of 1935. There he met and fell in love with a Romanian painter of noble blood, Princess Marie-Blanche (Balasha) Cantacuzene (1899–1976). After a summer and autumn spent painting and writing together in Greece, he moved with Balasha, her sister Elena (Pomme), and her sister's husband to Baleni, the Cantacuzene family home in Moldavia in southeastern Romania. The winter was passed at Baleni, reading, writing, conversing in French with the local "half-ruined" (*Words of Mercury,* p. 43) country people. Baleni would be his anchor for the next few years of traveling throughout the Balkans. He did some writing for magazines, and his translation from French of C. P. Radokanachi's *Forever Ulysses* was published in 1937 and sold well.

Some of Leigh Fermor's saddest and most poignant writing describes Romania in the sum-

mer of 1939 "while the peace of Europe disintegrated" (*Words of Mercury,* p. 45). In an introduction to the memoirs of the Romanian prince Matila Ghyka, *The World Mine Oyster* (1961), called "Rumania—The Last Day of Peace," he writes of the summer when "the evil omens multiplied" (reprinted in *Words of Mercury,* p. 51). There was a final blissful outing from Baleni in September 1939, a mushroom-picking picnic, before "the next day's news scattered this little society for ever" (p. 53). Leigh Fermor left for England to join the army, expecting to be back in a few months. "We none of us realized how great and how lasting the break would be," he wrote in 1990 (*Words of Mercury,* p. 45).

THE WAR HERO

Young Patrick Leigh Fermor joined the Irish Guards. At first there were letters from Romania, but though his friends sympathized with the Western Allies, by 1941 Romania was allied to Germany, and the letters stopped. Leigh Fermor was given a commission by the Intelligence Corps and stationed on the border of Greece and Albania to take advantage of his knowledge of the Balkans and the Greek language. As British liaison officer to the Greek army, he retreated to Crete with the Greek and British forces when the Germans invaded Greece in 1941. He took part in the Battle of Crete in May 1941 and was evacuated to Egypt when that battle was lost.

In June 1942, Leigh Fermor was sent back to occupied Crete by the British Special Operations Executive to become an underground liaison organizing and aiding the resistance movement. In the introduction to his translation of George Psychoundakis' memoir *The Cretan Runner* (1955), Leigh Fermor describes the British mission to occupied Crete. Of the qualifications for British officers, he states: "They were chosen from all over the army, their qualifications being willingness and suitability for that peculiar kind of warfare, and some acquaintance with modern Greek or with the ancient variety—a far greater help for the modern than is generally supposed" (*The Cretan Runner,* p. 10).

Leigh Fermor was remarkably well suited for the job. His gifts for friendship and language served him well, as well as his ability to march long distances in difficult conditions, to climb steep mountains, and to sleep anywhere, indoors or out.

The British officers would arrive by submarine or caique, establish a secret headquarters in the isolated mountains, and transmit news of German troop movements, relying on Cretan guides, helpers, and runners. "There were countless marches to the coast to meet secret craft. They brought in new agents or commando groups and evacuated stragglers or hunted Cretans for asylum or training in the Middle East" (*The Cretan Runner,* p. 13).

The story of the Cretan Resistance, including Captain (later Major) Leigh Fermor's exploits, is recounted by the Cretan runner George Psychoundakis, written after the war and translated by Leigh Fermor (known as Michali by his Cretan friends) in the early 1950s. Leigh Fermor planned and participated in the defection and flight of the Italian commander in Crete, taking him off the island by boat and seeing him safely to Cairo. Inspired by the success of this mission, he and his colleagues developed a daring plan: they would abduct the commander of the German occupation forces.

In February 1944, Paddy Leigh Fermor parachuted back into the mountains of Crete. With his second-in-command, William Stanley Moss, and the help of the Cretan Resistance partisans, they successfully kidnapped General Heinrich Kreipe in April 1944. Evacuating the general was extremely difficult, as the Germans threatened reprisals against locals aiding their escape, patrolled the island, and kept watch over the coastal beaches. Leigh Fermor, Moss, and their Cretan guides marched the general over the mountains, hiding in caves and sheepfolds. On May 14, 1944, Leigh Fermor and General Kreipe were picked up by a British torpedo boat and evacuated to Cairo. Major Leigh Fermor was awarded the Order of the British Empire, 1943, and a Distinguished Service Order, 1944.

Though he returned to Egypt safely after the escape from Crete, Leigh Fermor had contracted rheumatic fever and was ill for six months. While in Cairo, he met the gifted British photographer Joan Rayner. Born Joan Elizabeth Eyres Monsell in London on February 5, 1912, she had been married in 1939 to John Rayner, an editor at the *Daily Express*. Early in the war, she had worked as nurse, and then transferred to the ciphers departments of the British embassies in Madrid, Algiers, and finally Cairo. Joan's marriage to John Rayner, like many wartime marriages, did not outlast the war and was dissolved in 1947.

THE CARIBBEAN

When Paddy Leigh Fermor went home for his discharge from the service in 1945, Joan came with him. They would be lifelong companions. After the war, Leigh Fermor became assistant director of the British Institute in Athens, Greece. He was sent on a lecture tour around Greece, which was the first of many journeys on which Joan would accompany him. In October 1947, Paddy and Joan set off on an ocean liner for the Caribbean with the Greek photographer Costa Achillopoulo. Leigh Fermor had been commissioned to write captions for Achillopoulo's photographs, but a full-length book, *The Traveller's Tree* (1950), grew out of the original project.

The book was written partly in borrowed houses in France and England—Paddy and Joan had no fixed abode during the late 1940s—and partly at the Abbey of Saint Wandrille de Fontanelle in Normandy. Leigh Fermor would later write another short book, *A Time to Keep Silence* (published privately in 1953 and by John Murray in 1957) about his sojourn in this abbey.

Stanley Moss's book *Ill Met by Moonlight*, about Paddy Leigh Fermor's war exploits in the Cretan Resistance, was published in 1950 and established Leigh Fermor's reputation as a war hero. The publication of *The Traveller's Tree* the same year established Leigh Fermor as a writer to watch, as critics noticed his erudition, his modesty, and his style. The book won the Heinemann Literary Award in addition to its favorable reviews. His first and only novel, *The Violins of Saint-Jacques*, set in the French Antilles and clearly rooted in his Caribbean journey, was published in 1953.

A Traveller's Tree begins in the French Antilles and winds its way by boat and plane through a series of islands including Dominica, Barbados, Trinidad, Antigua, Saint Martin, and Saint Thomas toward Puerto Rico, Haiti, Jamaica, and finally Cuba. Everywhere Leigh Fermor observes and comments on scenes, history, politics, culture, atmosphere, language, anthropology, and literature of the place with humor, imagination, and torrents and catalogs of astonishing and highly readable prose. Leigh Fermor's party has charm and good contacts: they stay with local Creole aristocrats and planters as well as at inns in small fishing ports.

Leigh Fermor's imagination was captured by the story of Saint Pierre, the old capital of Martinique, which was destroyed by a volcanic eruption in 1902. Only one man survived the destruction, a condemned criminal who was saved by his stone cell in the city jail. The tale of *The Violins of Saint-Jacques* is told by dual narrators, one of whom is the sole survivor of the destruction of the imaginary island of Saint-Jacques in the French Antilles. As an elderly woman who has settled in a village in Greece, she tells her tale to the first-person narrator of Leigh Fermor's novella, who repeats it to the reader. Drawing on description and legend from his journey to the islands, Leigh Fermor paints a rich portrait of the life of the decaying Creole aristocracy, culminating in a dramatic carnival ball set against a backdrop of the volcanic eruption that destroys the island and its way of life forever. While Leigh Fermor's gift is for the rich detail that has free reign in his nonfiction, and his plot is heavy-handed to the point of cliché, the structure of the novella, with its dual narration and complex references to history and anthropology, as well as the connections with his travel narrative, make *The Violins of Saint-Jacques* a worthwhile companion to *The Traveller's Tree*.

A TIME TO KEEP SILENCE

The brief and lovely *A Time to Keep Silence* was first published as a series of magazine articles in 1953 and is both closely related to the writing of the Caribbean books and a key to the paradox of Patrick Leigh Fermor. Although never a believing Christian in the strict sense, Leigh Fermor seems always to have been drawn to aspects of the monastic life. As he writes in the author's introduction, his interest in monastic sojourns was "deeper than mere interest and curiosity, and more important than the pleasure an historian or an aesthete finds in ancient buildings and liturgy" (p. xvi). Rather, what drew him to extended stays in monasteries was "the discovery of a capacity for solitude and ... for the recollectedness and clarity of spirit that accompany the silent monastic life" (pp. xvi–xvii). Indeed, a young man who had undertaken a yearlong walking trip alone would certainly have a capacity for solitude, an ironic complement to Paddy Leigh Fermor's gifts for friendship and conversation.

Paddy and Joan were living in France in 1950, and the book is based on letters he wrote to Joan. He was trying to write, and the distractions of Paris were many. When he arrived at the Benedictine abbey of Saint Wandrille in Normandy, he was "in search of somewhere quiet and cheap to stay while I continued to work on a book that I was writing [*The Traveller's Tree*]," he explains in the opening pages of *A Time to Keep Silence* (p. 8). The search for a quiet place to write was to be a lifelong motif. Years later, David Mason, writing about his friendship with his neighbor Patrick Leigh Fermor in the memoir *News from the Village: Aegean Friends* (2010), would describe a talk given by Paddy Leigh Fermor at the Gennadius Library in Athens in 1997 titled "The Aftermath of Travel," discussing "the pursuit of the perfect refuge ... for getting the original journeys down on paper" (Mason, p. 66). Saint Wandrille worked its magic for Leigh Fermor. In the beginning he reports depression, restlessness, insomnia, and extraordinary lassitude, but soon he describes a transformation to "nineteen hours a day of absolute and god-like freedom. Work became easier every moment" (p. 23). He enjoys exploring the abbey, walks in the country, reading, the library; he admires the values, capacity for worship and prayer, gentleness and calm of the monastic community. Weeks pass, the work goes well, and when the time comes to leave he finds the reentry into the world of Paris painful. "The Abbey was at first a graveyard," he writes, "the outer world seemed afterwards, by contrast, an inferno of noise and vulgarity entirely populated by bounders and sluts and crooks" (p. 43).

The volume continues with essays on the great silence of the Cistercians at La Grande Trappe and the ruins of the rock monasteries at Cappadocia in Turkey. In the postscript, written three years after his time at the monastery, the reader learns that Leigh Fermor has often returned to Benedictine life. He is writing from a Benedictine priory in Hampshire. He has grown accustomed to the changes of tempo in entering and withdrawing from the monastic life. But what he loves, "the slow and cumulative spell of healing quietness—has lost none of its magic" (pp. 89–90).

THE 1950S: TRAVEL AND WRITING

Throughout the 1950s, Paddy and Joan continued their peripatetic life of travel and writing. Joan Eyres Monsell had a small independent income, and Leigh Fermor had his war reputation and the successful publication of the books about the Caribbean as well as translation and writing work for magazines. They had a wide international circle of friends, including the Duke and Duchess of Devonshire (Andrew and Deborah; the duchess was one of the well-known and famously beautiful Mitford sisters with whom Leigh Fermor kept up a correspondence published in 2008 as *In Tearing Haste: Letters Between Deborah Devonshire and Patrick Leigh Fermor*); Xan and Daphne Fielding (Xan Fielding had been Leigh Fermor's comrade in Crete; Daphne Fielding was one of Deborah Devonshire's closest friends); Ann and Ian Fleming; and many others. Through the hospitality of this circle of friends, Leigh Fermor had access to a number of houses that he would borrow to write in. Among them were the Devonshires' rambling, gothic Lismore Castle in Ireland and Dumbleton Hall in Gloucestershire, the home of Joan's mother's family. Leigh Fermor's abiding interest in architecture was nourished both by his travels and his opportunities to explore these houses in depth.

One of the projects on which Paddy and Joan worked together was the publication of George Psychoundakis' *The Cretan Runner: His Story of the German Occupation* (1955), translated and with an introduction by Patrick Leigh Fermor and illustrated by over a dozen photographs of the participants by Joan Eyres Monsell. Leigh Fermor discovered the manuscript in his friend's possession on a visit to Crete in the early 1950s and was immediately captivated. In his introduction, he calls the manuscript "a completely truthful account of Resistance life" (p. 15) told from the point of view of a native Cretan rather than a British officer. Even in the introduction to his translation, Leigh Fermor cannot resist a characteristic digression into the geography, history, mythology, customs, hospitality, language, and nature of the Cretan people.

Leigh Fermor was also involved in film work. In 1956, he was on location for the shooting of the film version of *Ill Met by Moonlight* (1957), which starred Dirk Bogarde as Major Patrick Leigh Fermor and was filmed at Pinewood Studios in England with location shooting in the Alpes-Maritimes in France and Italy and on the Côte d'Azur in France. The film was a highly romanticized version of the actual events, and Leigh Fermor was not particularly pleased with it. "There are scores of things dead wrong," he wrote in a letter to Deborah Devonshire (*In Tearing Haste*, p. 20). In 1957, he wrote the screenplay for the film *The Roots of Heaven* (1958), based on a Romain Gary novel and set in French Equatorial Africa, the story of an idealist who sets out to save the African elephant from extinction. On-site in Africa for the filming, Leigh Fermor worked with the Hollywood producer Darryl Zanuck, the director John Huston, and the actors Trevor Howard and Errol Flynn.

The 1950s were prolific years. *A Time to Keep Silence*, which had been privately printed in 1953, was released by the publisher John Murray in 1957. The many references in his letters to "scribbling away" from borrowed houses and retreats in the English and French countryside refer to the writing of his books about Greece, the first of which, *Mani: Travels in the Southern*

Peloponnese, came out in 1958. In the preface to *Mani*, Leigh Fermor writes from Hydra, thanking friends for hospitality in Normandy and more friends for the use of the house in Hydra where much of the book was written.

MANI

Mani was originally meant to be a chapter of a larger book about all of Greece and its islands, "a recapitulation of many former journeys" (*Mani*, p. 5). In the preface, Leigh Fermor describes the scope of the summary journey he undertook with Joan, starting in Constantinople, moving through Thrace and Macedonia, through the Pindus mountains to Epirus and Thessaly (the subject of a later volume, *Roumeli,* in 1966) to Athens, the Peloponnese, and the islands of Cyprus and Crete. The journey proceeds in typical Leigh Fermor style: "a matter of countless bus-rides and long stretches on horseback and by mule and on foot and on inter-island steamers and caiques" (p. 6). By the end, he writes, "the number of dog-eared and closely written notebooks I had filled up on the way was a forbidding sight" (p. 6). Rather than spread his material too thin, he decided to limit the geographical scope of his work, "to attack the country, rather, at certain chosen points and penetrate, as far as my abilities went, in depth" (p. 6). Here lies the paradox of Leigh Fermor's oeuvre: his interests are so wide-ranging, and his curiosity and gift for gathering "anecdote … superstition … talk and incident, nearly all of it odd or memorable" so extensive, that he finds it difficult to contain or organize it all into a coherent form. The result is astonishing in its breadth and depth of detail, but the work proceeded increasingly slowly as the years passed. Concentrating this book on the remote, small southern peninsular region known as the Mani allows Leigh Fermor "the luxury of long digressions" (p. 6).

A further purpose of *Mani* and later *Roumeli* is to capture these remote regions where an ancient way of life was still relatively undisturbed, yet already showing signs of being lost. Leigh Fermor writes, "Many things in Greece have remained unchanged since the time of the *Odyssey* and perhaps the most striking of these is the hospitality shown to strangers; the more remote and mountainous the region, the less this has altered" (p. 163). This idea of the Maniots as the descendants of the ancient Greeks of Homer and of myth is a notable connecting thread throughout *Mani*.

Patrick Leigh Fermor was an intrepid swimmer. *Mani* contains an incident where he unites this quality with his search for the connection to antiquity and myth in the region. He and Joan have commissioned a caique to take them around the tip of the peninsula, where there is a sea cave regarded as one of the mythical entrances to Hades. While the captain and Joan sail in slow circles and wait, Paddy Leigh Fermor dives overboard and swims into the cave, following it deeper into the rocky mountainside as it narrows and closes in around him. The swim into the legendary entrance to the Underworld is the opportunity for a digression on geology, geography, mythology, and the color of the water in Greece.

One of the remote villages Paddy and Joan encountered on the Mani journey was Kardamyli. It appears to have been love at first sight. Leigh Fermor's description of the "hamlet on the edge of the sea … unlike any village I had seen in Greece" (p. 34) is idyllic. Kardamyli's "quiet charm … grew with each passing hour" (p. 40). After years of borrowing houses, it was Paddy and Joan's desire to find a place in Greece to settle and build their own house. A few years later, Leigh Fermor would write to Devonshire that he had found the place. He writes, "The cliff is warrened with a great sea cave into which one swims, under stalactites and strange mushroom limestone formations. Not a house in sight, nothing but the two rocky headlands, an island a quarter of a mile out to sea with a ruined chapel, and a vast expanse of flittering water, over which you see the sun setting till its last gasp. Homer's Greece, in fact" (*In Tearing Haste*, p. 92). The plan, he continued, was to build a rambling house "with huge airy rooms, out of the local limestone." This would become the famous house at Kardamyli, on which construction began in

1964 and where the Leigh Fermors would live and offer hospitality to many for the rest of their lives.

RETURN TO ROMANIA

In a letter to Deborah Devonshire in 1961, Leigh Fermor writes that the Greek foreign minister Evangelos Averoff had read and liked *Mani* and invited him and Joan to stay at his house in Epirus, a wild and remote place in the mountains of northwestern Greece. "I took my courage in both hands (knowing he had just wangled an old friend of mine out of Rumania—more of this anon) and asked if he could do anything about my old love, Balasha Cantacuzene: and he has promised to, if he can! I can't believe it, though it may take a year or two … She always adored Greece, and would probably want to settle here. How wonderful it would be if she did make it! We haven't met for 22 years. She used to be so beautiful" (*In Tearing Haste*, p. 82).

Leigh Fermor continued to travel and write through the early 1960s, in Europe and from a home base in London he had established with Joan, Chester Row. He had hoped to write an account of his walk across Europe since before the war, but he was overwhelmed by the magnitude of the task and hindered by the passage of time and the loss of many of his journals. In 1965, he received a commission from *Holiday* magazine for a long article on the Danube, from Switzerland through the Iron Curtain, all the way to the Delta on the Black Sea. One purpose of the journey would be to jog his memory of his 1934 journey. Another purpose would be to try to contact Balasha and her family. He wrote to Devonshire from Chester Row that he was "scribbling like a maniac" to finish the book *Roumeli* (1966) in time to depart for the Danube journey, "filled with excitement and misgiving about Rumania and, if it's not compromising or dangerous for them, seeing old friends and loves unglimpsed for twenty-six years" (*In Tearing Haste*, p. 108).

He had learned from occasional letters and mutual friends that Balasha and her sister had been nurses during the war and that their land had been confiscated when Romania became a Communist state. In the late 1940s they were evicted from Baleni, and Balasha was imprisoned for trying to escape to Istanbul. Released from prison, she had lived in poverty, starving, in poor health. While in Romania in 1965, Leigh Fermor was able to make a brief visit, aided by Balasha's niece. "Mixing with foreigners incurred severe punishment, but harbouring them indoors was much worse; so the visit had to be made by stealth, at night, and on the back of a motorbike … We found them in their attic … it was as though we had parted a few months ago, instead of twenty-six years … It was a miraculous reunion" (*Words of Mercury,* pp. 46–47).

Contact was reestablished. The sisters were allowed a few "joyful visits to friends in England and France and Greece" (*Words of Mercury,* p. 47), but they resisted leaving their home permanently. In subsequent years they succumbed to illness; Balasha died in 1976.

ROUMELI

Where *Mani* is essentially a travel narrative with digressions, *Roumeli: Travels in Northern Greece* (1966) is a series of nearly independent essays related by their setting in northern Greece, drawing mostly on his travels with Joan in the 1950s but reaching back into his memories of the late 1930s as well. His focus is on the most remote and unusual tribes and regions and on the decline and passing of ancient ways of life. He writes of his first introduction to the region in 1935 and of the beginning of his love affair with Greece: "One of the great and unconvenanted delights of Greece … a direct and immediate link … between human beings … A stranger begins to realize that the armour which has been irking him and the arsenal he has been lugging about for half a lifetime are no longer needed. Miraculous lightness takes their place" (p. 58).

In the chapter titled "The Monasteries of the Air," Leigh Fermor picks up the thread of his great pleasure in monastic stays. He and Joan return to the Meteora, the group of monasteries perched on high rock pinnacles he had first visited in 1935. At this once-thriving monastic community, only a few monks remain in the mostly empty and ruined monasteries. Amid typically erudite digressions on ancient and recent history, legends of the saints, art and architecture, Leigh Fermor notes the passing of an ancient way of life which "has hardly changed since the early days of Byzantium" (p. 79), for better or worse overtaken by the materialism of the industrial West.

One entire chapter of *Roumeli* is a long digression on the differences between two aspects of the Greek character: the Hellene, referring to the glory of ancient, classical Greece, and the Romaic, referring to the "splendours and the sorrows of Byzantium" (p. 106). He concludes by returning to the thread that was woven into *Mani*: "the conviction that a stranger feels here that he is surrounded by people of ancient and civilized descent" (p. 123). He feels this conviction most strongly among the remote regions and simplest of people, "the lower one plunges in the economic scale" (p. 123).

To Leigh Fermor, as to the Greeks, "nothing to do with [Lord] Byron, even a pair of shoes, is wholly without interest" (p. 179). Roumeli is the territory Byron traversed, about which he wrote in *Childe Harold's Pilgrimage* (1812–1818), and where he died. One of the essays in *Roumeli* is the story of a quest undertaken by Paddy and Joan to recover a pair of shoes belonging to Byron that they have traced to the home of an elderly man in Missolonghi, the town where Byron died. Leigh Fermor must have felt a connection with Lord Byron, the attractive and intelligent young man, prematurely disillusioned with a life of pleasure, who set off on a series of travels and fell in love with Greece. Following in Byron's footsteps would be another recurring thread in the Leigh Fermor narrative.

KARDAMYLI

Paddy and Joan had been traveling, living, and working together since the 1940s. The years from 1964 to 1966 were occupied with building their house at Kardamyli in the Mani. Leigh Fermor described the house and its creation in an article for *Architectural Digest* in 1986 titled "Sash Windows Opening on the Foam." The article begins with a catalog of reference books, reflecting his wide inventory of interests and his love of conversation. "For if one is settling in the wilds," he writes, "a dozen reference shelves is the minimum; and they must be near the dinner table where arguments spring up which have to be settled then or never. This being so, two roles for the chief room in a still unbuilt house were clear from the start" (*Words of Mercury,* p. 126). Paddy and Joan pitched tents and lived on the site while they decided where the rooms would go. The house was built of local limestone by local workmen, conceived of their imagination and eclectic tastes with a mind to outdoor summer meals on the terrace and fine views of the sunset.

Paddy and Joan were married in 1968 in London. They never had children, but were often surrounded by friends and the children of friends. They also maintained a home in Worcestershire, and they split their time between Greece and England for the rest of their lives.

Leigh Fermor, the intrepid traveler and walker, was always a strong mountaineer. He spent the month of August 1971 in Peru, climbing in the Andes with his friend Andrew Devonshire and others. Some of the same friends planned a climbing expedition to Turkish Kurdistan in 1972 but changed their plans to the Pindus Mountains of northern Greece when the Turkish government denied permission for the Kurdistan trip. In 1976, Leigh Fermor climbed in the Himalayas and spent a month in India, writing and visiting scenes of his parents' and sister's life. An account of the Himalayan climbing expedition, "Paradox in the Himalayas," appeared in the *London Magazine* of December 1979–January 1980. His account of the Peruvian expedition, based on letters to Joan, was circulated among friends and fellow participants. Twenty years later it was published as *Three Letters from the Andes* (1991).

A TIME OF GIFTS

Leigh Fermor's account of his 1934 walk across Europe had been an unfulfilled project for forty years. It would prove to be his life's work. In 1974, he wrote to Devonshire: "A propos of the great virtue of my books being their non-appearance—beware! The present one is getting so long, Jock M [John Murray, his publisher] says it may have to be broken up into vols—so you can't count on it" (*In Tearing Haste,* p. 146). The first volume of the planned trilogy was published in 1977 as *A Time of Gifts: On Foot to Constantinople: From the Hook of Holland to the Middle Danube.* Partly reconstructed from memory, partly from old journals, and partly from his mature travels along the same path, the book is remarkable not only for his youthful enthusiasm and fearlessness but for its double point of view. The reader hears the voice of callow youth and at the same time the voice of experience looking back on a lost era.

A Time of Gifts opens with an introductory letter to Xan Fielding, his old comrade in Crete where "we lay among the rocks and talked of our lives before the war" (p. 5). The volume is dedicated to Fielding, "an attempt to complete and set in order, with as much detail as I can recapture, the earliest of those disjointedly recounted travels" (p. 6). Leigh Fermor continues with fifteen or twenty pages of engaging autobiography, bringing the reader to the point in his life where he embarks on the adventure.

Departing from London in December, there are many luminous descriptions of walking in snow and through wintry Brueghel-like landscapes in Holland and Germany. He describes the people he meets in bookstores, pubs, seaman's inns, and bargeman's lodgings. For the most part he is determined to walk, but he takes a barge trip up the Rhine. He spends Christmas and the New Year holiday with an inn family in Heidelberg, the first few days of January in a baroque palace at Bruchsal—his first exposure to such architecture—and is invited to an Epiphany party by some charming young female students in Stuttgart.

Leaving Stuttgart, the narrative goes into a long aside—one of many typical Leigh Fermor digressions—on poetry. When the road was dull, Leigh Fermor would recite poetry aloud to pass the time. The catalog, which he labels "fairly predictable" (*A Time of Gifts*, p. 83), is extensive, ranging through five hundred years of English and Irish literature, French, Latin, and Greek. There is a digression within the digression as he recalls an incident during the wartime abduction of General Kreipe. Waking up to a brilliant dawn in a Cretan cave, the captive general murmurs to himself the opening lines of one of Horace's Odes. Major Leigh Fermor, his captor, picks up where he breaks off and finishes the poem. It was a strange moment, says Leigh Fermor, "as though … the war had ceased to exist. We had both drunk at the same fountains long before; and things were different between us for the rest of our time together" (p. 86).

And so the journey continues from the Rhine to the Danube, the narrator moving between tales of the road and digressions on history, the arts, language, people, and the passage of time, what changes and what endures. The voice is primarily that of the youth who experiences the events, but occasionally the mature writer's voice is present, commenting on the youth and on the inevitable recognition that he has crossed a Europe that will never be the same.

Through southern Germany he travels to Austria: Salzburg and the Abbey of Melk. Leigh Fermor spends his nineteenth birthday with a hospitable count and countess to whom he had been given a letter of introduction in Munich. Then he is on to Vienna, where he stays three weeks, going door to door drawing portraits for cash to tide him over until his allowance arrives, and next into Czechoslovakia, where he comments on the intersection of the Magyar (Hungarian) and Slovak worlds, describing the typical costumes and characteristics of both cultures that exist side by side, and where he sees his first Gypsies.

At this point in the narrative, the raw material changes from detailed memory to actual diary entries. The youthful Paddy Leigh Fermor is at Bratislava, and the mature Leigh Fermor comments: "Recently—after I had set down all I could remember of these ancient travels—I made a journey down the whole length of the Danube ... and in Rumania, in a romantic and improbable way too complicated to recount, I recovered a diary I had left in a country house there in 1939" (p. 275). He must have been referring to his meeting with Balasha in 1965. The journal, he continues, must have been bought in Bratislava and records a host of information about his "travels in all the countries between Bratislava and Constantinople, whence it moves to Mount Athos and stops" (p. 275). So the writer decides to include passages of the direct youthful voice "dashed down at full speed" (p. 276).

At the end of March 1934, Holy Week and Easter arrived with the spring. Leigh Fermor is still dallying on the Slovakian side of the Danube. The volume is nearing its end. On Holy Saturday, he arrives at the bridge that crosses into Esztergom in Hungary. He lingers at the middle of the bridge, watching the storks' annual return from Africa. The bells of the basilica are ringing. A crowd is gathering for a grand Easter procession. The last lines of *A Time of Gifts* are haunting: "No-one else was left on the bridge and the few on the quay were all hastening the same way. Prised loose from the balustrade at last by a more compelling note from the belfries, I hastened to follow. I didn't want to be late. TO BE CONTINUED" (p. 316).

"HARD AT WORK ON VOL II"

A Time of Gifts was a tremendous success with critics and readers alike. In a letter to Deborah Devonshire in December 1977, Leigh Fermor mentions two book parties and "too kind words said and written about A T. of G" (*In Tearing Haste,* p. 156) and goes on to say, "I'm hard at work on Vol II" (p. 157). Volume 2 would be eagerly awaited by Leigh Fermor's publisher and his public, but did not appear until 1986. The writer had many distractions as always, including climbing in the Pyrenees and travels in Spain and Portugal with Joan, Xan Fielding, and Xan's new wife, Magouche. In April 1981 he wrote to Devonshire: "I'm getting a move on with this wretched book at last, after dragging my feet as usual. I long for it all to be finished, and me free.

I was an idiot to leave it all so long. It seems to be all right, thank goodness. I'm a bit nervous, after everyone being so nice about Vol. I" (p. 190).

Leigh Fermor wrote slowly. He wanted to get the details down correctly. There was another memory-jogging trip in 1982. He wrote a long letter to Devonshire in May: "Feeling I wanted to have another look at my 1934 itinerary for Vol II of *A Time of Gifts*, I flew to Hungary a fortnight ago" (*In Tearing Haste,* p. 200). He traveled to Budapest and the Great Hungarian Plain, finding it much changed, with most of his old friends either gone or great-grandmothers. He met Balasha's sister Pomme (Princess Elena Cantacuzene) in Bucharest, then moved on to Transylvania, but he could not bear the idea of returning to Baleni in Moldavia, the site of so many memories.

A week after returning from Hungary, Paddy and Joan returned to Crete, where they were feasted and honored by old friends in village after village. "I can't tell you how moving it was," he told Devonshire (*In Tearing Haste,* p. 202). In 1983, he flew to New York with one of his Cretan guides for celebrations and festivities to commemorate the forty-second anniversary of the Battle of Crete.

In October 1984, Paddy, Joan, and their friends Xan and Magouche Fielding journeyed to Greece, Istanbul, and Turkey. Leigh Fermor was drawn to the place on the Dardanelles strait (also called the Hellespont) where ancient Troy was located. This site is steeped in myth, legend, and ancient history. In 1810, Lord Byron swam across at its narrowest point. Leigh Fermor had long desired to swim across in the footsteps of the mythical Leander and his hero Lord Byron. At the age of nearly seventy, with Joan in a skiff alongside, and a couple of Turkish guides, he accomplished the feat in difficult currents, swimming for nearly three hours.

BETWEEN THE WOODS AND THE WATER

The long-awaited volume 2 of Patrick Leigh Fermor's walk across Europe, *Between the Woods and the Water: On Foot to Constantinople from the Hook of Holland: The Middle Danube to the Iron Gates*, was published in 1986, when he was seventy-one years old. The contrast between the youth making the journey and the mature man writing the book is even more marked than in *A Time of Gifts*. Like the previous volume, *Between the Woods and the Water* begins with an introductory letter to Xan Fielding. The tone is reflective; for the mature Leigh Fermor is all too aware of the fate of the world he passed through. He reminds the reader that he had set out "meaning to mix only with chance acquaintances and fellow-tramps" but found himself in Hungary and Transylvania

> drifting from one country-house to another, often staying for weeks or even months under patient and perhaps long-suffering but always hospitable roofs … The next decade swept away this remote, country-dwelling world and this brings home to me how lucky I was to catch these long glimpses of it, even to share in it for a while. A subconscious wisdom might almost have been guiding this stretch of the journey.
>
> (p. 5)

The narrative begins exactly where *A Time of Gifts* left off, on Holy Saturday 1934, on the bridge over the Danube between Slovakia and Hungary. Leaving the snowy landscapes of the first volume behind, Leigh Fermor relishes the spring weather as well as his hospitable companions. We find him in Budapest, staying with barons, musing on language and history. Then he sets off on a borrowed horse, his youthful enthusiasm captivated by the romance of the Great Hungarian Plain and Transylvania. The reader hears the voice of the exuberant youth when he is offered a glass of milk at a farmhouse and writes: "I sipped it slowly and thought: I'm drinking this glass of milk on a chestnut horse on the Great Hungarian Plain" (p. 42). Still riding Malek, the beautiful borrowed chestnut horse, he spends a night in a Gypsy camp. Making one of his leaps of historical connection, he muses that the few words of the Romany language that he recognizes are from the Hindi familiar to his Anglo-Indian upbringing.

The spring and summer pass in an idyll of country houses, picnics, conversation, browsing

in vast private libraries where he immerses himself in history and language, always making connections among cultures and eras. The Middle and Eastern Europe through which he was passing, and the fading aristocrats with whom he mingled, were still culturally influenced by the Hapsburgs and the Austro-Hungarian Empire. Therein lies the book's sadness, for the mature Leigh Fermor knows all too well the fate of this culture, having not only experienced the war but also borne witness to the effects of Communism during his later memory-jogging expeditions to the region. The mature man writes: "The tempo of my journey had slowed up, all sense of time dissolved, and it is only now, half a century too late, that I have sudden retrospective qualms about accepting so much hospitality, and they are not very severe. The industrial revolution had left these regions untouched and the rhythm of life had remained many decades behind the pace of the West … A blessed and happy spell descended" (p. 92).

Could it be possible that Leigh Fermor's memory of a journey undertaken more than fifty years earlier was so complete and detailed? Or is the tale embellished, perhaps even occasionally fictionalized, in the manner of an experienced storyteller? The journal begun in Bratislava, left behind in 1939, and recovered a generation later was certainly an aid to memory, but not as much as Leigh Fermor himself might have hoped. Resuming the journey after the "lotus-eating weeks" he comments, "luckily a few scribbled and remembered names are backed up by a collection of clear visions … though one or two of them, like undated lantern slides loose in a box, may have got out of sequence" (p. 178). Certainly the language and style is that of the mature Leigh Fermor, as well as the fully developed rich art of digression and deep catalog of historical associations.

Youthful high spirits return as Leigh Fermor resumes his interrupted journey. On foot in the foothills of the Carpathians, he remembers "the elation of being on the move again." "Travels like these are times of such well-being that spirits soar," he writes (p. 182). And later, drinking from a mountain stream: "I thought how glad I was, at that particular moment, not to be standing properly at ease on the parade ground at Sandhurst. Oxford would have been better; but this was best" (p. 205).

At the end of *Between the Woods and the Water*, we leave Leigh Fermor at the edge of the Balkans, on the border of a Bulgaria that had been part of the Ottoman Empire only fifty years earlier. He has seen the spectacular gorges of the Danube, his first mosque and his first Turkish settlement on the island of Ada Kaleh, and is stepping onto the deck of a steamer bound for the Iron Gates of the Danube. The final words are "TO BE CONCLUDED."

Though some readers found Leigh Fermor's long digressions and untranslated lapses into obscure languages tedious, most were delighted to continue the journey with him. Many were inspired. The volume won the Thomas Cook Travel Book Award in 1986, and the public looked forward to the conclusion of the trilogy.

HARD AT WORK ON VOLUME 3

In 1990, Leigh Fermor went to Romania again, sent by the editor of the *Daily Telegraph* to report on the aftermath of the fall of the Nicolae Ceausescu regime. This return to Romania, after a bloody revolution, with Balasha dead, was particularly heartbreaking. Writing about the old, lost friends from the happy days of 1934, in the 1990 article "Rumania—Travels in a Land before Darkness Fell," his tone is melancholy. The beautiful old manor houses seem to have shrunk. Their inhabitants are gone, their era ended. What the war began, Communism finished.

A brief appendix follows the conclusion of *Between the Woods and the Water*. In the 1970s and 1980s, two hydroelectric dams drowned the region of Danube gorges and the island of Ada Kaleh that Leigh Fermor had so much admired. His thoughts on what has been lost could be a metaphor for the lost happy times and the doomed friends of those years. Leigh Fermor worked on the third volume of the trilogy for the rest of his life, but he never brought it to publication. He was often encouraged, offered

and given clerical help, and asked why so many years passed between completed volumes. He had always been a determined and careful rewriter, sometimes taking months to return proofs to his publisher. He had given various replies, from "laziness" and dissatisfaction with his work (in a *Guardian* interview with James Campbell) to "wanting to get it right" (London *Times* interview with Nicholas Shakespeare), but it seems probable that the melancholy and loss grew simply too painful to contemplate as he grew older.

Travel, adventure, and the demands of friendship were always welcome distractions from writing. Though he would enter the contemplative life from time to time for the sake of work, Patrick Leigh Fermor was a man of action. He was by all accounts handsome, charming, cheerful, and generous. He loved conversation, food, wine, and laughter. He enjoyed house parties and company.

Leigh Fermor won numerous prizes and honors for his work; he became Chevalier de l'Ordre National du Mérite in 1992, Chevalier des Arts et Lettres in 1996, and Officier de l'Ordre des Arts et des Lettres in 2002. He was a member of the Academy of Athens and an honorary citizen of Heraklion, Crete, and Kardamyli, Greece. He was knighted by the British monarchy for service to literature and to British-Greek relations in 2004, at the age of nearly ninety.

Joan Leigh Fermor died June 4, 2003, at ninety-one years old after a fall at home in the Mani, and she was buried in the churchyard of her family home in Dumbleton, England. Patrick Leigh Fermor was losing his eyesight and had a successful operation for cancer in 2008. With the help of friends, he was continuing to work on the final volume of his trilogy at the time of his death on June 10, 2011, at the age of ninety-six. He had been writing in Greece, but at the last, when he was very ill, he expressed his wish to die in England, so he was flown to his home in Worcestershire. He was buried at Saint Peter's Church, at Dumbleton in Gloucestershire, on June 16, 2011, with his beloved wife, Joan.

In the 1990s, when he was in his eighties, Leigh Fermor had commissioned the British writer Artemis Cooper to write his official biography, with the caveat that it not be published until after his death. The book was expected to be published by John Murray, Leigh Fermor's publisher, by sometime in 2013. A draft of the third volume of Patrick Leigh Fermor's trilogy is reported to be ready for editing and is likely to be published posthumously.

"A Cave on the Black Sea," the article commissioned by *Holiday* magazine after the journey retracing his steps from the Danube to the Black Sea, offers a tantalizing taste of the final volume. Published in 1965, years before *A Time of Gifts*, the piece is set in December 1934 on "Europe's easternmost rim," the Bulgarian coast of the Black Sea only 150 miles from Constantinople. The descriptive language is breathtaking, the promise of the East palpable: "A promise of the Aegean and the Greek islands roved the cold Bulgarian air, sending a hint of their spell across the Propontis and the Bosporus to the shores of this huge barbarian sea" (*Words of Mercury*, p. 30). Losing his way in the dark, Leigh Fermor slips into an icy pool. Dragging himself along the shore with a cut forehead and broken boots, he staggers frozen and bleeding into a firelit cave populated by ragged Bulgarian shepherds, Greek fisherman, goats, and dogs, "an abode harmoniously shared by Polyphemus and Sinbad" (p. 33). He passes the evening singing and dancing, and sleeps among the Greek fishermen whose friendly warmth, he writes, "I had interpreted ... as a late symptom of Greek feelings towards Lord Byron's countrymen. I was right. Dimitri said as much. Uttering the words '*Lordos Veeron!*' he raised his bunched fingers in a gesture of approval. Greece and the Greeks ... were drawing nearer every day" (p. 38). As always for Leigh Fermor's reader, the narrator's past and his future intertwine with mythology, geography, language, and the joy of being alive.

How characteristic of Sir Patrick Leigh Fermor to die with a work in progress. Living life was always his passion—as a youth between the wars, as a war hero, traveler, and lover of friendship and life. Writing the life was more difficult, although the result is stunning. No wonder he found it difficult to get it right, for his work is far more complex than simply a record of events. As at home in the private library of a country house as on a mountain trek or swimming into the mouth of Hell, Leigh Fermor lived a life often in tension between the pleasures and distractions of society and the necessity of quiet and solitude to work. The complexity of his work is a testament to the complexity of his intellect and of his witness to the ebbing of an era.

Selected Bibliography

WORKS OF PATRICK LEIGH FERMOR

NONFICTION

The Traveller's Tree. London: John Murray, 1950.

A Time to Keep Silence. London: John Murray, 1957.

Mani: Travels in the Southern Peloponnese. London: John Murray, 1958.

Roumeli: Travels in Northern Greece. London: John Murray, 1966.

A Time of Gifts: On Foot to Constantinople from the Hook of Holland: From the Hook of Holland to the Middle Danube. London: John Murray, 1977.

Between the Woods and the Water: On Foot to Constantinople from the Hook of Holland: The Middle Danube to the Iron Gates. London: John Murray, 1986.

Three Letters from the Andes. London: John Murray, 1991.

Words of Mercury. Edited by Artemis Cooper. London: John Murray, 2003. (Anthology of prose, some previously unpublished in book form.)

TRANSLATIONS

Forever Ulysses. By C. P. Rodocanachi. New York: Viking, 1938. (Translated from the French.)

Julie de Corneilhan and *Chance Acquaintances*. By Colette. Paris: Fayard, 1941. (Translated from the French.)

Gigi, Julie de Corneilhan, and *Chance Acquaintances*. By Colette. New York: Farrar, Straus & Young, 1952. (Translated from the French, with Roger Senhouse.)

The Cretan Runner: His Story of the German Occupation. By George Psychoundakis. London: John Murray, 1955. (Translated from the Greek.)

OTHER WORK

The Violins of Saint-Jacques: A Tale of the Antilles. London: John Murray, 1953. (Novel.)

In Tearing Haste: Letters Between Deborah Devonshire and Patrick Leigh Fermor. Edited by Charlotte Mosley. London: John Murray, 2008.

CRITICAL AND BIOGRAPHICAL STUDIES

Campbell, James. "Scholar in the Wilds." *Guardian*, April 9, 2005 (http://www.guardian.co.uk/books/2005/apr/09/featuresreviews.guardianreview3).

Downing, Ben. "Philhellene's Progress: Patrick Leigh Fermor." *New Criterion* 19:9 (January 2001). Available online (http://www.newcriterion.com/articles.cfm/Philhellene-s-progress—Patrick-Leigh-Fermor-2268).

Lane, Anthony. "An Englishman Abroad." *New Yorker,* May 22, 2006, p. 58.

Mason, David. *News from the Village: Aegean Friends.* Pasadena, Calif.: Red Hen Press, 2010. (Mason's account of his years in Leigh Fermor's circle in Mani, 1980–1990.)

Moss, W. Stanley. *Ill Met by Moonlight.* 1950. Reprint. London: Buchan & Enright, 1985.

"Patrick Leigh Fermor (11 February 1915–)." In *Dictionary of Literary Biography.* Vol. 204, *British Travel Writers, 1940–1997.* Edited by Barbara Brothers and Julia Marie Gergits. Detroit: Gale, 1999. Pp. 68–81.

Shakespeare, Nicholas. "Walking Back to Happiness." *Times* (London), October 16, 1986, p. 17.

SORLEY MacLEAN

(1911—1996)

J. C. Bittenbender

A COMMANDING VOICE of modern Scottish Gaelic poetry, Sorley MacLean was a leading figure in the resurgence of interest in Scottish-language poetry that coincided with the Scottish literary Renaissance of the early and middle twentieth century. Along with Hugh MacDiarmid (a friend and influence on MacLean's own political poetry), MacLean helped to resuscitate interest in Scottish writing that had been neglected or overlooked during the preceding centuries of English cultural and political domination of Scotland. MacLean, in particular, was active in reclaiming Gaelic voices of the past that had either suffered negligence through a lack of translation into English or had not been adequately analyzed or critiqued in any meaningful way that would bring attention to a larger readership. In addition to identifying and recovering particular writers, MacLean celebrated lost folk songs and a number of older Gaelic poetic traditions, such as the pibroch, that were closely aligned with music and with the pipe-playing heritage of the Highlands and Islands of Scotland. In addition to his championing of a lost poetic past, MacLean produced volumes of his own finely tuned poetry that exhibit his love of Scotland and the Isle of Skye in particular. Through shorter lyrics as well as longer meditations in verse, MacLean reveals concerns and interests that range from a love of landscape and the natural world to politics, philosophy, and cultural identity. As his voice becomes more voluble in the crisis-torn period of the 1930s, he finds ways of joining his commentaries on contemporary issues with events and subjects from a Gaelic Scottish past (such as the Clearances that decimated the Highlands and Islands in the eighteenth and nineteenth centuries). If anything, for MacLean, cultural memory becomes for him a springboard to new poetic possibilities and offers poetic avenues that lead to a fresh awareness of the present moment.

BIOGRAPHICAL SUMMARY

Sorley MacLean (whose name in his native Scottish Gaelic language is Somhairle MacGill-eain) was born on October 26, 1911, on the island of Raasay, a small island that lies between the east coast of the Isle of Skye (part of the Inner Hebrides) and the mainland of Scotland. He was one of seven children born to Malcolm and Christina MacLean. His father, who was originally from Raasay, owned a tailoring business and his mother (whose maiden name was Nicolson) came from Skye. MacLean attended schools on Raasay and in Portree (the main town on Skye), where he studied English and Gaelic literature as well as classical works in Latin and French poetry. MacLean became a student at Edinburgh University and graduated in 1933 with a degree in English. In the years prior to the start of World War II, MacLean taught at a variety of schools on the Isles of Skye and Mull and in and around Edinburgh. In 1940 he entered military service and was sent to Egypt in 1941. He was seriously injured in the Battle of El Alamein in Egypt in 1942 and went back to teaching in Scotland after a period of hospitalization. During the early 1940s MacLean was getting much of his poetry published both in book form and in literary magazines and other periodicals. In 1946 he married Renee Cameron, and in 1954 he became headmaster of Plockton Secondary School where he remained until he retired in 1972. In his later years he moved back to Skye and served as a writer in residence at Edinburgh University; he received numerous awards and honorary positions from other institutions and societies, including the Gaelic College on Skye, Sabhal Mòr Ostaig. MacLean died of natural causes on November 24, 1996, in Inverness where he had been hospitalized. A wonderful biographical appreciation of MacLean can be found in the chapter titled "Sorley MacLean: The Man and His Work," by Joy Hendry, in *Sorley MacLean: Critical Essays,* published by Scottish Academic Press in 1986.

DÀIN DO EIMHIR *AND OTHER EARLY POEMS*

Many of MacLean's early poems were published in periodicals throughout the 1930s. His first collection of poems, titled *17 Poems for 6D* (a second edition with corrections, appearing in the same year, was titled *Seventeen Poems for Sixpence),* with lyrics in Gaelic, Scots, and English, was published by the Chalmers Press in 1940 along with poems by the Edinburgh poet Robert Garioch. A second volume, *Dàin do Eimhir agus Dàin Eile (Poems to Eimhir and Other Poems)* appeared in 1943, published by William MacLellan in Glasgow and illustrated by William Crosbie, a Scottish artist. Although the majority of these poems appeared in Gaelic some were translated into English. MacLean's own English translations of these poems (with the original Gaelic running on the opposite page) are preserved in *O Choille gu Bearradh/From Wood to Ridge: Collected Poems*, published in 1989 by the Carcanet publishing company in Manchester, England. (References to poems in this essay are taken from that edition.) Two sections within *O Choille gu Bearradh* contain poems that originally appeared in *Dàin do Eimhir*. *Dàin do Eimhir* is considered to be MacLean's finest collection of verse, and a number of highly regarded editions of this volume have been published since 1943. Notably, the first edition with all the poems translated into English was produced by MacLean's friend and fellow poet Iain Crichton Smith in 1971. An edition of *Dàin do Eimhir* published in 1999 (by Acair in Stornoway, Isle of Lewis) as *Eimhir* includes illustrations and additional essays by Smith and the editor Donald Meek. In 2002 an edition of *Dàin do Eimhir* was published by the Association for Scottish Literary Studies. The volume was edited by Christopher Whyte and includes new translations of some of MacLean's poems by Whyte in addition to commentaries and notes to accompany the poems. The 2002 edition also includes an excellent bibliography of works by and about MacLean and offers new insights into the publishing history of *Dàin do Eimhir*.

Dàin do Eimhir represents a sequence of mainly love poems in which MacLean weaves personal identity, love poems inspired by two separate women, reflections on the history of Scotland, current events unfolding in Europe, and MacLean's overarching passion for and celebration of the landscape of the Highlands and Islands of the west of Scotland.

In one of MacLean's earliest poems, "A' Chorra-Ghridheach"/"The Heron," he announces a number of the themes that will play an important role in his later work. The poem begins with the setting of a scene with no specific geographical location but one that reflects a more universal condition of the modern soul:

> A pale yellow moon on the skyline,
> the heart of the soil without a throb of laughter,
> a chilliness contemptuous
> of golden windows in a snaky sea.
>
> It is not the frail beauty of the moon
> nor the cold loveliness of the sea
> nor the empty tale of the shore's uproar
> that seeps through my spirit tonight.
>
> Faintness in fight,
> death pallor in effect,
> cowardice in the heart
> and belief in nothing.
>
> (p. 3)

The tone here exudes a sense of modern disillusion and a lack of faith. The speaker surveys the landscape with a sense of resignation, admitting that the healing power of nature and storytelling is not sufficient for what it seeks. The moon's beauty is "frail," the sea's loveliness is "cold," and the story of the "shore's uproar" is "empty." This bleak scene sets the stage for the entrance of the heron in the following lines:

A demure heron came
and stood on top of sea-wrack.
She folded her wings close in to her sides
and took stock of all around her.

Alone beside the sea
like a mind alone in the universe,
her reason like a man's—
the sum of it how to get a meal.

(p. 3)

The heron's purpose becomes joined with that of
the speaker, who goes on to connect his understanding of the troubled world that surrounds
him with the vision of the bird searching for
sustenance. MacLean takes a common scenario
out of the landscape and elevates it to a cosmic
level. The heron becomes "a mind alone in the
universe." Though the speaker appears to be one
with the heron, the speaker separates them
through expression of their shared vision: "I am
with you, alone, / gazing at the coldness of the
level kyle" (p. 5). Desire for some form of
enlightenment for the speaker becomes joined
with the acknowledgment that the heron possesses a "dream of rapture with one thrust" (p.
5), the strike into the water for food that becomes
the "straight, unbending law of herons" (p. 5).
That dream of rapture may be for something that
will disturb the "morose" contemplations of the
speaker, though the reader is left in the final
stanza with the "brain, heart, and love troubled"
(p. 5). This condition is described as a "sparkle"
and leads the reader to consider whether the
energy of the heron's rapture is a larger hope for
change and renewal.

"A' Chorra-Ghridheach" displays MacLean's
method of inhabiting the natural world with rich
observations that speak to the human soul. The
troubled aura that surrounds that poem may also
indicate the clouds surrounding MacLean and
other artists and intellectuals who were witnessing the disturbing changes coming to Europe as
the 1930s progressed. Many of MacLean's poems
from this period bear this imprint of concern and
anxiety. Another early poem, "Gaoir na h-Eòrpa"/
"The Cry of Europe," expresses MacLean's fear
and anger over the spread of fascism in Europe,
especially in Spain. The poem combines the
speaker's admiration for a particular woman with

the anguish of one who is witnessing political
turbulence in Europe:

Girl of the yellow, heavy-yellow, gold-yellow hair,
the song of your mouth and Europe's shivering cry,
fair, heavy-haired, spirited, beautiful girl,
the disgrace of our day would not be bitter in your
kiss.

(p. 9)

The mysterious girl becomes a refuge from the
forces that threaten the land, and as the poem
progresses the speaker increasingly turns to the
salvation offered by the object of his affections
as a shield from what is then happening in Spain
as Maclean writes his poem:

What would the kiss of your proud mouth be
compared with each drop of the precious blood
that fell on the cold frozen uplands
of Spanish mountains from a column of steel?

What every lock of your gold-yellow head
to all the poverty, anguish and grief
that will come and have come on Europe's people
from the Slave Ship to the slavery of the whole
people?

(p. 9)

In an essay titled "My Relationship with the
Muse," MacLean describes how the 1930s were
a difficult time for him as he contended with
crises that were personal, national, and philosophical in nature:

My mother's long illness in 1936, its recurrence in
1938, the outbreak of the Spanish Civil War in
1936, the progressive decline of my father's business in the Thirties, my meeting with an Irish girl
in 1937, my rash leaving of Skye for Mull late in
1937, and Munich in 1938, and always the steady
unbearable decline of Gaelic, made those years for
me years of difficult choice, and the tensions of
those years confirmed self-expression in poetry not
in action.

(*Ris a' Bhruthaich*, p. 12)

The confluence of hardship, conflict, and emotional turmoil in the poet's life at this time
contributed to the variety of themes that he addresses in his writing, and MacLean was adept at
bringing these strands into a dialogic relationship

with one another. This was a period of MacLean's life in which many difficult decisions needed to be made by the poet in terms of love and his involvement in European political movements. In "An Roghainn"/"The Choice," the poet seems to lament a lost love while also meditating on a decision to remain out of the conflict going on in Spain. He starts the poem with the image of a divided self:

> I walked with my reason
> out beside the sea.
> We were together but it was
> keeping a little distance from me.
>
> Then it turned saying:
> is it true you heard
> that your beautiful white love
> is getting married early on Monday?
>
> (p. 23)

The questioning tone continues throughout the poem, in which the speaker links the two conflicts of love and participation in the war in Spain:

> I did not take a cross's death
> in the hard extremity of pain
> and how then should I expect
> the one new prize of fate?
>
> (p. 23)

Here it seems as if the speaker's fate in love has been determined in part by his decision not to go to Spain to fight against the fascists. In order to stay in Scotland to support his family, MacLean had not followed his conscience to Spain, and this poem sensitively records the anguish of that decision. For this reason the speaker wonders, "how then should I meet / the thunderbolt of love?" (p. 23). There is an equation of passion here where one's love of conscience and political duty would have found reward in the love of the woman. However, the ending of the poem seems to reject the false dichotomy of the choice itself:

> But if I had the choice again
> and stood on that headland,
> I would leap from heaven or hell
> with a whole spirit and heart.
>
> (p. 23)

The critic Douglas Sealy has suggested that the poet's choices are responsible for the divided self, and there is a unifying effort with the final leap of the speaker into spiritual wholeness. In both "Gaoir na h-Eòrpa" and "An Roghainn," MacLean joins a European political and military crisis to the love of a woman in a way that enhances the understanding of both situations. He does this elsewhere in other poetry from this period, where his love of the Scottish landscape is often articulated alongside a concern for Europe, a critique of Scotland's past, and a lament for the dying Gaelic language. He allows his repertoire of experiences and concerns to inform and illuminate one another, such as in the early poem "Ban-Ghàidheal"/"A Highland Woman." As Joy Hendry points out, this may have been influenced by MacLean's time spent on the Isle of Mull. Here MacLean's observations of the effects of the Highland Clearances combine with commentary on the strict and often hypocritical nature of religion in Scotland:

> Hast Thou seen her, great Jew,
> who art called the One Son of God?
> Hast Thou seen on Thy way the like of her
> labouring in the distant vineyard?
>
> ....
>
> Thou hast not seen her, Son of the carpenter,
> who art called the King of Glory,
> among the rugged western shores
> in the sweat of her food's creel.
>
> This Spring and last Spring
> and every twenty Springs from the beginning,
> she has carried the cold seaweed
> for her children's food and the castle's reward.
>
> ....
>
> And Thy gentle church has spoken
> about the lost state of her miserable soul,
> and the unremitting toil has lowered
> her body to a black peace in a grave.
>
> (pp. 27–29)

Lines like these reveal MacLean's concern for the downtrodden of the remote parts of Scotland and especially those who suffer financial hardship at the hands of the wealthy landowners. The voice is biblical yet questions and critiques the church's appropriation of Christ for a cause that does not question economic and social injustice. The Highland Clearances of the eighteenth and nineteenth centuries involved thousands of Scots being forced off their lands by the British government both to suppress the clan system and to make way for rich landowners to profit from increased sheep farming. The tableau of the Highland woman bent under the hardship of life represents a victim of that event whose plight would be every bit as evident in the early twentieth century, when the lasting effects of the Clearances were still being felt across the land. Here too is the response of a church (likely Free Presbyterian or one with strict Calvinist leanings) that disregards the backbreaking work of the woman while yet criticizing her seemingly lost soul. His friend and fellow poet Iain Crichton Smith has written on MacLean's attitudes toward religion in this poem:

> It seems to me that MacLean's attitude towards religion is one of contempt since it does not deal with the real problems of poverty and the paradoxes on which the human mind is impaled. The movement, which seems to me to be almost wholly intellectual, of Auden from Freud and Marx to Christianity is not a course that MacLean has taken. The abstractionism of Auden, his hunger for ideas, his attempt to erect Love into a sort of metaphysical God, is much more superficial than MacLean's inward Highland knowledge of what Christ has meant to the woman with the creel.

("A Poet's Response to Sorley MacLean," pp. 47–48)

A similar attitude toward religion is articulated in "Calbharaigh"/"Calvary," where the immediacy of conditions in urban Scotland are drawn into focus by a speaker who urgently desires to redirect the vision and purpose of religion to where it is most needed, that is, to social and economic justice:

> My eye is not on Calvary
> nor on Bethlehem the Blessed,
> but on a foul-smelling backland in Glasgow,
> where life rots as it grows;
> and on a room in Edinburgh,
> a room of poverty and pain,

> where the diseased infant
> writhes and wallows till death.

(p. 35)

For MacLean, the religious hypocrisy of the church was matched by the economic, social, and cultural forces that had negatively impacted parts of early-twentieth-century Scotland. In the 1920s and 1930s MacLean became increasingly fascinated with Communism and increasingly repulsed by Fascism. His poetry from the 1930s and early 1940s often combines these political interests with reflections on events from the past that had profound effects on the communities of Scotland and particularly those located in the Highlands and the Western Islands. The Highland Clearances of the previous two centuries not only depleted the land of people (and healthy communities) but also had an immense impact on the preservation and continuation of the Gaelic language and culture. MacLean responds to these multiple deleterious effects on Scottish Gaeldom in a number of short poems that pave the way for his longer, epic poem, *An Cuilithionn*/*The Cuillin*. Another poem that contends with the Clearances is "An Saothach"/"The Ship," which takes the reader on board a vessel that is transporting those who have been removed from their land. Scottish history has recorded the travels and travails of those forced to leave Scotland through various forms of economic oppression, and other poets had written on this as well, but MacLean captures a modern idiom and sensibility as he alludes not only to events themselves but the lasting consequences of forced emigration.

The poem begins with the speaker addressing the ship itself:

> Will you ever put your head to sea,
> will you break a great proud ocean,
> pounding it with hard slender pinewood,
> with the threshing of your two shoulders?

(p. 29)

In a sense, here, the ship becomes a symbol for every Gael who is being transported away from their country of origin. There is a valedictory hope early in the poem that the ship will "defy the barbarous sea" and "oppress the rush of oceans" (p. 31), even though this is framed in a

SORLEY MacLEAN

questioning voice. The sea in this sense becomes emblematic of those political and economic forces that have battered the Gael while on land. However, the hopeful tone of the poem is soon submerged by the realities of what happened to many of those who left the shores of Scotland:

> Dust and ashes the great man
> forgotten in Moidart,
> his language exposed, his hand lost,
> the art and courage of his steering.

> The other ship is on an ocean rock,
> her men drowned, holes in her sides:
> when a darkening came she lost her way
> and the non-Gaels took her for a loan.
>
> (p. 31)

A few stanzas later a figure appears, "a man standing on a promontory, / a white halo of light around him, / words without pith or substance" (p. 33). It is unclear as to whether this figure represents the church, a politician, or simply the promise of escape from the oppression of the Clearances. Nonetheless the voice of the poem absolves this figure a few stanzas later before the true culprit is revealed:

> O poor fellow in your mist,
> you were not the means of the terrible thing;
> it was not you who made our villages desolate;
> it was not you who mutilated the head of our people.

> You did not drive man away for the sake of deer
> and the food of white sheep;
> you did not lay our house to the ground,
> reap our field and rot our boat.
>
> (p. 33)

The speaker then identifies the source of what has both caused the situation of emigration and led the ship to a future of despair with the lines "the pride of England on helm and sheet, / the paradise of England smothering you!" (p. 33). The poem surges ahead chronologically at this point through references to economic conditions and political movements then current in Europe:

> Her empire oppressing your sails,
> poverty slanting your course,

> the bourgeoisie, and their fustian,
> and their soul over your desire.
>
> (pp. 33–35)

McLean's interest in Communism and his experience of economic inequality is palpable in the later lines of the poem and in the envisioned promise of the final stanza:

> Will you ever put head to sea,
> will you leave a port of death,
> the murmur of the surge through the night
> but a red dawn on the horizon!
>
> (p. 35)

Although a number of MacLean's poems bear the stamp of the political, his most evocative poems are those that celebrate the natural beauty of the Hebrides. Shorter lyrics from his early period that focus on Highland scenery pave the way for the longer, epic tribute to the Isle of Skye that he will later pay with *An Cuilithion/The Cuillin*. Poems such as "Ceann Loch Aoineart"/"Kinloch Ainort" have been recognized as indicative of MacLean's abiding love for the landscape of the north and west of Scotland. In his introduction to *Sorley MacLean: Critical Essays,* the poet Seamus Heaney remarks upon MacLean's profoundly poetic sense of place:

> MacLean's responsibility is druidic. He stands at the centre, if near the end, of a world he embodies. Hence the effortless rhapsody of poems like "Ceann Loch Aoineart" and "Coilltean Ratharsair" thrives on the same nutrient love of place as the personal love-poems like "A' Bhuaile Ghréine" and "Tràighean." In all of them an urgency to name springs from a sense of crisis, either personal or communal. They return to hallowed spots and exemplary names with the same intent as Yeats when he repeated the roll-call of his Olympians: in order to resist the erosion of certain values, to maintain the dignity and continuity of a style of life and a way of feeling and behaving characteristic of the poet's caste.
>
> (p. 5)

MacLean paints his scenes so that they offer poetic panoramas in which the physical features connect in an interdependent fashion with the human, for instance in "Kinloch Ainort":

> A company of mountains, an upthrust of mountains,
> a great garth of growing mountains,

a concourse of summits, of knolls, of hills
coming on with a fearsome roaring.

(p. 37)

The speaker's voice here seems to increase in intensity and in awareness of the scene before him as the poem progresses. A spiraling of emotion can be detected by the reader as the mountains come into focus and expand in detail with each successive line. The landscape proceeds to take on more animal and human characteristics:

A rising of glens, of gloomy corries,
a lying down in the antlered bellowing;
a stretching of green nooks, of brook mazes,
prattling in the age-old mid-winter.

(p. 37)

Though they are not mentioned by name, one can see the highland deer as they merge with the land and the land takes on the characteristics of the deer. The words seem to caress the landscape and offer a somewhat erotic overtone in lines such as "impetuous thigh of peaks" (p. 37). While the speaker of this poem seems yet detached from what he is describing, the voice of "An t-Eilean"/ "The Island" shares an intimate experience with the geography on display, and in doing so again brings together themes of human love and love of place:

O great Island, Island of my love,
many a night of them I fancied
the great ocean itself restless,
agitated with love of you
as you lay on the sea,
great beautiful bird of Scotland,
your supremely beautiful wings bent
about many-nooked Loch Bracadale,
your beautiful wings prostrate on the sea
from the Wild Stallion to the Aird of Sleat,
your joyous wings spread
about Loch Snizort and the world.

(p. 57)

The island is Skye, and this poem expresses the deep connection MacLean has with the object of his love. The tone of admiration and deeply shared experience turns to one of concern as the poem progresses and the speaker reveals the suffering of the island and how history has left a seemingly incurable scar on the land:

Great Island, Island of my desire,
Island of my heart and wound,
it is not likely that the strife
and suffering of Braes will be seen requited
and it is not certain that the debts
of the Glendale Martyr will be seen made good;
there is no hope of your townships
rising high with gladness and laughter,
and your men are not expected
when America and France take them.

Pity the eye that sees on the ocean
the great dead bird of Scotland.

(p. 59)

In addition to the shared love, the speaker takes on the wounds that have been inflicted on Scotland, and particularly the Highlands, through the Clearances. This is not simply an observed pain but one that has been translated into the very being of the speaker-poet and clearly illustrates the manner in which MacLean's soul is integrated with the soul of the island, which includes history, landscape, and a sense of community that has been betrayed and oppressed. This commonly shared, dialogic relationship MacLean shares with the Highland and Island landscape permeates his poetry and can be seen on a grander scale in the long poem *An Cuilithion/The Cuillin,* composed in 1939.

MacLean's poetry shows the reader that yet another victim of the Clearances was music, including losses in the tradition of the harp or of the pibroch, a type of complex bagpipe playing that is an integral part of the cultural heritage of the west of Scotland and elsewhere in the Gaelic-speaking world. In an early poem titled "Craobh nan Teud"/"The Tree of Strings," the landscape becomes integrated with a harp that is experiencing "hardship" and "misery" (p. 49):

The tree of poetry
is in bands of steel,
in the cleft rocks,
in the notch of anguish;
the green foliage is
under the fierce abusive eye:
the Tree of Strings is
in the extremity of grief.

In the harp of Ruairi
and the pipes of the Patricks
is the loved tree of my talk,
in Patrick's unrest
is the paean beauty,
the serene lovely music,
the white crying music,
the music of my love and talk.

(p. 51)

Here the music is seen to be suffering from the same fate as the people of the Western Islands of Scotland who are forced to leave their country by the Clearances. The "Patricks" of the poem are two famous pipers from Scotland's past whose own music has done much to ensure the future of Gaelic culture: Patrick Mór MacCrimmon and Patrick Og MacCrimmon (father and son) served as official pipers for the MacLeods of Dunvegan (on Skye) in the seventeenth and eighteenth centuries. Patrick Mór MacCrimmon is usually credited with having written "Lament for the Children," a pibroch that is much revered in Scotland and is said to be an elegy for the elder piper's sons who were killed by a fever. MacLean pays tribute to these musicians through lines that make the art of pibroch reflective of the state of past and present Scotland as that land endures loss and hardship. In the third section of the poem MacLean joins the pipers, the harper Ruairi, Homer, Shakespeare, Deirdre (from Irish legend), and the Russian poet Alexander Blok as they collectively lament not only the circumstances of Scotland's oppressed state but that of Gaeldom and Europe. The "tree of strings" becomes a vision accessed by the speaker in other lands: "I saw the tree in a distant land / and its far sad music sore for me" (p. 53). In the end "Craobh nan Teud" becomes MacLean's modern lament for what is lost to culture through displacement, negligence, and political ignorance:

And eternal in the crying
quivering tormented novel words
the remote sad thought and feeling,
the sensitive fugitive who is eternal.

What put growing in this tree
a face lovely beyond every hymn,

a spirit gracious beyond all mortification,
beyond every anguish and joy of the tree.

(pp. 55–57)

The end of the poem exhibits the hope that music (symbolically represented by the tree of strings and the lovely face that dwells in its branches) will remain a sustaining influence that has the ability to unify communities even in the face of despair.

Another poem, "Oidhche Chiùin"/"Gentle Night," originally appeared in *Dàin do Eimhir* and highlights the influence on MacLean of the music of Scottish Gaelic culture. Here the poet engages with the pibroch tune "Maol Donn" ("the brown-polled cow"). As Christopher Whyte points out, this is an old tune that is often referred to in English as "MacCrimmon's Sweetheart." In his notes to the poem at the end of *O Choille gu Bearradh*, MacLean identifies the tune as a *ceòl mór*, or "big music"—"classical Scottish Highland pibroch, or music for bagpipes, with a theme and variations. Pibroch music is handed down from one generation to the next" (p. 315). As the poet's note seems to suggest, MacLean is himself the recipient of the song, and he makes new use of it in the context of "Oidhche Chiùin" not only in order to speak of his love for a woman but also to address issues of context regarding his own time and place. The speaker begins the poem by summoning a night that is tainted by contemporary suffering:

Come before me, gentle night,
starred blue sky and dew,
though there is not purged from any airt
the world's poverty and Spain's shivering cry …

(p. 139)

However, the following lines add to the description of the night, relating it to the poet-speaker's love and tying that in with the reputation of the pibroch: "a night when Maol Donn sings / a ceòl mór of gentleness on the mountain, / a night with my love in her beauty" (p. 139). It is as if by the invocation of the pibroch and all it represents from a Gaelic past the poet-speaker is able to relay the scope of his love for a woman that also encompasses a more universal love. The final lines bring the speaker into the poem more completely as he tells of what use he will make of the night he is summoning: "I will thoughtlessly comprehend / the piercing music of Maol Donn's theme" (p. 139). In a sense, this particular ceòl mór and the larger theme of the ceòl mór pibroch become talismanic in their ability to serve as unifying forces joining past and present together through a type of redemptive harmony. Poems like "Craobh nan Teud" and "Oidhche Chiùin" show MacLean's ability to create his own pibroch in verse that weaves the threads of time and theme together in a choral fashion.

MacLean frequently pays tribute to musicians from Scottish history who contributed so much to the development of Gaelic culture and who, in some fashion, serve as models for modern Gaelic poets such as MacLean. Another such case is that of "Uilleam Ros is mi fhìn"/"William Ross and I," in which MacLean acknowledges the Skye-born writer of love songs whose works had such a profound influence on MacLean's own love poetry:

> I am not at all related
> to William Ross though I pretended
> that my case is like his case,
> being jealous of the musical chiselling
> of words, which is a marvel in his poetry.
>
> (p. 189)

These lines reveal MacLean's own vision of poetry as a craft wedded to music. MacLean goes on to connect the plight of Ross, who lost his love to another man, with MacLean's own loss of a woman to a man in Ireland.

A longer, later poem, "Uamha 'n Oir"/"The Cave of Gold" (included in *O Choille gu Bearradh* within the section of poems written between 1945 and 1972) also pays tribute to the supremacy of music (and particularly pibroch) in the life of the Gael:

> A man went into the Cave of Gold
> and bewailed his lack of three hands,
> that two of them were not on the pipes
> and the other on the sword.
>
> (p. 283)

Here, in part 1 of the poem, MacLean is engaging with an old tale told of a piper named Mac-

Crimmons who entered a cave on the Isle of Skye and never emerged. In part 2 another piper enters the cave, and as the lines progress the reader sees the pipers confronting those forces that have been ranged against Gaelic traditions and island communities. At the conclusion of part 2, the pipers seem to question the usefulness and vitality of the "Black Chanter" whose music comes from a "poor bruised decrepit black mouth" (p. 293). However, in the final section, part 3, there is a transition in which the power of the pipes increasingly seems to supplant the power of the sword, as the different strains of music heard by the pipes fuses into a stronger message that is ultimately accessible to MacCrimmons:

> With no struggle but the plea of the music,
> he did not let go his pipe.
> The sword was useless,
> it was the music that strengthened his step,
> it was the music itself that strove.
>
> The pipe itself had the power,
> a kind of power in the lack
> of every mark that comes on the aspect
> of the dark Cave and dim sky
> and every colour and gilt that sun puts
> on sea and land and deed.
>
> (p. 297)

AN CUILITHION *AND LATER POEMS*

Influenced perhaps by the early-twentieth-century literary fashion for longer poems (and in particular Hugh MacDiarmid's epic *A Drunk Man Looks at the Thistle*), *An Cuilithion/The Cuillin* (1939) celebrates the mountains of the Isle of Skye. The poem offers beautiful descriptions of the landscape while simultaneously expressing political concerns about Nazi-plagued Europe of the 1930s. The poem also offers echoes of regret and anger related to the Clearances, the theme that similarly arises in MacLean's shorter poems. In the preface to *An Cuilithion* that appears in *O Choille gu Bearradh*, MacLean contextualizes the poem in terms of the time, place, and state of mind in which much of it was written:

> It was in the Spring or early Summer of 1939 that I started what was meant to be a very long poem

radiating from Skye and the West Highlands to the whole of Europe. I was regretting my rash leaving of Skye in 1937 because Mull in 1938 had made me obsessed with the Clearances. I was obsessed also with the approach of war, or worse, with the idea of the conquest of the whole of Europe by Nazi-Fascism without a war in which Britain would not be immediately involved but which would ultimately make Britain a Fascist state.

(p. 63)

MacLean goes on to explain that one perceived antidote to the European situation at the time was Communism as developed in Russia. However, although the poem is laced with a pro-Communist flavor, MacLean admits to a change of heart following Russia's harsh response to insurrection in Poland in 1944.

The poem starts with an invocation of Hugh MacDiarmid and "MacDonald" (perhaps of the MacDonald clan that is associated with the Isle of Skye):

Christopher Grieve, MacDiarmid,
had I the remnant
scraped from the dregs of a small third part
of your sharp profound wild spirit,
I would put the awesome Cuillin
in phosphorescence in the firmament,
and I would make the island shout
with a cry of fate in the skies.
And, glorious MacDonald,
if I had a third of your might,
I would keep our noble Cuillin
head on to the waves of Europe's battle.

(p. 65)

The landscape of Skye is featured prominently in the poem, and MacLean identifies particular mountains, valleys, and other geographical features as the poem progresses. Part 2 begins with descriptions of some of the mountains of the island:

The Sgurr Biorach the highest sgurr,
but Sgurr nan Gillean the best sgurr,
the blue-black gape-mouthed strong sgurr,
the tree-like slender horned sgurr,
the forbidding great dangerous sgurr,
the sgurr of Skye above the rest.

(p. 65)

The voice of MacLean's speaker often conveys an oral quality reminiscent of a medieval bard. This voice describes the island's geography in a manner that animates the topography and connects it with the human and natural world. A few lines later in part 2, MacLean moves from description to one of the larger themes of the poem: exile and the plight of Scots who were forced to leave Skye:

Multitude of springs and fewness of young men
today, yesterday and last night keeping me awake:
the miserable loss of our country's people,
clearing of tenants, exile, exploitation …

(p. 67)

This theme of the depopulation of Skye, and the Hebridean landscape in general, runs throughout the poem and often is raised alongside references to other European political and economic movements that are more particular to the early twentieth century. The tone modulates as the poem progresses and can often become visionary in nature:

I see townships that were in Brae Eynort
rivers with the pouring of bracken,
and I see the faint Twilight of the Gaels,
with its glimmer of bracken reaching heaven.

(p. 69)

Here too MacLean draws in the specific experience of Skye and its losses and joins it to the larger assault on the Gaelic way of life that would bring the displaced Scots into the same boat (literally in terms of forced emigration) with those from Ireland. The removal of the people from the land can be seen many times in the poem to be the result of economic forces involving the wealthy landowners, who cry out, "Lazy inefficient peasants, / oppress them, clear them and sweep them, / break them, drive them and rout them" (p. 73). This reflects MacLean's Communist leanings at the time he was writing the poem, and he frequently joins his claim against monied interests from eighteenth- and nineteenth-century Scotland with those of twentieth-century Russia and China:

And though another voice split the fog,
Lenin, Marx or MacLean,

Dimitroff or MacPherson,
Mao Tse-tung and his company,
the devilish revelry would drown
the voice of the wise and the cry of the tortured,
and the screeching noise would weary and oppress me,
while the great Cuillin reeled dizzily.

(pp. 73–75)

Here Lenin and Mao rub shoulders with MacLean and his compatriot James MacPherson, the eighteenth-century author, translator, and discoverer of the "Ossian stories," which were believed by some to be a source of Scottish Gaelic mythology (though others doubted their authenticity). Through the invocation of MacPherson's name in company with names of philosophers of Communist thought, MacLean is perhaps suggesting a shared identity in terms of socioeconomic oppression. The durability of the Cuillin (a collective name for the mountains on the island) can be seen through its transformation into a beacon of hope as the reader works through the remainder of the poem to the triumphant lines that form the conclusion (as the poem appears in *O Choille gu Bearradh*; there are suggestions that in fact the poem remained unfinished):

Beyond the lochs of the blood of the children of men,
beyond the frailty of plain and the labour of the mountain,
beyond poverty, consumption, fever, agony,
beyond hardship, wrong, tyranny, distress,
beyond misery, despair, hatred, treachery,
beyond guilt and defilement; watchful,
heroic, the Cuillin is seen
rising on the other side of sorrow.

(p. 131)

In *O Choille gu Bearradh,* poems from the period December 1939–July 1941 are collected in a section titled "An Tràigh Thathaich"/"The Haunted Ebb," which includes a number of poems that originally appeared in *Dàin do Eimhir.* The poems from this period of MacLean's career display a much more confessional tone. MacLean continues to develop his ability to establish a dialogic relationship between personal experience (and particularly his experiences of love and loss) and lovingly rendered descriptions of

island landscape. Here as well, the natural forces that form so much of the life of those living in the Highlands and Islands of Scotland become metaphors for love and loss, as in the poem "Muir-tràigh"/"Ebb," in which the tidal movements of the sea seem to correspond with the fluctuations of love:

I am not striving with the tree that will not bend for me,
and the apples will not grow on any branch;
it is not farewell to you; you have not left me.
It is the ebb of death with no floodtide after it.

Dead stream of neap in your tortured body,
which will not flow at new moon or at full,
in which the great springtide of love will not come—
but a double subsidence to lowest ebb.

(p. 141)

Another love poem, "Tràighean"/"Shores," is also directed to a lover, whom the speaker takes on a geographical tour of locations on Skye and other Hebridean islands while simultaneously expressing his emotions:

If we were in Talisker on the shore
where the great white mouth
opens between two hard jaws,
Rubha nan Clach and the Bioda Ruadh,
I would stand beside the sea
renewing love in my spirit
while the ocean was filling
Talisker bay forever:
I would stand there on the bareness of the shore
until Prishal bowed his stallion head.

(p. 141)

MacLean's love for the Hebrides, and particularly his home islands of Raasay and Skye, is intricately tied to the love he feels for the women he celebrates and grieves over in his poetry. The landscape he describes becomes animated and each locale has inherent animal or human features that the speaker associates with them. Some poems, such as "Camhanaich"/"Dawn," allow the loved one to become one with more universal aspects of nature such as the passage of night and day:

You were dawn on the Cuillin
and benign day on the Clarach,
the sun on his elbow in the golden stream
and the white rose that breaks the horizon.

(p. 157)

In a sense MacLean detects the indivisible nature of a type of love that is nurtured through attachment to a place and a culture and that projects itself outward through the love of another human. Seamus Heaney acknowledges the way Maclean expresses his love for the landscape in a complex manner that incorporates his cultural identity:

In a way, MacLean's relation with his landscape is erotic too, because the language of his poems of place has an amorousness and abundance about it which springs from the contemplation of the beloved contours. Contrary to the notion of the poet as one who gives to airy nothings a local habitation and a name, MacLean begins with names and habitations. He has an epic poet's possession of ground, founders, heroes, battles, lovers, legends, all of them at once part of his personal apparatus of feeling and part of the common but threatened ghost-life of his language and culture.

(p. 5)

The cohesion of that type of transcendental love is explored not only through MacLean's love poetry but through his verse that is concerned with other philosophical questions related to division, fragmentation and an ensuing unification. As seen earlier in "An Roghainn"/"The Choice," MacLean often contends with a divided self: "I walked with my reason / out beside the sea" (p. 23). In "An Sgian"/"The Knife," he also performs an interrogation of the self as he dissects his "stone of my love" (resembling in a way the "deep heart's core" of William Butler Yeats's "The Lake Isle of Innisfree") with the "knife of my brain" (p. 145):

As it increased in the number
of cut and brittle fragments,
so it took unity,
alone hard and taut.

(p. 145)

However, as the stone of love fractures it also unifies and becomes one with the landscape that surrounds it:

The stone that was cut
out of my own narrow spirit
was clipped to the greatness
that would contain the land of the world.

(p. 147)

Here the reader sees a unifying process that seems to be occurring at the same time as the stone fragments. The resulting "whole jewel" becomes the product of competing forces, and in some ways it seems as if MacLean is tapping into the modernist interest in unifying divided fragments of experience, an interest that finds expression not only in the poetry of T. S. Eliot but also in the various Scottish literary reactions against the concept of the "Caledonian antisyzygy," which had been espoused by the critic G. Gregory Smith in his 1919 book *Scottish Literature: Character and Influence*. Robert Crawford, in a 1990 review of *O Choille gu Bearradh,* indicates how "division, warring division, was to be MacLean's terrible muse" (p. 17). Hugh MacDiarmid's own reactions (as articulated in many poems and especially in *A Drunk Man Looks at the Thistle*) may have had an influence on MacLean, since both poets in addition to being friends often shared similar attitudes toward Scotland (though MacDiarmid was more of a Scottish Nationalist and MacLean displayed Communist sympathies).

Perhaps the most poignant and critically acclaimed poem from the section titled "An Tràigh Thathaich" is "An Tathaich"/"The Haunting," another contemplative poem about division in which the speaker is haunted by a face and a "tract of time" that offer unity:

A face haunts me,
following me day and night,
the triumphant face of a girl
is pleading all the time.

It is saying to my heart
that a division may not be sought
between desire and the substance
of its unattainable object ...

(p. 159)

The speaker reveals a great trust in the power of unity that works by way of memory. The face that haunts him cannot be affected by the passage of time, and the speaker realizes that even the arts of music and the "painted board" (p. 163) could not adequately capture the memory of the face of the triumphant girl. It is only the face and time itself that can accurately unify the "grace" (p. 159) and beauty that the speaker has come to recognize in the face. The speaker calls upon a "fourth dimension" (p. 163) that would allow for this wholeness of perception that would be even more powerful than music, art, or poetry to express this inability to be divided:

> O shapely human paean,
> is there a dimension in the universe
> that will give you a greater wholeness
> than music, board or lyric?
>
> (p. 165)

This poem, one of the last from *Dàin do Eimhir* to be included in *O Choille gu Bearradh,* shows the depth to which MacLean is capable of meditating on love. His poems offer a wide scope in terms of description, especially of landscape, and combine elements of philosophy, politics, history, and a concern for language. The integration and unification of these themes and concerns are evident as well in his later work.

The section that follows "An Tràigh Thathaich" in *O Choille gu Bearradh* is titled "Coilltean Ratharsair"/"The Woods of Raasay." This section is a longer stand-alone poem (though not as extensive as *An Cuilithion*) written in 1940 in which MacLean celebrates Raasay, the island of his birth and youth. As in *An Cuilithion*, MacLean uses the landscape of Raasay (and the mountains of Skye that loom in the distance) as a vehicle through which to meditate on a variety of themes. Here the predominant use of the landscape appears to be connected not only to memories of the speaker's youth but of the sources of his poetic inspiration. The poem is steeped in a mythic atmosphere. The speaker not only describes the landscape but addresses it as well in acknowledgement of what has been bestowed upon him by the woods and mountains:

> Straight trunks of the pine
> on the flexed hill-slope:

> green, heraldic helmets,
> green unpressed sea;
> strong, light, wind-headed,
> untoiling, unseeking,
> the giddy, great wood,
> russet, green, two plaitings.
>
> (p. 171)

The poem engages with the geography of the island, and the speaker pays tribute to the many sources of inspiration he has taken from the history and culture of the island. The "plaitings" of the first stanza develop into a theme of weaving, which carries through the poem as the speaker considers the attributes of the island and his experiences of what the island offers as strands that go into the construction of a larger fabric:

> The great wood in motion,
> fresh in its spirit;
> the high green wood
> in a many-coloured waulking;
> the wood and my senses
> in a white-footed rapture;
> the wood in blossom
> with a fleeting renewal.
>
> (p. 173)

These lines evoke images of a method of weaving to be found throughout the Gaelic-speaking world of western Scotland and Ireland, places that depend so much on the wool industry. "Waulking" is the traditional manner of weaving that includes using the rhythms of music and singing to aid in the movements of the weavers. Here the woods become the participants in the waulking as they join together the strands that form poetic inspiration. MacLean again illustrates the way he can capably invest the beloved geography of the west of Scotland with human attributes. What is also a major part of this description is the "motion" of a landscape that is never still and that always moves in harmony with the people who inhabit its woods and hills. These geographical features also command musical ability, as MacLean indicates in a later stanza:

> The wood of Raasay in its gentleness,
> joyful beside the Clarach,

the green variation on the pibroch theme
that the Cuillin makes with the waves.

(p. 179)

Nature itself seems to be in tune with the Gaelic tradition of pibroch, and MacLean again establishes the idea of the integration of Gaeldom with the natural world. The two entities are one and the same, and anything that stands in the way of their shared identity (such as the Clearances and other forms of political and linguistic oppression) tampers with the wholeness of the world.

Poems written by MacLean between August 1941 and April 1944 are collected in a section of *O Choille gu Bearradh* titled "An Iomhaigh Bhriste"/"The Broken Image." Although these poems continue the themes and interests of MacLean's earlier poems, particularly the love lyrics which are here best represented by poems such as "Uilleam Ros is mi fhin"/"William Ross and I" (mentioned earlier for its musical theme) and "Reothairt"/"Spring Tide," there is a transition as MacLean prepares to go off into military service and his eventual posting to Egypt in 1941. In "An Cogadh Ceart"/"The Proper War," the speaker addresses a loved one who has been lost to another and to a "wound" that has been inflicted by that other suitor. The speaker addresses a farewell message to the object of his affections as he takes leave to head to "Libya or Egypt" to take part in the "proper war" (p. 199). This conflict stands in contrast to the earlier war in Spain that MacLean did not go off to fight in. The distinction here is that Germany is a much greater threat to the whole of Europe (and this time the Communist Russia that MacLean admires is also under threat from Hitler) than that earlier conflict, and MacLean recognizes the propriety of his joining the forces to fight that enemy. The impossibility of his love for the woman recognized by critics as the "Scottish" woman—one of two women who serve as muses for much of MacLean's poetry throughout the 1930s and early 1940s (see Joy Hendry's essay in *Critical Essays* and Christopher Whyte's introduction to *Dàin do Eimhir*)—becomes part of a catalyst for his engagement in the larger political conflict:

I will not go to your cold bed,
that would not be useful, dear;
I'll rather get a tuft bed
in the comfortable sunny Desert,
or a gravel bed in a ditch,
in Libya or in Egypt.

(p. 199)

Coming toward the end of the "An Iomhaigh Bhriste," the poem paves the way for the section dated 1942–1943 and titled "Blàr"/"Battlefield," in which the poet offers some of the finest modern war poems ever written in Gaelic. Most notable is the poem "Glac a' Bhàis"/"Death Valley," which is often anthologized. Here the horrors of war and the effect they have on the combatants of both sides is sensitively rendered in ways reminiscent of the poetry of Wilfred Owen, Isaac Rosenberg, and other English poets of the First World War. The poem begins with an epigraph that states "Some Nazi or other has said that the Fuehrer had restored to German manhood the 'right and joy of dying in battle'"(p. 211). The speaker of the poem is then led to contend with the significance of that saying in light of his contemplating the dead body of a young German soldier in Africa:

Sitting dead in "Death Valley"
below the Ruweisat Ridge,
a boy with his forelock down about his cheek
and his face slate-grey;
I thought of the right and the joy
that he got from his Fuehrer,
of falling in the field of slaughter,
to rise no more ...

(pp. 211–213)

According to Joy Hendry, the poem's inspiration comes from Maclean's actual experience in 1942 of seeing his first dead German soldier in Egypt. Though the speaker of the poem cannot exactly place the political identity of the youth, there is one thing that becomes certain by the end of the poem and that is the nature of the misperception spawned by propaganda that equates death for a political ideal with human happiness:

Was the boy of the band
who abused the Jews

and Communists, or of the greater
band of those

led, from the beginning of generations,
unwillingly to the trial
and mad delirium of every war
for the sake of rulers?

Whatever his desire or mishap,
his innocence or malignity,
he showed no pleasure in his death
below the Ruweisat Ridge.

(p. 213)

The penultimate section in *O Choille gu Bear-radh* collects poems that MacLean wrote between 1945 and 1972. After being wounded in North Africa, MacLean eventually returned to Scotland and married Renee Cameron. He taught in Edinburgh and later served as headmaster at the Plockton Secondary School. His poetry from these years reflects many of the same concerns that he had expressed in his early verse, including an abiding sense of the diminishment of the force of the Gael that MacLean locates in a number of political blows to Scottish Gaelic culture. In poems that look to both the past and the present, he reveals an ongoing concern for threats to Gaelic culture in light of modern changes in Scotland. A poem titled "Cuil-Lodair 16.4.1946"/"Culloden 16.4.1946" recounts the defeat of Bonnie Prince Charlie's forces by the British in the battle of Culloden in April 1746. This was the final attempt of Charles Stewart and his Jacobite forces to reassert Scottish independence from Britain, and MacLean uses the two hundredth anniversary of the event as a springboard to make larger points about the suffering of the Gaels:

Was it the loss at Culloden
that brought the rotting in midwinter
that left the Gaeldom of Scotland
a home without people,
fields haunted by ghosts,
a pasture for sheep,
and that drove beyond the oceans
the worth that was in her people?

(pp. 221–223)

Here MacLean recognizes that the defeat of the Scottish forces was one of the blows that may have precipitated the gradual clearing of the Highlands by the British. Weakening the power of the clan system in Scotland was one of the goals of the Clearances, and MacLean extends the effects of this battle to the dispersion of the Gaels to other parts of the world. He concludes the poem with a sad assessment:

The distress of the Gaels
could be as it was
if the lost field of Culloden
had been a choice triumph;
but it was a breaking
to the race of the Gaels,
and there grew on this slope
only the withered tree of misfortune.

(p. 223)

Once again MacLean fashions descriptions of the landscape in a way that allows them to resonate with larger psychological and sociological themes. Here the health of the Gaelic culture is portrayed as a tree that has been deprived of sustenance and that grows on the "slope" of what may be the mountain of Scotland.

In what may perhaps be MacLean's most famous, haunting poem, "Hallaig," the speaker uses an ancient, almost bardic voice as he celebrates the landscape of his birthplace (the township of Hallaig is located on the east side of Raasay) and the nature of time. The poem begins with an invocation: "Time, the deer, is in the wood of Hallaig" (p. 227). The poem will return to this deer later, but the opening lines depict a window that is "nailed and boarded" through which at one time the speaker "saw the West." In what follows the speaker describes a transformation by which those he loved in the past have metamorphosed into the landscape:

... and my love is at the Burn of Hallaig,
a birch tree, and she has always been

between Inver and Milk Hollow,
here and there about Baile-chuirn:
she is a birch, a hazel,
a straight, slender young rowan.

(p. 227)

The poem then moves to Screapadal, another location on Raasay where MacLean (through the speaker) witnesses the enduring presence of the past through his ancestors who have become part of the landscape:

> In Screapadal of my people
> where Norman and Big Hector were,
> their daughters and their sons are a wood
> going up beside the stream.
>
> (p. 227)

The transcendental unity of the land with the people and their culture is here perceived by MacLean's speaker as he contemplates the history of Raasay as affected by the Clearances. In his essay "Sorley MacLean's 'Hallaig': A Note," John MacInnes establishes the scene that Mac-Lean uses in his poem:

> In 1846 John MacLeod, the chief of the MacLeods of Raasay (styled in Gaelic "Mac Gille Chaluim") sold the island to a pious gentleman from Edinburgh whose name was George Rainy. Rainy in effect introduced the Clearances to Raasay. Between 1852 and 1854 the entire population of twelve townships, ninety-four families in all, were driven from their homes, the majority of them being forced to emigrate to the Colonies. One of those townships was Hallaig.
>
> (p. 418)

As MacLean's poem continues the speaker sees the ghosts of the exiled islanders in the natural landscape that surrounds him. The men "lying on the green" and "the girls a wood of birches," "each one young and light-stepping, / without the heartbreak of the tale" (p. 229). The conclusion of the poem imagines the deer as time itself, stopped by a "vehement bullet" coming from the "gun of Love" (p. 229). Here the ghosts seem to inhabit a time that is pre-Clearance, and MacLean wants to freeze the scene before all of Gaelic culture (and the life of Raasay in particular) are utterly changed forever by the transportation of her people to another land. In the final line, even the blood from the deer "will not be traced while I live" (p. 229), since the bullet of love has the power to defeat the passage of time and the damage it has inflicted on Raasay.

Other notable poems from the 1945–1972 period include elegies for fallen Gaelic heroes, including MacLean's brother, Calum I. MacLean, who was a famous folklorist in Ireland and Scotland. Included as well is a tribute poem to William Butler Yeats ("Aig Uaigh Yeats"/"At Yeats's Grave"), and "Ard-Mhusaeum na h-Eireann"/"The National Museum of Ireland." Many of these poems articulate the shared Gaelic heritage of Scotland and Ireland, one that Mac-Lean acknowledges is under constant threat from outside forces.

The final section of *O Choille gu Bearradh*, "1972 and After," includes "Uamha 'n Oir"/"The Cave of Gold" (discussed earlier) and a poem about threats to the western islands, "Screapadal." The opening stanzas of this poem contain descriptions of the bucolic landscape of Raasay. However, Screapadal is another township on that island that was affected by the Clearances, and this poem, even more so than "Hallaig," implicates George Rainy and his contributions to the destruction of a way of life through the forced exile of the people of Raasay. Toward the end of the poem the focus shifts to more modern threats to the island in the shape of nuclear submarines that routinely ply the waters around Skye:

> There are other towers on the Sound
> mocking the tower that fell
> from the top of the Castle Rock,
> towers worse than every tower
> that violence raised in the world:
> the periscopes and sleek black sides
> of the ships of the death
> that killed the thousands of Nagasaki,
> the death of the great heat and the smoke,
>
> the death that would bring utter devastation
> even on the beauty
> that grew in Screapadal
> and is still there
> in spite of Rainy's bad deed,
> his greed and social pride.
>
> (p. 311)

The final poem in *O Choille gu Bearradh*, "Screapadal" confirms MacLean's abiding concern for the health and welfare of the communities of western Scotland. His reflections on the integrated nature of community and language form the foundation for his poetry, and they are every bit as evident in his later work.

In October 2011 a new edition of collected poems by MacLean was published by Polygon Books. This edition, titled *Caoir Gheal Leumraich (White Leaping Flame): Collected Poems in Gaelic with English Translation*, is edited by Christopher Whyte and Emma Dymock. In addition to providing the most complete edition of MacLean's poems to date, the volume also includes a biographical summary.

CONCLUSION

In his essay "A Poet's Response to Sorley MacLean," Iain Crichton Smith assesses the deep honesty that is evident in all of MacLean's work: "This is quite simply poetry which has been beaten out on the anvil of circumstance. There does not appear to be any strategies or artifices. The perplexities of life speak through it" (pp. 48–49). MacLean was adept at taking the diverse experiences of his own life and addressing them through poetry in a fashion that spoke to the reader or listener in a much more universal manner. His engagement with Scottish history often reflected the denigration and destruction of Gaelic culture that he lamented deeply. He sought to redress that situation through the unique quality of his own verse, which not only recaptured the natural beauty and cadences of the Gaelic poets and musicians who preceded him but also sought to harmonize their chords with more modern themes and concerns that were reflective of his own time. A masterful creator of love lyrics, he wrote what many consider to be the finest love modern poetic love sequence in Gaelic, *Dàin do Eimhir*. Though his poetic interests were wide-ranging, what is not lost in the rich mixture is MacLean's haunting, bardic tone that he inherited from his Gaelic forbears. He joins modern images, themes, and scenes with a voice that represents much older traditions. The strands MacLean weaves with his voice come to the reader in much the same way as the fabric of the land that is woven by the "waulking" weavers he celebrates in "Coilltean Ratharsair." His woven strands of verse will continue to entrance readers for years to come.

Selected Bibliography

WORKS OF SORLEY MACLEAN

POETRY

17 Poems for 6D: In Gaelic, Lowland Scots, and English. With poems by Robert Garioch. Edinburgh: Chalmers Press, 1940. (Published in a second edition with corrections in the same year under the title *Seventeen Poems for Sixpence*).

Dàin do Eimhir agus Dàin Eile. Glasgow: William MacLellan. 1943.

Poems to Eimhir. Translated from the Gaelic by Iain Crichton Smith. London: Victor Gollancz, 1971. (Published in the same year by Northern House, Newcastle upon Tyne, as part of Northern House Pamphlet Poets series, no. 15).

Reothairt is Contraigh: Taghadh de Dhàin 1932–72/Spring Tide and Neap Tide: Selected Poems 1932–72. Edinburgh: Canongate, 1977.

Poems 1932–82. Philadelphia: Iona Foundation, 1987.

O Choille gu Bearradh/From Wood to Ridge: Collected Poems in Gaelic and English. Manchester, U.K.: Carcanet, 1989. Reprint, London: Vintage, 1991. Corrected edition, Manchester, U.K., and Edinburgh: Carcanet/Birlinn, 1999.

Eimhir. With English translations by Iain Crichton Smith. Stornoway, Isle of Lewis, U.K.: Acair, 1999.

Dàin do Eimhir. Edited by Christopher Whyte. Glasgow: Association of Scottish Literary Studies, 2002.

Hallaig. Translated by Seamus Heaney. Sleat, Isle of Skye, U.K.: Urras Shomhairle, 2002.

Caoir Gheal Leumraich (White Leaping Flame): Collected Poems in Gaelic with English Translation. Edited by Christopher Whyte and Emma Dymock. Edinburgh: Polygon, 2011.

PROSE

"Realism in Gaelic Poetry." *Transactions of the Gaelic Society of Inverness* 37:80–104 (1934–1936).

"The Poetry of the Clearances." *Transactions of the Gaelic Society of Inverness* 38:293–324 (1937–1941).

"Aspects of Gaelic Poetry." *Scottish Arts and Letters*, no. 3:37 (1947).

"Notes on Sea Imagery in Seventeenth Century Gaelic Poetry." *Transactions of the Gaelic Society of Inverness* 43 (1960–1963).

"Old Songs and New Poetry." In *Memoirs of a Modern Scotland.* Edited by Karl Miller. London: Faber, 1970.

"Some Raasay Traditions." *Transactions of the Gaelic Society of Inverness* 49:377–397 (1974–1976).

"My Relationship with the Muse." *Chapman 16* 4, no. 3:25–32 (summer 1976).

"Some Thoughts About Gaelic Poetry." *Transactions of the Gaelic Society of Inverness* 52 (1980–1982).

Ris a' Bhruthaich: Criticism and Prose Writings of Sorley MacLean. Edited by William Gillies. Stornoway, Isle of Lewis, U.K.: Acair, 1985. (Contains most of MacLean's prose, critical writings, and book reviews that appeared in a variety of publications up to 1985.)

The Correspondence Between Hugh MacDiarmid and Sorley McLean. Edited by Susan R. Wilson. Edinburgh: Edinburgh University Press, 2010.

PAPERS

Sorley MacLean's papers were acquired by the National Library of Scotland in 1998. A catalog of these manuscripts may be accessed at http://digital.nls.uk/50years/1998.html.

BIOGRAPHICAL AND CRITICAL STUDIES

Batchelor, Paul. "*White Leaping Flame* by Sorley MacLean." *Guardian*, December 30, 2011 (http://www.guardian.co.uk/books/2011/dec/30/white-leaping-flame-sorley-maclean-review). (Review.)

Caird, J. B. "Sorley MacLean: A Personal View." In *Sorley MacLean: Critical Essays*. Edited by Raymond J. Ross and Joy Hendry. Edinburgh: Scottish Academic Press, 1986. Pp. 39–43.

Calder, Robert. "Celebration of a Tension." In *Sorley MacLean: Critical Essays*. Edited by Raymond J. Ross and Joy Hendry. Edinburgh: Scottish Academic Press, 1986. Pp. 155–163.

Campbell, Angus Peter, ed. *Somhairle: Dàin is Deilbh: A Celebration on the 80th Birthday of Sorley MacLean.* Stornoway, Isle of Lewis, U.K.: Acair, 1991.

Crawford, Robert. "War Poet." *London Review of Books*, May 24, 1990, pp. 17–18. (Review of *O Choille gu Bearradh/From Wood to Ridge*).

———. "Somhairle MacGill-Eain/Sorley Maclean." In his *Identifying Poets: Self and Territory in Twentieth-Century Poetry*. Edinburgh: Edinburgh University Press, 1993.

Devlin, Brendan. "In Spite of Sea and Centuries: An Irish Gael Looks at the Poetry of Somhairle Mac Gill-Eain." In *Sorley MacLean: Critical Essays*. Edited by Raymond J. Ross and Joy Hendry. Edinburgh: Scottish Academic Press, 1986. Pp. 82–89.

Gillies, William. "The Poet as Critic." In *Sorley MacLean: Critical Essays*. Edited by Raymond J. Ross and Joy Hendry. Edinburgh: Scottish Academic Press, 1986. Pp. 185–99.

Heaney, Seamus. "Introduction." In *Sorley MacLean: Critical Essays*. Edited by Raymond J. Ross and Joy Hendry. Edinburgh: Scottish Academic Press, 1986. Pp. 1–7.

———. "The Voice of a Bard." *Antaeus* 60:297–306 (spring 1988).

Hendry, Joy. "Sorley MacLean: The Man and His Work." In *Sorley MacLean: Critical Essays*. Edited by Raymond J. Ross and Joy Hendry. Edinburgh: Scottish Academic Press, 1986. Pp. 9–38.

Herdman, John. "The Ghost Seen by the Soul: Sorley MacLean and the Absolute." In *Sorley MacLean: Critical Essays*. Edited by Raymond J. Ross and Joy Hendry. Edinburgh: Scottish Academic Press, 1986. Pp. 165–175.

MacInnes, John. "Language, Metre, and Diction in the Poetry of Sorley Maclean." In *Sorley MacLean: Critical Essays*. Edited by Raymond J. Ross and Joy Hendry. Edinburgh: Scottish Academic Press, 1986. Pp. 137–153.

———. "Sorley Maclean's 'Hallaig': A Note." In *Dùthchas nan Gàidheal: Selected Essays of John McInnes*. Edited by Michael Newton. Edinburgh: Birlinn, 2006. Pp. 418–421.

MacNeacail, Aonghas. "Questions of Prestige: Sorley MacLean and the Campaign for Gaelic." In *Sorley MacLean: Critical Essays*. Edited by Raymond J. Ross and Joy Hendry. Edinburgh: Scottish Academic Press, 1986. Pp. 201–210.

Mac Síomóin, Tomás. "Poet of Conscience: The Old and the New in the Poetry of Somhairle MacGill-Eain." In *Sorley MacLean: Critical Essays*. Edited by Raymond J. Ross and Joy Hendry. Edinburgh: Scottish Academic Press, 1986. Pp. 109–125.

McCaughey, Terence. "Sorley MacLean: Continuity and the Transformation of Symbols." In *Sorley MacLean: Critical Essays*. Edited by Raymond J. Ross and Joy Hendry. Edinburgh: Scottish Academic Press, 1986. Pp. 127–135.

Ross, Raymond J. "Marx, MacDiarmid, and MacLean." In *Sorley MacLean: Critical Essays*. Edited by Raymond J. Ross and Joy Hendry. Edinburgh: Scottish Academic Press, 1986. Pp. 91–107.

Royle, Trevor. *The Mainstream Companion to Scottish Literature*. Edinburgh: Mainstream, 1993. P. 199.

Sealy, Douglas. "Out from Skye to the World: Literature, History, and the Poet." In *Sorley MacLean: Critical Essays*. Edited by Raymond J. Ross and Joy Hendry. Edinburgh: Scottish Academic Press, 1986. Pp. 53–79.

———. "Register of Gaelic Placenames in the Poems of Sorley MacLean." In *Sorley MacLean: Critical Essays*. Edited by Raymond J. Ross and Joy Hendry. Edinburgh: Scottish Academic Press, 1986. Pp. 223–230.

Smith, Iain Crichton. "A Poet's Response to Sorley MacLean." In *Sorley MacLean: Critical Essays*. Edited by Raymond J. Ross and Joy Hendry. Edinburgh: Scottish Academic Press, 1986. Pp. 45–51.

———. "Loss of Sorley MacLean Leaves a Great Gap" and "Introduction." In *Eimhir*. By Sorley MacLean. Translated by Iain Crichton Smith. Stornoway, Isle of Lewis, U.K.: Acair, 1999. Pp. 11–14, 15–18.

Stevenson, Ronald. "MacLean: Musician Manqué (and a Composer's Collaboration)." In *Sorley MacLean: Critical*

Essays. Edited by Raymond J. Ross and Joy Hendry. Edinburgh: Scottish Academic Press, 1986. Pp. 176–183.

Watson, Roderick. *The Literature of Scotland.* London: Macmillan, 1984. (Discusses Sorley MacLean at pp. 10, 443–447.)

Whyte, Christopher. "The Gaelic Renaissance: Sorley MacLean and Derick Thomson." In *British Poetry from the 1950s to the 1990s.* Edited by Gary Day and Brian Docherty. London: Macmillan, 1997. Pp. 143–169.

———. "Introduction." In *Dàin do Eimhir.* By Sorley MacLean. Edited by Christopher Whyte. Glasgow: Association for Scottish Literary Studies, 2002. Pp. 1–41.

———. "The Poetry of Sorley MacLean." In *Scottish Literature in English and Scots.* Edited by Douglas Gifford, Sarah Dunnigan, Alan MacGillivray, et al. Edinburgh: Edinburgh University Press, 2002. Pp. 655–670.

INTERVIEWS

Macdonald, Donald Archie. "Some Aspects of Family and Local Background: An Interview with Sorley MacLean." In *Sorley MacLean: Critical Essays.* Edited by Raymond J. Ross and Joy Hendry. Edinburgh: Scottish Academic Press, 1986. Pp. 211–222.

Nicolson, Angus. "An Interview with Sorley MacLean." *Studies in Scottish Literature* 14:23–36 (1997).

FILMS

Sorley MacLean's Island. Ogam Films, 1974.

Hallaig: The Poetry and Landscape of Sorley MacLean. Directed by Timothy Neat. Island House Film Workshop. Alva, Clackmannan, U.K., 1984.

Somhairle MacGill-Eain. Cuillin Films Earranta. Glasgow, 2002.

AUDIO RECORDINGS

Sorley MacLean Reads His Poetry at the SPLA/Verse Magazine Event for the "Auld Alliance," St. Cecilia's Hall. School of Scottish Studies, August 29, 1985. (Private collection.)

Joy Hendry Interviews Sorley MacLean. Scottish Poetry Library recording as part of the BBC Radio Scotland presentation "Scots Quair," 1990. (Private collection.)

15 Poems of Sorley MacLean: A Commentary. By Iain Crichton Smith, with readings by Sorley MacLean. Glasgow: Association for Scottish Literary Studies, October 2007. (Audio CD.)

WEBSITES

Scottish Poetry Library. http://www.spl.org.uk/. Offers links to works by MacLean and to biographical and bibliographical material.

Sorley MacLean Online. http://www.sorleymaclean.org. Maintained by the Sorley MacLean Trust. An excellent reference site that includes a biography, access to articles, bibliographies, photographs, and other valuable materials related to MacLean and his work.

NUALA O'FAOLAIN

(1940—2008)

Angela M. Garcia

NUALA O'FAOLAIN, THE prominent Irish journalist, novelist, and memoir writer, has in her autobiographical works and fiction left above all a legacy of truth-telling. Through a relatively short, twelve-year career as a book author, hers was a voice that broke a vast silence surrounding many personal issues relating to middle age, including fears of never being loved again, of invisibility. Her writing addresses taboos by questioning the absolute institutionalized power of both patriarchy and church—with experience and opinions that might be considered audacious, but were always thoughtfully grounded, never presented for their shock value. Especially in Ireland's national consciousness, O'Faolain's impassioned revelations and reflections reverberated beyond the literary sphere.

Exhibiting this brute honesty in her groundbreaking memoir *Are You Somebody* (1996), O'Faolain incidentally gave voice to countless others who—like her—suffered under the cruelties of neglect in the childhood home, and in Ireland within a society afflicted with the addiction to alcohol and among families at the mercy of the father's bidding. Upon publishing her story, the author drew a massive response from readers in Ireland and throughout the world; thousands wrote O'Faolain with their own sorrows or courageous experiences.

Gifted in the art of memoir, the author wrote in personal terms yet dealt with topics that necessarily linked to political and public life as well, often subversively. Much of O'Faolain's nonfiction is written with a hard-won feminist slant and sensibility, a feminism the author might equate simply with humanism. She demonstrates in her memoirs a deep consciousness of the movement she experienced predominantly in the 1960s and 1970s, a liberation movement that helped her to pursue her own prominent journalism career and to attain financial independence and mobility.

Thematically, the literature pivots upon the middle-aged or older woman's role in society, and in love. O'Faolain is open, and her willingness to risk facing almost any subject head-on—whether it be the uncertainty of feeling unloved, aging, or death—worked to break a certain silence in Ireland. The writing, most notably *Are You Somebody*, marked a watershed moment in the Irish memoir in overcoming insistent cultural repression regarding these and other taboo subjects, at the risk of discomfiting her audience. Instead she won them over with a warm, vulnerable, and unpretentious voice; her first memoir, a best seller in both Ireland and the United States, sold over a million copies around the world.

EARLY LIFE: DUBLIN

O'Faolain was born in Dublin on March 1, 1940, to Tomás and Catherine (Caitlin) O'Faolain. Much of her memoir writing, of course, summons and uses her life as her work's key material. It takes memories and expounds on them, interprets them, trying to make sense of the flotsam of life. In her writing, she keeps in mind the non-Irish and contemporary audience as she makes clear that 1940s Ireland might seem a century ago to a modern man or woman. As she reenvisions her past, O'Faolain fills in with deft strokes the family dynamics and societal strictures that she believes irrevocably shaped her life at the time of writing. Some of these accepted paradigms she sees as sadistic—accepted cruelties of Irish culture of the 1940s and 1950s such as physical abuse or neglect. In examining her life, she sorrowfully admits that she arrived a little too late to reap the fruits and adopt the thinking of the global feminist movement—that, on the contrary, despite her multiple affairs with men, she would fall back into 1950s feminine behaviors, including dependence and obsessive jealousy, decades into the future—indeed, well into her sixties.

Yet the author clearly counts herself as a beneficiary of social change. This complexity of a feminist coming of age in a time that seemed a century ago presented a potent mixture particularly in traditional, late-blooming Ireland. In her groundbreaking memoir *Are You Somebody* (1996), she sets the stage for her feminist beliefs, exploring how she is both like and unlike her mother, Catherine. One looming difference was domesticity. O'Faolain clarifies that her mother, "because she fell in love ... and ... married, ... was condemned to spend her life as a mother and homemaker. She was in the wrong job." Like her mother's mother, she "never went out, never had money, never stopped having children" (p. 10).

Indeed, the harshness of her childhood experience—in particular, the neglect by her mother, the one whom she expected to fulfill the role as caregiver and a primal source of parental love—seems to have indelibly marked O'Faolain's life and writings. That core emptiness or unfulfillment left her a voice that could be alternately clinical, passionate, humorous, marveling, or caustic, always full of life, but essentially starved for affection. O'Faolain states, after unsentimentally describing how the teacher looked down upon her own dirty cardigan and spoke badly about the mother who sent her to school that way: "She was to have thirteen pregnancies altogether: nine living children" (p. 10). Three became "ferocious alcoholics" (p. 14).

But her mother had at least one overarching positive influence and habit as well. Catherine's obsessive reading served O'Faolain well throughout her life; her love of books and comfort in reading, she says, was the most useful thing she brought out of her childhood. She may not have modeled love, but she modeled literacy. And yet O'Faolain recognizes that theirs was reading as a defense—from parents, from husband (in her mother's case), or from the world in general. And that this reading was compounded by a

dangerous habit, an addiction to alcohol. This compulsion for Catherine to drink alone in a pub as she read was later echoed in O'Faolain's own solitary tendency to settle down with a book accompanied always by a glass of wine.

O'Faolain's family moved about a dozen times during her youth, according to her sister Deidre Brady's memoir of these years, *Thank You for the Days* (2005), with most of the writer's earliest literary memories focusing on their coastal home near Malahide, north of Dublin, where she remembers the incessant roar of the sea. In O'Faolain's recollections, her father as a public figure, a well-known journalist, was largely absent from the children's lives while her mother—living off the pittances she would ask from him in order to care for the large brood—would escape to her fiction and neglect child-rearing duties.

As the second-oldest of nine children, she grew up playing with siblings and friends in woods, fields, and shores she describes as bleak, and peppered with the holes where the Irish townspeople dug and lived during the famine: the nineteenth-century era of Ireland's deep psychic suffering as a nation and the historical period O'Faolain explores in her 2001 novel *My Dream of You*. Considering that O'Faolain dubs "1940s Ireland ... a living tomb for women," it is no surprise that O'Faolain's father laid the pathway for her later journalistic prowess and fame (p. 11). A true career man, he also ruled the family in a distracted fashion, engaging at the same time in a discreet but persistent sexual affair on the outside. This ultimately resulted in his having another, secret family, with another son born to his mistress beyond his nine children.

O'Faolain's father figured as a preeminent social journalist who forsook his Irish nomenclature to rename and remake himself as the anglicized Terry O'Sullivan, writing for the *Sunday Press* and later creating the *Dublin Evening Press* gossip column "A Dubliner's Diary." O'Faolain describes him as a "dapper, smallish" man who "transcended the cautiousness of (his) background" but who, along with his wife, had lost the values of the generation that preceded his. He used "a natural charm and courtesy" to keep other people at a distance (p. 21). A car and discreet driver composed the major tools of his trade, when he would daily prowl the country and be gone until midnight, pecking at his typewriter at the office in order to drop names and record the gossip and social goings-on.

As he gradually became a media celebrity, with that role's attendant power and glamour, Sullivan was awarded with the perks the business trade would bestow: the best hotel rooms, food, drink, and so on. His career and persona remained largely a secret from his family, and O'Faolain recalled how he would come and go at a moment's notice, at his own discretion, even on Christmas Day—when, she noted, he could not bear to linger the entire day with his growing family but would leave for some vague destination, pub or party, during the latter half of the day. He named one of his daughters after his mistress.

Meanwhile, his wife, who apparently feared him and subsisted with her children on very little money, hardly enough to survive, continued to stay at home. The only money she ever made for herself came from a few book reviews she wrote for a local paper, but she kept the cuttings all her life. She was a frequent patron of both library and pub; she read incessantly and drank regularly. Her passive escapades into the romantic were not lost on her daughter, who—like the other siblings—were deeply imprinted by her habits and resented the lack of breakfast, bedding, clean clothing, love: all the symptoms of persistent neglect. She treasured the few book reviews she had published in the newspaper, the only money she earned herself; otherwise, she was dependent on her husband for the trickle of funds he would allow her.

The neglect abided amid strains of culture the father infused into it, whether that was hearing the Irish language or *Swan Lake* on the gramophone. To the outside world, the family looked middle class and respectable enough, although neither parent was a practicing Catholic, only the children. Yet somehow they maintained an illusion of a family.

Frequenting pubs and parties was her father's mainstay, but always he would go alone. So while others assumed the family was well-to-do, O'Faolain's mother, deprived of funds for necessary items and services, and to pay the bills, soon fell into a pattern of pub visits and progressively regular inebriation. She increasingly retreated to her books for escape, her life wasting away, while the father kept a mistress and illegitimate son elsewhere in Dublin, with all of prominent Dublin turning a blind eye. In *Are You Somebody*, O'Faolain reports only minor exceptions to her father's willful ignorance of his children's lives. She notes occasional physical abuse, which included beating his wife and the boys, the sudden slapping of the grown girls—but she admits there was also sometimes a loving gesture or message of concern.

In her second memoir, *Almost There* (2003), she concedes—after unearthing old letters—that he phoned her and gave her money from time to time. That book suggests that some degree of paternal involvement and affection did exist, but that she had dismissed or forgotten about it. She also admits that her father took her mother on a few overseas vacations near the end of their lives, and she posits that there may have existed a benevolent side to his willful ignorance, in that his denial of his wife's drinking made it possible to preserve her dignity.

The family had moved to Clontarf, in Dublin, by the mid 1950s: a deeply formative period in her mid-teens when, O'Faolain points out, women felt destined for marriage, so the emphasis was on courting. The "career tools," then, were "manner, figure, clothes, carefully judged liberties allowed to this boyfriend or that" (p. 33). In contrast to her oldest sister, who was largely considered the beauty of the family, second-born Nuala O'Faolain was seen as the smart or brainy one, as she excelled academically. And as one of the oldest, she was expected to mind the younger siblings, taking them around in prams. Yet it was she who posed a challenge to her parents at the age of thirteen, when she began to discover the boys, or sometimes men, at the nearby dances—"a sweaty, shuffling mass of solid eroticism" she recalls—and stray with them into dark alleys afterward (p. 31).

But amid all this depression, repression, and neglect that formed the pattern of O'Faolain's childhood days in Clontarf—a pattern for her future days, too, which she traces back to this time—one major intervention interceded. The girl was deemed a problem child by the nuns—she was likely to get herself pregnant, tempted as she was by her awakening sexuality by boys and men at and after late-night dances.

And so presently, the late-night, adolescent forays into sexuality that she details in *Are You Somebody* threatened to develop a reputation that would discomfit her father and his position, as he snapped at her that she resembled a mill girl. There was also the very real danger of becoming pregnant, which meant either giving the child up for adoption or taking a ferry trip to England for a secret abortion, which was illegal in Ireland. Not only was abortion illegal, but it carried a huge stigma; it was unspoken, a taboo in Catholic Ireland. Finally, the nuns in town—her teachers, who knew everything—called her father to let him know that she was being dropped off at home by a married man after the dances. She was thirteen and knew nothing except that she was crazy about him. They told her father to take her away from the school.

Thus, although it was a financial hardship for the family, which had to pay for many children's educations, O'Faolain was sent off on her fourteenth birthday to a well-reputed Irish language–centered girls' boarding school, St. Louis' Convent in County Monaghan, on the border of Northern Ireland. She was bought a trousseau to take with her—"napkin rings, … shoes, a dressing gown, a hairbrush—things no one in the family had ever had before" (p. 32). Thus began another world, and a transformative one for her, which O'Faolain writes about fondly, recounting no bouts of homesickness.

The Catholic education, administered in Irish by nuns, granted O'Faolain a deep look into a world not witnessed before, a world she refers to liberally in her autobiographical works, and a world that was a refuge from her family home—although, at the same time, its shattering divergence in values, celestial and cerebral, seemed miles away from the world she knew out there, which was the world of the body.

A CAREER AMID CHANGING TIMES

O'Faolain, who always excelled academically, met the challenges of this new world. She earned strong marks on her leaving certificate and consequently was accepted into University College Dublin, where she studied English. Distracted by the freedom her small apartment allowed her, the author ended up dropping out of school for a year or so and working at odd jobs, before a doctor patron, a friend of the family, helped finance her second chance at finishing her degree there. She took this opportunity to complete her studies, living in what she terms squalid conditions.

At times, she moved in and out of literary Dublin, bohemian-style, for example, sharing a mutual friend's front room with the poet Patrick Kavanagh or mucking about with the novelist John McGahern. Significantly, she takes a feminist viewpoint of this period: "The 'literary Dublin' I saw lied to women as a matter of course and conspired against the demands of wives and mistresses. Outside the home, in the circles where academics and journalism and literature met, women either had to make no demands, and be liked, or be much larger than life, and feared" (p. 70).

O'Faolain recollects that when she was a young woman, she knew no married women who wrote, and she deems publishing at the time "a man's world" (p. 70) preceding the era of women's mutual support, feminist presses, and the like that would soon follow. The author categorizes herself as a literary-minded person during this period rather than a real writer. She recognizes how the culture was "terribly dependent on drink" and how "there was too much public anecdotal life and not enough personal lyric life" (p. 70). Drink, she also recalls, ruined man men and women, writers or not, their lives stabbed with repeated humiliations until they abandoned the drinking life, so central to the social-intellectual milieu.

During this time she had met her first real boyfriend, whom she names Michael in the memoir. He was married but separated (it was difficult and took years to get a divorce at the time). He helped to teach her about culture; with his influence, she began a lifelong love affair with classical music. As a young woman in her early twenties, she hoped to marry him, but the vague promise of a wedding was never to materialize.

After earning her undergraduate degree, O'Faolain went to England and attended the University of Hull to focus on medieval prose romances, but at twenty-one, she felt lonely in Hull, away from Michael, who had remained in Ireland. However, upon rejoining Michael in Dublin to work toward an Oxford University scholarship, she found that the prospect of marriage to him remained elusive. In her memoir she focuses on the love relationship over the university experience, in accordance with her priorities. For what truly mattered to her, as she consistently notes, are the personal affairs, when she felt herself to be most alive. Not the degrees.

Finally she did well enough on an examination in English literature to be granted a scholarship to Oxford University. As a college undergraduate in Dublin, O'Faolain had devoured Scott Fitzgerald and Ernest Hemingway novels, but also Rosamund Lehmann and Daphne du Maurier, so the English literary pantheon represented glamour for her. She humorously recounts in *Are You Somebody* how she longed to be blasé about wealth, longed to be troubled and rich. Still unpretentious and without tourists, Oxford in 1963 promised shades of this lifestyle.

O'Faolain tried her hand at directing drama productions at Oxford; she was vastly inexperienced but she managed to talk her way into the student position: a foretelling of her career as television program director in England and Ireland. She became director of the Dramatic Society at Oxford, a sixties feminist breakthrough in this bastion of English intellectual tradition. But her most compelling personal development was a relationship with a male student whom in the memoir she calls Rob. They had plans eventually to marry, until O'Faolain, stunned by a remark warning her off the marriage by her father (who rarely takes an interest in her affairs), decided to call off the wedding.

O'Faolain emerged from Oxford with a bachelor of philosophy degree in English, mainly having studied nineteenth-century literature. Then she returned to UCD to work as a lecturer in English. Later she taught adults at Morley College, an adult education college, also in Dublin.

By the mid 1960s, more liberal changes were brewing in Irish society. Censorship was being lifted both in film and book publishing in once-provincial Dublin. Drugs began to infuse the culture. O'Faolain traveled to Morocco with a gay male friend and indulged in hashish, then returned to her professorial post. Tellingly, she emphasizes the importance of self-preservation at this time.

Later she was accepted for a position with the British Broadcasting Corporation in London, where she began a career making programs for the BBC's Open University. By this time, the 1970s, she was living with Rob again, but she would have drunken fights with him, showing up to work with a black eye. Jealousy was a major factor, as he was seeing another woman. Once again, O'Faolain terminated the long, sometimes long-distance relationship.

She traveled intensively during this time to places including Prague, Florence, Tehran, and New York City, and she interviewed authors including Norman Mailer, John Betjeman, John Berger, and Seamus Heaney. Rather than filming these as mere interviews, she was able to be creatively suggestive in her use of images and locations to illustrate a complex concept or argument. With John Berger, she writes, she was truly able to collaborate. He was also one of the married men with whom she had an affair, never giving a thought to the wife involved. In her later years, she would question this glaring flaw in her feminism: the inability to empathize with the other, "legitimate" woman whom she also was cheating. Repeatedly, in the personal affairs she describes in her writing, she plays the other woman and never the wife. She would remain unmarried all her life.

Later she switched to work on a BBC program called Open Door, an informal documentary television unit in which O'Faolain produced shows that represented diverse elements of society—for example, a show on transsexuals. Most significantly for her, however, in 1973 she filmed a piece on "the Troubles" then brewing and erupting in Northern Ireland. She found the project exciting and edifying, and she was "thrilled, not horrified" (*Are You Somebody,* p. 124) to be reporting from the bullet-ridden war zone of Derry.

A few years later she returned on assignment to film portraits of life in the village of Crossmaglen and the Shankill Road area of Belfast in Northern Ireland for a "general educational" unit of the BBC, but she remembers herself being "as ignorant as English media people" (*Are You Somebody,* p. 125). Her instructions were to leave politics out of the program about these areas that were at the center of occupation and violence during the Troubles, and the result, for O'Faolain, became necessarily ridiculous. During this time she wrote book reviews for the *London Times* and guest lectured. She spent time in Tehran to help plan an open university unit there.

She reconnected with Rob again, ten years after they had met, and for a time they shared a country cottage in woods outside of London, near a village train stop called Wrabness. Rob finally left her after the peaceful year there, still seeing another woman. His note read, "Back Tuesday."

A RETURN TO IRELAND

In 1973, O'Faolain marked a return to her home country through a renewed interest in Irish language, literature, and song. She calls this a turning point in her life. After engaging herself intellectually and emotionally with the Brian Merriman Summer School in rural County Clare, she found herself reconvening with her Irish sense of self and the sense of community implicit in Ireland, particularly the Irish town or village.

While there, she opened up emotionally, often weeping to the old songs sung in Irish. She heard conversations in Irish and experienced larger-than-life personalities. Later, the summer school convened in Ennis and then West Clare. O'Faolain, who was feeling reconnected with Ireland as her home, decided to move back by January 1, 1977. She had been granted a temporary position as producer for Radio Telefis Eirann (RTE), the national broadcasting service of Ireland. Through her work with RTE she was able to experience a huge range of different towns, each with their own flavor. (At the age of nearly forty, she also learned to drive during this period.)

In Ireland, O'Faolain felt herself freed of the "rigid class structure" of England. The Irish, she felt, were not "cowed and classified from birth" (*Are You Somebody,* p. 148). For fifteen years she lived with Nell McCafferty, a woman who was a prominent journalist and playwright from the North. In *Are You Somebody,* she devotes a chapter to their travels abroad, when they were happiest adventuring on walking holidays and reading with each other. It reads as a tribute to her former partner, and her lament of the end of the relationship is genuine but somewhat restrained in comparison to her depiction of the breakups with men in her youth.

But all was not idyllic in her reengagement with her home country. O'Faolain realized she was "on the edge of alcoholism" upon returning to Ireland in her late thirties, a time of particular vulnerability for her. The gentleness of the floating pub life, and this quiet time with self, also gave her a sense of purity within the emptiness, "a perfection of melancholy" (*Are You Somebody*, p. 152).

In 1980, after burying her father, O'Faolain checked herself into a psychiatric hospital; she describes a breakdown during which she continued to hear her father's voice. It was six months before she felt she had recovered fully enough to enjoy the small things in life again. Travel again became central both to her personal life and to her career. In fact, she valued the love for the many small places in Ireland, which she inherited from her father, as she too traveled extensively for her journalistic career; she savored the small towns, each with its own character, and the various festivals, events, and traditions to be covered.

Indeed, if there is something O'Faolain unqualifiedly glories in, in nearly all her works, it is travel, whether in Ireland, Athens, Italy, or Dubrovnik. She sees this venturing out in quest of new sensory experiences as a time when one falls back on one's own resources, as living most vividly. The passages seize upon the landscape and architecture and rhapsodize about these different places, full of hope and the promise of adventure, no matter the age of the adventurer. She speculates that what reading was to her mother, travel is for her. Indeed, O'Faolain presently helps to gather her family together through a travel vacation. She would organize and truly come to treasure these annual gatherings of her once-fragmented family, as her siblings with their husbands and wives spent time together in Italy every year.

In the late 1980s she experienced an unexpected stroke of luck, which O'Faolain came to see as serendipitous. The writer had landed a guest spot on a radio show, in which she invoked "the physical beauty of the seaside places north of Dublin when (she) was a child" (*Are You Somebody,* p. 20). This in turn would lead to an invitation to write a weekly opinion column for the *Irish Times.*

On the radio program she brought to life that "sparkling world" in its idyllic wildness, how much had been lost, yet tried to explain that modern Ireland was a "much, much better place than it used to be" in spite of the beauty lost to development (p. 23). Presumably, she was thinking of the quality of life for women, and the rights of women. Her columns attracted bagfuls of letters from readers, as they tackled such controversial issues in Ireland as domestic violence and homophobia. She spent a year in Belfast documenting the Troubles, but she was assigned to give a personalized glimpse of the political. Later she would decry the tone of authoritative righteousness she felt forced to use in her writing. As with her stints at the BBC and RTE, at the *Irish Times* she felt herself again in a male-centered world.

RUNAWAY SUCCESS

In the mid 1990s a colleague encouraged O'Faolain to publish a selection of her columns in book form. She was asked to write an introduction that would give some background or lead-in to the journalism. But this lead-in, meant to provide the personal context for the public opinions she espoused, exploded into a personal revelation. And so this Irish and American best seller, with the American edition subtitled *The Accidental Memoir of a Dublin Woman,* arrived at its unexpected extraordinary success—truly accidental because it began as a mere preface to the "real" work of newspaper writing.

An epilogue to the 1998 edition of *Are You Somebody* records the explosive national reaction to her 1996 memoir. O'Faolain recounts how, after an appearance promoting the book on the nation's most popular late-night talk show, *Late Night with Gay Byrne,* an appearance she noted as exceptionally honest, there was such a demand for the book that booksellers had to sell the books directly from the boxes, with no time to even stock them on the shelves.

The wild, almost fairytale popularity summoned by *Are You Somebody,* a book typed out in two months in a cottage in County Clare, was evidence of how effectively it hooked readers both in Ireland and America. O'Faolain noted that she was able to start her life anew through this breakthrough, that the literary success gave her a rebirth. The question "Are you somebody?" she explains, refers to the question the author was often asked on the street, since she was seen regularly as an interviewer on television. It proves a rich meditative lead-in, a koan that holds multiple meanings, and it transforms into a question O'Faolain essentially asks herself in the work: Am I worth something? The issue of self-worth becomes pivotal when reflecting on a life of romantic love lost, and parental love perhaps never really felt or believed. It also elicits a turbulent volume of an "answer."

Critics too heaped their praises. The novelist Colm Tóibín raved that it was "likely to become a classic of Irish autobiography" in a *Times Literary Supplement* review. Others took pains to distinguish the volume from the sheafs of celebrity tell-all memoirs for its genuineness, and they hailed it as a remarkable literary achievement. In a jacket blurb for the book, the novelist Roddy Doyle clarified the importance of place: "Writing about herself, Nuala O'Faolain has also written about Ireland. It is a cruel, wounded place—and this book has become an important part of the cure."

The memoir juxtaposes a successful public life with an emotional roller coaster of a private life rooted in a psychic discontent. O'Faolain's unhappiness seems to stem from the inability to sustain a lasting relationship, and it is this vulnerability that ultimately leaves a raw emptiness in the writer's soul. And yet the sincerity in her accounting, this headstrong mapping out of fragile emotional suffering, proves riveting to the reader; in particular (as she notes in *Almost There: The Onward Journey of a Dublin Woman*, a second memoir published in 2003) she seemed to strike a chord in recording the neglect of the parent.

The work, "an emotional episode, somehow, in public life, in Ireland," stayed twenty weeks at number one on the best-seller list in that country (*Are You Somebody*, p. 189), and it was a *New York Times* bestseller as well. The success of the first book resulted in a rumored seven-figure advance for her second, a history with commentary, *My Dream of You*, for which she embarked on a seventeen-city book tour. By 2001, she was commuting between Manhattan and a Dublin apartment. Instead of her earlier column, she was commissioned to write a weekly piece for the Saturday supplement to the *Irish Times*, a shorter, more personal version of her former column, "Regarding Ireland."

But with another book contract, O'Faolain was happy to be able to resign from her column writing. In her second memoir, *Almost There*, she trains her focus on America, where she has met a man through a personal ad on the Internet, a dating website. First she expounds upon the affair with the older married man in Irish hotels. Next the writing moves gradually toward her summer in the Adirondacks, where she spends weekends with John Low-Beer, a divorced man with partial custody of his eight-year-old daughter. From 2002 until her death, O'Faolain lived much of

the time with him, and in 2003, they registered as domestic partners.

All three of her first books were on the *New York Times* best-seller list. Critics noted the strength and originality of her work and its significance in tackling themes largely unexplored in Irish fiction.

The work to follow, *The Story of Chicago May* (2005), was based in history like her second book, this time following a turn-of-the-century Irish girl, born in 1871, who becomes a prostitute and petty thief in the big untamed American cities of Chicago and New York, as well as the cities of Paris and London. The book openly exposes its research with statistics, court records, newspaper accounts, and the like. And the life uncovered, and imagined (for this is also ultimately a fictional account), is a fascinating one, although perhaps more problematic for the reader in its structure. Some readers found the author's account of her research intrusive and resented the digressions, connections, and associations O'Faolain made in regard to her own life, friends, and family. Yet for other readers she effectively accomplishes the feat of bringing a silenced feminine voice to life, and honoring Chicago May's complexity. O'Faolain won the 2006 Prix Feminina prize for the novel.

A VOICE ON THE THRESHOLD

In Manhattan at the end of February 2008, at age sixty-eight, O'Faolain noticed a loss of feeling on the right side of her body. She went to the emergency room of a local hospital, where a CAT scan and x-rays were performed; they showed several tumors in her brain and lungs. True to herself in refusing any naïveté or self-delusion concerning her condition, and treasuring her quality of life, she made the choice to refuse a course of chemotherapy that would have extended her life for a short time, saying that life was no longer worth living when she could not appreciate the small things such as reading (though she could still feel music, she noted).

She decided to return to Ireland from New York to die. In her final reunion with her siblings in Italy, she attended in a wheelchair. Thanks to a friend with a private plane, she was able to travel to Paris, Madrid, and many other beloved European venues in the quick three months that passed before she died. When her life ended in a Dublin hospice, on May 9, 2008, the news of her death was a shock to many of her friends and acquaintances, as she had just given a national radio interview three weeks before.

In April 2008, O'Faolain had broken another taboo in speaking on Irish radio, RTE, candidly about her terminal illness and her impending death. In the interview she described undergoing a humiliating, depersonalizing wait, for hours on a stretcher, before being informed of her metastatic cancer by a staff member rushing past. That was the way she'd heard the diagnosis. The cancer quickly spread from her lungs to her brain and liver.

O'Faolain explained her decision to return home to Ireland to die, to the community she considered her family. As an atheist, she calmly but sorrowfully stated that she anticipated no afterlife after her death. The interview exposed more the mourning of an unfinished life, more upset and anger, than fear.

The wrenching interview, conducted by her journalist friend Marian Finucane, valiantly addressed the subject of death like no other interview ever broadcast by RTE. In a weakened voice, O'Faolain admitted that she was afraid and said that "all goodness went out of life" once she was diagnosed with terminal cancer. For that reason, she refused chemotherapy, in anticipation of the further deterioration of her life's quality. The interview does not try to cushion the blow for any listener, to speak bravely of her travails. Instead she sharply catalogs the small aesthetic pleasures that are diminishing for her since the diagnosis. For instance, she explains that she no longer could read the work of Marcel Proust that had consoled her all her life. Poignantly, plaintively, O'Faolain voices—almost arguing—how she feels cheated by the sudden events that have conspired to change, to destroy, her life: the unspeakable pain of having to leave the world behind. "I thought there would be me and the world, but the world turned its back on me, the

world said to me that's enough of you now and what's more we're not going to give you any little treats at the end" (Finucane).

The capacity to marvel at nature had left her; however, Franz Schubert's "Death and the Maiden" in concert, she was relieved to note, was still able to touch her. Nevertheless, while she said prayers during her life to a vague spiritual presence, she could not and would not take a step that would be false to herself ("I can't be consoled by mention of God. I can't"), even when darkness was falling all around her. She did not move toward traditional religion at this point, but instead chose to meet her fate in the hereafter fully as herself, leaving her faith to be directed upon the beauty of nature and goodness of animals as always.

Allusions to death haunt O'Faolain's work in a sometimes serious but often self-mocking way, in that she would fretfully exaggerate small symptoms and believe she had cancer. So it is almost as though her worst nightmare had come true, had come back to haunt her. The Schubert piece that Kathleen DeBurca listens to in *My Dream of You* was composed while he was dying. Miss Leech, the librarian, is dying of cancer. Kathleen's close friend Jimmy has just died, and her boss's mother dies during the course of the story.

All the fear of aging gathered in *Almost There* and in *Best Love, Rosie* (2009)—a posthumously published novel—encapsulates the fear of dying, and she references the potential cause being cancer as well. In *Best Love*, Rosie's former lover Leo is thin and slowly dying. But Rosie—unmarried and childless—finds her strength in friends (rather than end bitterly as lovers, she salvages a friendship with Leo) and mainly in the aunt who was a mother to her, the only mother she knew. She also finds spirit and strength in refurbishing an old cottage by the sea, and in the nameless, homeless dog she finds there: she is motivated in how it needs her.

Critics agree upon O'Faolain's singular bravery and vividness of voice, infused upon everyday life. Daphne Merkin in her 2001 *New York Times* interview "A Thorny Irish Rose" called her a "hurtling life force" (p. 25). Her last interview was no exception: "It amazed me, Marian, how quickly life turned black, immediately almost. For example, I lived somewhere beautiful, but it means nothing to me anymore—the beauty" (Finucane). Even in her dying, she gives permission to others to be distressed, to grieve openly, to rage. She talks about what others are afraid to talk about.

As for Ireland, "the country suffered a collective existential crisis" in the wake of the interview, according to the *Guardian*'s June Caldwell. The response to this frankness about death stunned O'Faolain. Many faithful readers wrote to her after the interview. This helped her, she said, to piece together some of the little fragments of her life.

STYLE, TONE, AND THE INFLUENCE OF PROUST

Stylistically, O'Faolain embraces a collage of elements or genres in order to remain true to her subject, whether it is herself or a woman from history. Both memoirs weave past and present, with two stories running side by side, and switch place and person in a stream-of-consciousness fashion. O'Faolain intersperses colorful, engaging anecdotes throughout the books that work to illustrate the time and place, and she incorporates the honest storm of emotions whirling through the different stages of her life.

The writer often tells sad stories in her intimate, conversational tone, but she seldom sustains that note of melancholy in the nonfiction writing. As in *Are You Somebody*, a matter-of-fact observational stance tends to calibrate or moderate the reports, almost journalistic, and mostly unsentimental in its plain talk. In this sense the heartfelt cries of sorrow, the suffering when it is allowed to rush out, is more deeply felt by the reader—as are the moments of ecstatic and sensual passion. At the same time, O'Faolain needs to make herself the target of her own research. As a writer, she values reflection upon and analysis of her younger self's choices, as well as dissection of her middle-aged struggles with loneliness and aging. And whether these stories and memories coalesce may remain for

the reader to decide; the overall effect of the memoir is one of a unified whole, whether or not the author considers that her life possesses this quality.

When working with nonfiction, she imagines a story based on extensively detailed research, and she tends to merge the research process into the story—to create a new story. The method of discovery might be imagined, as in the fictional research process of Kathleen DeBurca in *My Dream of You* (based on O'Faolain's actual research—the documents quoted are real). Or, alternatively, the author records her own digging up of facts as part of the narrative, as in *The Story of Chicago May*, called a "history with commentary" in the frontispiece to the next novel, *Best Love, Rosie*. The effect, then, even in her historical fiction, is also semiautobiographical, though the effect can also be structurally intrusive for readers who might dislike the personal digression and the mixing of these two genres.

O'Faolain's historical novels are hefty with research, but the imagination that infuses the life of a woman in history lightens and invigorates both stories. As the "history with commentary" tag indicates, these books are difficult to pin down, since they can be classified neither as strict biography nor pure historical fiction. Both follow two women of polar opposite classes through passions and privations and bring to life the social mores and trappings of a certain milieu.

Both also examine divisions. Her first novel homes in primarily on the division between English or Anglo-Irish and nationalist Irish tribes, a rift of both culture and class as depicted in famine times; *My Dream of You* offers a multi-layered examination of social injustice, focusing on the victimization of the poor and women. In this work, the immorality of the English in their evictions and starvation of the Irish is implicit in the details. Moral blame is also quietly laid upon the husband and landlord William Talbot for his ejection of his wife out of their home and, after the court proceedings brought against her, into an asylum in England. Any immorality on the part of the alleged adulterer, Marianne Talbot, is not the focus. Rather the focus in on the loneliness, disempowerment, and sensual starvation that leads to her passion. Stylistically, *I Dream of You* sits in no comfortable genre. In the work, authentic quoted documentation from historical research (as it is discovered by the narrator) is interspersed with the historical fictionalization or novelization of events. So O'Faolain balances fiction and nonfiction, while also balancing these two time periods, 1840s and 1990s.

Injustice in *Chicago May* centers upon the life of a woman seemingly condemned to prostitution in order to survive and gain financial independence, a profession it is difficult for her to reject even in advanced middle age, when she is trying to reform. The book takes a feminist-humanist stance, in that May allegedly becomes the victim of her former lover, who is a professional burglar. Originally she tries to defend him from a prison sentence, but after his release, she apparently fears him. (Then when she, along with an accomplice, strikes back, she herself is condemned to a decade in prison.) Here the research is the author-narrator's, not the protagonist's, as she dramatizes May's life events.

This work also introduces O'Faolain's view of the contrasts between Ireland and the United States in the early twentieth century. Both her second memoir, *Almost There*, and the posthumously published *Best Love, Rosie* (the closest to a traditional novel that she wrote), would continue an examination of the differences in character of these two nations in a contemporary setting, as O'Faolain herself commuted between Manhattan and her oceanview cottage in County Clare from her mid fifties onward. Arguably, *Best Love* introduces more of a bantering, humorous tone than any of her other longer works. It is perhaps more aligned in tone to the voice in some of her *Irish Times* columns, with more of an eye toward amusement and entertainment of the audience.

O'Faolain has been called a reader's writer, and her own reading life formed an essential part of her being. A particular influence she names throughout her voracious reading life was Marcel Proust; she would devour *Remembrance of Things Past* and other writings by the Frenchman repeatedly throughout her lifetime. While her journalistic life eventually centered on twenty

years of commenting on public affairs, this lifelong influence of Proust's may have compelled her to choose the memoir as a preferred and most powerful form of expression.

Fintan O'Toole, a columnist for the *Irish Times* for over thirty years, commented on her connection to Proust in terms of her opinion columns. After all, the years of writing columns were what forged her writing voice from her first memoir. O'Toole's insight could apply equally to her later prose, fiction or nonfiction:

> In her fashioning of a public "I," [O'Faolain found] a kind of intimacy with her readers through which those large questions and emotions could be filtered and humanized. She forged that miraculous literary self that was at once immediately personal and yet sufficiently capacious to register the movements of the great outside world.

> In this regard, Nuala's devotion to Marcel Proust was not accidental. She learned from him how to construct a coherent sense of self in writing, one that could be intimate and immediate but also infinitely expansive. Often her columns started, and remained, with herself, but brought political and moral issues within the frame of her own vibrant emotion and luminous intelligence.

> (*A Radiant Life*, p. 301)

O'Toole further links her columns with her memoir *Are You Somebody*, when he elaborates, "Her deep reluctance to write that book suggested that, at some level, she understood the way it took apart the self that made her one of the greatest columnists ever to inhabit the English language" (p. 302). Equating or defining the art of memoir with the analysis as a breaking apart or fragmenting of self shows the danger that can be implicit in working within this genre, and it provides the reader with an enlightening filter through which to absorb O'Faolain's meditations.

CATHOLICISM IN ARE YOU SOMEBODY: A DIVIDING OF BODY AND SOUL

Division also loomed large in O'Faolain's spiritual life as she grew up in an Irish 1950s culture where the paradigm was Roman Catholic and church was still heavily intertwined with state. Although she had to forget, when away at school, "what (she) knew about bodies" (*Are You Somebody,* p. 33), O'Faolain calls her being sent to the convent school "the biggest single stroke of luck in [her] life" (p. 36).

Like most boarding schools at the time, hers was a Catholic school run by nuns. O'Faolain, much to her own surprise, adapted and enjoyed these years, despite the rules and restraint. She reveled in the routine and order she found to be missing in her chaotic home life. Although her beloved fiction was forbidden there, she would desperately read the French novels that young visiting French teachers would have in their possession. Again, though she knew little Irish when she entered—"couldn't read it and could barely speak it … I was half-gagged all the time," she received top marks in examinations there and top marks as well when she did her leaving certificate in Irish (p. 30). In fact, students were made to study English through Irish.

However, on holidays O'Faolain continued to explore the wild contrast between her ancient-seeming convent and the beginning of the rock-and-roll revolution and would emerge at night "pale from smoking, hollow-eyed from silent explorations with boys in bus shelters" (p. 33). Her sisters were working. She also offered to quit school and work at the local department store, but she was sent back to the school again after every holiday: a "cerebral place" where "we might as well have been disembodied spirits for all the attention that was paid to our bodies" (p. 33). So the chasm between the spiritual and academic, and the forbidden sensuality that beckoned—prevalent in all of Irish Catholic culture—only deepened the more for a teenage boarding-school girl. For much of the year, bodily desires were hidden away, never to be referred to in decent conversation.

And yet O'Faolain takes pains to point out the same-sex romantic forays that were permitted, if not encouraged: events that gave school its "tingling excitement," when "any luxury was most intensely felt" (p. 34). This experience also marked a time when the romantically inclined young girls would have "crushes" on older boarders, in her case a sixth year. She approaches the subject clinically, like an anthropologist reporting

a practice that no longer exists, and at the same time defensively, as a nun there who is still her friend as she writes warns her, exasperatedly, not to come out with all this information.

The author begins by imagining the patriarchal derision that would greet her revelation: "The emotions we felt as schoolgirls were volatile and exaggerated and they have always been despised by the world. But they were not trivial. They were a grounding in the affective dimension that was to matter most to us all our lives" (p. 35).

Here O'Faolain reiterates the prime importance of love and relationship over career, over everything in life. She emphasizes that this long custom, complete with its own special vocabulary, was not trivial, not a substitute for a similar experience with boys, but an emotional learning experience: "learning appropriateness, learning control, learning to differentiate our selves from the other selves around" (p. 35). The author marvels at how students traditionally would bestow gifts and letters on the beloved, typically an older girl but sometimes one of the teaching nuns themselves, the hanging around for weeks with the focus and obsession on her, and finally the excitement of being thanked by the loved one.

O'Faolain also emphasizes that although the phenomenon is hushed and taboo in present-day Ireland—when she sees the women years later, she knows they would "faint with shame" if she introduced the subject (p. 36)—there is nothing to be ashamed of. (She is only ashamed of her acts of stealing the gifts when she had no money or for stealing bread from the refectory because she was hungry.) Part of the reason she delineates this is that her mother was expelled for a similar crush, and was devastated to the point that it changed her life, perhaps a motivating factor for her psychological drive inward and her addiction to drink: her sheer self-destructiveness and isolation. Additionally, O'Faolain notes, they never had guests at home, and her mother was disowned by or in no communication with her family; so the children had no maternal relatives that they knew of. But, as was to be expected during these times in Ireland, she never spoke of it.

This also provokes her own life decision: her refusal to express shame at any part of her life, whether it be frowned upon by society or not, from her promiscuity as a young woman in 1960s London (she prefers the term "availability," but avows that she never could say no to a man's offer) or her bisexuality in middle age.

There may exist a Catholic reserve, however, in her recounting of her bisexuality, after fifteen years living with the preeminent journalist Nell McCafferty from Derry. O'Faolain never labels herself as such. She chooses not to detail this life stage, her longest relationship, except in describing their travels and conversational exchanges. Yet, while she depicts her former partner as more of a companion and with none of the graphic glimpses from her sensual life with various boyfriends, she does break a great taboo for literary Ireland. Even in reporting these confidences, including her emotions and a few details surrounding their breakup, she lifts another stone from the wall of silences, secrecies, and denials that she feels damaged her through her family life. Likewise, O'Faolain removes any shame from her neediness and emotional pain, and thus implicitly models and encourages frankness while she validates others' isolation, abandonment and suffering.

At the end of the book, the forays and relationships dissolve, as she turns to reporting how she spends Christmas alone—counting them at seven successive deliberately solitary Christmases—with her dog Molly, for whom she expresses unchecked devotion and affection. She writes about her holiday hike in emotional detail, sparing the reader none of the shades of isolation that wash over her—as seemingly deliberately isolated as a nun with a vow of silence.

In her memoir, O'Faolain dismisses any real relevance the nuns have in the contemporary, secular world, mocking their advice "that in whatever situation I might find myself I should think what the Virgin Mary would have done and do the same" (p. 37). And in her later writings she neither embraces nor outright rejects church doctrine. She thinks for herself. She sees abor-

tion as a deeper question than the heated debate would have one assume—that extensive reflection *is* in fact necessary, and discourages reactiveness. Meanwhile chinks appear in the armor of the church as allegations and revelations of sexual abuse begin to be reported in her country.

And therefore both in her columns for the *Irish Times*, which drew a large response in letters to the editor over the years, and in her memoirs, O'Faolain takes on the cloak, in some sense, of reteaching the new morals of a new age to her Irish readers. And she does not mince words in her Catholic country. In a column on a convent's alleged cruelty to orphans in their care, she writes: "People are reluctant to face the truth. But I believe the truth is that what lay behind the cruelty perpetrated on children in care was Catholicism itself. It developed the concepts of sexual wickedness and maternal sin which were used to facilitate the expression of sadism" ("Schools and Sadism," in *A Radiant Life*, p. 88).

Except for an impulse to pray her gratitude to an unnamed deity, she is basically secular in private and in public life. The author rejects any concept of an afterlife, as she emphasized in the interview given a month before her death, by metastatic brain cancer.

AN HONEST VISION OF AN INCONSISTENT FEMINISM

Whether she is writing memoir or a novel or historical fiction, O'Faolain poses staunch questions regarding humane and equal treatment of women, young, middle-aged, or elderly, at work or at home. In an *Irish Times* column her declaration could hardly be more explicit: "I look on the feminist project as the great project of my time on earth, and I'm happy that I've lived to see it have some success. A baby girl born in many parts of the world, including Ireland, has a much better chance today than she would ever have had before of using the whole of her unique self's potential during her life" ("As for Love," in *A Radiant Life*, p. 139).

With her mother as the prime model, the writer equates motherhood—or childbearing, as she often refers to it—as well as domesticity, with servitude. O'Faolain, after all, observed firsthand her mother's misery as she slaved away for her offspring and, later, for her unfaithful husband. And this was branded into the daughter's psyche. Her mother's suffering, only partially numbed by drink, haunts O'Faolain throughout her writing, right up to the end of her second memoir, *Almost There*, when the ghost of her mother is revealed as a pervasive presence in the daughter's life, even after her mother's death.

Even when the daughter is at an age the mother never reached, a lamentable maternal force continues to impress upon O'Faolain, always on the edges of her mind. In *Almost There*, when O'Faolain is allegedly on the brink of happy companionship, the mother figure still makes herself felt: a sad image perpetually anxious but also perpetually rejecting the home, moving out toward the pub. O'Faolain declares that her mother's unhappiness seems more real than her own happiness, and—upon careful reading—the dismissal of the mother she imagines at the end is only thrust forward as a tantalizing proposal or possibility—a "why not" she asks herself. Why not close the door on my mother once and for all? She never truly exorcises that spirit of desolation.

In most of her work, nonfiction or fiction, O'Faolain examines the "difficulties intrinsic to being a woman" (*Are You Somebody*, p. 81). The author, who sees herself as a typical product of Ireland in the 1950s, largely accepted traditional boundaries and struggled with her nontraditional choices. Only strict societal norms prevented her from openly cohabitating with her boyfriend. She was prepared to marry if she discovered she was pregnant. In fact, she wanted to marry, period, and has called that the career goal for girls of this era.

She quotes her twenty-year-old self, or at least the being that offered herself to her boyfriend Michael at the time, with all her hopes and dreams. In clinically observing and analyzing her younger self through the letters, she notes how she quietly urges marriage. But around the same time she cites letters received from her mother—who bemoans the mess that engulfs her as well as the chronic lack of money—and notes that she does see the dangers of that institution, and she indeed tends to emulate artists and women who were unmarried. O'Faolain is able to marvel at the disconnect between the ideal of her own marriage versus her mother's often miserable domestic reality.

Meanwhile, a later letter from her grandfather deplores the idea of her marrying her second boyfriend, Rob, and advises her to see her clergyman for counseling. Her father, too, in a rare moment of personal interest, warns her away from him, saying they will only be divorced. Lovers' letters are also quoted, sometimes to illustrate the prevailing belief system of the time, such as what a woman can humbly give a man, in which he lists all the attributes of a loving, self-effacing woman: "the sieve for his ideas and enthusiasms, the moderator of his superfluous angers, the soft bosom of his hard days, his scourge to action—or his dangler of promised sweetmeats" (p. 53). The author uses this as blatant evidence of earlier, patriarchal times. From this material are forged the bars of the patriarchal mental prison, from which O'Faolain works a lifetime, only half-successfully, to free herself.

At the end, in her opinion, she is glad she never bore children because "under the old system it was so easy to rear children badly. The child wouldn't have properly survived" (p. 84). In addition, she points out that women were not financially independent. She can recollect only one woman who had bought her own house with her own earnings from this period, and very few women instructors or professors at UCD.

O'Faolain says of her affairs with married men that the decade it took before change came was too late in correcting her faltering, unconscious moral sense. "The fog I had been wandering in was so dense that it took me ages to make my way half out of it. Which is where I am now" (p. 85). The memoir form itself becomes a means to light her way out of the fog and into clarity of thought and moral integrity—a means through which the shroud might be lifted, to grant the self new life.

This fog imagery is echoed in the airborne imagery that ends *Are You Somebody*, following the upfront craving for a partner, a relationship to write about rather than the self's means of preservation. She remarks on the brokenness of the variegated ruins of history that lie patched about her perch above the Atlantic, including a prehistoric burial site, an abandoned village from the famine, a church and holy well and a pile of shells, all stemming from representing separate shards of history. O'Faolain uses these as metaphors for her own unconnected bits and strands of history, moments without a progression or product. Yet the metaphor does lend her memories an eternal, if fragile, quality, as she sees positivity, even personal redemption, in the emptiness before her: "But in front of me there is a vista: empty, but inexpressibly spacious. Between those two—landscape of stone and wide blue air—is where I am" (p. 188). And so through her reading, the scene is transformed into a prospect of readiness and anticipation of some measure of personal happiness once more, if conjured from air. (Later, however, O'Faolain questions her motive for this ending, and its authenticity—did she just want to find closure?)

Lamentably, in her opinion, the fog in which she wanders prove so dense that the prefeminism patterns engrained in her beliefs and behavior repeat themselves in middle age and beyond, as recorded in *Almost There*, in which the author conducts an affair with an older married man. In this second memoir, O'Faolain delineates a passionate and illicit liaison, secretly arranged in a string of hotel rooms.

As always, the admittedly empowering force of feminism in her public life, in her career, is fraught with contradiction in private. While she avidly joined women's right marches through the 1970s, O'Faolain admits that her personal life did not usually mirror these societal strides by women. The men with whom she had affairs, usually married men, often charmed her but ultimately treated her dismissively. "I did see what I was doing. But I didn't want to respond to the feminist call to self-respect. I wanted to know Harry," she writes of one of her married lovers, "and the conditions of knowing him were not negotiable" (*Are You Somebody*, p. 134). And yet apparently the author's own boundaries were always movable; she adjusted them to fit the circumstance of the relationship, for the sake of passion, even when this meant loneliness, abjection, and depression: a demeaning of the self. In Ireland in 1977, she felt that even the Merriman Summer School "could reflect the awkwardness and shyness and sudden cruelties that continue to deform social intercourse between the sexes" there (p. 147).

O'Faolain comments on how gratifying it was in the 1980s to attract the attention of a "dominant, difficult" personality but reflects that "the relationship was too embedded in an old culture to be invigorated by women's-movement thinking. That old culture had come crashing down, but we were wandering among its ruins, picking through its fragments" (p. 138). Nevertheless, the influence of the movement grew for her and continued to enlighten and strengthen her.

Professionally in both the BBC and RTE establishments, the men seemed to run the show, using a "rough, macho management style often in play just underneath the good manners of formal management" so that women felt and were excluded (p. 138). However, with the feminist movement attracting wide interest, she was able to pioneer a series called *Women Talking* as well as the *Women's Programme* on RTE, the latter of which featured shows on topics including "incest, prostitution, abortion, women's pay and employment, contemplative nuns, health issues, Unionist women and their views on Southern women" (p. 149). A later series for RTE, *Plain Tales*, focused on giving voice to older women and the issues relevant to their own lives. The series won the 1985 Jacob's Award for Irish television program of the year.

FEMINISM IN FICTION: MY DREAM OF YOU

How much has the Irish woman's (or any woman's) situation genuinely changed in the past 150 years? The reader is led to ask herself this question in observing Kathleen, the contemporary protagonist-narrator, struggle with her own middle-aged, modern feminist woes, as she figures out her role, her power, within an unexpected new love relationship. At the same time,

Kathleen both provides powerful details of the Great Hunger and lays out a dramatic, singularly Irish period piece that highlights as well the gentry woman's plight in nineteenth-century Ireland.

The historical characters O'Faolain chooses to fictionalize represent instances of woman's strength and suffering in Western history. Although she certainly does not gloss over the starvation and agonies of the Irish during the famine, her literary focus is the historical figure of Marianne Talbot in *My Dream of You* (2001). Marianne is a wealthy landlord's life, completely part of the Anglo-Irish establishment of the 1840s and one who flinches at the starving beggars crying out in Irish to her in her passing carriage. The Talbot pantry is full, while the Irish outside are begging for a handout, eating grass.

Yet O'Faolain shows Marianne—while heavily privileged—to be, in fact, enchained herself by her husband, William, who dictates everything from the household rules to their lovemaking. The wife and mother is essentially a prisoner in her own house; her husband has decided, while evicting hundreds of Irish families from their homes, that it is unsafe for his own wife to travel elsewhere. Marianne is portrayed as having no real friends; only the servants are her familiars, and they are culturally (and linguistically) alien to her, as they speak Irish. She allies herself only, perhaps a bit desperately, to her small daughter Mab.

What O'Faolain admires is the reckless passion and bravery Marianne Talbot demonstrated in having an affair with the Irish groom of the household, a man with his room housed alongside the stable. Yet even this alleged affair becomes dubious in the telling. The book, after presenting a romantic story surrounding the couple, true to the documents found and new evidence presented, allows for multiple versions of the story, with multiple detailed possibilities. At the end, after the main plot is offered, suggesting the tryst between the lady of the house and the groom (Richard Mullan), none of the details are presented as solid fact, and O'Faolain swiftly bursts the romantic balloon she has so fully imagined. Documents, including interviews with servants (each of whom may have a motive for lying in their testimony), emerge that imply that there might have existed no affair at all, the affair might have been set up, or else an affair took place with another man; O'Faolain conjectures this mystery man as possibly the clergyman who took Marianne into custody after the scandal.

Regardless, Marianne Talbot's shared material wealth and upper-class status could not save her. Kathleen, through dogged library research, highlights court documentation evincing that the wife was thrown out of the house by her husband and treated as a common criminal, which was the custom at the time, entirely within the legal rights of her husband. "Richard Talbot thought to secure his wealth and his name by driving her insane. But she was punished for nothing ... He crushed Marianne, and it turned out there was no greater meaning to it than the crushing of a butterfly" (*My Dream of You*, p. 355).

Eventually Marianne was taken to England and placed in a mental institution (all the facts proving this patiently documented) for her alleged adultery. It is quite a saga with suspense between developments. A mental break is imagined to have occurred after the incident, and then the gradual loss of sanity and sensibility in the environs of the institution. According to the documents, a cousin, John Paget, discovers where she is residing, removes her from the place, and takes her into his own family home. There is no trace of her life discoverable on record after the fortuitous rescue, and the character dissolves into the anonymity that is the fate of so many billions of women in history. O'Faolain's characterization of Marianne as a butterfly underlines her essential fragility and vulnerability, and perhaps her purity alongside her ruined mind.

However, the novel's postscript belongs to Kathleen who, as a latter-day Marianne, serves to not merely assuage but positively redeem Marianne's loss. The marvelous triumph of *My Dream of You*'s Kathleen DeBurca is the contemporary answer to the nineteenth century's dilemma of a woman depending on a man, no matter the passion. Shay, a sixty-something married man who long ago immigrated from Ireland to England for work in landscaping, but now feels drawn back toward his homeland, has promised a passionate extramarital relationship. He proposes to fly into Ireland from England, pay for her cottage, and see her at regular intervals. She imagines and reimagines this scenario of waiting, but finally (and it takes all her strength of character) leaves a message turning him down. She finally decides she wants more than another submissive role in a relationship where she would be always the one waiting, waiting—while the man conducts himself and makes the decisions on his own terms. The power differential is ultimately too much; Kathleen decides that she honors herself too much to play that game in her advanced middle age. And that claiming of power ultimately becomes the counterpoint to the institutionalization and insanity of her alter ego, Marianne, and Marianne's utter loss of power.

The end of the novel brings a stark reminder of the prefeminist past, and revives a maternal theme once again, as Kathleen recalls another horrific incident of womanhood versus patriarchy, this time involving the Catholic Church in the late twentieth century, when she was twenty. She recounts a memory of when her mother was in labor with yet another child and, as an older woman, was at risk of dying in childbirth. The mother shrieks in agonies of pain. Yet the church that runs the hospital, and the husband who agrees with church doctrine, will not allow her morphine because they want to protect the baby. Only Kathleen tries to fight for her mother's freedom to have an abortion, or at least to have morphine administered in a Protestant hospital:

> I tried to explain that Mammy had never got a break, that she'd always been pushed around that she was dying for no reason, dying young, leaving her kids before she'd got anything back from them, for no better reason than she was a woman in a country run by bad old men.

> Them and their unborn babies! I choked. Them and their rules for the womb! I could accept that she's dying, if she wasn't screaming in pain …

> All night

(p. 492)

PLIGHTS OF AGING: SEEKING PASSION IN ALMOST THERE *AND* MY DREAM OF YOU

In *Almost There* (2003), the writer continues to grapple with aging and, indeed, attests that she watches the small deteriorations of her body as though they were happening to someone else. At the same time, she faces looming questions of how to find sexual fulfillment and companionship at this stage of life.

O'Faolain is living in Manhattan. At a friend's suggestion, she uses an Internet dating site; she meets John, a lawyer, and spends summer weekends with him in a resort outside of New York City, where she lives and writes. But the old ghosts are still with her. Although she wishes to learn "ordinary, daily love" (p. 274), in a lengthy tirade, revealed largely through quoted dialogue at the end of the book, she openly demonstrates her rage and immaturity but mainly outright jealousy of her lover's eight-year-old daughter, and his affection toward her. In this sense, the focus is not on her partner, John. He is not the center of the anecdotes.

Almost imperceptibly, out of natural descriptions of the summer landscape, and contented dog walks and swims at the pier, the book spirals into open rage and jealousy of the daughter at the end. O'Faolain's self-admitted turbulence and blazing between opposite emotions is in evidence. This emerges in a crescendo of intensity, so uncontrolled that it seems primal and rooted in the author's rage at her own neglect by her parents as a child. Dialogues are replayed, in which her lover tries to assuage her insecurities, but to no avail. And though she recognizes the jealous monstrousness that has possessed her, O'Faolain is unable to do anything to tame that loose energy and ammunition.

She is plainly aghast and ashamed of herself, and states as much, but no therapy seems to keep her anger in check. This flood of anger and bewilderment she recognizes as crucially linked to her own childhood experience of parental neglect: the opposite of what she witnesses in the father-daughter relationship before her.

Her remonstrations and sharp barbs meet only vague confused soothing noises from her lover, so nothing is quelled, nothing transformed. A block is formed between them. The jealousy is chronic, static, and comes from a deep core of her being. The suffering associated with her own childhood neglect appears to be the root of her rage, rage that now threatens a new love affair. Although she admits bouts of fondness for the girl's innocence and radiance, she also sees her as manipulative, and she contends that she didn't anticipate a child being involved. At sixty-one, O'Faolain has no desire to learn how to be a mother.

And yet mostly *Almost There* serves as a companion piece for, or a writer's journal of the process of writing, *My Dream of You*. The greater part of the book, the first part, delivers an extended annotation on the real-life, passionate, but also ultimately thwarted, love affair that inspires the yearning Kathleen's affair in *My Dream of You*.

In exposing her affair with a fatherly, older married truck driver named Joseph in *Almost There*, O'Faolain exposes much of the true-life basis for the events underlying the contemporary half of her fictional account, in which the protagonist, Kathleen, has an affair with Shay, an Irish landscaper who had immigrated to England decades before. Their plight, as it reflects the educated class and the working class, both Irish in this case, echoes the imagined passion of the nineteenth-century Anglo-Irish wife, Marianne Talbot. Marianne, as a woman, represented part of the tiny population of the well-to-do landowner elite during the famine. And yet she was mansion-bound, trapped by her gender into submission to her husband's complete power. Kathleen, a career woman, seems powerful in comparison—but in their private lives the women share similar weaknesses and vulnerabilities, even living 150 years apart.

While respectfully evoking the horror of the legendary, not-so-distant suffering of the famine—the grimmest Irish historical period, which is stamped into the Irish psyche—*My Dream of You* also articulates the turmoil of the contemporary middle-aged, single and childless, working woman in Ireland. Kathleen herself is forty-nine, a reflective woman who is quite capable of managing her life, but ripe for an affair at the cusp of her half-century birthday. Having recently retired from her travel journalism career in London, and deeply grieving over the death of her best friend, Jimmy, she stands at a crossroads in her life.

The crisis in her life occurs when Jimmy dies unexpectedly in his sleep in his thirties, of a heart attack. (That her solidarity lies with a gay male friend rather than a woman also loosely aligns with events in *Almost There*, when a younger gay male friend in Dublin takes her under his wing and looks after her.) Afterward she speaks to Jimmy, implores him, cries to him, asks for advice, and mainly misses his presence dreadfully, both his cynical cheer and his routine puncturing of her self-delusions and drama. She also misses his warm, physical presence. Kathleen speaks to Jimmy as though he were her private deity, and this way she is able to articulate her passion but also her private pain and her fears about the deterioration of the body and approach toward death:

> Jimmy, I want to make love with this man all day every day forever and he feels the same about me.
>
> There was silence from Jimmy.
>
> Jimmy, I'm fifty. Two of my bottom teeth are wobbling. Coffee gives me heartburn. I dye my hair. Even if a few men want me when I'm going through my fifties … I won't want them. I'll sleep with anyone who asks me the same as always, but … it was ashes, Jimmy. It was lonely as hell. This is my only chance to be kept soft and warm by a true lover … All that time that I can never have back again, Jimmy! And maybe nothing, nothing till I die, if I can't have this!
>
> (p. 424)

The author readily incorporates weaknesses, mainly self-doubts, into her female protagonists. A self-deprecating humor leavens the aging love-less angst. O'Faolain also focuses on a topic rare in fiction, the subject of the passionate love affair of a middle-aged *woman*, warts and all. She does not shirk from the sagging skin or the dentures.

When, serendipitously, after getting off a ferry, Kathleen meets her lover Shay, she feels she has been given another chance at love, decades after her young experiences. She believes she has finally found a soul mate in Shay, who is equally smitten. They begin speaking in a pub, where she spots him, average looking and ordinarily dressed, by the counter. He approaches her and they end up going home to her cottage together, but he leaves in the morning, saying he is going out for orange juice, and does not return. His note explains that if he didn't leave then, he would never be able to go at all.

Thus the affair is set in motion.

Although the affair changes Kathleen's world, the author awards her a brave and difficult decision: not to wait for Shay in Ireland but rather to give him up. This taking control of her future is a move away from passivity and a triumph for the character—a message that Kathleen wants more than this second-best role out of her life. In a sense, O'Faolain evokes a coming-of-age story arising at fifty, rather than the teenage years.

O'Faolain herself is less successful at ending her own passionate years of trysts. She reveals that she tries meeting her former lover abroad, where he has retired with his wife, but he is ill, and there is no future for them. She is forced to turn around and travel home. The rapturous secret meetings belong to the past, and to memory. Rather than coming to any kind of fruition, they lead to nothing.

Almost There seems at first glance a promising, hopeful title, but, again, the final pages are in fact not promising, more a foretelling of the battles to come, in a relationship where she feels she can never be Number One, but will always be second to the daughter. Even in O'Faolain's final interview, she remains unapologetically unmaternal, ungrandmotherly, and she makes clear that she doesn't want to sit around watching a fourteen-year-old do her homework. And the gist of her second memoir is that the relationship, tugged in two directions demanding of the same man's love, does, predictably, suffer.

THE LURE OF AMERICA: CHICAGO MAY

For O'Faolain, her first move to Manhattan after the success of *My Dream of You* was a watershed because she felt she wasn't able to write fiction in Ireland, where she was told she wasn't good enough. She noted the pessimism in Ireland, while in New York City she felt the hopefulness and opportunity of America. Her second memoir gives a glimpse into her relationship with an American man.

For her next two novels, O'Faolain features America as part of the setting. She felt drawn to a place where she could remake herself, writing fiction as she said she never could in Ireland. America was a land of capped teeth and always staving off old age, looking a decade or two younger than an Irish counterpart. For the most part, O'Faolain embraced the opportunity America offered—even as she saw through its foolishness and naïveté. It was an antidote to Irish cynicism, after all. In 2005 she cohosted the Saint Patrick's Day Parade along with Frank McCourt and other Irish authors, and she could laugh off the Irish stereotypes Americans projected through that day and that event.

The Story of Chicago May (2005) interposed the author's own research into the biography of the Irishwoman May Duignan, a gangster who moved from rural Ireland to Chicago and also operated in New York and other big American cities, as well as in London and Paris. O'Faolain portrays the prostitute's life in these decades and the financial independence it granted her. Crooks and criminals, denizens of the underworld, look after each other, keeping their code. But at times they also betray each other. She describes Chicago May's failed relationship with another Irish-born criminal, Eddie Guerin, the heists they attempted, and how difficult it was for May to give up her profession even after a decade of incarceration, since she was unable to keep herself with a low-paying, regular job, especially when her identity was discovered.

The author quotes from Chicago May's own memoir to emphasize her fear of Guerin. At the same time, a Berkeley police chief, August Vollmer, comes to her rescue by suggesting that the famous May write about her adventurous life. She remains in correspondence with this patron until the end of her days. In a similar vein, O'Faolain herself had benefited several times from patronage, for example that of the doctor who helped her return to university for her last year after she had dropped out of UCD.

Chicago May had written her own autobiography, which O'Faolain quotes, but it describes events with little to no introspection. So O'Faolain conjectures and speculates upon the psychological underpinnings of the notorious character, sometimes using letters as her clues. Chicago May also spent two years in a French women's prison and ten years in an English women's prison, so there is a gritty realism to her story, reminiscent of Stephen Crane's *Maggie: A Girl of the Streets* (1893).

Chicago May's true life passion was Charley Smith, another criminal who had served time. The two were able to spend five months living together in London. With him she attempted to kill Guerin upon his release from jail, which resulted in her English incarceration. Decades pass after that, but at the end of her life, when she lay dying in America, it was he who sat by her side and cared for her.

So Chicago May, like O'Faolain, traveled back and forth seamlessly between the Old and New Worlds. At one point in the narrative, she chooses to return to visit her family in their rural Irish village—the family she had stolen from and run away from at eighteen—despite her notoriety as a lady of the night. But O'Faolain remarks that there is no real going home for May. Her new life has little in common with the Ireland she has sailed away from, with its small-town concerns. Chicago May is a woman at once familiar with police and judges, anonymous men in parks, and fellow jailbirds and criminals.

Similarly, at the end of her life there is no real epiphany, moral or otherwise, for May. But she has survived life on her own terms and, like O'Faolain, in advanced middle age, she becomes an author for the first time. O'Faolain helps the reader to imagine a soul for her, through her fears and her triumphs. And at the end of her life, her truest friendship, curiously, is with a Berkeley police chief, who encourages her to write and with whom she faithfully corresponds as she herself tries to reimagine a life for herself.

Chicago May died on May 30, 1929, from complications of an operation on her fallopian tubes. She had been hospitalized for several weeks in Philadelphia, and she died on the day she was supposed to marry Smith. She had never possessed a home of her own. O'Faolain puts May's life in the context of a deeply embedded fear of sexuality in Ireland:

> At the time May died, and for at least another half-century, Ireland was fully in the grip of an institutionalized fear of women; that is, of sexuality. One Irish male in fifty, then, was a Catholic priest: three-quarters of all men between twenty-five and thirty-four were single; there had been a fourfold increase in a decade in admissions of men to mental hospitals, and Ireland had the lowest birth rate in Europe. The clergy worked obsessively at controlling sexuality by diktat and by propagating disgust. In my lifetime, little girls were not allowed to participate in athletics because they would have had to change their clothes near boys.
>
> (pp. 294–295)

O'Faolain recounts that in an orphanage near May's locality in the 1960s, thirty-five abandoned babies housed in a convent died in a fire, one reason being that the nuns didn't want the firemen to see themselves or the girl children in their night attire. In 1984, again in the vicinity, a teenage girl died trying to deliver her baby alone, using nail scissors. Both she and the full-term baby died.

O'Faolain suggests that times have not changed nearly as much as we would like to believe. "These examples of the deformed attitude to the female body that was the result of poverty, ignorance, and the influence of a celibate clergy could be multiplied by hundreds and even thousands of examples, great and small" (p. 296).

Thus the escape from this fear of sexuality, which might prove lethal to body and soul, could manifest itself as an Irish- or any woman's journey to America, especially in the past but even today. With May, the immigrant becomes a prostitute and petty thief, but also a memoirist. While she shows initial loyalty to Guerin by serving time in a French jail, her defining qualities become reinvention and survival; she even experiences a modicum of long lost love from Smith at the poignant end of her life.

FRIENDSHIP AND SOLITUDE

The bittersweet ties between women in O'Faolain's literature seem to involve more emotional ups and downs than the relationships between protagonists and male friends, particularly gay male friends. In *Best Love, Rosie,* O'Faolain describes the problematic but essentially loving relationship between Rosie and the aunt who raised her, Marinda—or as she is called, Min. Min, to Rosie's chagrin, does not behave as a sixty-nine-year-old ought, and instead, as a free spirit, she absconds to America and stays there, making her way around the country working at cleaning or laundering, with a Mexican immigrant friend. Min is a radical aunt whose own life had been subjugated to the rearing of her dead sister's children since the age of fifteen, and at last she is able to realize her own hopes and dreams of emigrating, traveling about, and generally living her life for herself. She crows, over the phone to Ireland, that she has never been happier.

By contrast, despite her career, men occupied center stage in Rosie's life, and she herself notices the patterns: how her sense of well-being would depend on how her love relationship at the time was faring. At the time of the writing of her first memoir, at age fifty-five, O'Faolain significantly sees her plight as nearly chronic and permanent. Although she allowed for occasional half-hearted glimpses of hope that she might find a meaningful sexual relationship as well as companionship with somebody, she continued to view her advanced middle age as a liability.

When relationships are not center stage in her work, it is often the changes in her own body that take the spotlight. O'Faolain does not shirk from cataloging the shocking minor changes that all add up to her apparent physical demotion or degradation in the eyes of men, and thus in her own eyes: the graying of the eyebrows, the plumping of the stomach, looser skin at the face, neck, and arms. She experiences a disgust at witnessing some sexual attraction between older couples. She is bewildered to find that she no longer attracts the lingering glances of men; similarly, in *Best Love, Rosie*, the protagonist notes that when she walks into the bar, the men glance up into the mirror and then settle back down to their drinks, as if she were not worth bothering with—she is only another invisible, older woman. Beneath notice. Unremarkable. The character finds herself unable to accept this new reality.

Though muted at times, much of the underlying pathos, even agony, in O'Faolain's works comes from struggling to come to terms with her new and undefined place in society, when she is no longer viewed as a sexual being. This is ironic, since her career in journalism is intellectual and culturally stimulating, and the Western feminist viewpoint is that this ought to give her self-esteem and fulfillment. But in these personal diaries, the work, no matter how prestigious or famous, falls into the background. It never seems to impact her general happiness—except, notably, for the widely flung travel assignments the jobs afford O'Faolain.

Like Kathleen DeBurca and Marianne Talbot, Chicago May and Rosie are presented as essentially solitary characters. Kathleen does make friends with the town librarian who helps her research the time period and people: Miss Leech never married, is proud and well-loved in the place, and fiercely independent; at the end of the novel, she is dying of cancer. And Rosie does make space in her life for friends, although she seems to treasure the dog she rescues just as deeply. Rosie's closest link is to her mother figure, Min, the aunt who has looked after her since she was a baby, but now the aunt, who decided in her sixties to abscond to America, has found her own inner vagabond. In her poverty, she is gleeful at finally having the freedom to experience the traveling life Rosie always had. They share intermittent phone calls.

Meanwhile Rosie's closest e-mail friend in Seattle, a friend from her youth who it turns out is gay and a grandfather, Markey, also becomes a confidante. They share a mission, to write a self-help book about surviving middle age, and Rosie is to come up with ten tips. The humor is probably more evident here than in any of O'Faolain's works, as her grimness and morbidity, quoting Rainer Maria Rilke for example, elicit groans from her Americanized friend on the other side of the Atlantic. No death! Americans don't like death! He teasingly, but sincerely, warns her to keep it cheerful and positive if she wants to sell her little book in the United States. The glib results are entertaining, and create a lighter mood than the other work, perhaps also because there is almost no explicit historical research apparent.

With her trademark clinical observations trained on her own life experience, O'Faolain notes that she had a man's career—university professor, television producer and broadcast journalist, newspaper reporter—but in her personal life fell prey to her mother's muted and unfulfilled desire for passion, and passionate companionship. Fulfillment may be proximal but it seems an ever-moving line.

CONCLUSION

Although many have commented on O'Faolain's fierce intellect, others have failed to give equal credence to her fierceness of heart, and determination and talent for survival in a world where she often felt alone.

Her work not so quietly asks whether, in her fifties and sixties, she must give up all hope of romance or companionship. Where did I go wrong? Will I never find love? Will anyone out there have me? These recur as the vital and universal questions, articulated multiple ways as O'Faolain sorts out the dark folds of her past and deliberately sets aside ego for more scouring honesty—eyes wide open, to examine a life.

But it is not only the cri de coeur against merciless time and aging that marks O'Faolain's literature, although this theme sometimes seems to eclipse the others in its rising. Equally, she celebrates the life spirit that rages toward the light. The narrative role is always to celebrate, often through humor, the beauty and joy that life brings: whether through friends and family, or nature and animals, particularly the dogs and cats on which she poured much of her affection. The end of her final novel, *Best Love, Rosie,* swings upward, reflecting that "love is at the centre. Remember that, now that you have to start again … Loving, and being loved, comes in infinite

shapes and patterns. Who knows what it will look like next time? Remember that" (p. 446).

Selected Bibliography

WORKS OF NUALA O'FAOLAIN

MEMOIR
Are You Somebody: The Accidental Memoir of a Dublin Woman. New York: Henry Holt, 1996. (Published in Ireland as *Are You Somebody? The Life and Times of Nuala O'Faolain.* Dublin: New Island, 1996.)
Almost There: The Onward Journey of a Dublin Woman. New York: Riverhead, 2003.

NOVELS
My Dream of You. New York: Riverhead, 2001.
Best Love, Rosie. Dublin: New Island, 2009. London: Arcadia, 2009.

OTHER WORK
The Story of Chicago May. New York: Riverhead, 2005. (History with commentary.)
"The Times That Were in It." *Michael Hartnett Memorial Lectures,* 2007; http://www.eigsemichaelhartnett.ie/michael-hartnett-memorial-lectures.html. (Lecture.)
A Radiant Life: The Selected Journalism of Nuala O'Faolain. London and New York: Abrams, 2011. (Journalism.)

CRITICAL AND BIOGRAPHICAL STUDIES
Caldwell, June. "She Gave a Voice to Irish Women." *Guardian,* May 13, 2008, section G2, p. 18.
Edwards, Bob. "*Morning Edition* Interview with Nuala O'Faolain." *National Public Radio,* March 14, 2001 (http://www.npr.org/programs/morning/features/2001/mar/010314.ofaolain.html).
Finucane, Marian. "Nuala O'Faolain Interview: 'I don't want more time. As soon as I heard I was going to die, the goodness went from life.'" *Independent.ie,* April 13, 2008 (http://www.independent.ie/national-news/nuala-o-faolain-interview-lsquoi-donrsquot-want-more-time-as-soon-as-i-heard-i-was-going-to-die-the-goodness-went-from-lifersquo-1346206.html).
Merkin, Daphne. "A Thorny Irish Rose." *New York Times,* February 18, 2001, pp. 22–25 (http://www.nytimes.com/2001/02/18/magazine/a-thorny-irish-rose.html?scp=1&sq=Merkin,%20Daphne.%20%E2%80%9CA%20Thorny%20Irish%20Rose&st=cse).

Nolan, Yvonne. "The Girl of Her Dreams." *Publishers Weekly,* March 12, 2001 (http://www.publishersweekly.com/pw/print/20010312/26167-the-girl-of-her-dreams-.html).

Tóibín, Colm. Review of *Are You Somebody*. *Times Literary Supplement*, November 29, 1996, p. 15.

Wachtel, Eleanor. Canadian Broadcasting Company radio interview with Nuala O'Faolain. *Writers and Company* (http://podcast.cbc.ca/mp3/writersandco_20090812_18181.mp3), 2003.

"Writer Nuala O'Faolain Dies." *RTE Ten*, May 10, 2008 (http://www.rte.ie/ten/2008/0510/ofaolainn.html).

PHILIPPA PEARCE

(1920—2006)

Abby Mims

As one of the most beloved children's writers of the late twentieth century, Philippa Pearce wrote fiction that has touched generations of children and adults alike. She is known for helping to shape what is considered the "golden age" of British children's literature and is widely recognized for her love of children and reverence for the power of their imaginations. Pearce's work builds from her high respect for her audience, and as a result, she works with themes often avoided by other children's writers, such as bullying relatives, disappointment, poverty, fear of the old and infirm, and the reality of our own mortality. Never one to water down reality, she is not known for traditional happy endings; instead she captures the realistic moments that occur during the ups and downs of childhood. In tackling these more difficult topics, she often plays with the patterns of growth and transformation in her stories, focusing particularly on the journey from childhood to adulthood. Within this journey is the inevitability of change and how time passes differently as we grow older. Much of her skill lies in an ability to capture the intense emotions of childhood on the page, with its oft-heightened perceptions and dramatics.

Her most famous work is *Tom's Midnight Garden* (1958), the winner of the Carnegie Medal in 1959, a young adult novel that was later adapted for radio, stage, and the movie screen. In writing this book, Pearce and the time-traveling Tom Long became to previous generations of children what J. K. Rowling and Harry Potter are to more recent ones. In this magical novel, Pearce wanted foremost to explore the concept of adults having once been children. In doing so, she gives Tom a mystical garden that only he can travel to, where he watches a child his own age grow up quickly, over a period of several days. When he meets her again in his "real" life, she is an old woman, yet he realizes this does not change the heart of their friendship. Pearce returns to relationships between the young and the old again and again in her work, highlighting the gap of understanding that universally exists. Many of her adult characters are terrible at relating to the young people around them, while her child protagonists are often shown the wisdom of adults when they least expect it.

Pearce is also skilled at creating vivid, three-dimensional characters in her work. Her heroes and heroines are written as relatable, flesh-and-blood people, often struggling with their own wants and desires as they learn the lessons inherent in growing up. From a boy who desperately dreams of a dog of his own, whose rich fantasy world leads him to disaster in *A Dog So Small* (1962), to a girl who befriends a talking mole only to have to sacrifice their friendship in order to secure his freedom in *The Little Gentleman* (2004), to a young woman who is determined to find out the truth about her father's death and inadvertently exposes years of family secrets in *The Way to Sattin Shore* (1983). Pearce's solutions to her stories' dilemmas are never simple, never pandering, and never black and white; she allows her protagonists to live in the shades of gray that reflect real life.

Many critics note the sophistication of Pearce's writing for a younger audience, as she incorporates a plethora of symbols and metaphors to symbolize the process of become a young adult. A pinecone stands in for the loss a child suffers when his parents divorce; a rope swing encompasses the major anxieties of childhood; an imaginary dog forces a boy to leave his childhood behind. In turn, setting figures prominently in her works, often functioning as a character unto itself. Pearce famously used both the English countryside and the mill house of her own childhood as backdrops for *Minnow on the Say* (1955) and *Tom's Midnight Garden*, while *The Way to Sattin Shore* was inspired by her time living near the Suffolk Estuary. Rivers and other bodies of water are nearly ubiquitous in her novels, representing to Pearce the very current of life itself, forever moving forward, no matter the events that befall our lives. She also very much uses her own experiences and that of her family in her stories, and she wrote many of her books with her daughter Sally in mind, and later, her two grandsons.

Perhaps it is these personal aspects of her fiction that help her connect with such a wide audience of readers, but Pearce also possesses a keen understanding of human nature, which shines through all her works. Known to have a soft, yet deliberate manner, she also had strong opinions about the minds and hearts of children, preferring to talk to them over adults most of the time. She understood them on a level that most adults do not; she was quoted as having said, "People think how carefree children are. Children have different cares, and cares particularly which they don't want to articulate" (Nettell, p. 29). It is this attitude that allowed her to delight children of all ages with her novels, short stories, and picture books for nearly five decades, until her death at the age of eighty-six, in 2006.

BIOGRAPHY

Philippa Pearce was born on January 23, 1920, the youngest of four. She grew up in Great Shelford, a village in Cambridgeshire near the upper edges of the River Cam. Her father was a flour miller, as his father before him had been, and Pearce's father raised his family in the Mill House just as he had been raised. The house was built in the nineteenth century next door to the mill itself, and the sprawling countryside around it provided a childhood full of outdoor adventures. In the afterword to *Minnow on the Say* she writes, "We had a wonderful place to grow up in, to love ... We swam in the river, fished (with worms), boated, and—in a hard winter—

skated on flooded water-meadows" (p. 242). And indeed, the river, the mill, the meadows, and the sprawling landscapes of the English countryside recur in Pearce's books, her settings often sketched as if directly from her memories.

Pearce started elementary school later than most, at the age of nine, due to nephritis, a kidney disease. As a result, her early childhood was spent alone, reading books and writing. In particular, she was struck by the story of *Black Beauty*, and after reading it, she became a lifelong vegetarian, maintaining a passion for the humane treatment of animals. She later attended the Perse School for Girls, where she was awarded a scholarship to study English and history at Girton College in Cambridge. Although all three of her siblings earned scholarships to universities, Pearce was the first of her family to complete higher education. Initially, she majored in English, but switched to history before graduation. Until she reached the university, she attended Baptist church services with her mother, and was a Noncornformist. However, her exposure at Girton caused her to lose her faith and also break her vow of abstinence.

World War II was still under way when Pearce finished her formal education, graduating with a degree in history in 1944. Instead of joining the military, she became a civil servant for the Board of Trade and Ministry of Information. She worked there until the end of the war, before moving on to the BBC Radio Schools Broadcasting Department. She spent the next thirteen years at the BBC, writing, adapting, and producing scripts. She would later comment that her training in broadcasting served her writing well, given the word limits and pared-down style that radio demanded. It never occurred to Pearce to write fiction until the summer of 1951, when she was confined to the hospital while suffering from tuberculosis. During her convalescence, she wrote down every aspect she could recall of her favorite childhood canoe trip, and these recollections were the basis for her first novel, *Minnow on the Say*. In the late 1950s, her family had to sell the Mill House, and Pearce was desperate to record every bit of it on the page. Imagining that the land around it would most likely be broken into parcels and developed, she took copious notes on the house and its surrounding walled gardens, which three generations of her family had enjoyed as children. These documents, along with stories remembered and adapted from her father's childhood, formed the novel *Tom's Midnight Garden*, which won the Carnegie Medal in 1959. (*Minnow on the Say* had earlier been a runner-up for the medal.)

After these early publishing successes, in 1959, Pearce moved on from the BBC in the hopes of learning more about children's education. She had edited and adapted a variety of children's books for the radio, works from the likes of Rosemary Sutcliff and Clive King, and as a result, she developed strong theories regarding children's literature. Pearce made no secret of the fact that she abhorred young adult fiction with a moral message. She respected the intelligence of those who read her work, and their innate sensibilities, saying, "Children have never taken to improvement through books. They have a healthy instinct for inattention, especially when they detect the unpalatable flavour of Truth in what should be a delightful tissue of lies. … [Messages] kill stories stone dead" ("Obituaries," *Telegraph*, December 27, 2006).

In this spirit, she took an editorial post with the Clarendon Press for a few years, later becoming a children's book editor with André Deutsch. She also continued to write and produce radio for both children and adults, including a weekly radio program, "The World of Books." Despite her early literary successes, the years after *Tom's Midnight Garden* were plagued with difficulty. Her next book, *A Dog So Small*, was turned down by Oxford University Press for being too dark and melancholy. It was eventually published by Kestrel Penguin in 1962 and became a critical success. It was lauded for its tender portrayal of a lonely child who eventually lets go of his rich fantasy life in order to embrace reality.

During this time, Pearce met and married Martin Christie, a fruit grower who had been a Japanese prisoner of war. Tragically, Christie died two years later, shortly after the birth of their daughter, Sally. Raising the child alone took a toll on Pearce's writing, as she no longer had the time she once had to write. However, she started her life anew a few years later and relocated to London with her daughter. In 1968, Pearce collaborated on writing the childhood memoirs of Major Sir Brian Fairfax-Lucy, titled *The Children of the House* (1968). The book focuses on his parents, a pair of impoverished aristocrats who are struggling to maintain their quality of life and in consequence sacrifice the unity of their family. Their children are left isolated and without love, and they turn to the household servants for guidance and affection. The book met with positive reviews, the *New York Times* writing, "The simplicity, truth and lack of emphasis in this story are virtually Chekhovian, and it is a stouthearted reader who will not weep" (B.W.).

During the 1970s, Pearce produced several volumes of new work, if at a much slower pace than she was accustomed to. She focused on short fiction, and published two collections for children, *The Elm Street Lot* (1969) and *What the Neighbours Did* (1972). Both books were recognized for their uncanny ability to view the world through the eyes of children with great humor, and without a trace of condescension. Her next work, *The Battle of Bubble and Squeak* (1978), a close-to-home account of a family's battle with a pair of unruly gerbils, won Pearce the Children's Whitbread Award in the year of its publication.

Eventually, Pearce returned to the country and lived in a small cottage built by her grandfather near the Mill House. She and Sally had plenty of company there, housing a small collection of animals that included hens, goats, a pony, a dog, and a cat. There, into the 1980s and 1990s, she continued to craft tales that incorporated aspects of her life. She diverged somewhat from her usual subject matter in 1983, when she published *The Way to Sattin Shore*, another runner-up for the Carnegie Medal. The novel is deeply psychological, a dark exploration of a daughter's attempt to understand her father's mysterious death. In 1989, Pearce and Brian Fairfax-Lucy published a rewritten version of *The Children of the House*, retitled *The Children of Charlecote*.

It was several years before Pearce produced another novel for children, but in the interim years she published dozens of stories, including *Lion at School and Other Stories* (1985), *Who's Afraid? and Other Strange Stories* (1986), *Here Comes Tod!* (1992), and *The Rope and Other Stories* (2000). In 2004, she published *The Little Gentleman*, the tale of the relationship between a little girl and a mole, heralded for its deft exploration of the fleeting nature of childhood, the inevitability of death, and the freedom inherent in real love. Her final book, *A Finder's Magic*, inspired by her two young grandsons, was published posthumously in 2008.

YOUNG ADULT NOVELS

Pearce's first novel, *Minnow on the Say* (1955), is based around a memorable canoe trip she herself went on as a child. Set in England on the River Say in the 1930s, the tale focuses on two twelve-year-old boys, their unlikely friendship, and a search for buried treasure. The story is told through the perspective of David Moss, the middle child of a housewife and a bus driver, who finds an abandoned canoe near his father's landing on the river. His father tells him he cannot keep the canoe; he must go looking for its owner. The owner, twelve-year-old Adam Codling, finds David first and accuses him of stealing it; once this misunderstanding is resolved, it's revealed that Adam is a very poor orphan, being raised by his aunt in his grandfather's house. They are all living on his grandfather's meager pension, and because of their financial situation, Adam may be sent to live with distant cousins in Birmingham.

Adam goes on to confide to David that at one time, the Codlings possessed a fortune, part of which, rumor has it, is buried along the River Say. The only clue to its location is a four-line poem, which has taunted the Codlings since the Tudor days, and so the two boys embark on a hunt for this treasure in the hopes of keeping Adam's family intact. They shortly christen their canoe *The Minnow* and begin a summer of treasure hunting, with the river and its landscape serving as a stunningly beautiful backdrop.

While the plot may sound somewhat formulaic, Pearce is praised for providing believable characters, along with suspense and twists of fate that prove surprising. One of Pearce's greatest gifts is for creating rich, complex characters in her stories, especially children. *Minnow on the Say* is no exception, as the loyal David is contrasted against the more impulsive Adam, and the adults also play important roles in the book's narrative arc. Pearce doesn't shy away from deeper themes here, writing an especially poignant portrait of Adam's grandfather, a man paralyzed by grief after losing his only son in the Great War. In his advanced age and confusion, he doesn't realize that the boy who lives with him isn't his son, but is his grandson. Pearce writes,

> Before Mr. Codling's eyes, [the moon] brought the vision of a moonshine-ghostly boy: Adam was no longer a stranger with red hair, but a familiar-seeming boy with a head silver-fair—a boy as fair as John Codling had been. ... "John," he called softly and warmly, "John!".... Joy made his voice ring out, loud and strong, as it had not sounded for many years.
>
> (pp. 130–131)

Tragedy seems to follow this family, as Adam's mother died soon after his father, as a result of her own grief; his grandfather dies at the end of the previous scene. His Aunt Dinah leads the family with her strength, yet she too seems resigned that they will never recover the ancient family fortune. However, in true Pearce form, the boys' adventures become about more than finding buried treasure, and the book remains an exploration of friendship and the realities of poverty, mourning, and greed. It also established what would be for Pearce a long pattern of incorporating the emotional and physical landscape of her life into her stories.

Pearce's second novel, *Tom's Midnight Garden* (1958), has been heralded as one of the best children's books of the twentieth century. It is widely recognized as one of the most complex novels ever written for young adults, and it remains a gorgeously well-written fantasy, which encompasses the universal themes of growth, transformation, and childhood rites of passage.

The story begins when Tom is sent to live for the summer of 1958 with his relatives, Aunt Gwen and Uncle Alan, who live in a flat that was once part of a grand mansion. His parents send him away for fear that he will catch the measles from his brother. Tom is anything but happy about this decision, resentful that he will miss months of playing with his sibling in their beloved backyard. His aunt and uncle have no children and therefore have a hard time understanding how to relate to Tom; because he might be contagious they also keep him inside at all times. As a result, he is lonely, isolated, and bored from the very first days of his convalescence, and also disappointed that the flat doesn't have a yard to play in when he recovers. Given his lack of physical activity, he does not sleep well at night and often lies awake listening to the sound of the grandfather clock in the foyer. After several evenings of waking up in the middle of the night, Tom ventures downstairs, only to hear the clock strike thirteen. As this happens, the mansion is magically transformed to its former glory, complete with a lush and beautiful garden just outside the back door.

When Tom ventures into the garden, he sees it is full of people from the 1890s, but they are ghostly in appearance, and they either ignore him or pass right through him. Eventually, he meets a young girl named Hatty, an orphan who lives with her oppressive aunt, indifferent cousins, and a gardener named Abel, the latter of whom fears Tom is some kind of evil spirit. Tom and Hatty become friends, yet each night he visits her she is a different age—sometimes older, sometimes younger, but always changed. Tom remains the same age, however, which causes within him a crisis of sorts. Is any of his experience real, or is it all a dream? Is Hatty a ghost or is he? With all these questions in mind, and the length of his stay at the house growing shorter, Tom continues to visit the garden as part of an existential quest. As he travels there night after night, Pearce vividly establishes this particular dream world that belongs exclusively to children. She writes,

> There is a time, between night and day, when landscapes sleep. Only the earliest riser sees that hour; or the all-night traveller, letting up the blind of his railway-carriage window, will look out on a rushing landscape of stillness, in which trees and bushes and plants stand immobile and breathless in sleep—wrapped in sleep, as the traveller himself wrapped his body in his great-coat or his rug the night before.

> This grey, still hour before morning was the time in which Tom walked into his garden.

(p. 36)

His friendship with Hatty deepens with each encounter, until the night when Hatty appears much older than Tom, at age nineteen and distracted by a suitor her own age. She effectively ignores Tom, and he leaves the garden confused and hurt. When he returns to the garden the following night, both it and Hatty have disappeared. Tom is heartbroken, knowing he will soon return to his family and never have another chance to find her. The next day, just as he is about to depart, his relatives implore him to pay a visit to the elderly landlady who lives upstairs, Mrs. Bartholomew. Within their conversation, she reveals to Tom that she is Hatty, grown old, and reassures him their adventures in the garden did indeed take place. Unlike his aunt and uncle and perhaps his own parents, she speaks to him with a depth and sensitivity he hasn't experienced with other adults. The book ends several years later, when Tom is an adult and has returned to the flat where he experienced the magic garden. In doing so, he finds the tree where he and Hatty carved their initials, leaving him with no choice but to embrace all that is mysterious and unexplained in life.

Pearce uses many symbols throughout the book, particularly in terms of the notion of time. The grandfather clock functions most pervasively in this sense, and we are immediately alerted to it on the book's first few pages. It is a forbidden object (it belongs to Mrs. Bartholomew, and Tom is told not to touch it), yet the family depends on it to keep time in the flat, although it rarely strikes the right hour. It also serves as Tom's only strange company the few first nights in the flat. Alone and unable to sleep, he focuses on the sounds it makes: "Yes, you could hear it striking, very distinctly; you could count the strokes. Tom counted them, and smiled condescendingly: the clock was wrong again in its striking—senselessly wrong" (p. 8).

Pearce lends a slightly ominous quality to the clock's errant striking, and to the clock itself, as the inscription on its face reads "Time No Longer," which is taken from the Book of Revelations. However, the clock also provides Tom's passage to the garden, to a land of childhood innocence. It seems that Pearce means for the grandfather clock to speak for the contrary nature of time, its elusiveness as well as the exacting nature inherent in timekeeping. Perhaps, too, the clock is keeping time on how long children can remain pure and innocent, as Tom's garden contains several allusions to the Garden of Eden. This secret paradise not only contains a gardener named Abel (assumed by Tom to have a brother named Cain), but the garden itself disappears once Hatty reaches adulthood, seeming to signify the loss of innocence that naturally follows one's journey out of childhood.

Pearce also uses the narrative to play with the vast differences in how children and adults view time. Tom notices that no time seems to pass while he is in the garden, and time literally stands still in his real life when he is there; the grandfather clock shows the same time when he enters the garden as when he leaves it. This is a statement on the whole of childhood, given that children have little to no sense of time until a certain age, and only then does the adult world encroach and force them to live by the clock. Curious about the nature of time, Tom asks his uncle to explain the concept to him. In typical adult fashion, his uncle diagrams time in a linear way, and Tom doesn't understand. To compensate, Tom uses his own abstract logic to make sense of what happens to him in the garden. He ponders his uncle's shortsightedness, noting that his relative "had taken for granted that there were twenty-four hours in a day—twice twelve hours. But suppose, instead, there were twice thirteen? … He could be in bed for ten hours and still have an hour to spare—an hour of freedom" (pp. 15–16).

Pearce is nearly always juxtaposing the young and the old in her work, and Tom's relationship with his uncle stands in contrast to the connection he feels with Mrs. Bartholomew. Their conversation bridges the gap between young and old, as she speaks to him with much more depth and sensitivity than the other adults around him. When he leaves her, he hugs her as if she were the younger version of herself. Tom is transcending time again with the discovery that their friendship exists both in the past and the present, no matter how old Hatty has grown. Pearce appears to be telling the reader that age doesn't separate us, our attitudes and preconceived notions do.

In all, *Tom's Midnight Garden* is a touching, suspenseful story of mystery and magic wrapped around the experience of making the first steps from child to adult. It seems that as Tom matures in the narrative, so does the complexity of Pearce's prose, as if she expects her reader to develop right alongside her protagonist. In the same vein, many reviewers have noted that Pearce does not rely on the "cheap tricks" of some mystery writers—using the wind in the trees to explain away the sounds of a ghost in the attic, for example. She strives instead to provide the reader with a resolution that is satisfyingly complex, remaining intensely concerned with preserving the "reality" of the fantasy she has created. In this novel in particular, Pearce sets up clear rules in terms of what can and cannot happen to Tom in the magical garden, so the reader is all the more willing to play along. This kind of literary finesse is what has caused so many young readers to identify with Tom, as he is just like any other child: a bit bored, a tiny bit lonely, and constantly longing for adventure.

Pearce's next book, *A Dog So Small* (1962), is a darker take on childhood, one that was initially rejected by publishers for being "too depressing" for children. The protagonist of the story, Ben, thinks of nothing but dogs, all day and all night: large breeds, small breeds, and everything in between. It is his greatest wish to have a dog of his own, although he knows how impractical this is, as he and his family live in London. However, hope arrives in the form of his grandfather, who promises him one for his birthday. We meet Ben on this very disappointing morning, just as he receives not a real dog, but a placard of a Chihuahua named Chiquito, stitched in wool. Feeling cheated and angry upon receiving this gift, Ben vows to never visit his grandparents again.

Of course Ben does visit them again, and when he does, Chiquito suddenly comes to life in his mind as a fearless companion of sorts, one who can lead him on all kinds of adventures. At first, they embark on these experiences only in his dreams, as the dog only comes to life when Ben's eyes are closed. As time goes on, however, Ben retreats into their world by covering his eyes, and he begins to prefer his imagination to reality. Eventually, this game leads Ben to wander into a busy street with his eyes closed, and a car hits him. Seriously injured, he is sent to live with his grandparents to recuperate. While there he discovers that his grandparent's elderly dog, Tilly, is pregnant, and he will be taking a puppy home with him. Unfortunately, Ben's expectations are that the dog will be just like Chiquito, and he is surprised and crestfallen when the puppy has a personality entirely its own. Although Ben contemplates getting rid of the dog before he goes home, they eventually form a lasting bond.

In this short character study, Pearce explores many of the negative emotions children must experience in order to mature and grow: first and foremost, that fantasy can be taken too far, and that the land of make-believe must be sacrificed in order for one to become an adult. She also lays bare the reality that sometimes adults promise things they can't deliver, and that often, when a person receives what they have been longing for, it may bring with it a mixed bag of unrealistic expectations and disappointment.

In Pearce's next book, a lively battle is wrought between two gerbils and a family, the animals seemingly winning at every turn. Pearce wrote the story specifically for her daughter, Sally, and admits that most everything she chronicles in *The Battle of Bubble and Squeak* (1978) happened in her own life: gnawed curtains, family strife, and predatory neighbor cats. Pearce begins by giving us Alice Sparrow, a widowed mother of three who discovers in the middle of the night that her son Sid has procured a pair of gerbils from a boy at school. Although she tells Sid in no uncertain terms that his stepfather will return the animals, she wrestles with the decision. Pearce provides clear insight into her mindset, as Alice sits drinking tea in the darkness and

thinking. "She didn't like animals. … [the children] were like their father. … No doubt, if he had lived, the house would have swarmed with cats, dogs, rabbits, guinea pigs, hamsters, budgerigars, and canaries in yellow clouds" (p. 10).

Sid is upset enough at this that he wishes for the house to explode and then his own death, but he settles on smashing a bowl of bacon fat on the kitchen floor after his parents have gone to work. Unexpectedly, his stepfather brings the gerbils back to the house that night, as Sid is guiltily cleaning up his mess. Once Alice realizes the gerbils might not be going anywhere, she realizes that the battle is on between her and these furry creatures. She makes many attempts to get rid of them, and when she seemingly succeeds, Sid runs away for the afternoon. In a particularly poignant scene, Sid's stepfather finds him in the woods near their house and confides that he had mice growing up; he promises to buy Sid more gerbils. Luckily for Sid, the gerbils are returned the next day, courtesy of a mother much like Mrs. Sparrow. In the end, the entire family has become attached to Bubble and Squeak, with Mr. Sparrow even going so far as to bring a few mice home to keep them company.

In a realistic and touching manner, Pearce gets to the heart of the conflict within a family and the various compromises that must be made in order to maintain balance within a household. *The Battle of Bubble and Squeak* was successfully received by both readers and critics, going on to win the 1978 Whitbread Award.

Pearce's writing took a darker, and some critics say less successful, turn in her 1983 novel *The Way to Sattin Shore*. The protagonist of the story is Kate Tantor, who must journey through the secrets of her family in order to unravel the truth about her father's mysterious death. Kate is a reflective ten-year-old, who has always been told that her father drowned on the day she was born. She lives with her mother and grandmother in a peaceful, ordinary home, although her grandmother rules the household in a stern and quiet way. In turn, Kate has learned not to question them about her father's past, but she is left no choice when a letter arrives that hints he might still be alive. When she presses her mother and grandmother for answers, they refuse to provide them. In order find the answers she needs, Kate travels a few towns away to the Sattin Shore, where the rest of the Tantors live.

At the heart of this novel is a gruesome family tragedy, covered up for many years. Kate eventually learns it was her Uncle Bob who died, not her father. Her father, Frank, tried to save Bob from drowning, but he left him too close to the incoming tide when he went for help, and Bob drowned on the Sattin Shore in six inches of water. Since the brothers had not gotten along well and had fought over Kate's mother in the past, rumors began to circulate that Frank had always wanted Bob dead. When the body is misidentified as Frank's, and it's assumed both brothers have died, he and his wife's family decide that he should leave the village in order to protect his wife and child. Frank agrees, given his difficult relationship with his mother-in-law and the sense that these rumors would eventually ruin his marriage. Once the truth is revealed, Kate goes straight to the heart of the matter, speaking the truth of so many families. Pearce writes, "Such a muddle! Such a mess! Everybody hating everybody else … Everybody afraid … Everybody pretending what isn't true" (p. 133).

Pearce does provide us with a hard-won happy ending, however, with scrappy Kate inspiring in her father the courage to return home. Kate has a powerful moment of insight about their relation to one another while she watches him with her mother. Pearce affords her the clarity of an adult as she writes, "And there was her father looking at her … It seemed only now that she had time to look at him long and carefully and think: So this is my father. I am partly like him; I am partly him" (p. 170).

Deftly written, Pearce's novel delves deep into the emotional pains and secrets that often hold families together and can often tear them apart. Kate's journey is at once tender and touching and her character arc gains power as Kate's understanding of the world widens and matures.

With her next novel, Pearce once again uses everyday settings as a place where unexpected magic can happen. *The Little Gentleman* (2004) tells the story of Mr. Franklin, a retired school-master who is injured in a fall. He asks his housekeeper's daughter, Bets, to do him an odd favor; she is to go out to the meadow and read out loud from a text about earthworms, written by none other than Charles Darwin. As she reads, a mole appears in front of her and casually begins discussing his experiences with earthworms. He prattles on about how he delights in eating them and details the special larder he keeps for their storage underground. Bets is surprised, but not alarmed, and she continues to read to and chat with this "little gentleman" daily, reporting back their conversations to Mr. Franklin.

Soon after meeting, Bets and the little gentleman form a bond of trust, as he declares he will no longer speak to Mr. Franklin. (While Mr. Franklin and the mole have spoken before, the mole is aware that what Mr. Franklin would like most is to capture him and keep him caged for his own entertainment.) He requests she continue to read to him, specifically the poems of Alfred, Lord Tennyson. Through their daily meetings, it is revealed that a spell was cast on the mole nearly 250 years before that both made him immortal and able to speak. He is also responsible for creating the divot in the hill over which King James III's horse stumbled, causing the king's death. The mole was later taken to Scotland as a kind of talisman for the cause, but once the movement collapsed, his goal was to return home. After much digging and a few centuries, he has returned to Mr. Franklin's meadow.

As their friendship deepens, the mole confides in Bets that his greatest sadness is in regard to his immortality; all his friends eventually leave him. After much discussion, he also tells her that there is a spell she could conduct that would return him to his natural state, although he warns her that this would be the end of their friendship, as moles detest human beings. In a gesture of true friendship, Bets offers to weave this magic regardless, if it means the little gentleman will be happy.

Before she does this, though, Pearce deepens the nature of the story by giving the mole the ability to shrink Bets and make her part mole, so that she is able to follow him into his underground world. Pearce describes Bets's intense experience in this dark place, which appears to read as her first awareness that her life, unlike the mole's, will not continue forever. Pearce writes,

> She followed, but she was often lingering like a traveler in a strange land, wanting to miss nothing: the layers of curious smells, none of them offensive to a girl who was also part mole; the heavy silence and then the minute sounds of movement; the feel of the earth above, below, around. They were now certainly much deeper underground than they had been before.
>
> She had dawdled, and suddenly she was no longer aware of the mole ahead. That friendliness had gone. She seemed to have entered—or had it come up around her?—a kind of hollow, booming blacker-than-blackness that now filled the tunnel from side to side, from floor to top. It was like a huge wave, a high tide, an ocean that flowed around her and through her.

(p. 147)

Acting altruistically, Bets does eventually release the mole from the spell of immortality, so that he can live a normal life and be free. Inherent in this act is not only Bets's growing maturity; it is recognition of the mortality that we all must face. With this deceptively simply tale, Pearce sheds light on the transitory nature of childhood and life itself.

Pearce's final novel was published in 2008, two years after she died. The book was written in honor of her grandsons Nat and Will, and il-lustrated by their "other grandmother," Helen Craig. Reviewers and readers were intensely fond of *A Finder's Magic*, as many threads from her previous successful books appear here, most evidently magic, adventure, and the bonds of family. The book works as a mystery and a puzzle of sorts, as readers familiar with her other tales will recognize the pattern of clues she leaves behind: a boy and his real/unreal dog, minnows in a pond, a ghost on a swing, and of course, a river.

Pearce again gives readers an emotionally distressed boy, Till, who after waking from a dream receives a message from an elusive stranger about his lost dog, Bess. While standing just outside Till's garden gate, the aptly named Mr. Finder tells the boy they can find old Bess,

Till will just have to follow his lead. Mr. Finder then encourages him to cross over into Gammer's Meadow with him, but it takes Till several tries before he can pass through, as the gate gives him electric shocks each time he tries to open it. The meadow eventually leads them to Miss Gammer and Miss Mousy, two spinster sisters who live in a giant house there, and this strange hodge-podge of characters set out to find Till's beloved dog, Bess.

The search begins with some magic on the part of Mr. Finder, as, after quizzing the boy about Bess's habits, likes and dislikes, and so forth, he asks Till to retrieve one of the dog's toys. Mr. Finder embeds a message of help into the toy, which, when tossed gently at other animals, allows them to speak to Mr. Finder telepathically and answer any questions he poses. None of them are much help, aside from the heron who lets Mr. Finder know that the dog barks too much, scaring no one but annoying everyone. They then stumble upon a mole, who tells them he felt strange footsteps on the earth above him the day before. This revelation proves a red herring, as does an experiment with Miss Grammar's cat, and they must go to the spinster sisters for help. Just as Till is beginning to doubt Mr. Finder's honesty, they find the dog unexpect-edly, in the hands of another kind of "finder," one who keeps what he finds.

While it is at once a lighthearted fantasy, the book is imbued with a haunting quality that does not allow the reader to dismiss it as a simple children's story. Although the plot isn't as complex as some of Pearce's other works, the genuine nature of her characters still shines through.

SHORT STORIES

In addition to her novels, Pearce published several collections of short stories, including: *What the Neighbours Did, and Other Stories* (1972), *The Shadow-Cage, and Other Tales of the Supernatural* (1977), *The Elm Street Lot* (1969, expanded edition 1979), *Lion at School, and Other Stories* (1985), *Who's Afraid? and*

Other Strange Stories (1986), *Here Comes Tod!* (1992), and *The Rope and Other Stories* (2000). These tales range from the realistic to the supernatural, and as always seek to connect to young readers through adventure and mystery while remaining loyal to a range of childhood emotions. Although many of her stories contain elements of the supernatural, Pearce simultaneously keeps one foot in realism while capturing the sense of the mysterious, the unknown, and the unsaid in the everyday. Much as she does in her novels, in these pieces she combines hard-to-forget characters with an innate sense of timing and tension, providing both entertainment and satisfaction in a few short pages. Reviewers have often commented that the sophistication and adult world in many of her stories could easily lend themselves to readers of years far beyond childhood.

In *Familiar and Haunting: Collected Stories* (2002), which contains nearly all the stories she ever published, she separates the book into two sections, titling one "Stories" and the other "Hauntings." Among the stories that fall into the more realistic realm is "Fresh," a tale Penelope Farmer of the *New York Times* called "introspective, reminding me of the strangeness and intensity of Philippa Pearce's earlier work." Indeed, Pearce's eye for detail and scene-setting can be seen in the story's first two paragraphs:

> The force of water through the river gates scoured to a deep bottom; then the river shallowed again. People said the pool below the gates was very deep. Deep enough to drown in, anyway.
>
> At the bottom of the pool lived the freshwater mussels. No one had seen them there; most people would not have been particularly interested in them, anyway. But if you were poking about among the stones in the shallows below the pool, you couldn't help finding mussel shells occasionally. Sometimes one by itself; sometimes two still hinged together. Gray-blue or green gray on the outside on the inside, a faint sheen of mother-of-pearl.
>
> (p. 113)

Pearce writes this straightforward, slightly haunting piece from the point of view of a preteen boy, Dan Webster. He and his younger cousin, Laurie, are exploring the river detailed above, catching what they can in a jam jar for Laurie to bring back to London with him. When they find a live mussel, Dan tells Laurie that if they put it in the jar it won't survive until Laurie leaves for London, but Laurie is not easily thwarted. Eventually, the two agree to leave the mussel (aptly named Fresh for the freshwater it's been caught in) trapped in a makeshift habitat they've crafted out of a carton. They stick the carton in the tree roots, allowing Fresh the river water it needs to survive. Both boys are preoccupied with the mollusk for the next few days, and the night before his cousin is to leave, Dan sneaks from his house and goes to the river in a dreamlike state. He stands in the muddy banks and contemplates freeing the creature forever, but in the end he doesn't. His younger cousin is none the wiser when they return the next day and capture Fresh. Dan is gruff when Laurie thanks him for the mussel; Pearce is then giving us perhaps the first moral dilemma that Dan has wrestled with and the formation of his more adult conscience.

Her writing takes a more domestic slant in "In the Middle of the Night." The story details the coincidental late night meeting of four siblings in the kitchen, and showcases in particular Pearce's knack for detail and humor. Charlie is the first to leave his bed, as he cannot sleep for the worry that a fly has flown into his ear and is stuck there. He ventures downstairs for some water and a snack, only to find one sister in the living room comforting the dog and another already in the kitchen. The eldest decides they will make potato cakes and also wake the youngest sibling, on the premise that if they are caught, the punishment will be lighter if the baby of the family is present. They eat happily together, the youngest falling asleep after eating what he's renamed the dish, "paradise cakes." The next morning, his recounting of the night and his mother's missing mashed potatoes threaten to expose the children's adventure, but their father manages to keep their mother at bay. A light-hearted tale, Pearce deftly slides into the minds of children here, providing them with adventures that can be found in their own home.

In "The Rope," the recurring image of a dangling rope in a boy's dreams causes him to wake up shrieking; Pearce disorients the reader for a few paragraphs before it is clear what so frightens him. Seamlessly, Pearce gives us a coming-of-age piece revolving around a boy's anxiety that he won't be able to cross over the neighborhood lake on a rope swing, in front of all his friends. Instead of the usual happy ending one might expect from a children's story, Pearce lets the boy dangle on said rope for nearly two pages, leaving him hovering over the water, unable to reach the opposite shore. His only choice is to humiliatingly let go in front of everyone. She writes, "Suddenly, hanging there helplessly, he saw; he knew. He knew that nothing and nobody could save him now–unless he could save himself. He must do it immediately. At once" (p. 9). Within her character's anxious thoughts, Pearce gives us an unexpected lesson in self-sufficiency, and in the end, despite his perceived failure, his friends and family support his display.

In "Inside Her Head," Pearce revisits a favorite theme, the ways in which the young and the old relate. Inflicting her protagonist Sim Tolland with the most familiar of childhood ailments, the chicken pox, she pits him against his own boredom and discomfort, smack in the middle of summer. He is then visited by old Mrs. Crakenthorpe, whom he imagines will inflict even more suffering upon him by boring him silly. However, Mrs. Crankenthorpe turns the visit into an adventure of sorts, sharing with Sim a story from her childhood. She was just as sick and bored as he is now, she tells him, and decided to climb the famous elm tree on the block, which is now only a stump. Her tale grows as she tells it, and Sim contributes some details, including impossible heights and fire trucks. The old woman has effectively shown him the power of his imagination to free his mind from boredom. The lesson Pearce seems to be teaching us is that the world is limitless inside your own head; you just have to be willing to go there.

Perhaps the most feared event in a child's life, the divorce of his or her parents, is explored in "The Fir Cone." It's a realistic presentation of the anxieties and tension that occur when a family splits up, as Pearce gives us harried and stressed parents and an anxious little boy. The story opens with Charlie and his mother cleaning out a cupboard that is full of old toys and junk, and Charlie finds a fir cone there that reminds him of a happy memory of his parents together. He carries it with him to visit his father in London and uses it as a way to soothe himself about the changing dynamics of his family. His father is short with him during lunch, and Charlie leaves the fir cone on the table in the restaurant, which causes him to feel even more out of sorts. When his father drops him off, Charlie feels defeated and alone until one of his siblings reminds him of the song they sang during the outing where Charlie first found the fir cone. Guiding himself back through the memory, Charlie realizes he can hold onto the good moments with his parents even in the face of their impending divorce.

Pearce has also written a handful of more serious reality-based stories, including the vignette "Black Eyes." At the heart of the story lies the familiar tension between two young relatives who are strangers, yet expected by adults to get along famously. Jane, the protagonist, is anxiously awaiting the arrival of her cousin Lucinda for the weekend; she imagines her to be blue-eyed, chubby, and shy. Lucinda is the opposite of her imaginings, complete with jet black hair, eyes as black as licorice, a mother she claims is a witch, and a teddy bear she says has the power to make bad things happen. As the weekend goes on, Lucinda alternatively taunts and teases Jane, going so far as to create scenarios wherein Jane's parents are emotionally or physically hurt. Jane attempts to tell her parents how cruel Lucinda is, but they don't believe her. As Lucinda is about to return home in the final pages, she takes Jane's teddy bear to the train station with her instead of her own. In a panic, Jane and her father race to the station to switch them back. Her father retrieves the stuffed animal, much to Jane's relief. As Jane watches the train pull away, she sees Lucinda toss the teddy bear out the car window, where it perishes in traffic. This final act by Lucinda causes Jane to feel empathy for her cousin, and as her father explains that Lucinda lives in a very unhappy home, a more mature understanding transpires for Jane.

The story "Who's Afraid?" runs along similar plot lines, as Pearce explores the resonance of small childhood moments. Joe is so terrified of his cousin Dicky that he considers killing him in order to preempt the impending bullying he fears will take place at their great-grandfather's birthday party. At the party, Joe is forced to play a frightening game of hide-and-seek with Dicky, and he finds refuge in a room where he discovers his great-grandmother in her wheelchair. Joe startles her, and he takes her hand to calm her, forgetting his own fears for a moment. Pearce writes, "He wanted her to know that he meant her no harm; he wanted her to say, 'This is a small hand, a child's hand. You are only a child, after all'" (p. 126). She returns this gesture of kindness with one of her own, making ghost noises in order to scare off Dicky. Joe slips out of the room soon after, never speaking, as he doesn't know what to say to an old woman. He reflects on this moment a year later, when he hears that she has died, and he wishes he had thanked her.

In terms of her more supernaturally based stories, Pearce nearly always grounds them in a solid reality before twisting the plot to her needs. A classic example is "The Running Companion," which starts innocently enough by detailing the intense runs Mr. Adamson takes every day. Pearce quickly paints a picture of a man who is not well liked and full of resentment and anger, and a grown man who still lives at home with his mother and crippled brother. Most of his rage is directed at his brother; Mr. Adamson feels he was neglected because their widowed mother had the disabled brother to take care of. His lack of empathy for his sibling has hardened inside of him and become the running companion of the story's title. Pearce cleverly personifies this hatred, making it feel to Mr. Adamson that it is "just behind him or at his very elbow, a person. Was it monster or man? Had it a heavy body, like his own, to labor uphill only with effort, or had it a real runner's physique, lean and leggy?" (p. 233). When their mother passes away, it is implied that Mr. Adamson's companion gets the best of him, and he pushes his brother down the stairs. The story now told by his neighbors is that

Mr. Adamson was so calloused that he stepped over his brother's body in order to go for a run, but he soon feels another runner is following him along his course. In attempting to outrun this thing behind him, everything he cannot face, he runs harder than he ever has in his life. In a twist of fate, he makes the mistake of turning around to see what has been chasing him and dies on the spot of heart failure.

In a similarly dark ghost story, Pearce explores an uncle's death in "The Dog Got Them." Although a fairly straightforward ghost story, pieces of the reality of alcoholism and the trauma it causes are woven into Pearce's narrative When Andy hears his uncle Joel is ailing, his aunt Enid will not allow her nephew to see him. Joel dies shortly thereafter, and it is revealed that Enid suffered with him through hallucinations and tremors of alcohol withdrawal for months, and the experience was a waking nightmare for both of them. In the weeks following Joel's death, Aunt Enid acts strangely, continuously attempting to keep entities no one else can see out of her house—in trying to chase them out one night, she falls and breaks a hip. Her family comes to stay with her during her convalescence; they also hope to try to get to the bottom of her strange behavior. The family's first night there, Andy wakes in the middle of the night and sees two giant rats in the corner, poised to attack. When he wakes up they are gone, and Enid tells him they were Joel's long-dead pet rats; apparently these are the entities that she'd been seeing for weeks. The family then leaves the dog in the bedroom to get rid of their spirits, and he successfully chases them away.

In a decidedly unnerving tale, Pearce uses an ordinary glass bottle to create a haunting in "The Shadow-Cage." A farmer, Ned Challis, often finds artifacts in his field near a place called Whistler's Hill, where it is rumored witches once lived. One day, he finds a green stopped bottle that he gives to his daughter. She loans it to the neighbor boy, Kevin, who feels inexplicably drawn to it and keeps it with him at all times. He buries it beneath the jungle gym at school a few days later, afraid it will break while he is playing. He forgets to bring it home with him, and wakes in the middle of the night with an overpowering urge to retrieve it. He finds the bottle where he left it, but as he tries to leave he hears strange whistling sounds and is paralyzed, trapped in the jungle gym's shadow made by the moon. His terror rises as the sounds grow closer, but just as the noises are upon him, Ned rescues him. They agree to keep the secret of what's happened, but Ned takes the bottle to be inspected at the local museum. In the end, Ned gives the bottle to his daughter, after it has been unstopped and cleaned. The girl feels it nearly shines of innocence; she decides to fill it with flowers. Instead of leaving the reader on that note, however, Pearce tells us that the museum found traces of human blood inside the bottle, leaving no doubt that darker forces once resided on Whistler's Hill.

Even though there is a ghostly haunting in "His Loving Sister," the realistic plot points of this tale are frightening enough on their own. The narrator recounts the tragic story of his childhood best friend's family, the Phillipses. Two siblings, Lizzie and Billy, were orphaned young, and Lizzie has taken care of Billy her whole life. Even though she eventually marries and has children, she still lives with Billy and tends to his needs while he runs the local repair shop in town. Lizzie is close to the narrator's mother, and the narrator's best friend is Lizzie's son, Steve. The narrator's father doesn't care for Billy, telling his son he is a dishonest businessman and a shady character in general. One foggy night, Lizzie's husband and three children are killed in a car crash, and it is rumored that Billy fixed the brakes and caused the fatal accident, because he wanted Lizzie all to himself again.

With this story, Pearce shows us the darker side of sibling relationships along with the impact of grief on a community. She accurately sketches the range of reactions and confusion that come with sudden death: the narrator is in shock for years afterward, his mother became permanently sad, his father angry, and Lizzie faded into a shadow of her former self. Although Lizzie never accuses her brother publicly of murder, she moves to Canada soon after to live with a distant relative. A few years later, the narrator's mother hears that she has returned to their town, ostensi-

bly to live with her brother. By now, even the narrator's mother admits Billy was responsible for the deaths of Lizzie's husband and children, and she is in disbelief that her friend would return. When his mother takes the narrator to visit Lizzie at the repair shop, they catch a glimpse of her out back, but she then disappears. They run into Billy instead, who looks like a ruined man. He tells them Lizzie died in Canada ten days before of a broken heart, but yes, she is there—haunting him. The tale in turn haunts the narrator for the rest of his life, as he grapples with the evils inherent in human nature and the swiftness with which death can take those you love.

As a whole Pearce's stories, whether realistic or supernatural in nature, show the same daring and skill apparent in her longer works. Her characters are constantly brushing up against the reality of disappointment, anxiety, grief, and death in both childhood and life, and the ways Pearce has them respond to these events consistently resonates with deep emotional truth.

CONCLUSION

Pearce achieved a high degree of success in the nearly five decades of her writing career. In addition to garnering the Carnegie Medal and the Whitbread Award, she was a member of the Royal Society of Literature and was awarded the Order of the British Empire in 1997 for her services to children's literature. In addition to her writing, she was also known for mentoring and editing scores of emerging writers, and she was a regular at conferences and on the lecture circuit. Pearce was passionate, funny, and honest in her writing and in life, and she worked tirelessly at her art, which she felt was one of the highest callings she could have pursued. She continued to write, lecture, and publish to the delight of children of all ages until her sudden death of a stroke in 2006, at the age of eighty-six.

Pearce was able to set herself apart from many children's writers with her ability to detail the very real struggles of childhood with a unique honesty and integrity. Unafraid to put her young characters in proximity to danger and heartbreak, she speaks at once to the truths of life and the adventures all children crave. Her respect for her audience is perhaps what has made her work lasting, along with her ability to step inside the mind of a child and write flawlessly from that perspective. This, along with her ability to weave her own life into her stories, makes her work personal and universal all at once. As Frank Contrell Boyce writes, "All Pearce's books have this strange, unobtrusive power. They seem like simply fantasy or adventure stories, but somehow they never leave you. Her secret was she put so much of herself in them" (p. 11).

Selected Bibliography

WORKS OF PHILIPPA PEARCE

NOVELS

Minnow on the Say. London: Oxford University Press, 1955.

Tom's Midnight Garden. London: Oxford University Press, 1958.

A Dog So Small. London: Constable, 1962.

The Children of the House. With Brian Fairfax-Lucy. London: Longman Young Books, 1968. Reissued as *The Children of Charlecote*. London: Gollancz, 1989.

The Battle of Bubble and Squeak. London: Deutsch, 1978.

The Way to Sattin Shore. London: Kestrel, 1983.

The Little Gentleman. New York: Greenwillow, 2004.

A Finder's Magic. London: Walker Books, 2008.

SHORT STORY COLLECTIONS

The Elm Street Lot. London: British Broadcasting Corporation, 1969. Expanded ed. Harmondsworth, U.K.: Kestrel, 1979.

What the Neighbours Did, and Other Stories. London: Longman Young Books, 1972.

The Shadow-Cage, and Other Tales of the Supernatural. Harmondsworth, U.K.: Kestrel, 1977.

Lion at School, and Other Stories. London: Viking Kestrel, 1985.

Who's Afraid? and Other Strange Stories. London: Viking Kestrel, 1986.

Here Comes Tod! London: Walker Books, 1992.

The Rope and Other Stories. London: Puffin, 2000.

Familiar and Haunting: Collected Stories. New York: Greenwillow, 2002.

PICTURE BOOKS

Mrs Cockle's Cat. Illustrated by Antony Maitland. London: Constable, 1961.

The Squirrel Wife. Illustrated by Derek Collard. London: Longman Young, 1971.

Beauty and the Beast: A Re-Telling. Illustrated by Alan Barrett. London: Longman Young, 1972.

Emily's Own Elephant. Illustrated by John Lawrence. London: MacRae, 1987.

The Toothball. Illustrated by Helen Ganly. London: Deutsch, 1987.

Freddy. Illustrated by David Armitage. London: Deutsch, 1988.

Old Belle's Summer Holiday. Illustrated by Bill Geldart. London: Deutsch, 1989.

The Little White Hen. Illustrated by Gillian McClure. London: Deutsch, 1996.

Amy's Three Best Things. Illustrated by Robin Bell Corfield. London: Puffin, 2003.

CRITICAL AND BIOGRAPHICAL STUDIES

Boyce, Frank Cottrell. "A River Runs Through It." *Guardian*, November 29, 2008, p. 11. (Review of *A Finder's Magic*.)

B. W. "*The Children of the House*." *New York Times Book Review*, November 3, 1968, p. 38.

Farmer, Penelope. "What the Neighbors Did." *New York Times Book Review*, January 20, 1974, p. 8.

Mark, Jan. "Light at the End of the Tunnel." *Guardian*, October 15, 2004, p. 33. (Review of *The Little Gentleman*.)

Nettell, Stephanie. "Obituary: Philippa Pearce: One of the Finest Children's Writers of Her Generation." *Guardian*, January 1, 2007, p. 29.

"Obituaries: Philippa Pearce." *Telegraph*, December 27, 2006.

Sheean, Ethna. "Search on the River Say." *New York Times Book Review*, May 4, 1958, p. 32. (Review of *Minnow on the Say*.)

———. "While the World Slept." *New York Times Book Review*, November 1, 1963, p. A48. (Review of *Tom's Midnight Garden*.)

Tucker, Nicholas. "Philippa Pearce: Author of 'a Masterpiece of Children's Literature' in *Tom's Midnight Garden*." *Independent*, December 23, 2006.

ADAM PHILLIPS

(1954—)

Julie Ellam

THE WRITINGS AND interests of Adam Phillips are varied and difficult to summarize; his style favors the opening up of multiple interpretations and the deconstruction of absolutes such as "truth." He is a psychoanalyst and a professor of literature, and both of these professions leave traces throughout his output; the theories and work of the psychoanalysts Sigmund Freud and D. W. Winnicott are primary evident influences. Phillips' literary background also resurfaces in his writing as he moves between the language of the psychoanalyst and the literary critic with ease. The roles of language and the unconscious in our lives are significant subject matters for him and ones that he uses readily.

Although he is a renowned editor and reviewer, he is most available to the reading public as an essayist. His essays have been collected in a number of volumes and are always marked by their literary references and a seemingly light but thorough knowledge of the subject in hand. Tickling, flirting, excess, love, monogamy, and kindness are just some of the thematic concerns that he returns to implicitly and explicitly. Generally, his essays discuss areas that have been neglected or overlooked but are nevertheless vital in our lives.

An understanding of psychoanalysis gives a key to his writing, and despite (and also because of) his alliance with this profession, it is often questioned in his essays. He challenges the received concept of the expert, most notably in *Terrors and Experts* (1995), with paradoxical expertise and invites readers to appreciate the uncertainty of interpretation over absolute authority. In keeping with this methodology, he suggests readings and asks questions of hitherto accepted wisdoms rather than claiming to know the answers. His writing style is at times playful and ironic and also occasionally moving, and this is most apparent when he focuses on particular case studies. This may be because when such studies are referred to there is a shift from the abstract to a more vivid account of human relations.

As well as writing essays, reviews, and criticism, he has edited editions of the work of other authors, including *Charles Lamb: Selected Prose* (1985); *Walter Pater: The Renaissance* (1986); *John Clare in Context* (1994), with Hugh Haughton and Geoffrey Summerfield. He selected and introduced *The Penguin Freud Reader* (2006); and he is the series editor of new Freud translations published by Penguin Modern Classics. He also cocurated an art installation and wrote an accompanying book titled *The Concise Dictionary of Dress* with his partner Judith Clark and in collaboration with the London-based art production company Artangel in 2010. He is a regular contributor to the *Observer*, the *New York Times,* and the *London Review of Books*. The range of knowledge that he draws on confirms the advocacy he makes in his essays, of the importance of adults remaining curious for what he calls "the good life." The definition of this term is comparable to good mental health but is not interchangeable with it, as he consistently resists using such phrasing. The implication is that the use of "good life" is an admittance of how subjective a state good or bad mental health is.

Adam Phillips was born September 19, 1954, in Cardiff, Wales. His parents, Eric and Jacqueline Phillips, were second-generation Jews of Russian and Polish descent. In *Promises, Promises* (2000) he makes a rare excursion into autobiography in chapter 23 ("Christopher Hill's Revolution and Me"). He explains how his parents "very determinedly, wanted to protect their children from struggle; to make the struggle for survival, which had been the project for them and their parents, seem like a thing of the past." He describes them as "fervent socialists with a passion for the Bloomsbury group" and also gives an insight into his grandparents. Their survival, he writes, was "to us" "heroic," but for them, "it was itself demeaning that they had had to suffer such heroism. Their history had been an insult to their often good-natured natural snobbery" (p. 329). He attended the public school Clifton College in Bristol and studied English literature at St. John's College, Oxford. From his days at Oxford, he counts Professor John Carey as a lasting influence on his understanding of literature and psychoanalysis. Following this, he underwent child psychoanalytic training at the Middlesex Hospital, in the Child Psychiatry Department, as well as at the Tavistock Clinic and the Hampstead Clinic. After qualifying, he worked at Guy's Hospital and the Camberwell Child Guidance Clinic, and he also worked in the Charing Cross Hospital in the Department of Child Psychiatry. He was the principal child psychotherapist at the latter establishment from 1990 to 1997.

He left the National Health Service and his work of treating children to work with adults in a private practice after leaving Charing Cross Hospital. In an interview with Fisun Güner, he explains that he changed over to treating adults in private practice because of both the deterioration of conditions in the area he was working and because he now has three children and he found it increasingly difficult to "listen to the terrible things" that can happen. He expands on this with the clarification that when he first started working in the field of child psychiatry he thought he would be able to "listen to anything" but that as a father he found it to be just too painful. In his practice, Phillips has counted the writers Will Self and Hanif Kureishi among his patients. In 2006, he accepted employment for a six-year-term as a visiting professor in the English Department at the University of York.

Although Phillips has more than fifteen book-length publications to his credit and has also edited several books, his work to date has received little critical coverage in articles or wider studies. As of 2011, his influence on the present and future of literature is difficult to gauge, but readings of his main collections demonstrate that his work is likely to be of enduring interest to students of literature and psychoanalysis. Michael Payne recognizes the problems of measuring the lasting impact of a living author but also encapsulates an overview of Phillips' work that many admiring reviewers have shared: "There is a pervasive sense of undefensive, available presence throughout Phillips' books, in that he is as open and available to his readers as he is to his patients. That is surely why reading him is like a form of therapy" (p. 7).

Not all reviewers have shared this pleasure, and it is fair to say his style has the effect of dividing opinion. Elaine Showalter is one of his more prominent negatively critical readers. Bearing in mind that her methodology has often taken the route of material politics and a faith in truth and justice, it is possible to see that Phillips' work, as influenced as it is by a combination of Freudian theory, post-structuralism, and the uncertainties of truth (among other considerations), might be regarded as being at odds with her political position. The reviewers Peter Lomas and Carol Tavris show a similar disquiet for, respectively, his work's perceived superficiality and for its elaborate generalizations.

ON KISSING, TICKLING, AND BEING BORED

Phillips wrote a book-length study, *Winnicott*, which appeared in 1988. This gives an insight into the work and practice of this famed child psychoanalyst, who is recognized for the significance he gives to the mother-child relationship and the concept of natural development. Phillips' next book, *On Kissing, Tickling, and Being Bored* (1993), is the earliest of the collections of essays that readers are most likely to associate him with. The introduction to these essays gives a useful template for his later work, as he sets out his view of psychoanalysis and the worth it has for the analyst and analysand: "Psychoanalysis—as a form of conversation—is worth having only if it makes our lives more interesting, or funnier, or sadder, or more tormented, or whatever it is about ourselves that we value and want to promote; and especially if it helps us find new things about ourselves that we didn't know we could value" (p. xvii).

In this 1993 volume, Phillips gently unravels and prods at the idea that psychoanalysis is a science, which is an approach that recurs in his subsequent texts. By asking us to think of psychoanalysis as a conversation, and by asking us to think it has a limited value rather than being an absolute cure for, for example, conflict, boredom, or sadness, he deconstructs the profession of psychoanalysis. That is, the privileging of psychoanalysis as a science and, therefore, an authority is destabilized but not dismantled. The sovereignty of psychoanalysis is undermined while its influence and value are both questioned and upheld. Phillips is being true to his standard, which queries the validity of absolute truth; his work demonstrates a reluctance to offer what he sees as the false comfort of an absolute cure.

The uses of psychoanalysis are explained as being "an evolving and relatively new story," and so for Phillips psychoanalysis can give us "new lines on things that matter to us (like kissing, tickling and being bored)" (p. xvii). The claim that these subjects "matter to us" is reiterated with the choice of essays and the title, but this is also a useful indication of Phillips' playful style. He teases his readers in the way that his subjects of choice might not immediately seem of paramount importance, but in looking at what matters to us, he highlights areas that have been previously left out of the debate.

This introduction also brings up what Phillips calls the "inspiring contradiction" in Freud's work (p. xviii); the interpretation of contradictions as being "inspiring" is one that colors Phillips' writing; he generally tends to look for contradictions and he embraces rather than criticizes them. More specifically, he sees a significant contradiction between the idea of development, which can indicate progress, and the unconscious, which is "by definition the saboteur of intelligibility and normative life-

stories" (p. xix). In psychoanalytic theory the unconscious is a predominant site of interest no matter the school of psychoanalytic thought. In *A Glossary of Contemporary Literary Theory*, Jeremy Hawthorn draws on William Empson's point that Charles Darwin, Karl Marx, James George Frazer, and Sigmund Freud all contributed to an understanding that we do not have complete control over our desires and actions: "Freud's development of a theory of the Unconscious is part of a general movement of thought that places a great emphasis upon the individual or collective mind's dark or hidden areas" (p. 370). The ramifications of accepting the influence and unknowability of the unconscious is that logically for Phillips this stands in tension with the concept of developing and progressing, and, it is implied, improving or not improving. By pointing out the contradiction that takes place when holding on to both of these concepts at once, which is an aspect of psychoanalysis, he indicates how the theory in its general sense is necessarily contradictory too. He does not level this as a criticism but as a point that must be understood. The by-product of this recognition is that contradictions do not have to be solved, and it is acceptable to live with a paradox. The ability to live with contradictions and to hold on to them rather than solve them is written into Phillips' essays consistently, and understanding this is intrinsic to comprehending his style and the contents of his books.

As promised, these essays consider kissing, tickling, and boredom—as well as fear, composure, and obstacles. Rather than presume his readers have prior knowledge, Phillips often takes recourse to the *Oxford English Dictionary* to define the actions, states, or objects he is exploring. There is a history of the definition of "worrying," for instance, and this is not offered definitively but as a means to instigate a discussion. It is explained that worrying has previously been associated with hunting and persecution (p. 50). It is also an "ironic form of hope" (p. 56).

In chapter 7, "On Being Bored," he explains that this has "rarely been written about," and he goes on to give this neglected area an airing he thinks it deserves (p. 71). The boredom of the child and the adult are juxtaposed and differentiated, and for both groups he examines the limitations and possibilities that come with being bored. For the child, he allows for the spaces this creates: "While the child's boredom is often recognised as an incapacity, it is usually denied as an opportunity" (p. 73). He also suggests boredom can be interpreted as a "mourning of everyday life" (p. 75), and a form of protection (p. 82). In addition, he warns that the danger for the adult is that boredom "will turn into waiting," and so it may turn into stasis (p. 82).

ON FLIRTATION

In Phillips' 1994 book *On Flirtation,* flirting is introduced as a trope for considering the uncertainties of our lives. By looking at flirting and, in turn, uncertainty, the template of the progress narrative is also depicted as a myth. The potential offered by flirting is that it offers excitement and contingency, but when faith in progress is adhered to, according to Phillips, flirtation has been deemed as a threat and is made "acceptable only as a means to a predictable end" (p. xvii).

The narrative of progress is further deconstructed in chapter 4, "Success," as Phillips flirts with the problems of success and living in the future. He cites John Stuart Mill's disillusionment at the age of twenty when he realized he would not be completely satisfied if he fulfilled his aim of being a great reformer. Success, it appears, is not enough in and of itself to create happiness, and the notion of progress, the idea of there being a direct linear line to happiness, is similarly found to be an illusion.

Flirtation, Phillips argues, represents another way of thinking that allows for chance, instead of being based in hope for progress. He offers the view that "if it can be sustained," flirtation can be "a way of cultivating wishes, of playing for time. Deferral can make room" (p. xix). He explains ambivalence and "therefore self-doubt" as being "integral" to psychoanalysis, and so it is understandable that flirtation is used as a means to allow for the deferral of meaning as well as fixity (p. 148). The allusion to deferral may be

also read as an invitation to make room for post-structuralism and the work of theorists such as Jacques Derrida, as deferral moves us toward the concept of *différance*, which simply put is to both differ and defer meaning. Contingency is also broached as a value to live by in chapter 11, titled "Cross Dressing," which contains the warning that "if we cultivate unbearable choices, we create impossible lives" (p. 130).

TERRORS AND EXPERTS

In *Terrors and Experts* (1995), Phillips focuses on the role of the expert, mainly in psychoanalysis, and he destabilizes the authoritative position of the so-called expert. Although critique of authority is an ongoing interest in Phillips' writing, it is amplified here as he deconstructs the profession he is famously associated with. As Phillips unpacks the authority of the psychoanalyst in the way he questions what constitutes an expert, he similarly critiques the absolutes of truth. In this way the expert is logically exposed as perhaps not inexpert but at least diminished.

He returns to earlier comparisons, establishing the process of psychoanalysis as being similar to the process of sharing a conversation. He also argues that elitism and mental health should be mutually exclusive, and he prefers using the term "the good life" to refer to mental health. By warning against the psychoanalyst assuming the role of expert, he undermines the associated link between psychoanalysis and science and also the objectivity that is presumed to come with psychoanalytic practice. He concludes the text (perhaps paradoxically) with a (prescriptive) final point that argues that too much definition and prescription is not the role of psychoanalysis: "At its best, psychoanalysis can show us both what we have in mind, and what we mind about, and the relationship, if any, between them. But it cannot tell us who we can be. It can tell us, though, that prescription begins when curiosity breaks down. Too much definition leaves too much out" (p. 104). While refusing to offer up psychoanalysis as a panacea, he simultaneously gives clues as to what the good life might be in the last two sentences of this quotation. Lack of curiosity and "too much definition" are to be avoided.

He asks us in the preface to consider that "there may be terrors but there are no experts" (p. xvii). Prior to this, he asks the psychoanalyst to ask him- or herself, "What kind of person do I want to be?" (p. xvii). The terrors comes in love and in the disillusion that there are no experts, including psychoanalysts. In this context, terror is associated with uncertainty and with the recognition that absolutes are a myth.

A desire for the authority of the expert is seen, he argues, in the way children treat their parents "as though they were experts on life" and suggests we are capable of continuing to desire such an expert in adult life (p. 1). The relationship between the expert and terror should not be underestimated, he suggests, as the expert is able to allow terror to uphold the authority he or she assumes: "The expert constructs the terror, and then the terror makes the expert. If you are part of the solution you are part of the problem" (p. 14). The warning is that the unassailable psychoanalyst will assume authority through dependency and through the prescription that limits the potential of the patient seeking help. Phillips' resistance to absolute authority is evident as is the connection he makes between power and how it is maintained.

Peter Lomas' review of this work for the *Times Literary Supplement* begins with an expression of sympathy for the readers and for Phillips for not being sure of "the claims of the psychotherapist" in a world of increasing specialization, and he also sees that Phillips' "indictment is made with acuteness and verve." Lomas criticizes the work, however, for what he perceives as a lack of depth in its arguments; although Lomas regards the prose as fluent, he points to a lack of engagement and a preference on Phillips' part for style over substance. For Lomas, "the feel of the consulting room" and "the nitty-gritty of the everyday struggle of the therapist to keep his or her head above water" is not touched upon (p. 28).

Lomas clarifies his position by looking to the chapter on the psychoanalyst Sándor Ferenczi, which he sees as the "most interesting," and he compares the work of Ferenczi with that of Phillips. As Phillips outlines, Ferenczi experimented with "mutual analysis," as he was interested in the fear he had of his patients. By doing this, we are told, he was showing there was no shame in the process of analysis, or, "rather, it was a shame, and therefore worth thinking about" (*Terrors*, p. 32). Lomas cites this as an invitation to Phillips to also be more involved in his writing with such self-revelations and to perhaps be more personal.

THE BEAST IN THE NURSERY

The eponymous allusion for Phillips' 1998 volume appears in the coda to *The Beast in the Nursery*, as the author makes a summary of sorts, elaborating on the contradictions embedded in Freud's ambition that psychoanalysis "should become a science." Phillips unravels the difficulties of this desire as such, saying that "the dreamer and the child, as he described them, kept reminding him that there were other ways of doing things. In Freud's allegory the modern individual is the site for this conflict between the dreamer and the scientist, between the child and the realist, between the beast and the nursery" (p. 115). The reference to the beast and the nursery, rather than the beast in the nursery, leads the reader to interpret the title as an advocacy of living with conflict and viewing contradiction as enabling the good life.

This preference expressed in the coda for holding on to a contradiction rather than trying to solve it is a reworking of the themes of the book's earlier chapters. In chapter 1, for example, Phillips looks back to Freud's early papers and explains how Freud made the case that "we should all be essentialists trying to be pluralists, and pluralists trying to be essentialists." He goes on to say "there is no way of having it without having it both ways" and we are in danger of becoming like "Freud's 'civilized' children" who lose interest in curiosity and "may become too eagerly too old for pleasure" (p. 33). The reference to the beast in the nursery may be understood in this light as an invitation for readers to recognize and accept the contradictions that have shaped us rather than dismissing them as childish and of the past.

In chapter 3, "A Stab at Hinting," Phillips describes psychoanalysis as "a theory of hinting" (p. 63), and this is a useful means for understanding his thought processes here and elsewhere. He looks to the writing of John Keats, Henry James, and Ludwig Wittgenstein and to how they "insist" on the value of hinting because of the unintentional creativity they may inspire. Chapter 1 also refers to James and to what "interest" might mean, "and how we manage, or plot, to lose it" (p. 11). The poet, novelist, and philosopher are used to expand the theory of hinting that Phillips suggests and so includes the literary and the philosophical within the sphere of psychoanalysis. He also distinguishes between two types of psychoanalysts: ones who "turn hints into orders" and others who try to "turn orders into hints" (p. 77).

Phillips also uses this book to once more challenge the concept of progress, and in doing so he criticizes what he sees as the "reactionary" aspect of psychoanalysis, which has promoted this "dismayingly comforting" way of thinking (p. 37). He associates the idea of progress with the stoical belief in trying to "make the most of it," and he describes this as a "class-blind, politically pacifying and apparently a-historical myth of human development" (p. 38). In this pithy statement, he demonstrates an awareness that "making the most of it" is an unequal proposition depending on where one falls in the class strata. For those in poverty, with limited opportunities and facing prejudice, the demand for stoicism would seem an unequal one, since those who are not faced with economic restrictions and cultural apartheid have less to put up with. Making the most of it, he suggests, is an unfair demand that fails to recognize the hierarchies in society.

This engagement with an overtly political critique is rare in Phillips' work, an observation later raised by Elaine Showalter in her largely negative review of Phillips' 2002 book, *Equals,* in the *Guardian.* She wonders if Phillips has so often received sparkling reviews because the critics are intimidated by his style and knowledge. She emphasizes what she regards as too much

impersonality on his part, in this work that is concerned with equality, and she understands this as demonstrating a resistance to engaging his readers. She also wonders "about the value of an equality that depends so much on stylistic one-upmanship."

The preference for suggesting and hinting, and for questioning absolutes, that Phillips depends on may be read as in keeping with a style that is influenced by psychoanalysis and post-structuralist thinking. Furthermore, a reader who is influenced by more materialist theories will inevitably be critical of a perceived lack of political immersion. Left-leaning politics are present in Phillips' writing, but they are more subtle than obvious, and this in itself may be regarded as a fault in the view of readers and reviewers who expect a more concrete analysis of psychoanalysis and equality in society.

In keeping with this style, *The Beast in the Nursery* is cautious rather than overt in the manner it takes up the point of the difference between suggestion and instruction. This is exemplified in the contrast Phillips makes between the work and followers of Winnicott and Melanie Klein. This comes when he considers the work of Winnicott to be more suggestive and less instructive than that of Klein and Kleinians, and the preference for Winnicott is made apparent.

The Beast in the Nursery was followed by *Darwin's Worms* (1999), which draws on the work of Darwin and Freud to form a discussion about death. The reviewer Frank Kermode asserts that Phillips "weaves the counsel of these sages together with much art, for it is part of his plan to make the contemplation of death an enjoyable, even a sublime, experience" (p. 7). Kermode's essay for the *London Review of Books* also explains the general relevance of Phillips' work and he examines how Phillips' writing style refreshes ideas from the past. For instance, Phillips writes about the human experience of grief and the way humans seem to be more strongly grief stricken in comparison to other animals; Kermode points out that Walt Whitman touched on this same observation (roughly a century ago) but not in the same way, and the perspective and the elegant form of expression that Phillips offers are illuminating. Grief in humans is explored with the advantage of knowledge of earlier writings, as he expands on the way we view death.

PROMISES, PROMISES

The relationship between literature and psychoanalysis is a dominant feature of *Promises, Promises* (2000), a collection of twenty-eight chapters. This relationship is an often implicit aspect of Phillips' writing, but in *Promises, Promises* he voices a desire for symbiosis between the two. The dedications to his former English literature teachers emphasize the bond, in his opinion, and he explains the importance of why psychoanalysis should not and cannot be taught in a vacuum:

> Read in isolation from its cultural context—as it is in most psychoanalytic training—it can seem to be rather more of a specialism, rather more of a privileged language than it in fact is or could ever be. Psychoanalysis cannot make any useful sense if it is not seen as entirely of a piece with its culture, however adversarial it is, or claims to be.
>
> (p. xii)

He also points out that, starting with Freud, the so-called father of psychoanalysis, there has been "a certain unease" between literature and psychoanalysis and with writers and writing and "that has been integral to the history of psychoanalysis" (p. xiii). Freud's work is sprinkled with literary allusions and myths; perhaps most famously his theory about the "Oedipus complex," a cornerstone of psychoanalysis, is named after a king from Greek mythology. Freud's followers continue to interpret this, from *The Interpretation of Dreams* (1900), as a useful framework for looking at family relationships. The rivalry between the father and son, the son's desire for the mother, and the ensuing love triangle is a well-established story that psychoanalysts have returned to repeatedly as a useful framework for looking at family relationships.

Phillips' engagement with literature is expressed in a number of reviews for outlets such as the *London Review of Books* and in conference papers, which are reproduced in *Promises, Promises*. "Winnicott's Hamlet," which is chapter 4, exemplifies the preference Phillips has for using literature to read psychoanalysis and vice versa. It begins with an epigraph from "The Decay of Lying" by Oscar Wilde, which refers to Hamlet's proclamation of art holding a mirror up to nature, and it goes on to cite Freud protesting "rather too much" at Arnold Zweig's request to be his biographer (p. 72).

Phillips looks at how Freud, Ernest Jones, and Winnicott have looked back to Shakespeare in various ways and to *Hamlet* in particular: "When Shakespeare turns up in psychoanalysis, it is often *Hamlet*—and when *Hamlet* turns up, the play is usually used to say something about knowing and truth, about its difficulty, its impossibility, its uncertain status and definition" (p. 79). Phillips resists the temptations of the progress myth and so avoids drawing a line straight from Shakespeare to Freud to Winnicott. This means he also misses a direct confrontation with the story of the anxiety of influence, and in so doing he avoids making a simplistic reading of the Oedipus complex. Instead of discussing the Oedipus complex in a reductive manner, Phillips draws on the work of a possible father-figure Winnicott and his references to *Hamlet* in 1950, where Winnicott talks about truth and knowledge. Phillips also looks to Winnicott's 1966 work on the "To be or not to be" speech, which attempted to re-describe Freud's theories of bisexuality.

Phillips' indebtedness to his predecessors, if not father-figures, comes in his references to his unacknowledged debts (from Winnicott to Jones), which has echoes of guilt attached to it, as guilt is another way of reading indebtedness. Even though Phillips mainly sidesteps a direct discussion of the Oedipus complex and the rivalry between father and son, he invokes it tacitly through the references to *Hamlet* and in the explanations of Freud's conflicting relationship to Shakespeare.

Nicholas Fearn's 2001 overview of Phillips' work points to the essays in *Promises, Promises* to argue that Phillips' light touch might lead to his work having no lasting legacy, nor (it is implied) a traditionally therapeutic effect. In *Promises, Promises*, says Fearn, Phillips has written that "he thinks of literature and psychoanalysis as 'forms of persuasion.' Accordingly, he avoids the therapeutic vocabulary—of 'shyness,' 'depression' and 'low self-esteem'—in favour of 'language that's more productive, language that goes on to produce more language'" (p. 18). Fearn argues, however, that the validity of psychoanalysis is in its seeking to cure "by helping us to understand how we represent our lives." He writes that Phillips' "literary talents" mean he is "well-equipped to help construct these representations," but he also describes what he sees as Phillips' shortcomings: "Because in Phillips' work psychoanalysis does not hold out the prospect of coming to know or understand things that are true about oneself and others, it becomes, in the words of one academic, a 'cultural experience rather than a clinical one'" (p. 18).

Phillips followed *Promises, Promises* with *Houdini's Box: The Art of Escape* (2001). This volume looks at four different escape artists as well as considering the concept of escape in and of itself. Harry Houdini and Emily Dickinson are among the escapees, and death and fear are central thematic concerns in the book. It is also at one with Phillips' ongoing emphasis that escape—rather than conclusions and finitude—should be valued. The possibility of escape, after all, allows for change and a different type of freedom.

GOING SANE

In choosing the title for his 2005 book, *Going Sane,* Phillips takes a typically playful approach, making a familiar phrase unfamiliar to remind us how madness takes precedence in Western culture. His preface explains that "sanity" is an idea that has rarely been considered in print; he makes the case for his decision to write a book-length study of sanity because it has never been "systematically studied or defined" (p. 3).

Early in part 1 of *Going Sane*, Phillips references the anti-psychiatrists of the 1960s and 1970s, including R. D. Laing, as a means to explain the changing history toward perceptions of madness in the psychiatric profession and to give Phillips' text a foundation from which to develop. In Phillips' interpretation, the anti-psychiatrists took the approach that "madness was an authentic response to the horrors of contemporary life; to be sane in a world like this was to be out of touch with reality" (p. 25). The reviewer Michael Wood points out that although Phillips draws on the anti-psychiatric movement, he is careful to not "glamorise madness" and "clearly marks his distance" from his predecessors (p. 17). That is, in contrast to his predecessors Phillips chooses to focus on sanity rather than madness; in this vein, he notes that, historically, "no one is famous for their sanity" (p. 35) and that it is "striking" that the sane "do not declare themselves" (p. 42).

In part 2, he considers the concept of "original madness" and the ideas of Erasmus, for example, who wrote of us as being born insane. For Winnicott, says Phillips, sanity as adults may mean not experiencing things as intensely as when we were younger: "Our sanity can be the way we sever our connections to the feelings and experiences that matter most to us. The sanity we seek out as a refuge from fear can also be a way of starving ourselves. Winnicott is encouraging us to take on our own turbulence" (p. 95). Phillips also advocates this perspective. Just as he refuses to take the definition of sanity for granted, he also asks what we mean by "development," and he wonders, "What exactly is supposed to develop in development?" (p. 99). This reference to Winnicott, and his questioning of the received view that development implies linear growth and advancement, highlights a perspective that Phillips shares with him. Through Winnicott and Phillips, the readers are encouraged to similarly question the stability of the meaning of linearity and progress in development.

Going Sane also considers Christianity as an influence on Western perceptions of redemption and sanity, and Phillips argues that redemption and sanity have been aligned historically by certain Christian strains of thought. This leads him back to his conceptualization of the myth of progress, as redemption is linked to ideas of development. He regards "ersatz Christianity" as being where "sanity equals love," and he suggests that this version of sanity may be "an attempt to medicalize morality" (p. 113).

In this study of what development in relation to sanity may mean, he also claims that desire contradicts ideas of development and of being able to find one's way through unpredictability: sanity "highlights and muffles this contradiction" (p. 114).

He regards narrow definitions of sanity as destructive and is, therefore, critical of a strict interpretation. He points out the necessity of having a fluid understanding of this term, as a restricted view "allows us neither our full range of emotional reactions to situations—whether terror, bewilderment or ecstasy; nor our most effective forms of self protection against them" (p. 178).

Going Sane gives space to what Phillips calls three "modern psychiatric diagnoses" and offers persuasive interpretations that seeming pathologies may at least in part be understood as forms of self-protection (p. 160). He looks at childhood autism, schizophrenia, and depression, and in each case he explains the fears that may lie within the person who has been diagnosed. He refers, for instance, to the "absent presence" of an autistic child: "The autistic child lives as if there is no world, no meaning, no pleasure and nothing to do except those things they have to do to stave off the terror of being alive" (p. 166). In his review, Michael Wood relates that he will be haunted by the use of such "delicate and compassionate metaphors" in this consideration of how an autistic child might feel (p. 17).

For reviewers and readers searching for less deconstruction and more instruction from Phillips, the final pages of *Going Sane* may give the answers that they have been searching for, as he attempts to widen the readers' understanding. In part 3 he takes the unprecedented step of offering what he calls a "blueprint for a contemporary sanity," and he refers to Winnicott's view "that madness is the need to be believed" (p. 220). Phillips regards sanity as an "antithetical" word, and he interprets it as "keeping opposites in play" as well as keeping alive "our more haunting conflicts and confusions" (p. 222). He contemplates the nature of being superficially sane

versus being deeply sane, and he debates the way adaptation is the "religion" of the superficially sane—whereas, he says, for the deeply sane adaptation is "experienced as a form of corruption" (p. 223).

His "blueprint for a contemporary sanity" allows for the sane to prefer the provisional over order and patterns. The sane do not need to take revenge, he says, because for them revenge is "an attempt to coerce agreement" (p. 229). Dissatisfaction can be an "inspiration" rather than a "refuge," for the sane have found ways of taking pleasure in problems; pleasure is preferred over the moral stance.

The sane "prefer listening to speaking," he says, but they also recognize the need to speak too (p. 229). They think the desire to be unique or special "is the secret saboteur of our liveliest pleasures," because they feel no need to be rescued from anonymity; being ignored can be a freedom, and being left out does not have to be experienced as isolation (p. 230).

Phillips argues that the sane person has not consented "to the modern redemptive myth of relationships." Relationships for the sane are seen as experiments, and what the experiment is for or about does not have to be clear: "For the sane, so-called relationships could never be subject to contract." Acknowledgments for the sane are preferred over principles, and these "can never be formalized" (p. 231). The sane are also aware of luck and coincidence, and of the unconscious and the work of the forbidden. Frustration is an aspect of life, and it is also preferable to take risks rather than perpetuate a secure way of living for just the sake of security.

Toward the end of his list, Phillips associates kindness with sanity and so offers an early view of his 2009 book, *On Kindness* (2009). *Going Sane* questions the nostalgia that keeps telling stories about blame, and Phillips suggests the "new sane person" wants "a new story about kindness" (p. 238). Living with sanity, according to Phillips, is a way of being open and respectful with ourselves and others, and of coping with ambiguity and ambivalence and frustration. It is also about not adhering to the binary oppositions where one element in the binary is favored over the other: "so instead of sanity as seeming to be a choice between conformity and self-assertion, between sincerity and authenticity, between duty and desire, the sane person would want, ideally, to incorporate each of these into a repertoire rather than make the grand gesture of choosing between them" (p. 245).

Phillips also uses this blueprint to reexamine what has been regarded as human nature; he implies that this is at least difficult if not impossible to quantify. Because he looks at alternative definitions of being sane and mad, it follows that human nature is not a fixed entity or easy to summarize.

The reviewer Carole Tavris says that *Going Sane,* as its essential thesis, attempts to resolve the question of why sanity has not had as much focus as madness in previous psychoanalytic writings. But Tavris asserts that this question is easily explained; she argues that the reason social scientists and psychiatrists have "shied away" from defining happiness or sanity is because "these are moral and philosophic concepts, not psychological or medical ones." She queries the distinction Phillips makes between being "superficially" and "deeply" sane, and she also laments, "The book is full of the kind of psychoanalytic generalizations that may cause the reader temporary insanity" (p. 4). Tavris is unimpressed by the way the text shifts between pointing out the delimiting effects of categorization while also asking for fluid rather than fixed definitions of sanity.

In contrast, Wood largely accepts the central premise of *Going Sane,* and he praises what he describes as some of the "wonderful writing" on display: "I shall not soon forget locations/locutions like 'the no man's land between the tantrum and the grudge' or the proposition that 'strung out between romance and pornography it is no longer clear what men and women want to use each other for'" (p. 17).

Going Sane ends with a poignant reading of sanity, and it is one that finally but only temporarily pins down how understanding our reactions to humiliation may be a key to understanding madness and sanity: "sanity should not be our word for the alternatives to madness; it should refer to whatever resources we have to prevent humiliation" (p. 245).

Phillips' next two books were *Side Effects* (2006) and *Intimacies* (2008, written with Leo Bersani). *Side Effects* turns the concept of so-called bad side effects on its head, and it continues to explores areas that Phillips endows with interest. Among the book's seventeen chapters are "The Forgetting Museum," "Paranoid Moderns," and "Needing to Know When It's Over." *Intimacies* is structured around four chapters and has the dialogue of psychoanalysis as one of its concerns. Phillips and Leo Bersani have engaged with both the process of psychoanalysis and optimism about the future with an element of intimacy in order to write a new story about it. In the book's preface, Phillips describes how the writing came about and highlights the collaborative nature of the project. He explains that Bersani wrote the first three chapters and he responded with questions, and Bersani wrote the conclusion with his points in mind. The "loose ends," we are told, have been left in "and the reader can read the book as it was written" (p. viii).

ON KINDNESS

On Kindness (2009), written with the feminist historian Barbara Taylor, looks at kindness from a point of view that is both psychoanalytic and historical. The authors suggest that to analyze kindness, it is also necessary to consider hatred: "Hatred is our primal form of self-protection, a closing off from everything that threatens us" (p. 65). The authors are not attacking hatred, though; instead they are offering a glimpse of the emotion that appears to run counter to love and kindness. Binary thinking, where love would be opposed to hate, for example, is deconstructed to highlight the uses of hate. This in turn disavows the marginalization of feelings we might ordinarily think of with guilt. The authors describe hatred as "one of our methods of survival" (p. 65), and they explain that it is also useful for defining pleasure: "Hatred is both our means of sustaining our pleasure and a pleasure in itself. If we can't hate we can't be happy" (p. 67).

In contrast with this measured view of hatred and the refusal to condemn it, kindness is ultimately affirmed as desirable. "People think that they envy other people for their success, money, fame," the book concludes, "when in fact it is kindness that is most envied, because it is the strongest indicator of people's well-being, their pleasure in existence" (p. 114).

Earlier in the book, however, the authors outline the problems people have in showing or experiencing kindness. They explain our relationship to kindness and the lack of trust we may have in its efficacy by rooting it in the child's relationship with his or her parents: "Every child wants to cure their parents of whatever makes them unhappy, and every child fails at this. That experience alone can make the child begin to doubt the value of his kindness, because it isn't magic" (p. 69). The breakdown of the value of kindness is also referred to in the use of the theme of sexual jealousy, and in a passing nod to *Othello*, as this emotion is seen as running "the risk of being the death, or the murder of kindness." The volume goes on to make a connection between jealousy, hatred, and kindness, and illustrates how self-hatred (and being unkind to oneself) and jealousy are often inseparable: "The origins of self-hatred are often to be found in failures of kindness" (p. 63). Once more, Phillips (with Taylor) has written about a subject that appears to be so familiar that it has been passed by, and his explanations of why we value kindness and the reasons we have difficulties with it are expressed clearly for the lay reader who is not a part of the psychoanalysis profession.

ON BALANCE

In the 2010 volume *On Balance*, Phillips examines the expectations we attempt to live up to in terms of "balance" and "excess." This work offers a defense of excess and looks at how we are caught up in thinking we are too imbalanced, too excessive, because the normative value in Western society is balance.

He begins by introducing John Stuart Mill's point that "the idea of balance can unbalance us" (p. xii). He also explains that balance is associated with order, and that order has been posited as good and achievable in the dominant ideology, "so the essays in this book are about the balancing acts that modern societies involve us in" (p. xiii). The book's nine main sections have several more subsections, with no noticeable symmetry. Sleep, W. H. Auden, the truant mind, and a celebration of the writing of W. G. Sebald are some of the essay topics.

Phillips discusses our reactions to the excessive behaviors of others and how these reactions may reveal a paradoxically excessive position on the part of the one making the judgment. He argues using the theories of Jacques Lacan that such reactions expose something of ourselves and our own conflicts. The judgment of the excesses of others is telling, also, says Phillips, in that there is something "God-like" inherent in it (p. 48). He points out that excesses give insights into what we lack: "Our excesses are the best clues we have to our own poverty; and our best way of concealing it from ourselves" (p. 48). He destabilizes the preference for balance further when he proposes that it is "impossible to overreact" (p. 31).

In "Enough Is Enough," an essay in the first main section, "Five Short Talks on Excess," he looks at appetite and satisfaction. Instead of criticizing behavior generally regarded as excessive—that is, as greed—he interprets it as "a form of despair" (p. 16) and suggests that "an addiction is an unformulated frustration" (p. 17). Crucial to this point is the faith we learn to have in the goal of satisfaction and balance, a value that he goes on to query. Phillips expands his argument about appetite and satisfaction by referencing Franz Kafka's story "The Hunger Artist," in which Kafka's performance faster explains that he starves himself in public because he cannot find the food he likes.

Phillips asks whether satisfaction "is rather more elusive than this suggests" and whether satisfaction is more "radically misleading": "If sex, for example, didn't have to satisfy us it might give us more pleasure" (p. 20). He draws a link between satisfaction and the avoidance of frustration, and he wonders if people in "affluent countries" have been encouraged to be "phobic of frustration" (p. 19). Within environments of affluence and capitalism, Phillips implies, consumers have learned that satisfaction should be possible and without it we should be unhappy.

In the essay "Celebrating Sebald," Phillips takes an overview of responses to the work of W. G. Sebald, which has received near universal critical praise—excessive and unwarranted praise, according to the dissenting reviewer Michael Hoffman. Phillips examines the idea that "celebration resists language in a way that suffering does not" (p. 243). The theme of celebration in Sebald's writing is used as a means to continue the thread of Hoffman's original point and in the process the concept of celebration is analyzed too.

The melancholic drift of Sebald's work is spotted with references to celebration, and Phillips argues that in his writing, in certain places, "celebration is like mourning" in that they share the form of "play-acting" (p. 251). Phillips extends this to ask what it is that is being acted. He looks at the "horrifying history" of the Holocaust and how Sebald "did and didn't live through it" (p. 252); Phillips notes how this period in German history comes in again and again in Sebald's books as the thought of complicity (and playacting) is returned to. In this reading of Sebald's writing, Phillips tries to go deeper with the analysis of the words by considering what celebration is and how Sebald explores the past by avoiding "explicit formulation" and resisting "being polemical" (p. 250).

OTHER WORK

Aside from his roles as psychoanalyst and professor of literature, Phillips is primarily identifiable as an essay writer. In a 2010 essay for the *Guardian* newspaper, "Over the Moon: Adam Phillips on the Happiness Myth," he spells out the drawbacks of the pursuit of happiness. He refers to the U.S. Declaration of Independence and its assurance of the unalienable right to pursue hap-

piness as a counterpoint to his premise that happiness is not and should not be regarded as a right. His argument appears to be contentious, apolitical even, but as he states his case with three persuasive points: The first point is that happiness is subjective, and so the idea of collective happiness is bound to be untenable in that not everybody will be able to agree on what happiness is. His second point is that "bad things," such as cruelty and humiliation, can make some people happy. His final reason is that some people like being unhappy, and unhappiness may, for some, in fact be "the registration of injustice or loss" (p. 2).

The superego, as the conscience, also has a part to play in our levels of happiness, and Phillips refers to one of "Freud's more horrifying ironies" that the pursuit of pleasure "incites, calls up, the super-ego." The authority of the superego means that our pleasures are supervised by our conscience. This means that pleasure is often limited by this inner policeman. He clarifies this with the simplified phrasing that "there is no such thing as a free lunch" when the super-ego is involved.

The definitions of happiness, unhappiness, and satisfaction are also examined when he refers back to Winnicott's paper "The Deprived Child," in order to explore the mother and child relationship, the meaning of satisfaction, and the idea that the entangled child has the right to steal from the mother before disentanglement and separation. In the case of the child stealing, Phillips explains, it is the person, the mother, that is being actually sought out and not the stolen object. Because the stolen object is not the mother, however, the child remains unsatisfied and still wants what she or he does not have.

Phillips correlates this understanding of the pursuit of happiness with addiction and capitalism: "In this sense, consumer capitalism is a system tailor-made for deprived children." Consumer capitalism holds out the promise of satisfaction, but from Phillips' perspective it exploits and thrives on the individual's sense of lack (of the mother) and offers only a temporary substitute for the absence the adult is trying to compensate for. As it is just a temporary fix for the consumer and the addict, the consumer continues to buy and spend in the pursuit of an unachievable but promising happiness.

Monogamy (1996) collects aphorisms on subjects associated with this often idealized relationship. There are 121 separate entries, and the vast majority of these are between a few sentences long and up to half a page. Only occasionally is an entry extended over two pages, as with a discussion on being left out and being left in. Infidelity, jealousy, and being in a couple are just some of the other subjects that are treated.

In a 1997 interview with Dwight Garner of the online magazine *Salon*, Phillips was quick to point out that although he questions the truth of monogamy, the book does not set out to condemn it: "Monogamy seems to me peculiarly difficult to talk about in a way that, as it were, moves the story on or modifies our ideas about it," Phillips said. "And this suggests to me that it's a very powerful, quasi-sacred idea. This book is not at all promoting the value of infidelity." But he says that the book was meant to demonstrate how difficult it is to "describe and redescribe this thing that a lot of us take for granted." The final words of *Monogamy* are a rumination on promises, and they remind us once more to not take for granted the most traditional of family values: "Monogamy and infidelity: the difference between making a promise and being promising" (p. 121).

As the editor of *The Penguin Freud Reader* in 2006 and of the Penguin Modern Classics translations of Freud's work, Phillips took on a task of making Freud's writing accessible to the public that received considerable attention in the literary reviews in broadsheet newspapers. The translation of Freud's work began with the publication of *Civilisation and Its Discontents* in 2002 and the series is made up of fifteen volumes of various texts. In his introduction to the *Reader*, he explains that his aims are "to enable the curious, who are by definition not the converted, to discover what, if anything, is so haunting about Freud's writing" (p. viii). He has devised the book in such a way as to encourage the readers to dip in and jump around the text "for when Freud begins to bore or irritate us" and it is set out "from end to beginning," so "that spurious

sense of linearity can be lost" (p. xv). Included in the 2006 volume are the selections "An Outline of Psychoanalysis," "Fetishism," "Mourning and Melancholia," and "Humour."

The Concise Dictionary of Dress was an exhibition as well as a publication, and it has since taken form as a multimedia experience through the website of the Artangel company, where photographs and videos give extra layers of access and insight. The exhibition comprised eleven installations produced by the fashion curator Judith Clark, but the definitions for the installations were written first by Phillips. The definitions were used as a form of inspiration to the imagination; Phillips originally wrote more than eleven definitions for the project, and Clark selected from among them. The installations also drew on the stock of the Victoria and Albert Museum and its storage site of Blythe House.

For an idea of how this concept transpired into an exhibition, it is useful to look at one of the definitions, "Conformist," and how this inspired the choice of an installation based around the work of the nineteenth-century artist, socialist, and author William Morris. As Phillips explains on the website, "Conformist" is invoked in a less pejorative sense than we may be used to, and he points out that we are all conforming to a point of view even when we say we are not. He implies that Morris is useful for reclaiming a more positive sense of this word because Morris' art asked for a conformity to certain high standard in its creation. Conformity in this instance invites us to consider the value of workmanship.

CONCLUSION

In *Promises, Promises*, Phillips criticizes psychoanalysis for being "notably reclusive," and in his explanation for this claim it is possible to find a justification for his writing: "Psychoanalysis at its best should be a profession of popularizers of interesting ideas about the difficulties and exhilaration of living" (p. xiv). His agenda as a writer is, it is apparent to say, to open up psychoanalysis to the wider reading public and beyond the community of specialists. Showalter's previously cited review argues that his style tends to be that of "one up-manship," and it is debatable, of course, whether his work is universally popular in or outside the worlds of psychoanalytic specialists or academia. However, his writing consistently marks a shift away from that of an insular academic writing only for fellow academics as he attempts and often succeeds in broaching everyday subjects such as boredom, fear, and excess in order to question the negative judgments we make of ourselves and others. His writing is by necessity an inclusive way of working, and perhaps as inclusive as it is possible to be given the complexity of the ways of thinking that he writes about.

Selected Bibliography

WORKS OF ADAM PHILLIPS

PRIMARY TEXTS

Winnicott. London: Fontana, 1988.

On Kissing, Tickling, and Being Bored. London: Faber and Faber, 1993.

On Flirtation. London: Faber and Faber, 1994.

Terrors and Experts. London: Faber and Faber, 1995.

The Beast in the Nursery. London: Faber and Faber, 1998.

Darwin's Worms. London: Faber and Faber, 1999.

Promises, Promises: Essays on Literature and Psychoanalyis. London: Faber and Faber, 2000.

Houdini's Box: The Art of Escape. London: Faber and Faber, 2001.

Equals. New York: Basic Books, 2002.

Going Sane. London: Hamish Hamilton, 2005.

Side Effects. London: Hamish Hamilton, 2006.

Intimacies. With Leo Bersani. Chicago: University of Chicago Press, 2008.

On Kindness. With Barbara Taylor. London: Hamish Hamilton, 2009.

The Concise Dictionary of Dress. With Judith Clark. London: Violette Editions, 2010.

On Balance. London: Hamish Hamilton, 2010.

OTHER WORKS

Monogamy. London: Faber and Faber, 1996. (Collection of aphorisms.)

The Penguin Freud Reader. Selected and with an introduction by Adam Phillips. London: Penguin, 2006.

"Over the Moon: Adam Phillips on the Happiness Myth." *Guardian*, September 4, 2010, p. 2.

The Concise Dictionary of Dress. Cocurated with Judith Clark. Installation at Blythe House (repository of the Victoria and Albert Museum), April 28–June 27, 2011. (See http://www.artangel.org.uk/projects/2010/the_concise_dictionary_of_dress for links to photographs and video interview with Adam Phillips.)

SELECTED EDITIONS AS EDITOR

Selected Prose. By Charles Lamb. London: Penguin, 1985.

The Renaissance: Studies in Art and Poetry. By Walter Pater. Oxford: Oxford University Press, 1986.

John Clare in Context. With coeditors Hugh Haughton and Geoffrey Summerfield. Cambridge, U.K.: Cambridge University Press, 1994.

CRITICAL AND BIOGRAPHICAL STUDIES

Fearn, Nicholas. "The New Statesman Profile." *New Statesman*, April 23, 2001, p. 18.

Garner, Dwight. "Monogamy." *Salon.com,* (http://www.salon.com/1997/02/19/monogamy/), February 19, 1997.

Güner, Fisun. "TheArtsDesk Q & A: Psychoanalyst Adam Phillips." *TheArtsDesk* (http://www.theartsdesk.com/visual-arts/theartsdesk-qa-psychoanalyst-adam-phillips), April 17, 2010.

Kermode, Frank. "Complicated Detours." *London Review of Books*, November 11, 1999, p. 7.

Lomas, Peter. "Terror of Simplicity." *Times Literary Supplement*, May 3, 1996, p. 28.

Payne, Michael. "What Difference Has Theory Made? From Freud to Adam Phillips." *College Literature* 32, no. 2:1–15 (spring 2005).

Showalter, Elaine. "Caring, but Little Sharing." *Guardian* (http://www.guardian.co.uk/books/2002/jul/06/highereducation.booksonhealth), July 6, 2002.

Tavris, Carole. "Shiny People Laughing." *Times Literary Supplement*, June 17, 2005, pp. 3–4.

Wood, Michael. "Haunted by Kindness." *London Review of Books*, April 21, 2005, pp. 17–18.

SECONDARY TEXTS

Hawthorn, Jeremy. *A Glossary of Contemporary Literary Theory*. London: Hodder Arnold, 2000.

JAMES ROBERTSON

(1958—)

Helena Nelson

JAMES ROBERTSON IS widely known as a Scottish novelist and champion of the Scots language. Nonetheless, the first few years of his life were spent in England. He was born on March 14, 1958, in the Kentish town of Sevenoaks, several hundred miles from the country with which he would develop such strong affiliation. His father, John Trevelyan Robertson, had served as a junior officer in the Royal Artillery during World War II (stationed first in India, where he was seconded to the Indian Army, and later in occupied Germany) and, following a Cambridge degree after the war, worked as a sales manager for John G. Stein, a company that made refractory bricks used in the lining of furnaces. His mother, Katherine Elizabeth Scott, had trained as a primary school teacher in Roehampton College, London. They were parents with a high regard for education: their house was full of books.

On both sides, however, the ancestry was Scottish. Katherine's parents were originally from Dundee, John's father was from Ross-shire, and though the grandparents had moved to England like their children, there was never any doubt about their native origins. As a result, when John Robertson moved his young family to Bridge of Allan near Stirling in 1964, there was a feeling—especially for the six-year-old James—that they had returned "not in a haze of exile, but really going home, like a nail into wood" (*Close & Other Stories*, pp. 10–11).

The youngest of three children, James quickly developed a habit of scribbling stories and poems, and drawing cartoons, while developing a passion for Westerns, first in book form and later in films. He had a particular sympathy for the "underdogs" of history, the Native American peoples, the Zulus, the Maoris. He knew he wanted to be a writer and he knew what he wanted to write—Westerns.

His childhood in Bridge of Allan was happy and privileged. The Robertsons had a comfortable income, with access to beautiful countryside, local libraries, and an excellent education. Early schooling for James and his older brother was at Hurst Grange, a privately funded school in Stirling, while his sister attended a girls' establishment closer to home. At Hurst Grange, Robertson received a thorough grounding in academic subjects, as well as Presbyterian Christianity. The head teacher, Tim Brown, taught Latin and English and encouraged creative writing in his pupils—even those who wanted to write Westerns. Robertson's sources of inspiration were historical, and his appetite for fact-based stories led him to commence a multivolume saga based in a U.S. cavalry outpost in Arizona.

There was undoubted parental support for his literary endeavors: at ten years old, the budding novelist was presented with a portable typewriter as a Christmas gift. The Robertsons lived in a large house, and the writer of the family had a room on the attic floor, where he typed away to his heart's content. He was reading voraciously and making weekly visits to the local library in Bridge of Allan, as well as periodic forays to the main library in Stirling. Though he remained loyal to Western writers such as Louis L'Amour, he quickly extended his tastes to classic novelists: Jane Austen, Thomas Hardy, George Eliot, Robert Louis Stevenson, P. G. Wodehouse, among many others. "Books," he later observed in an autobiographical essay, "have always been hugely important to me, a kind of backdrop against which the rest of my life has played out" ("Becoming a Writer," p. 347).

By the age of thirteen, he was a boarder at Trinity College, Glenalmond. The school was not as good as Hurst Grange, but since he excelled at history and English, and was also good at athletics and rugby, he settled in well. He continued to write in his spare time. By the age of sixteen, he had completed at least two books—one a Western, another a history of the Plains Indian wars. He was also writing poems and short stories, some of them quirkily influenced by surrealist painters and writers. He approached publishers with his work (his intention to be a professional writer burned brightly), but his manuscripts were returned.

In Scottish high schools at this time, the study of literature and history was almost exclusively *English* literature and *English* history. The young Robertson's experience was no exception, apart from the obligatory annual exposure to Robert Burns, the national bard. In his final high school year, he secured good examination passes in history, English, and French and was ready to go on to university. As the son of a Cambridge graduate, he was persuaded to stay on at school to do the Oxford and Cambridge examinations, although he had already developed significant unease with what he saw as an unfairly privileged system of education. Offered a place at his father's former college, he decided to turn it down: "Cambridge would be too much like Glenalmond for my liking—more cloisters and public school boys and, perhaps, more networks of snobbery and elitism" ("Becoming a Writer," p. 348). In 1976, Robertson commenced a degree in history at Edinburgh University, where his older brother was studying agriculture.

Up to this point, an exclusive education in an all-boys boarding school had kept the young writer from the "real world." At last he had arrived in a more egalitarian environment. While studying, he took a part-time job in the Safari Park at Blair Drummond, near Stirling. For a little while, writing receded into the background. But not for long.

In 1978, two events had a profound effect on him. First, he had the opportunity to study at the University of Pennsylvania for a year, as part of an exchange program. This time at an Ivy League school in Philadelphia opened new horizons, and allowed him to see Scotland from a distance— and for the first time to view it as a land of possibility, rather than restriction. Secondly, his journey to the United States coincided with the death of a legendary Scottish poet: Christopher Murray Grieve, better known by his literary pseudonym "Hugh MacDiarmid." MacDiarmid had a public reputation as a fiery radical—both in writing and in politics—although Robertson had read very little of his work. Paradoxically, it was in America that Robertson began to search out the great man's writings, and as soon as he returned to Scotland at the end of the year, he immersed himself in MacDiarmid's poetry and ideas. For the first time, Robertson began consciously to investigate "Scottish literature," "a literature that nobody had told [him] even existed" ("Becoming a Writer," p. 350). It was inspirational: he began to write poetry again, and the Scots tongue seemed to him a medium through which he could express feelings that had no other outlet.

It may be helpful at this point to place the writer's life in a political and historical context, since this is the backdrop to three of his four novels. Back in 1964, when Robertson was transported from Kent to Scotland as a child, he was moving to a country that had once been an independent sovereign state and had never forgotten that fact. Although the Act of Union in 1707 had united Scotland and England under the name "Great Britain," the move had proved unpopular north of the border, and the words of the 1320 Declaration of Arbroath had not been forgotten— Robertson quotes from this in his own young person's history of the Scottish parliament: "for sae lang as a hunner o us bide alive, we will niver naewise knuckle tae English rule" (*A Scots Parliament*, p. 23).

This concept of domination by the English, in political, linguistic, and cultural terms, recurred as a central concern with Scottish writers, not least from the mid-nineteenth century onward. By the 1920s, the poet and political agitator Hugh MacDiarmid spearheaded a Scottish cultural "renaissance" and was one of the driving forces behind the setting up of the Scottish National Party (SNP) in 1934. (The SNP later expelled MacDiarmid as a Communist.) MacDiarmid's poetry in Scots was a complex personal, moral, and political symbol. The power of the Scottish National Party was slow to develop, but in 1967 it took its first seat in the London parliament; after the second of two 1974 elections there were eleven Scottish MPs in Westminster; and by 1978, it looked as though devolved government in Scotland was not only possible but likely. In March 1979, in the spring of James Robertson's exchange year in Philadelphia—his absence overseas prevented him from voting—a referendum on political devolution was held. It failed to secure sufficient support, and the prospect of "home rule" receded for another two decades. Meanwhile, SNP members of the U.K. parliament, in protest at this result, withdrew their support from the Labour government, precipitating a vote of no confidence, a general election, and the loss of most of their seats. This was the year that a Conservative government, led by the first British female prime minister, Margaret Thatcher, came to power and James Robertson returned to Edinburgh, completing his history degree in 1980 with first-class honors.

Politically, therefore, things were disappointing to the young Scottish writer: the Conservative government represented privilege and capitalism, and it opposed devolved government for Scotland. However, he had several unpublished novels to his name: his apprenticeship as a writer was well under way. Deciding he needed more experience of the world, he traveled with a friend to Australia. Well-paid work was easy to find there. He also spent a couple of months in New Zealand. Returning to Scotland late in 1981, he assumed he would easily find employment: he was wrong. By the early 1980s, the United Kingdom was in the grip of a capitalist recession. Living with his parents again, he wrote another novel (which remained unpublished) and had poems in both English and Scots accepted by a range of literary magazines. Finally, he found paid work as a sales representative for the publishing firm Cassells, selling travel guides and phrase books.

The influence of MacDiarmid had not diminished. Robertson had become increasingly involved with Scottish cultural activity, deliberately strengthening the literary connections he knew were essential for a writer. He began to write for the leading arts and political magazine *Radical Scotland* and was accepted for doctoral study at Edinburgh University, researching the way Scottish history had been interpreted and reinterpreted over the centuries. This quickly led him to Sir Walter Scott, the historical novelist par excellence—and at this point he realized he need look no further. His final thesis was titled "The Construction and Expression of Scottish Patriotism in the Works of Walter Scott."

Meanwhile, Robertson was extending his experience of both publications and the book trade. He was working part-time in the Edinburgh branch of Waterstone's booksellers, and he had become the literary editor of *Radical Scotland*. He was writing poems, articles, and short stories. In 1987, he won third prize in Glasgow University's McCash Competition for poetry in Scots. That same year he married Anne Millar, a young woman he had met while he was a postgraduate student; she shared his cultural and political interests.

After completing his doctorate in 1988, Robertson transferred to the Glasgow branch of Waterstone's, where he became assistant manager. At the same time, he was continuing to write short fiction. His first significant publication was a short story collection titled *Close & Other Stories*, published by B&W Publishing (later renamed Black & White Publishing) in 1991. But by this time, the strain of combining a full-time job with the life of a writer was proving intolerable. The marriage, too, had been less than successful.

Publication of *Close* put Robertson in a position to apply for a writing residency. To his surprise and delight, he was successfully appointed as the first writer in residence in Hugh MacDiarmid's old cottage at Brownsbank near the Borders town of Biggar. Robertson gave up his job in the bookstore and moved into the isolated little property—on his own. Inside the cottage, he was surrounded by MacDiarmid memorabilia; outside there was an uninterrupted vista of farm fields. During his two years there, he completed a second collection of short stories (*The Ragged Man's Complaint*, 1993) and a first poetry collection (*Sound-Shadow*, 1995), as well as taking on a number of editorial tasks. His marriage was at an end, but his life as a full-time professional writer had begun.

SHORT STORIES

It is easy to see short stories as five-finger exercises completed in preparation for the "bigger" work. In Robertson's case, however, the short fiction is not so easily dismissed. In *Close & Other Stories*, he is already a confident writer, unafraid to present tales with potency out of proportion to their length. In "Rabbit," for example, the first-person narrator offers a straightforward meditation on death. Though little more than six hundred words long, the tale captures a voice, a character, and a situation with the succinct immediacy of a poem. The tone is wry, shrewd, and emotionally reticent: "There are in society those who are called achievers; and there are the rest of us" (*Close*, p. 40). It is a voice that recurs in Robertson's work.

The stories in *Close* draw on the settings Robertson has known well, not only Scotland but the United States and Australia. There is black humor—for instance, one serial killer is a bookseller, who takes revenge on the book-buying public because "Poetry is dead. It died, I think, with Eliot, the only modern poet whose lines I can remember" ("True Crime," *Close*, p. 52). There are elements of the magical and surreal, too—for example, in "Home Maintenance" the stresses in a marital relationship are increasingly evident in the way the bathroom and kitchen faucets keep tightening; and in "Bottle," the alienated main character lives inside a gigantic futuristic "bottle bank," collecting glass bottles as they are thrown inside for recycling. The short stories foreshadow themes (and sometimes characters) that Robertson will continue

to explore in greater depth: the responsibility (and often the isolation) of the individual; loving human relationships; and the living past, which is never wholly divisible from another central concern—the identity of Scotland itself.

A second collection of stories, *The Ragged Man's Complaint*, was issued in 1993, during the first year of the Brownsbank residency. It followed logically from the first: a similar (but not repetitive) blend of situational, reflective, or bizarrely surreal tales. There is more dialogue in this collection, though, and much of it is in Scots, including the dramatic monologue "Surprise, Surprise," which is in a consistently Scots voice. Increasingly, a concern with Scotland's identity asserts itself: it arises clearly in "The Mountain," "Portugal 5, Scotland 0," and "Republic of the Mind," in which the female character, Kate, reflects on Scotland before devolution:."that curious limbo … that place between what they had and what they sought. They were whole people but they were less than whole because of how their country was" (*The Ragged Man's Complaint*, p. 148).

Robertson had become increasingly interested in the idea of Scots as a literary language. In the second year of his MacDiarmid residency, he approached a number of contemporary writers (Irvine Welsh was among them) with the idea of a collection of stories entirely in Scots. He assembled twenty-eight of these and *A Tongue in Yer Heid* (1994) was born. In the introduction to this volume, Robertson outlines the case for Scots as a language in its own right. Old English developed two branches. One of these grew from the Saxon dialect south of the Scottish border into the English we know today. The other developed from the Anglian branch in the north and became Scots. "A writer's decision to reject English forms in favor of Scots ones is," observes Robertson, in his introduction to *A Tongue in Yer Heid*, "a political decision. The motive may be oppositional or affirmative, or both, in terms of class, culture or nationality, but it is inherently political" (p. xiii). For James Robertson, culture and politics are inseparable.

JAMES ROBERTSON

SOUND-SHADOW

Another product of the residency was Robertson's first collection of poems, *Sound-Shadow*. Published in 1995 by B&W Publishing, eleven of the forty-one poems are in Scots. The use of that language does not, however, correspond noticeably with the strongest writing, with the possible exception of "Makar o the Warlds," a lyric homage to MacDiarmid, which captures a voice both simple and genuine, referring to the great man's own poems as:

> ... perfite
> Wee sangs, arcin across the universe
> Like space-ships,
> Like starns.
>
> (*Sound-Shadow*, p. 50)

The language of the most intense poems here is English, as in "Fragment of an Autobiography" where

> A new-found anger knotted at the neck of my
> exclusive education
> And I began to deconstruct and reconstrue.
>
> (p. 18)

There's an attractive feeling here for the weight and placing of words, nicely exemplified by the angry elegance of the parallel verbs in "deconstruct and reconstrue." Even the poems in English, nevertheless, are lightly peppered with Scots words, such as "douce" (sweet) and "stour" (dust). The form is mainly free verse with traditional first-word capitalization, but there are also some metrical, rhyming pieces, as well as three sonnets in Scots. "A Space Between the Years" (p. 55) draws on a familiar theme—"Why does the past refuse to say goodbye," while "Into Exile," one of the most successful poems in the book, captures again the narrative voice of an isolated, but not unhappy, man:

> As I go into exile
> I look back and see
> Oban losing touch with me.
> And behind Oban, Lorn,
> Scotland, the world I suppose.
> They are wrapped in a pocket
> Of me crossing to Mull,

In a small pouch carrying them away from themselves.
> I hold them as I lean at the side of this boat,
> Looking down at the sea in its fight with men.
> And casually, carefully, I empty them in.
>
> (p. 26)

On this journey to a Scottish west-coast island, the poet synthesizes concepts and pebbles, geography and identity, and he does this without compromise or easy resolution. Ideas open and they remain open. In the lengthy poem "The Blues at Brownsbank," Robertson refers to

> Scots words still thick on the land, rough, kind,
> capable
> Language enduring against the odds, douce, dour
> cratur—
> This is one way of listening out for the future.
>
> (p. 63)

Past, present, and future—the overlapping layers of time: this would continue to be a powerful preoccupation, together with the idea of the Scots language as an enduring symbol of Scotland's individual spirit.

At this point in his career, Robertson had had stories and poems published, while undertaking editorial work of various kinds. But he had an idea for a tale set in seventeenth-century Scotland, a novel that would pull his various preoccupations together. To help support himself while undertaking the background research and writing, he began doing radio abridgments of classic novels, and he applied for a Scottish Arts Council bursary. While waiting to hear whether his application had been successful, he bumped into a former sales rep contact from his bookstore days, who floated the idea of a book of ghost tales—something of this sort, he suggested, would always be easy to sell. He put Robertson in touch with an editor, and within a year *Scottish Ghost Stories* was researched and written. Published by Warner Books in 1996, the volume proved commercially successful: it was reprinted seven times and as of 2011 it was still in print. Meanwhile, the Scottish Arts Council agreed to help fund research for his novel. *The Fanatic*, which appeared in 2000, turned out to be not only the first Robertson novel to find a publisher but also a novel that won him a sizeable readership.

JAMES ROBERTSON

THE FANATIC

Scottish Ghost Stories is not a serious literary text; it is a highly readable set of tales, written in standard English to suit a wide readership. Nonetheless, it does have links with *The Fanatic*. The second chapter of *Ghost Stories* deals with "The Wizard of the West Bow," Major Thomas Weir, one of the strictest Scottish Presbyterians of the seventeenth century, who, by his own account, fell prey to the Devil, committed a number of abominations, and, following his trial for heresy, was burned alive. Weir plays a crucial role in *The Fanatic,* too, as does James Mitchel, mentioned in the same chapter of *Ghost Stories*. Mitchel is the radical "Covenanter" who occupies center stage of Robertson's novel, while the old town of Edinburgh is the main setting.

The Fanatic is not, however, a straightforward historical novel. It crosses two time periods; it is an ambitious and complicated work, reflecting Robertson's sense of the past as a living presence in both spirit and structure. Each chapter is headed with a location and a date, the first being in 1677, the second 1997, and so on. Two main plot threads intermingle, but there are several subplots too.

The historical thread covers most of James Mitchel's life, from his experience as a boy in 1645 after the Battle of Philiphaugh to his execution in 1678. This is the period of the "Covenanters," the Scottish people loyal to the Presbyterian National Covenant of 1638, which formally rejected the Book of Common Prayer imposed on them by King Charles I as well as the idea that the Stuart monarchy had any sort of "divine right" to control the church. To the Covenanters, the only head of the Presbyterian Church was Jesus Christ, and many of them were prepared to fight and die for that belief. It was a time of faction, civil war, and brutal battles. Superstition mingled with religion; Highland warred with Lowland. The Devil was believed to walk the streets (Major Thomas Weir was one of his victims), and witches were hunted down and executed. In this setting, Robertson's seventeenth-century protagonist, James Mitchel, is driven by his fanatical (but genuine) dedication to the cause: he attempts to kill Archbishop Sharp, once a defender of the Covenant and now a turncoat: "Nobody was loathed by an entire people as Sharp was" (*The Fanatic*, p. 3).

Meanwhile, another set of characters establish their own tensions in modern Edinburgh. Carlin (the name, in Scots, means "old hag" or "witch"), the failed postgraduate history student who has lost his way in life, agrees to take on the job of ghost on one of the tourist ghost tours of the city. Garbed in a black cloak, with "magic" staff and wig, he is briefed to reenact the part of a phantom Major Weir, equipped with a spoof rat on a string. But Carlin already feels the past is tangible: "He could stretch his fingers and feel it, the shape of it. It was like having second sight in reverse." Worse still, it is "a hole at the back of his mind through which anything might come" (*The Fanatic*, p. 24).

Carlin's past life troubles him. An isolated person, he has good reason to find human closeness difficult. A young publisher, Jackie Halkit, has initiated his involvement in the ghost tours, but when she attempts to make personal contact with him, he resists. He isn't even convinced by his role as ghost. Something drives him to investigate the man he is impersonating, and the research into Weir leads him to Mitchel, the eponymous fanatic. Carlin is on a quest: he is looking for "the truth" about the past in order to understand something about his own present.

The chapters swing between the seventeenth and twentieth centuries. Sometimes a chapter will even cover two time periods, although both will either be historical or roughly contemporary. It is a complex mechanism, invoking an intricate network of minor characters. For example, Mr. MacDonald, an elderly librarian in the National Library of Scotland, assists Carlin in his research into Weir and Mitchel. MacDonald gives him access to a little-known manuscript, allegedly by Sir John Lauder, titled "ANE SECRET BOOK." Through this medium, Lauder, a man of intelligence and dignity, periodically provides potent first-person narrative.

However, MacDonald himself has ghostly traits, as does the secret manuscript, while Carlin, who cannot talk freely to human beings about personal matters, has long exchanges with his own mirror, conversations that add vitality and comic resonance. In this way, the narrative style varies dramatically—from fairly formal "English" commentary (sprinkled with Scots words) to broad contemporary Scots dialogue in Carlin's mirror conversations, and finally (in the manuscript extracts) to formal, elegant, seventeenth-century Scots. This creates a rich linguistic texture, without alienating a reader for whom Scots is not familiar.

Two particular aspects of the novel are compelling. One of these, as mentioned above, is the psychological state of Carlin—his partly anguished, partly comic exchanges with his talking mirror. The other is the intense drama of scenes from the lives of James Mitchel, Thomas Weir, and his sister Jean. Robertson has the ability to re-create a period incident and make it wholly believable. Elements of horror often make it even more riveting—the torturing of James Mitchel, for example, or the visit by Mitchel's wife to see her husband imprisoned on the tiny Bass Rock island. Although the central fascination (via Carlin and Lauder) is with Mitchel's mental state, mini-studies of female characters are also powerful. Mitchel's wife, for example, plays a tiny but emotive role, while Jean Weir (Major Weir's hapless sister) almost takes center stage at one point in the book, having two entire chapters of her own.

If there is a weakness in this novel, it is that the twentieth-century personages, with the exception of Carlin, are less "real." Hugh Hardie, who runs the ghost tours, is forgettable, and Jackie Halkit, though she has a more important role, is significantly less convincing than her female historical counterparts. But *The Fanatic* is a powerful and compelling read. It reflects accurately on a period of Scottish history sometimes termed "the killing time"; it accomplishes a dramatic pacing that keeps the reader riveted; it resists facile resolution about what is real and what is not; and it even brings the narrative wholly into the political present: at the end of the novel, people on the streets of Edinburgh are celebrating the results of the 1997 general election, which heralded the end of the Thatcher era and opened the door to Scottish devolution.

ROBERTSON AS PUBLISHER

In *The Fanatic*, Jackie Halkit works for a small independent publishing house. In his publications since 1991, Robertson had worked closely with editorial personnel at B&W Publishing (which had become Black & White Publishing), and in the 1980s he had worked for Cassells. In the late 1990s, as he searched for a publisher for *The Fanatic*, he took a somewhat unusual step for a novelist: he launched his own pamphlet imprint. He was living in the Fife village of Kingskettle at the time, and he named his new imprint Kettillonia. One intention with Kettillonia was that it would allow him to publish the sort of writing that did not easily find a publisher. He had himself just won the McCash prize for a six-part poem in Scots, and he had another sequence of poems in English inspired by Alfred Hitchcock characters and films. Such material was too lengthy for a magazine, too short for a book. However, he could, and did, publish it himself in chapbook form. But Kettillonia had wider ambitions. It aimed to "put original, adventurous, neglected and rare writing into print," with the catchphrase "Keep your finger on the pulse of Scottish writing" (www.kettillonia.co.uk).

The first few Kettillonia publications included Robertson's Scots verse translation of the eighteenth-century Gaelic poem "Là a' Bhreitheanais" ("The Day o Judgment"), by Dùghall Bochanan (Dugald Buchanan); *The Gravy Star,* extracts from a novel by Hamish MacDonald; *Temples Fae Creels,* by Andrew McNeil; Matthew Fitt's *Sair Heid City* (extracts from a novel in Scots); and Robertson's own *I Dream of Alfred Hitchcock,* all in 1999. The pamphlets were unusual and varied. Sales, even in bookstores, did remarkably well. The imprint was, and continues to be, a visible manifestation of Robertson's warm relationships with other writers in Scotland and overseas—he has also published Scots translations of the Chinese writer Yang Lian and, more recently, a book-length collection of poems by the Guatemalan poet Humberto Ak'Abal.

But Kettillonia is not Robertson's only foray into publishing. The friendship with Matthew

Fitt, which first started when Robertson published Fitt's short story "Stervin" in *A Tongue in Yer Heid*, had continued and flourished. The two writers shared a common interest in the use of Scots, especially as a literary language. As Robertson's Brownsbank residency came to an end in 1995, Fitt was appointed his successor. In 1996 the two men began to discuss an ambitious venture that would bring Scots language and literature into the classrooms of Scottish schools, still indubitably dominated by "English" literature. After several years of planning, proposals, and funding applications, and the involvement of a third team member, Susan Rennie, this idea finally materialized in August 2002 as a publishing imprint titled Itchy Coo.

"Itchy Coo" can be translated into English as "itchy cow." "Coo" is one of the most widely used and familiar Scots words, and it was simply and humorously reflected in the kicking cow logo. But "itchy coo" has a wider meaning too: it captures the idea of anything that causes a tickling sensation, precisely the sort of effect that was needed to get more Scots texts into homes and schools in Scotland. The three Itchy Coo originators, Robertson, Fitt, and Rennie, had formed an organization called Dub Busters, and on the advice of the Scottish Arts Council, they then formed a partnership with Black & White Publishing, the independent firm that had published Robertson's early stories and poems. Itchy Coo's formal aim was to provide a range of high-quality texts and other resources in Scots for use in school education at all levels. The subtext was to develop appreciation and confidence in the use of Scots by working closely with teachers and young people. It was a gargantuan task, but within the first two years, the new imprint had published sixteen titles, supported by a website and schools liaison program. As time went on, Fitt did most of the schools work, Robertson most of the editing. (Susan Rennie left the project in 2002.) The illustrator Karen Sutherland contributed outstandingly attractive artwork, and Itchy Coo books began to occupy prime positions in the children's section of all Scottish bookshops.

As of 2011, Itchy Coo had published thirty-seven titles, from which more than 250,000 books had sold. In terms of international sales of children's books, this is a relatively trivial number, but in terms of children's books in Scots, it is a remarkable achievement, in both cultural and political terms. In less than a decade, the status of Scots as a reputable language for learning had been raised significantly. Children's classics by Roald Dahl and A. A. Milne had been translated into Scots, not to create rivalry between versions but to enrich the reading experience on every level. At all points in its history, the enterprise has had a sense of exuberance, commitment, and excitement.

And yet, while all this was going on, James Robertson wrote, among other things, three novels, the first of which was *Joseph Knight*.

JOSEPH KNIGHT

Robertson began researching the real historical person known as "Joseph Knight" in 2000. Just under three years later, the novel was published to considerable acclaim, winning the Saltire Book of the Year award. The tale is prefaced by some words from the Nigerian novelist and poet Ben Okri: "Nations and peoples are largely the stories they feed themselves. If they tell themselves stories that are lies, they will suffer the future consequences of those lies. If they tell themselves stories that face their own truths, they will free their histories for future flowerings." In pursuing the truth about Joseph Knight, Robertson explores a less than praiseworthy period of history, in which European landowners, many Scotsmen among them, exploited the slave trade to make huge profits in the sugar plantations of the West Indies.

The real Joseph Knight was born in Africa and sold in Jamaica to John Wedderburn, who brought the slave with him to Scotland in 1769. Knight had been favored by his owner: he had learned to read and write, and no doubt to form his own opinions of his condition. Meanwhile, there was growing opposition to the slave trade in Britain: the case of James Somersett at the English Court of the King's Bench in 1772 had already confirmed that a slave, once in England, could not be forced by his master to leave the country again, and although the judgment stopped short of ruling on the legality of slavery itself, it was widely interpreted as effectively making it unlawful in England and Wales. At the same time, the international abolitionist movement was slowly gaining strength. Knight could read: he knew about the English court case and believed he could assert similar rights under Scottish law. Seeing himself as an employee, rather than an enslaved man, he demanded wages from Wedderburn, who refused; when Knight sought to leave his service, Wedderburn immediately had him arrested. Knight pursued his rights through the Scottish courts and had a ruling in his favor at the Sheriff's Court in Perth. Wedderburn appealed the decision but was ultimately defeated at the Court of Session in Edinburgh, Scotland's highest civil court. Because the Scottish judges looked at the whole question of slavery and not just the specifics of Joseph Knight's case, their decision effectively established the fact that slavery in Scotland was illegal.

James Robertson's novel commences in 1802. Sir John Wedderburn is in his seventies reflecting on his life and the regrettable decline of the slave trade. He recalls Toussaint L'Ouverture, the "barbarous savage" who "had learned the slogans *liberté, egalité* and *fraternité*" from the French revolutionaries and "had the outrageous idea of applying them to Negroes" (*Joseph Knight*, p. 5). As he considers his own mortality, he broods about his own former slave, Joseph Knight, who escaped from him nearly a quarter of a century previously. Through his solicitor, he has commissioned a private detective, Archibald Jamieson, to find Knight—to discover what happened to him after the court case. However, Jamieson has failed in his quest. "A man like that surely does not just disappear?" says Wedderburn incredulously (p. 8). That, nevertheless, is precisely what Knight has done.

Although Jamieson has failed, he continues his quest unpaid. The plot, therefore, is driven by this search for the mysterious Joseph Knight, just as the plot of *The Fanatic* was driven by Carlin's search for Major Thomas Weir. Jamieson needs

to understand why Knight was so important to Wedderburn and, ultimately, to himself.

The novel progresses, by means of flashback chapters, to survey the period of Scottish history from 1746 (the Battle of Culloden) to 1802, the focus of each section being to shed light on the Wedderburns, the background to the Jamaican slave trade, and finally the significance of Joseph Knight. The time frame (just short of sixty years) is much shorter than that used in *The Fanatic,* and as a result the plot lines work more cleanly. Actual historical events are seamlessly mixed with scenes of pure invention, and the reader rarely loses a sense of direction (the scenes where Scottish lawyers interact with James Boswell and the celebrated Dr. Johnson are the only point where momentum falters). As in *The Fanatic,* Robertson re-creates gruesome scenes from the past with riveting intensity—for example, the terrible defeat of the Jacobite rebels by government forces:

> Briefly the enemy's guns also fell silent. But then they began again, this time loaded with grapeshot, withering sprays of lead pellets that ripped through the clans like scythes through a field of oats. To stand and take this, after everything else, was intolerable. First the MacLeans, then all the Highlanders still surviving in the centre and right, threw off their plaids, gripped their claymores and staggered forward through the bog, screaming into the grapeshot gale as they went. They left behind a carpet of bodies and body parts. When they were halfway across the moor the Government infantry's muskets opened up on them.
>
> (p. 39)

This horrible vision haunts the subsequent life of Wedderburn, just as their father's death by hanging and disembowelment haunts his younger brother. These are the men of a generation who go on, in Jamaica, to dominate, enslave, and rule, exporting their massive wealth to Scotland, while themselves becoming characterized by repressed emotion and inability to love.

The scenes in Jamaica are equally powerfully depicted, not least the terrible punishments of the black slaves who rebel in 1760 and are brutally executed:

The gibbet was shaped like a huge H on the platform. From the crossbeam were suspended three contraptions like seven-foot-high birdcages. Cuffy and the other two were given some bread and cheese and a mug of grog each, then they were strung up in chains within these cages and hoisted above the crowd. There they were to hang, without further food or water, naked except for loincloths, through the blazing days and the humid, mosquito-thick nights, until they died.

(p. 121)

Parallels to the Christian crucifixion are obvious and troubling. When Wedderburn returns to Scotland he finds "there were many aspects of life in Jamaica that, back in Scotland, were better disguised, glossed over or suppressed" (p. 164). It is as though he has left a fantasy world to live in the real one, bringing just one token with him to prove it had all really happened. The token is eighteen-year-old Joseph Knight.

But things are changing. The philosophical ideas of the Enlightenment have become increasingly prevalent, and some of their finest proponents are in Edinburgh (the philosopher David Hume plays a background role). The theatrical climax is Knight's Court of Session case, in which the advocates John Maclaurin, Allan Maconochie, and Henry Dundas argue the case in favor of Knight, while Robert Cullen, James Ferguson, and Ilay Campbell defend Wedderburn's position as "owner." Interestingly, Knight's legal team, with whom the contemporary reader is most likely to sympathize, speak an elegant, beautifully phrased Scots: "We submit that, leavin aside aw the niceties o written law, whether there or here, there is a natural law frae which stem oor first principles o morality and justice, and that that natural law finds slavery utterly repugnant" (p. 296).

However, when the worthy lawyers defending Wedderburn's rights articulate their case, they speak in English. This sounds, by contrast, specious and manipulative. One of them even mocks the use of a Scots word (*deave*, meaning to annoy or weary):

Like my learned and emphatic friend Mr Dundas, I do not wish to *deave* your lordships with arguments you have already read at length. Nonetheless,

I must repeat what was said earlier: Joseph Knight is so far from being a *slave*, as that term is generally understood, that one must wonder what oppression it is from which he seeks to free himself.

(p. 307)

It is a powerful piece of writing. Though climactic, it is, however, by no means the end of the novel.

Robertson employs a number of narrators, as well as his own third-person account. Each brings us, it seems, a little closer to the mysterious Mr. Knight, and at last the concluding chapter allows Knight himself to speak directly to Jamieson. He has found a place in Scotland where his own history and the history of Scotland itself can meet and make sense: he has joined the coal miners of Fife. In the blackness of a mine all men are equal. Besides, it was the miners who sent money to help him fight his court case years before. We share Knight's thoughts as he connects the Scots heroes (William Wallace and Robert the Bruce) with the heroes of his own race, such as Toussaint L'Ouverture, those who fought for freedom from slavery. And Knight reflects on freedom, the sense in which he and his comrades both are and are not "free": "It might not be much, life, but he wanted it all the same, all he could get of it, so death would have to wait" (p. 372). The twist, of course, as Knight rejoices in the fact that he is "alive and here and now," is that he is really not alive at all, though the fiction is sufficiently powerful for his statement to feel true.

Joseph Knight tells a story that faces a nation (Scotland) with its own thorny truth: namely, that the Jacobite rebellion (which led to Wedderburn's father's execution) was regarded as noble and heroic, while Joseph Knight, who fought another historic battle, has been largely forgotten. In one sense, therefore, the novel seeks to restore a balance. It presents Scotland as, on the one hand, a country of willing slave owners and, on the other, a land that embraced enlightened change, a country where even the ordinary working people (the miners) supported a former black slave from what few resources they had.

THE TESTAMENT OF GIDEON MACK

Carlin, in *The Fanatic*, is unable to cope with closeness; Joseph Knight never reveals his true African name to his wife (although he loves her). These are novels from an author whose own marriage had failed. By the time Robertson was beginning the research for his third book, however, a new relationship had begun, one that would lead to a happy, stable marriage to Marianne Mitchelson in 2006. Perhaps this has something to do with the very different treatment of the central character in *The Testament of Gideon Mack,* which appeared in that same year. Although Gideon Mack is no less emotionally isolated than his literary predecessors, there is no doubt we are in the company of a novelist who is having fun: the whole idea of fiction has become a glorious playground. In fact, "truth" is the central theme of a story narrated entirely through more than one manifestly unreliable first-person narrator.

"The Testament," to which the title refers, forms the main part of the novel, sandwiched between a prologue and epilogue from the "publisher," who is apparently presenting the late Gideon Mack's autobiographical manuscript to the public. The setting is the Scottish east coast town of Monimaskit, where Mack was minister of the local church in the early years of the twenty-first century. Monimaskit is fictitious, as are Keldo Woods, the River Keldo, and the terrifying rock chasm the "Black Jaws." The curious reader, looking up names and geography on the Internet, will quickly find themselves at www. scotgeog.com, a site that at first appears serious and authoritative, and which even discusses the "real" town for which "Monimaskit" is the literary name: the presumed publisher has, after all, admitted that he has been "obliged to alter some of the names of the people and places involved in these affairs" (*The Testament of Gideon Mack*, p. 385). The website also makes reference to a local historian (another source of crucial information in the novel), Augustus Menteith. Menteith is a worthy Scottish name, but neither Augustus Menteith nor his useful book exists. Robertson deliberately intermingles fact and invention, in such a way that the reader quickly enters a world that seems real, a necessary setting for a tale where ordinary people come face to face with the supernatural.

The Testament of Gideon Mack is the only one of Robertson's novels so far to be recounted entirely in the first person, though the voice of the narrator is not Gideon Mack alone: at start and finish, the "publisher" introduces and concludes the tale in person. As a result, a sense of authenticity is established immediately, further assisted by the fact that the main narrator is a church minister. However, Mack is a cleric who has never believed in God. He has successfully concealed his own lack of faith from his congregation and fellow ministers. His life, therefore, has been in one sense a lie, and his "testament" (the title has deliberately biblical connotations) represents the document in which he finally tells "the truth." It is a story, however, that necessitates a willing suspension of disbelief: Mack falls into a river gorge, is carried underground by the force of the water, and spends three days in the company of the Devil, an interestingly modern individual. Of course, Mack may be mad, or he may be lying, or the publisher may have invented the manuscript. At least, these are the questions readers find themselves faced with, before remembering that everything, including the scotgeog.com website, has been fabricated by James Robertson.

The characterization, nonetheless, is entirely credible, and the relationships in the tale are plausible and compelling. The contemporary background, too, is the same one that has formed the backdrop to Carlin's experiences in *The Fanatic*. References to real political events in the United Kingdom place Mack's life in a context that is accurate and recognizable. Even Mack's birth date—March 17, 1958—means he is (or was) only three days younger than his living author. His "testament," therefore, sets his personal story in the context of the second half of the twentieth century, a period in which Scotland has become increasingly secular: Mack's loss of faith conforms to the national trend. At the same time, the novel creates its own legend, and there is no reason to suppose traditional Scottish attraction to tall tales and superstition has declined in any way.

In many ways, this is the most straightforward of Robertson's novels, even though its manipulation of fact and fiction is so elaborate. It could almost be one of the short stories from *Close*, allowed to run its full course. It recounts a dramatic sequence of events, involving one main protagonist, a love interest, a twist, and an ending that raises more questions than it answers, in the best tradition of a good ghost story. As always, the style (no matter who is telling the tale) is persuasive and readable. The evocation of scenery is intensely visual and the conception very much in the spirit of earlier Scottish novelists, such as Walter Scott, Robert Louis Stevenson, James Hogg, and John Buchan. The history of the land in which the tale is set is also never far away. At one point, for example, Gideon Mack encounters a bumblebee, unexpectedly flying out of a chest of drawers. It precipitates the following reflection:

> History. You can't get away from it. What the bee made me think of was one of those things that is half-myth, half-history: Archbishop Sharp, dragged from his coach on a moor in Fife by nine vengeful Covenanters, pushed to his knees and slaughtered. When they ransacked the coach they opened the dead man's snuffbox, and a bee, his supposed familiar—for Sharp, they believed, was not just their enemy and persecutor but a warlock who counted Satan among his friends—escaped from it and drifted away over the heather.
>
> (p. 169)

This tiny detail—the bee present at Sharp's death in 1679—is like a magnet attracting belief. It may not be true, but it *feels* true. It is unlikely someone today will believe Archbishop Sharp was a warlock, but we want to believe in the bee, just as we want to believe in that insect in Gideon Mack's house, and in the fact that Mack emerged from the river gorge wearing a different pair of shoes from the ones he fell in with (in all traditional tales of magic, the central character returns with some small sign that it was not all his imagination). It is a poetic technique, essentially, to pin a complex and searching idea to a tiny and apparently simple symbol, a visual

reality that will be remembered after much else is forgotten.

On the scotgeog.com website, there is an interview with the author (presumably Robertson interviewing himself), in which he refers to the real events that form the backdrop to this novel, "running from the Second World War through to the re-establishment of the Scottish parliament and the invasion of Iraq." Robertson goes on to suggest "the story of how the country changed politically and culturally in the second half of the 20th century would be a great subject for a big, sprawling, panoramic kind of novel." This precisely describes his next book, *And the Land Lay Still*.

AND THE LAND LAY STILL

If *Gideon Mack* is, in some ways, like a single extended short story, *And the Land Lay Still* (2010) resembles Chaucer's *Canterbury Tales*, a set of stories and characters connected by their journey through a common setting of time and place. The book is presented in six "parts," each the length of a novella and each preceded by a second-person meditation. The style of the meditations owes much to another influential Scottish novelist, Lewis Grassic Gibbon (1901–1935), employing sparse punctuation and exploiting rolling prose rhythms:

> *And the sea breathing its endless breaths around it, in out in out in out, great white waves crashing on black rocks, exhausted waves flopping flatly on deserted beaches, weed washing back and forth in bays and inlets, and fish eels lobsters seals ebbing and flowing in the tidal inhalations, exhalations, and sometimes a seal watching you, ten twenty thirty minutes an hour, submerging then resurfacing, always watching you, coming closer, keeping a distance, and you watching the seal, pacing it along the shore, connected but never connected, always apart.*
>
> (*And the Land Lay Still*, p. 1)

These italicized passages allow us into the mind of Jack Gordon, a character who abandons his home and family in part 2. It takes some time to realize whose thoughts we are sharing, and the style of Jack's thoughts creates a surreal effect, as though the voice behind the expression has stepped out of time. Jack (like Carlin, Joseph Knight, and Gideon Mack) is a misfit, a man who cannot belong in the human society of the land he loves.

But the novel also has much warmer, more accessible characters, the first of which is Michael Pendreich, who is trying to sort out the archive of his father's photographic work. Like a number of other individuals in this novel, Michael's father, Angus, is a storyteller. His work creates a visual narrative of Scotland over fifty years—or at least that's how his son sees it. Meanwhile, the novel itself recounts the key events in half a century of Scottish social and political history, assembled through the intricately connected lives of some of its people.

Following the various plot elements, many of which seem radically disparate at first, the reader needs to maintain faith that the novelist will assemble the "jigsaw pieces" in due course. Michael's task, it appears, is to make "the connections, more of them even than he can know or imagine" (p. 671). The first three parts are almost self-sufficient in terms of character and theme. By part 4, however, different elements and characters start to overlap. This is also the point where the reader is most at risk of confusion, because everything is set against real events in Scotland between roughly 1950 and 2008. It is a novel in which private lives and public life meet, in which imaginary characters talk about real events, in which even Angus Pendreich's photographs seem familiar, drawing as they do on familiar iconic images. It is a novel with a bit of everything: passion, violence, murder, rape, sexual despair, sexual reorientation, espionage, counterespionage, love. The country in which everything is set—Scotland—becomes a state of mind, which the contemporary reader is invited to inhabit.

Like *Gideon Mack*, this novel also plays with the blurred lines between truth and fiction. One of the main characters, Jean Barbour, is (among other things) well-known for her ability to spin a yarn, and two of her traditional (but beautifully contemporary) tales are shared in part 1. Jean is attracted to the idea of "a story with no beginning, no middle and no end," which is perhaps even "the story we're in" (p. 42). This is patently the story Robertson himself is also grappling with. Through character and event, he reviews the long-term effects of World War II and the subsequent slow period of change, culminating in devolved government in Scotland and a new sense of nationality. Although this is not an autobiographical novel, it is, in many ways, the story of James Robertson's own life.

Jack Gordon, the voice of the meditations, keeps a pocket of stones, and as he tramps the roads of Scotland with no identity and no apparent purpose, he finds

> the stones had no purpose, they were just a story. You kept the story going. That was what you had to do. You picked the stones up where you found them and you took them on, and every so often you laid them down again. You were making a pattern but you didn't know what the pattern was. You didn't know where you were in the pattern of where or how or if it would end.
>
> (p. 145)

Meanwhile, the more cynical Ellen Imlach, a journalist and another storyteller, tells Mike Pendreich, "All stories are lies, Mike. The secret is to work out how big the lie is. That's why we keep believing in a thing called truth. It doesn't exist but we can't help looking for it. It's one of the most endearing of human failings" (p. 539). Finally Michael himself addresses this idea in his speech to the assembled crowd at the exhibition of his father's photographs. "Trust the story. That's all. Trust the story," he says, recalling something Jean Barbour told him. Then he continues:

> Whatever else we put faith in will, in the end, betray us or we will betray it. But the story never betrays. It twists and turns and sometimes it takes you to terrible places and sometimes it gets lost or appears to abandon you, but if you look hard enough it is still there. It goes on. The story is the only thing we can really, truly know.
>
> (p. 646)

In this huge novel, a mammoth overview of life and times in Scotland over half a century, the reader shares an attempt to make sense of what is "really" going on psychologically and politically, and at the same time, becomes intensely involved with the life stories of a number of characters. The emphasis on story, though, and the sense of the land as an enduring "character" (shared with a nod to Lewis Grassic Gibbon), shows Robertson asserting his vocation as a national storyteller, taking his place in a literary tradition. His ability to tell a cracking tale is undoubted. What makes him particularly distinctive is the strong sense that he himself is grappling with the "truth" of what is going on, trying to make honest sense of a tale in which he is not only narrator but participant.

In 2011 Robertson was still mid-career as a novelist. After a book like *And the Land Lay Still*, it was impossible to predict where he might go next, though hard to contemplate anything that will not have Scotland as its geographical and psychological setting. Robertson's writing life has subsumed many roles. Through interaction with Black & White Publishing, and subsequently Kettillonia and Itchy Coo, he has been a publisher, editor, and translator. He has completed significant quantities of light verse in Scots for younger readers, his sense of fun immediately apparent in this context. He has also translated two of A. A. Milne's children's books into Scots versions (*Winnie-the-Pooh in Scots* in 2008 and *The Hoose at Pooh's Neuk* [*The House at Pooh Corner*] in 2010), as well as a book by Roald Dahl. This is perhaps a unique sideline for a major novelist, though not as disconnected from his other writing as may first appear. After all, the history teacher Billy Lennie, in *And the Land Lay Still*, is bringing up his children to speak the three languages of Scotland: Gaelic, English, and Scots. Passing on the richness of language is a matter both of heritage and love. We can see this clearly in Robertson's memorable rendering of Roald Dahl's *Fantastic Mr Fox* as *The Sleekit Mr Tod* (2008). The Scots version communicates sheer delight in the vitality of living Scots. For example, just after Mr Fox has narrowly escaped death at the hands of the three evil farmers (Boggis, Bunce, and Bean), Mrs Fox comforts him in the loss of his fine tail. Dahl's original English version reads:

Down the hole, Mrs Fox was tenderly licking the stump of Mr Fox's tail to stop the bleeding. "It was the finest tail for miles around," she said between licks.

"It hurts," said Mr Fox.

"I know it does, sweetheart. But it'll soon get better."

(Fantastic Mr Fox, p. 15)

Meanwhile, Robertson's Scots version goes as follows:

Doon the hole, Mrs Tod wis doucely lickin the dock o Mr Tod's tail tae stench the bleedin. "It wis the maist fantoosh tail for miles aroond," she said atween licks.

"It's sair," said Mr Tod.

"I ken it is, ma crowdie-mowdy. But it'll soon mend."

(The Sleekit Mr Tod, p. 15)

It's easy to see how children relish such words as "fantoosh" and "crowdie-mowdy," easy to see how Scottish educationalists would see such work as enriching for young readers—in fact, for *any* readers. The sheer exuberance of sound and rhythm reminds us of Robertson's other writerly function, as poet. His public presence as a novelist has overshadowed that side of his work, but it should not be forgotten.

ROBERTSON AS POET

In 1993, when Robertson took up post as MacDiarmid writer in residence, he looked like someone who might become primarily known as a poet. In the early 1980s, he had placed poems in all the leading Scottish poetry publications. His position as literary editor of *Radical Scotland* had brought him into regular contact with poetry and poets. He had won a prize in the McCash Competition for poetry in Scots in 1987, had poems in the Mercat Press *New Makars* anthology in 1991 (the same year that *Close* was published), and followed this up with his first collection, *Sound-Shadow* (discussed earlier). The impulse toward poetry, though it gradually took a backseat in publication terms, did not go away. One of Robertson's first Kettillonia pamphlets was *I Dream of Alfred Hitchcock* (1999), a set of thematically linked pieces, connected by works of the legendary film director. This sequence is almost entirely in English (the voice of the Scottish crofter from *The Thirty-Nine Steps* is one of two exceptions). It exploits dramatic monologue, using both free verse and formal structures. It has a sense of playfulness, combined with fine control of phrase and cadence. The title poem, for example, concludes:

> […] In the final cut he was just
> That fat laborious figure passing by, seemingly
> Irrelevant. His little joke, his last laugh.
> For with that bouquet he stamped his mark on everything
> I was about to see, as if to say,
> You may dream but you do not dream alone,
> You dream with me.
>
> (*I Dream of Alfred Hitchcock*, p. 4)

As Kettillonia continued to expand its list, it included a pamphlet of Robertson's sonnets, commissioned by the Stirling Smith Museum and confirming the author as a skilled formalist. Three of the seventeen poems in *Stirling Sonnets* (2001) are in Scots, and they are the ones that most clearly lift off the page. For example, there is "Dougal Graham on War." Graham was a disabled man of diminutive stature—the first known literary war reporter, born and bred in Raploch, the "rough" side of the city of Stirling. After witnessing the Jacobite defeat at Culloden in April 1746, he self-published and sold his *History of the Late Rebellion* in rhyming verse. In Robertson's sonnet he sounds remarkably modern (Scots is the only language in which this sonnet could convey its inimitable "bite"):

> I wis a hard wee bastart—had tae be:
> ill health and iller maisters made me teuch.
> But five fuit tall an Raploch-bred's eneuch
> tae cairry ye throu maist adversity.
> [*wis* = was, *maisters* = masters, *teuch* = tough, *eneuch* = enough]
>
> (*Stirling Sonnets*, p. 13)

In the same year, another Kettillonia pamphlet carried Robertson's translations from Baudelaire, *Fae the Flouers o Evil* (*Les Fleurs du mal*). The last of these metrically formal poems, "End o the Day," invokes the Scottish eighteenth-century poet Robert Fergusson, who becomes the speaking voice consigning himself to the shades:

> Ma body wearies for release,
> Ma hert wi heavy dooms is fou,
> Ma trauchelt spirit griens for peace:
> I hap ma banes in your daurk plaids
> An lay masel at lenth in you,
> O shades, O caller, caller shades.
> [*Hert* = heart, *fou* = full, *trauchelt* = troubled, *griens* = yearns, *hap* = wrap, *banes* = bones, *plaids* = blankets, *caller* = cool, refreshing]
>
> (*Fae the Flouers o Evil*, p. 28)

It seems Robertson's lyric voice may be increasingly finding its natural place in Scots rather than in English, and perhaps this offers a resolution to a common "problem." Contemporary U.K. writers, perhaps more now than at any other time, face the challenge of finding a diction at once both modern and appropriate to poetry. Since the 1930s, a number of Scottish writers, from Hugh MacDiarmid and William Soutar onward, have found Scots a medium that can be both ancient and modern, both traditional and exuberantly alive.

This, of course, is not a new phenomenon. In editing *Selected Poems* (2000), by Robert Fergusson (1750–1774), Robertson remarks that the bard "saw no dilemma in writing in both languages" (p. 13). Neither did James Robertson see such a dilemma when in 2004 the fruits of a new writing residency were shared—another inaugural appointment—this time at the Scottish Parliament building in Edinburgh. *Voyage of Intent* (2004), compiled during the residency, contains both sonnets and essays. The eleven sonnets purport to be similar to "snapshots of the Parliament a few weeks after its official opening" (*Voyage of Intent*, p. 11). They are a wonderful complement to the various prose sections from other works dealing with matters of Edinburgh politics, a consistently fine set of sonnets. Each of the eleven, whether in English or Scots, conveys a sense of mastery and precision. They have flowered at a unique time in history, and that fact is manifest in every word, every line. The final sonnet, the title poem, ends:

> For in the end a Parliament is not
> a building, but a voyage of intent,
> a journey to whatever we might be.
> This is our new departure, this is what
> we opted for, solid and permanent,
> yet tenuous with possibility.

(p. 24)

Voyage of Intent may be a slender volume, but it is an essential companion to anyone pursuing an interest in Robertson's work, as is his 2009 Kettillonia poetry pamphlet, *Hem and Heid*. This publication, which collects "ballads, sangs, saws, poems" in Scots, reminds us that Robertson's poetry, like mica in granite, has continued to gleam even as the prose works have dominated. *Hem and Heid* includes more than one ballad, an obviously attractive medium for a writer drawn to narrative forms. The pamphlet also includes translations from French and Spanish into Scots, as well as a sequence in six voices, all of them Scots, about the repatriation of a Lakota (Sioux) Ghost Shirt, returned by Glasgow's Kelvingrove Museum to South Dakota in 1999. "The Bluidy Sark," which won the University of Glasgow Mc-Cash Prize for poetry in Scots in 1999, focuses preoccupations that have been with Robertson from the start. When he sat at his typewriter in his attic bedroom at the age of ten, planning his history of the Plains Indian Wars, this image from "The Bluidy Sark" must have been in his head:

> ... a photograph that's hauntit me
> Since I wis nine or ten: a deid man in the snaw,
> A seik auld man in aw-through-ither claes,
> Hauns raxed oot tae grup at naethin, ice-stiff
> Whaur the bullets foondert him: still and on he lies,
> Auld Big Foot, deid a century and mair,
> Aye frozent there,
> Aye ettlin tae rise.
> [*deid* = dead, *snaw* = snow, *seik* = sick, auld = old, *aw-through-ither* = messy, jumbled, *hauns* = hands, *raxed* = stretched, *grup* = grip, *naethin* = nothing, *whaur* = where, *foondert* = felled, *mair* = more, *aye* = always, *ettlin* = trying]

(*Hem and Heid*, p. 32)

At some point, Robertson's poetry will surely be collected in a substantial volume. It complements his prose writing in a way that nothing else quite could. In *And the Land Lay Still*, the gatherings at Jean Barbour's house evoke an essential aspect of Scots culture—its multifaceted nature: story-telling, debate, poetry, painting, photography, singing. Just as all the characters in this complex novel are linked, so James Robertson's writing, in all its various forms, connects.

Of all contemporary novelists in Scotland, Robertson must surely be foremost in consciously staking a claim to his place in the Scottish literary tradition, though he does not do this lightly. From William Dunbar to Edwin Morgan, the influences are there, weaving their way through his writing, sometimes almost invisibly. Like Sir Walter Scott, he reanimates historic events. Like Scott, too, he has taken on the role of publisher, collecting and disseminating the work of other Scottish writers. Even in the elaborate notes from the "publisher" in *The Testament of Gideon Mack* there is mischievous allusion to Scott. But at different times in different books most of the great names of Scottish writing come to mind—James Hogg, Robert Louis Stevenson, John Buchan—as well as the fact that many of them wrote both prose and verse.

Robertson's 2010 novel, *And the Land Lay Still*, has three dedicatees, all now dead. One of them is Jean Bonnar, to whom the poem "Oot o This Life" in *Hem and Heid* is also dedicated. Although Robertson's work is still far from complete, "Oot o This Life" offers an attractive sense of quietus. It is both traditional and modern; its use of Scots is in perfect harmony with the lyric voice; and somehow it matches the meditations of Jack Gordon as he wanders farther and farther north, until he is finally ready to die. It is the sort of poem that will prove durable in the literary tradition, a poem that could have been written at any time in the last three hundred years, and perhaps, therefore, a fitting note on which to conclude:

> Oot o this life ye maun mak a life,
> Syne oot o this life ye maun gang;
> And the mak o it micht be bruckle or haill

And the span o it short or lang,
And the sun micht shine or the rain ding doun
And yer days be lown or thrang,
But oot o this life ye maun mak a life,
Syne oot o this life ye maun gang.
[*mak* = make; *oot* = out; *maun* = must; *syne* = then; *gang* = go; *mak* = making; *micht* = might; *bruckle* = fragile; *haill* = strong and healthy; *lang* = long; *ding doun* = beat down; *lown* = calm; *thrang* = full of bustle, stress]

(*Hem and Heid*, p. 5)

Selected Bibliography

WORKS OF JAMES ROBERTSON

Short Stories
Close & Other Stories. Edinburgh: B&W, 1991.
The Ragged Man's Complaint. Edinburgh: B&W, 1993.
Scottish Ghost Stories. London: Warner, 1996.

Novels
The Fanatic. London: Fourth Estate, 2000.
Joseph Knight. London: Fourth Estate, 2003.
The Testament of Gideon Mack. London: Hamish Hamilton, 2006.
And the Land Lay Still. London: Hamish Hamilton, 2010.

Poetry
The New Makars: The Mercat Anthology of Contemporary Poetry in Scots. Edited by Tom Hubbard. Edinburgh: Mercat Press, 1991. (Poems from a variety of contemporary Scots poets.)
Sound-Shadow. Edinburgh: B&W, 1995.
I Dream of Alfred Hitchcock. Kingskettle, U.K.: Kettillonia, 1999.
Fae the Flouers o Evil: Baudelaire in Scots. Kingskettle, U.K.: Kettillonia, 2001.
Stirling Sonnets. Kingskettle, U.K.: Kettillonia, 2001.
Voyage of Intent: Sonnets and Essays from the Scottish Parliament. Edinburgh: Scottish Book Trust and Luath Press, 2004.
Hem and Heid: Ballads, Sangs, Saws, Poems. Newtyle, U.K.: Kettillonia, 2009.

Selected Work for Children and Young Readers
A Scots Parliament. Edinburgh: Itchy Coo, 2002. (A history of Scotland's Parliament from its medieval origins to the present day, written in Scots.)

King o the Midden: Manky Mingin Rhymes in Scots. Edited by James Robertson and Matthew Fitt. Edinburgh: Itchy Coo, 2003.

Translations into Scots
Là a' Bhreitheanais/The Day o Judgment. Kingskettle, U.K.: Kettillonia, 1999. (Translation from the Gaelic of the poem by Dùghall Bochanan/Dugald Buchanan.)
The Sleekit Mr Tod. Edinburgh: Itchy Coo, 2008. (Translation from the English of Roald Dahl, *The Fantastic Mr Fox*, London: Puffin Books 1974; reissued with new illustrations by Quentin Blake in 1996. The Itchy Coo version reproduces the 1996 illustration and pagination.)
Winnie-the-Pooh in Scots. Edinburgh: Itchy Coo, 2008. (Translation from the English of A. A. Milne, *Winnie-the-Pooh*.)
The Hoose at Pooh's Neuk. Edinburgh: Itchy Coo, 2010. (Translation from the English of A. A. Milne, *The House at Pooh's Corner*.)

As Editor
Hugh Miller: Scenes and Legends of the North of Scotland. Edinburgh: B&W, 1994.
A Tongue in Yer Heid: A Selection of the Best Contemporary Short Stories in Scots. Edinburgh: B&W, 1994.
Dictionary of Scottish Quotations. With Angela Cran. Edinburgh: Mainstream, 1996.
Selected Poems. By Robert Fergusson. Edinburgh: Birlinn, 2000.

Other Work
"Becoming a Writer." In *Spirits of the Age*. Edited by Paul Henderson Scott. Edinburgh: Saltire Society, 2005. Pp. 339–352. (Autobiographical essay.)

Selected Kettillonia Publications
Ak'Abal, Humberto. *Drum of Stone*. Newtyle, U.K.: Kettillonia, 2010. (Selected poems with translations in English by Rosemary Burnett and in Scots by James Robertson.)
Fitt, Matthew. *Sair Heid City*. Kingskettle, U.K.: Kettillonia, 1999. (Extracts from a novel in Scots.)
Lian, Yang. *Whaur the Deep Sea Devauls: A Sequence and Other Short Poems*. Newtyle, U.K.: Kettillonia, 2005. (Scots translations from the Chinese by Brian Holton and Harvey Holton.)
Macdonald, Hamish. *The Gravy Star*. Kingskettle, U.K.: Kettillonia, 1999. (Extracts from a novel by MacDonald.)
McNeil, Andrew. *Temples Fae Creels*. Kingskettle, U.K.: Kettillonia, 1999.

Correspondence and Manuscripts
The National Library of Scotland has drafts and typescripts of *The Fanatic*, *Joseph Knight*, and *Gideon Mack*.

CHARLOTTE TURNER SMITH

(1749—1806)

Marianne Szlyk

CHARLOTTE TURNER SMITH IS one of many authors whose literary reputation has benefited from the rise of feminist literary criticism and its reappraisal of women's writing. It is true that early-twentieth-century scholars examined Smith's work both on its own terms and as part of a larger context. Most notably, they examined her novels as an influence on Jane Austen's fiction and an object of the later novelist's satire. Smith herself would not become central to scholars' mapping of literary fields until much later; as Jacqueline M. Labbe points out in her introduction to the 2008 volume *Charlotte Smith in British Romanticism*, in 1971, the scholar Bishop C. Hunt, Jr., "could only conclude that Smith was the lesser artist, despite the clear affinities" (p. 3) between Smith's work and William Wordsworth's and despite the male poet's acknowledgment of Smith's influence. Then in 1986, Dale Spender counted Smith in a catalog of female predecessors to Jane Austen. Citing Smith's portrayal of her protagonists as well as her engagement with politics, Spender grouped her with other neglected authors, some of whom, like Aphra Behn, are now central to eighteenth-century literary studies. In 1995, David Perkins' second edition of his *English Romantic Writers*, a popular college-level anthology, included Smith in its infusion of female poets and essayists. This event occurred alongside more sustained critical scrutiny of women's writing within Romanticism and Stuart Curran's 1993 scholarly edition of Smith's poetry. Curran, in his introduction to *The Poems of Charlotte Smith*, presents this once obscure author as "the first poet in England whom in retrospect we would call Romantic," drawing readers' attention to her impact on Wordsworth and other poets (p. xix). More recently, in her introduction to *Charlotte Smith in British Romanticism* (a collection of essays by various scholars),

Labbe argues that Smith is key to an understanding of Romanticism. She also advocates scrutiny of Charlotte Smith's writing in various genres (poetry, novels, children's literature, plays, and letters), which will in turn enable readers to gain a fuller understanding of her accomplishment as an eclectic Romantic-era author. Conversely, the absence of a multiple-genre approach may have limited scholars' understanding of these achievements, as Labbe indicates in her introduction.

More importantly, the rise of Smith's literary reputation reflects the ongoing evolution of literary studies itself, a phenomenon that is partially but not wholly due to feminist scholarship. In 1965, Harrison R. Steeves characterized Smith as "[no] more than a respectable bread-and-butter novelist with an appraising eye for literary vogue" in *Before Jane Austen*, a survey of the eighteenth-century novel (p. 317). The superficiality of this characterization reflects the mid-twentieth century's mapping of the literary field with the art-novel at its center. Feminist scholars have transformed this map so that it is more sensitive to women writers and readers' concerns as well as to the conditions under which writers and publishers produced work and readers consumed it. This transformation has in turn affected what can be considered literature. As Labbe has maintained, reading Smith's work in multiple genres alongside each other is essential to understanding it. The presence of her poetry in her novels is a prominent feature; however, one must also juxtapose Smith's novels with her children's literature, a genre that has not always been considered literary, as well as her letters. Moreover, Smith herself believed that her poetry was her best and most significant work. The fall of formalism may also have bolstered Smith's literary reputation, as her novels' distinguishing features include not only poetry but also substantial stretches where another character's story interrupts the main narrative. In other words, her novels did not have "the unity of design" that Gary Kelly sought in his groundbreaking 1976 study, *The English Jacobin Novel, 1780–1805,* even though they clearly possess the political and autobiographical elements that he was interested in (p. 12). Writing eleven novels in fourteen years (to name only one of the genres she worked in), supporting a large family, Smith was prolific, producing uneven work, whereas more highly regarded novelists like Elizabeth Inchbald and Jane Austen wrote fewer books, enabling them to spend more time on each. Furthermore, scholars' greater willingness to consider literature within its political and historical context has made Smith a more interesting writer even when, as in *The Banished Man* (1794) or *The Young Philosopher* (1798), to name two of her later novels, she appears to contradict the positions dramatized in her earlier novels. These actions, conversely, caused earlier critics like Steeves to view her politicized writing as merely following a "literary vogue." Finally, the dynamic and contested boundaries between British literature's "long eighteenth century" (1660–1815) and its Romantic era (1780–1830) have also elevated Smith's literary reputation. In her introduction to *Women, Revolution, and the Novels of the 1790s* (1999), Linda Lang-Peralta draws readers' attention to previous conceptions of these novels (including Smith's) as "strangely-shaped formations [in] a desert area generally to be avoided for the sake of the manicured gardens of Enlightenment literature or the well-marked peaks of Romanticism" (pp. ix–x). Given this perspective, Smith's works were marginalized. By contrast, if one views the late 1700s and early 1800s as a contested, dynamic, and therefore transitional period, Smith's writing becomes much more interesting.

THE LIFE OF CHARLOTTE TURNER SMITH

Smith was born in London on May 4, 1749, to Nicholas and Anna (Towers) Turner, a young couple who, as their daughter's biographer Lo-

raine Fletcher notes, had fallen in love and been able to marry because of his elder brother's death and the subsequent inheritance. Similarly opportune events often conclude Charlotte Smith's novels, especially *Emmeline: The Orphan of the Castle* (1788) and *The Old Manor House* (1793). Like the happy couples in these novels, Nicholas and Anna also spent much time in the country as he owned two estates and other properties there. Their Suffolk estate, Bignor Park, would be especially significant to Charlotte, whose poetry later celebrated the nearby River Arun. However, Anna died giving birth to a son, also named Nicholas, when Charlotte was three and her sister Catherine Anna was two. Grief-stricken, Charlotte's father traveled in Europe while his unmarried sister-in-law Lucy Towers raised his children at Bignor Park and later in London. He would be away from his family for several years and did not return until Charlotte was in school. He also gambled, and subsequently had to marry a wealthy woman to pay his debts.

Charlotte was a lively, precocious child who was particularly interested in reading, writing, drawing, and botany and, in Stuart Curran's words, "received the best of what then passed for a girl's education" (1993, p. xix). While at school, she received drawing lessons from the landscape painter George Smith (no relation to the man she later married). Botany drew her closer to her beloved countryside, and she would recommend this science through her writing for children. Surprisingly, she left school at the age of twelve. Loraine Fletcher indicates that Nicholas Turner's financial troubles led him to keep her at home. These troubles also caused him to sell Stoke Place, his property in Surrey. Nevertheless, Charlotte was tutored at home, and then entered society at age thirteen, all of which involved a significant outlay of money. A more typical age for a young lady to attend adult parties would have been sixteen or seventeen. (In comparison, from the same era, Frances Burney's Evelina is eighteen when the events of the novel occur, as later is Jane Austen's Fanny Price when the Crawfords wonder whether or not she is "out" in society.) Charlotte's early marriage, at fifteen to Benjamin Smith, occurred as a result of her father's remarriage, as stepmother and stepdaughter did not get along. By the time Charlotte was eighteen, she had given birth to two children, her first having died while she had been pregnant with her second. Late in her life, when discussing her marriage with her correspondent Sarah Rose, she stated that she had been "sold a legal prostitute in my early youth" (*The Collected Letters of Charlotte Smith*, 2003, p. 625). She also crossed out her last name, Smith, in signatures to later letters, signifying her contempt for her husband.

Charlotte's marriage moved her to a very different milieu, as her husband was the son of a successful London merchant. The first, fragmentary letter in *The Collected Letters of Charlotte Smith* recounts her mother-in-law's constant criticism in a lighthearted way. It nevertheless shows her frustration with the woman's praise of "the [merchants' wives in the West Indies], whose knowledge of housewifery she is perpetually contrasting with my ignorance" (p. 2). In addition, Charlotte began married life in a relatively urban section of London, rather than in the countryside, and she was constantly pregnant, bearing twelve children in twenty years and burying three of them by 1786. In 1767, after the death of her first child and the near-death of her second, her father-in-law allowed her to leave the city for Southgate, which was close enough that her husband could rejoin the family on the weekend. He often did not, pursuing pleasures incompatible with both family life and business. An early biographer, Mary Hays, notes that Charlotte's retreat from her marriage permitted devotion to motherhood and learning, sometimes simultaneously, for she read while nursing her children or rocking the cradle. However, by 1771, Charlotte and her growing family left this idyll for a larger house in Tottenham, a suburb of London. There her family responsibilities (which involved serving as clerk and confidante to her father-in-law, Richard, as well as raising her children) overwhelmed the time that she had carved out for herself in Southgate. By this point, her mother-in-law had died, and Richard had remarried Charlotte's aunt. Lucy's motives for this relationship were complicated, as Fletcher

observes in *Charlotte Smith: A Critical Biography*. The well-meaning Lucy would remain involved in her niece's life, even after Charlotte separated from Benjamin in 1785.

Richard Smith died in 1776, setting off a chain of events that would compel Charlotte to become a professional writer. Intending to protect his grandchildren from their father, Richard had written his will in such a way that his other family members, namely his sons-in-law, Thomas Dyer and John Robinson, refused to settle it for years. They furthermore sued Benjamin Smith for his mismanagement of the estate, and this suit forced him first into debtor's prison and then to life abroad and in Scotland, first with Charlotte and family, and then with his mistresses and their children. Debtor's prison was clearly traumatic for her. Shortly after she separated from her husband, her response to her failed marriage was to fight for her children's inheritance and write for a living. Her career as a writer began with the successful first volume of *Elegiac Sonnets* (1784), which revived a once-outdated form and invoked the natural world that nourished yet could not satisfy her. After translating two French works, she turned to the novel. Her first effort, *Emmeline* (1788), was successful, appearing in four British editions, two American editions, and one French translation during her lifetime. From 1791 on, Charlotte became acquainted with left-wing writers and thinkers based in Brighthelmstone (now Brighton). As a result, beginning with *Desmond* (1792) and continuing until her career's end, her novels weighed in even more decisively on political and social issues, bringing both gravitas and immediacy to her variations on the courtship plot and the gothic novel. She then became the object of conservative ire, which served to deflate her literary reputation, especially after her death. She would publish eleven (or twelve, if one counts her uncompleted *Letters of a Solitary Wanderer* of 1800–1802) novels, four books of poems (including nine editions of the first volume of *Elegiac Sonnets*), five works for children, one play, and one nonfictional narrative in the years until her death in 1806. All the while, she managed her career, battled with lawyers and the trustees of her father-in-law's estate as well as with her brother and sister, educated not only her children but also her grandchildren, mourned the loss of her adult children Augusta Anna and Charles, and lived with serious illness, probably arthritis and either uterine or ovarian cancer.

Charlotte Smith died on October 28, 1806, in Surrey. She pursued her vocation to the end, as two books—the now critically acclaimed *Beachy Head* (1807) and the other a natural history for children written with her sister, Catherine Anna Dorset—appeared after her death. Her husband had died months earlier in debtor's prison. Richard Smith's estate would not be settled until 1813, and even then none of Charlotte and Benjamin's surviving children received anything from what remained after thirty-seven years of legal wrangling.

ELEGIAC SONNETS

The two volumes of *Elegiac Sonnets and Other Poems* can now be considered the centerpiece of Charlotte Smith's own career, particularly as her poetry has gained more prominence within Romantic studies, reflecting her literary ambitions. She continued to work on these poems, starting with the first edition in 1784 (titled *Elegiac Sonnets and Other Essays*) adding a second volume in 1797, and finally attempting to produce a third in 1806. In these poems, Smith gives voice to a number of speakers while maintaining a consistently mournful tone. Her speakers include not only ones presumed to be herself but also characters from her novels and other figures such as Petrarch and Johann Wolfgang von Goethe's Werther. The variations in these poems reflect individual differences. To choose two examples, both from *Elegiac Sonnets*, the theme of Sonnet 40, a piece later included in her novel *Emmeline*, is very much like that of "To Spring." Yet Sonnet 40's slower pace and ocean imagery arise from the languor of its speaker, *Emmeline*'s Lady Adelina Trelawny, whereas "To Spring," a sonnet whose speaker may be the author, bristles with vivid imagery of birds, flowers, and other greenery, the nature that offers "the power to cure all sadness—

but despair" (1993 ed., p. 18) Smith maintains this dichotomy between nature's power and its impotence in many of the sonnets, but not all. In Sonnet 21, Smith's Werther excludes the natural world to focus on his emotional turmoil, "the path that leads me to the grave" (1993 ed., p. 27). Even when he goes to this world to find solace, as in Sonnet 22, his descriptions are less vivid than elsewhere in Smith—or in the passage from Goethe's novel that Smith quotes in her footnotes. This quality reflects his psychological state, which he succumbs to and Lady Adelina does not. Smith also gives voice to characters whose sorrow is less pervasive and more occasional. Lady Adelina's brother, Godolphin, a naval officer who ultimately marries Emmeline, reveals himself through "his" sonnets published in *Elegiac Sonnets*. *The Banished Man*'s Mrs. Denzil contributes a satirical view of Brighthelmstone in Sonnet 64, denying its ability to cure melancholy despite "romantic rocks that boldly swell" or "tepid waves, wild scenes, or summer air" (1993 ed., p. 56).

Smith also uses her sonnets to place herself in a network of literary relations that her constant novel writing and her family's legal troubles may have prevented her from assuming in real life. In "To Miss C—on being desired to attempt writing a comedy," she defends the tone and subject matter of her poetry against the suggestions of an unnamed "ever partial friend" (1993 ed., p. 32). Other addressees include her one-time literary mentor and friend William Hayley. In Sonnet 19, she compares her poetry, "a simple band design'd / Of 'idle' flowers that bloom the woods among" (1993 ed., p. 25) to his, embodied by "The laurel wreath [...] woven with myrtles by the hands of Taste" (1993 ed., p. 25). Elsewhere, in Sonnet 64, written in the voice of a fictional character, she embeds a quote from his "Epistle to a Friend on the Death of John Thornton" (1790) just as she embeds quotes from John Milton or Shakespeare in other poems. Even after their later estrangement, and even as she cast aspersions on Hayley's recent poetry, Smith often mentioned to Sarah Rose her wish that she had been able to show her later works to him. Smith's frequent apostrophes to Suffolk's River Arun may also be placed in this category as they also invoke the playwright Thomas Otway and the poet William Collins as well as childhood and the natural world. Similarly, she takes on the persona of Petrarch in several sonnets and elsewhere celebrates Penshurst, the subject of Ben Jonson and Edmund Waller's poetry. Stuart Curran indicates another, more pervasive strategy: her use of quotations from her extensive knowledge of English and other European literatures including Latin ("Intertextualities," 2008, p. 179). Furthermore, as the poet who revitalized the sonnet for a new generation, she contributed to a network of literary relations between older poets such as Petrarch and John Milton and newer poets such as Wordsworth, John Keats, and the Victorians who followed in their path.

OTHER POETRY

Given the political elements present in her novels and her writing for children as well as her ambitions for her poetry, it is surprising that Charlotte Smith wrote only one overtly political long poem, *The Emigrants* (1793), a two-part, blank-verse work that advocates for the French who sought refuge in England during the Revolution. Her emphasis is on mothers and their children as well as on the clergy. In the first book of *The Emigrants*, set during November 1792—that is, after the September Massacres and the fall of the monarchy but before the king's trial—she depicts the refugees as they arrive on the English shore. She displays surprisingly less irony and animus than one would imagine. The speaker's praise for England's charity and skepticism about liberty mediates her call for reform. Above all, a proto-pacifist, she advocates for peace. Her footnotes maintain her respect for the Catholic clergy, which may have surprised readers of her novels, especially *Celestina* (1791) and *Desmond*, where she had criticized their abuse of power. However, the clergy she depicts are in a much more humbled position than those who appear in her novels, including her later *Letters of a Solitary Wanderer* (1800–1802). In *The Emigrants*, she juxtaposes "[him] of milder heart, who was indeed / The simpler shepherd in a rustic scene"

(1993 ed., p. 141) and "the wandering Pastor [who] mourns […] / His erring people" (1993 ed., p. 142) with an individual higher up in the hierarchy who "[dwells] on all he lost—the Gothic dome, / That vied with splendid palaces" (1993 ed., p. 140) and his political influence. These members of the clergy, in turn, mix with Smith's archetypal sorrowful mother and "her gay unconscious children, soon amus'd" (1993 ed., p. 142), all of whom arouse the speaker's pity and her call for political reform in England. This sorrowful mother, however, recalls the French court where, echoing yet subverting Edmund Burke, "Beauty gave charms to empire" (1993 ed., p. 143). This mother's recollection of Versailles does not invoke the scorn that Smith's novels reserved for glamorous women. Her perspective is also distinct from the matter-of-fact way that mothers in Smith's writing for children view their former participation in the social whirl. Then, in the second book of the poem, set in March 1793, after the former king's execution, the speaker again contemplates the exiles' camp and conjures up the horrors that have occurred in France. Characteristically, she admits that the reviving spring cannot make up for the horrors that the exiles have endured, not to mention her own legal troubles. Pitying both Louis XVI's family in its prison and the farm worker in Britain, she concludes that happiness may not be found on earth; nevertheless, she calls for "the reign of Liberty, Reason, and Peace" (1993 ed., p. 163).

Even though Charlotte Smith would continue to weave political and social commentary in her novels and writing for children, her other, later, poems value aesthetics and morality over political engagement. Her aesthetic engagement, as Judith Pascoe notes, relies on a minutely particular, scientific gaze, and therefore, it may be considered a stance within cultural politics for particularity and against transcendence. Smith's poems written for *Conversations Introducing Poetry: Chiefly on Natural History* (1804) emphasize the natural world, elevating study of this world to a means of learning important moral lessons. "The hedge-hog seen in a frequented path" encourages its readers to treat wild animals with kindness rather than tormenting them (1993 ed., pp. 183–184). "The early butterfly" promotes empathy as the speaker describes the fate of an insect in spring (1993 ed., pp. 184–185). Perhaps the most overtly political is "To the fire-fly of Jamaica, seen in a collection," which presents the insect alongside various figures, including a slave escaping from his or her master (1993 ed., pp. 204–207). Smith's later *Beachy Head* (1807), a posthumously published work, expands on this emphasis while adding depictions of historical scenes to its vast canvas. This extensive, perhaps incomplete, poem begins as *The Emigrants* does, with the speaker entering her vantage point above the English shore. However, this speaker sees farther in space and in time. Her vision includes not only the shoreline itself but also the relics of Roman culture in Britain and a succession of fleets from present-day merchant ships to the Dutch and English ships at war with the French to the Norman invasion. She recalls her own childhood spent exploring the countryside near the River Arun as well as archetypal, fictional characters who find solace in nature. One man even composes poetry to that effect, which we read. As in *The Emigrants*, she questions whether humans can be happy on earth, but in this later poem, her answer is inconclusive, embracing both the pleasure that a recluse finds in writing poetry and the sorrow that a girl and her brother find as they grow up. One wonders how she might have finished this poem, and Curran speculates that either Smith's sister or her publisher Joseph Johnson may have edited it significantly in order to prepare it for publication. As her last letters on literary business reveal, this final poem marked a new type of poetry for her, transcending her earlier sonnets. Critics today praise her continual evolution as a poet, even, as Curran does, contrasting it with, by implication, the absence of such evolution in Wordsworth and Samuel Taylor Coleridge's work.

EARLY NOVELS (UNTIL 1791)

Of Charlotte Smith's novels, her first three are probably the most conventional, each being a variation on the courtship plot as seen from the young woman's perspective. *Emmeline: The Orphan of the Castle* (1788) is in fact the object of Jane Austen's satire both in her juvenilia and her early novel *Northanger Abbey* (1818). In *Jane Austen and the War of Ideas* (1975), Marilyn Butler suggests that Austen's discomfort with Smith's novels stems from her Christian conservatism; this stance calls for self-scrutiny and requires characters to mistrust their individual perceptions, instead testing them against an objective reality. Conversely, Smith's protagonists must trust themselves as they are tested throughout the course of the novels. Emmeline, for example, must trust her judgment that her cousin Delamere is too self-indulgent and volatile. It does not matter that marriage to Delamere would be desirable, rescuing her from poverty and social isolation or that his family eventually supports this marriage, hoping that it will gloss over attempts to cheat her out of her inheritance. In Smith's next novel, *Ethelinde; or, The Recluse of the Lake* (1789), the protagonist must discount seemingly credible evidence and believe that her fiancé, Montgomery, is alive. Celestina in the 1791 novel of the same name must also remain faithful to her fiancé, Willoughby, even though he appears to have abandoned her to marry a wealthy cousin. Unlike Austen's fallible heroines, Smith's heroines in these three novels are never wrong, despite all appearances and despite the opposition of older but wiser characters who recommend conventional solutions to the young women's problems—that is, marriage to a wealthy man whom they do not love. Furthermore, both Ethelinde and Celestina learn that they cannot seek refuge with family or friends. Ethelinde's experience with her various relatives is especially trying, particularly when her guardian's wife attacks her reputation, claiming that Ethelinde has seduced her husband. Paradoxically, this same woman is neglecting her children to have an affair with a dissolute nobleman. Ultimately, Ethelinde finds her best and surest refuge with her fiancé's mother. As a reading of Smith's entire body of work shows, the protagonists' self-confidence replicates their author's armor, which enabled her to live her unprotected, unconventional lifestyle.

A close reading of these three, relatively conventional novels reveals more individuality and even idiosyncrasies. The men whom Smith's heroines marry are generally poorer and of lower social status. Ethelinde's fiancé must work for a time in India in order to earn enough to live even a simple life with her in England. Each novel dramatizes the opposition between urban or suburban society and a more humane, rural community, and each couple chooses the latter. At the end of *Celestina*, both of the heroine's rejected suitors become part of this community with Celestina and Willoughby at its center. *Emmeline* and *Celestina* both include Smith's poetry written in the voice of various characters. Smith's insertion of her poetry is not simply a means of "puffing" it but is an entry into the consciousness of her characters and a means for them to communicate with each other. One key sonnet in *Emmeline* reveals the depth and strength of Godolphin's emotions: his "exhausted heart, / [...] calm, tho' wretched; hopeless, yet resign'd" (2003 ed., p. 386). This sonnet addressing the "mournful sober-suited night" (p. 386) enables the reader to realize that the speaker's attachment to Emmeline is deeper and more persistent than those of her other suitors. Overhearing his poem also enables her to recognize her attraction toward him even though she cannot yet act on it (p. 388). All three early novels contain Smith's detailed description of the natural world. Much of *Ethelinde* is set in the Lake District, a rural region later associated with Wordsworth's poetic retreat from urban society. *Celestina*'s array of settings enables Smith to describe a wider variety of interesting landscapes. In Europe, Willoughby wanders among the rugged mountain landscape and the many wildflowers that the narrative indicates, using their scientific names. Similarly, descriptions of the Hebrides' haunting landscape and hardscrabble life underscore Celestina's physical and emotional isolation even as she attempts to build a new life. Her sonnets written on this island reveal her resourcefulness in handling her emotions, whereas an earlier sonnet written near her home on the southwest coast of England and to a young woman who has died exhibits her abject sorrow.

In "Narrating Seduction: Charlotte Smith and Jane Austen," Jacqueline M. Labbe also points out that Smith was able to include more "adult" elements in her early novels than her unmarried contemporaries were because of her marital status. For example, Emmeline befriends Lady Adelina, who has become pregnant after an extramarital affair. Although Lady Adelina experiences a mental breakdown, she survives the birth of her child, and, after her dissipated first husband dies, it is probable that she will marry her child's father, Fitz-Gerald. Coincidentally, her poems that Lady Adelina shows to Emmeline humanize her and foreshadow her eventual recovery, for she is able to craft her poems and articulate her sorrow to others. A second example comes from Smith's second novel, *Ethelinde*. Sir Edward Newenden is unhappily married to an affluent, alcoholic woman, and Smith sympathetically presents his struggles to suppress his love for the young heroine even as she cares for his neglected children. A third "adult" element, which Kristina Straub points out in her introduction to *Celestina,* is the protagonist's friendship with Vavasour, her libertine suitor. Straub notes that they are able to talk with and even advise each other. Furthermore, as critics have recognized, these three more conventional novels also bear within them Smith's social criticism. Eleanor Rose Ty emphasizes Smith's balancing act through which she avoided alienating readers. In *Emmeline*, the presence of various failed marriages alongside the courtship plot exemplifies this. Similar marriages in *Ethelinde* and *Celestina* serve an equivalent function. Judith Davis Miller adds that Smith's later, more overtly critical, novels grew from her initial attempts at social criticism. *Celestina* particularly shows how Smith's novels would continue to develop. This novel's setting, characters, and plot establish a continuum between contemporary France and England; the novel includes narratives by Jessy Woodburn, a young girl forced to become a maid in the city, and Mrs. Elphinstone, a woman growing conscious of her husband's failings, and the last volume contrasts Celestina's perspective and Willoughby's. This multiple narrative augurs *Desmond* (1792), an epistolary novel chiefly but not exclusively from a young man's perspective as he grapples with the French Revolution and his love for a woman in an abusive marriage. Curiously, while he wanders in rural France, Willoughby mentions "hearing, at a distance, the tumults, with which a noble struggle for freedom … agitated the capital, and many of the great towns of France" (*Celestina*, 2004 ed., p. 473), foreshadowing the highly topical setting of Smith's next novel.

MIDDLE NOVELS (1792–1794)

Written and published in a very short space of time, Smith's novels *Desmond* (1792), *The Old Manor House* (1793), *The Wanderings of Warwick* (1794), and *The Banished Man* (1794) occupy the most tumultuous segment of the French Revolution, the period leading up to and including the Reign of Terror. Prior to July 1792 when *Desmond* was published, the English public tolerated support of the French Revolution. Edmund Burke's 1790 *Reflections on the Revolution in France* was clearly influential, but radical authors were able to respond to his argument. Smith is one of these responders, for, as editors Antje Blank and Janet Todd point out in their introduction to a 2001 edition of the novel, in the letters that make up *Desmond* both the title character and Geraldine refute what Smith appears to have considered common misconceptions inspired by Burke. Yet, by the time Smith wrote the last novel in this brief period, *The Banished Man*, her argument had drastically changed. Events such as the August 1792 massacre of the Swiss Guard, Louis XVI's trial and subsequent execution, and the 1794 treason trials in Britain had reversed public opinion, especially among those who bought and published books. In addition, Smith's family had grown to include her son-in-law Alexandre de Folville, a French exile. Most importantly, conditions in France had made the optimistic ending to *Desmond* incredible and Desmond and Geraldine's defense of the Revolution unconvincing to most readers. Even in 1792's more liberal climate, Smith's usual publisher, Thomas Cadell, had refused to handle this novel, and she was forced to work with a different firm. She would not return to Cadell until 1794's *The Banished*

Man. Smith's reliance on her publishers made this rupture especially significant.

Read today, these next four novels are particularly interesting and demonstrate Smith's achievement as a novelist. These novels' plots, characters, settings, and themes are more directly engaged with politics and social issues. The masculine perspective within the narrative has become more important, building on *Celestina*'s incorporation of Willoughby's perspective into the narrative. As a result, the courtship plot is transformed from Smith's first three novels, and the "adult" elements seem more integral and less gratuitous. *The Wanderings of Warwick,* for example, is motivated by Warwick's jealousy and suspicion, which in turn arises from Isabella's having left her elderly fiancé for him. Therefore, he fears that she will leave him if she finds a man offering her both wealth and attractiveness. An even more compelling example from *Desmond,* which Blank and Todd touch on, is Geraldine Verney's grim loyalty to her husband even as he attempts to prostitute her to a French nobleman who has lent him considerable sums of money. The world of this novel is also one in which the title character is able to have an affair with Josephine, a married French woman who then bears his child, even as he maintains a Platonic relationship with Geraldine, the woman he eventually marries. Critics have speculated about the role that Desmond's liaison with Josephine plays in Smith's narrative, particularly if one reads this novel as following certain conventions that we expect from women's novels from this period. However, although her audience did criticize Desmond's liaison with Josephine, they were otherwise comfortable with the rest of the novel. The scholar Katherine Binhammer cites a contemporaneous conservative critic in the *Critical Review* who supports Smith's right to discuss politics in a novel intended for women.

A profitable discussion of Smith's novels might begin with *Desmond*, as Amy Garnai's 2009 volume *Revolutionary Imaginings in the 1790s* does, highlighting its importance to Smith's reputation as a radical novelist as well as its grounding in her politics. One key question is the extent to which the young Lionel Desmond is a mouthpiece for Smith's views and the female protagonists in the earlier novels are not. The period of *Desmond*'s composition and its publication marks the high point of Smith's political activism. In addition, it is the first of her novels to include a preface from the author. It is true that this may be a response to contemporaneous criticism of the novel, as the preface is from the second edition (1792). One may also wonder who would have been a suitable dedicatee for a novel that calls for an end to titles of nobility. Nevertheless, in this preface Smith acknowledges her novel's politicization, its difference from her previous novels, and her "apprehension which an Author is sensible of on a first publication" (*Desmond*, 2001 ed., p. 45). She grounds her novel in "conversations to which [she has] been a witness" (p. 45), referring to her association with French exiles and English liberals in Brighton but not to her own letters or conversation. In comparison to Smith's earlier novels, the epistolary nature of this novel presents the title character's perspective as more subjective, mediated by the letters of his mentor, Bethel, and, of course, those of Geraldine, enlightened by his travels and his conversation with Bethel and his friend Montfleuri, as opposed to the earlier protagonists' centrality and impermeability. In her 1993 study *Unsex'd Revolutionaries,* Eleanor Rose Ty underscores the distancing effect of epistolarity, for she considers the novel to be Smith's means of examining evidence about the French Revolution and its potential for reforming England. Katherine Binhammer argues that this type of novel permits Smith to avoid revealing her political position. Yet to some this examination is very partial, as each of the letter writers is either radical or, as in Bethel's case, tolerant of radical arguments. One wonders how Desmond's friend, Montfleuri, would have fared after the execution of the more moderate revolutionists or whether he would have become a wary exile like the protagonist of Smith's *The Banished Man* (1794). One may also question, as Blank and Todd do, whether Geraldine is the author's surrogate or even mouthpiece. Smith was noted for her inclusion of autobiographical elements in her writing, and the unhappily married woman makes

an inevitable appearance in her novels. In Geraldine's case, her failed marriage has not only given her empathy for the French but allowed her to see political conditions more clearly. Like her author, she must rely on her own judgment, which she does in her observations on the French people and the countryside, made in a letter to her sister Fanny. Ironically, as Binhammer observes, the novel's ending will force her to rely on Desmond's judgment, rather than on her own. Just as Desmond and Bethel's political discussions distance Smith's novel from her earlier works in this genre, the presence of Geraldine and the courtship plot make this prose work a novel rather than a political dialogue in the style of Burke's *Reflections.*

The Old Manor House (1793) and its short sequel, *The Wanderings of Warwick* (1794), may be considered a retreat from *Desmond*'s extensive engagement and a return to her previous conventional novels. This novel and novella are set during the 1770s, and as Jacqueline M. Labbe suggests in her introduction to the 2002 edition of *The Old Manor House*, Smith was responding to criticism of *Desmond* when she chose the more historical setting of these later novels. *The Wanderings of Warwick* is more avowedly commercial, written to take advantage of the popularity of *The Old Manor House*. This quality may have lessened Smith's emotional investment in this tale, as she and her publisher John Bell disputed whether or not she had written enough to fulfill her contract with him. *The Old Manor House* builds on what Smith had achieved in her previous novel, *Desmond*. It continues her project of social criticism; this time, as Labbe points out in her introduction, she addresses the injustice of Britain's property law and inheritance in a subtler way than she had addressed the French Revolution and gender issues before. Once again, the protagonist is a young man, Orlando, which allowed Smith to move beyond the confines of the Rayland estate and English society to America, the site of a successful revolution. Unlike Desmond, Orlando is younger, poorer, and more accepting of convention. He writes poetry from time to time as an outlet for his emotions, much as characters like Godolphin or Celestina in previous novels have done. A younger son, he stands in contrast to his debauched brother Philip. Orlando, on the other hand, is willing to be guided by his cousin Mrs. Rayland and his father, even if he may play each against the other. This willingness to accept their constraints probably makes him more acceptable to readers than Desmond was. After all, the earlier hero was free to do what he wanted, when he wanted, traveling to France to investigate the Revolution and dally with other men's wives. As Stuart Curran states in the general introduction to the Pickering & Chatto edition of Smith's novels (2005–2007), she may have recognized that readers could not stomach the latter. Orlando's beloved Monimia, a beautiful young girl whom he educates, is more acceptable as well, her submission to him is more credible than Geraldine's to Desmond, and the dangers that she faces are more conventional within a novel. *The Old Manor House* also draws on popular gothic elements, beginning with the estate's landscape and the omnipresence of the past but also leading to Monimia's confinement and later Orlando's journey back to England, where friends and family are unable to recognize him. This novel continued to be reprinted through the nineteenth and twentieth centuries and, at one point, was even subtitled *Monimia and Orlando*, highlighting their love story. However, other critics like Sir Walter Scott and, more recently, Anne Henry Ehrenpreis have viewed the "true" romance as the relationship between Orlando and Mrs. Rayland.

The Banished Man (1794) has also been considered a retreat, but it is clearly a response to a very different political situation. The French Revolution had devolved into a bloody civil war in which the Jacobins overcame the Girondistes, the less vengeful faction that the English radicals tended to support. By this time, the English had turned inward in response not only to the political turmoil in France but also to conservative efforts to quash radical calls for reform in Britain, the war with France, and an ongoing famine. The English economy was also in transition between an older model and a new one, twenty years into what would be known as the industrial revolution. Again, as with *Desmond*, Smith joins a preface to her novel, but this preface refers to her personal situation more than to the content of her novel. Her later digression "Avis Au Lecteur," placed midway through volume 1, discusses the content more in depth. This novel may indeed mark a breaking point for her. The year 1794 was a productive yet stressful time for her personally, marking the beginning of her daughter Augusta Anna's physical decline. Amy Garnai speculates about the extent to which *The Banished Man* reflected Smith's evolving opinions and to which it reflected her understanding of the changed marketplace. She notes that Smith frequently refers to this novel as "gothic" as if to align it with a then-current trend and thereby gloss over outdated elements of the work.

The novel itself begins at a German castle under siege from the French army. There the French émigré D'Alonville, together with his dying father, seeks refuge with Madame de Rosenheim and her daughter, the wives of German officers who are fighting elsewhere. Throughout the course of the novel, D'Alonville continues to be on the move, crisscrossing Europe and England. Eventually, he is tutor to a nobleman's sons; this position forces him to conceal his marriage to Angelina (who is then propositioned by a friend of his employer's family). He finally settles in Verona with his English wife and her mother, Mrs. Denzil, a stand-in for the author. Unlike Smith's previous protagonists, D'Alonville is a monarchist and a staunch enemy of the Revolution, calling attention to the ways in which political change has destroyed France. *The Banished Man* can be considered a reversal of *Desmond's* advocacy of revolution. Whereas the earlier novel narrates the process of Desmond's attempt to convert Bethel to political radicalism, the later novel depicts D'Alonville's conversion of his English friend Edward from a sunny liberalism to a more in-depth understanding of political realities. *The Banished Man* is also a reversal of actual events—namely Augusta Anna's death in Bath. The ending allows D'Alonville and Angelina, who may represent Alexandre and Augusta Anna de Folville, to become part of a larger community in Verona. The reader can imagine that Angelina flourishes physically as Augusta Anna did not, for, in his last letter to Edward, D'Alonville describes her as "the goddess-nymph of this delicious country [Italy]" (1795 ed., p. 377).

LATER NOVELS (1795–1802)

In her introduction to Charlotte Smith's letters from 1795, Judith Phillips Stanton states that with the first two novels in the period 1795 to 1802, Smith truly returned to the type of novel she had written in the 1780s and early 1790s, that is, before *Desmond*. The novels *Montalbert* (1795), *Marchmont* (1796), *The Young Philosopher* (1798), and *Letters of a Solitary Wanderer* (1800–1802), however, reflected the changes that had occurred in England, in Europe, and in the author since *Celestina* had appeared in 1791, including the political changes detailed above. Ill health and the ups and downs of the battle over Richard Smith's estate had decreased Smith's output. For short stretches, she retired from writing: at one point because she believed that the estate was about to be settled, at another because her still-growing family demanded her time and attention. (Smith raised several of her grandchildren despite her straitened circumstances.) She also began to work in other genres, not only poetry but also children's literature, an increasingly popular category that drew other literary figures such as William Godwin. Novels may have been too taxing to write, although, in the last two years of her life, Smith's letters to Sarah Rose mention that she is working on an unknown novel that did not survive. The marketplace also was a factor. Smith's main publishers, Cadell and Davies, rejected at least two of her manuscripts: an earlier draft of *Montalbert* (then titled *Rosalie*) and one of her works for children. Smith's letters during this period complain about the poor market for books; however, at this point, she was also competing with more popular, conservative writers like Jane West as well as the serious-minded Maria Edgeworth and Anna Leticia Barbauld.

Overall, though, *Montalbert* and *Marchmont*, appearing in 1795 and 1796, reveal that Smith had lost her bounce and optimism. Whereas her earlier novels rewarded protagonists like Emmeline or Orlando for their perseverance and integrity, the later novels' heroines' tenacity receives more ambiguous rewards. In *Montalbert*, the title character is impulsive and jealous. He precipitously courts Rosalie Lessington, a young woman abandoned by her adoptive family, and demands that they marry secretly and travel to Italy together, where he then abandons her. Without family, she is forced to rely on Walsingham, a kindly young Englishman. Upon Rosalie's return to England, her reliance on him leads to serious consequences for her when she is stripped of her child and abandoned. She cannot return to her birth mother, who is dead. *Marchmont*'s title character is hotheaded; he alienates the lawyer who was supposed to help him with his case, which forces Marchmont and his wife, Althea, into debtor's prison. Otherwise, Althea is fairly resourceful, having chosen to help Marchmont's sisters with the shop that they open briefly rather than continue living with her diabolical stepmother after her father's death. Compared to the endings of Smith's earlier novels, those of *Montalbert* and *Marchmont* are ambiguous. Although Rosalie and Althea are each reunited with the men they love, their mates are imperfect in a way that even Willoughby or Warwick was not. Then again (as Amy Garnai's comments on *Marchmont*'s theme of legal injustice suggest), earlier characters like Willoughby, Warwick, or even Orlando did not face the obstacles that Marchmont does.

Smith's next novel, *The Young Philosopher* (1798), was written during a comparatively optimistic time. The impact of Augusta Anna's death had begun to lessen, although Smith would continue to mourn her daughter for the rest of her life. The battle over Richard Smith's estate seemed to be drawing to a close. She may also have been refreshed by her work in other genres: her beloved poetry, children's literature, and even drama. Within the next year, she would retire from writing for a brief period. Accordingly, this next novel is more successful—even, in Loraine Fletcher's words, "patchily brilliant" (p. 266). Its structure, however, is more complicated. The novel's title references George Delmont, a younger son who has chosen to be a farmer rather than to be either a minister or a lawyer, professions that, he argues, harm people. He also refuses to be a local politician, citing his unsuitability for negotiating with others. The first volume is somewhat dilatory. Several chapters follow the family of Dr. Winslow, who are stranded at Delmont's farm and serve as fashionable foils to him. Smith even spends some time on the courtship of Dr. Winslow's ward, Miss Goldthorp, and Delmont's cynical elder brother, Adolphus. Then, from the end of the first volume on, the narrative follows Laura Glenmorris and her daughter, Medora, two American women who are in England to fight for an inheritance. Almost all of the second volume is devoted to Laura's story as she tells it to Delmont. In the "present" day, Medora and Delmont fall in love, but she is kidnapped and her mother has a nervous breakdown, resulting in her forced confinement. The novel contains gothic elements, especially in Laura's story, although Medora's kidnapper is revealed to be Captain Darnell, the sleazy brother of a lawyer employed by the other side in the inheritance suit, and the persons behind Laura's subsequent forced confinement are censorious spinsters, her mother's friends. Finally, Laura and Medora each escape from their kidnappers, and Laura's niece resolves the suit by offering to share her inheritance with Medora. Delmont and the Glenmorris family then leave England. Eleanor Rose Ty compares this ending to that of Voltaire's *Candide* (1759), observing that the return to America of Delmont and the Glenmorris family enables them to live outside the law that governs British society. This utopian ending underscores Smith's distaste for the legal system.

Charlotte Smith's final fiction, *Letters from a Solitary Wanderer* (1800–1802), is perhaps closer to a collection of tales, linking it with her earlier translation *The Romance of Real Life* (1787). Published in five volumes, *Letters* had two publishers, as the first, Sampson Low, died in 1800, and his firm then went out of business. Smith was unhappy with the second publisher, Longman and Rees, for she disliked the quality of its paper and printing. At this point in her career, she was increasingly debilitated, and her

family's financial situation forced her to sell her library in 1803. These factors may have affected the composition of this work. The first volume is relatively cohesive, retelling the story of a Catholic family destroyed by its patriarch's dependence on his spiritual advisors. This story differs from Smith's other novels in the refusal of the family's sole survivor, Edouarda, to marry the man who rescues her, because she fears passing on her father's mental illness to any children she might have. The second, more fissured, volume presents the story of a couple who, before their marriage, are caught up in a slave revolt in Jamaica as the woman, Henrietta, seeks to escape an arranged marriage that she likens to being sold in slavery. They are rescued by her uncle, an enlightened and benevolent character similar to Walsingham from *Montalbert* or Armitage from *The Young Philosopher*. The next volume is the type of historical narrative that would become popular in the early nineteenth century. It follows the efforts of Corisande to find her father, a French Huguenot nobleman imprisoned in the aftermath of the St. Bartholomew's Day massacres. Along the way, she encounters various historical figures including Margaret of Valois and Margaret's estranged husband, Henry of Navarre, who alternately help and hinder her in her quest. Returning to the end of the eighteenth century, the fourth and fifth volumes are more intertwined; the fourth tale, about Leopold and Gertrude, a Hungarian nobleman and his English wife, spills over into the fifth volume. There the narrator seeks out Gertrude's sister, Leonora, whose husband has brought her to the wilds of Ireland because he cannot pay his substantial debts. Once she and her children are rescued from a Catholic mob, she in turn tells the story of another character, who, with her mother, was disinherited for supporting her brother, himself a supporter of the French Revolution. The fifth volume concludes as Leonora, her children, and her friends prepare to leave Ireland and join Gertrude and her husband in Switzerland. Originally, according to Loraine Fletcher, Smith had intended to finish her novel with the story of the narrator of the previous volumes, but she did not write this last volume. Fletcher says that the twentieth-century editor Jonathan Wordsworth praised the first three volumes of this work for its descriptive writing, re-creating a variety of landscapes from the north of England to Jamaica. He also found continuities between Smith's heroines in this work and those of her earlier novels. In *Revolutionary Imaginings in the 1790s,* Amy Garnai examines *Solitary Wanderer* with an eye to considering Smith's writing holistically instead of isolating her works by genre. *Letters from a Solitary Wanderer* also reflects Smith's continued interest in gender politics and the impact of imperialism on individuals as well as her desire to transcend national borders that she considered parochial.

SMITH'S SURVIVING PLAY

Early on in her career, Smith mentions her ambition to write for the theater. One letter to William Hayley is even written in the form of a brief skit. Another letter to an unknown recipient, possibly the playwright and theater manager George Colman the Elder, discusses revisions to a comedy. However, no published play survives from this early period, nor is there any record of a performance. Smith's only surviving play is *What Is She,* a talky comedy performed from April 27 to May 2, 1799 at Covent Garden and published that year by Longman and Rees. Even then, Judith Phillips Stanton indicates in her notes to Smith's *Collected Letters* that Smith's surviving correspondence does not mention it. This play appears to have been more read than performed, as at least three editions were printed. Published anonymously, it also shows a direction that Smith chose not to follow. However, as Catherine Anna Dorset's memoir of her sister states, she was also clever and cheerful, characteristics that predominate in this comedy, which emphasizes wit and character over plot. At its center is Mrs. Delville, a mysterious woman who has retreated to the country and refuses to marry. Disguised as Mr. Belmont, a gentleman seeking a position, Lord Orton courts her. Other characters surrounding this couple are Lord Orton's sister and the men who pursue her, a ridiculous would-be author and her tradesman husband, a lawyer who

imitates Lord Orton, and a prickly uncle who turns out to be the father of Mrs. Delville's late husband. Unfortunately, as a playwright, Smith appears to have shown poor timing. According to the chronology posted at the website for British Women Playwrights Around 1800, 1799 appears to have been the last year until 1807 when the British theaters staged a significant number of plays by women. From 1800 to 1806, fewer plays by women were staged, and more were "closet" plays, that is, plays that were published rather than performed. In 1801, no plays by women were performed, and in 1802, only one, Mary Berry's *The Fashionable Friends,* reached the stage. As Ellen Donkin has observed about unsuccessful female playwrights in the late eighteenth century, Smith's lack of acting experience may have held her back at a time when the theater had become more professionalized than ever before. Indeed, even the most successful female playwright of this time, Elizabeth Inchbald, a former actress herself, faced difficulties, particularly once John Philip Kemble retired as manager of the Drury Lane theater.

CHILDREN'S LITERATURE

A devoted mother, Smith had always been involved in the education of her children, and later in life, she raised her son Nicholas' son and daughter. Literature for children also became a popular field, drawing other novelists. Later in Smith's career, she was perhaps more credible as an author of educational books, for, as she jokes to Sarah Rose, as a fiftyish novelist, she would be "twaddl[ing] about love with spectacles on my nose … growing as foolish in my old Age as some certain good Ladies of *more eminent fame*" (*Collected Letters,* p. 646, emphasis hers)—referring to her contemporaries Sophia Lee, the author of *The Life of a Lover* (1804) and the poet Anna Seward, whom Smith ridiculed. Moreover, that same letter indicates that her publisher Joseph Johnson preferred her "making Childrens books" (p. 646). Smith's was probably not an isolated example, as Devoney Looser's *Women Writers and Old Age in Great Britain, 1750–1850* reveals through its discussion of other authors like Frances Burney and Maria Edgeworth.

Smith began her career as an author for children with *Rural Walks, in Dialogues, Intended for the Use of Young Persons* in 1795, the same year that she published *Montalbert* and that her daughter Anna Augusta died. Her daughter's last illness was a particularly stressful time for Smith, as she believed that had she been able to access her late father-in-law's money, her daughter (and perhaps even her infant who had died in 1794) might have survived. Nevertheless, unlike *Montalbert*, *Rural Walks* is calm and restrained. It follows the widowed Mrs. Woodfield's education of her three daughters and her niece Caroline. Having grown up in London and abroad, Caroline is initially scornful of the quiet that her cousins enjoy. Mrs. Woodfield could be regarded as a revision of the older but wiser, often unhappily married, woman often seen in Smith's novels—such as *Emmeline*'s Mrs. Stafford, *Celestina*'s Lady Horatia Howard, or *The Banished Man*'s Mrs. Denzil. It is not clear why Mrs. Woodfield and her daughters lead their quiet life. Mrs. Woodfield may be closer to the mother of *Ethelinde*'s Montgomery, a widow who is able to provide the heroine with a rational, rural retreat from society. Among the qualities Smith wishes to instill in her readers, she says in her introduction to the first edition of the book, are the repression of discontent and "the necessity of submitting cheerfully to such situations as fortune may throw them into" (1795 ed., p. iii). This discontent may include resentment of a husband's ill-treatment and economic inequity within marriage, which Smith does not mention, just as much as it includes Caroline's boredom and her cousin Elizabeth's scorn for her fellow partygoers. However, the sequel to *Rural Walks*, 1796's *Rambles Farther: A Continuation of Rural Walks,* covers Mr. Halesworth's courtship of Caroline, which may provide readers with a model. This courtship, though, is not free from drama, as Caroline tests her fiancé when she flirts with Lord Landeville, and Mr. Halesworth later produces a mysterious child for her to raise. Stuart Curran suggests in his general introduction to the 2005 Pickering & Chatto edition of Smith's works that this child may well be Mr. Halesworth's own. Alternately, the presence of this child may be a means of initiating Caroline into motherhood, the aspect of marriage that Smith appeared to have valued most, and thereby protecting her character from a relapse into the thoughtless life that she enjoyed before *Rural Walks* began. In an essay on writing for girls, "Lost Needles, Tangled Threads: Stitchery, Domesticity, and the Artistic Enterprise in Barbauld, Edgeworth, Taylor, and Lamb," Carol Shiner Wilson suggests that it may be worth reading this plot twist alongside Anna Leticia Barbauld's "Live Dolls," in which an aunt uses a poor woman's child to teach her wealthy niece to be less selfish and extravagant.

Focusing on the courtship plot in *Rambles Farther* distracts the reader from a fuller understanding of Smith's writing for children. *Rural Walks* and *Rambles Farther* are works of moral education. Mrs. Woodfield spends much time reasoning her pupils out of their character flaws. She also encourages her pupils to study natural history and drawing as well as to engage in charity. A number of scenes take place in the presence of the rural poor, enabling Smith not only to open her readers' eyes to the poverty among them but also to encourage them to assist others. Stuart Curran has observed that Smith's writing for children is far more culturally diverse than most such writing at that time. Ella, a new character introduced in *Rambles Farther*, grew up in the West Indies and brings with her a native servant, Mimbah, whose dialect Smith reproduces. Ella and Mimbah's presence allows Mrs. Woodfield to introduce geography, patriotism, and slavery, but it may also reflect Smith's ongoing involvement with Richard Smith's estate and her sons' involvement in the business of the British Empire. Carol Shiner Wilson indicates that Smith's books were unusual in their emphasis on natural history and outdoor activities; most books emphasized indoor activities, namely sewing for others and fighting one's tendency toward disorder. As with *Desmond*, Smith's publishers at first rejected *Rambles Farther*, but (according to Judith Phillips Stanton's annotation in *Collected Letters*), they reconsidered their decision once Georgiana, Duchess of Devonshire, a patron of Smith's, intervened.

With *Minor Morals*, published in 1798, the same year as *The Young Philosopher*, Smith follows a new family, Mrs. Belmour and her several nieces and nephews whose mother has recently died. Sophy, the eldest daughter, resembles Caroline from the previous books; moreover, she has been at a fashionable boarding school, and part of her aunt's project is to correct the flaws that she has acquired from this schooling. Once again, the family lives in rural retirement, and their lessons include the importance of charity, poetry by John Milton and William Cowper, and natural history. The children also receive moral education; for example, Smith devotes a considerable chapter to a comparison between two sisters in order to instill readers' respect for one girl's industry encouraged by her grandmother's disdain. Unsurprisingly, the grandmother's favorite becomes the victim of an unhappy marriage and must rely on her sister for moral and financial support. The volume concludes with the story of Zulmine, the Turkish wife of a neighbor, reflecting the occupations of Smith's sons but also her own desire to transcend parochialism. It is interesting to contrast Zulmine's seemingly easy assimilation into Mrs. Belmour's circle with the difficulties that D'Alonville faces and that ultimately cause him to leave England in *The Banished Man*—or with those that Smith faced in advocating for her French son-in-law, Alexandre de Folville.

Smith concluded her career as a writer with a series of other works for children. *Conversations Introducing Poetry* was published in 1804. Written once she had sold her library, this book relies on poems by Smith and her sister, Catherine Anna Dorset, as it follows Mrs. Talbot's education of her children George and Emily. Many of the poems included in this book concern the natural world as children would observe it, and much dialogue touches on economic disparity between the very wealthy and the less well-off. Mrs. Talbot instructs her children in how to negotiate the snobbery of the wealthy and quietly ameliorate their injuries to the poor without alienating the former. In 1805 Smith also produced two volumes of *A History of England: From the Earliest Records to the Peace of Amiens, in a Series of*

Letters to a Young Lady at School; Smith's fellow radical novelist Mary Hays completed the series with a third volume in 1806. Smith's last work in this genre was *A Natural History of Birds*, which appeared in 1807, after her death. In her last letters, she expressed her concern over the delay of the book's publication. Poems from these last works appear in Stuart Curran's 1993 edition of her poems, making them more accessible and again demonstrating how Smith's work continued to evolve from its beginnings in her *Elegiac Sonnets*. The scholar Dahlia Porter, for example, has argued that *Conversations Introducing Poetry* influenced her later *Beachy Head*, a book-length poem written for adults and now considered to be one of her finest pieces. This is not surprising, given Smith's incorporation of poetry in her novels and her sonnets whose speakers are characters from these same novels.

Selected Bibliography

WORKS OF CHARLOTTE TURNER SMITH

POETRY, PLAYS, AND CORRESPONDENCE

What Is She? London: T. N. Longman and O. Rees, 1799.

The Poems of Charlotte Smith. Edited by Stuart Curran. Women Writers in English 1350–1850. New York: Oxford University Press, 1993. (This collection includes the ninth edition of *Elegiac Sonnets, Volume 1* (1800); the second edition of *Elegiac Sonnets, Volume 2* (1800); *The Emigrants*; poems from *Conversations Introducing Poetry* and *A Natural History of Birds* ; and *Beachy Head.*)

The Collected Letters of Charlotte Smith. Edited by Judith Phillips Stanton. Bloomington: Indiana University Press, 2003.

NOVELS IN MODERN EDITIONS

The Banished Man. Kessinger, n.d.

Marchmont. 4 vols. Gale Ecco Print Editions, n.d.

Montalbert. 3 vols. Gale Ecco Print Editions, n.d.

The Wanderings of Warwick. Gale Ecco Print Editions, n.d.

The Old Manor House. Edited by Anne Henry Ehrenpreis. New York: Oxford University Press, 1969.

Letters of a Solitary Wanderer. New York: Woodstock Books, 1995. (With an introduction by Jonathan Wordsworth.)

The Young Philosopher. Edited by Elizabeth Kraft. Eighteenth-Century Novels by Women. Lexington: University of Kentucky Press, 1999.

Desmond. Edited by Antje Blank and Janet Todd. Peterborough, Ontario: Broadview Literary Texts, 2001.

The Old Manor House. Edited by Jacqueline M. Labbe. Peterborough, Ontario: Broadview Literary Texts, 2002.

Emmeline: The Orphan of the Castle. Edited by Loraine Fletcher. Peterborough, Ontario: Broadview Literary Texts, 2003.

Celestina. Edited by Loraine Fletcher. Peterborough, Ontario: Broadview Editions, 2004.

Ethelinde; or, The Recluse of the Lake. 5 vols. Boston: Elibron Classics, 2005. (Facsimile reprint of the 1790 2nd ed.)

The Works of Charlotte Smith. 14 vols. Edited by Stuart Curran. Volume editors: Adriana Craciun, Stuart Curran, Kate Davies, Elizabeth Dolan, Ina Ferris, Michael Gamer, M. O. Grenby, Harriet Guest, Jacqueline Labbe, D. L. Macdonald, A. A. Markley, Judith Pascoe, Judith Stanton, and Kristina Straub. London and Brookfield, Vt.: Pickering & Chatto, 2005–2007. (Vol. 1: *Manon l'escaut; or, The Fatal Attachment* (1786) and *The Romance of Real Life* (1787). Vol. 2: *Emmeline: The Orphan of the Castle* (1788). Vol. 3: *Ethelinde; or, The Recluse of the Lake* (1789). Vol. 4: *Celestina* (1791). Vol. 5: *Desmond* (1792). Vol. 6: *The Old Manor House* (1793). Vol. 7: *The Wanderings of Warwick* (1794) and *The Banished Man* (1794). Vol. 8: *Montalbert* (1795). Vol. 9: *Marchmont* (1796). Vol. 10: *The Young Philosopher* (1798). Vol. 11: *Letters of a Solitary Wanderer* (1800–1802). Vol. 12: *Rural Walks* (1795), *Rambles Farther* (1796), and *Minor Morals* (1798); *A Narrative of the Loss of the Catherine* (1796). Vol. 13: *Who Is She?* (1798), *Conversations Introducing Poetry: Chiefly on Subjects of Natural History* (1804), and *The Natural History of Birds* (1807). Vol. 14: *Poems*; including both volumes of *Elegiac Sonnets and Other Essays* (1784, 1797), *The Emigrants* (1793), and *Beachy Head, and Other Poems* (1807).

First Editions

Emmeline: The Orphan of the Castle. 4 vols. London: Thomas Cadell, 1788.

Ethelinde; or, The Recluse of the Lake. 5 vols. London: Thomas Cadell, 1789.

Celestina. 4 vols. London: Thomas Cadell, 1791.

Desmond. 3 vols. London: G. G. J. and J. Robinson, 1792.

The Emigrants. 2 vols. London: Thomas Cadell, 1793.

The Old Manor House. 4 vols. London: J. Bell, 1793.

The Wanderings of Warwick. London: J. Bell, 1794.

The Banished Man. 4 vols. London: T. Cadell, Jr., and W. Davies, 1794.

Montalbert. 3 vols. London: E. Booker, 1795.

Marchmont. 4 vols. London: S. Low, 1796.

The Young Philosopher. 4 vols. London: T. Cadell, Jr., and W. Davies, 1798.

Letters of a Solitary Wanderer. 3 vols. London: S. Low, 1800–1801.

Letters of a Solitary Wanderer. 2 vols. London: T. N. Longman and G. Rees, 1802.

Writing for Children

Rural Walks, in Dialogues, Intended for the Use of Young Persons. 2 vols. London: T. Cadell, Jr., and W. Davies, 1795.

Rambles Farther: A Continuation of Rural Walks, in Dialogues, Intended for the Use of Young Persons. 2 vols. London: T. Cadell, Jr., and W. Davies, 1796.

Minor Morals, Interspersed with Sketches of Natural History, Historical Anecdotes, and Original Stories. 2 vols. London: S. Low, 1798.

Conversations Introducing Poetry: Chiefly on Subjects of Natural History. 2 vols. London: J. Johnson, 1804.

A History of England: From the Earliest Records to the Peace of Amiens, in a Series of Letters to a Young Lady at School. 3 vols. London: Richard Phillips, 1805–1806. (The third volume was written by Mary Hays.)

A Natural History of Birds, Intended Chiefly for Young People. London: J. Johnson, 1807.

CRITICAL AND BIOGRAPHICAL STUDIES

Binhammer, Katherine. "Revolutionary Domesticity in *Desmond*." In *Women, Revolution, and the Novels of the 1790s*. Edited by Linda Lang-Peralta. East Lansing: Michigan State University Press, 1999. Pp. 25–46.

Blank, Antje, and Janet Todd. "Introduction." In *Desmond*. Edited by Antje Blank and Janet Todd. Peterborough, Ontario: Broadview Literary Texts, 2001. Pp. 7–33.

Butler, Marilyn. *Jane Austen and the War of Ideas*. Oxford: Clarendon Press, 1975.

Curran, Stuart. "General Introduction." In *The Works of Charlotte Smith*. Vol. 1: *Manon l'escaut; or, The Fatal Attachment* (1786) and *The Romance of Real Life* (1787). Edited by Michael Gamer. London and Brookfield, Vt.: Pickering & Chatto, 2005. Pp. vii–xxvii.

———. "Intertextualities." In *Charlotte Smith in British Romanticism*. Edited by Jacqueline M. Labbe. London and Brookfield, Vt.: Pickering & Chatto, 2008. Pp. 175–188.

———. "Introduction." In *The Poems of Charlotte Smith*. Edited by Stuart Curran. Women Writers in English 1350–1850. New York: Oxford University Press, 1993. Pp. xix–xxix.

Donkin, Ellen. *Getting into the Act: Women Playwrights in London, 1776–1829*. New York: Routledge, 1995.

Dorset, Catherine (Turner). *Charlotte Smith*. In *Celestina*. Edited by Loraine Fletcher. Peterborough, Ontario: Broadview Editions, 2004. Pp. 574–599.

Ehrenpreis, Anne Henry. "Introduction." In *The Old Manor House*. Edited by Anne Henry Ehrenpreis. New York: Oxford University Press, 1969. Pp. vii–xxvi. Ehrenpreis reads Smith's novel alongside male eighteenth-century novelists like Henry Fielding and Tobias Smollett. More recent scholarship tends to rely on female writers for its comparisons.

Fletcher, Loraine. *Charlotte Smith: A Critical Biography*. New York: Palgrave, 2001.

Garnai, Amy. *Revolutionary Imaginings in the 1790s: Charlotte Smith, Mary Robinson, Elizabeth Inchbald*. New York: Palgrave Macmillan, 2009.

Hays, Mary. "Mrs. Charlotte Smith." In *Emmeline: The Orphan of the Castle*. Edited by Loraine Fletcher. Peterborough, Ontario: Broadview Literary Texts, 2003. Pp. 507–518.

Kelly, Gary. *The English Jacobin Novel, 1780–1805*. Oxford: Oxford University Press, 1976.

Kraft, Elizabeth. "Introduction." In *The Young Philosopher*. Edited by Elizabeth Kraft. Eighteenth-Century Novels by Women. Lexington: University of Kentucky Press, 1999. Pp. ix–xxii.

Labbe, Jacqueline M. "Introduction." In *The Old Manor House*. Edited by Jacqueline M. Labbe. Peterborough, Ontario: Broadview Literary Texts, 2002. Pp. 9–29.

———. "Introduction." In *Charlotte Smith in British Romanticism*. Edited by Jacqueline M. Labbe. London and Brookfield, Vt.: Pickering & Chatto, 2008. Pp. 1–11.

———. "Narrating Seduction: Charlotte Smith and Jane Austen." In *Charlotte Smith in British Romanticism*. Edited by Jacqueline M. Labbe. London and Brookfield, Vt.: Pickering & Chatto, 2008. Pp. 113–127.

Lang-Peralta, Linda. "Introduction." In *Women, Revolution, and the Novels of the 1790s*. Edited by Linda Lang-Peralta. East Lansing: Michigan State University Press, 1999. Pp. ix–xv.

Looser, Devoney. *Women Writers and Old Age in Great Britain, 1750–1850*. Baltimore: Johns Hopkins University Press, 2008.

Mann, David D., and Susan Garland Mann, eds. "Chronological List of Plays by British Women Playwrights, 1770–1823." University of Montreal: British Women Playwrights Around 1800 (http://www.etang.umontreal.ca/bwp1800/chronology.html), December 1, 2000. (From *Women Playwrights in England, Ireland, and Scotland, 1660–1823*. Edited by David D. Mann and Susan Garland Mann. Bloomington: Indiana University Press, 1996. Pp. 403–417.)

Miller, Judith Davis. "The Politics of Truth and Deception: Charlotte Smith and the French Revolution." In *Rebellious Hearts: British Women Writers and the French Revolution*. Edited by Adriana Craciun and Kari E. Lokke. SUNY Series in Feminist Theory and Criticism. Albany: State University of New York Press, 2001. Pp. 338–359.

Pascoe, Judith. "Female Botanists and the Poetry of Charlotte Smith." In *Re-Visioning Romanticism: British Women Writers, 1776–1837*. Edited by Carol Shiner Wilson and Joel Haefner. Philadelphia: University of Pennsylvania Press, 1994. Pp. 193–209.

Porter, Dahlia. "From Nosegay to Specimen Cabinet: Charlotte Smith and the Labour of Collecting." In *Charlotte Smith in British Romanticism*. Edited by Jacqueline M. Labbe. London and Brookfield, Vt.: Pickering & Chatto, 2008. Pp. 29–44.

Steeves, Harrison R. *Before Jane Austen: The Shaping of the English Novel in the Eighteenth Century*. New York: Holt, Rinehart, and Winston, 1965.

Straub, Kristina. "Introduction." In *The Works of Charlotte Smith*. Vol. 4: *Celestina*. Edited by Kristina Straub. London and Brookfield, Vt.: Pickering & Chatto, 2005. Pp. vi–xii.

Ty, Eleanor Rose. *Unsex'd Revolutionaries: Five Women Novelists of the 1790s*. Toronto: University of Toronto Press, 1993.

Wilson, Carol Shiner. "Lost Needles, Tangled Threads: Stitchery, Domesticity, and the Artistic Enterprise in Barbauld, Edgeworth, Taylor, and Lamb." In *Re-Visioning Romanticism: British Women Writers, 1776–1837*. Edited by Carol Shiner Wilson and Joel Haefner. Philadelphia: University of Pennsylvania Press, 1994. Pp. 167–190.

Wordsworth, Jonathan. "Introduction." In *Letters of a Solitary Wanderer*. New York: Woodstock Books, 1995.

MEERA SYAL

(1961—)

A. M. Sánchez-Arce

MEERA SYAL IS a British comedian, writer, singer, journalist, producer, and actor. She became famous for being part of the team that created the comedy series *Goodness Gracious Me*, first broadcast on BBC radio and then an extremely popular television series. Syal is extremely well-known in the United Kingdom, and although some commentators insist in referring to her as British Asian she believes that this label is reductive. Besides her popularity in the media as an actor, comedian, and journalist, Syal has also written and produced extensively for film and television. She has published two novels, *Anita and Me* (1996) and *Life Isn't All Ha Ha Hee Hee* (1999).

SYAL'S LIFE

Meera Syal was born Feeroza Syal on June 27, 1961, in Wolverhampton, Staffordshire (currently the East Midlands), in the United Kingdom. Her parents, Surenda Syal and Surinder Singh, had moved to England from New Delhi shortly before her birth in 1960 and were an accountant and a teacher respectively. Originally from the Punjab (northwest India), Syal's family was marked by the Partition of India in 1947. Her father's family was one of many forced to flee from their home in Pakistan. Surenda Syal's father felt that since they were Hindu they would be safer in India than Pakistan and moved them from Lahore (Pakistan) to New Delhi (India). Meera's parents met at college in New Delhi in the 1950s and saw each other for seven years without their parents' knowledge because of their different religious backgrounds; Surinder was Sikh. The couple finally married in 1958 and moved to England in 1960.

Syal grew up in Essington, a small former coal-mining village near Wolverhampton. Toll-ington, the fictional setting of Syal's first novel, *Anita and Me* (1996), is based on Essington, including the fact that the village used to have an economy based on (now closed) mines, the proximity of major motorways, and the large pond in which one of the characters nearly drowns. The Syals were still living there in 1968 when Enoch Powell, the Conservative MP for Wolverhampton South West, gave his infamous "Rivers of Blood" speech, which forecast the destruction of the British nation because of immigration. Powell, who as health minister had toured the Caribbean in the early 1960s to encourage immigration to Britain at a time when the country had a need for skilled labor, was by 1968 espousing views that immigration would generate violence in the United Kingdom and urging the government to encourage immigrants to go back to their countries; Powell's standpoint fell just short of requiring repatriation. Furthermore, Powell did not consider people of color who were born in Britain as being British—in his view, to be British was to be white. Powell's anti-immigration stance was confined to immigration by nonwhite people; his words fueled racism and made it more acceptable to express openly racist views. Powell's speech and its effects feature in *Anita and Me*.

The family moved to Bolxwich. Syal completed primary school and passed the 11-plus exam, gaining entry to Queen Mary's High School for girls in nearby Walsall, a grammar school. She then went to the University of Manchester, where she studied English and drama. During her final year at university she cowrote *One of Us* (1983), a one-woman play, with her friend Jacqueline Shapiro. Syal won the National Student Drama Award for her performance in *One of Us* and took the play to the Edinburgh Fringe Festival, where she was spotted and offered a job at the Royal Court Theatre in London. She had planned to continue her studies with a masters degree but decided to take the job and start professional acting. Syal worked at the theater for seven years before she received a call from the BBC in 1992 to write a three-part television series, *My Sister Wife*, which kick-started her career writing for radio and television and then led to writing screenplays and producing films. Syal's versatility is exemplified by her becoming part of a girl band called Saffron in 1988 (other band members were the late pop singer Nazia Hassan and the actor Rita Wolf). In 1989 Syal married the journalist Chandra Shekhar Bhatia, with whom she had a daughter. They divorced in 2004 after a separation of more than four years. In 2005 she married her frequent collaborator Sanjeev Bhaskar and had a son.

The year 1996 was important in Syal's career as *Goodness Gracious Me* started airing on BBC Radio 4 and *Anita and Me* was published to wide acclaim. The novel won the Betty Trask Award, awarded to first novels (either traditional or romantic rather than experimental) written by authors resident in a current or former Commonwealth country under thirty-five years of age. It was also a finalist for the Guardian Fiction Prize. *Anita and Me* is frequently included in school and university syllabuses, and it was adapted for cinema in 2002 by Syal herself (directed by Metin Hüseyin). Syal also took on a minor part in the film, that of the strong-minded Auntie Shayla.

Syal had written her first screenplay, *Bhaji on the Beach*, in 1993 for BBC Channel 4 television. Cowritten with its director, Gurinder Chadha (famous for *Bend It Like Beckham*), *Bhaji on the Beach* could be called a chick flick with political teeth. It is still referred to as a watershed in the representation of Asian and British Asian women in television. Syal was awarded an MBE (Member of the British Empire) in the Queen's New Year's Honours List of 1998. She has also received a Media Personality of the Year Award at the Commission for Racial Equality's annual Race in the Media awards (2000) and a Nazia Hassan Foundation Award (2003).

In 1999 Syal published a second novel, *Life Isn't All Ha Ha Hee Hee*, the story of three girlfriends in their thirties, which was adapted as a television miniseries for the BBC in 2005. Syal cowrote the first two episodes with Abi Morgan and starred as one of the three friends, Sunita, who is a college dropout, social worker, mother, and unhappy wife. Throughout the 1990s and 2000s, Syal has continued her television and film work, participating and writing in numerous television series and shows; she also wrote a Bollywood-themed musical, *Bombay Dreams*, with Andrew Meeham for Andrew Lloyd Webber (London 2002–2004 and Broadway 2004). She wrote a play titled *Generation Next* scheduled for production in the National Theatre's 2012 Connections Plays season, and in 2011 she was writing a pilot script for an original serial, *Heal Me*, set in Scotland for Touchpaper/BBC. She was also working on her third novel.

Academic criticism of Syal's work is not easy to come by. Two essays on the novel *Anita and Me* were published in 1999: Berthold Schoene-Harwood's article "Beyond (T)race: Bildung and Proprioception in Meera Syal's *Anita and Me*" and Rocío G. Davis's essay "India in Britain: Myths of Childhood in Meera Syal's *Anita and Me*." Since the late 1990s, Meera Syal's work has had growing critical attention in the form of articles and essays, and Syal is also often included in books about postcolonial literature, British literature, and women's writing. However, there is little sense of an accumulation of knowledge because most publications do not build on the insights of other critics. Although Syal has been widely reviewed and interviewed in the media, scholarly work on her books has until recently been relegated to the margins, being published by university presses with little or no marketing power or as small sections on books about British Asian or postcolonial literatures. Although this dispersion of scholarship on Syal means that articles and essays on her novels have not always been visible, her work continues to inspire and provoke analyses, particularly in relation to issues of identity, postcolonialism, and British women's writing.

ANITA AND ME

Anita and Me (1996), Syal's first novel, is a semi-autobiographical work that takes the form of a bildungsroman; the main character develops and matures over a period of two years, from the ages of nine to eleven. It tells the story of Meena, a preadolescent girl living in Tollington, a small village (loosely based on Syal's own village of Essington) on the outskirts of Wolverhampton, as she makes the transition between primary and secondary school. Like many girls, Meena dreams of being rich and famous, wants to be accepted by the popular girls in her neighborhood (in particular Anita Rutter, the "Anita" of the title), feels insecure about her body, and is becoming increasingly curious about relationships and sex. So far, so predictable. But Meena's situation is exacerbated by the fact that her parents are immigrants from India and her family is ostensibly the only nonwhite, foreign family in the whole village. At the end of the novel, it is revealed that this is not actually the case, as a Punjabi man and a French woman own the Big House in the village and were the owners of the mine that used to employ most of the village men.

Meena's insecurities are those of a preadolescent, but normal feelings of being different and wanting to fit in are surrounded by episodes where it is clear that in Meena's society she is actually treated as being different. Although she is allowed to fit in, this is not necessarily easily achieved or devoid of repercussions. Meena the adult narrator clearly knows this, but Meena the child character, for much of the novel, does not. Episodes that Meena the child does not fully understand are presented to readers so that they can make judgments that the character cannot. This kind of divided narratorial perspective is used in classics such as Charlotte Brontë's *Jane Eyre* (1847) and is also present in one of the key intertexts of *Anita and Me*: Harper Lee's modern classic *To Kill a Mockingbird* (1960). Graeme Dunphy's essay "Meena's Mockingbird: From Harper Lee to Meera Syal," offers a detailed analysis of how *Anita and Me* draws on *To Kill a Mockingbird*, particularly in relation to plot structure, characterization, use of flashback, and

the context of postcolonialism. The novel's use of a first-person narrator with two points of view successfully juxtaposes the child-like perspective that dominates most of the story and the more complex adult perspective of Meena's world, which is first encountered at the beginning of the novel in what could be called a prologue (but is not actually given a title). Rocío Davis calls this a "double vision" and describes it in the following way:

> It is the interplay of two focal points, that of the experiencing child and that of the observing or reminiscing adult which tend to evolve to offer a double vision: the child's experience and the adult narrator's use of that experience. The adult narrator often takes advantage of the imagining, the creating, the remembering, the retelling of the child's perspective to focus the experience of personal or communal identity from the very beginning.
>
> (p. 141)

The voice of the adult narrator develops throughout the novel and finally comes into its own at the very end, as Meena comes to terms with the events that lead to Anita's sister, Tracey, nearly drowning, and she decides not to take revenge on Anita and her boyfriend Sam by accusing them of pushing Tracey into the pond. The adult narrator voice thus bookends the narrative and makes us aware of its presence throughout. The main *Bildung* element in the novel is Meena's development of a nuanced perception of her surroundings, including the social and racial tensions that affect the way people treat each other; she also comes to an understanding of her own family and cultural legacy in the context of forging her own identity.

In his 1999 article on Syal, Bertholde Schoene-Harwood suggests that Meena, as the child of immigrants, is outside the frame of bildungsroman and that her attempts to integrate into Tollington reflect a desire to "succumb totally to English society's frame of *Bildung* and thus be fixed in a definitive cultural location" (p. 161). This analysis is based on thinking about cultures as fixed and separate, as well as the assumption that a bildungsroman depicts the development of an individual from ostracism to social integration, and that the protagonist's identity does not change from beginning to end. Integration, however, is not an essential trait of formation novels. James Joyce's *A Portrait of the Artist as a Young Man* (1916), Thomas Hardy's *Tess of the d'Urbervilles* (1891), and Johann Wolfgang von Goethe's *Sorrows of Young Werther* (1774), for example, depict the protagonists' personal growth as conditional on their discomfort with, or rejection of, their society. Meena presents readers with a similar development that makes her more aware of the fault lines present in her social surroundings, including racial prejudice. In his 2004 volume *Black British Literature: Novels of Transformation*, Mark Stein disagrees with Schoene-Harwood's conclusions about Meena and states:

> While it is accurate that *Anita and Me* is decidedly *not* an uncritical celebration of "hybridity," of "syncretism," and of "in-betweenness," it seems incautious to assume that Meena can transcend "race" beyond "trace" in a society where race remains highly significant and racism deeply entrenched. Meena learns to survive in such a society, and her lessons are crucial precisely because of her phenotype and the heightened visibility it entails.
>
> (p. 52)

Stein is right to ask for caution and remind readers that Meena's "difference" is highly visible. It is impossible to pass, as her skin color marks her out as alien in her society.

This depiction of British society as racist is counterbalanced by the narrative point of view, as described by Roger Bromley:

> The village and its inhabitants are only seen from the perspective of the narrator and they are often constructed as figures in a Dickensian gallery of working-class stereotypes, identified in terms of what Barthes called the semic code, a major device for thematising persons, objects or places. A reverse stereotyping or caricaturing takes place as the controlling gaze is Asian British.
>
> (p. 145)

Meena's "Asian British gaze" is providing an alternative story; hers is an authored story that looks back at white narratives about migration and race, as well as projecting the same scrutinizing gaze onto white working-class England. Of course, this type of narrative is still within the comfort zone for many readers as it confirms the late twentieth- and early twenty-first-century rhetoric about racism in Britain as being the preserve of poor working-class people. Syal tackles this misconception in the preface to the novel (and also in *All Isn't All Ha Ha Hee Hee*). But one must not forget that Meena's is also the gaze of the lower middle class looking at the disenfranchised, the working class, and those outside the class system (the long-term unemployed living on benefits).

Anita embodies those living outside the class system. She is the most popular girl in the neighborhood (or the Yard, as the novel puts it), and Meena is obsessed with her. Three years Meena's senior, Anita is twelve when we first meet her and fourteen at the end of the novel. She represents what Meena thinks she wants: she is the older girl, self-assured and occupying what looks like her rightful place in the children's microcosmic world of the Yard. She is also, in Meena's mind, beautiful and exciting to be with. However, the narrative shows readers that beneath Anita's exterior is a teenager deeply affected by her family background, particularly her mother's disaffection and final abandonment. Anita is seen by Meena at first as tough, a born leader. Gradually, this image of Anita is revealed to be a construction of Meena's (and, in a way, Anita's) own fantasies, as Anita is seen more and more as not clever enough to see through social situations—as, for example, when she thinks that Sam Lowbridge's racist outburst at the village fête is great rather than misguided or wrong—and is finally portrayed as someone clinging desperately to a boyfriend, Sam. Anita is unable to fathom why Sam may be attracted to Meena: "She was muttering to herself scrabbling round urgently for more missiles. 'You wanna chuck me for her? Her! Yow like her better? Her! Her?'" (*Anita and Me*, p. 314). Anita's response to seeing Meena and Sam kissing is childish. It also reflects an important feature of the novel; it is difficult to pinpoint whether there is active racism in the community or merely ignorance and thoughtlessness.

Anita's exclamations of surprise and disbelief show that she sees Meena as a poor choice and herself as much superior. Her disbelief is shown through the repetition of "her" as a question and with exclamation marks. The question is, why does Anita think herself better? The unspoken (and unwritten) word here could be "race." In Anita's eyes, we might surmise, Meena could never be equal to (let alone better than) her because Anita is white and Meena is not. Any actual racism here is difficult to pinpoint, however, since it is slippery and not spelled out. Anita could well be thinking that Meena is younger and not as attractive as herself, for example. Graeme Dunphy mentions a similar sense of unease in two other passages: in one of these, Anita's mother, Deirdre, does not invite Meena in for dinner; in the other, a boy feels relief on realizing that he could have been paired with Meena (so he had not gotten the worst girl after all). Dunphy explains:

> The reader fills in the gaps and wonders what Meena does not, whether an anti-Asian intolerance is lurking behind the scenes. We have already identified as a feature of Syal's humour that the reader understands things in Meena's report which Meena herself misses; here the same technique is employed without humour to highlight prejudice and discrimination. Of course, we cannot know this for certain. … But precisely this is the insidious nature of racism, that it is often subliminal, and this can be far more damaging to the victim's self-esteem than outright hostility. On the one hand, when prejudice is present it is impossible to pin it down and achieve clarity, while on the other hand this uncertainty may cause the victim to see discrimination even where it is not in fact present.
>
> (p. 653)

Dunphy's is a perceptive analysis of the way the novel deals with insidious prejudice and racial discrimination. This apparently friendly but nevertheless hostile environment exacerbates Meena's problems in developing a sense of self and her attempts to erase her difference (in this case, race) and resemble Anita.

The invisibility of minorities in the 1960s in the United Kingdom and the absence of role models in the media (for example in television or in the teenage magazine *Jackie* that the girls read) can be seen as social elements that would exacerbate Meena's desire to conform to the normative whiteness that prevails in her village. Meena starts to hate her body and feel embarrassed to be in public with her family (who are clearly "foreign" in her and other people's minds):

> I had never wanted to be anyone else except myself only older and famous. But now, for some reason, I wanted to shed my body like a snake slithering out of its skin and emerge reborn, pink and unrecognisable. I began avoiding mirrors, I refused to put on the Indian suits my mother laid out for me on the bed when guests were due for dinner, I hid in the house when Auntie Shaila bade loud farewells in Punjabi to my parents from the front garden, I took to walking several paces behind or in front of my parents when we went on a shopping trip, checking my reflection in shop windows, bitterly disappointed it was still there.
>
> (*Anita and Me*, p. 146)

Meena's desire to fit into Tollington by adopting a "Yard accent" (the predominant accent in her white, working-class Midlands village) has evolved into something unhealthy: "Meena's desire for recognition leads her to obliterate herself. Using [Franz] Fanon's terminology, she has 'epidermalised' inferiority without questioning it, wishing to be visible as a human being by becoming less 'visible' in terms of difference" (Sánchez-Arce, p. 119). This desire to "obliterate herself" reaches a high point in her deliberate horse-riding accident, an accident that is the direct result of hearing Anita boast of kissing Sam and watching him and his gang attack an Asian man. This final act of self-effacement is also the beginning of Meena's liberation from Anita and Sam. She uses her four months in the hospital to distance herself from them, and she completes that distancing at the end of the novel, when she rejects the option of lying to get them into trouble with the police. Meena has outgrown Anita and the Yard; she is ready to move house and go to grammar school. Of course, Anita and Sam are still there in Meena's childhood memories and fantasies. This can be seen in the title of the novel itself, where Anita takes precedence over Meena and is the only named character. Meena is only present through the pronoun "me."

The use of "me" is significant because it is not just a stand-in for "Meena." It affirms the adult-narrator Meena's developed identity through affirming her subject position. However, it can also be seen as a sign of Meena the child's uncertainty as to her identity; she is not a fully-fledged Meena, just a "me."

Burcu Kayışçı's article "Where Is Home? Where Are Roots? The Politics of Multiculturalism in *Anita and Me* and *White Teeth*" examines how the novel problematizes notions of Englishness and national identity as fixed. Kayışçı argues that both *Anita and Me* and *White Teeth* favor "flux over fixity and multiplicity over unitary interpretations of identity" (p. 41). James Procter also discusses Englishness in a comparative section on Syal and Hanif Kureishi in his book *Dwelling Places: Postwar Black British Writing*, this time in relation to suburban space. Procter sees Tollington as the suburbs and argues that the novel represents a retrenchment into a mythological Englishness (which is seen as rural and white by the villagers) as its partly rural setting is threatened by the motorway and property developers. At the same time, Procter also highlights the fact that Syal's narrative and its protagonist belong firmly in an English tradition:

> This focus on white communities and cultures allows … Syal to provincialise Englishness, revealing and satirising the "smallness," the *ethnicity* of working-class Brummie or middle-class south London life. Yet while these fictional "ethnographies" of provincial England allow Syal and Kureishi to poke fun at and distance themselves from "native" white culture, their accounts also betray the extent to which the protagonists participate in and *belong* to this culture.
>
> (p. 128)

The critical works by Kayışçı, Procter, Sánchez-Arce, and Schoene-Harwood consider similar issues in relation to Syal and *Anita and Me*, but they do so from different perspectives and reach different conclusions. Whereas Schoene-Harwood places the text outside the framework of the bildungsroman and of Englishness, Kayışçı shows how the novel dismantles those notions of a fixed cultural identity. Sánchez-Arce argues that the novel is indeed a bildungsroman and examines the conflict within Meena as a result of cultural tensions, tracking her moving away from rural-suburban England toward a developed self. Finally, Procter emphasizes the narrative's pull toward Englishness within the framework of black British writing. Kayışçı, Procter, and Sánchez-Arce analyze Syal outside the frame of first-generation narratives, suggesting that there is a huge difference between migrant writing and writing by second-generation writers who do not necessarily have (or want) a narrative of return to the homeland. England is their birthplace and they have to negotiate their identities here with everything they have, including their parents' original culture, the receiving culture, and the culture they make up for themselves. Dunphy also highlights Meena's status as a second-generation migrant who "has to cope with a confusion of identities and find her own place within them" (p. 649). He also divides migrant literature into immigrant literature and emigrant literature, depending on whether the focus is on the country of arrival or the original country. This is a useful distinction that nevertheless shows how critical discourses of postcolonial and migrant writing are themselves confused, for it would be much easier simply to class Syal's writing as English or British.

Humor and irony play an important part in *Anita and Me*, which is an extremely funny novel. Some of its humor, however, can make readers feel uncomfortable at times. In a way, this is one of the characteristics of good comedy; it creates discomfort while exploiting social prejudices. Rocío G. Davis analyzes the novel's "ironically humorous mode" (p. 142) in her discussion of how the child-narrator is a metaphor for the search for self-definition. Dunphy discusses how Syal's narrator is funny about both middle-class Indian and white working-class British cultures and suggests that Meena's position in between both of them allows her to do this. He also explains that the humor in the novel is sometimes reliant on the fact that readers can understand situations better than Meena the child, and so they may be amused at events recounted from Meena the child's point of view when she has missed the point herself.

Sánchez-Arce discusses the narrative strategies of the novel and the doubling of Meena as the adult narrator and the child character. The fact that the narrator is the adult Meena is most apparent in the prologue to the novel due to the prevalence of an ironic stance. The adult Meena's ironic stance as helps distance the narrator from the events of her childhood. Sánchez-Arce analyzes the prologue as a declaration of principles that should warn readers not to read the rest of the story as a true story, because Meena cannot be trusted as a narrator:

> I've always been a sucker for a good double entendre; the gap between what is said and what is thought, what is stated and what is implied, is a place in which I have always found myself. I'm really not a liar, I just learned very early on that those of us deprived of history sometimes need to turn to mythology to feel complete, to belong.
>
> (*Anita and Me*, p. 10)

This warning at the end of the prologue implies that Syal's semiautobiographical novel cannot be taken at face value, that "Meena inhabits the space between language and meaning, between words and what they suggest. She is a story-teller who creates her own myths … playing in and with the overlapping interpretations provided by different frames of reference" (Sánchez-Arce, p. 115). Humor, then, is key to unraveling too easy an idea of *Anita and Me* as testimony or autobiography. Earlier in the prologue, Meena has already thrown readers into confusion by using her ironic stance to undermine traditional (some would say, stereotypical) migrant narratives, the narratives more typical of first-generation migrants that provided an inadequate template for second-generation writers. These stereotyped narratives have become the staple of postcolonial fiction and are extremely familiar so Meena (and Syal by extension) is able to use them to point to the fact that they are what is expected of her:

> I do not have many memories of my very early childhood, apart from the obvious ones, of course. You know, my wind-swept, bewildered parents in their dusty Indian village garb standing in the open doorway of a 747 … living in a shabby boarding house room with another newly arrived immigrant family, Polish, I think it would be quite romantic … I slept in a drawer, probably, swaddled in back copies of the *Daily Mirror* … Of course, this is the alternative story I trot out in job interview situations or, once or twice, to impress middle-class white boys who come sniffling around, excited by the thought of wearing a colonial maiden as a trinket on their arm.
>
> (*Anita and Me*, pp. 9–10)

The adult Meena is scathing about social expectations about her. These include assumptions about a life story of immigration from a rural (code for poor and backward) country, lack of education (code for unskilled economic migrants), and poverty in crowded conditions (code for the common fear that England is being "swamped," to use former prime minister Margaret Thatcher's infamous terminology in 1978, clearly influenced by Enoch Powell's 1968 rhetoric in the "Rivers of Blood" speech).

The opening pages set the tone for the whole novel. We encounter an ironic stance. At first the narrator—an adult Meena who recounts childhood events—takes the reader in with stereotypical stories of immigration. It is only after a page that she reveals that she is inventing her memories. Meena ironically appropriates "obvious" memories only subsequently to undermine them. This presents itself as a satire on society's values, Meena's jocular piling up of anecdotes revealing the absurdity of many assumptions underlying white liberal thinking. The narrative is carefully structured to maximize the effectiveness of Meena's revelation that all these "memories from early childhood" are only "alternatives" that she puts forward for approval, knowing that they are expected of her.

The reader is taken in by familiarity of these stories and the apparently harmless down-to-earth tone. But the tales become increasingly unbelievable, and the reader begins to suspect something by the time Meena recounts how her mother "count[ed] the kicks from the daughter inside her" (*Anita and Me*, p. 9). Is this Meena's sister? If not, how can Meena have any "memories" of the time before she was born? Or is Meena ironically referring to a supposedly common memory pool shared by all migrants and their children; the narratives of exile and displacement told in novels and poetry first, more recently on television and film? Meena identifies two types of audience who wish to be taken in by such stories: interviewers and white middle-class boys. But other readers may also feel rebuffed if they start reading the account without questioning it.

Syal is also commenting on literature and postcoloniality, particularly the pegging down of nonwhite British writers and artists to a specific set of narratives that they are expected to produce. This relates to the search for authenticity (read honesty, testimony, and truth for example) in writings by nonwhites and is directly linked to what Dean MacCannell termed "staged authenticity" (p. 91) in a 1973 article reproduced in his book *The Tourist: A New Theory of the Leisure Class*. MacCannell's notion of staged authenticity is crucial to readings of Syal and other writers considered postcolonial, for they sometimes rely on a readership of what might be termed literary "tourists," who have an interest in "the 'real life' of others" (MacCannell, p. 91) and therefore encourages writers to calculatingly display themselves as "the real thing." Meera's "alternative story" is precisely an example of this staged authenticity, as can be seen by its formulaic nature.

Meena is providing a narrative that fits in with expectations of what her life would be like. At the same time, she is also undermining this and providing a different life story, one that she sets up as truer and more believable. By extension, this is also what Syal as an author is doing in her semiautobiographical work. Nevertheless, one should ask the question: is any of these staged authenticities truer than any other one? The answer is yes and no. Whereas the details of Meena's childhood as recounted in *Anita and Me* are close to Meera Syal's own life, the act of autobiographical narration is still staging this authenticity and, in effect, providing an alternative staged authenticity for the new generation. Susheila Nasta points toward this performativeness in relation to British Asian writers who, she says,

are both *British* and *Asian* and deliberately inhabit a range of different staged identities along a shifting spectrum which defines the particular histories of their individual lives. They are not caught between, in a state of never-ending becoming, but strategically invent a series of alternative locations, as a means to assert both their presence, and their difference from Anglo-British lives.

(p. 186)

Therefore, *Anita and Me* is a novel in which structural irony is set up by the narrator herself, although her younger self in the rest of the novel knows nothing about it. The preface could even be described as an example of Romantic irony, where the self-conscious narrator is making us aware that she is creating a fiction. This is perhaps the reason why sometimes readers tend to forget the existence of this preface, concentrating instead on Meena's childhood recollections and skipping over the ambivalent adult narrator.

Syal's untitled preface undermines from the outset a reading of *Anita and Me* in terms of identity politics, yet all interpretations to date have examined identity. This is not wrong in itself as long as it is recognized that the novel is not a straightforward source of historical or sociological material. In a sense, Syal is having it both ways. She has written a coming-of-age novel that relies on a narrative of adjustment and confrontation within a racially prejudiced setting, but she is also telling readers not to fall for this type of narrative. The name of the protagonist, Meena, should warn us further. The slippage between "Meena" and "Meera" is obvious, and this tends to reinforce autobiographical readings. However, Meera is itself a stage name, an artistic name, so in reality Meena is at least twice removed from the writer. The fact that Syal has chosen a name that corresponds to her artistic name rather than her given name is telling. Meena's irony is aimed at her personal situation; Syal's could be projected toward a whole society. Even the slippage from Meera to Meena points in this direction. Whether this is intentional or not, Syal's double brings us back to the introductory remarks on the author and the discussion of doubleness and the authorial persona. The success of *Anita and Me* as a narrative lies with Meena's voice, which is in turn a product of Syal's authorial self. In spite of the semiautobiographical nature of its content, the form of the novel makes readers aware of its own artificiality while at the same time performing so convincingly that it is credible, if not technically real.

LIFE ISN'T ALL HA HA HEE HEE

If *Anita and Me* invites both literary and sociological interpretations, Syal's second novel, *Life Isn't All Ha Ha Hee Hee* (1999) has elicited mainly the second type of reading. It tells the story of three friends in their thirties. The scholar Susanne Reichl analyzes the paratexts (cover, dedication, and so forth) in *Life Isn't All Ha Ha Hee Hee* and *Anita and Me* and suggests that in *Life Isn't All Ha Ha Hee Hee* they exclude a male readership and encourage a feeling of sisterhood among women while also making the point of addressing women who know Punjabi directly. Indeed, *Life Isn't All Ha Ha Hee Hee* could easily be labeled a British Asian *Sex and the City*, relocated from New York to South East London. Its three main characters—Chila, Sunita, and Tania—are sketches of women in their thirties: the quiet, passive, girl ready for family life; the high achiever whose academic life went wrong after she fell in love and who is now unhappily married with two children who take up all her time; and the cynical media "chick" who is lonely in spite of a string of boyfriends and a glamorous job. Although the action takes place when the women are in their thirties, their individual sections provide details of their childhoods, when their friendship started.

The novel opens with Chila's marriage to a desirable (rich and handsome in the context of the novel) bachelor, Deepak, despite the fact that most people, including her mother, had written her off in terms of marriage prospects. Chila slots into the traditional role of the housewife and puts up with Deepak's demands and infidelities until she finds out that he is having an affair with her best friend, Tania. Even then, she only leaves him when she realizes that Deepak is with Tania as Chila is giving birth to their first child. At the end of the novel, a confident Chila has patched up her friendship with Tania but not her marriage, and she is about to go on holiday to India with her son.

Whereas Chila's story is one of conformity to traditional social norms, Tania's is one of rebellion against them. She breaks with her family to pursue a career in the media instead of looking after her widower father, and she rebels against expectations of her as an "Asian woman" from her community and her bosses. Tania's actions are the catalyst for the breakup of Chila's marriage and the exposure of Sunita's as unhappy, as well as for the friendship of the three women to be put on hold temporarily. A television filmmaker, Tania ropes in her friends to appear in her documentary about happy British Asian couples, only to use editing and camerawork to expose their lives as unhappy and pathetic. Chila and Sunita are humiliated in public, and they witness Tania's betrayal of Chila in kissing Deepak. The documentary makes Sunita realize that she must change herself and her marriage dynamics. She loses weight and starts going out more. At the end of the novel there is a glimmer of hope for her relationship, as she is going on a holiday abroad with her estranged husband. Reconciliation of the three friends takes place when Tania prevents Deepak from kidnapping Chila's son (by stealing and burning his passport). Child kidnap is a recurrent theme in Syal's work. It featured in *Bhaji on the Beach* and also in the harrowing story of Jasbinder Singh in *Life Isn't All Ha Ha Hee Hee*.

Life Isn't All Ha Ha Hee Hee can be placed firmly in the chick-lit genre. The genre of the novel has led many reviewers to see it as a representation of Asian women in general. As noted in the discussion of staged authenticity in relation to *Anita and Me*, it seems almost a requirement for a British Asian writer to refer to certain themes related to their perceived background, and much is made by critics of this expectation and of the way the themes reflect a different or new society. In Syal's case, given her public persona as a comedian, the expectations about her work extend also to being funny and dealing with women's issues.

The narrative in *Life Isn't All Ha Ha Hee Hee* is framed by an omniscient, third-person narrator who allows us glimpses into each of the women's first-person narratives of the past. These first-person narratives throw light on different aspects of the friendship between the three women. However, some reviewers note that the three first-person narrators merge into a common voice. Susan Chacko, for example, reviewing the novel on the Sawnet (South Asian Women's Network) website, notes that "although the women are very distinct when described from the outside, their voices when they speak for themselves are not all that different. Sunita and Tania, in particular, sound awfully similar. Still, even if they all had one voice, I thoroughly enjoyed that voice." Chacko praises the novel's content: "In the background lie the classic dilemmas about culture—Asian vs. Brit vs. a new amalgam—and parents and sex and marriage. But when Syal describes them, they sound fresh and perceptive and original, and often, funny." Paradoxically, Syal's emphasis on sociorealism may have produced a novel with multiple narrators which do not provide the narrative with different voices, whereas the more ironic, mythical style of *Anita and Me* introduces multiple points of view using a first-person narrative.

Susanne Reichl's experience of the novel's voices is quite different from Chacko's:

> The three women portrayed in *Life Isn't All Ha Ha Hee Hee* are rounded characters. ... Their language reflects this heterogeneity: whereas Chila uses a number of Punjabi words, most of them for food or festivities, Tania hardly ever does, and Sunita usually flags them with a critical comment on her language use. This of course reflects the women's different stances towards their parents' traditions, despite their friendship.
>
> (p. 144)

Şebnem Toplu's article "The Trajectory of the Hybrid Self" argues that Syal "confront[s] traditional narrative styles" and "allows [her narrators] to voice their individual hopes and frustrations polyvocally" (p. 95). But Toplu here refers to the overall narrative structure of the novel, whereas Chacko is concerned with the individuality of each narrative voice. So although the text is polyvocal—that is, it has several narrators—their voices may not be distinctive enough.

Another criticism of Syal's style in *Life Isn't All Ha Ha Hee Hee* is that it contains clichés. Melissa Denes, for example, suggests that

> Syal's book wants to deal in grown-up issues, but large sections read like superior teen fiction—Judy Blume in knockabout mood. The jokes are very good, and Syal writes with practised ease ... It is surprising, then, to find her indulging a purple streak: when she is not being ironic, she is unfashionably sentimental and there are some swooningly awful descriptions [of] female-bonding and of sex.
>
> (p. A4)

Denes' rather blunt comments are mostly to do with the form of the novel, which fulfills many readers' expectations of comedy attached to Syal's authorial persona. Both novels are full of situations and one-liners that might belong in a comedy sketch. However, whereas in *Anita and Me* the comedy is closely checked by irony and subtle turns of phrase, the second novel frequently relies on well-known stereotypes and situations: "Believe me, for single Asian girls, there is no such thing as safe sex. When you ask a guy if he's got protection, what you mean is, has he got tinted windows, safety locks and a baseball bat in the boot, in case of passing brothers?" (*Life*, p. 28).

Although reviewers' praise has largely focused on the novel's thematic rather than formal innovativeness, some scholarly articles and essays warn against straightforward sociological readings of the novel. For instance, Christiane Schlote rejects the idea of interpreting the characters in Syal's novel as representative of South Asian or British Asian communities as a whole (p. 76) and highlights the heterogeneity of these communities. Writing in the same journal issue, however, Toplu argues that "multicultural writers' in-between state is highly reflexive in their works" (p. 93) and dismisses Zadie Smith's claims that "to reduce writers to the role of representatives who are expected to delegate, or speak on behalf of a particular community, is to curb their artistic freedom" (cited Toplu, p. 93). Toplu goes on to argue that in the novel Syal "discusses serious points about the choices women face today, locating her protagonists as British women with Indian backgrounds living in London" (p. 94).

Toplu's assessment is partly right; Syal is offering a variety of examples of British Asian women in their thirties as would befit British Asian–themed chick lit. As Schlote remarks, Syal relies on "mainly female characters, whose racial, gender and class identities go beyond binary theories of absolute difference of absolute universality and who are marked attempts to escape predetermined cultural, gender or social roles imposed on them" (p. 77). This is an important and welcome development since British Asian women's characters—whether in television, film or literature—are scarce and limited. In a 1994 interview with Shirani Sabratnam, Syal herself commented on the paucity of roles for Asian actresses in the context of discussing her first screenplay, *Bhaji on the Beach*: "It's frustrating for actresses anyway; but for Asian actresses, we are limited to wives in arranged marriages and parts in Raj epics. I realised that actresses didn't have any power to change: but writers, by creating good scripts can do so regardless of race" (p. 6). This was clearly still a concern for Syal in 1999, as the character Tania sarcastically talks about how "it was quite a relief to peel off the labels randomly stuck on her forehead somewhere around 1979, which read 'Culture Clash Victim—Handle with Care' or 'Oppressed Third World Woman—Give her a Grant'" (*Life*, p. 54). Tania's voice here and on other occasions is extremely similar to that of the adult Meena in *Anita and Me*. Both narrators bemoan the fact that they are subject to expectations created by stereotypes or narratives of immigration. Like Meena, Tania also invents a past for herself when it suits her, using an ironic stance:

> When I get asked about racism, as I always do in any job interview when they're checking whether I'm the genuine article (oppressed Asian woman who has suffered), as opposed to the pretend coconut (white on the inside, brown on the outside, too well off and well spoken to be considered truly ethnic), I make up stories about skinheads and shit through letterboxes, because that's the kind of racism they want to hear about. It lets the nice interviewer off the hook, it confirms that the real baddies live far away from him in the SE postcode area, and he can tut at them from a safe distance. I never tell them about the stares and whispers and the anonymous gobs of phlegm at bus stops, the

creaking of slowly closing doors and the limited view from the glass counter (we never get as high as the ceiling), which all scar as deeply as a well-aimed Doc Marten.

> (*Life*, pp. 142–143)

Tania uses these well-known stories in an ironic way, exposing what has come to be expected of "genuine article[s]," employing a refreshingly sarcastic tone, and then she delivers a well-timed punch line about not even getting close the oft-mentioned glass ceiling for women and ethnic minorities, a punch line that is directly aimed at the implied audience (the interviewers). Toplu argues that *Life Isn't All Ha Ha Hee Hee* is very different from early migrant writing such as that of Sam Selvon, a first-generation British Caribbean writer famous for *The Lonely Londoners* (1956). Toplu states that Syal's novel is not tackling racism as obviously as writing by first-generation migrants and notes that the passage where Tania talks about job interviews (quoted above) is "the unique explicit reference to racism in Syal's fiction which signifies the sophisticated twist from Selvon" (p. 96). It might be argued that, just like in *Anita and Me*, Syals' immersion of the protagonists in a subtly racist environment which is only occasionally signposted is a product not of Syal's sophistication but of her perceptive analysis of how racist discourses come in many shapes and of how racist expression may have changed in certain quarters to become more subtle than views expressed in the 1950s and 1960s but no less damaging.

Despite Toplu's claim that the novel reflects "the choices women face today," the women in the novel are actually not given much in the way of choices, as they all retreat into tradition as a way of dealing with their lives. As it is usually the case with chick lit and chick flicks, there is only an illusion of diversity and choice. Much as with the illusion of diverse voices through the use of multiple narrators, the use of different female protagonists does not necessarily lead to a diverse range of character outcomes or opening of options for women characters. Dave Gunning makes this argument in his 2010 volume, *Race and Antiracism in Black British and British Asian Literature*:

Ultimately, Syal's novel moves towards an affirmation of the value of "traditional" cultures to her protagonists, but does so carefully, with an awareness of the limits to which this acceptance should stretch. The novel explores those aspects of British Asian ideologies that may be subjected to critique, particularly regarding gender relations; it searches for ways to renegotiate relationships with tradition in order to circumvent these oppressions. However, by the end of the novel, the heroines achieve personal and social stability through reaching back to tradition and affirming the "Asian" aspects of their plural heritage. Syal's cultural conservatism is at least as important as her critique of the repressions operating within the field of ethnic delineation.

(pp. 113–114)

On the surface, Syal's British Asian characters are innovative creations; she presents us with two working women, one of whom is also married and with children, and a housewife who leaves her husband. These are women who have friendships, lives, and personalities outside traditional roles. Nevertheless, the novel pulls toward a resolution of their problems by suggesting that they go back to their roots. This is particularly the case with Chila, who plans a trip to India, and Tania, who gets involved in community projects and acts dutifully toward her father at the end of his life. Sunita's future is more uncertain, as she has forged a life for herself but is still trying to work things out with her husband.

Simulation (here used in the way defined by French philosopher Jean Baudrillard) is a key theme in *Life Isn't All Ha Ha Hee Hee* and is intrinsic to its narrative production. Baudrillard talks about how postmodern culture relies so much on models that it has lost touch with the real world. For him, representation currently precedes and determines the real and this leads to a lack of distinction between reality and representation. *Life Isn't All Ha Ha Hee Hee* is aware of its own simulated status, the fact that it is itself a representation that is itself based on other representations more than on reality itself, and deals with the subject in different ways. Simulation in the novel is best exemplified by the characterization of Chila, who of the three friends is the most compliant with tradition. She builds a "traditional," good-girl image for herself,

which she relates to a safe, stable life. Even at school, she prefers the special class, where she cuts and pastes all day, to normal lessons with other children. We are not told this, but Chila is probably conforming to educational bias against black children, who were often believed to be less intelligent. She is not only darker than her friends, but she is also a refugee from Africa and therefore is triply disadvantaged as Asian, African, and female. She represses any outstanding quality she may have in order to avoid problems, concentrating instead on composing collages of the perfect home, made out of magazine cuttings:

> I suppose it didn't help that my education was spent in the prefab hut at school cutting out stuff from old Argos catalogues. I always did the same picture: My Perfect House. I'd cut round beds and dining tables and pine kitchen units and pink chaises-longues and I'd arrange them into rooms and I'd always leave a space in the hallway for me to stand. Just me. And a cat if I could find one, though I was never very good with cutting round the ears, really fiddly.

(*Life*, p. 29)

Simulation is at the heart of this passage, which foretells Chila's later marriage and setting up of a house with Deepak. The older Chila is just like the young girl who cuts and pastes illustrations of furniture and arranges them into a model of what her "perfect" house would be, moving on to shaping her home according to the model. Thus Chila's home is not a real home even though it contains real things and has real walls; it is a reproduction of a representation (the magazines), a copy of a model that has never existed in reality. The problem is that her "model" home turns out to be inhabited by an unfaithful husband as well. Toward the end of the story, Chila has the house to herself, her son replacing the cat of her childhood version. The home she lives in is as constructed as the cardboard house of the collage, both literally and in terms of cultural identification. Life imitates simulated reality, with the "perfect" house in the collage hiding the fact that "real," simulated homes are in the community. Chila wants to feel safe so she refuses to judge the teachings she receives from her family, or to judge almost anything for that matter. Chila's character could also be said to be a simulation. She is conforming to the stereotype of the perfect British Asian daughter and wife, the "model" British Asian woman.

Syal portrays Chila as a conformist who is a victim of the identity she feels safe representing. Chila's cultural identification with her constructed "home" could be seen as Syal's take on the "chick lit" genre, which she has given a particular British Asian twist. In terms of style, the novel is a collage, a collection of different narratives that are pasted together by the omniscient narrator, the voices of the characters being diverse pieces of "literary" furniture cut from other genre novels. Individual sections also read like a combination of different linguistic clichés, as we saw above.

Sara Upstone's theories about humor and irony in Syal, however, point to a much more productive use of simulation. She explains that

> Syal's comedy is less about being funny than about a survival mechanism that re-creates events so that their negative aspects are not entirely disabling. If there is sometimes laughter in this, then it only signifies that the emotion being obscured is perhaps particularly negative … Our popular image of Syal is a woman who makes us laugh. But we need also to look beyond this laughter. This looking underneath is perhaps difficult when the obvious content is so dynamic and engaging. … Undertake this searching and we discover how close laughing is to crying.
>
> (p. 138)

Humor cannot be separated from the serious issues that Syal addresses in her two novels. Indeed it is their use of humor and irony that marks the novels out as different. *Anita and Me* is a much more optimistic novel than *Life Isn't All Ha Ha Hee Hee*, as in the former book the child-protagonist believes that she is leaving the racist world of Tollington for the better. Nevertheless, the narrator checks these fantasies, and the ending is perhaps too neat to ring true. Upstone mentions how implausible it is for a Punjabi-French couple to own the Big House in Tollington and the mine. The final showdown between Meena and Sam, when Meena lets him kiss her, occupies the frame of teenage fantasy not dissimilar to

that of Jane Austen's *Pride and Prejudice* or even to comic-strip stories such as those in the teen magazine *Jackie*. *Life Isn't All Ha Ha Hee Hee* is thus perhaps a grown-up corrective to *Anita and Me*'s fantasy. The humor is still there, as is the irony, but although the protagonists seem at first able to change their situations, they cannot. These are the laughs prompted by the clown's tears. In this respect, Syal's work as a comic is extremely relevant to her fiction.

DRAMA, FILM, AND TELEVISION WORK

Meera Syal's output of drama, film, and television work as an actor, producer, and writer is extensive, and this work has helped shape her authorial persona and the expectations attached to her novels and other writings. She has worked on feature films by renowned directors such as Woody Allen and Stephen Frears, and she has appeared in some of the most popular television soap operas and other series in the United Kingdom, such as *Absolutely Fabulous, Bad Girls, The Bill, Doctor Who, Goodness Gracious Me, Holby City,* and *The Kumars.* She has also appeared regularly on radio and television programs, and she has adapted *Anita and Me* as a feature film (2002) and *Life Isn't All Ha Ha Hee Hee* as a three-part television drama (2005).

Syal's writing career started with a play rather than fiction. *One of Us* (1983) was cowritten with Jacqueline Shapiro and was first performed at the Edinburgh Festival in 1983, with Syal in the lead role. It won the National Student Drama Award that same year. It tells the story of a young Asian woman who leaves home because she wants to be an actor; she becomes obsessed with her white friend Carol, but she is finally reunited with her family, her mother in particular. Much like *Anita and Me,* the story is a journey of self-discovery and rebelliousness. It also features the themes of personal erasure and the desire to fit into the dominant culture, which the novel expands upon: Carol could well be thought of as a precursor of Anita Rutter. *One of Us* was crucial to Syal's career because it was her first significant acting role and led to her being offered an acting job in London. Although the script is unpublished, it seems likely that this piece of early writing could throw light on Syal's development of recurrent themes in her novels and other writing. It is also a powerful early example of Syal's use of a frequently ignored point of view, that of a young British Asian woman. Possibly because of this focus, Syal was asked by the BBC in 1992 to write a three-part television series titled *My Sister Wife*, a drama on Pakistani marriage in which she also starred, that exploded stereotypes about British Asian women. This led to a television film for Channel 4, *Bhaji on the Beach* (directed by Gurinder Chadha), in 1993.

Bhaji on the Beach is a critique both of racism in Britain in the 1980s and early 1990s and of the ideal of womanhood in British Asian (particularly Punjabi) communities. The film is a comedy told in a combination of social realism à la Ken Loach (a well-known British director who makes mainly social realist films) and parodies of Bollywood films. Reviews such as Ann Hornaday's for the *New York Times* highlight the film's convergence of feminism and postcolonialism. However, as Hornaday explains, even as Chadha and Syal are subverting expectations about British Asian women, they are also poking fun at bombastic feminist thought that forgets women themselves. A case in point is that of the director of the Asian Women's Centre in Birmingham, Simi, who takes the group of nine very different women to Blackpool (an English seaside resort similar to Atlantic City) and on arrival says to them: "It's your day! Have a female fun time!" Although this is exactly what the trip and the film (clearly targeted at women audiences) involve, the exhortation is out of place.

The film shows that these women are all very different—in contrast to the way television or film parts for Asian women in Britain at that time usually cast such women as essentially the same—and it also analyzes how the experience of diaspora affects different generations of British Asian women. While the younger generation of Asian women in Britain are painfully aware of the conflicting demands made on them by the normative "British" majority and their "British Asian" community, middle-aged women escape through fantasy or try to enforce an ideal of Indian femininity with the support of the older generation. These portraits are juxtaposed to that of a wealthy woman visiting from Bombay, who is shown in dress and behavior to be both less stuck in tradition and deeply shocked by the conditions under which the others have to live, including racism and the patriarchal rule that is enforced by the women themselves as well as by most of the men.

Syal and the film director Chadha could therefore be said to be turning a critical eye outward to British society and inward to British Asian communities, though this distinction is flawed because a critique of British society is actually also an internal critique. It is easy to forget that many of the characters (certainly all the young ones) are actually British. This is stated visually in the first establishing shot, a right-to-left tracking shot of shop fronts in a mixed Birmingham neighborhood that starts with a quintessentially "British" shop, the butchers, and continues showing swastika graffiti on the shutter of a closed shop, a grocery with a variety of fruit and vegetables from around the world, and a newsdealer run by one of the main characters. The direction of the tracking shot may already be said to upset typically Western reading strategies (left to right), although there is a variety of left-to-right and right-to-left languages in India and Pakistan.

In some quarters *Bhaji* has been criticized for being too harsh on British Asian men; it could be argued that the film is harsh on most men, not just British Asian ones. But not all men are portrayed negatively, and criticism of both men and women who enforce gender stereotypes comes through in this film that exposes patriarchal rule and received notions of femininity as damaging both to men and women. One of the main plot lines, that of the abusive husband who tries to kidnap his son, is a case in point. The husband is seen clearly to be in the wrong, but clearly, too, family and social pressure contribute to his inexcusable behavior. Some of the older women's reactions to the wife seeking a divorce are also held up for criticism, as are the extended family's living arrangements with multiple generations living under the same roof and wives treated as servants.

The plot line of *Bhaji on the Beach*, though highly melodramatic, was used by Syal in later work, particularly in *Life Isn't All Ha Ha Hee Hee*, in the story of Jasbinder Singh, who appears on the fringes of the narrative. Jasbinder divorces her husband, who subsequently kidnaps their children and kills both them and himself. This is the background to the thwarted kidnap attempt by Deepak. Jasbinder's husband is the typical abuser who considers his wife and children as property and cannot think of them as being anywhere else but with him. His crime and suicide highlight issues of male proprietary feelings and the way women are made to feel guilty even when they are the victims: "Gurpreet Singh told his wife if he could not have the children, no-one would, and that this was her punishment for destroying her family" (*Life*, p. 215). Syal's repetition of this plot line marks her concern about this issue and is echoed by Jasbinder's speech in the novel:

> The courts tell me this was an act of passion, a tragic event. I want this event called what it was, murder. I have been blamed for this. People say it was my karma, my fate for leaving my husband. But no-one will blame him. … This court ruling must be overturned, for all the other women out there, like me. For Leila Khan, who was stabbed to death when collecting her children from a custody visit. For Priya Kumar, whose ex-husband kidnapped her son and has been missing for five years. For Jyoti Patel, who let her ex-husband take her children on holiday and when he returned …
>
> (p. 216)

Internal critique of Britain and, within it, British Asian communities is the main focus of all of Syal's work. Syal is best known for being part of the team that wrote *Goodness Gracious Me*, a comedy sketch show that was originally on BBC Radio 4 (1996–1998) and was later televised on BBC 2 (1998–2001). The sketches were unlike anything previously shown on British radio and television. They exploded Indian stereotypes by making fun of them, particularly in relation to the clash between British and Indian cultures in modern Britain. Many of the sketches explored the conflict between traditional Indian culture and modern British life. Some reversed the roles and viewed the British from an Indian perspective, while others poked fun at Indian stereotypes.

Characters, themes, and plotlines recur in Syal's oeuvre whatever its format and media. Syal's preoccupations are firmly placed on her English and diasporic background and focus attention on ordinary people in extraordinary circumstances. Syal may be best known as a comedian, but she asks important questions about what it is to be English, British, Asian, or a combination of the three. She also focuses particularly on women (some would say British Asian women) and critiques patriarchy in Britain and, within Britain, in the British Asian community. Her work may be considered funny, but she is dead serious.

Selected Bibliography

WORKS OF MEERA SYAL

NOVELS AND PLAYS

One of Us. With Jacqueline Shapiro. First performed at the Edinburgh Festival, 1983. (Despite its success and the fact that it launched Syal's career as an actor and writer, this play has never been published.)

My Sister Wife. In *Six Plays by Black and Asian Women Writers*. Edited by Kadija George. London: Aurora Metro, 1993.

Anita and Me. London: Flamingo, 1997. (This edition is the source for all quotations in the text.)

Life Isn't All Ha Ha Hee Hee. London: Doubleday, 1999.

SELECTED SCREENPLAYS AND MUSICALS

Bhaji on the Beach. Feature film directed by Gurinder Chadha, 1993.

Anita and Me. Feature film directed by Metin Hüseyin, 2002.

Bombay Dreams. Bollywood-themed musical, cowritten with Andrew Meeham for Andrew Lloyd Webber. London 2002–2004 and Broadway 2004.

Life Isn't All Ha Ha Hee Hee. BBC television miniseries, 2005. (Syal cowrote the first two episodes with Abi Morgan.)

Generation Next.. Written for the National Theatre's 2012 Connections Plays season.

FILMS AND TELEVISION SERIES BASED ON SYAL'S WORK
Anita and Me. Feature film directed by Metin Hüseyin, 2002.
Life Isn't All Ha Ha Hee Hee. Television miniseries, 2005.

CRITICAL AND BIOGRAPHICAL STUDIES

Bromley, Roger. *Narratives for a New Belonging: Diasporic Cultural Fictions.* Edinburgh: Edinburgh University Press, 2000.

Chacko, Susan. *"Life Isn't All Ha Ha Hee Hee* by Meera Syal." *Sawnet* (http://www.sawnet.org/books/reviews.php?Life+isn%27t+All+Ha+Ha+Hee+Hee), February 16, 2009.

Davis, Rocío G. "India in Britain: Myths of Childhood in Meera Syal's *Anita and Me.*" In *On Writing (and) Race in Contemporary Britain.* Edited by Fernan Galván and Mercedes Bengoechea. Alcalá de Henares, Spain: Servicio de Publicaciones de la Universidad de Alcalá de Henares, 1999. Pp. 139–146.

Denes, Melissa. "The Temptations of Television." *Guardian Review,* November 13, 1999, p. A4. (Review of *Life Isn't All Ha Ha Hee Hee*).

Dimarco, Danette, and J. Sunita Peacock. "The *Bhadramahila* and Adaptation in Meera Syal's and Gurinder Chadha's *Bhaji on the Beach.*" *Mosaic* 41, no. 4:106–178 (2008).

Dunphy, Graeme. "Meena's Mockingbird: From Harper Lee to Meera Syal." *Neophilologus* 88, no. 4:637–659 (2004).

Gunning, Dave. *Race and Antiracism in Black and British Asian Literature.* Liverpool: Liverpool University Press, 2010.

Hornaday, Ann. "In *Bhaji on the Beach,* Feminism Meets the Diaspora." *New York Times,* May 22, 1994, p. 29.

Hussain, Yasmin. *Writing Diaspora: South Asian Women, Culture, and Ethnicity.* Hampshire, U.K.: Ashgate, 2005.

Kayışçı, Burcu. "Where Is Home? Where Are Roots? The Politics of Multiculturalism in *Anita and Me* and *White Teeth.*" *Interactions* 19, nos. 1–2:41–52 (spring–fall 2010). (Special issue, "The Role of Female Voices in Constructing Fictional Maps of Contemporary Britain.")

MacCannell, Dean. *The Tourist: A New Theory of the Leisure Class.* Berkeley: University of California Press, 1999.

Nasta, Susheila. *Home Truths: Fictions in the South Asian Diaspora in Britain.* Houndmills, U.K.: Palgrave, 2002.

Procter, James. *Dwelling Places: Postwar Black British Writing.* Manchester, U.K.: Manchester University Press, 2003.

Reichl, Susanne. *Cultures in the Contact Zone: Ethnic Semiosis in Black British Literature.* Trier, Germany: Wissenschaftlicher Verlag Trier, 2002.

Sabratnam, Shirani. "Meera Syal: The Fun in Comedy." *Artrage,* February–March 1994, p. 6. (Interview.)

Sánchez-Arce, Ana María. "Invisible Cities: Being and Creativity in Meera Syal's *Anita and Me* and Ben Okri's *Astonishing the Gods.*" In *Cities on the Margin, on the Margin of Cities: Representations of Urban Space in Contemporary Irish and British Fiction.* Edited by Philippe Laplace and Éric Tabuteau. Besançon, France: Presses Universitaires Fran-Comtoises, 2003. Pp. 113–130.

Sandapen, Sheila Françoise. "Being Black, Becoming British: Contemporary Female Voices in Black British Literature." PhD diss., Indiana University of Pennsylvania, 2009 (http://dspace.lib.iup.edu:8080/dspace/bitstream/2069/192/1/Sheila+Sandapen.pdf).

Schlote, Christiane. "No Leisurely Stroll Through Arab and Punjabi London: Transnational Cityscapes in Hanan Al-Shaykh's *Only in London* and Meera Syal's *Life Isn't All Ha Ha Hee Hee.*" *Interactions* 19, nos. 1–2:75–92 (spring–fall 2010). (Special issue, "The Role of Female Voices in Constructing Fictional Maps of Contemporary Britain.")

Schoene-Harwood, Berthold. "Beyond (T)race: *Bildung* and Proprioception in Meera Syal's *Anita and Me.*" *Journal of Commonwealth Literature* 34, no. 1:159–168 (1999).

Stein, Mark. *Black British Literature: Novels of Transformation.* Columbus: Ohio State University Press, 2004.

Toplu, Şebnem. "The Trajectory of the Hybrid Self." *Interactions* 19, nos. 1–2:93–109 (spring–fall 2010). (Special issue, "The Role of Female Voices in Constructing Fictional Maps of Contemporary Britain.")

Upstone, Sara. *British Asian Fiction: Twenty-First Century Voices.* Manchester, U.K.: Manchester University Press, 2010.

Vogt-William, Christine. "Rescue Me? No, Thanks! *A Wicked Old Woman* and *Anita and Me.*" In *Towards a Transcultural Future: Literature and Society in a "Post"-Colonial World.* Edited by Geoffrey V. Davis, Peter H. Marsden, Bénédicte Ledent, and Marc Delrez. Amsterdam: Rodopi, 2004. Pp. 373–387.

RICHARD CHENEVIX TRENCH

(1807—1886)

Matthew Sperling

RICHARD CHENEVIX TRENCH is undoubtedly a significant figure in mid-Victorian intellectual and religious life, but there is no clear consensus on where the center of his significance lies. John Bromley's 1959 critical biography, which is the only book-length study of Trench's life and work to date, gives equal weighting to four of Trench's vocations, as philologist, poet, theologian, and archbishop. For church historians and students of the British Empire in the late nineteenth-century, what matters is Trench's role as the final archbishop of Dublin at the time of the disestablishment of the Church of Ireland. For historians of theology, Trench's writings on the parables, the proverbs and the Gospels are among the most important examples of mid-Victorian exegetical scholarship, and they exemplify the traditionalism and resistance put up by British theologians to the radical threats posed by new continental scholarship. For readers of poetry, Trench's work represents vividly the transition from a strongly Wordsworthian late Romantic mode to a Victorian one; while his work as sonneteer, elegist, and narrative poet has a strength and memorability that is its own. His literary, critical, and editorial work, on sacred Latin poetry, on the English sonnet, and on the Spanish Golden Age dramatist Pedro Calderón de la Barca, represents a small but significant contribution to nineteenth-century literary culture. For students of social and cultural history, Trench is a figure whose name recurs in the biographies of many of the most eminent Victorians of his time, from his early days as one of the Cambridge "Apostles" onward, and his friendships with men such as Alfred Tennyson, Frederick Denison Maurice, John Kemble, Thomas Carlyle, and Samuel Wilberforce show

his centrality in Victorian literary, religious, and political life. Historians of linguistics, meanwhile, have highlighted Trench's popularizing philological works of the 1850s as his key contribution (these remained in print and were used in schools for many decades), along with his crucial role in the foundation of the great *Oxford English Dictionary*—he is popularly reputed as the "Father of the *OED*."

This is enough achievement to have filled several lifetimes, and the fact that one man did it all testifies not only to the scale of his abilities but also to the remarkable, prodigious energy of mid-Victorian Britain. Trench is an emblematic figure: an eminent Victorian whose life and works seem deeply entrenched in the conservative ideology, the moral seriousness, and the grief-touched sentimentality of his time. Yet his writings are so strongly marked by the spirit of the age, which runs deep into the body of their vast learning and diligence, that even when the worldview contained in them seems to us objectionable or outdated, they retain the power to instruct, amuse, and surprise, through the trenchantness, wit, and seriousness of their claims.

This article will chiefly be dedicated to Trench's work as philologist, poet, and religious writer, for it is here that he is of most interest to students of Victorian literature and culture; but his life was a remarkably long and full one, with much to tell us about one of the most crucial periods of British history.

LIFE

Trench's mother, Melesina Phillipa St. George (née Chenevix, 1768–1827), the granddaughter of Richard Chenevix, bishop of Waterford, came from a family of Huguenot origin, while his father, Richard Trench, Sr. (1774–1860), came from a prominent family of the Anglo-Irish aristocracy. By Trench's own account, his mother was the strongest formative influence on his character and early years. Something of the piety of the household Trench grew up in is expressed in his mother's posthumously published pamphlet, *Thoughts of a Parent on Education* (1837), which tells us that "the first object of education is to train an immortal soul" (Bromley, p. 1). But Melesina was also a cosmopolitan and sophisticated women, as is evidenced by the diaries and personal writings collected in *The Remains of the Late Mrs. Richard Trench*, the publication of which Trench arranged in 1862, many years after her death. On reading these accounts of foreign travel and high society life in revolutionary and Napoleonic Europe, Thomas Carlyle remarked on the "clear, pure, lucid English lady-soul" that emerged brightly from their pages (Bromley, p. 2). While relishing her meetings with the great and the good, Melesina characteristically views postrevolutionary Paris with some doubtfulness: "A revolution does not seem to be favourable to the morals of the people" (Bromley, p. 10). After the early death of her first husband from consumption, Melesina remarried at the age of thirty-five, to Richard Trench, at the English embassy in Paris in 1803. Before they could return home, however, war was renewed between Britain and the Napoleonic Empire, leaving them effectively interned in Paris for several years (though the conflict seemingly failed to stop Parisian high society from continuing much as normal). While there, the Trenches suffered the sad loss of two children in infancy—the grief of child mortality is a recurring theme in Melesina's writings and would likewise become a theme in the life and writings of her son. Permission to return home was finally granted in 1807, and it was on a visit to Ireland in that year that Richard Chenevix Trench, their third son, was born.

In Trench's early years, several keynotes of his character emerge already. He entered preparatory school in 1816, and Harrow three years later. His character was pugnacious: one schoolmate

reports on his abilities as a cricketer ("not much of a batsman, but a safe long-stop" (Bromley, p. 15)), while Charles Wordsworth, nephew of the poet, records an early scrap:

> Richard Trench and I fell out over a game of quoits. He lost his temper, flew into an Irish rage, took up a quoit and threw it at my head. Such an outrage called for instant chastisement and I am afraid it must be said that I administered it, as boys are wont to do, rather too savagely; for the next day he had to go to London to see a dentist in order to have his teeth, which had suffered in the fray, put to rights. Who would have supposed that such an encounter could ever have taken place between the future sedate and amiable Archbishop and the future advocate of reconciliation among Christians?
> (Bromley, p. 15)

The most important facets of his character already emerging, however, were his scholarly and literary abilities. Early favorites, under his mother's influence, included Percy Bysshe Shelley and Aeschylus, while his mother records that the young Trench's "craving for books" was so great by age fifteen that "he cannot take an airing without arming himself against ennui by one or more volumes," and that he "delights in referring, collating, extracting," and "luxuriates in the idea of finding fifteen readings of the same passage in Scripture" (Bromley, p. 18)—a habit of mind that would later serve well his capaciously learned and cross-referenced books of English word lore and biblical scholarship.

In 1827 Melesina Trench died, marking the end of the first phase of Trench's life. But the second phase had already begun, for in 1825 he entered Trinity College, Cambridge, immediately becoming a member of the celebrated "Cambridge Conversazione Society," later to become known as the "Apostles." In the long history of the Apostles, the nature of the society fluctuates between seriousness and snobbism, earnestness and cultish homosexual preciosity, but at this early stage their numbers included several young men who would go on to become some of the most distinguished and important figures of their time. Trench's fellow Apostles included Alfred Tennyson, later poet laureate; his great friend Arthur Hallam, who was to die tragically young in 1833 and inspire Tennyson's greatest poem, *In*

Memoriam A. H. H. (1850); F. D. Maurice, one of the greatest Anglican churchmen and theologians of his time; and the writer and poet John Sterling, the subject of a memorable biography by Thomas Carlyle (1851).

Trench was by temperament inclined to keep his distance from the more outgoing and unconventional members of the Apostles; in a letter of 1828 he describes them, with some raising of the eyebrow, as a "gallant band of Platonico-Wordsworthian-Coleridgean-anti-Utilitarians." His acquaintance with Tennyson was never especially close, and it seems touched by a degree of early poetic rivalry, but Trench nonetheless takes credit for a role in inspiring one of Tennyson's finest poems, "The Palace of Art" (1832). As Alfred Tennyson himself recalls, in the 1897 *Alfred, Lord Tennyson: A Memoir* written by his son Hallam Tennyson, "Trench said, when we were at Trinity together, 'Tennyson, we cannot live in art'" (vol. 1, p. 85). The poem, with its strong opposition between the moral and the aesthetic, was provoked by Trench's remark, while the dedicatory lines, beginning "I send you here a sort of allegory," are addressed to him (although some dispute remains as to when Trench and Tennyson first met). In his scholarly and unspectacular way, Trench led an active literary life among the Apostles. He ran a journal titled *The Translator*, where he first ventured translations of his favorite poet of the Spanish Golden Age, Pedro Calderón de la Barca, on whom he would publish a book many years later, and he tried his hand at writing a verse tragedy in the Calderón manner, with the title "Bernardo del Carpio." It was never staged, although the manuscript, which he destroyed in 1864 upon his consecration as archbishop of Dublin, circulated privately.

After he left Trinity, taking the bachelor's degree in 1828, Trench traveled widely on the continent. In subsequent years he would downplay the Apostolic phase of his life—largely because of the adventurous and ill-advised involvements it led him into in 1830–1831. Trench's growing love for Spanish literature and culture gave rise to several distinguished poems around this time, including the sonnets "On a Picture of Madrid, by Murillo" and "Gibraltar" ("England, we love thee better than we know"), the latter reminiscent of Robert Browning's "Home-Thoughts, from Abroad." But his visits to the country also convinced him of the darker side of its social and political life, and fostered in him, as in other young men of his generation and acquaintance, a hope for its revolutionary emancipation from the cruel reign of King Ferdinand VII, though this was not without a sense of foreboding: "I do not think Spain has any chance of escaping a bloody and terrible revolution," he wrote in a letter of 1829 (Bromley, p. 29). His sympathies were drawn to the group of fifty or so Spanish liberals who were at this time exiled in London, and in a pair of sonnets, "To the Constitutional Exiles," Trench gives guarded encouragement to their cause. He was not alone in this sympathy, and the bolder character of John Sterling in particular served to ignite the political passions of the idealistic young Apostles, so that Trench, Tennyson, and Hallam, among other Cambridge men, were drawn in to action. Soon a plan was being hatched for a revolutionary expedition against Cadiz, with the exiled Spaniards, under the leadership of General José Torrijos, backed by English money and volunteers, and with the hope of gaining popular support in the form of uprisings in the north of the country. In retrospect, the expedition looks a fiasco—the suicidal folly of a ragtag army, backed by what Carlyle, in his *Life of John Sterling* (1851), sardonically calls "one or two young democrats of Regent St" (Bromley, p. 36) who hope to win the overthrow of a powerful despot, and yet on arrival utterly fail to gain support from the Spanish. The youthful idealism and the radical commitment to justice of the whole episode are matched by its blundering and naïveté. University friends back home joked of "Dick Trench" taking an inept turn as continental revolutionary, but for others of his acquaintance the Spanish adventure had a deadly ending: after a final, desperate attempt to ignite a coup was foiled at Malaga, a number of the rebels, including the Englishman Robert Boyd, were captured and executed by firing squad in December 1831.

The excitement promised by the Spanish adventure speaks to a more general sense of aimlessness and futility for the young Trench at this time. His sense of vocation was weak. In 1830 he writes of "twenty-three years of existence squandered away," with "the riddle of existence" weighing heavy upon him, in his lack of "happiness and moral elevation" (Bromley, p. 32); and the summer of 1831, after his return from Spain, was a time of ennui and spiritual unease. His reading included Jakob Böhme, the seventeenth-century German theologian whom Trench refers to as "the mystic cobbler," and Blaise Pascal's *Pensées* (1669), but apart from this he felt himself veering into "sheer bankruptcy." He was forgetting his Greek; he was writing no poems; and his "troublous and disordered existence" was lacking in all vitality: "I have given over despairing and reading Shelley, and am beginning to acquiesce in things just as they are; in brief, subsiding into a very respectable worldling" (Bromley, pp. 43–44).

Two things held promise for him: the prospect of marrying his cousin Frances Mary Trench, and the prospect of taking holy orders. One of his courting gifts to Frances was a copy of Samuel Taylor Coleridge's *Aids to Reflection* (1825)—a rather unpromising choice of romantic gift, perhaps, but one that indicates the serious-mindedness of the young couple. Frances's reaction to the gift is not recorded, but they married in May 1832, and a first child, Francis, followed in 1833. Their long and happy marriage brought seven sons and five daughters, but three of the boys died before their time; their firstborn, eight-year-old Francis, died in 1841—a source of terrible, lifelong grief for Trench, and the spur for his *Elegiac Poems* (1843)—and later they faced the tragic double blow of their sons Arthur and Richard dying as young men in 1860–1861 while away in India. Richard died on the thirty-fourth anniversary of Melesina's death; 1860 was also the year in which Richard Trench, Sr., died, age eighty-six. Family bereavement and child mortality were of course more common for the Victorians than they are for us; nonetheless they gave to Trench's adult life a near-constant undertow of grief and suffering.

These were years of growth: Trench was ordained deacon in 1832, and that year was also significantly marked by a meeting with Samuel Taylor Coleridge, the great Romantic poet and conservative sage, at Highgate. Coleridge, one of the great talkers of his day, spoke of the radical arguments on the dating of scripture being made by modern biblical scholars on the Continent, but Trench's orthodoxy was steadfast: "me he did not shake in the slightest degree" (Bromley, p. 48). After a period of ill health spent convalescing in Italy through much of 1834–1835, he was ordained as a priest in July 1835, and in this year his first book of poems, *The Story of Justin Martyr, and Other Poems*, was published. (It was to be followed by four subsequent books in the next seven years, before vocational commitments slowed Trench's poetic output; *Poems,* a two-volume edition of his collected lyrics, appeared in 1885.) The next phase of Trench's life was chiefly given over to quietly filling his priestly duties in various Hampshire parishes: Curdridge from 1836; Alverstoke from 1841; Itchenstoke from 1844. It was in 1836 that he came into the ambit of Samuel Wilberforce, the son of the great abolitionist William Wilberforce. Samuel's reputation has suffered posthumously, in particular following his humiliation in 1860's Oxford Town Hall debate on evolution with Thomas Henry Huxley (when "Soapy Sam" turned his wit to ask whether it was through his grandmother or grandfather that Huxley was descended from a monkey), but he was a formidable character, reputed as the greatest public speaker of his day, and was one of the key movers in the nineteenth-century Anglican Church. Wilberforce, who rose to be bishop of Winchester, was the key influence on Trench's church career, repeatedly and successfully maneuvering in "the church scramble" to secure preferments for him. Trench's close connection to Wilberforce sealed his growing orthodoxy. For the remainder of his life, to the occasional regret of his more adventurous friends from Cambridge days, he would strike a somewhat stiff and austere figure. The poet pursuing the revolutionary cause seemed long gone.

In 1845, the pace of Trench's ecclesiastical career quickened: upon Wilberforce's appointment as bishop of Oxford, he asked Trench to be his examining chaplain, a role of significant academic importance; then in 1846 Trench became professor of divinity at King's College, London, before finally rising to be dean of Westminster in 1856. As the dean, Trench's major achievement was the innovation of Sunday evening services, which succeeded in drawing greater numbers of Londoners to the Abbey. Although he was acknowledged as a superb writer of sermons and lectures, it seems that Trench was not altogether successful as a public speaker: contemporaries found his "deep sepulchral tones" very difficult to make out in the large setting of Westminster, with "words hurried into one great indistinct utterance" (Bromley, p. 135). It was in these years that Trench also established his reputation as a theologian and philologist—as his poetic output shriveled, his scholarly and ecclesiastical output blossomed. His *Notes on the Parables of Our Lord* (1841) and *On the Study of Words* (1851) were the first major books in a steady stream of writings in these fields (discussed more fully below), and when he joined the London Philological Society in 1857, he became the key player in moves to initiate work on what would become the *Oxford English Dictionary*.

In 1863 Trench reached the height of his ecclesiastical career in being offered the opportunity to be become archbishop of Dublin. Again Wilberforce was a prime mover in securing the position for Trench and in convincing him to take it. Trench had doubts. His relationship to Ireland, the land of his birth, had never been easy: after the end of a brief spell in the country in 1833 he declared himself "glad to be quit of Ireland" (Bromley, p. 44) although in 1847 he had traveled back there to work selflessly in famine relief, which left him exhausted and fevered. Upon being offered the archbishopric, he wrote to Wilberforce to explain that "England is my world, the land of all my friends" and to warn of his deficiency in qualification for such a post: "I have few or no gifts of government, little or no power of rallying men round me." But Wilberforce would not be dissuaded by such vacillations, and in 1864, after some further agonizing

over whether to accept the role, Trench was consecrated archbishop. Friends including F. D. Maurice wrote to congratulate him upon the news—and yet Maurice's letter sounded a note of reservation, for he remembered Trench saying many years earlier "that no one could wish to be a bishop who was not a hero or a madman."

It was at this point that Trench burned the cherished manuscript of "Bernardo del Carpio," his attempted undergraduate tragedy. Such literary ambitions, it seems, would no longer be appropriate to the dignity of his office. In a way, Trench's interest to the student of literature and intellectual history fades out in these years, as he becomes chiefly an actor in ecclesiastical history; and yet the story that ensued in Trench's Dublin years has its own drama. Whether Trench was hero or madman to take on the role, it is clear that the archbishopric presented him with challenges and controversies the likes of which he had never faced before.

Trench came to the post at a time when the Church of Ireland was the subject of fierce political unrest, which was now reaching a head and which threatened its very existence. The move toward its disestablishment is today seen by most historians as inevitable, but in its day it excited fierce passions on both sides of the debate. It was William Gladstone, the great Liberal Party leader, who finally forced reform through. In 1868 he campaigned and won election as prime minister (his first stint in the office) under the banner of "Justice for Ireland," and he immediately set to implementing a program of reform for what he, along with many others, saw as the unjust conditions of the Irish Church. The overwhelming majority of the nation were of course Catholic: the 1861 census reported that only 9 percent of the nearly six million population of Ireland were members of the Anglican Church; and yet, because Anglicanism was the established church, the whole community was subject to an oppressive taxation system, paying a tithe toward the upkeep of that church. (From 1830–1836 this had provoked a campaign of civil disobedience by the incensed Catholic peasantry, known as the "Tithe War"; a Royal Commision report on the Irish Church in 1868 reveals that £364,000 of its

£581,000 annual net revenue came from the tithe.) The church was controlled by Parliament in Westminster, with the queen appointing its bishops. The contentions surrounding Gladstone's policy were fierce and long-running, and Trench, a naturally retiring and somewhat shy figure, suffered a world of troubles, finding himself plunged into political contention and badly out of his element.

In Trench's view, the movement for disestablishment was a work of party politics and was not borne out by the beliefs and desires of the Irish people: "Whatever energy there is in the assault on the Irish Church is in England, and not here," he argued, and he described Gladstone as "a dreamer of dreams" (Bromley, p. 168). With the perspective of hindsight, this seems an implausible view for him to have reached, and there can be little doubt that Trench's deep commitment to establishment orthodoxy led him to see only that which he wanted to see; but Trench was uncompromising in his views, and once the likelihood of the course of events became clear, he was fierce and steadfast in his negotiations for the best terms for disestablishment. He was deeply concerned for the future of Protestantism in Ireland:

> If you overthrow the Irish Established Church you will put to the Irish protestants the choice between apostasy and expatriation, and every man among them who has money or position will, when he sees his Church go, leave the country. If you do that, you will find Ireland so difficult to manage that you will have to depend on the gibbet and the sword.

Such pessimism for the future did not hold sway, and in 1869, after lengthy struggles in the House of Lords, Gladstone's "Irish Church Act" ("An Act to put an end to the Establishment of the Church of Ireland") was finally passed through Parliament, coming into force on January 1, 1871. The Anglican Church would no longer be the state church in Ireland, and it would receive no more compulsory tithes; it would also send no more representatives to the House of Lords.

For Trench, this defeat was dispiriting. He felt that the House of Lords had let down the Church of Ireland with shaming weakness: "A House of statesmen, or at least one which embraced so many statesmen, should have formed a juster estimate of what was within its reach to accomplish" (Bromley, p. 191). But there was little time for such retrospective grievances, for the question of how the disestablished church was to be reconstructed so as to avoid total collapse was most urgent.

Seeking relief from the controversy, in summer 1870 the Trenches holidayed in the Tyrol, but more misfortune was in store. First the explosive drama of the Franco-Prussian War forced them into a swift detour, and then Trench and his daughter Edith endured a terrifying cow attack near Innsbruck, although the archbishop characteristically managed to find a religious reassurance in the incident: "we were set upon by a cow, both of us knocked down, and only that the proverb 'God gives short horns to the wicked cow' was fulfilled in the creature, we might have been much hurt. As it was, by God's good Hand upon us, we escaped with some bruises and torn clothes" (Bromley, p. 202).

On his return, the work of drawing up a constitution for the disestablished church, and revising its prayer book, took up his energies. As a devout High Church man, he was determined that the prayer book should undergo no radical changes and that the bishops should retain a significant degree of power in the synod, where other parties wanted them to be subordinate to the clergy and to the lay members: after tenacious and tedious struggles over these issues, he was eventually successful in both of his aims, though not without making himself a good many enemies. All were agreed, however, that Trench was a formidable and statesmanlike presence.

Trench's health at that point was declining. In November 1875, while crossing the Irish Sea, he slipped in a gangway on deck and broke both his kneecaps, leaving him pained and disabled for the remainder of his life. And in 1884 he finally gave way to the inevitable, and resigned his position on the grounds of "feebleness of body." It was not to be a long retirement: in March 1886 he died in London, aged seventy-eight, and was buried in Westminster Abbey. On his deathbed he is reported to have said, "I have cared for a good Greek play as much as for most

RICHARD CHENEVIX TRENCH

things, but it does not do to die upon" (Bromley, p. 224).

PHILOLOGICAL WRITINGS

Although they occupied only a relatively small portion of his life, all appearing during the 1850s, Trench's philological writings are felt by many to be his largest legacy. His early passion for "referring, collating, extracting" has been noted, and in his four books of English word lore—*On the Study of Words* (1851), *English Past and Present* (1855), *On Some Deficiencies in Our English Dictionaries* (1857), and *A Select Glossary of English Words Used Formerly in Senses Different from Their Present* (1859)—this passion bears abundant fruit. All four books are replete with rich and well-sifted matter from the complex and contested history of English semantics, and Trench's striking, memorable, and accessible discussions of the history of language communicate the qualities and significances of their chosen examples with persuasive force—even where Trench's interpretations seem deeply entrenched in mid-Victorian conservative religious ideology.

The first and most substantial of Trench's books on language, *On the Study of Words*, was published in 1851, and at the time of his death thirty-five years later the book had never been out of print, passing through nineteen editions in his lifetime. In the decades after his death several revised editions, updated by later scholars, appeared both in Britain and the United States, until in 1927 George Sampson produced an edition (returning to the first, 1851 text) in the J. M. Dent "Everyman" Library, confirming the book's classic status. In these years, Trench became an authority in schools and universities, his books becoming almost synonymous with the study of words. Several sets of study questions on the content of his book were published, for use by students, and the book was widely taught. Writing in 1943, the distinguished English short story writer and critic V. S. Pritchett recalls reading *On the Study of Words* as a schoolboy:

One of my happier memories of English as it is taught at school is of an hour in which the masters woke us all up by drawing on Archbishop Trench's delightful lectures on words and their derivations. To reveal that things, especially familiar things, are not what they seem, is a sure way of getting keen attention. I do not know how original Trench was as a philologist, but he was entranced by the strangeness of words. They were more than a passive and well-thumbed coinage to him.

(Pritchett, p. 252)

Trench, and his visionary sense for the "strangeness of words" and their power, thus became a strong and formative influence on many literary writers. *On the Study of Words* was first presented as a series of lectures for the students of the Diocesan Training School in Winchester, and it comprises a short preface followed by six lectures: "Introductory Lecture," "On the Morality in Words," "On the History in Words," "On the Rise of New Words," "On the Distinction of Words," and "The Schoolmaster's Use of Words." The lectures are animated throughout by their pedagogic purpose and by the belief that words are indeed the "living powers" that Coleridge claimed them to be. Trench wishes to communicate to his hearers and readers the excitement of his own awakening to the vitality of words, which was "like the dropping of scales from his eyes, like the acquiring of another sense, or the introduction into a new world" (p. 2). He takes Ralph Waldo Emerson's insight that "language is fossil poetry" and extends its reach to include also "fossil ethics" and "fossil history" (p. 4), and throughout the book the evocative poetry of his instances is bound fast to his instructive purposes.

Trench's signal contribution to the discourse on language was to place the moral and social history of sense-change at the center of historical semantics. This is starkly clear in the chapter "On the Morality in Words," where Trench judges "man" to be "fallen, and deeply fallen, from the heights of his original creation," and finds the evidence for this fallenness and progressive debasement in language:

Like everything else about him, it bears at once the stamp of his greatness and of his degradation, of his glory and of his shame. What dark and sombre threads he must have woven into the tissue of his life, before we could meet such dark ones running

323

through the tissue of his language! ... It needs no more than to open a dictionary, and to cast our eye thoughtfully down a few columns, and we shall find abundant confirmation of this sadder and sterner estimate of man's moral and spiritual condition. How else shall we explain this long catalogue of words, having all to do with sin or with sorrow, or with both? How came they there? We may be quite sure that they were not invented without being needed, that they have each a correlative in the world of realities. I open the first letter of the alphabet; what means this "Ah," this "Alas," these deep and long-drawn sighs of humanity, which at once we encounter there? And then presently follow words such as these, Affliction, Anguish, Assassin, Atheist, Avarice, and twenty more...

(pp. 26–27)

The 1850s were an exciting and a decisive time for English scholarship on language. It is traditionally held by historians of linguistic thought that England had lagged somewhat behind the Continent, after the decisive turn taken with the discovery and classification of Indo-European at the beginning of the nineteenth century by men such as Friedrich von Schlegel, Rasmus Rask, and Franz Bopp. But by the 1840s the methods of the new philology had been imported and were starting to take hold, and the formation in 1842 of the London Philological Society, the first such body in the world, signaled the energetic ambitions of Victorian philology. It is perhaps fair to say that the major contribution of the English to the discourse on language comes not in any theoretical advancements or even in any very detailed technical contributions to the emerging discipline of linguistics (though it had not yet acquired that name), but instead in the forms of a lexicographical scholarship of unparalleled depth and scale, and of the creation of a popularizing discourse on "the history of the language."

It has been convincingly argued that nationalist ideology is at work here. The discourse of "the history of the language" was created at a time of national crisis, and just as Trench wrote a number of poems in response to the Crimean War of 1853–1856, so we might regard his tributes to the genius of the English language, and the deep sense of a common heritage they foster, as a sort of "war work." Trench was deeply patriotic, and in fact somewhat martial in character, and in his

second book of popular philology, *English Past and Present*, his calls for a patriotic understanding of the binding, unifying force of the English language become explicit: "The love of our native language, what is it in fact, but the love of our native land expressing itself ...?" (pp. 13–14)

It was Trench's third philological work that, although the shortest of the four, had perhaps the most dramatic worldly outcome. In 1857 Trench delivered a historic paper, spread over two nights, to the Philological Society, of which he had recently become a member. "On Some Deficiencies in Our English Dictionaries" was the decisive influence on the formation and execution of what eventually became the *Oxford English Dictionary*, of which Trench may rightly be regarded as the founding father. In 1858 Trench proposed the motion that moved the Philological Society to initiate work on a new dictionary, and in the same year, along with Herbert Coleridge (the grandson of Samuel Taylor Coleridge), whose dictionary work was cut short by his death at age thirty, and Frederick Furnivall, Trench was appointed to the "Unregistered Words Committee" set up to begin and oversee the collection of materials that would go toward the dictionary's compilation.

Trench's vocational commitments in the next years prevented him from taking a full role in the execution of the dictionary, but if it were not for the calls from Westminster and Dublin, it is likely that we would today know Trench, and not the great James A. H. Murray, as the *OED*'s crucial editor. (It is also likely that the dictionary would thus have been completed several decades earlier than it eventually was.) But even if Trench could not carry out the work himself, nonetheless the dictionary was constructed along the lines suggested by his pioneering paper. In *On Some Deficiencies*, he established the principles of inclusiveness and descriptivism that were to be the hallmark of the dictionary, in setting out his "true *idea* of a Dictionary":

A Dictionary ... is an inventory of the language: much more indeed, but this primarily, and with this only at present we will deal. It is no task of the maker of it to select the *good* words of a language. If he fancies that it is so, and begins to pick and choose, to leave this and to take that, he will at once go astray. The business which he has undertaken is to collect and arrange all the words, whether good or bad, whether they do or do not commend themselves to his judgment, which, with certain exceptions hereafter to be specified, those writing in the language have employed. He is an historian of it, not a critic.

(pp. 4–5)

Although Trench did not invent such ideas, which were in some degree derived from Henry George Liddell and Robert Scott's English version of Franz Passow's German-Greek lexicon, and from methodological analogies with the collection of data in natural sciences, nonetheless he stated them most convincingly. The key principles are inclusiveness, which is to say that the lexicographer's only duty is "to make his inventory complete," and descriptivism (rather than prescriptivism), which is to say that the lexicographer must only describe usage as it exists and has been recorded, and must not enter his judgments upon the merits and demerits of that usage. Trench's simultaneous commitment to pure descriptivism in lexicography, and to a strict moralism in his interpretation of historical semantics, has sometimes perplexed or even offended critics of his work. How could the two positions be compatible? But the vision of moral decline and slippage he sees inscribed in language change in no way impairs the accuracy and scruple of Trench's compilation and classification of the evidence from which such moralizing inferences were made. The point of assembling evidence as objectively and carefully as possible was in order to be able to draw the most accurate moral conclusions from it.

Trench's fourth and final philological book, the *Select Glossary of English Words Used Formerly in Senses Different from Their Present* (1859), makes good upon the arguments laid out in *On the Study of Words* and *English Past and Present* by gathering abundant data, arranged alphabetically, to illustrate the vicissitudes and byways of English historical sense-development. It is therefore perhaps less important than its three predecessors, but it nonetheless contains a remarkable collection of materials, arranged and narrated with characteristic partiality, learning, and vigor. This approach is well evident in the

Johnsonian exclamation he comes out with, for instance, in his entry for the word "knave"— "How many serving-lads must have been unfaithful and dishonest before 'knave,' which meant at first no more than a boy, acquired the meaning which it has now!" (pp. 107–108)—or in the cautionary tale of moral descent that Trench finds in the sense-changes undergone by the word "libertine":

A striking evidence of the extreme likelihood that he who has no restraints on his belief will ere long have none upon his life, is given by this word "libertine." Applied at first to certain heretical sects, and intended to mark the licentious *liberty* of their creed, "libertine" soon let go altogether its relation to what a man believed, and acquired the sense which it now has, a "libertine" being one who has released himself from all moral restraints, and especially in his relations with the other sex.

(p. 112)

The *Select Glossary*, in common with all four of Trench's philological works, provided a rich quarry for the lexicographers, with almost all of the many thousands of pieces of quotational evidence that Trench assembles taken straight up into the dictionary as the basis for entries. In addition, Trench's works are often cited themselves: in the first edition, there are more than six hundred quotations from his works.

Trench's theologically inflected moralism toward language change has sometimes been fiercely criticized by historians of linguistics, for it directly contravenes the canon of modern linguistics that insists that the linguist should be an impartial observer and descriptor of his or her field, making no judgments upon value. In a broader sense, the reputation of Trench's philological work has not benefited from the large trend in linguistics since the late nineteenth century, by which the work of those scholars dedicated to scholarship that is lexicological (that is, word-based, rather than, say, grammar-based or phonetic) or diachronic (that is, historical, rather than structural) has been retrospectively sidelined. But in his own time, and for decades thereafter, Trench's books made up part of the reading of all educated readers in Britain, and they represent a substantial contribution to mid-Victorian intellectual life. Through the *Oxford*

English Dictionary, moreover, his philological work extends its influence over all speakers and writers of English down to the present day.

POETRY

When Trench's collected *Poems* was issued in 1885, its two volumes were divided thematically, in typical nineteenth-century fashion. This followed the pattern established by his *Poems: Collected and Arranged Anew*, published in 1865. The large number of lyrics and sonnets he composed, and the somewhat smaller number of narrative poems, were arranged in roughly chronological groupings, with separate sections for "Poems from Eastern Sources," "Elegiac Poems," and "Poems Written During the Russian War 1854, 1855." Although Trench can fairly be described as only an "occasional" poet after around 1850, nonetheless his output was steady and cumulatively large, and, as those groupings suggest, he was adept in a number of modes.

Trench's poetry has not fared well in the century-plus since his death. A survey of major anthologies illustrates his neglect: although he was anthologized in Palgrave's *Golden Treasury* in the late nineteenth-century, and although his work was known to the small educated readership of his day, his name is now almost entirely absent even from the largest historical collections of Victorian poetry. His poetry is unread and unremembered, and at this late stage a revival of interest seems unlikely for several reasons. Trench's short lyrics and sonnets, although skillfully made, are formally conventional and often resemble no more than a stage-paste of the bourgeois religious and social pieties of the age. His narrative poems ply a now deeply unfashionable mode of orientalizing, late-Romantic genre painting, as in "The Death of Justin Martyr" or "The Steadfast Prince." His sense for the natural language of the English landscape and his elegiac melancholy have none of the innovative force of his model for the former, William Wordsworth, or his contemporary in the latter, Tennyson.

And yet immersion in Trench's poetry speaks vividly to a sense of the reality of the nineteenth century. It has been said that all art bears the imprint of its historical period, and the greatest art is that which is most deeply marked; if this is so, the *un*timelessness of Trench's period-piece work is part of his distinction. An untitled lyric of some force and memorability, from the "Elegiac Poems," will bear this out:

> O life, O death, O world, O time,
> O grave, where all things flow,
> 'Tis yours to make our lot sublime
> With your great weight of woe.
>
> Though sharpest anguish hearts may wring,
> Though bosoms torn may be,
> Yet suffering is a holy thing;
> Without it what were we?

(Poems, vol. 2, p. 240)

Here we find the preponderance and ponderousness of Victorian melancholy well caught by Trench's too-heavy stresses. The repeated exclamation "O" weighs down the first line into a leaden succession of what could almost be eight stressed syllables in a row, and just when we think the completed line-unit has released us from its chains, we get another "O," for good measure, followed in short order by "flow" and "woe." Altogether, the first stanza's phonetic pattern reduces to a continuous moaning of innumerable Os, sounding like someone groaning with grief, head in hands, and looking like a row of puncture marks, or nails driven in to the pained flesh of the page (O, O, O, O). And yet from here, the poem's ambition is to persuade that "our lot" is still somehow "sublime," not only with this woe but, more than that, because of this woe. The second stanza effects the leap to this piece of wisdom through bare syntactical assertion: "Yet suffering is a holy thing," we are told. The mystery of God's inscrutable mercy is left in place by the irrefutability of that claim. The argument here is content-free—deliberately so, for Trench had no wish to rationalize the experience of faith, and to ask for the proof of the proposition would be beside the point. Suffering simply "is" a holy thing, and the surface of the poem is torn and punctured (holey) by its own emphatic and excessive language; and somehow the Christian experience has to be concluded into a "whole," the mental strain of which is carried by the appalling, and yet on some level brilliant, plunge into banality in Trench's final line.

Trench's contemporaries admired his work. In 1836 Trench reported that "Wordsworth's principal praises of it were that it was very thoughtful and (which he prizes highly) the language was choice and pure," and in 1839 he had the privilege of a meeting with the master: "I met him at breakfast this morning ... walked a little about town with Wordsworth, and he talked over with much kindness my two books of verse" (Bromley, p. 73). If this sounds like the self-serving account of the young tyro overly keen to hear a positive response from his hero, we find a less biased account in the positive review of Trench's first book, *The Story of Justin Martyr*, published in the *Athenaeum*, which praises the poems for "the purity of the thoughts they contain and the selectness of the language in which these are clothed," and goes on to say that "in all of them we find true feeling and grace of expression ... and a charity and gentleness of spirit" (Bromley, p. 60).

Such qualities are strongly evident in one of Trench's best-known poems, "A Walk in a Churchyard," a work very much in the manner of Wordsworth's contributions to the *Lyrical Ballads*, and particularly reminiscent of "We Are Seven." The poem begins with a simple and homely location shot:

We walked within the Churchyard bounds,
My little boy and I–
He laughing, running happy rounds,
I pacing mournfully.

"Nay, child! it is not well," I said,
"Among the graves to shout,
To laugh and play among the dead,
And make this noisy rout."

(*Poems*, vol. 1, p. 21)

But the speaker of the poem soon realizes his unwiseness, in checking the child's exuberance out of mere solemnity. Nature was performing no respectful mourning rituals in the graveyard, but instead shone the "same azure vault of love" upon that patch as upon everywhere. So why should the boy mourn? After nine stanzas of deliberation

on this theme, the poem arrives at this conclusion:

Oh no, the glory earth puts on,
The child's unchecked delight,
Both witness to a triumph won—
(If we but read aright,)

A triumph won o'er sin and death,
From these the Saviour saves;
And, like a happy infant, Faith
Can play among the graves.

(pp. 23–24)

Such are the strengths of Trench's best poems. But he had his own reservations about his work. In a footnote to his first book, with a classic case of the young poet's simultaneous embarrassment and self-advertisement, he described the poems as "the expression of states of mind in which I would not now ask others to sympathize, and from which I am thankful myself to have been delivered" (Bromley, p. 60). When his second book, *Sabbation, Honor Neale, and Other Poems* came out in 1838, he admitted, "I am not sanguine about it making its way" (p. 70). And this worry was rather confirmed by the response of his friends. As his friend from Trinity days, J. W. Blakesley, said, "We all think that the clergyman has swallowed up the poet" (p. 70), and Trench broadly conceded the point, admitting the minor ambitions of the work:

Alas! it is not my own choice that makes me rather hop upon the nearest twig than take a flight to the high mountain, but a consciousness of the weakness of my wings ... What can I do but be thankful that I can carve a cherry-stone (which is the image I would rather use than yours of cutting a gem) so as to please a few friends? ... One thing however I will promise, that I will not allow the subjective, the moods of the mind, so serious a preponderance over that which is daily rising more in value in my mind, the objective in poetry.

(pp. 70–71)

Trench's friend W. B. Donne had a different objection, on the grounds of Trench's subject matter, which he raised upon publication of Trench's next two volumes, *Genoveva* and *Poems from Eastern Sources* (both 1842):

I am rather dismayed at the title, "principally from Eastern sources." I am in dread of parables, allegories, apothegms in verse, instead of broad pencillings of nature, and narrative. Trench keeps bad company. I do not mean that he drinks and drives coaches. But instead of reading Sophocles and Dante he fills his brain with quaint poets and mystics, and is more anxious to impress a moral than to create and stamp beautiful images. This which is very creditable to him as a Divine is the wrong course for a poet.

(pp. 79–80)

There is no doubt some justice in this criticism too. But it would be wrong to dismiss Trench's longer narrative poems and his reworkings of allegories drawn from exotic sources, for viewed in their clearest light, they richly combine the responsibilities of the churchman and the instincts of the poet.

This part of Trench's poetic output is equally bedded in Anglican theology. Trench's longer poems have overarching ecclesiastical themes, and strong doses of religious instruction, affirming again and again the faith found through suffering and the inevitability of pain in human life. In Trench's first book, the title poem, "The Story of St. Justin Martyr" (1835), unfolding in rhymed couplets, pictures the saint retreating from life in a "miserable mood" into solitude and deep reflection. This reflection turns toward Justin's thwarted ambitions: when young, he desired to "repel the heavy weight, / The load that crushed unto the ground / The servile multitude around" and to live a life without sin, pure in the eyes of God (*Poems*, vol. 1, p. 2). But he has failed: his "feeble flight" has fallen into "baffled purpose, wasted years, / My sin, my misery" (p. 4). He confesses his sins to the ruined city he contemplates, before an elderly man appears besides him and offers wisdom to assuage his despair. Justin's fault, the old man offers, was his ambition: "a purpose and a loftier aim / Than the blind lives of men may claim" (p. 7). Trench's voice comes through the comfort offered by this mysterious man as he affirms the inevitability of pain, suffering, and sin in human life. It is the "richer soil" of the eternal life in God's kingdom that is the object of human life, its redemption and purpose. In this lesson the image of the ruined city is no longer a prompt to nihilism, but

an assurance that though we are born into sin, human life is eternally couched in the rivers of God's "influences"—Trench the word collector here playing with the multiple senses of "influence" as the starlight pouring from the heavens, the flowing of one river into another, and the moral guidance of the scriptures, which guides our actions. God's influence passes over our cracked mortal vessels, like the sun rising over the ruined city, in the climactic image of the poem:

A rich dissolving splendour poured
Through rent and fissure, and restored
The fall'n, the falling, and decayed,
Filling the rifts which time had made,
Till the rent masses seemed to meet,
The pillar stand upon its feet,
And tower and cornice, roof and stair
Hung self-upheld in the magic air.

(pp. 10–11)

Trench's next major long poem, "Honor Neale" (1838), extends this moral enquiry. It relates the tragic, but redemptive tale of the Irish girl Honor Neale through the reports of friends who had met her mother, and through the words of the mother herself. Trench sketches her descent into illness with careful simplicity. Honor shows a deep reverence of the "pure doctrine and lore of Christ," but "slow to learn" (*Poems*, vol. 1, p. 155), she is withdrawn from her school in order to participate actively in the rural life of her family, laboring earnestly but with difficulty in the fields. As the burdens of her new life weigh on her, Honor becomes ill, suffering too much to leave the house. Through this suffering, she is spiritually elevated:

But if through gracious teaching from on high,
And through that lengthened discipline of pain,
In Spirit she grew fitter for her change,
In body she grew weaker day by day.

(pp. 156–157)

Her suffering continues; and in inverse proportion she is brought closer to God and the scripture she struggled with at school. Before her death, she requests the counsel of a priest. In the exchange with the priest, Trench emphasizes

Honor's innocent conscientiousness: she asks forgiveness for leaving an orphan girl whom she labored with "out alone in all the cold" while she warmed herself inside (p. 161). The priest is surprised and gratified by the weight with which this "little sin" has burdened the young girl, remarking that he wished to have left life with Honor's innocence. She dies soon after; her mother absorbs the burden of suffering, but learning from Honor's example, she is able to express gratitude to the God who "called her out of this poor sinful world, / And took her to Himself" (p. 163).

The argument of "Honor Neale" addresses the problem of suffering, which is shown to have its virtues in heightening spirituality and in bringing the sufferer closer to God. A similar theme is found in the more complex "Genoveva" (1842), loosely sharing the same plot as Robert Schuman's later opera of the same name. "Genoveva" unfolds (again in rhyming couplets) the story of the eponymous wife of Count Sigfried, who is called away to join Charles Martel's crusade against the Saracen invasion of Europe. Left alone, Genoveva is betrayed into a false adultery by one whose advances she thrice spurns. Fearing death, she flees to the forest—wherein, with her infant, she comes to terms with her suffering through a series of visions. Dante (for whom Trench later proclaimed his strong admiration in "The History of the English Sonnet"), lurks large behind the image of the forest as a place of religious turmoil. It is in this place of suffering, where seems "Dark the earth, forlorn of love, / But, oh! Darker heaven above" (*Poems*, vol. 1, p. 240), that the virtue of suffering asserts itself. An angel presents her with the cross, the "choicest blessing, costliest boon" (p. 245), a symbol of the gift of suffering. It is an "angelic comforter": the reminder that suffering is a gift God "keepeth for his friends" (pp. 245–246). It comes alive and speaks, assuring her that to "Look on Me / and looking, so / Learn to bear thy present ill" (p. 247). As Genoveva is able to affirm her faith through bearing of her suffering, Count Sigfried returns, and the two are united as she approaches his hunting party, looking for sport in the forest. They both return together to

Sigfried's kingdom. But with her spirit refined by the ascetic exile in the woods, Genoveva no longer holds any interest in the pageantry and show of ceremony, nor earthbound life:

> She doth meekly undertake
> All life's tasks for his dear sake;
> Yet evermore she did seem
> Like one moving in a dream.
>
> (p. 257)

She passes from the world in Trench's poem like water disappearing into steam. Count Sigfried learns her indifference to "his old ancestral towers / His twice desolated bowers." He erects "in the deep recess / Of a pathless wilderness" a church and altar to Genoveva, and mirrors the example of her life. Trench has him satisfy his thirst from the same water she drank in her exile, and there in God he "finds perfect peace" (pp. 261–262).

LITERARY-CRITICAL WRITINGS

Trench's literary-critical contributions, though a minor part of his output, often swam against the contemporary current. In the anthology of poetry he edited in 1868, *A Household Book of English Poetry*, Trench confesses an initial fear that the best poetry of the nation had already been brought together in Palgrave's *Golden Treasury*—a volume that "so occupied the ground that there was no place for one who should come after" (p. v). But Trench is discontented with the current state of anthologies, which, he argues, have by and large "failed to leave the impression of being the result of investigation … into the treasures of our English poetry" (p. vi); and this process of investigation is a defining feature here. Explanatory notes that explore the critical context and elucidate some of the allusions within the collected poems are attached to the end of the volume, in part as evidence of Trench's own research and investigation. These glosses are also informed by a consideration for general readers, who "capable of an intelligent interest … have yet had neither time nor opportunity for special studies of their own in it" and who "rely … on the hand-leading of others" (p. xi). But even the studied reader of poetry will find these notes valuable, not least for the intentionally wide and eclectic range of texts brought together. The *Household Book*, as Trench tentatively argues, "lays claim to a certain originality" (p. vii) in its gathering of poems that have fallen out of critical favor, poems "which deserve much better than that complete oblivion into which they had fallen" (p. viii), and the willing reader will find rich pickings there.

Recovering and reassessing forgotten or devalued poetry is a frequent theme in Trench's critical work. It animated his critical and translation work on Calderón, which culminated in the 1880 second edition of Trench's study of the dramatist, published as *An Essay on the Life and Genius of Calderón*; and in the earlier *Sacred Latin Poetry, Chiefly Lyrical* (1849), it animated his gathering-together of poems of the early church, which had undeservedly, he argues, been given "hard measure" (p. 49). Trench admires this poetry for aesthetic and historical reasons. In the preface, he writes that "we are untrue to our position as a church, that is, as an historical body" (p. vii); and this volume beds the poetry it presents in the development of Latin poetry as an organ of the church and the divine Word. Trench highlights two distinct but equally important developments that led to the birth of this poetry: the "disintegration of the old prosodical system of Latin verse, under gradual substitution of accent for quantity" (p. 2) and the implementation of rhyme as a means of producing melody. These developments are part historical, part spiritual. Spiritually, antiquated metrical patterns, Trench argues, were not suited for the exultation that the Gospels had inspired. He likens the Latin language and its metrical binds to a garment that wrapped too tightly around a body. The new religious spirit demanded a more flexible language, one that would allow thought and feeling to be expressed in the form of its own necessity, by its own demands, and not forms pressed onto it from outside. Trench is careful, however, to root this into a historical context. The old system of quantity had "involuntary associations" with "heathen worship" (pp. 13–15); the introduction

of liturgical singing with its accentual melodies, Trench asserts, was a move to cleanse the church and its worship of these connotations. The greater use of rhyme—an accompanying feature to the accentual quality of Latin poetry—shared similar intertwined spiritual and historical well-springs. For Trench, rhyme became popular because of its "universality" (p. 41). It did not invoke barbarism, nor the "over-refined ingenuity of a late and artificial [age]" (p. 41). But it appealed to a man's "craving after and deep delight in, the rhythmic and periodic" (p. 43) by communicating the sense of order and purpose that was to be found in the Gospels, in the idea of the Divine itself. Trench ingeniously supports the "elevating and solemnizing power" of rhyme with evidence from "language ... the most unconscious witness, set its seal, having in the Latin but one and the same word, for the solemn and the recurring" (p. 44). So Latin poetry was born: the stuffiness of prosody giving way to a rapturous freedom of necessity, where sense and sound were brought together; and rhyme giving way to a law of comfort and order, in which "to move according to law is felt to be the freest move of all" (p. 44).

Sacred Latin Poetry concludes with an evocative appeal to recover "much which appears trite" but which "was yet very far from being so at its first utterance" (p. 49). Trench extends his critical program of championing poetry that has fallen out of favor in the essay "The History of The English Sonnet," collected as the foreword to Trench's 1884 edition of the sonnets of Wordsworth, his first poetic master. The sonnet, Trench notes, is unpopular with the reader but is a favorite form for the poet. He argues that this division in taste is a result of the strict rules of sonnet composition, which force a poet to refine his sentiment and polish his thought: the sonnet leaves "loose nebulous vapour ... compressed and rounded into a star" (p. 5). The rest of the lecture plays out as an at times playful, but always loving, tour through these stars. In the "rapid progress through that province of Poet's land" (p. 17), Trench isolates some of the key figures and moments in the development of the form. Henry Howard, Earl of Surrey, is credited for bringing the sonnet from Italian shores to English land.

Once there, the sonnet was cradled in its development by Sir Philip Sidney, whose forms were left "wanting in that foundation of moral dignity," and by Edmund Spenser, whose work with the sonnet "was a little tedious" (p. 7). Trench then arrives at Shakespeare, and in deep admiration he declines to pursue the "mystery" at the heart of his sonnets, being "so heavily laden with meaning, so double-shotted" (pp. 8–9). Trench celebrates the aesthetic and, perhaps surprisingly, the moral triumph of Shakespeare's sonnets. Citing sonnet 129 ("Poor soul! The centre of my sinful earth"), Trench asserts that there are few sermons where can be learned "lessons so solemn and so profound" (p. 10).

After Shakespeare, John Donne is admired for his Christianity and John Milton for his "austere grandeur" (p. 15). With the death of the latter, the first age of the sonnet closes, before Wordsworth begins the second age: a "central figure" who "turned the Sonnet to a new use" (p. 23) by creating poems of successive sonnets, breaking with the tradition of the sonnet as an isolated form. Admiring nods are then given to John Keats and his "grandly recorded" poem "On First Looking into Chapman's Homer"; and Coleridge is passed over in favor of his son, Hartley, whose sonnets spoke a "sad self-reproach for a wasted life which haunted him" (p. 27). But the most significant figures in the sonnet's history are assessed to be Shakespeare, Wordsworth, and Milton. It is of these men primarily that Trench speaks when he concludes that the sonnet, as a vehicle for the "loftiest, purest, tenderest, best" thoughts, is one of English poetry's "richest inheritances" (p. 31).

RELIGIOUS WRITINGS

Trench carried the rigor of his philological work into his dense and learned theological writings. His first book-length theological work, *Notes on the Parables of Our Lord* (1841), surveys the parable stories of the Gospels while keeping an analytical eye trained on the trends of secondary interpretation. It is largely a synthesis and representation of previous, in particular patristic, scholarship: "I have been astonished to find how seldom an original and independent collection of materials has been made by commentators," Trench wrote in a letter at the time (Bromley, p. 66). The opening sections of the *Notes* give a close dissection of the importance of the "parabolical element" (p. 27) in Christ's teaching and the varieties of ways in which this element is misconstrued, dampened, and misread. For Trench, the parable is the superlative form of teaching. It rises above the myth, allegory, fable, or proverb through its power not only to illustrate, but to provide "in some sort proof," and to reach into the "harmony unconsciously felt by all men" (pp. 18–19).

Language is the grounds on which to explain the parables. Trench admonishes the mystic tradition, which has attempted to escape language through imageless meditation and to gain divine knowledge *via negativa*, or through negation. There is a "power and mystery, of the truth and falsehood of words" that exercises itself through parables (p. 26). It would be reckless, Trench advises, to treat the word as a shell and discard it once we have found the kernel of divine truth hidden there. The human word and divine meaning are like the body and soul: "the outer covering is not to fall off and perish, but to become glorified, being taken up by, and made translucent with, the spirit that is within" (p. 27). The parable, then, is useful in its harmony of form and content. The unity of the divine meaning in human language, Trench contends, is the achievement of parable. Christ knew this to be true: "to create a powerful impression, language must be recalled, minted and issued anew," and Christ "gave no doctrine in an abstract form, no skeletons of truth, but all clothed, as it were, with flesh and blood" (p. 27).

So the Gospels give us the flesh and blood of Christ's parabolic teaching. But how are we to make these bodies breathe? Parables are outwardly fair in form, but even fairer within—and interpreting them faithfully is a matter of discipline and delicacy for Trench. He rhetorically poses the question, "How much of them is significant?" (p. 32), before surveying two contrasting methodologies. The approach of "modern times" is sketched, in which the narrative detail of the parable is treated as perfunctory, and is to be discarded once the teaching is discovered (p. 32). Trench is obviously contemptuous of this fast-and-loose approach to detail, but he is sensitive also to the dangers of picking a parable apart too closely: interpretation that fails to remember that a knife is "not all edge, nor a harp all strings" (p. 34) has the potential to be nothing more than an exercise in ingenuity, where any and every sort of meaning may be furnished forth by incidental, misconstrued detail.

Trench then commits himself to a path between these two extremes: rigorous, but delicate with the narrative furnishings of the moral teaching; not cavalier with the stories themselves, but also not needlessly pedantic and stretching. A combination of Augustinian discipline and devotional care, Trench believes, will lead to the true interpretation that is "not always easy to be discovered, yet being discovered, easy" (p. 39). His treatment of the well known Samaritan parable (Luke 10:30–37) reflects this balance. It moves between a close reading of the minutiae and the larger religious significance of the lesson of charity and love. Finding the metaphoric key that easily opens the lock, Trench explores the significance of the opening of the parable: "A certain man went down from Jerusalem to Jericho." Careful not to disregard the physicality of going down and up from the two cities, he notes the respective lays of Jerusalem and Jericho as well as the common parlance of coming up and going down (p. 253). The typical Trenchian move here, however, repeated in his treatment of other parables, is the gentle extrapolation from detail into a wider spiritual picture. Only where it is "absolutely needful" (p. 260) does Trench probe. He weaves the idea of going down from Jerusalem to the "profane city" with the going down of the Fall: the traveler is "personified human Nature, or Adam" who is left "grievously wounded, left full of wounds ... every sin a gash from which the life-blood of his soul is copiously flowing" (pp. 258-9). Through equating the traveler's going down with man's descent into sin, through this close examination of detail, Trench is able to reach "the deeper interpretation ... reserved for the future edification of the Church" (p. 258): that below the lessons of love and charity, the Samaritan parable teaches us that Christ, our Samaritan, activates through love our faith in him.

Another inroad into faith and the teachings of Christ is examined by Trench in *Notes on the Miracles of Our Lord* (1846). These *Notes* are more combative than the work on parable. As well as creating a survey of critical argument surrounding the significance of miracles, Trench is writing against the increasing popularity of "utterly maimed and imperfect" "Evidences Of Christianity" (p. 33)—circulated pamphlets placing what Trench perceived as too strong a focus on miracles, at the expense of doctrine. Through careful argumentation, Trench moves to restore Christian doctrine to its place of priority in the consideration of miracles. In order to do this, he first offers some remarks on the definition of the miraculous. He is not trusting of the "most shallow and fallacious" assertion that all of nature is miraculous (p. 16). Wonderful though nature is, perceiving it as a miracle relies on the basis of a "dead mechanical view of the universe": The clock-maker makes his clock and leaves it; the ship-builder builds and launches his ship and others navigate it; but the world is no curious piece of mechanism which the Maker makes and then dismisses from his hands, only from time to time reviewing and repairing it (p. 17).

In fact, asserts Trench, nature hides God: we find nature everywhere—and so commonplace is its "voice" that we might forget the God behind and above it. Through the miraculous, Trench maintains, God introduces the particular into nature—God reminds us that he is there. Having defined the miraculous in this way, Trench goes on to consider it as an "ethical act" (p. 32). Ethical is used here insofar as a miracle "must witness" to doctrine (p. 33). Doctrine is its test; Trench is disparaging of the use of miracles to test the authenticity of doctrine. This has no theological validity, he argues, while considering the negative psychology of a deep reverence for miracles, rhetorically asking "that if men are taught that they should believe in Christ upon no other grounds than because he attested his claims by the works of wonder ... how shall they consistently refuse belief to any other, who shall come attesting his claims by the same?" (p. 33). If too strong an emphasis is placed on miracles, Trench contends, the Christian faithful will be lost to any religion that can claim miracles in its favor.

This is not to say that miracles are not important, says Trench. He defends the miracle from what he believes are its foremost detractors: the Jewish; the "heathen" in Celsus, Hierocles, and Porphyry; the pantheistic in Baruch Spinoza; the skeptical in John Locke and David Hume; the argument from relativity in Friedrich Schleiermacher; the argument from rationalism in Heinrich Paulus; and the historico-critical attacks from Thomas Woolston and David Strauss. Trench had made a detailed study of Strauss's controversial *Life of Jesus* (1835–1836), in order the better to combat the new continental exegesis, and had earlier come to this conclusion in a letter to John Sterling:

> The idea and aim of the book is not, I think, in the main to overthrow Christianity, though could he make out his points it would be equivalent to an overthrow, but to turn it from a historical religion in which the facts are and contain the doctrine into a philosophy, which shall be equally valuable whether the facts in which it has hitherto been implicitly involved but which now he asserts cannot stand the test of close examination, be true or not.
>
> (Bromley, pp. 65–66)

In his *Notes on the Miracles*, Trench finds in all rationalizing attacks on the miraculous aspects of Christianity a consistent envying of the man who has had his faith in doctrine bolstered by the miraculous. From this platform, he moves to prove the "mutual interdependence" of "the miracles proving the doctrines and the doctrines approving the miracles" (p. 81). Trench's focus is telling in the way he unpacks the miracle of two blind men given sight by Jesus. He highlights the importance of the fact that these two blind men were "earnest"; Jesus walked from them, Trench argues, to test the authenticity of their faith (p. 161). Once that authenticity is proved, Jesus performs the miracle healing. Jesus' words on healing the men—"According to your faith be it unto you"—are then explored by Trench as indicative of the mutual relationship between miracles and doctrine: "faith, which itself is nothing, is yet the organ of receiving everything" (p. 161). Faith in doctrine as the test of miracles, and not in miracles as the test of doctrine, is the key idea behind the exegesis of this miraculous healing. This is captured in Trench's final image of doctrine as "the bucket let down into the fountain of God's grace without which the man could not draw up out of that fountain; the purse, which though itself of the coarsest material, does yet enrich its owner by that which it contains" (p. 161)—an image that also illustrates the combination of poetic vision and deep faith running through all of Trench's writings.

Selected Bibliography

WORKS OF RICHARD CHENEVIX TRENCH

PHILOLOGICAL WRITINGS

On the Study of Words: Five Lectures Addressed to the Pupils at the Diocesan Training School, Winchester. London: John W. Parker, 1851.

English: Past and Present: Five Lectures. London: John W. Parker, 1855.

On Some Deficiencies in Our English Dictionaries. London: John W. Parker, 1857; 2nd ed. 1860.

A Select Glossary of English Words Used Formerly in Senses Different from their Present. London: John W. Parker, 1859.

POETRY

The Story of Justin Martyr, and Other Poems. London: Edward Moxon, 1835.

Sabbation, Honor Neale, and Other Poems. London: Edward Moxon, 1838.

Genoveva: A Poem. London: Edward Moxon, 1842.

Poems from Eastern Sources: The Steadfast Prince, and Other Poems. London: Edward Moxon, 1842.

Elegiac Poems. London: Edward Moxon, 1843.

Poems from Eastern Sources: Genoveva, and Other Poems. London: John W. Parker, 1851.

Alma, and Other Poems. London: John W. Parker, 1855.

Poems: Collected and Arranged Anew. London: Macmillan, 1865.

Poems. 2 vols. London: Macmillan, 1885.

Literary-Critical Writings

Sacred Poems for Mourners. (As editor.) London: Rivington, 1846.

Sacred Latin Poetry, Chiefly Lyrical. (As editor.) London: John W. Parker, 1849.

Life's a Dream: The Great Theatre of the World: From the Spanish of Calderón: With an Essay on His Life and Genius. London: John W. Parker, 1856. Rev. ed. *An Essay on the Life and Genius of Calderón: With Translations from His "Life's a Dream" and "Great Theatre of the World."* London: Macmillan, 1880.

A Household Book of English Poetry. (As editor.) London: Macmillan, 1868.

Plutarch: His Life, His Lives, and His Morals: Four Lectures. London: Macmillan, 1873.

"The History of the English Sonnet." In *The Sonnets of William Wordsworth Collected in One Volume.* Edited by Richard Chenevix Trench. London: Suttaby, 1884.

Religious Writings

Notes on the Parables of Our Lord. London: John W. Parker, 1841.

Exposition of the Sermon on the Mount: Drawn from the Writings of St. Augustine, with Observations and an Introductory Essay on His Merits as an Interpreter of Scripture. London: John W. Parker, 1844. Expanded and rev. ed. *St. Augustine as an Interpreter of Holy Scripture.* London: John W. Parker, 1851.

Notes on the Miracles of Our Lord. London: John W. Parker, 1846.

The Star of the Wise Men: Being a Commentary on the Second Chapter of St. Matthew. London: John W. Parker, 1850.

On the Lessons in Proverbs: Being the Substance of Lectures Delivered to Young Men's Societies at Portsmouth and Elsewhere. London: John W. Parker, 1853.

Synonyms of the New Testament: Being the Substance of Lectures to the Students of King's College, London. London: Macmillan, 1854.

Studies in the Gospels. London: Macmillan, 1867.

Lectures on Medieval Church History: Being the Substance of Lectures Delivered at Queen's College, London. London: Macmillan, 1877.

Brief Thoughts and Meditations on Some Passages in Holy Scripture. London, 1884.

Sermons New and Old. London: Macmillan, 1886.

Papers

Trench's letters and papers are widely dispersed between several archive sources, principally Hampshire Record Office, Winchester; Lambeth Palace Library; National Library of Ireland; Queen's College, London; British Library; Bodleian Library, Oxford; National Register of Archives; and Trinity College, Cambridge.

CRITICAL AND BIOGRAPHICAL STUDIES

Aarsleff, Hans. *The Study of Language in England, 1789–1860.* 1967. 2nd ed. London: Athlone Press, 1983. (Includes discussion of Trench as a philologist.)

Aarsleff, Hans, and Robert W. Burchfield. *The Oxford English Dictionary and the State of the Language.* Washington, D.C.: Library of Congress, 1988. (Includes discussion of Trench as a philologist.)

Bayne, Ronald. "Trench, Richard Chenevix (1807–1886)." *Dictionary of National Biography: From the Earliest Times to 1900.* Edited by Leslie Stephen and Sidney Lee. Vol. 19. London: Smith, Elder, 1909.

Bromley, John. *The Man of Ten Talents: A Portrait of Richard Chenevix Trench, 1807–86, Philologist, Poet, Theologian, Archbishop.* London: Society for Promoting Christian Knowledge, 1959.

Cooke-Trench, T. R. F. *A Memoir of the Trench Family.* London: Privately printed, 1897.

Crowley, Tony. *The Politics of Discourse: The Standard Language Question in British Cultural Debate.* London: Macmillan, 1989. New ed. *Standard English and the Politics of Language.* Basingstoke, U.K.: Palgrave Macmillan, 2003. (See chapter 2, "Archbishop Trench's Theory of Language: The Tractatus Theologico-Politicus.")

Harris, Roy. "Introduction." In *On the Study of Words.* By Richard Chenevix Trench. London Routledge/Thoemmes Press, 1994. (Part of the series *British Linguistics in the Nineteenth Century.*)

Milne, Kenneth. "Trench, Richard Chenevix (1807–1886)." *Oxford Dictionary of National Biography.* Edited by H. C. G. Matthew and Brian Harrison. Oxford: Oxford University Press, 2004.

Pritchett, V. S. "Books in General: *On the Study of Words* by Richard Chenevix Trench." *New Statesman and Nation*, October 16, 1943, p. 252.

Silvester, James. *Archbishop Trench, Poet and Divine: A Sketch of His Life and Character.* London: Society for Promoting Christian Knowledge, 1891.

Tennyson, Hallam. *Alfred, Lord Tennyson: A Memoir.* 2 vols. London: Macmillan, 1897.

Trench, Maria, ed. *Richard Chenevix Trench: Letters and Memorials.* 2 vols. London: Kegan, Trench, 1888.

Trench, Melesina. *The Remains of the Late Mrs. Richard Trench: Being Selections from Her Journals, Letters, and Other Papers.* Edited by Richard Chenevix Trench. London: Parker, Son, and Bourne, 1862.

CUMULATIVE INDEX

All references include volume numbers in boldface roman numerals followed by page numbers within that volume. Subjects of articles are indicated by boldface type.

E.

"F.

"Homage to the British Museum" (Empson), **Supp. II:** 182
"Homage to William Cowper" (Davie), **Supp. VI:** 106
"Homages" (Hart), **Supp. XI:** 123
Homans, Margaret, **Retro. Supp. I:** 189
"Home" (Beer), **Supp. XIV:** 4
"Home" (Burnside), **Supp. XIII:** 14–15
"Home" (Carson), **Supp. XIII:** 66
"Home" (Ewart), **Supp. VII:** 37
"Home" (Fallon), **Supp. XII:** 106
Home (Storey), **Supp. I:** 408, 413, 417
"Home Again" (Montague), **Supp. XV:** 214
Home and Beauty (Maugham), **VI:** 368–369
Home and Dry (Fuller), **Supp. VII:** 70, 81
"Home at Grasmere" (Wordsworth), **IV:** 3, 23–24
Home Chat (Coward), **Supp. II:** 146
"Home Conveyancing Kit, The" (Wallace–Crabbe), **VIII:** 320
"Home for a couple of days" (Kelman), **Supp. V:** 250
"Home for the Highland Cattle, A" (Lessing), **Supp. I:** 241–242
"Home from Home" (Delanty), **Supp. XIV:** 65, 67
Home Front (Bishton and Reardon), **Supp. IV:** 445
Home Letters (Disraeli) **IV:** 296, 308
Home Letters of T. E. Lawrence and His Brothers, The (Lawrence), **Supp. II:** 286
"Home Maintenance" (Robertson), **Supp. XIX:** 268
"Home Thoughts from Abroad" (Browning), **IV:** 356
"Home Thoughts Abroad" (Newman), **Supp. VII:** 293
Home Truths (Maitland), **Supp. XI:** 163, 170–172, 175
"Home [2]" (Thomas), **Supp. III:** 405
"Home [3]" (Thomas), **Supp. III:** 404
Home University Library, **VI:** 337, 391
Homebush Boy (Keneally), **Supp. IV:** 344, 347
Homecoming, The (Pinter), **Supp. I:** 375, 380, 381; **Retro. Supp. I:** 225–226
Homecoming: Essays on African and Caribbean Literature, Culture, and Politics (Ngũgĩ), **VIII:** 214, 224
Homecomings (Snow), **VII:** xxi, 324, 329, 335
"Homemade" (McEwan), **Supp. IV:** 389, 391, 395
"Homemaking" (Kincaid), **Supp. VII:** 229
Homer, **I:** 236; **II:** 304, 347; **III:** 217, 220; **IV:** 204, 215
Homeric Hymns (tr. Chapman), **I:** 236
"Homesick in Old Age" (Kinsella), **Supp. V:** 263
"Homesick Paterson, Live at the Blue Bannock, Thurso" (Paterson), **Supp. XVII:** 216
"Home–Thoughts, from Abroad" (Browning), **Retro. Supp. III:** 17

"Homeward Prospect, The" (Day Lewis), **Supp. III:** 129
Homeward: Songs by the Way (Russell), **VIII:** 280, 282
Homiletic Fragment I, **Retro. Supp. II:** 301–302
"Homilies from Hospital" (Lochhead), **Supp. XVII:** 143
"Homogenic Attachment, The" (Carpenter), **Supp. XIII:** 43
"Homogenic Love: And Its Place in a Free Society" (Carpenter), **Supp. XIII:** 41, 42–43
Hone, Joseph, **VI:** 88
Hone, William, **IV:** 255
"Honor Neale" (Trench), **Supp. XIX:** 328–329
Honest Man's Fortune, The (Field, Fletcher, Massinger), **II:** 66
Honest Whore, The (Dekker and Middleton), **II:** 3, 21, 89
Honey for the Bears (Burgess), **Supp. I:** 191
"Honey from Palaiochora" (Constantine), **Supp. XV:** 78
Honeybuzzard (Carter), *see Shadow Dance*
Honeycomb (Richardson), **Supp. XIII:** 182, 183, 189
Honeymoon Voyage, The (Thomas), **Supp. IV:** 490
"Honeymooneers, The" (Sampson), **Supp. XVIII:** 299–300
Hong Kong House, A: Poems 1951–1961 (Blunden), **Supp. XI:** 34, 38
"Hong Kong Story" (Nye), **Supp. X:** 201–202
"Honora, an Elegy" (Seward), **Supp. XVII:** 230
Honorary Consul, The (Greene), **Supp. I:** 7, 10, 13, 16; **Retro. Supp. II:** 164–165
Honour of the Garter, The (Peele), **I:** 205
Honour Triumphant; or, The Peeres Challenge (Ford), **II:** 88, 100
Honourable Deceivers, The; or, All Right at the Last (Trotter), **Supp. XVI:** 287
"Honourable Estate, An" (Gunesekera), **Supp. X:** 86
Honourable Estate: A Novel of Transition (Brittain), **Supp. X:** 41–43, 46–47
"Honourable Laura, The" (Hardy), **VI:** 22
Honourable Schoolboy, The (le Carré), **Supp. II:** 301, **313–314,** 315; **Retro. Supp. III:** 2 to **Retro. Supp. III:** 221, 219
Hood, Thomas, **IV:** xvi, xx, **251–267,** 311
Hood's (periodical), **IV:** 252, 261, 263, 264
"Hood's Literary Reminiscences" (Blunden), **IV:** 267
Hood's Own (Hood), **IV:** 251–252, 253, 254, 266
Hook, Theodore, **IV:** 254
Hooker, Richard, **I:** **176–190,** 362; **II:** 133, 137, 140–142, 147
Hoop, The (Burnside), **Supp. XIII:** 13, 14
Hoors (Burke), **Supp. XVIII:** 2, 4, 13–14

"Hooymaand/Hay Month/July" (Hadfield), **Supp. XVIII:** 113–114
"Hope" (Cornford), **VIII:** 105, 112
"Hope" (Cowper), **III:** 212
Hope (Deighton), **Supp. XVIII:** 62, 64
Hope, A. D., **Supp. VII:** **151–166**
"Hope Abandoned" (Davies), **Supp. XI:** 97
Hope for Poetry, A (Day Lewis), **Supp. III:** 117, 119
Hopes and Fears (Yonge), **Supp. XVII:** 271–272, 273
Hopes and Fears for Art (Morris), **V:** 301, 306
Hopkins, Gerard Manley, **II:** 123, 181; **IV:** xx; **V:** ix, xi, xxv, 53, 205, 210, 261, 309–310, 338, **361–382; VI:** 75, 83; **Supp. II:** 269; **Supp. IV:** 344, 345; **Retro. Supp. II:** 173, **185–198**
Hopkins (MacKenzie), **V:** 375n 382
Hopkinson, Sir Tom, **V:** xx, xxxviii
Horace, **II:** 108, 112, 199, 200, 265, 292, 300, 309, 347; **IV:** 327
"Horae Canonicae" (Auden), **Retro. Supp. I:** 12–13
Horae Solitariae (Thomas), **Supp. III:** 394
"Horatian Ode . . . , An" (Marvell), **II:** 204, 208, 209, 210, 211, 216–217; **Retro. Supp. II:** 263–264
"Horatius" (Macaulay), **IV:** 282
Horestes (Pickering), **I:** 213, 216–218
Horizon (periodical), **Supp. II:** 489; **Supp. III:** **102–103,** 105, 106–107, 108–109
Hornby, Nick, **Supp. XV:** **133–146**
Horne, Richard Hengist, **IV:** 312, 321, 322
Hornet (periodical), **VI:** 102
Horniman, Annie, **VI:** 309; **VII:** 1
"Horns Away" (Lydgate), **I:** 64
Horse and His Boy, The (Lewis), **Supp. III:** 248, 260
"Horse at Balaklava, 1854" (Carson), **Supp. XIII:** 66
"Horse Dealer's Daughter, The" (Lawrence), **VII:** 114
"Horse–Drawn Caravan" (Murphy), **Supp. V:** 329
Horse–Eaters, The: Poems and Satires, Third Series (Clarke), **Supp. XV:** 26
"Horse, Goose and Sheep, The" (Lydgate), **I:** 57
Horse Underwater (Deighton), **Supp. XVIII:** 57–58, 59, 60
Horseman's Word, The (Morgan, E.), **Supp. IX:** 166
"Horses" (Muir), **Supp. VI:** 204–205"Horses" (Muir), Supp. VI: 204–205
Horse's Mouth, The (Cary), **VII:** 186, 188, 191, 192, 193–194
Hoskins, John, **I:** 165–166, 167
"Hospital Barge" (Owen), **VI:** 454
Hostage, The (Behan), **Supp. II:** 70, **72–73,** 74
Hostage, London: The Diary of Julian Despard (Household), **Supp. XVII:** 81
Hostages to Fortune (Braddon), **VIII:** 49

"V.